Human Societies

An Introduction to Macrosociology

Human Societies
An Introduction to Macrosociology

NINTH EDITION

Patrick Nolan
University of South Carolina at Columbia

Gerhard Lenski
University of North Carolina at Chapel Hill

DOMINICAN COLLEGE LIBRARY
Blauvelt, New York 10913

DISCARDED

Paradigm Publishers
Boulder • London

129186

All rights reserved. No part of the publication my be transmitted or reproduced in any media or form, including electronic, mechanical, photocopy, recording, or informational storage and retrieval systems, without the express written consent of the publisher.

Copyright © 2004 by Paradigm Publishers

Previous editions copyrighted by The McGraw-Hill Companies, Inc., 1970, 1974, 1978, 1982, 1987, 1991, 1995, and 1999.

Published in the United States by Paradigm Publishers, 3360 Mitchell Lane Suite C, Boulder, Colorado 80301 USA.

Paradigm Publishers is the trade name of Birkenkamp & Company, LLC, Dean Birkenkamp, President and Publisher.

Library of Congress Cataloging-in-Publication Data

Nolan, Patrick, 1947–
   Human societies : an introduction to macrosociology / Patrick Nolan, Gerhard Lenski. — 9th ed.
      p. cm.
Includes bibliographical references and index.
   ISBN 1–59451–023–7 (pbk. : alk. paper)
   1. Macrosociology.   2. Social evolution.   3. Social systems—History.
I. Lenski, Gerhard Emmanuel, 1924–   II. Title.
   HM490.N65 2004
   301—dc22   2003021641

Printed and bound in the United States of America on acid free paper that meets the standards of the American National Standard for Permanence of Paper for Printed Library Materials.

Designed and Typeset by Straight Creek Bookmakers
07 06 05 04   2 3 4 5 6 7 8 9

ABOUT THE AUTHORS

Patrick Nolan is Professor of Sociology at the University of South Carolina at Columbia. He received his Ph.D. in sociology from Temple University, where he was an NDEA Title IV Fellow. He has been teaching introductory sociology for more than a quarter century, and he has published a number of papers on macrosociology and societal evolution written singly and in collaboration with Gerhard Lenski. He was coauthor of the sixth, seventh, and eighth editions of *Human Societies,* and he is author of its *Instructor's Manual* and *Student Study Guide.*

  Gerhard Lenski is Alumni Distinguished Professor Emeritus of Sociology at the University of North Carolina at Chapel Hill. He is also the author of *The Religious Factor* and *Power and Privilege.* He is a fellow of the American Academy of Arts and Sciences, a former Guggenheim Fellow, an IREX Senior Faculty Exchange Fellow, and a recipient of the American Sociological Association's Career of Distinguished Scholarship award.

For Lou and Ann

CONTENTS IN BRIEF

Chapter 13

Chapter 14

Chapter 15

Chapter 16

CONTENTS

PART TWO Preindustrial Societies

PREFACE

Change—*extremely rapid social change*—is the most important fact of life today. Today's world is a vastly different place from the world of twenty-five or fifty years ago, and the world of the next half century will almost certainly be greatly changed from our world today. Yet this will be the world in which most of today's students will find themselves. This means that the most important things they should be learning are the things that can help them anticipate the changes that lie ahead and prepare themselves for them.

Human Societies attempts to address this need in two ways. First, it offers students a framework for understanding human societies, and more especially for understanding the forces responsible for the more fundamental kinds of social change. To do this, we begin in Chapters 1 to 4 with an examination of the basic elements of this framework as found in ecological-evolutionary theory. We then show that this theoretical framework helps to explain the emergence, development, and, in some cases, the extinction of the various types of societies that men and women have created over the centuries and millennia. We believe that this broadly comparative and historical approach offers students a fresh and far more challenging perspective than is provided by texts that focus almost entirely on the students' own society.

Second, *Human Societies* offers students a model of how to use evidence to evaluate the validity of ideas and opinion. We do not ask students to accept our views on societies and social change because we claim to be authorities, but rather because we present a systematic body of evidence to support our claims. We believe it is important for students to understand the role of empirical evidence in evaluating ideas and opinions about the social world. In this vein, we encourage instructors and students alike to become acquainted with the data sources identified in the text and in the accompanying *Instructor's Manual* and to use these sources to test their own ideas about human societies or to challenge ours.

This volume is the ninth edition of *Human Societies,* but the first with Paradigm Publishers and the first in paperback (except for an earlier international edition for use overseas). We had long hoped to have a paperback edition of *Human Societies* available for American and Canadian students because of the greatly reduced cost, and we are pleased that our new publisher shares our view. We are especially appreciative of the strong interest and support provided by the president of Paradigm Publishers, Dean Birkenkamp, and his staff in the preparation of this volume.

No chapter is entirely unchanged in the present edition, and in a number of chapters the changes are substantive and significant. All of the changes are identified in the *Instructor's Manual* (available on request from the publisher), and we strongly recommend that instructors who have used previous editions, as well as those who are using *Human Societies* for the first time, consult it before preparing their course materials or making class assignments.

We invite your comments, reactions, and suggestions regarding *Human Societies*. You can send them to Patrick Nolan at the Department of Sociology, the University of South Carolina, Columbia, S.C. 29208, e-mail pnolan@sc.edu; or to Gerhard Lenski, P.O. Box 409, Hansville, WA, 98340, e-mail Aglenski@earthlink.net.

ACKNOWLEDGMENTS

It is not possible to acknowledge adequately all our intellectual debts in the brief space available here. But many who read this volume will recognize our debt to Thomas Malthus, Charles Darwin, Herbert Spencer, Karl Marx, Max Weber, Thorstein Veblen, Albert Keller, William Ogburn, V. Gordon Childe, George Peter Murdock, R. H. Tawney, Sir Julian Huxley,

George Gaylord Simpson, Leslie White, Julian Steward, Amos Hawley, Marvin Harris, William H. McNeill, and Bruce Mayhew, among others. The citations that appear at the end of this volume should be regarded as further acknowledgments of indebtedness and appreciation.

Many social scientists and a few biologists have been kind enough to provide critical comments on, and suggestions for, one or more of the eight editions of *Human Societies* thus far. The social scientists include Brian Aldrich, Francis R. Allen, E. Jackson Baur, Rae Lesser Blumberg, Steve Borgatti, William Brustein, Woody Carlson, Robert Carroll, William R. Catton, Jr., Ronald Cosper, Timothy Crippen, David Featherman, Thomas Feucht, George Furniss, Walter Goldschmidt, Robert Bates Graber, J. Patrick Gray, Gareth Gustafson, Thomas D. Hall, Amos Hawley, Paul Heckert, John Hofley, Joan Huber, Holly Hughes, Larry Hunt, Donald Irish, Peter Kivisto, Philip Marcus, Robert Miller, Peter Peregrine, Ross Purdy, Leo Rigsby, Ellen Rosengarten, David Rowlee, Norman Storer, Jacek Szmatka, Theodore H. Tsoukalas, Wout Ultee, Charles K. Warriner, Norbert Wiley, and Everett K. Wilson. The biologists include Alfred E. Emerson, Richard E. Lenski, and Edward O. Wilson. We extend sincere thanks to each of them for valuable suggestions, but remind readers that the final responsibility for the contents is ours alone.

We also thank Phillip Butcher and Ben Morrison of McGraw-Hill for their many years of friendship and their support for *Human Societies*.

Patrick Nolan
Gerhard Lenski

PART ONE

THEORETICAL FOUNDATIONS

1

The Human Situation

Imagine a huge photo album filled with pictures of human life beginning 100,000 years ago. Imagine, too, that each of its 1,000 pages provides a record of life in a different century.

What would such an album be like, and what might you learn from it?

After the initial excitement of viewing the first few pages with their photographs of life in the Stone Age long, long ago, you would probably find the pages that followed terribly repetitive, even boring. In fact, throughout the first half of the album and beyond, hundreds of pages would be filled with the same kinds of pictures—scenes of people physically indistinguishable from ourselves, though naked or clad in animal skins, huddled around fires in front of caves or beside rude shelters made of branches and leaves, fashioning simple tools and weapons from stone, wood, and bone, hunting with wooden spears, foraging for edible plants, nursing infants, and performing a limited number of other basic tasks. Fascinating though the first of these pictures might be, you would soon tire of the repetitiveness and might begin to flip pages in search of something new and different.

Roughly halfway through the volume, if you were still attentive, you would gradually begin to see occasional indications of innovation and change. For example, you might see for the first time a photograph of people burying someone who had died. Later, you would slowly find increasing evidence of other new activities. Occasionally, you might see a photograph of people painting on the walls of caves or engaging in strange new rituals unlike anything you had seen before. Other innovations would gradually appear, especially new kinds of tools and weapons—spoons, saws, needles, bows and arrows, oil lamps, even crude dugout canoes. Shortly before page 900, you would begin to see people trapping and netting fish, harvesting wild grains with stone sickles, weaving baskets, taming wild dogs and sheep, and, yes, even drinking beer.

Not until the last hundred pages, however, would you find the first photographs of people farming, and it would be another twenty or thirty pages before you would see any real towns. A little after page 950, you would find views of the construction of the great pyramids of Egypt, and later still, you would begin to see the first pictures of individuals whose names you would recognize: Moses on page 967, Aristotle on 976, Cleopatra on 979, Jesus on 980, Mohammed on 986.

Although signs of innovation and change would be growing, you would not find evidence of really rapid social and cultural change of the kind to which we are accustomed until you got to the end of the album. There, crowded into the *last three pages,* you would see for the first time everything from the first steam engine to the first jet engine, the first computer, the first television, and the first nuclear weapons—all those inventions and discoveries that are so important in our lives today.

This journey through the past is bound to raise questions in the mind of any thoughtful person. Why, for example, did the Stone Age last so long? Was life so satisfying that people had no interest in finding different ways of doing things? But, if that was true, why did they eventually begin to change?

The historical record also raises questions about the more recent past and about conditions today and in the years ahead. What has caused the explosive acceleration of the rate of change in the recent past, and should we expect even more rapid change in the years ahead? If so, what kind of world awaits us in the twenty-first century?

There are other questions, too. Has all the change of the recent past been worth it? Are we better off today than our forebears were a century or more ago, or have the costs outweighed the benefits? Finally, and most important of all, can we do anything to control the process of change and to maximize its benefits and minimize its costs?

Questions like these force us to recognize how much we are like poorly prepared astronauts on a fleet of spaceships, hurtling at fantastic speeds on an uncharted course filled with unknown hazards. Our ships are the societies in which each of us lives—American society, Canadian society, Dutch society, Chinese society, Polish society, Nigerian society, Brazilian society, and all the rest. Each of these extraordinarily complex social systems is moving rapidly into new and uncharted realms, and most of us, like ill-prepared astronauts, have as yet only the most limited understanding of these systems on which our survival and well-being depend.

Presidents, prime ministers, and other leaders continually assure us that they understand the situation and have matters firmly under control. But a moment's reflection reminds us that neither they nor their predecessors planned or willed the world that exists today. Like the rest of us, they have repeatedly been caught off guard and swept along by unanticipated changes and developments.

In a world like this, all of us have a vested interest in learning all that we can about the societies in which we live and the others with which we share the planet. Above all, we need to prepare ourselves for the changes that lie ahead.

Fortunately, we are not without resources. A branch of modern science known as **sociology*** has made the study of human societies its chief concern. Its basic aim is to understand human societies and the forces that have made them what they are. Although many important questions remain to be answered, considerable progress has already been made, and the aim of this volume is to provide a summary of, and introduction to, what has been learned thus far.

Much of the work of sociologists is devoted to the study of one or another of the many different component parts of societies (e.g., individuals, families, communities, classes) and to its specific features and problems (e.g., crime, race relations, religion, politics). The study of these components and features of societies is sometimes called *micro*sociology.

Macrosociology, in contrast, focuses on human societies themselves. Although it, too, is concerned with individuals, families, classes, social problems, and all of the other parts and features of societies, it analyzes them *in relation to the larger social systems—the societies—of which they are part.* The difference between macrosociology and microsociology is much the same as the difference between the study of complex mechanical systems, such as spaceships, and the study of one of their component parts, such as their booster engines or life-support systems.

This volume takes the *macro*sociological approach. Our primary concern, and the focus of our analysis, will be human societies themselves. This does not mean that we will ignore their components; that would be impossible. It does mean, however, that when we consider their component parts and various features, we will treat them as what they are: parts of larger and more inclusive social systems.

Two other characteristics of this book should be noted. First, its approach to the study of human societies is **historical** and **evolutionary.** We must examine societies over an extended period of time if we are ever to understand the critical processes of societal change and development. Experience has shown, moreover, that the broader the span of time we consider, the better we can understand the most basic processes of change in human life.

*For definitions of this and other terms used in this volume, see the Glossary, pp. 360–367.

Second, our approach to the study of human societies is **comparative.** Comparison is the basis of science. An understanding of anything depends on comparing it with other things. To understand an individual chimpanzee, for example, scientists compare it with other chimpanzees. To understand chimpanzees as a species, they compare them with other apes, and to understand apes, they compare them with other primates and other mammals. In every comparison both the similarities and the differences are used to draw inferences about why things are as they are. Only by repeated comparisons are we likely to build a reliable store of knowledge about the world of nature and all that it contains. This is true whether our concern is with atoms, galaxies, robins, chimpanzees—or human societies.

In making comparisons, the most important task for scientists is to discover *differences that make a difference.* In medicine, for example, the aim is to discover the actual causes of diseases, not just their symptoms. The same is true in other sciences: the goal is to discover the causes of things.

This search for the causes of things leads to the development of theory. **Scientific theories** are explanations of various aspects of the world of nature; they are explanations of why things are as they are. Theories also provide a coherent set of principles that form the basic frame of reference for a field of inquiry.

One of the most important characteristics of scientific theories is that they are **falsifiable.** This means that they are stated in such a way that they can be tested and shown to be wrong, if indeed they are wrong. To win acceptance in the scientific community, a theory must withstand repeated tests and must be supported by a substantial body of observations that are consistent with its explanation of relationships.

Sometimes it seems as though science is merely the patient accumulation of facts. But facts by themselves are meaningless; they explain nothing. For scientists, the collection of facts is the means to a much more important end, namely, the development and testing of theories designed to explain some aspect of the world of nature.

Our study of human societies in this volume is guided by such a theory—**ecological-evolutionary theory.** As its name suggests, this theory is concerned with two things. First, it is concerned with the relations among the parts of societies, and with the interactions between societies and their environments. Second, the theory is concerned with the evolution of societies—how and why they change and how these changes create differences among societies.

HUMAN SOCIETIES: THEIR PLACE IN NATURE

Often in the past, and still today, many people have thought of human societies as though they stood apart from the world of nature that science studies. This is easy to do, because modern industrial societies are much like giant cocoons that stand between us and the surrounding environment. As a result, we seldom encounter anything that has not been processed and transformed by human actions. Nevertheless, the first premise of ecological-evolutionary theory is that *human societies are a part of the* **global ecosystem** *and cannot be adequately understood unless this fact is taken fully into account.*[1]

As many scholars have observed, the world of nature is structured like a system of wheels within wheels. Larger things are made up of smaller things, and these in turn are made up of still smaller things. Figure 1.1 provides a greatly oversimplified view of the structure of the world of nature as understood by modern science. Subatomic particles, such as protons and electrons, form the lowest level. These are combined in various ways to form atoms, such as carbon and radium. Atoms in turn are organized into molecules, such as water, salt, amino acids, and proteins.*

*Though Figure 1.1 does not show it, molecules constitute multiple levels in the hierarchy, because some of the simpler molecules, the amino acids, for example, are building blocks for more complex and more inclusive molecules such as proteins.

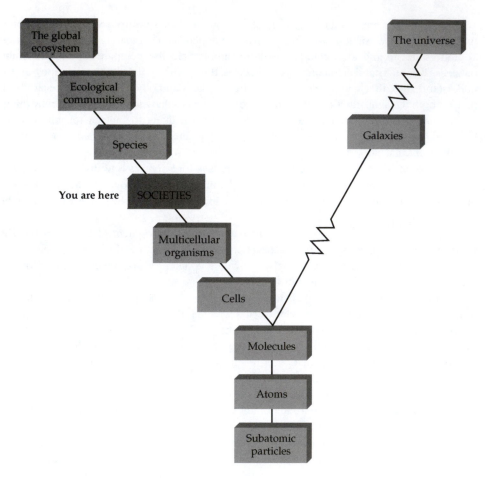

FIGURE 1.1 *Levels of organization in the world of nature.*

Once we go beyond the level of molecules, we encounter the important division between living and nonliving things. Since our concern is with human societies, there is no need to consider all the levels of nonliving matter. Suffice it to note that the structure leads by degrees to the level of the giant galaxies that wheel through space and ends with the universe itself.

Societies, however, are part of the biotic world: they are one of the ways in which *living* things are organized. More specifically, they are a form of organization found in many species of multicellular organisms.

This brings us to the question of why some species are organized into societies while others are not.

Societies as Adaptive Mechanisms

The development of the societal mode of organization has been called "one of the great steps in evolution, as important as the emergence of the cell, the multicellular organism, and the vertebrate system."[2] Actually, societies evolved not once but a number of times, independently, and in widely scattered parts of the animal kingdom. According to the biologist E. O. Wilson, four groups of animals are especially noteworthy with respect to the development of social organization: (1) the colonial invertebrates (such as corals, sponges, and Portuguese man-of-wars); (2) the social insects (ants, termites, and many species of wasps and bees); (3) many species of nonhuman vertebrates, especially mammals, birds, and fish; and (4) humans.[3]

Why did so many and such diverse species develop this particular mode of organization? Quite simply, because being organized this way helped the members of these species survive. In other words, the societal mode of life became common in the animal kingdom for the same reason that wings, lungs, and protective coloring became common: they are all valuable **adaptive mechanisms.**

But societal organization is different from adaptive mechanisms that enable species to perform some particular activity—the way wings, for example, enable creatures to fly, or lungs enable them to exchange oxygen and other gases with the air. What distinguishes social species from all the rest is a characteristic that has the potential for being used in a great variety of ways: an enhanced capacity for cooperation.

To those who study animal behavior, "cooperation" means simply that the individuals in a given species associate with and interact with one another for their mutual benefit. It does not mean they cooperate in every activity, nor does it imply an absence of competition and conflict.

The types of cooperative activities in which the various social species engage include reproduction, nurture of their young, securing food, and defense against predators and other dangers.* Some social species rely on cooperative behavior in almost every area of life; others are less involved in, or less dependent on, social activities. But every **social species** benefits substantially from the fact that its members are genetically programmed to solve at least some of their problems by acting together instead of individually.

A Definition of Human Societies

Once we recognize that human societies are adaptive mechanisms involving cooperative activities among their members, we are close to a definition of these important entities. There is, however, one other essential consideration that must be taken into account.

Human societies have within them many kinds of smaller groups, such as families, communities, political parties, and religious groups, and these subgroups are also adaptive mechanisms involving cooperative activities among their members. Thus, our definition needs to specify that human societies are *autonomous* groups—groups that are not subject to the political authority or control of any larger, more inclusive group.** In short, *a human population is considered a society to the degree that it is politically autonomous and its members engage in a broad range of cooperative activities.*

This definition obviously applies to American society, Russian society, or Brazilian society, but not to an American labor union, Russian Jews, or the city of Rio de Janeiro. None of the latter is autonomous; each is subordinate to the larger society of which it is a part. Similarly, the population of Germany constitutes a society, but German-speaking people as a whole, scattered among several societies (e.g., Germany, Austria, Switzerland), do not; the population of Saudi Arabia constitutes a society, but Arabs as a whole and Muslims do not.

Sometimes unusual circumstances make it difficult to say whether a group of people is or is not a society at a particular point in its history. Uncertainty is most likely to arise when a small society is gradually absorbed by a larger and more powerful one. Consider the Inuit (Eskimo) of northern Canada, for example. Not very long ago these people lived in numerous small settlements, each one largely self-sufficient and each one free of outside political control. Gradually, however, the Canadian government began asserting authority over these groups. At the same time, the Inuit were becoming increasingly involved in economic relationships with Canadians and were drawn into the complex web of cooperative ties that is Canadian

---

*Even nonsocial animals display cooperative activity in the area of reproduction (i.e., they reproduce sexually). But a species is not classified as "social" if its cooperative activity is limited to this single, though important, area.
**Clearly autonomy is a matter of degree. For instance, in today's global economy no society is completely free of the economic influences of other societies. Nonetheless, they still maintain considerable political autonomy, especially over their domestic affairs.

(a)

(b)

Societies evolved not once but a number of times, independently, and in widely scattered parts of the animal kingdom: (a) living star coral, (b) honeybee workers and their queen, (c) a pride of lions, and (d) Yagua society in Brazil.

(c)

(d)

society. Because these developments occurred slowly over an extended period, it is impossible to say precisely when a given Inuit group ceased being a society and became, instead, part of Canadian society. Then, many years later, there was a rare reversal in this common pattern of large societies swallowing smaller ones; the Inuit were granted their own homeland, Nunavut ("Our Land"), and thereby regained much of their lost autonomy from the Canadian government.[4]

UNDERSTANDING HUMAN SOCIETIES: BASIC ASSUMPTIONS

That human societies are part of the larger world of nature is not simply a truism to be acknowledged and then forgotten; it is a fundamental fact that must be reckoned with and taken fully into account in any serious effort to understand them. At the same time, however, human societies are not merely one more kind of society with a few new wrinkles added. On the contrary, many of their most important characteristics are unique.

In studying human life and human societies, it is easy to emphasize one of these aspects of the human situation to the neglect of the other. Ecological-evolutionary theory, the theory that guides our study of human societies, avoids this by starting with three basic assumptions. First, because human societies are part of the world of nature, they are all influenced by their **environments** in a variety of ways. Second, because human societies are part of the world of nature, their members, like the members of every other species, are endowed with a **genetic heritage** that profoundly influences their actions. Third, this genetic heritage enables the members of human societies—and them alone—to create **cultural heritages,** and it is this that gives human life its unique qualities. If we neglect or ignore any of these three factors, our understanding of human societies will necessarily be flawed.

Human Societies and the Environment

To say that every human society is dependent on its environment and that this environment profoundly influences it raises an important question. Exactly what does the term **"environment"** mean?

This term refers to *everything that is external to a specified population and that has any effect on it*. Thus, for whales, the oceans and the varied forms of life they contain, together with the air above them, the ships that sail on them, and the toxic wastes that pour into them, constitute the environment, just as tropical forests and the countless species of plants and animals they contain are the environment of monkeys.

For a human society, the environment includes such things as the soil, mineral and water resources, climate, terrain, plants, animals, and other features of the territory it occupies. In addition, its environment includes any other human societies with which its members come into contact or which influence it in any way. In other words, every human society must adapt not only to a *biophysical* environment but to a *human social* environment as well. Its welfare and even its survival depend on its success in adapting to both.

In thinking about the environment, we need to recognize at the outset that it presents both opportunities and threats. Thus, while a society depends on its environment for all the material necessities of life (i.e., food, water, shelter, etc.), that same environment also harbors deadly enemies. The biophysical environments of some human groups have contained many kinds of large and deadly predators, and the environments of even the most technologically advanced modern societies continue to harbor countless species of harmful viruses, bacteria, insects, and rodents. Moreover, the efforts of human groups to cope with their environments, can, in turn, alter those environments and create new problems. Societies can hunt valuable animals into extinction and they can pollute their air and water.

The social environment also poses both opportunities and threats. Contact between societies can produce mutually beneficial exchanges of goods and information, or it can produce death and destruction. We live today in a global economy where goods, services, and people literally flow around the world, but in the twentieth century alone, hundreds of millions of people lost their lives, were wounded, or were driven from their homes as a result of war. And even when war is avoided, societies can be threatened and harmed by other societies through other means, such as disease, atmospheric pollution, economic competition, or political subversion.

Human Societies: Their Genetic Heritage

In the efforts of societies to cope with the challenges of their environments, their most basic resource has always been the vast store of information contained in the genes of their members. For the **genes** with which each of us is endowed at the moment of conception contain the information that is essential for life itself, and for everything we do from breathing and walking to learning and communicating.

Until the past century, however, no one even knew of the existence of genes, far less imagined the enormous influence they exert on every living thing from the simplest one-celled animals to humans. Even today many people fail to recognize, or badly underestimate, their importance.

As biologists have discovered, every species has a genetic heritage uniquely its own. This heritage is the product of an evolutionary process that has been going on for more than 3 billion years. Because of it, each member of a species is endowed with a vast store of *chemically coded information* which it receives from its parents or parent.*

Individuals have no control over the information stored in their genes. Yet this information guides and shapes the life of every living thing, in much the same way that the information built into the design of a modern computer influences the computer's operations, and the information stored in our brains affects our feelings and our actions.

Like every other species, we humans possess a unique and distinctive heritage that influences every aspect of our lives. Like the information we carry in our brains, the information stored in our genes is a *product of experience*. Unlike the kinds of information we learn, however, it does not result from our personal experience. Rather, it is the result of the experiences of countless generations of our ancestors. Through the interaction of the biological processes of mutation, sexual recombination, and natural selection, every species gradually accumulates its own distinctive store of useful genetic information.

To understand our species' genetic heritage, we need to bear in mind the nature of our ancestry. We are members of the anthropoid suborder (which also includes the great apes and monkeys), which is part of the **primate order,** which is part of the mammalian class, which, in turn, is part of the vertebrate division of the animal kingdom. This means that we are more closely related and genetically more similar to other **anthropoids** than to the rest of the primate order, to other primates than to other mammals, to the rest of the mammalian class than to other vertebrates, to the rest of the vertebrate division than to other animals, and to other animals than to plants. It also means that our basic adaptations resemble those of primates and mammals more closely than those of other, less closely related species.

When we compare ourselves with the other anthropoids and especially with our closest kin of all, the great apes (e.g., chimpanzees and gorillas), the range of common traits is striking (see Table 1.1). To begin with, there are the many traits that we and they share with most other mammals, such as warm-bloodedness, body hair, lungs, four limbs, a relatively elaborate brain, the ability to learn and communicate, and, in the female, mammary glands

*Some species reproduce asexually and these individuals therefore have only a single parent.

Depression: Product of Interaction of Heredity and Environment

Recent research provides yet another striking example of how human life is shaped by the interaction of genetics and environment. In a study to determine the causes of clinical depression in a sample of 847 young adult New Zealanders, researchers collected data on their subjects' DNA and on their exposure between the ages of 21 and 26 to seriously stressful experiences, such as a death in the family, unemployment, debt problems, trouble in intimate relations, homelessness, disabling injuries, and physical or sexual abuse.

What they found was that those subjects who had inherited the *short* version, or allele, of the gene 5–HTT from *both* of their parents and who experienced four or more seriously stressful experiences were two-and-a-half times more likely to suffer clinical depression than those who inherited the *long* allele from *both* parents. Those with the short allele were also nearly three times more likely to have considered or attempted suicide. Another striking finding was that those who had two copies of the long allele and had been exposed to four or more seriously stressful experiences were no more likely to suffer from clinical depression than persons who had not experienced *any* seriously stressful experiences.

This study is yet one more in a growing body of evidence that human life—both individually and collectively—is shaped by the combined influence or interaction of genetics, or heredity, and environment, and that neglect of either can only impoverish our understanding of human life.

Source: *New York Times*, July 18, 2003, article, based on report in the journal *Science* of the same date.

that secrete milk for the nurturance of offspring. In addition, we and the other anthropoids share to varying degrees such physical traits as upright posture, flexible arms and hands, separated fingers and opposable thumbs, prolonged immaturity of offspring, greater reliance on stereoscopic color vision than on smell, and a high order of intelligence, as well as such behavioral similarities as the abilities to deceive one another, form coalitions, and play.[5]

One cannot compare humans with other species in this way without recognizing the extent to which basic patterns of human life are rooted in our genetic system. For it is not just a matter of similarities between our anatomy and physiology and that of the other primates: it is also a matter of behavioral tendencies and predispositions. If we humans are capable of cooperation and live in societies, it is not because we choose to be social creatures, but because of our genetic heritage. Similarly, if we rely on learning as a basic mode of adaptation to the world we live in, it is not because we decided it was the best thing to do, nor did we invent learning. Rather, it is an expression of our mammalian and primate heritage.

Learning is the process by which an organism acquires, through experience, information with behavior-modifying potential.[6] This means that when it comes to solving problems, an animal that can learn is not completely dependent on **instinct** (i.e., the behavioral repertoire provided by its genetic heritage). Instead, its own experiences become a factor shaping its behavior. In the case of humans and some of the higher primates, the evolution of the forebrain has reached the point where they are able to store such a wide range of memories that they can learn by **insight;** in other words, they can analyze a situation in their minds and thereby avoid the time-consuming, costly, and often painful process of trial and error.[7]

The adaptive value of the ability to learn is greatly enhanced when animals live together in groups. This gives the individual more opportunity to observe, and to communicate with, others of its kind. In effect, social animals benefit from the experience of their fellows as well

TABLE 1.1 Physical Characteristics Shared by Primates, Including Humans

- Independent mobility of fingers and toes
- A wraparound first digit in both hands and feet (thumb, big toe)
- Replacement of claws by nails to support the digital pads of the last phalanx of each finger and toe
- Teeth and digestive tract adapted to an omnivorous diet
- A semierect posture that enables hand manipulation and provides a favorable position preparatory to leaping
- Center of gravity positioned close to hind legs
- Well-developed hand-eye motor coordination
- Optical adaptations that include overlap of the visual fields that provide precise three-dimensional information on the location of food objects and tree branches
- Bony orbits that protect the eyes from arboreal hazards
- Shortening of the face accompanied by reduction of the snout
- Diminution of the sense of smell in those active in daylight
- Compared to practically all other mammals, a very large and complex brain in relation to body size

Source: Adapted from Monroe Strickberger, *Evolution* (Boston: Jones and Bartlett, 1990), p. 384.

as from their own individual experience. Social life thus multiplies the amount of information available to a population. In the words of two leading students of primate life, "The [primate] group is the locus of knowledge and information far exceeding that of the individual member. It is in the group that experience is pooled."[8]

The adaptive value of the ability to learn is also greatly enhanced among primates by the prolonged physical immaturity of their young. The young of most species are genetically equipped to fend for themselves from the moment of birth. For mammals, however, there is a period during which the young depend on sustained contact with one or both parents. In the

All mammalian species have a marked capacity for learning. Among anthropoids, this is enhanced by the prolonged physical immaturity of the young: chimpanzee family, with older sister nuzzling younger brother in mother's arms.

case of the anthropoids, this period of dependence is especially prolonged, a fact that is linked both with their enhanced capacity for learning and with their dependence on the societal mode of life.

But what makes us so different from those anthropoid apes—chimpanzees and gorillas—with whom we may share more than 99 percent of our genes?[9] After all, only we build skyscrapers, set off nuclear explosions, philosophize, compose symphonies, and travel in space. The explanation is that at some point in the evolution of one anthropoid line there occurred a series of genetic changes that, although few in number, had revolutionary consequences for behavior. The most critical changes altered the structure of the brain and shifted the center of vocalization to the neocortex, or newer part of the brain, where learning takes place and learned information is stored. Thus, thanks to relatively minor genetic changes, our remote ancestors acquired the capacity to create a radically new mode of adaptation—**culture**.*

Culture: A New Mode of Adaptation and a New Kind of Heritage

Unlike the genetic heritages of other species, ours enables us to create culture.** This makes it possible for us to adapt to our environments and satisfy our needs in totally new and remarkably varied ways.

Because culture is such a basic and critical part of human life, we need to understand precisely what it is. Unlike the information that every species passes from one generation to the next through its genes, culture is *learned* information, and it is passed from person to person and from generation to generation by means of **symbols.**

What are symbols that they have made such a difference to our species? After all, the members of other species also communicate among themselves, using **signals** to share information. Both signals and symbols are *information conveyers.* But there is a vital difference: the meaning of a signal is wholly or largely determined by the genetic makeup of the individuals who use it; the meaning of a symbol is not.

The best way to understand this distinction is to look at examples of the two kinds of information conveyers, beginning with signals.[10] Animals signal with movements, sounds, odors, color changes, and so on, and the signals they produce vary greatly in the amount of information they convey. The simplest type of signal is one that is used in only a single context and that has only one possible meaning—the sexually attractive scent released by a female moth, for example. In contrast, some species are able to transmit more complex information by varying the frequency or intensity of a signal or by combining different signals simultaneously or in sequence. Thus, a foraging honeybee returns to her hive and performs the "waggle dance" to direct fellow workers to the food source she has located.[11] By varying the movements and vibrations that comprise the dance, she communicates enough information about direction and distance to enable her sisters to land remarkably near the target, and at the same time adds a comment on the quality of the food supply and the state of the weather.

In some species, especially birds and mammals, the use of and response to signals are partially learned. The young of certain species of birds, for example, must learn some ele-

---

*This is a classic example of what is known as the "threshold effect," in which a small change in one thing has a big effect on something else—as when someone walks for miles in a pouring rain without any improvement in his situation and then takes one or two additional steps and enters a building and completely escapes the downpour.

**To avoid confusion, it should be noted that we define culture as shared *symbols* rather than shared *behavior* (see page 31). Thus, learned behaviors that are shared and passed on in other primate societies (e.g., food washing) would not be classified as culture by our definition.

With symbols, every society has developed its own rich and distinctive heritage to supplement its genetic heritage: the flag of Canada.

ments of their territorial songs from adults.[12] We, too, learn to modify and use genetically based signals in different ways. Thus, we learn to pretend to yawn to indicate boredom. But whether simple or complex, and whether or not learning is involved, a signal is an information conveyer whose basic form and meaning are genetically determined.

Symbols, by contrast, are not genetically determined. The ability to create and use symbols does depend on genetics, but the form of a symbol and the meaning attached to it do not. Thus, a symbol is *an information conveyer whose form and meaning have developed within a community of users.*

Humans share the ability to create symbols with no other species. Various kinds of animals from plow horses to circus seals have been trained to recognize, respond to, and even use, after a fashion, a number of symbols. Chimpanzees and gorillas have proved to have a remarkable ability in this regard, learning to use up to 750 different symbols, even combining a few of them to convey more complex meanings.[13] None of these animals, however, has ever created a symbol, that is, has ever deliberately assigned its own meaning to a gesture, sound, or object. Rather, the symbols they use were designed by humans and taught to them. What is more, these creatures show not even the rudiments of language development in the wild.[14] Thus, while their accomplishments are impressive, they cannot compare with humans. For we not only quickly master the language of the group into which we are born but we also are capable at a very early age of devising new symbols and even entire symbol systems. Small children invent names for their stuffed animals and sometimes go on to make up "secret codes." And at least one case has been documented in which a set of twins, first thought to be retarded because no one understood their speech, proved to have invented an entirely original and complex language by which they communicated with one another.

We can appreciate the significance of symbols only when we understand the degree to which symbolic meanings have been unleashed from our species' genetic endowment. Take the sound of the third letter of our alphabet, for example. We use that sound to refer to the act

Fifteen Ways to Say "I Love You"

Because the connection between the sounds people make and their meaning is arbitrary, different languages use different combinations of sounds to express the same idea. Thus, every language has its own distinctive way of saying "I love you." In some languages, the phrase varies slightly when a woman addresses a man; these variants are shown in parentheses.

Arabic: Ana b'hibbik (Ana b'hibbak)
Cambodian: Bon sro lanh oon
Chinese: Wo ai ni
Danish: Jeg elsker Dig
English: I love you
French: Je t'aime
German: Ich liebe dich
Hebrew: Ani ohev otakh (Ani ohevet otkhah)
Hindi: Maiñtumheñ piyar karta huñ
Hungarian: Szeretlek
Italian: Ti voglio bene
Japanese: Watakushi-wa anata-wo aishimasu
Korean: Tangsinul sarang hä yo
Navaho: Ayór ánosh' ní
Russian: Ya tebya liubliu

Source: Charles Berlitz, *Native Tongues* (London: Panther, 1984), p. 54.

of perceiving (to see), to a bishop's jurisdiction (a see), and to a large body of water (a sea), as well as to the letter itself. Spanish-speaking people, meanwhile, use it to say "yes" and "if," and French-speaking people to say "yes," "if," "whether," and "so." Obviously there is no logical connection between these various meanings, nor is there any genetically determined connection between the meanings and the sound. They are simply arbitrary usages adopted by the members of certain societies.

Further evidence that symbols are determined by their users and not by genes is the ease with which we alter them. When English people of the thirteenth century said, "Fader oure that art in heve, i-halged bee thi nome," they meant to say—in fact they did say—"Our Father who art in heaven, hallowed be Thy name,"[15] and when Chaucer wrote "Hir nose tretis, hir yen greye as glas," he meant to say—in fact, he did say—"Her nose well-formed, her eyes gray as glass." English-speaking people have simply altered many of their symbols since his day. Slang is created by the reverse procedure: the symbol itself remains unchanged, but it is given a new meaning. The words "bread" and "dough," for example, have both come to be used to refer to money.

Although linguistic symbols are the most basic and important, they are not the only kind we use. Anything to which humans assign a meaning becomes a symbol. Thus, the cross has become a symbol of Christianity; the maple leaf is a symbol of Canada. Every nation in the world today has a flag to represent it, and standardized symbols communicate basic traffic directions on highways.

Because they are not genetically determined, symbols can be combined and recombined in countless ways to form symbol systems of fantastic complexity, subtlety, and flexibility. The only limits are set by the physical characteristics of those who use them, that is, by the efficiency and capacity of the human brain and nervous system and the accuracy of our

The difference between a human mind without symbols and the same mind with them is eloquently described in Helen Keller's account of her early life.

senses. And symbol systems help to overcome even these limitations. For example, our species' memory (i.e., its capacity for storing information) has been greatly increased by the use of written symbols and written records.

In the final analysis, the importance of symbol systems lies not in what they are, but in what they have made it possible for our species to become. Although we are all born into the human family, we become fully human only through the use of symbols. Without them, we are unable to develop the unique qualities we associate with humanness. For symbols are more than a means of communication: they are tools with which we think and plan, dream and remember, create and build, calculate, speculate, and moralize.

The difference between a human mind without symbols and that same mind with them is eloquently described in Helen Keller's account of her early life.[16] She became both deaf and blind before she learned to talk. By the age of seven, after years without meaningful communication with other people, she had become very much like a wild animal. Then, a gifted teacher, Anne Sullivan, began trying to communicate with her by spelling words into her hands. Helen learned several words, but she did not yet comprehend the real significance of symbols. Finally, in a moment that both women later described in moving terms, Helen suddenly realized that *everything* had a name, that *everything* could be communicated with symbols! In her own words, she felt "a thrill of returning thought." At last, the world that exists only for symbol users began to open to her.

Miss Keller's experience helps us understand why the ancients, in their accounts of creation, so often linked the beginning of language with the beginning of the world. One of the oldest written texts from Egypt, for example, tells how Ptah, the creator of the world and the greatest of the gods, "pronounced the names of all things" as a central part of his act of creation.[17] Language also figures prominently in Chinese and Hindu creation myths. The book of Genesis tells us that the first thing Adam did after he was created was to name all the beasts and birds; and the Gospel According to St. John opens with the lines "In the beginning was the Word, and the Word was with God, and the Word was God." Significantly, the original Greek for "word" was *logos,* which meant not merely word, but meaning and reason. And *logos* is the root of our own word "logic," and of the suffix *-logy,* used to denote science, as in biology or sociology.

The German scientist Alexander von Humboldt once said, "No words, no world," and it is true that the human world, the world of human societies, would not exist without words. Without words and other symbols, human societies would differ little from the societies of other primates, for they would lack their most distinctive feature: culture. *With* symbols, every society has developed its own rich and distinctive heritage to supplement its genetic heritage.

In the chapters that follow, we will explore in detail the impact of these cultural heritages and see how they have influenced human life. First, however, we need to pull together the several elements of our analysis to this point.

HUMAN SOCIETIES: THE BASIC MODEL

The aim of ecological-evolutionary theory, as we have seen, is to understand why human societies are the way they are. Like every theory, it starts with certain assumptions. It assumes that human societies are both part of the world of nature and, at the same time, unique in a number of fundamental ways.

One of the tools that can help us in analyzing societies and in constructing theories about them is a technique known as *modeling,* which expresses hypothesized cause-and-effect relationships in a detailed and explicit manner. Modeling compels us to be precise about the relationships involved in a theory—more precise than we might otherwise be. One way of doing this is to construct models in the form of mathematical equations that express these relationships. This method is used widely in physics and economics, and sometimes also in sociology. Another method, and one that is especially well suited to *macro*sociology, expresses relationships by means of visual diagrams.

In the chapters that follow, we will present a number of models in diagrammatic form as a means of summarizing various aspects of ecological-evolutionary theory. Since some of the relationships involved are complex, some of the models will also be complex.

Our first model, however, is quite simple. But it is extremely important because it identifies the most basic determinants, or causes, of the characteristics of human societies as understood by ecological-evolutionary theory. As Figure 1.2 indicates, this theory asserts that all of a society's characteristics are ultimately due to just three things: (1) the influence of its biophysical and social environments, (2) the influence of our species' genetic heritage, and (3) the influence of prior social and cultural characteristics of the society itself. The double arrows

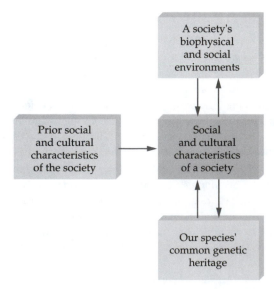

FIGURE 1.2 *Basic ecological-evolutionary model of the determinants of the characteristics of human societies.*

in the model also indicate that human societies are not just affected by, but also affect, the environment and our species' genetic heritage.

In the chapters that follow, we will *amplify and extend* this basic model, adding greater detail. In Chapter 2, for example, we will examine the middle box on the right side of Figure 1.2 to see just what those characteristics are. In Chapter 3 we will see why and how human societies change. This will provide us with the information we will need in Chapter 4 to "map" the principal types and varieties of societies that have evolved over the course of the last 100,000 years.

From that point on we will examine each of the major types of societies and see how the forces of change have transformed human societies over the course of history. Throughout the process, we will gradually extend our basic model by incorporating into it, and into our theory, the more interesting features and complexities of human life.

One point to bear in mind is that ecological-evolutionary theory, like all theories, is subject to refinement and modification as new facts become known and new evidence uncovered. For example, while we know that our species' genetic heritage influences human societies in countless important ways (e.g., cultural systems could not exist without it), it is still impossible at this point to determine many of its more specific effects (e.g., whether differences in mathematical ability between men and women are genetically determined), and opinions often differ. Recent advances in the science of genetics, however, promise to clarify our understanding of this issue in the years ahead, and research in various other areas will almost certainly lead to other refinements and improvements.

Excursus: A Brief History of Sociology

Before going further in our analysis of human societies, it may be well to pause and take a closer look at sociology itself—its origins and history, its recent trends and current status. This brief excursus also provides an opportunity to consider the relationship between sociology and the other social sciences.

Though sociology is a relatively recent addition to the scholarly world, its roots can be traced back to the writings of Plato and Aristotle. Philosophers were already then speculating about societies—comparing one with another and trying to understand the forces that shaped them.

The more immediate origins of modern sociology, however, lie in the sixteenth, seventeenth, and eighteenth centuries. This was a period in which the peoples of western Europe, especially the educated minority, were confronted with a tremendous amount of new information that could not be assimilated into traditional belief systems. They learned that the earth was not, as they had long supposed, the center of the universe. And they also learned, through the discovery of whole new continents populated by peoples with cultures radically different from their own, that western Europe was not the center of the earth. At the same time, European societies were themselves changing. The Protestant Reformation had divided western Europe, and the bitter religious wars that followed undermined much of the moral and intellectual authority of the clergy. Meanwhile, urban populations were growing in size and influence. All this led to the questioning of older theories and to renewed speculation about the nature of human life.

Among the consequences were two more or less independent developments, which laid the foundation for modern sociology. The first of these was the revival of interest in the systematic study of man and society, fostered by writers such as Thomas Hobbes, John Locke, A. R. J. Turgot, Jean-Jacques Rousseau, Adam Ferguson, John Millar, Adam Smith, and Thomas Malthus. Before the eighteenth century ended, these men and others had established the independence of social theory from theology and had laid the foundations of the modern social sciences. Some of them even went so far as to identify the phenomenon of sociocultural evolution— long before Darwin's day—and to formulate explanations for it.[18]

During this same period, others began making systematic, quantitative studies of various social phenomena. Birth and death rates were an early object of research; later there were studies of class, family income, jury verdicts, election results, and a variety of other phenomena. Sometimes those who were involved in developing theory were also involved in research, though usually this was not the case. By the end of the century, the quantitative tradition was firmly established; ties to theory were still imperfectly developed, but a basis had been established for the eventual integration of these two essentials of science: theory and research.[19]

The term "sociology" first appeared in the 1830s in the writings of a Frenchman, Auguste Comte. As a result, Comte is often referred to as the founder of modern sociology. This is an unmerited honor, however, since his writings were in an already established tradition and his own contributions were not that important.

The most famous nineteenth-century sociologist, and the most influential in his own day, was an Englishman, Herbert Spencer. Through his writings, which were translated into nearly all of the major languages, he brought sociology to the attention of the educated classes throughout the world. Like others before him, Spencer was profoundly interested in sociocultural evolution, though he saw it as merely one manifestation of a universal cosmic process linking the physical, biotic, and human worlds. Interest in evolution was stimulated even more in that period by the writings of Charles Darwin, a contemporary of Spencer.

Karl Marx was another major contributor to the study of human societies in the nineteenth century. Unlike Spencer, he stood apart from the emerging discipline of sociology, with the result that the relevance of his work to the discipline went unrecognized for many years. With the passage of time, however, this has changed. One reason has been the belated appreciation of the importance of the material base of human life—people's need for food, shelter, and the like, and the techniques for meeting these needs. Marx also called attention to the ubiquity of conflict in human societies and its role in producing social change.

Ironically, despite its European origins, sociology found more rapid acceptance in the United States. A number of leading American universities established professorships even before the end of the century, and by the early decades of the twentieth century, many institutions had established full-fledged departments of sociology. During the period between the two world wars, sociology continued to expand in the United States but declined in Europe, partly because of attacks by totalitarian governments, especially in Germany and the Soviet Union, partly because of greater resistance to change and innovation by the faculties of European universities. As a result, sociology became primarily an American enterprise.

Following World War I, sociology underwent a number of important changes. Under American leadership the discipline became increasingly concerned with contemporary American society. Interest in other societies declined, as did interest in the historical dimension of human experience. To a large extent these changes reflected the desire of a new generation of sociologists to make the discipline more scientific. The result was a greatly heightened interest in field research,

especially studies of local communities and their problems—crime, poverty, divorce, juvenile delinquency, illegitimacy, prostitution, the problems of immigrants, and so forth.

With this shift in interest, sociologists gradually abandoned the earlier evolutionary approach. In part, this was because of criticisms leveled against it, but primarily it was because the older approach seemed irrelevant to the concerns of the newer generation. Sociologists were forced to find a substitute for evolutionary theory—some new theoretical approach that could organize the growing but diffuse body of information on American society. By the late 1930s, *structural-functional* theory emerged as the apparent successor to evolutionary theory.

Structural-functional analysis is, in effect, the sociological counterpart of anatomy and physiology in biology. Like anatomists, structural-functionalists are concerned with the identification and labeling of the many different parts of the things they study and with the structural relations among them (e.g., the structural patterns formed within business organizations, families, etc.). Like physiologists, they are interested in the functions each of the parts performs. Just as physiologists are concerned with the functions of organs, such as the liver, heart, and spleen, structural-functionalists are interested in the functions of institutions, such as the family, and of moral rules, such as the taboo against incest. The theory has been criticized, however, for its emphasis on order and stability, and its relative neglect of conflict and change.

Since World War II, sociology has grown substantially not only in the United States but also in Europe, Japan, and Canada, and it has begun to take root in other areas as well. During the Stalin era, sociology was outlawed throughout the communist world. Later, however, restrictions were removed and there is now a lively interest in the subject throughout eastern Europe and even in China. This growth of sociology in other countries has reduced the unhealthy concentration of the discipline in the United States that characterized the decades of the 1930s and 1940s.

Another notable development has been the movement of sociology beyond the confines of the academic community. Prior to the 1940s, sociologists were employed almost entirely by universities and colleges. Beginning in World War II and continuing to the present, there has been a growing demand for their services by government, industry, and other kinds of organizations.

Several research traditions are active in sociology today. Foremost among them are: (1) symbolic interaction/constructionism; (2) structural-functionalism; (3) Marxist/conflict; and (4) ecology/evolutionism. The first is primarily concerned with microsociological issues and focuses on the means by which individuals make sense of their social situations. The second, as we have already noted, is primarily concerned with the mutual interdependence of the parts of societies. Marxist/conflict theorists, on the other hand, emphasize societal conflict and the role it plays in transforming societies. Ecological-evolutionary theory, the theory that guides this book, focuses on the relationships between the parts of society and how the relationships of societies to their environments (both social and biophysical) are affected by and affect their development.

Our advocacy of the ecological-evolutionary perspective is based, in part, on the fact that it incorporates valuable elements from each of the other perspectives. It is concerned with interdependence and order (structural-functionalism) as well as conflict and change (Marxist/conflict); and it provides an understanding of the changing social *context* within which people interact and create a meaningful world (symbolic interactionism/constructionism). More important, it is not simply an eclectic or uncritical blend of these elements; it provides an integrative framework that enables one to see the relations among all of the varied aspects of human societies. In fact, as will become apparent in the following chapters (especially Chapters 10 through 16), one of its distinguishing characteristics is its view of industrial societies and their future prospects; it is neither as pessimistic about present social conditions, nor as optimistic about their future possibilities, as are many Marxist/conflict theories.*

Despite continuing disagreements, sociology has made substantial progress. In our view, two of the more important developments have been the increasing use of quantitative techniques and the revival of interest in *macrosociology*. The first of these was a natural outgrowth of efforts to achieve greater precision in describing social phenomena and greater rigor in analysis. This trend was given an enormous boost by the invention of computers, which enable researchers to handle large amounts of data and carry out complex statistical analyses that would otherwise be impossible.

The revival of interest in macrosociology has come about for a number of reasons. Above all, there is a growing recognition that the most pressing problems of our time—war, the distress of Third World nations, the problem of poverty, environmental degradation—are all macroorganizational problems that require macrosociological theory and research if solutions are to be found. Moreover, there is a growing recognition that many microorganizational problems and develop-

ments—the changing role of women, the changing nature of the family, "globalization," immigration and cultural diversity in industrial societies—cannot be understood adequately, or dealt with effectively, unless they are viewed within the context of broader societal trends. One response to this renewal of interest in macrosociology has been a revival of interest in societal development and change and the formulation of ecologically oriented developmental theories of the kind that provides the foundation and framework for the present volume.[20]

Sociology and the Other Social Sciences

The study of human societies has never been exclusively a sociological concern. All the social sciences have been involved in one way or another. Most of the others, however, have focused on some particular aspect of the subject. Economics and political science limit themselves to a single institutional area. Human geography studies the impact of the physical and biotic environments on societies. Social psychology is concerned with the impact of society on the behavior and personality of individuals.**

Only sociology and anthropology have been concerned with human societies *per se*. That is to say, only these two disciplines have interested themselves in the full range of social phenomena, from the family to the nation and from technology to religion. And only these two have sought to understand societies as entities in their own right.

In matters of research, there has been a fairly well-established division of labor between sociology and anthropology. Sociologists have, for the most part, studied industrial societies; anthropologists have concentrated on preliterate societies. This division of labor has made good sense, since the skills needed to study a remote tribe in the mountains of New Guinea are very different from those needed to study a modern industrial society.

From the standpoint of teaching and the development of theory, however, the separation of sociology and anthropology has been far less satisfactory. Many problems, especially those involving long-term evolutionary processes, require the contributions of both disciplines. Ignoring either leads to incomplete analyses and biased interpretations. As a consequence, there has been a long tradition of intellectual "borrowing"

---

*The chapters that follow contain both descriptions and explanations. It is worth noting, therefore, that even where there is some disagreement among scholars about *why* certain features exist or develop, there is general agreement about *what* features exist. Theories may provide different explanations of the "facts" in these cases, but generally agree on what they are.

**It should be noted that social psychology is a hybrid that can be found in both sociology and psychology departments. In sociology departments the emphasis tends to fall on the impact of the group on the behavior of individuals, whereas social psychologists in psychology departments are more concerned with questions concerning the determinants of personality and the impact of various personality types on group performance.

between sociology and anthropology, and this volume stands in that tradition.

With the revival of evolutionary theory, scholars in these fields came to recognize that both disciplines were neglecting agrarian societies—those societies that occupy the middle range in the evolutionary scale between primitive preliterate societies and modern industrial societies. More recently, therefore, both sociologists and anthropologists have undertaken research on these societies in Southeast Asia, the Middle East, and Latin America.

The growing concern with agrarian societies has also led to increased cooperation between sociologists and historians. Since history is the study of written records of the past, historians are the experts on agrarian societies of earlier centuries. Much of the older work by historians, with its heavy emphasis on the names and dates of famous people and events, is of limited value to students of human societies. But that discipline has been changing too, and historians today are much more concerned with the social processes and patterns that underlie the more dramatic, but often less significant, events on which their predecessors focused. As a result history and sociology have become more valuable to each other.

This trend toward interdisciplinary cooperation is evident today in all the social sciences, and even beyond. Scholars are coming to recognize that no discipline is sufficient unto itself. To the degree that any field cuts itself off from others, it impoverishes itself intellectually. Conversely, to the degree that it communicates with other disciplines, it enriches itself and them.

2
Human Societies as Sociocultural Systems

One of the fascinations of human societies is their diversity. In any other social species, despite some variation caused by differences in their environments, one society is remarkably like the next in size, complexity, and the activities of its members. This is hardly surprising, of course, in view of the fact that one society is also remarkably like the next in its genetic heritage and that this heritage determines the great majority of the species' characteristics.

Why, then, are human societies, which *also* have similar genetic heritages, so different from one another in so many ways? Why are some huge and organizationally complex, while others are small and simple? And why are the activities of their members often so varied? Why, for example, are the members of some societies warlike, while the members of others are relatively peaceful? Why are some puritanical in relations between the sexes, while others are much more permissive?

The explanation of the tremendous variations among human societies is that their common genetic heritage enables them to develop very different cultural heritages. Without their cultures, human societies, too, would all be essentially alike. But with culture comes an extraordinary potential for diversity.

Because our societies, unlike those of other species, have both a social *and* a cultural dimension, sociologists and other social scientists often refer to them as **sociocultural** systems. This contraction of the two words is partly a convenience. But it is more than that: it is a reminder that the social and cultural aspects of human life are inextricably intertwined.

HUMAN SOCIETIES AS SYSTEMS

The term **system,** which we have just linked with "sociocultural" and which appears frequently in sociological writing, is a simple word with a profound meaning. It can be applied to a wide variety of things, many of them in the world of nature. There are physical systems, such as the solar system, star systems, weather systems, and systems of lakes and rivers. Every living organism is a system. And there are systems *within* organisms (digestive, reproductive, etc.), systems *of* organisms (**populations, societies**), and systems that include organisms and their environments (**ecosystems**). Then there are the systems created by humans: mechanical systems (cars, pianos), political systems, linguistic systems, mathematical systems, irrigation systems, and transportation systems. In every instance, "system" refers to *an entity made up of interrelated parts*.

The key word in this definition is "interrelated." In the words of one expert, a system is a "bundle of relations."[1] For this reason, what happens to one of the component parts of a system has implications for other parts and for the system as a whole. Too much beer in the stomach has repercussions for the brain, for example, just as the alignment of an automotive system's wheels affects its steering. Francis Thompson, the poet, captured the systemic qualities of the universe itself in his line "Thou canst not stir a flower without troubling of a star."[2]

Mechanical devices, such as a watch, are nearly "perfect"
systems.

The meaning of the concept *system* is best understood, however, if we focus on a smaller, more specific "bundle of relations," such as the mechanism of a watch. In working order, this entity is a mechanical system. Each of its components (gears, dial, hands, etc.) is also an entity—and each remains an entity even if the mechanism is dismantled. But when the relations among these components have been destroyed, the entity that is *the system* ceases to exist. A system, then, is clearly more than the sum of its parts: it is the sum of its parts *plus all of the relations among them*.

Systems vary greatly in the degree to which the functions of the parts are coordinated with one another and with the functioning of the system as a whole. Using this as a criterion, mechanical systems are some of the most nearly "perfect" systems known. Consider the watch mechanism again. Each component exists, and each functions, for one purpose only: the purpose for which *the system* exists and functions (i.e., to mark the passage of time). Moreover, each component relates only to the other parts of its own system, and its operation is totally dependent upon theirs.

It should come as no surprise, then, to note that, insofar as *systemic* qualities are concerned, the societies of some species resemble a watch more than they resemble human societies. The activities that go on in the honeybee's social system, for example, are as beautifully coordinated as gears and dials: they all serve the interests of the system (i.e., the society as a whole) and demonstrate a nearly total interdependence among the parts. The bee's genetic heritage is clearly a blueprint for a harmonious social system.*

The situation is quite different in human societies. For one thing, the coordination among their component parts is often poor. For another, their components do not always function in ways that are conducive to the well-being of the system itself (i.e., the society). For example, their members are individualistic and often self-assertive, resist efforts to coordinate and control their behavior, and do not readily subordinate their needs to the needs of the group. In short, a genetic blueprint that is very different from the honeybee's, but just as compelling, *prevents* human societies from achieving the strict ordering of relations that characterizes some systems.

There must, however, be enough **cooperation** among the members of a human society, and the various parts of the system must function smoothly enough, for *the basic needs of the system itself* to be met. The alternative is the dissolution of that "bundle of relations" that is the society.

This creates problems, because the needs of the system and those of its members are not necessarily the same. For example, an individual does not have to have children in order to satisfy his or her basic survival needs, but a society is doomed if it fails to produce new members to replace each older generation as it dies off. Similarly, individuals can violate their society's laws and moral codes and survive, even prosper; but no society can endure unless it fights such violations and keeps antisocial and disruptive behavior in check.

In response to the multiplicity of needs of both individuals and societies, untold numbers of social and cultural answers have evolved. Although these answers have always been imperfect, they are fascinating in their diversity and complexity.

THE FIVE BASIC COMPONENTS OF HUMAN SOCIETIES

To understand how these social and cultural answers develop, we need to consider the five basic components that are present in every human society: (1) **population,** (2) **culture,** (3) **material products,** (4) **social organization,** and (5) **social institutions.** Although we will examine each one separately, these components cannot actually be isolated from one another. Because they exist only in interaction with one another in a society, it is impossible to discuss any one of them without reference to the rest. We will, however, disentangle them as best we can.

Population

Population, the first basic component of society, is a term that refers to *the members of a society considered collectively.* In analyzing human societies, there are three aspects of population that must be taken into account: (1) the **genetic constants,** (2) the **genetic variables,** and (3) the **demographic variables.**

Genetic Constants   The genetic constants of a population are those characteristics that reflect our species' *common genetic heritage.* As the word "constants" implies, these traits are the same for every society and, for all practical purposes, the same from one generation to the next.

---

*Virtually all members of bee, ant, and wasp (*Hymenoptera*) societies are sisters who because of their reproductive process **(haplodiploidy)** share three-fourths of their genes. Thus their individual biological interests (preserving and passing on their genes) are largely indistinguishable from their collective interest (survival of the group). In contrast, the most closely related humans (other than identical twins)—parents and their children, and siblings—share only one-half of their genes, aunts/uncles and nieces/nephews one-quarter, cousins one-eighth, and others even less. It is not surprising, therefore, that there is a greater divergence of "interests" and a greater potential for conflict in human societies.

Specifying the genetically based traits that are shared by people everywhere is not an easy task. First, there is simply no way that scientists can observe and study the biological component of human life without cultural influences getting in the way.

The second problem in drawing up a list of our common genetic traits lies in the complexity of genetics itself. Scientists are still a very long way from fully understanding the subject. One thing that is clear, however, is that most observable traits—for example, a physical characteristic or behavioral tendency—do not result from the action of a single gene, but rather from the interaction of *a number of different genes*. Any given gene, meanwhile, usually affects not just a single trait, but a *number of different traits*. To compound the problem further, the influence of genes on development can be modified by environmental factors.

Several illustrations may help to make the complexity of the problem clear. First, despite much debate it is still not clear whether the difference in performance of men and women on certain kinds of aptitude tests (e.g., spatial reasoning) is the result of early cultural influences, of genetics, or of some combination of the two. Similarly, sexual orientation, long considered to be entirely the product of cultural influences, is now suspected of being, at least in part, the result of hormonal influences on the fetus during pregnancy. And schizophrenia, autism, and other mental and emotional illnesses once blamed entirely on poor parenting and other cultural factors may have a basis in genetics and fetal development.[3]

Obviously, there is a great deal we do not understand about the influence of genes on human life. We know enough, however, to put to rest the once-popular **"tabula rasa"** hypothesis.[4] Proponents of this view claimed that the minds of newborn infants are like blank slates, totally devoid of content, and that human thought and action are due entirely to social and cultural influences experienced after birth.

This idea has long had great appeal because, if it were true, it should be possible for careful social planning to eliminate most of the ills of the world. If societies can make people selfish, cruel, and aggressive, they should also be able to make them kind, compassionate, and caring.

Today, however, after more than a century of disappointments resulting from efforts to fundamentally alter human behavior, and because of insights provided by the new sciences of genetics and primatology, it is clear that people and their societies are profoundly influenced by the genetic heritage of our species *as well as* by their cultures.[5] The unattractive aspects of human life, no less than the attractive ones, inevitably reflect this ancient evolutionary heritage and seem destined to remain a part of the human scene for a long time to come.*

With these cautions and considerations in mind, what can be said about the genetic constants?

First, *all humans have the same basic needs*. These include such obvious physical requirements as the need for food, water, sleep, warmth, and oxygen—needs that must be satisfied for people merely to survive. Individuals also need to be a part of some society. This is especially important during the early formative years: human babies are born in a state of extreme immaturity and helplessness compared with most other animals. In fact, during the first year their physical development includes processes such as brain growth and bone hardening that are part of the *fetal* development of other primates.**[6] Maturation proceeds at an unusually slow pace, and humans require a much longer time than members of other species to reach maturity and the greater "self-sufficiency" that adulthood brings. But even as adults, they are still dependent on society.

---

*This does not mean, of course, that nothing can be done about the unpleasant aspects of human behavior. Every society takes steps to discourage and suppress them, but both modern history and our knowledge of genetics indicate that there are limits to what societies can achieve in this regard (e.g., see Chapter 15).

**The reason humans enter the world in this immature state is apparently due to brain size. At birth the human brain is only 23 percent of its adult size, whereas for chimpanzees and rhesus monkeys it is 41 percent and 65 percent, respectively.[7] If human infants were to develop in the womb the additional months it would take for them to become more mature, their greater head size would make birth impossible.

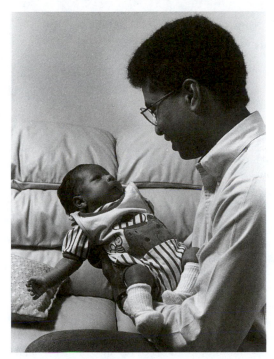

Human babies are born in a state of extreme immaturity and helplessness compared with most other animals: a father and one-month-old son.

In addition, there are a variety of other genetically based **drives** whose satisfaction, while not essential for survival, motivate the actions of individuals. These vary in importance and intensity from individual to individual and from stage to stage within the life cycle. They include such things as our sexual drive, our need for play, the need for new experience, and the need for respect and affection from others.*[8]

Second, *the members of every society have the same basic physiological resources for satisfying their needs and desires*. These include such obvious things as eyes, ears, hands, legs, teeth, bowels, heart, brain, and so on. The brain is an especially impressive resource: it provides us with the means of recording information equivalent to the content of a thousand twenty-four-volume sets of the *Encyclopaedia Britannica* and is far more densely packed with information than any computer.[10] In addition, we are genetically programmed for the automatic performance of a variety of activities (e.g., digestion, ovulation, circulation, growth) and have many invaluable reflexes and response sets (e.g., we automatically draw back without conscious thought when touching something hot).

Third, because of their genetic heritage *humans are motivated to optimize pleasurable experiences and minimize painful and unpleasant experiences*. This is a trait that we share with the rest of the animal world. Although an individual's definition of pleasure and of pain may be modified to some degree by experience (see point 5 below), the extent to which this is possible is usually quite limited.

Fourth, in their activities, *humans economize most of the time, seeking the optimal return for their expenditure of resources*.[11] This is because their needs and desires almost always

---

*Newborn infants, for example, have a decided preference for visual variety and contrast in their surroundings and a "bias to explore" that is manifest from the moment of birth. Newborns also have such a powerful need for social contact and the stimulation it provides that when this is denied, their health often suffers and they may even die.[9]

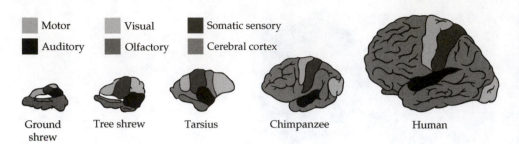

Source: J. R. Napier, Nature, vol. 196, pp. 409–411.

FIGURE 2.1 *The human brain is an impressive resource: it can record as much information as 1,000 twenty-four-volume sets of the* Encyclopaedia Britannica. *Compare the size of the cortex of humans with that of other primates.*

exceed their resources. Thus, to maximize the satisfaction of needs and desires, economizing is essential, especially when the costs involved are high. Failure to observe this basic principle can only lead to frustration, disappointment, and unfulfilled needs and desires.

Fifth, *humans have an immense capacity for learning, and for modifying their behavior in response to what they learn.* Learning is not merely a process of remembering what happened and when; it is also a process of evaluation based on the association of things and events with experiences of pleasure and pain. Patterns of action that prove painful tend not to be repeated while those that are pleasurable tend to be reinforced. Because of their remarkable capacity for learning, humans enjoy far more freedom from the constraints imposed by genetically programmed behaviors that so restrict the lives of most animals. Thus, they are able to devise alternative patterns of action for most of the situations that confront them—a fact that has proved both a blessing and a curse.

Sixth, *humans everywhere develop a variety of derivative needs and desires that reflect their experiences as members of society.* Because these experiences vary from society to society and from individual to individual within a given society, the nature and intensity of our derivative needs also vary. All of us, however, tend to develop at a minimum the need or desire to possess things, to give and receive affection, to express ourselves, to be respected, to have emotional and aesthetic experiences, and to discern order and meaning in our lives.

Seventh, *humans have the capacity to create and use symbol systems and to develop cultures.* This uniquely human ability is dependent on a variety of genetically based attributes, including such organs of speech as lips, tongue, palate, sinuses, and vocal cords. Equally important, however, are peculiarities of the human brain, specifically those areas of the cerebral cortex that control speech and abstract thought (see Figure 2.1).[12] Most linguists now believe that, despite the many differences among the 3,000 spoken languages humans employ, there is a single underlying structure that is shared by all and is part of our common genetic heritage.[13]

Eighth, *our species' heritage includes powerful emotions and appetites inherited from distant prehuman ancestors.* The structure of our brain reflects its long evolutionary heritage. This is because as new components developed they did not replace, but were entwined with and added on to, existing ones. Thus, the highest level, the cerebral cortex, which houses our ability to reason, is layered around and interconnected with the more primitive levels, which house our emotions. The precise nature of the relations between these components has yet to be determined, but it is obvious that our actions and thoughts are often powerfully influenced—both positively and negatively—by such emotions as fear, love, and rage.*[14]

---

*This helps explain why advertisements for everything from automobiles and beer to politicians so often appeal to emotions rather than to reason. Advertisers are betting millions that emotions will override reason when people make purchasing and voting decisions.

Ninth, and finally, *humans have a highly developed sense of self and are powerfully motivated to put their own needs and desires ahead of those of others, especially when the stakes are high*.[15] In part, especially early in life, this is instinctive and genetic, but it is also a product of learning.* No two individuals can possibly share exactly the same set of experiences over the course of their lives, and since experience shapes both our values and our perceptions of ourselves, a highly developed awareness of self and self-serving behavior become unavoidable. As recognition of this gradually penetrates our consciousness, the distinction between self and others grows increasingly salient. Meanwhile we are discovering that actions that are pleasurable to others are not always pleasurable to ourselves, and *vice versa*.

Because of this divergence of interests, competition and conflict are endemic in human societies, though their form, intensity, and nature vary depending on circumstances. This does not prevent us from cooperating with one another, since most of us discover in infancy and early childhood that the benefits of cooperation usually exceed the costs. Thus, enlightened self-interest ensures a substantial amount of cooperation in every human society.

As many great novelists and poets have recognized, however, a powerful tension is built into the very fabric of human life: *Homo sapiens* is, by nature, both a social animal and an individualistic, self-centered animal. It is this more than anything else that creates the drama in human life, and the uncertainties. And it is this which justifies one early sociologist's characterization of human societies as systems of "antagonistic cooperation."[16]

Genetic Variables   In addition to the core of traits which all humans share and which make up the major portion of everyone's genetic heritage, each of us also has thousands of genes that are absent, or occur in somewhat different forms, in other individuals. Because these genes are not distributed equally among societies and their populations, there are *variable* aspects to the genetic heritage of human societies. These include skin color, hair texture, eye shape, blood type, incidence of color blindness, taste sensitivity, and susceptibility to various diseases, to name a few of those that have been identified thus far.[17] The *direct* impact of these variables on the life of human societies appears to have been of limited importance. However, because of social and cultural responses to them, such as ethnic **stereotyping** and **prejudice,** their indirect effects have often been substantial.

Although prior to the modern era human populations in different regions of the world had no direct contact with one another and therefore could not interbreed for long periods, no fully human group was ever isolated long enough, or became genetically differentiated enough, to become a separate species. During prolonged periods of isolation, however, human populations did become genetically differentiated in a number of highly visible ways, such as skin, hair, and eye color; hair type; body build; and shape of face and head. These differences, which tend to be interrelated, eventually became the basis of our modern concept of race. A *race* is simply a part of the human population in which some combination of these highly visible traits occurs with a frequency that is appreciably different from that of other parts of the human population. Racial differences, it may be noted, are found in many species, not just in humans.[18]

Members of modern societies often have difficulty appreciating the adaptive value of racial characteristics, because we no longer depend on them for our survival or well-being. When we encounter unpleasantly strong sunlight, for example, we adapt *culturally:* we create artificial shade or we apply artificial "pigment" to our eyes (sunglasses) and to our skin (suntan oil). Throughout most of human history, however, a population's *genetic* attributes were its primary means of adapting to the hazards of its environment, and even minor variations in

---

*The genetic basis of this becomes obvious when we compare human societies with the societies of the social insects.

Human populations became genetically differentiated in a number of highly visible ways during prolonged periods when interbreeding was not possible: compare the height, body build, hair type, and skin color of the Eskimo with the Masai tribesman from Kenya.

relevant characteristics, such as the ability to store body fat as an insulation against extreme cold, could determine which individuals survived and which did not.

This explains why many genetic variables, from skin color to body and facial form, are not randomly distributed across the globe, but occur in discernible geographical patterns.[19] For example, the pigment in our skin determines how dark it is and protects underlying cells from exposure to ultraviolet light. Darker skin is universal in hot, sunny regions, with the heaviest pigmentation of all in the African Sudan, where solar radiation is the most intense and constant.[20] In contrast, light pigmentation in countries with limited sunshine facilitates the synthesis of vitamin D, which protects a person against rickets.[21]

The "sickling gene," found chiefly in populations of Africa, the Middle East, and India, in areas where a particularly deadly form of malaria occurs, provides a somewhat different illustration of the adaptive value of genetic variables. An individual who inherits this gene from *both* parents will develop sickle-cell anemia, a disease that is normally fatal before adulthood. But a far greater number of people in the population inherit the gene from only one parent, develop only mild symptoms of the anemia, and are highly resistant to certain virulent forms of malaria. As a result, in areas with a high incidence of malaria, the sickling gene has had great adaptive value: more individuals derive a benefit—resistance to malaria—

than suffer a cost—death from sickle-cell anemia—and the trait, therefore, persists in the population.[22]

Most genetic variables are not as easy to identify as the ones we have discussed so far. This is because most of our characteristics result from the action of more than one gene and are not determined by genes alone. Genes provide the potential, but the reality is determined by the interaction of genes and environment. Complicating matters, environment also includes the intrauterine environment of the prenatal period, even the preconception experience of sperm and egg. This interaction of genetics and environment has been dramatically illustrated many times, as in the case of Jewish children born in Israeli kibbutzim and Japanese children born in America who, because of better diets, tower over parents born in the ghettos of Europe and in Japan. It is clear that most biological characteristics, from longevity to musical aptitude, are shaped by both genes and environment. But so far, at least, efforts to separate the two and measure their relative influence have proved frustrating and unprofitable.

One thing has been clarified, however: the relation between racial and nonracial genetic variables. Studies have been made, for example, of color blindness and blood characteristics, which are variables that can be precisely identified and are minimally affected by environmental factors, and whose gene frequency in a population can therefore be accurately calculated. When the distributions of these genes are plotted geographically, they cut across racial lines. For example, the frequency of the gene for type B blood is essentially the same among the south Chinese, Russians, and west Africans.[23] Findings like these make it clear that the traits used to define race are an extremely limited set of variables that are not correlated to any appreciable degree with other genetic variables that have been carefully analyzed.[24]

Demographic Variables   The demographic properties of a population include such things as its size, its density, how it is dispersed or concentrated (e.g., to what extent its members are concentrated in a few areas or spread out more evenly over its entire territory), the patterns of migration into and out of the society, its composition in terms of age and sex, and its birth and death rates. These characteristics, like certain clusters of genes, vary from one society to another. But these variations, unlike most genetic variations, have direct, demonstrable, and far-reaching consequences for human societies.

Population size is the most variable of the demographic properties of human societies, which have ranged in numbers from 20 members or less (in some preliterate societies of the recent past) to more than 1.3 billion (China's current population). Variations in other demographic characteristics often appear insignificant beside such variations in size. For example, two societies with stable populations (i.e., neither growing in size nor declining) and with annual death rates of 14 per 1,000 and 40 per 1,000, respectively, may not seem very different. But this variation actually means that the average life expectancy at birth of the members of the first society is seventy-one years, and of the second only twenty-five years!

In later chapters we will have frequent occasion to consider demographic variables, since they play an important part in the evolution of human societies. By contrast, we will have very little to say from here on about the genetic variables discussed in the previous section, since there is little to indicate that they have played a significant role in societal evolution.

Culture

The second basic component of every sociocultural system is **culture,** *a society's **symbol systems** and the information they convey.* As we saw in Chapter 1, **symbols** are information conveyers that enable us to handle information in ways that are impossible for other creatures. We can *extract* more information from an experience (i.e., learn more) because symbols permit us thought processes denied other species. We can also *share* more information, because symbols enable us to express so much of the subtlety, complexity, and diversity of our experiences. We can, in fact, do more with information *whatever* is involved: in recording it, accumulating it, storing it, combining it, or applying it, symbol users have a fantastic advantage over signal users.

The symbol systems and store of information that comprise a society's culture are like a foundation laid down by previous generations. Because each new generation has this base on which to build, it can avoid repeating many of the experiences of earlier generations. If a group has already learned how to make and use fire, or invented the plow, or devised a system of numbers, its members need not repeat the time-consuming and often difficult process by which that particular element of culture was first acquired. Instead, they can address new challenges, which may result in further enrichment or modification of their culture.

We will examine both of the basic parts of culture in some detail, beginning with symbol systems.

Symbol Systems   The most basic symbol systems in any society are its spoken **languages.*** No matter how many other symbol systems a society creates, these are the ones that bear the major burden of transmitting information among them.

At the heart of every spoken language is an enormous set of social conventions, or customary practices, that constitute its vocabulary and grammar. The vocabulary is a set of sounds with meanings attached to them, and the relationship between a sound and its meaning is embedded in the history of its use by those who share that language. To those who speak English, the word "bed" means a place to sleep, not because of any logical or necessary connection between the sound and the activity, but because this is the convention that has evolved in English-speaking populations. Similarly, grammatical conventions tell us how words must be combined if they are to be meaningful and intelligible to others. Thus, it means one thing to say, "The bear ate Jack," something quite different to say, "Jack ate the bear," and nothing at all to say, "The ate bear Jack."

Until we study a foreign language, most of us have the impression that there is something natural—even inevitable—about the way our own society and its language separate experience and thought into the bits of meaning we call words, and that learning another language is only a matter of learning the sounds another society applies to those same "units of experience." Yet as people conversant in two or more languages are well aware, words in one do not necessarily have a simple equivalent in the other. Americans and Russians were reminded of this some years ago during talks between President Kennedy and Chairman Khrushchev. Kennedy repeatedly said that the Russians should not miscalculate the will and intentions of the American people, and every time the word "miscalculate" was translated, Khrushchev flushed angrily. Kennedy later learned that the Russian language has no precise equivalent of this word, and the translator had seized on a Russian word, normally applied to a small child or uneducated person, meaning "unable to count." Khrushchev naturally assumed that Kennedy was implying he was not very bright!**[25]

One reason languages separate experience into different units is because the experiences of the people who *create* and *use* the languages are so different. For example, gauchos, the famous horsemen of the Argentine prairies, distinguish among 200 different colors of

---

*Many societies have, or have had, two or more languages. Even those with a single language have often had multiple dialects that were mutually unintelligible.

**In another incident during the "cold war," tensions between the Soviet Union and the United States were very high and focused on the city of Berlin where many feared World War III might break out at any moment. To assure citizens of Berlin that he and the United States supported them, President Kennedy said, "Ich bin ein Berliner," thinking he was saying "I am a Berliner." Unfortunately inserting the article "ein" into the sentence changed its meaning, and what he said, literally, was "I am a jelly doughnut"![26]

horses, but use only 4 words for all the plants known to them: *pasto,* fodder; *paja,* bedding; *cardo,* wood; and *yuyos,* all others.[27] Meanwhile, the Inuit (Eskimo) use numerous expressions to refer to the various phenomena that we call simply "snow." For instance, they distinguish among dry-wind-driven snow, dry-packed-suitable-for-cutting-into-blocks-and-building-igloos snow, and ice-crust-surface snow.*[28] In yet another part of the world, the Dugum Dani, Stone Age horticulturists on the island of New Guinea, have seventy different words that refer to sweet potatoes, their staple crop,[30] and in the Middle East, Arabic is reputed to have a thousand expressions for "sword," indicative of that culture's stress on poetry and emphasis on synonyms and figures of speech.[31] English is a language rich in numbers and units of measurement, perfect for describing and recording mathematical and scientific data. In short, a language reflects the needs, concerns, and experiences of those who use it.

Another reason languages differ in the way they categorize and classify experience is the haphazard and spontaneous manner in which they evolve. Consider the evolution of the word "bureau," for example. A bureau was originally something made of baize, a thick green cloth. Because these bureaus were often put on writing tables and chests of drawers, the word was eventually extended to mean the furniture as well as the cloth. Later, because many government offices were equipped with bureaus, or writing tables, the offices themselves came to be known by that term (e.g., the Federal Bureau of Investigation).[32]

This process of change in language is so much a matter of chance that it is unlikely that the same pattern would occur in two societies. Even if two societies begin with the same language, as when a small group separates from the parent group to settle a new territory, linguistic differences are bound to develop unless an extremely high level of communication is maintained between them. There is no better example of this in the modern era than in the differences between English as it is spoken in England, Australia, Canada, Jamaica, and the United States. To Australians, for example, "Don't come the raw prawn" means "Don't try to put one over on me," and "Fair and dinkum" means "True and honest."

So far we have discussed spoken language as if it were merely a neutral and passive vehicle for transmitting information. But as political leaders, propagandists, and advertisers have long recognized, individual words often acquire, through the process of association, powerful emotional connotations that enable them to convey more than is embodied in their formal definitions. Words like "communist," "racist," and "sexist," for example, have such strong negative associations for many Americans that they respond unthinkingly to the emotional content of these symbols. Words can also acquire strong positive associations, and these, too, may be used to manipulate emotions. For example, linking kinship terms with organizations, as in "Mother Russia," "Mother Church," or "Uncle Sam," can stimulate warm feelings of affection.

Supplementing its spoken language, every society uses conventional gestures and facial expressions whose meanings are evident to members of the group. This second kind of symbol system, **body language,** should not be confused with such facial expressions and body movements as our involuntary reaction when we touch something hot, or the way we pucker up when we taste something bitter. These are genetically determined signals. True body language is symbolic, just as words are, for the form and meaning of the gestures and expressions are determined by those who use them. Consider, for example, the shrug of the shoulders. Various groups use it to convey indifference, uncertainty, or a lack of information on the subject in question, with the specific meaning being indicated by the context in which it is used.[33]

A third kind of symbol system in many societies is *written language,* a relatively recent development in human history. Some of the oldest written records in existence today were

---

*It is worth noting that these are not really different words but complex combinations of terms.[29] The point being made, however, is simply that these differences in snow are of considerable importance for Inuit life, whereas they attract little attention in a society practicing a different technology.

*Two sides of a limestone tablet found in Iraq, bearing some of
the oldest known writing (about 3500 B.C.). Included are
symbols for head, hand, foot, threshing sledge, and several
numerals.*

prepared thousands of years ago by temple authorities in Mesopotamia to enable them to keep a record of business transactions.[34] These priests were stewards of their god's resources, and when they loaned out his animals or grain, it was imperative to get them back again. Even though the priest who made a loan might die, the god expected it to be repaid. To keep track of their god's property and thereby avoid his wrath, the priestly community devised a primitive system of writing that involved a mixture of numerals, pictographs, and ideograms.

The arbitrary and symbolic nature of this writing is clear. Even when a pictograph (essentially a picture) was used to represent a bull, it was a stylized representation that excluded many of the animal's features that might have been included. Moreover, the same features were used consistently, indicating that conventional forms of notation had already been established. From a very early date, the pictograph of a jar came to represent a certain quantity of grain, rather than the jar itself. And finally, among these early examples of writing are a number of ideograms, which are "pure" symbols, since they are completely arbitrary and based solely on convention. They lack any visual resemblance to the objects they represent, just as the dollar sign bears no resemblance to the currency it symbolizes.

As new uses for writing were discovered, new efforts were made to translate spoken language into written form. At an early date kings and princes recorded their military triumphs for posterity, priests their sacred rites and traditions. At first, as the Mesopotamian priests' experience makes clear, a society's written symbols could express only a small part of what was possible with its spoken symbols. Gradually, however, written languages developed until they were able to convey the same information as spoken ones, and writing came into its own as a means of storing information, for communication across the barriers of space and time, and eventually as a medium of artistic expression, education, and entertainment.

As societies have acquired more information, it has often become necessary to go beyond such basic symbols as letters and numerals. Thus, new symbol systems have evolved that greatly facilitate the handling of specialized kinds of information. For example, musicians devised musical notation so they could express the information that they create and use, and mathematicians and scientists developed a wide variety of symbol systems to express abstract ideas, complex numbers, and so on. The specialized symbol systems now found in modern societies include languages for the deaf, the blind, engineers, stenographers, computer scientists, and others too numerous to mention.

Over the course of history, the relative importance of the three basic types of language—body, spoken, and written—has altered considerably. Body language, including symbolic gestures and facial expressions, may well have been dominant among our very early ancestors, declining only when true speech evolved. Then, until quite recently, spoken symbols remained the primary means of transmitting information from one person to another and from one generation to the next. With the invention of the printing press and the subsequent spread of literacy, written language steadily increased in relative importance, largely because it could overcome space and time, the historic barriers to communication. During the last century, thanks to such devices as the telephone, radio, motion pictures, and television, spoken language, too, has overcome those barriers, altering the balance once again. And in the most recent, most dramatic development of all, a great variety of languages have been created for computers, enabling them to handle fantastic amounts of information of diverse kinds. More important than these shifts in the relative importance of different types of language, however, is the fundamental trend that has persisted from early prehistoric times: *the continuing expansion of old symbol systems and the creation of new ones have steadily increased the capacity of human societies to handle information.*

Information   Cultural information is *knowledge acquired through experience and conveyed through symbols.* A society's information is, in effect, a product of its experience: its experiences in the remote past and in the recent past; its experiences with its environment and within itself. Needless to say, no society's culture preserves every experience of every member throughout its entire history. Rather, a society gleans what it or its more influential members consider valuable and attempts to preserve it.

Because every society has a unique past, every culture is unique. We can say this another way: out of diverse experience, diverse information emerges. This means that human societies not only have different amounts of information on a given subject; they frequently have different "facts" as well. Since we know that human senses and intellect are limited and fallible, this should be no surprise. Even hard scientific "facts" must often be revised in the light of later research.

Cultural information is not limited to the kinds of ideas whose truth or accuracy is capable of being proved or disproved, however. It includes a group's total perception of reality: its ideas about what is real, what is true, what is good, what is beautiful, what is important, what is possible. When we discussed symbol systems, we saw that they, too, are so rooted in subjective experience that even individual symbols may become "units of experience"—which explains why a word like "mother" can be so emotionally charged. We also saw that the kind of information conveyed by symbol systems ranges from historical and statistical data to concepts of deity, attitudes toward horses and plants, characteristics of snow, poetic inclinations, even music itself. Cultural information includes, quite literally, *everything humans are capable of experiencing and able to convert into symbolic form.*

Because all human societies have certain fundamental kinds of experiences in common, because their members all have the same basic needs to satisfy, and because all societies have the same system needs, all cultures include information on certain basic subjects:

- Every culture has a substantial store of information about the **biophysical environment** to which the society must adapt, including its plant and animal life, its soils and terrain, its mineral resources and water supply, its climate and weather conditions.
- Every culture includes information about the group's social environment, the other human societies with which the group has contact.
- Every culture contains information about the society itself: its origin, its people, its heroes, its history.
- Every culture contains information that seeks to explain the ultimate causes of things and events.
- Every culture has information that enables the members to cope with recurring problems, from feeding themselves to resolving intragroup conflict.
- Every culture contains information that guides individuals in making judgments about what is good, what is right, and what is beautiful.
- Every culture has information created solely to satisfy culturally activated and intensified needs, such as the desire for artistic expression, for example, or for ritual.

All cultures contain information created solely to satisfy culturally activated and intensified needs, such as the desire for artistic expression and social rituals: Balinese dancers performing the sacred dance drama of The Witch and The Dragon.

Although this list is neither exhaustive nor detailed, it conveys something of the breadth of culture.

Much of the information contained in cultures is ideological in nature and results from efforts to make sense out of human experience.[35] For **ideology** *is information used to interpret experience and help order societal life.* Because humans are users of symbols and creatures of culture, life can be overwhelming. We think, feel, hope, enjoy, and suffer as no other creatures can. We imagine what we cannot know and yearn for what may not exist. We live simultaneously in three worlds: the past, the present, and the future. We alone, apparently, live out our lives aware that death is inevitable. To make things more difficult, we create for ourselves a profusion of cultural alternatives, in the face of which our genetic heritage is an inadequate guide. It is not surprising, therefore, that as individuals we need help in interpreting experience, finding meaning, and making choices. And, as we have seen, societies need help in regulating and ordering their collective life.

Medieval Christianity is a good example of a highly developed and comprehensive ideology, the kind that answers virtually all of these individual and societal needs. At its center was a vision of a universe inhabited by many kinds of spiritual beings (seraphim, cherubim, humans, demons, devils, etc.) mostly under the dominion of God. God was perceived as the King above all earthly kings, but because His authority was challenged by Satan, the prince of evil, people were confronted with a choice as to which to serve. Those who chose God (who would ultimately prevail) were obliged to accept the Church's doctrines and conform to its code of morality. The latter enjoined Christians to be charitable to one another, honest, sober, hardworking, monogamous (better yet, celibate), obedient to all in authority, and regular in devotions and worship. Since no one could adhere perfectly to these requirements, the Church provided opportunities for people to confess their sins, do penance, and obtain absolution.

When we look closely at medieval Christianity, we find the three basic elements that comprise *every* ideology. First, there is a system of **beliefs** about the kind of world we inhabit. Second, there is a system of general **moral values** that emanate from, or are justified by, those beliefs. Finally, there is a system of **norms** that apply those general values to specific situations and spell out how the members of the group are to act in various circumstances, what they should and should not do.

There are two basic kinds of norms in every society, and they have evolved in very different ways. Some are part of official or legal codes of conduct that are enforced by an authority, such as a government, a church, or other organization. We refer to such norms as *laws, regulations,* or *rules,* and they are sometimes accompanied by explicit statements of the sanctions that will be used to punish those who violate them. A city ordinance, for example, may specify a fine of $25 for littering streets or sidewalks.

In contrast, many norms are informal and unofficial, and violations of them are not officially sanctioned. Thus, every society and every subgroup in a society, from corporations to families, have many informal rules, or **customs,** which define for the members acceptable and unacceptable behavior. Customs apply to such diverse things as modes of dress, hairstyles, food preparation, the selection of marriage partners, the performance of various tasks, proper grammar, and attitudes toward children or older people—to name only a few. These informal norms are as important in shaping behavior as more formal ones. Norms and their related **sanctions** (i.e., rewards and punishments) are basic components of every system of social control.

Sometimes it is difficult to determine, or even to imagine, how certain elements of ideology originated, or what they can possibly tell us about the past experience of a society. This is true, for example, of one of the central beliefs of Hinduism, the belief in the sacredness of the cow. The boxed insert explains how this seemingly strange belief has, for centuries, helped the members of Indian society cope with some of their basic and recurring problems in a highly adaptive way.

In very small societies, all of the members usually have common beliefs and values. In larger and more complex societies, however, this is rarely the case. People in different occupational groups, different kinds of communities, and different classes have different interests and different experiences, and these inevitably lead to different beliefs, different values, and different norms. Not infrequently, these differences cause conflicts between the people involved. In extreme cases, as in modern Bosnia and the United States at the time of the Civil War, such conflicts may threaten the very existence of a society.

Another crucial body of information in every culture is **technology.** This is *information about how to use the material resources of the environment to satisfy human needs and desires.* Compared to ideology, technology seems rather prosaic and uninteresting. Historians and social scientists have tended to ignore it,[36] and until recently people seldom came to blows over the relative merits of different technologies. As we will see in coming chapters, however, the influence of technological information on the course of history and on the process of societal change and development has been greatly out of proportion to the recognition usually accorded it.

In every society, a large component of technological information concerns food: where and how to grow it or get it and how to process it for consumption or storage. There is also information about the other material resources available to the society and how they may be converted into useful forms—into fuel for heat, cooking, and other purposes; into clothing and shelter; into tools, weapons, ornaments, houses, factories, toys, and other things the group or its members need or value.

Because a distinctive body of information tends to build up in response to each set of human needs, we sometimes speak of various technologies in the same society, such as a military technology or a communications technology. Often, however, we speak of a society's technology in the singular, because there is an underlying unity to this store of information. The principles of **metallurgy,** for example, are used in virtually every area of technological activity in a modern industrial society.

India's Sacred Cows: The Adaptive Value of an Ideology

In a society where tens of millions of people go to sleep hungry every night, devout Hindus, who constitute the vast majority of India's population, would not dream of killing any of that country's 54 million cows. To a Hindu, even the killing of a human being is not thought to be as great a sacrilege as is the killing of a cow.

Marvin Harris, a leading proponent of ecological-evolutionary theory, examined this seeming paradox in an effort to find a rational explanation. He rejected the view that an ideology evolves arbitrarily, unrelated to the rest of societal life or to the experiences of its members in the past. Rather, he suspected that any belief that has been as widespread and as persistent as the Indian taboo against slaughtering cows for food must have significant adaptive value for the society.

In a book titled *Cows, Pigs, Wars and Witches: The Riddles of Culture*, Harris reported the results of an analysis of this subject. He found that the cow is of enormous economic value to the members of Indian society. A peasant's cow is, in effect, a factory that provides food (milk, butter); fertilizer; fuel for cooking (dried manure is excellent for this purpose, producing a clean, low heat); flooring material (a paste of manure and water hardens into a smooth surface that holds down dust and can be swept clean); and, most important of all, oxen to pull the peasant's plow. Harris also found that less than 20 percent of the food consumed by Indian cattle is edible by humans. In short, the cow converts substances of little worth to the peasant into extremely valuable products.

Although Indian peasants recognize that a living, productive cow is vastly more valuable to them and to their children than the same cow consumed as food, it would be only natural for them to ignore this fact when they are desperately hungry. The religious taboo against killing cows is a powerful cultural mechanism that helps to protect these animals even in times of famine and thereby preserves an invaluable resource. In short, Hinduism's conception of the cow as sacred is based on the experience of countless generations of the Indian people, and it has served them well.

Although it has caused some problems, especially in the industrial era, Hinduism's conception of the cow as sacred has served the Indian people well over the long course of their history.

Material Products

The third component of human societies consists of *the things they produce or obtain through trade*. These products of technology range from perishable items that are consumed within days or even hours, as with many foods, to things that endure for centuries, such as pyramids, cathedrals, and plastic containers. They range, too, from utilitarian objects like hammers and houses to frivolous items like boom boxes and Frisbees.

Energy is easily the most vital product of societal activity, since without a continuous input of it, all activity would come to a halt: even thought requires energy! Food is the most basic source of energy. In societies today the energy resources of food are supplemented by energy obtained from animals, from wind and water, and, in modern industrial societies, from mineral sources (coal, petroleum, natural gas, and uranium).

Many of the material products of human labor are meant only for consumption. Some, however, are created to facilitate the production of other products. These are known as **capital goods** and are a major determinant of a society's wealth. The more capital goods a society possesses, the more goods it is able to produce.

The first capital goods were simple tools and weapons made of stone, wood, and bone which enabled our early ancestors to produce such essentials as fire, food, shelter, and more tools and weapons. Later, as the store of cultural information increased and as new environmental resources became available, the character of tools changed. Metals became especially important because they combined strength and durability with malleability. With the domestication of animals, an important new kind of capital good was created. In more recent times, new and enormously productive capital goods have been created in the form of large industrial complexes that utilize sophisticated machines and instruments and are powered by the recently discovered **inanimate forms of energy.**

Social Organization

The fourth component of every society is *the network of relationships among its members*. These relationships make it possible for members to satisfy both their own individual needs and the needs of the society as a whole. The latter include the need to replace members who die or leave the group and to equip their successors with the many skills needed to make

Material products of culture that are used to produce other goods are known as capital goods: a paper manufacturing plant on the Penobscot River near Bangor, Maine.

them productive, contributing members of the group; the need to produce and distribute essential goods and services; the need to hold in check conflicts within the group so that vital relationships can be maintained; and the need to protect members from external threats, whether from the biophysical environment or from other human societies.

Systems of social organization are influenced to some extent by biological differences among the members. Social relationships in all mammalian societies, for example, are organized to take account of age and sex differences. Human societies, however, rarely stop there. In most instances they go much further, developing elaborate kinship networks and other complex social arrangements that reflect cultural influences. Thus, when we think of social organization we must think of it as a product of the interaction of culture and people.

Individuals   Every society must cope with a constant turnover in its membership. Older members die and are replaced with newborn infants.* This creates a major problem: although these infants have the same basic genetic resources as the individuals who died, they lack their cultural resources. In other words, none of them knows anything about their society's store of information on matters ranging from religion to technology. Everything must be learned. To put it another way, raw, ignorant "recruits" must somehow be transformed into productive and responsible people who can work cooperatively with others and make a contribution to the group's welfare.

The means by which societies do this is known as the **socialization** process. This is a complex process that begins as soon as the infant is capable of discerning that its actions generate reactions by others, and that some of those reactions are pleasant while others are not. Sometimes these reactions are conscious, purposive efforts by parents and others to influence or train the child. But often they are simply unplanned, spontaneous responses—the response, for example, of weary parents who are awakened repeatedly by a cranky baby.

Over time, even very young children begin to anticipate the responses of other people and to adjust their behavior accordingly. At this point, they have begun to absorb the culture of their society and to internalize its norms and values. This process continues throughout an individual's life, and comes to include the conscious acquisition of countless skills that can range from brushing one's teeth to programming computers.

The socialization process is never entirely successful in any society. The "concern for self" which is part of our genetic heritage, together with the individuating nature of learning, combine to limit the extent to which people are able to subordinate their personal interests to those of society. All of us are able to rationalize at least some violations of our society's norms. ("It was just a little white lie." "Everybody exceeds the speed limit here.")

Most of the time, however, most individuals, by the time they reach adulthood, conform to their society's standards, partly because of their desire to obtain the rewards and avoid the penalties that can be expected, and partly because they have come to accept their society's standards as their own. In short, they have become contributing members of their society, individuals who are able to fulfill their duties and meet their responsibilities.

Social Positions, Roles, and Statuses   Individuals who occupy positions in a social structure are expected to fulfill a number of social roles. These roles emerge and develop in response to recurring needs and problems in societies. Young children, for example, require care and attention, and the roles of mother and father have evolved in response to this need. In large and complex societies, there is a continuing need for political leadership, and a variety of roles, ranging from school board member to president or prime minister, have developed in response.

---

*To varying degrees, membership turnover also involves individuals who migrate from one society to another. Emigration and immigration, however, do not alter the basic nature of the problem of member turnover discussed in this section.

Roles in society, like roles in the theatre, *have distinctive behavioral expectations and requirements attached to them.*[37] Thus, just as a woman may play the role of Juliet on the stage, so she may "play" the roles of wife, mother, and doctor in her home and community. In both instances, people expect her to act in certain ways and not in others, simply because of the roles she occupies. When she meets those expectations, she is applauded or rewarded. When she fails to meet them, she is criticized, or worse.

The behavioral requirements and expectations that are attached to "real life" roles are the **norms** we discussed on page 37. As we saw then, they may be quite formal, as in the laws forbidding theft and murder, or they may be informal, as in a neighborhood's expectations concerning property maintenance. They may involve fundamental moral issues, or they may involve the minutiae of etiquette. Norms also vary in their scope. Some apply to everyone, as in the law forbidding bigamy in the United States; others apply to only a few, as in rules governing the conduct of members of the Canadian Parliament.

As we will see in later chapters, roles change as societies change. New roles are added and older ones disappear. Even when roles persist, their content often changes. Thus, prior to the development of modern technology, the feeding of infants was entirely the work of women. Today, this is a responsibility often shared with men.

It is also important to recognize that roles differ greatly with respect to the prestige or social honor accorded them. For instance, people in industrial societies hold the occupational role of medical doctor in higher esteem than that of garage mechanic.[38] Successful hunters and good storytellers are held in similarly high regard in hunting and gathering societies. Such rankings are referred to as **statuses,** and, as we will see later, status differences are important in motivating people to fill certain roles in societies, and they can affect people's access to scarce and valued social resources.

Groups   In most societies, individuals are organized into a variety of units we call groups. These range from small family units and cliques to giant corporate entities of various kinds. In popular usage, the term "group" is often applied to any aggregation of people, regardless of their other characteristics. Sociologists, however, limit the term to *an aggregation whose members (1) cooperate to satisfy common, or complementary, needs; (2) have shared norms; and (3) have a sense of common identity.*

As this definition suggests, human aggregations differ in their degree of "groupishness." While some aggregations clearly qualify as groups (e.g., Jehovah's Witnesses) and others just as clearly do not (e.g., all redheads in the United States), many are borderline (e.g., Americans of Irish descent). This last example reminds us that the degree of "groupishness" of an aggregation is not permanently fixed. Aggregations may take on more of the qualities of a group, or they may lose some. Their members may come to work together more closely; develop new, stronger, and more generally shared norms; and acquire a stronger sense of common identity; or just the opposite may occur, as has happened with Irish Americans during the last hundred years.

Even after we exclude such aggregations as redheads, the concept "group" still includes such a wide variety of organizations that it is necessary to differentiate among them. The most familiar way of doing this is by their basic function in society. Thus, we differentiate between families, churches, schools, political parties, and so forth.

Sociologists have also found it useful to differentiate among groups on the basis of their size and the intensity of the social ties among their members. Small groups in which there are face-to-face relations of a fairly intimate and personal nature are known as **primary groups.** Primary groups are of two basic types, **families** and **cliques.** In other words, they are organized around ties of either kinship or friendship. Larger, more impersonal groups are known as **secondary groups.**

Roles in society are like roles in the theatre: both have distinctive behavioral expectations attached to them. Balcony scene from Shakespeare's Romeo and Juliet.

Classes   Inequality is a fact of life in every human society. Some individuals always control more of the society's resources than others do and enjoy more than their share of its benefits. Human societies differ greatly, however, in the amount of inequality present among their members. In some it is minimal, in others it is enormous. In larger and more complex societ-ies, where inequality is always substantial, individuals can be divided into **classes,** or **strata,** on the basis of their relationship to various social and cultural resources, such as political office, wealth, occupational skills, education, and legal status (e.g., free persons versus slaves). Taken together, all of the classes on a given dimension constitute a **class system.**[39]

Sociologists and others often find it is enough simply to distinguish between the upper, middle, and lower strata of a society. For some purposes, however, more precise distinctions are needed. Thus, in discussing societies of the past, we often distinguish between nobles and commoners or between free persons and slaves. Similarly, in discussing contemporary societ-ies, we often refer to the working class, the professional class, political elites, and others. In each instance the class or stratum is defined on the basis of *some important attribute* (e.g., legal status, type of job, education) *that is the same for all members of the class and that influences their access to power, privilege, and prestige.*

Stratification   Viewed as a whole, all of the statuses and class systems of a society constitute its system of stratification. And, as we will see in the following chapters, stratification systems vary dramatically in a number of important ways. For instance, in some societies the differences in wealth, power, and prestige between those at the top and those at the bottom of the stratification system are quite small, while in others they are quite large. In some the great majority of people are concentrated near the bottom, while in others more are in the middle range. In some the people who are privileged with respect to one dimension of inequality are privileged with respect to all dimensions, while in others, people who are high on one dimension may be at the middle or near the bottom on others.

Not surprisingly, stratification is one of the major sources of conflict within societies. No system of distribution can satisfy everyone, since there is no obviously "right" or "fair" way to distribute power, privilege, and prestige. For example, it is equally reasonable, in the abstract, to assert that a given product should be distributed on the basis of (1) how much a person needs it, (2) how much effort a person invests in producing it, or (3) how much skill a person contributes in producing it, to name only three of the possibilities.

Even if the members of a society employed just one of these principles in allocating its rewards, disputes would still be likely. If members applied the principle of effort, for example, they would have to measure and compare effort. Should it be calculated by the hours spent on the job, by the foot-pounds of energy expended, or by how hard a person tries? Or, if the group used the skill criterion, they would have to measure and compare such dissimilar skills as those of a nurse, a computer programmer, and a diplomat. In brief, there is no obviously "right" way to allocate rewards in human societies, and conflict over the rules and results of distribution, therefore, is virtually inevitable.

Because of systems of stratification, not everyone has an equal voice in decision making within societies. On the contrary, in many societies a few individuals have vastly more influence on societal policies than others. We need to keep this in mind whenever we discuss the policies and actions of such societies: while leaders make decisions on behalf of, and in the name of, the entire society, most members of the society have usually never been consulted. This is true even in societies with multiparty representative political systems and free elections.

Social Institutions and Institutional Systems

Social institutions and **institutional systems** are the last of the five basic components of human societies. These differ from the other components we have considered in one important respect: they are *combinations of the other four components*. In other words, they bring together population, culture, the material products of culture, and social organization (see Figure 2.2).

A British sociologist once described social institutions as "frozen answers to fundamental questions."[40] Although it is an exaggeration to call them "frozen" answers, institutions are durable and persisting elements of sociocultural systems. For purposes of definition, we may think of them as *durable answers to important and persistent problems*.

One reason for their durability is that their value to society is impressed on individuals at an early age. Thus, we grow up thinking of them as natural and inevitable. Another reason for their durability is that the different elements of institutional systems are intricately intertwined and it is often impossible to change one element without being compelled to change countless others, making the cost of change too great.

All societies develop numerous "durable answers." Among those found in modern industrial societies are such things as: marriage, the jury system, secret-ballot elections, private property, religion, and rights of privacy.

For many purposes, sociologists are less interested in specific social institutions than in institutional systems. As the name implies, *institutional systems are systems of interrelated institutions*. Five such systems are of major importance in the study of human societies, and much of our analysis in later chapters, especially Chapters 5 to 15, will be organized around them.

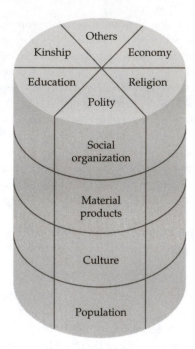

FIGURE 2.2 *Relations among the basic components of human societies. Each major institutional system brings together people, culture, the material products of culture, and social organization.*

The first is **kinship,** which structures such things as the obligations and responsibilities among relatives, marriage choices, and relations between spouses. The second is the **economy,** which centers on the production and distribution of valued goods in a society. The third is the **polity,** which focuses on the distribution of power and collective decision making. The fourth is **religion,** societal beliefs and practices regarding things considered sacred. Fifth, and finally, **education** is the system that prepares people to assume productive roles in society.

These are like major slices of the sociocultural "pie." Each provides answers to a set of interrelated, important, and persistent problems that confront every society. Kinship is the oldest of these systems, but all of them have existed for thousands of years and all seem likely to continue for as long as human societies endure.

THE WORLD SYSTEM OF SOCIETIES

Before we conclude this discussion of human societies as sociocultural systems, there is one more system that needs to be considered. Every human society is, itself, part of a larger and more inclusive sociocultural system that sociologists have come to call the **world system of societies.**

Throughout history, human societies have established and maintained relations with one another. They have met at water holes, traded goods, exchanged ambassadors, sent out missionaries, fought wars, translated books, exacted tribute, and in countless other ways developed and maintained a network of social and cultural ties. During much of the past, direct ties were limited to neighboring societies, since direct relations with distant societies were not possible. But even then, *indirect* relations existed. Society A maintained ties with society B, which, in turn, maintained ties with society C, and so on throughout the system. No society was ever totally cut off from the world system of societies for long, since even the most isolated societies had occasional contacts with others. With advances in transportation and communication during the last 5,000 years, relations between societies increased greatly and direct relations have been established between societies far removed from one another. As a result, the world system of societies has grown more integrated and more complex and has come to exercise an ever-increasing influence on the life of individual societies.

Institutions are durable answers to important and persistent problems: trial by jury in England, Central Criminal Court, Old Bailey.

3

The Evolution
of Human Societies

Evolution is a term that refers to long-term directional patterns of change that scientists have discovered throughout the world of nature. Today different groups of scientists are engaged in the study of cosmic evolution (the evolution of the universe as a whole), biological evolution (the evolution of living organisms), and sociocultural evolution (the evolution of human societies).

Sociocultural evolution, like biological evolution, is a complex process involving three basic sets of forces: (1) forces of **continuity** that act to preserve from generation to generation much of the existing store of information and many or most existing arrangements; (2) forces of **innovation** that produce new information and new arrangements; and (3) forces of **selection** that determine which elements survive and which are eliminated.*

After we examine each of these forces individually in some detail, we will consider the interplay among them and the directional changes they have produced in the world system of human societies of the past 10,000 years.

FORCES PROMOTING SOCIAL
AND CULTURAL CONTINUITY

Evolutionary change in a society is a *cumulative* process. Even in a society that appears to be changing rapidly, most elements of culture and social organization remain unchanged for extended periods. In modern industrial societies, for example, where rates of change are among the highest the world has ever known, many elements of culture are hundreds of years old, and some, such as the alphabet, the calendar, the numeral system, certain religious beliefs and practices, and basic techniques of farming and metallurgy, are thousands of years old. The same is true of many elements of social organization, such as the roles of prime minister, king, queen, priest, and rabbi, and the even older roles of mother, father, husband, wife, child, cousin, and grandparent.

There are a number of reasons for the persistence of social and cultural elements in a society.

One major reason is that, in the absence of a clearly better alternative, people will continue to do what works. For instance, in simple societies, through generations of experience, people have developed effective tools, technologies, and strategies for coping with their environments. Any alternative or change, therefore, is likely to be *less effective* than what it would replace, and diminished results would quickly lead any potential innovators to return to "tried and true" ways.

Cultural elements are also preserved if they are perceived by enough people as useful in answering their individual or personal needs.** This explains the persistence of many

*See the excursus at the end of this chapter for a more detailed comparison of sociocultural and biological evolution.
**This does not mean that human societies strive to satisfy the needs and desires of all their members equally or impartially. On the contrary, as we have seen (page 43), all societies are more responsive to the needs of some of their members than to the needs of others.

elements of art, music, literature, and religion, and the persistence of a great variety of customs and norms, including even such antisocial patterns of behavior as speeding or illicit drug use.

In more complex societies, there are additional reasons. For example, in class-stratified societies, fundamental technological or social change is likely to affect the amount and distribution of valued goods. As a result, classes and groups that would lose benefits are likely to resist, and since they generally have more power and more resources than those that would gain, they are often able to delay or prevent change from taking place.*

Sometimes elements of culture are preserved not because they are superior solutions to problems but simply because they ensure *standardized behavioral responses* in situations where these are essential. For example, although driving a car on the right side of the road is inherently neither safer nor easier than driving on the left, this choice cannot be left to individuals. Every society must have a norm to ensure that all of its drivers follow the same procedure.

Another cause of continuity is the *cost involved in changing*. Change can be expensive; it would cost billions of dollars, for example, for Americans to change to the metric system. Change can also be costly in terms of time and energy, since it takes both to learn new rules and techniques and new ways of relating to others and performing one's job.

The **socialization process** is also a tremendous force for continuity within societies. As we saw on page 40, this is the process by which individuals learn the culture of their group and acquire the skills that enable them to become functional members of their society. Through this process the members of a society acquire the belief that their culture is a precious resource and worth preserving. During their prolonged immaturity, children are obliged to master many of the most basic elements of their culture. This is essential for their survival, and their only road to any degree of independence. Before they learn to talk, for example, children are almost totally dependent on other people; after they master their society's language, they have an invaluable tool to help them get what they want. The same is true of other elements of culture: it pays the child to master them. Thus, the desire of members of the adult generation to preserve their culture by transmitting it to their offspring is more than matched by their offspring's eagerness to learn it, especially during the formative years. Since this cycle necessarily repeats itself as each generation matures, the result is a tremendous force for continuity.

These efforts to pass culture on to the next generation are reinforced by **ideologies.** One of the chief functions of ideology is to preserve valued insights of the past. Since these insights usually include the belief that the existing social order is a moral order that ought to be preserved, a society's values, norms, and leadership acquire an aura of the sacred and thus become less vulnerable to efforts to alter them. Ironically, even revolutionary ideologies like Marxism eventually acquire a sacred and conservative character: once they win acceptance, they too become a force for continuity and for resistance to change.

Finally, *the systemic nature of human societies* is a major force for continuity. This is because most of the elements in a sociocultural system are linked to other elements in such a way that change in one area often makes change in other areas necessary. As a result, the members of a society do not adopt change casually, especially when they are aware of how extensive—and expensive—that change may ultimately be. When Sweden shifted to driving on the right-hand side of the road, for example, this "simple" change meant not only that cars and other vehicles had to be redesigned, but also that traffic signals and road signs throughout the country had to be relocated, traffic laws revised, and the deeply ingrained habits of millions of people altered. Similarly, as more women with young children have become employed in many societies, it has been necessary to create expensive new child care systems.

---

*We will also see that in complex stratified societies, the potential for innovation is affected by the distribution of information in societies (e.g., see Chapter 7).

Although rates of change in modern industrial societies are among the highest the world has ever known, many elements of their cultures are hundreds or even thousands of years old: Jewish boy reading from scriptures more than 2,000 years old.

FORCES PROMOTING SOCIAL AND CULTURAL CHANGE

In spite of the strength of the forces promoting social and cultural continuity, some change occurs in every society. Even in the simplest and most tradition-minded societies, gradual changes occur in such things as the pronunciation of words, and legends are altered inadvertently as they are transmitted by word of mouth from one generation to the next. Social and cultural change is of two basic types. Sometimes it involves the addition of new elements to the existing system; sometimes it involves a new combination of existing elements.

Forms of Innovation

Social and cultural innovation takes various forms. Often it takes the form of borrowing from other societies, a process known as **diffusion.** This occurs more often than most of us realize. In fact, there is good reason to believe that most elements in most sociocultural systems have been borrowed from other societies.

Many innovations, of course, are independently produced within society. These are of several types. **Alterations** are the least important. These are innovations whose adaptive value is no greater than that of the things they replaced, as in new styles of dress or new musical fashions. Alterations are often unintentional, as in gradual changes in the pronunciation of words or inadvertent errors in the transmission of stories and legends.

Discoveries and inventions are much more important types of innovations. **Discoveries** provide the members of a society with new information that has adaptive value, while **inventions** are new combinations of already existing information.[1] Thus, Columbus was a discoverer, while Gottlieb Daimler, who built the first automobile, was an inventor. What Daimler did was to combine in a new way a number of things that were already part of the technological heritage of western societies (e.g., the gasoline engine, the carriage body, running gears, the drive shaft, brakes). The "only" thing that was new about the automobile was the automobile itself. As we will see shortly, we must understand the nature of inventions if we are to understand why societies differ in their rates of innovation and change, and why these rates have changed over the centuries.

Causes of Innovation

Persius, a Roman poet, once wrote of hunger as "the teacher of the practical arts and the bestower of invention." Plato put the matter even more succinctly when he described necessity as the mother of invention.

One does not need to be a social scientist to recognize the stimulus that *hunger and other human needs* provide. Throughout the ages, men and women, prodded by unfulfilled needs and desires, have dreamed of ways of satisfying them. Most dreams have remained just dreams, but sometimes individuals have transformed them into realities and something new and useful has been added to the sum of human knowledge.

Because of culture, human needs and desires seem limitless. Each problem that is solved and each need that is satisfied seem to generate new needs and new desires as people come increasingly to take the satisfaction of their former needs and desires for granted. This is the basis of the so-called revolution of rising expectations that was such a striking feature of life in the twentieth century. Despite the fact that standards of living have risen more in the last century than in any previous century, discontent and dissatisfaction have probably never been greater. Recognition of this important aspect of human nature has led some observers to note that while Plato was certainly correct in his observation that necessity is the mother of invention, it is also true that *invention is the mother of necessity.* In other words, the process of innovation and change seems to feed on itself so that once it is set in motion it tends to continue, and even to accelerate.

While most of us have no trouble recognizing how unsatisfied needs influence the innovative process, we are likely to overlook the role of *chance,* or accident. Based on our experience as members of a modern industrial society, we tend to think of inventions and discoveries as products of planning and forethought. Yet from earliest times to the present, chance has been an important factor in the innovative process. Thus, in a primitive society,

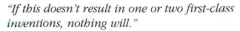

"If this doesn't result in one or two first-class inventions, nothing will."

someone with a high fever may dream of a visit by a long-dead grandmother and awaken to find the fever abated. Nothing would be more natural under the circumstances than for the individual to assume that the "visit" was the cause of the cure and, in future illnesses, to pray to the grandmother for help. Should such prayers sometimes be followed by cures, the practice might well spread and eventually become a permanent feature of the society's culture.

Chance has also played an important role in *technological* innovation. Random strikes by lightning, for example, were almost certainly an important part of the process by which humans first learned about fire and became aware of its uses and dangers. More recently, the great scientist Louis Pasteur discovered the principle and technique of immunization only after he accidentally injected some animals with a stale bacterial culture of chicken cholera. When the animals unexpectedly survived, it occurred to Pasteur that weakened bacteria might immunize against the very disease that the bacteria, at full strength, were responsible for. Similarly, a key problem in the development of modern photography was solved when Louis Daguerre put a bromide-coated silver plate into a cupboard where, unknown to him, there was an uncovered container of mercury. When he returned the following day, he found that a latent image had begun to develop and correctly surmised that fumes from the mercury were responsible.[2]

While these and many other examples illustrate the role that chance has played in the innovative process, it would be a mistake to suppose that chance *alone* is responsible in most of these cases. Conscious, purposive action is also involved. Not just anyone could have made the discoveries made by Pasteur and Daguerre. Each man was already working on a problem about which he was highly knowledgeable, and each was a member of a society that already possessed a substantial store of relevant information.

Many changes in human societies arise in response to *changes in either their biophysical or social environments*. Archaeologists have found, for example, that changes in climate in the past (e.g., global warming following the last Ice Age) led to changes in diet, in technology, and probably in other societal characteristics as well.[3] Similarly, changes in the social environment (e.g., increasing contacts among societies or the rise of expansionistic and militaristic neighbors) can create new problems for societies and lead to social and cultural innovations of various kinds.

Finally, one often overlooked cause of change has been *human fecundity*. Human populations, like other populations, are able to produce many more offspring than environmental resources can sustain. In other species, this merely leads to high death rates among the young, except in those rare instances when a genetic mutation or environmental change enables a population to utilize some new resource. Human societies, however, are able to respond to population pressures with cultural innovations. *Ideological* changes in customs or in laws, for example, may cause people to delay the age at which they marry, or legitimate such practices as abortion. Alternatively, *technological* changes may provide the population with better methods of contraception, or enable them to produce more food to keep a growing number of children alive and well.

Variations in the Rate of Innovation

When we compare different societies, we find that they produce innovations at greatly different rates. Some, such as American society, have had extremely high rates of innovation. In many others, the rate of innovation has been negligible.

There are a number of reasons for such variations, but one of the most important is *the amount of information a society already possesses*.[4] One of the most important forms of innovation—invention—is the act of combining already existing elements of culture. This means that a society's potential for invention is a mathematical function of the number of elements, or amount of information, already present. Table 3.1 illustrates this principle. It shows how various numbers of units, or elements, of information can be combined. Although two units

TABLE 3.1 Number of Combinations Possible for Various Numbers of Units

No. of Units	Total Number of Combinations									
	2 at a Time	3 at a Time	4 at a Time	5 at a Time	6 at a Time	7 at a Time	8 at a Time	9 at a Time	10 at a Time	Total
2	1	0	0	0	0	0	0	0	0	1
3	3	1	0	0	0	0	0	0	0	4
4	6	4	1	0	0	0	0	0	0	11
5	10	10	5	1	0	0	0	0	0	26
6	15	20	15	6	1	0	0	0	0	57
7	21	35	35	21	7	1	0	0	0	120
8	28	56	70	56	28	8	1	0	0	247
9	36	84	126	126	84	36	9	1	0	502
10	45	120	210	252	210	120	45	10	1	1,013

can be combined in only one way, three units can be combined in four ways, and four units in eleven ways. In other words, *the addition of each new unit more than doubles the number of possible combinations.* Thus, a mere fivefold increase in the number of units from two to ten leads to a *thousandfold* increase in the number of possible combinations, and when the number of units reaches twenty, over a million combinations are possible!

Of course, not all elements can be combined in a useful way. It is difficult, for example, to imagine a useful combination of the hammer and the saw. The number of potential combinations, therefore, is much greater than the number of fruitful ones. This does not affect the relationship between the number of units and the number of combinations, however.

One indication of the importance of the existing store of information is the frequency with which two or more individuals sharing the same body of information, but working entirely independently, have made the same invention or discovery at about the same time. More than half a century ago, two sociologists compiled a list of 148 of the independent inventions and discoveries, and there have been more since then.[5] The list includes:

Sunspots: Fabricius, Galileo, Harriott, Scheiner, 1611
Logarithms: Napier, 1614; Buergi, 1620
Calculus: Newton, 1671; Leibnitz, 1676
Nitrogen: Rutherford, 1772; Scheele, 1773
Oxygen: Priestley, Scheele, 1774
Water as H_2O: Cavendish, Watt, 1781; Lavoisier, 1783
Telegraph: Henry, Morse, Steinheil, Wheatstone and Cooke, 1837
Photography: Daguerre and Niepce, Talbot, 1839
Natural selection: Darwin, Wallace, 1858
Telephone: Bell, Gray, 1876

A second cause of variations in the rate of innovation is population size.[6] Because every member of a society has somewhat different needs and abilities, the more people there are, the more new ideas and information are likely to be produced. Larger populations are also likely to generate problems, and, because they tend to be organizationally more complex, are likely to generate more varied patterns of social interaction, leading to more new customs, norms, laws, and other kinds of information required to control and regulate relationships. In the case of technological innovations, the more people who are aware of a problem and looking for a solution, the more quickly it will be found, other things being equal. Since societal populations vary so greatly in size, this is another factor of considerable importance.

Third, the stability and character of a society's environment can also affect the rate of change. There is greater pressure for social and cultural change in an unstable or changing environment than in a stable one. This is true with respect to both the biophysical and the social environment.* Any change in the latter that upsets the balance of power among societies (e.g., large-scale migrations, empire building, a new weapons system) is an especially potent force for further innovation and change.

The potential for development and change can also be severely limited by environmental factors. For example, desert and arctic societies have been unable either to develop the techniques of plant cultivation themselves or to adopt them from others. The absence of vital resources, such as an adequate water supply or accessible metallic ores, can also hinder innovation, as can endemic diseases and parasites that deplete people's energy.[7] Topography has played an important role in shaping patterns of intersocietal communication. Oceans, deserts, and mountain ranges have all prevented or seriously impeded the flow of information between societies, while navigable rivers and open plains have facilitated it. Considering the importance of diffusion, enormous differences in the rate of innovation can be explained by this factor alone.

A fourth factor influencing the rate of innovation in a society is *the extent of its contact with other societies*. The greater its interaction, the greater its opportunities to appropriate their innovations. In effect, contact enables one society to take advantage of the brainpower and cultural information of other societies through the process of *diffusion*. The importance of diffusion was beautifully illustrated some years ago by an anthropologist, Ralph Linton, who wrote:

> Our solid American citizen awakens in a bed built on a pattern which originated in the Near East but which was modified in Northern Europe before it was transmitted to America. He throws back covers made from cotton, domesticated in India, or linen, domesticated in the Near East, or wool from sheep, also domesticated in the Near East, or silk, the use of which was discovered in China. All of these materials have been spun and woven by processes invented in the Near East. He slips into his moccasins, invented by the Indians of the Eastern woodlands, and goes to the bathroom, whose fixtures are a mixture of European and American inventions, both of recent date. He takes off his pajamas, a garment invented in India, and washes with soap invented by the ancient Gauls. He then shaves, a masochistic rite which seems to have been derived from either Sumer or ancient Egypt. . . .

Linton followed this individual as he went through his daily round of activities using cultural elements most of which originated in other societies. As the day comes to a close and "our friend has finished eating," Linton wrote,

> he settles back to smoke, an American habit, consuming a plant domesticated in Brazil in either a pipe, derived from the Indians of Virginia, or a cigarette, derived from Mexico. If he is hardy enough he may even attempt a cigar, transmitted to us from the Antilles by way of Spain. While smoking he reads the news of the day, imprinted in characters invented by the ancient Semites upon a material invented in Germany. As he absorbs the accounts of foreign troubles, he will, if he is a good conservative citizen, thank a Hebrew deity in an Indo-European language that he is 100 per cent American.[8]

A fifth factor influencing the rate of innovation is *the systemic nature of sociocultural systems*. Because the various components of these systems are interdependent, a change in any one of them generates pressure for change in others. The invention of the automobile, for example, created the need for many new laws and for the construction of a vast new highway system. More important still, it led to the transformation of cities by encouraging the growth and spread of suburbs and the construction of thousands of new suburban shopping centers, which often have weakened or destroyed older business districts in the centers of cities. In addition, the automobile spawned a tremendous number of other changes in the business world, including the fast-food industry, motels, and the trucking industry, to name but three. The negative conse-

---

*It is worth repeating that environmental change is often the result of previous human activities.

quences of widespread automobile use have also spurred innovations.* For example, the noxious by-products of gasoline combustion have encouraged development of a number of pollution control devices, and leaking underground gas tanks from abandoned gasoline stations have led to new (microbiological) methods of decontaminating underground water.

Not all cultural innovations generate the same degree of pressure for change in the rest of the system. Some create very little pressure for further change, while others generate tremendous pressure. A new style of painting, for example, may have no impact on society outside a small circle of artists and critics. A new political movement, on the other hand, can have far-reaching consequences, depending on the number of people who join it and the seriousness with which they take it. But one kind of innovation that never fails to have far-reaching consequences is change in a society's *basic subsistence technology*. For reasons that will become clear shortly, changes in subsistence technology have ramifications that are felt in almost every other area of life.

Sixth, the rate of innovation is greatly influenced by *"fundamental" innovations*. Not all discoveries and inventions are of equal importance: a few pave the way for thousands more, while the majority have little effect.[10] The invention of the plow and the steam engine and the discovery of the principles of plant cultivation, animal domestication, and metallurgy were all fundamental innovations. So, too, were the inventions of writing and money.

Sometimes a fundamental innovation will cause the rate of innovation to rise because it involves a principle that can be applied, with minimum effort and imagination, in hundreds, even thousands, of different areas. This was true, for example, of the steam engine, metallurgy, printing, and the silicon chip. Sometimes, however, an invention or discovery is considered "fundamental" because it so drastically alters the conditions of human life that hundreds or thousands of other changes become either possible or necessary. This was the case with the principle of plant cultivation, which, as we shall see in a later chapter, led to revolutionary changes in every area of human life.

A seventh factor influencing the rate of innovation is *the society's attitude toward innovation*. In many societies there has been such a powerful ideological commitment to tradition that innovation of any kind has been discouraged.[11] In contrast, most modern societies have a strongly positive attitude toward innovation and change.

Though the problem has not been studied as carefully as it deserves, a society's attitude toward innovation seems to be greatly influenced by its prior experience. A society that has benefited from change in the past is usually more receptive to innovation than a society that has not. Attitudes toward innovation also vary according to the nature of the dominant ideology in a society. Some ideologies generate a very conservative outlook and oppose change; Confucianism is an example of such an ideology. Capitalism, in contrast, has been much more supportive of innovation and change.

Before we leave the subject of the rate of innovation, it is important to note a tendency that is especially evident where technological innovation is concerned: it tends to occur at *an accelerating pace*. Figure 3.1 illustrates this speedup for human societies as a whole during the period from 1000 A.D. to 1900 A.D. The majority of societies have never experienced such an acceleration. But those that have experienced it have influenced human history out of all proportion to their numbers.

The explanation of the acceleration is that *each new bit of useful technological information acquired by a society increases the probability it will acquire still more*. This is partly a function of the potential of technological elements for being recombined in new ways. But more than that, technological advance tends to reinforce several of the other basic factors that influence the rate of innovation. Throughout history, for example, advances in a society's subsistence technology, themselves engendered by increasing population and population

---

*This is not unusual. In fact, many technological innovations are the direct result of problems caused by the adoption of earlier technological innovations (e.g., see Chapter 9).[9]

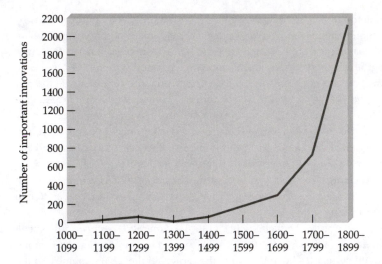

FIGURE 3.1 *The number of important technological innovations by century, 1000 A.D. to 1900 A.D. Technological innovation tends to occur at an accelerating rate, because each new element increases the probability of acquiring more. See also Table 5.1, page XX.*
Source: Adapted from Ludwig Darmstaedter and Rene DuBois-Reymond, *4000 Jahre Pionier-Arbeit in den Exakten Wissenschaften* (Berlin: Stargardt, 1904).

density, have led to further growth in population size. This growth in population, in turn, often elicited further innovations. Similarly, technological advance and population growth have led to increased intersocietal contact, resulting in greater diffusion and thus enhancing the rate of technological innovation.

In short, technological innovation and advance tend to make *further* innovation and advance increasingly likely. It is hardly surprising, therefore, that societies in which this happens come to be increasingly different from societies in which it does not.

FORCES OF SELECTION

Intrasocietal Selection

Selection operates at two levels in sociocultural evolution: *within* societies and *among* them. **Intrasocietal selection** occurs when members of a society choose one way of doing things rather than another. For instance, in the distant prehistoric past, our ancestors began to cultivate plants and domesticate animals and gradually abandoned their earlier practices of foraging for wild fruits and vegetables and hunting wild animals. Although such choices are generally based on what appear at the time to be rational considerations, they are always made on the basis of limited and imperfect knowledge, and therefore sometimes produce disastrous and unintended consequences in the future. This was certainly the case when wealthy Romans chose to use lead, instead of pottery, for their cooking utensils, dishes, and water piping, and when Europeans adopted the Native American practice of smoking tobacco.

Because of social and cultural innovations, societies are often faced with choices between competing alternatives. Earlier in this century, for example, the members of many societies were confronted with a choice between the horse and carriage and the new "horseless carriage." Gradually, the horseless carriage, or automobile, as it came to be known, replaced the older means of transportation.

Intrasocietal selection often occurs imperceptibly, as one element of technology gradually replaces another: in the early decades of the present century, the horseless carriage gradually replaced the horse-drawn carriage in industrial societies.

The process of selection is like the process of innovation in that it too can be rational and deliberate, as in the adoption of the automobile and the rejection of the horse and buggy. But, again, as in the process of innovation, chance, limited information about long-term consequences, and irrational factors may play a part.

Although it is, of course, the members who make the choices which shape and alter their society, everyone does not have an equal voice. "Who decides" depends on the kind of decision involved and the nature of the power structure involved. For example, the teenaged members of an industrial society may choose, at one level, which songs become hits, but their range of choices has already been substantially narrowed by the people who control the music industry and who pay disc jockeys to promote certain records and otherwise manipulate the selective process. Similarly, all of the members of a democratic society may have equal opportunities to cast their votes for public officials, but the choice among candidates has already been substantially narrowed by elites in the mass media and the political system.

This raises the question of whether or not a society's culture and social organization can be considered optimally adaptive. While much of it *is* adaptive for the society as a whole (i.e., it helps satisfy basic needs of the system or its members), many elements have been selected by and for the benefit of special segments of the society and are "adaptive" only, or largely, for them. Thus, the process of selection may result in the retention of many elements that are *nonadaptive* or even *maladaptive* for the society as a whole. Drug pushers and users select elements which they find rewarding, but which create serious problems for society as a whole (e.g., crime and illness). Similarly, others make decisions to use maladaptive or harmful products, such as sugar-coated cereals, tobacco, and alcohol.

Intersocietal Selection

Intersocietal selection occurs when a society ceases to exist as an autonomous entity. This can be the result of conquest or absorption by a more powerful society, or disintegration as a result of a natural disaster, environmental change, food crisis, or epidemic disease. Throughout human experience, but especially over the past 10,000 years, societal extinction has been the result of contact and conflict among societies, and warfare and disease, either singly or in concert, have played the most important role.[12] As a result, larger, more technologically ad-

The Great Paradox

Despite the tremendous changes that have occurred in human life during the last 10,000 years, the majority of societies changed very little during their entire existence. In other words, contrary to what we might infer from the changes that have occurred in the world system of societies—or from our own experience—rapid social and cultural change has been the exception rather than the rule until recently. In most societies, life changed very little from one generation to the next, or even from one century to the next.

When first considered, this paradox seems to be a contradiction, but actually it is not.* A system can change greatly even if most of its parts do not change—if the parts that fail to change are simply eliminated from the system.

This is exactly what has happened in the world system of societies. The great majority of individual societies changed very little during the course of their existence, but almost none of those societies survived into the present century. Almost all of the societies that *have* survived have been that small minority that have changed, and changed greatly.

Table 3.2 provides a simplified illustration of what has happened in the last 10,000 years. Of the ten hypothetical societies in the illustration, only two changed from Time 1 to Time 4. During the course of their existence, the other eight did not change at all in terms of size. Nevertheless, as the bottom line of the table shows, the size of this hypothetical world system steadily increased, and by Time 4 it was almost eight times larger than it had been in Time 1.

As this illustration suggests, *a process of selection has been at work in the world system of societies, favoring larger, more powerful societies at the expense of smaller, less powerful ones.* As we will see later in this chapter and elsewhere, this process has favored those societies that have been most successful in accumulating useful information relevant to subsistence activities. When societies have come into conflict with one another over territory and other vital resources, those that have been technologically more advanced have usually prevailed.** Thus, even though the vast majority of individual societies have resisted social and cultural change, the world system of societies has been dramatically transformed.

It is obvious, therefore, that we have to consider both change and continuity (i.e., the absence of change) if we are to understand human societies. Both have been profoundly important in the evolution not only of the world system of societies but of individual societies as well.

*It should be noted that this is the nature of a paradox; it is an *apparent* or *seeming* contradiction, rather than an actual one.
**There have been exceptions, of course, as when more-advanced societies have waged wars far from home and when their vital interests were not involved. This happened in the American war in Vietnam, for example.

TABLE 3.2 The Great Paradox Illustrated: While the Majority of Societies Have Remained Unchanged throughout Their Existence, the World System of Societies Has Changed Tremendously

Society	Population Size			
	Time 1	Time 2	Time 3	Time 4
A	100	1,000	2,000	5,000
B	100	500	1,000	2,500
C	100	100	100	100
D	100	100	100	100
E	100	100	100	*
F	100	100	100	*
G	100	100	*	*
H	100	100	*	*
I	100	*	*	*
J	100	*	*	*
World system total	1,000	2,100	3,400	7,700

*This society no longer exists.

vanced and militarily powerful, and more disease-experienced societies have prevailed, and they have come to constitute an ever larger proportion of the world system of societies.

The key to the major changes that have occurred in the world system of societies in the last 10,000 years is the process of intersocietal selection that has drastically reduced the number of societies.[13] Were it not for this process, in which the units that survive (or become extinct) are entire societies, human life would not have changed nearly as much as it has.

The process of intersocietal selection presupposes the existence of differences among societies. Such differences were inevitable once the human population began to spread out geographically and occupy new and different kinds of environments. Chance also contributed to the process of societal differentiation, so that even when two societies confronted similar environmental challenges, they did not respond in exactly the same way. Differences in vocabulary provide a good example of this: even when all societies were confronted with identical experiences, such as birth and death, or the differences between males and females, they created different symbols to represent them. More important still, different beliefs developed to explain and interpret these experiences, and varied norms evolved to guide behavioral responses.

Not all the differences that have developed among societies have been equally important from the standpoint of intersocietal selection. Differences that influenced societal growth and development have been especially important, because *societies that have grown in size and developed in complexity and military power have been much more likely to survive and transmit their cultures and institutional patterns than societies that have preserved traditional social and cultural patterns and minimized innovation* (see Figure 3.2).

The reasons for this are obvious. To survive, societies must be able to defend their populations and territories against a variety of threats. These include the ravages of epidemics, natural disasters of other kinds, and, above all, threats from other societies. One only need consider the history of the United States, Canada, Australia, Brazil, or the former Soviet Union to see what happens to smaller and less developed indigenous societies (i.e., the American Indians, the Australian aborigines, and various tribal groups in Siberia and Soviet Asia) when they compete for territory with larger and more technologically developed societies. Larger societies have greater manpower and can more easily absorb military casualties. In addition, their more advanced technology has military applications, so that their soldiers have more deadly weapons, better logistical support, and greater mobility. Finally, their more complex

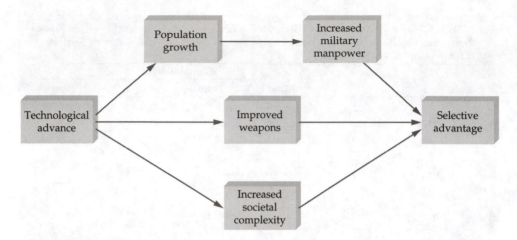

FIGURE 3.2 *Model of the effects of technological advance on the process of intersocietal selection.*

patterns of social organization can easily be adapted to military needs and this, too, provides an important competitive advantage. Thus, while it would be a mistake to suppose that more-developed societies always prevail over their less developed rivals, the odds are strongly in their favor.

Intersocietal selection is not always a violent process. Sometimes societies collapse simply because of insufficient support from their members. This is especially likely to occur when a less developed society comes into contact with one that is much more highly developed.* Many members of the less developed society become impressed with the wealth and power of the more advanced society and either migrate to it or begin to adopt its customs. If these tendencies become widespread, the institutional fabric of the less developed society begins to fray and a process of societal disintegration begins. There are a number of well-documented cases of this in India, where primitive tribes in the hill country have simply disintegrated and their former members have been absorbed into Indian society.[14]

SOCIETAL GROWTH AND DEVELOPMENT

Most societies change little during the course of their existence. Occasionally, however, significant changes have occurred. Some societies have grown substantially. Some have shifted from a nomadic way of life to permanent settlements in villages, and some have shifted from a predominantly rural mode of life to a predominantly urban one. Such changes have usually been accompanied by important changes in social organization—substantial increases in organizational complexity, marked increases in the division of labor, and significant increases in social inequality. In short, some societies have experienced a process of substantial growth and development while others have not.

How can we explain such a profound difference in the experience of societies?

We have already considered the basic factors that cause innovation in a society and those that affect the rate of innovation. Now we need to look at cultural innovation from a somewhat different angle and ask the further question, Do all kinds of new information have the same potential for societal growth and development, or do certain kinds of innovations have a greater potential than others?

---

*This can also be the result of the spread of an epidemic disease which breaks down and disrupts the operation of the simpler society (e.g., the Aztecs' after contact with the Spanish).

Victims of bubonic plague in Florence, Italy, in the 14th century. New and deadly diseases can profoundly alter long-term developmental trends, such as the growth of population. The bubonic plague killed between a quarter and a half of Europe's population in just a few years.

Subsistence Technology's Role in Sociocultural Evolution

Technology, as we have seen, is that part of a society's store of cultural information that enables its members to convert the resources available in their environment into the material products they need or desire—food, clothing, shelter, and all the rest. But information alone is not enough: *energy* is also needed if natural resources are to be converted into things that humans need.[15] In fact, without some source of energy, information is useless, since even the least demanding of activities, such as thinking, require energy.

Subsistence technology is the term used to refer to those elements of a society's store of information that enable it to obtain the energy its members require, and it is no exaggeration to say that subsistence technology provides the key to understanding societal growth and development. Specifically, *advances in subsistence technology are a necessary precondition for any significant increase in either the size or the complexity of any society.*

Societies that depend on hunting and gathering as their chief means of subsistence cannot sustain populations nearly as large as those that depend on farming; and those that depend on slash-and-burn horticulture, a more primitive method of farming, cannot sustain populations as large as those that depend on plow agriculture. These differences in the limits set on the size of a society by its subsistence technology are matched by differences in the limits set on other aspects of societal development, such as the extent of the division of labor, the degree of social inequality, the size and complexity of communities, the wealth of the society and its standard of living, and the power of the society over its biophysical environment and over other societies. In short, *technology defines the limits of what is possible for a society.*[16]

Within the range of options made possible by its technology, a society's choices are often influenced by the relative economic costs of the various alternatives. China's technol-

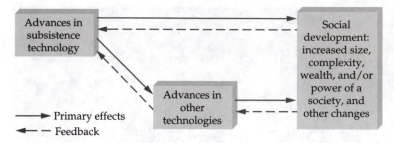

FIGURE 3.3 *Model of the effects of advances in subsistence technology on other technologies and on societal development.*

ogy, for example, makes the production of automobiles and the construction of a highway system possible, but its decision makers have opted instead for less costly solutions to their society's transportation needs: mass public transport and private bicycles. In a world in which resources are never sufficient to meet all of the demands for goods and services, differences in cost can never be ignored by societies, and they are compelled to adopt one of the less expensive solutions much of the time. Thus, in addition to determining the limits of the possible for a society, *technology also affects the choices that are made by influencing the costs of various alternatives.*

Advances in a society's subsistence technology are also important because *they stimulate advances in other kinds of technology.* For example, advances in subsistence technology tend to be accompanied or followed by advances in other productive technologies and in the technologies of transportation, communication, and defense, all of which contribute to societal growth and development (see Figure 3.3).

Technology's critical role in societal growth and development is not surprising when we consider that a society's tools and machines are, in effect, the functional equivalent of improvements in the basic organs with which its members are endowed—eyes, ears, voice box, arms, legs, brain, nervous system, and the rest. Microscopes, telescopes, and television all extend the range of our vision, just as telephones and radios extend the range of our hearing, and bicycles, automobiles, and airplanes increase our mobility. Where technological advances have occurred, they have enabled the members of societies to act as if they had acquired a new and improved genetic heritage—improved sight, more acute hearing, new powers of locomotion, and so forth. Thus, technological advances—especially advances in subsistence technology—are functionally equivalent to the important kinds of changes that occur in the course of biological evolution.

One important feature of the process of societal development that should not be overlooked is indicated by the feedback loops shown in Figure 3.3. Feedback is a special kind of causal relationship. It is one in which a part of the effect produced by the initial cause or event reverts back to, and alters, its source. For example, illness may cause a loss of appetite, and the resulting failure to eat may then aggravate the illness. Advances in subsistence technology stimulate advances in other technologies and lead to growth in the size and complexity of a society. But these developments, once they have occurred, usually increase the probability of further advances in subsistence technology.* Population growth, for example, increases the number of potential innovators and, although few individuals ever make an invention or discovery of practical value, the greater the number of potential innovators in a society, the greater tends to be the rate at which innovations occur. Thus, as this example suggests, *once the process of societal development is set in motion, it can become self-sustaining.* While this is not inevitable, the probabilities of continued development clearly increase.

*There are exceptions, as we will see in Chapter 7.

Societal growth and development, while advantageous to societies in many ways, are not unmixed blessings. They create new problems and these often lead to changes that many members of society would prefer not to make—changes in beliefs and values, changes in patterns of social organization, changes in institutional arrangements. Among preliterate societies, for example, technological advance often leads to population growth, and population growth necessitates changes in social organization. Such societies must choose either to split up into smaller independent groups in order to preserve their traditional kin-based system of governance, or to remain united but adopt a more authoritarian political system that is dominated by a small elite minority. Not surprisingly, they will generally continue to "fission" into smaller groups until they are prevented from doing so.[17]

Ideology's Role in Sociocultural Evolution

Whenever its technology presents a society with a range of options, its beliefs and values—the core elements of ideology—always come into play. These often have little or no effect on societal growth and development, as when people choose one style of clothing in preference to another, one form of entertainment rather than another, or even one form of marriage over another. Sometimes, however, ideologies do have a substantial effect, as when they dispose people to accept and even welcome change or, conversely, to view it negatively.[18] Western capitalism, for example, has been far more supportive of new ideas and innovations of many kinds than was Soviet Marxism.

When the beliefs and values involved are felt to be sufficiently important, a society may reject the most economic solution to its needs in favor of a solution that is ideologically preferable. The United States, for example, has chosen to make private automobiles and an extensive system of superhighways a major part of its solution to its transportation needs, reflecting not only the influence of powerful gasoline and automotive lobbies, but the individualism of its members and their desire for ease and freedom of movement as well.

Ideologically based decisions that affect a society's basic institutions may have extremely grave consequences. In eastern Europe, for example, countless decisions by Communist leaders over the years eventually led to a political and economic crisis of such proportions that the members of these societies rose up in mass revolt. And in a number of Third World societies, deeply ingrained beliefs about the value of large families continue to promote high rates of population growth that make it virtually impossible for the living conditions of all but a small minority of the people to improve.

Since one of the important consequences of technological advance is that it increases the range of options available to societies and their members, such advance leads to greater scope for the exercise of beliefs and values. Advanced societies today have far more choices available to them than societies of the past, and they are much freer to apply diverse ideologies in making their decisions. This does not guarantee happy results, of course, as the bitter experiences of Nazi Germany and the Soviet Union remind us.

A MODEL OF THE EVOLUTION
OF THE WORLD SYSTEM OF SOCIETIES

We can now construct a model of the evolutionary process that explains the basic trends in the world system of societies in recent millennia. Numerous cultural traits—occasionally augmented by discoveries, diffusion from other societies, and inventions—pass through the filter of intrasocietal selection. Items that people continue to use and pass on are preserved, those that are abandoned or superseded become extinct. In addition whole societies and their streams of cultural traits pass through a filter of intersocietal selection. Societies that effectively cope with their biophysical and sociocultural environments continue to exist as autonomous

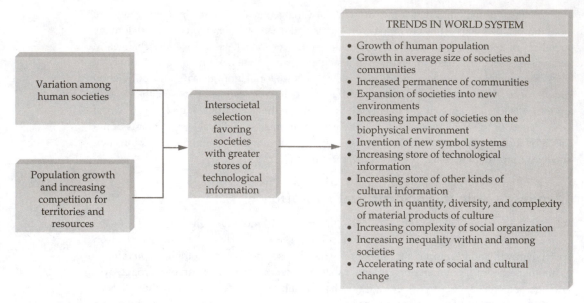

FIGURE 3.4 *Model of the causes of the evolution of the world system of societies.*

systems, those that don't either break up or are incorporated into other systems. Although societies with large effective bodies of cultural information are more likely to survive and pass on their traits, as the earlier citation from the anthropologist Ralph Linton showed, diffusion allows much of the cultural information of systems that fail to survive to be preserved and passed on within the world system of societies.

   Because technologically advanced societies have had the advantage in this process of intersocietal selection, *their characteristics have increasingly come to be the characteristics of the world system as a whole* (see Figure 3.4). Thus, because technologically advanced societies tend to be larger than other societies, the average size of societies has been increasing for the last 10,000 years. Similarly, because technologically advanced societies are structurally more complex than other societies, the trend in the world system has been in the direction of increasingly complex societies. The same logic applies to all of the trends shown in Figure 3.4.

   There is, of course, nothing inevitable or unalterable about these trends. A number of factors could disrupt them. For example, a deadly new disease could sweep through human societies and, in a short period of time, reverse many of the trends of the last 10,000 years. The Black Plague of the fourteenth century had this effect in a number of societies, and it is not inconceivable that something comparable could happen on a global scale.* An unpredictable catastrophe involving the biophysical environment could also reverse the trends of history, as could a war fought with modern military technology. Both nuclear and biochemical warfare have the potential for producing a global catastrophe, and there is no technological antidote for either. Ecological-evolutionary theory clearly provides no grounds for complacency regarding the future.

*Although the plague caused immeasurable human misery, the dramatic depopulation of Europe produced by its cyclical recurrences may actually have fostered economic change and technological innovation. For instance, since plague killed people but did not destroy property, it increased per capita wealth among the elite. It also greatly reduced population pressure on the land and other resources, increased the bargaining power and earnings of surviving peasants, and spurred a number of labor-saving innovations, such as firearms.[19]

Although we cannot predict the future, we can say that, so far, the process of intersocietal selection has favored technologically advanced societies. Like the old game of musical chairs, it has eliminated first one, then another, of the less developed societies. The result is a world system that, with the passage of time, increasingly consists of what were once the exceptions—innovative and developing societies.

Excursus: A Comparison of Biological and Sociocultural Evolution

In recent decades, our understanding of biological evolution and sociocultural evolution has advanced dramatically. It is now clear for the first time that *both types of evolution are based on records of experience that are preserved and transmitted from generation to generation in the form of coded systems of information.* In the case of biological evolution, the record of experience is preserved and transmitted by means of the genetic code. In sociocultural evolution, the record is preserved and transmitted by means of symbol systems. Both the genetic "alphabet" and symbol systems provide populations with the means of acquiring, storing, transmitting, and using enormous amounts of information on which their welfare and, ultimately, their survival depend. Thus, *symbol systems are functional equivalents of the genetic alphabet.*

It is hardly surprising, therefore, that there is a fundamental similarity in the way the two evolutionary processes operate. Both processes involve random variation and selective retention.[20]

Despite these similarities, there are a number of important differences in the way the two systems of evolution operate. Some of these are of special significance for students of human societies, such as the difference that results from the way information is transferred and spread in the two evolutions. The only way genetic information can be transmitted is through the process of reproduction. Because different species cannot interbreed, they cannot share genetic information with one another.* Thus, biological evolution is characterized by continued differentiation and diversification, a process much like the branching of a tree or shrub. Cultural information, by contrast, is easily exchanged between the members of different societies. Not only can human societies exchange information, but two or more can merge into a single system—the equivalent, were it possible, of the merging of separate species in biological evolution. Thus, sociocultural evolution is likely to eventuate in even fewer and less dissimilar societies than exist today.

This is related to a second important difference. In biological evolution, the emergence of more complex species of plants and animals has not had the effect of eliminating, or reducing the number of, simpler species. One-celled organisms thrive alongside, and indeed *inside,* complex multicellular organisms. In sociocultural evolution, on the other hand, the emergence of new and more-complex kinds of societies has usually led to the extinction of older, simpler ones, as illustrated by the destruction of thousands of small American Indian societies since 1492. Thus, while biological evolution produces the pattern of a richly branched shrub, sociocultural evolution approximates the pattern of a pine tree that gradually loses its lower branches as new, higher branches appear and overshadow them.

A third important difference involves a population's ability to incorporate into heritable form the useful information its members have acquired through the process of individual **learning.** In sociocultural systems, this is easily done; it is, as we have seen, the basis of their evolution. But it has no counterpart in biological evolution. Prior to Darwin biologists believed that something analogous *did* occur in the biotic world. Jean-Baptiste Lamarck, Darwin's most famous predecessor, argued that if an organism continually repeated a certain action, not only would this produce structural change in the organism, but the change would be inherited by its offspring.[21] It has long since become clear that biological evolution does not work that way: giraffes do not have long necks because their ancestors stretched day after day to reach high leaves, but because short necks were a liability in their ancestors' environment; animals with the genes for short necks were unable to survive and reproduce. In the cultural world, however, a kind of Lamarckian evolution *does* occur. Just about anything a population learns and considers worth preserving can be incorporated into its cultural heritage.

Springing from the easy flow of cultural information among societies and the ease with which it is incorporated into heritable form is yet another way in which sociocultural evolution differs from biological: it has given rise to much higher rates of change in our species. An evolution whose mechanism is genetic change is necessarily a slow process in a species that has a long generation span and relatively few offspring. But cultural information, relative to genetic, can be rapidly acquired, exchanged, recombined, and accumulated, with the result that substantial alterations in a

*Closely related species do occasionally interbreed, as when lions and tigers produce "ligers" or "tiglons." These hybrids are usually sterile, however, at least in the animal kingdom, and therefore their importance in the process of biological evolution has been minimal.

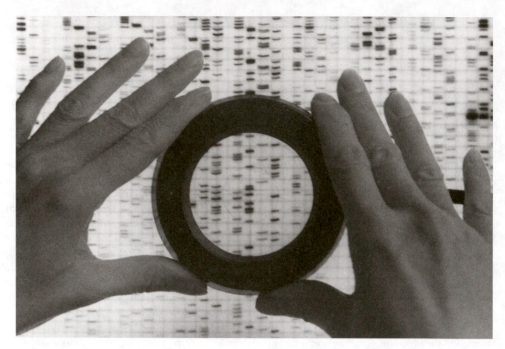

In biological evolution, information is preserved and transmitted by means of the genetic code: scientists are developing an ever more detailed map of human genetic information.

society's culture may occur within a single generation. Moreover, sociocultural evolution does not require that every society go through step-by-step sequential stages of development, as in biological evolution. Rather, a society may compress or even skip stages.[22] In the Third World today, for example, some nations have gone directly from human porters and pack animals to trucks and airplanes as the primary movers of goods, bypassing the stage of dependency on wagons and railroads that was part of the evolutionary experience of those societies in which the newer methods of transportation were first developed.

Finally, sociocultural evolution may have a greater potential than biological evolution for being brought under rational human control. So far, however, this process has hardly begun. One of humanity's most urgent tasks in the years ahead is to increase our understanding of the dynamics of sociocultural evolution so that we can find ways to control its direction and make it more responsive to human needs and ideals.

4

Types of Human Societies

The basic aim of science, as we have seen, is to explain how the world works. To this end, scientific research—whether it is focused on butterflies, galaxies, or human societies—looks for patterns and regularities in the world around us. This requires countless observations designed to reveal how things resemble one another, how they differ, and why—*a process of systematic comparison*.

CLASSIFYING HUMAN SOCIETIES

Over the years this process of comparison has given rise to many systems of classification in the various sciences. The periodic table in chemistry and the Linnaean taxonomy and its successors in biology are two of the more familiar. Such systems help us make sense of the wealth of data generated by research and serve as guides to scientists, suggesting new comparisons for study and new lines of research. But most important of all, these systems of classification have stimulated the development of theories that explain the patterns and regularities that have been discovered.

The system of classification that we will use in studying human societies is based on the **subsistence technologies** they employ. The origin of this system, like the origin of ecological-evolutionary theory itself, lies in the work of seventeenth- and eighteenth-century European scholars who responded to the discovery of less developed societies in the New World, Africa, and Asia by rethinking age-old questions about human origins and history. This led some of them to compare societies and try to classify them. A number of them even recognized the crucial importance of subsistence technology and based their systems of classification on it.[1]

The system of classification used in this volume grows out of that early work. It divides human societies into ten basic categories, with individual societies classified on the basis of their *primary mode of subsistence:*[2]

    Hunting and gathering societies
    Simple horticultural societies
    Advanced horticultural societies
    Simple agrarian societies
    Advanced agrarian societies
    Industrial societies
    Fishing societies
    Maritime societies
    Herding societies

A system of classification is most useful when it is simple, reliable, and objective,* so that the classification of cases is as unambiguous as possible. A society is classified as a hunting and gathering society only if the hunting of wild animals and foraging for uncultivated

---

*Objective and reliable in the sense that different observers using the classification criteria would place cases in the same categories.

Members of a twentieth-century society of hunters and gatherers: Australian aborigines singing sacred songs in preparation for an important ritual ceremony.

plant foods are its primary means of subsistence. Horticultural societies are societies that cultivate plants but do not have plows.[3] Advanced horticultural societies use metal tools and weapons, while simple horticultural societies have only wood and stone ones. Agrarian societies also cultivate plants but in addition have and use plows. Advanced agrarian societies use iron tools and weapons, while simple agrarian societies use only copper and bronze, which are softer and less plentiful metals (see Table 4.1).

Industrial societies are the newest type of society and technologically the most advanced. The distinguishing feature of these societies is their heavy dependence on machine technology and on the *inanimate* sources of energy—coal, petroleum, natural gas, and nuclear power—that drive the various machines. Because of their highly advanced technology, industrial societies are the most powerful and productive societies the world has ever seen.

Over the course of history, the majority of people have lived in one or another of the six kinds of societies described above. Some, however, have lived in societies that do not fall

TABLE 4.1 Criteria for Classifying Primary Types of Human Societies

Type of Society	Plant Cultivation*	Metallurgy*	Plow*	Iron*	Inanimate Energy Sources*
Hunting and gathering	-	-	-	-	-
Simple horticultural	+	-	-	-	-
Advanced horticultural	+	+	-	-	-
Simple agrarian	+	+	+	-	-
Advanced agrarian	+	+	+	+	-
Industrial	+	+	+	+	+

*The symbol + means that the trait is widespread in the type of society indicated; the symbol – means it is not.

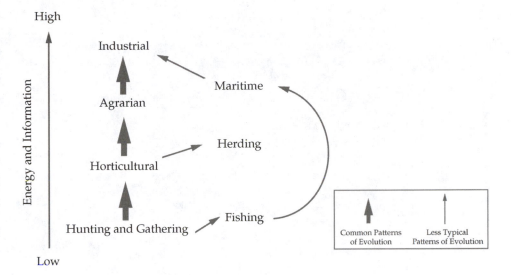

FIGURE 4.1 *Levels of technological development and patterns of evolution.*

neatly into any of these categories. For example, many today in Asia, Africa, and Latin America live in what are commonly referred to as "less developed" or "developing" societies. These are, in effect, *hybrid* societies, combining elements of modern industrial technology with traditional horticultural or agrarian technology.

Finally, in addition to all the others, there are three kinds of societies that have evolved in response to special or unusual environmental conditions. In semiarid regions, for example, as in the Middle East and North Africa, farming has not been possible, and in order to survive people have been forced to rely on the herding of livestock (sheep, goats, camels, etc.) as their basic means of subsistence. Elsewhere, peoples that have lived along the shores of rivers, lakes, or oceans have often found it advantageous to adopt fishing or overseas trade and commerce as their principal means of subsistence.

As Figure 4.1 indicates, the various societal types differ from one another not merely in terms of the kind of subsistence technology they employ but also in their overall level of technological development: agrarian and maritime societies, for example, are technologically on about the same level of development, and both are far more advanced technologically than hunting and gathering societies.

In the chapters that follow, we will examine each of the major types of societies. In Chapters 5 through 7, we examine in turn hunting and gathering, horticultural, and agrarian societies. In Chapter 8, we consider more briefly the environmentally specialized types of societies. In Chapters 9 through 13, we examine in considerable detail modern industrial societies; and, finally, in Chapter 14, we examine two kinds of hybrid societies, industrializing horticultural societies and industrializing agrarian societies.

SOCIETAL TYPES THROUGH HISTORY

Throughout most of human history, everyone lived in hunting and gathering societies. This period of relative social and cultural uniformity ended only within the last 10,000 to 12,000 years.

The first new type of society to emerge was fishing society (see Figure 4.2). Though the practice of fishing seems to have begun thousands of years earlier, fishhooks, nets, traps, boats, and paddles had to be invented before any society could make the shift from hunting and gathering to fishing as its *primary* means of subsistence.[4]

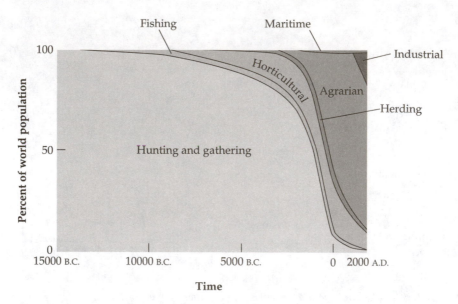

FIGURE 4.2 *Societal types through history: changes in size reflect the growth or decline in numbers of each of the societal types.*

Simple horticultural societies probably came next; they first appeared in the Middle East between 10,000 B.C. and 8000 B.C. and were well established 10,000 years ago.[5] Though people began to use copper within the next 1,500 years,[6] it was not until nearly 4000 B.C. that metal tools and weapons became common enough in any of these societies to permit us to call them *advanced* horticultural.[7]

The plow was invented late in the fourth millennium, and this innovation also occurred in the Middle East.[8] By 3000 B.C. it was used widely enough by societies in Mesopotamia and Egypt to justify labeling them simple agrarian.

Iron was discovered early in the second millennium B.C. but, like copper, did not become the dominant material in tools and weapons for a long time.[9] Thus, the first advanced agrarian societies did not appear until the early years of the first millennium B.C.

The origin of herding societies remains something of a mystery. Evidence of the domestication of sheep and goats dates from about 9000 B.C., but evidence from the earliest site suggests a hybrid technology.[*10] While we cannot say for certain when any society first came to depend on herding as its chief means of subsistence, it was probably sometime after horticultural societies appeared.

Minoans on the island of Crete, around 2000 B.C., were apparently the first people to rely on overseas commerce as their basic means of subsistence.[12] Maritime societies also flourished in Europe during the Middle Ages. Currently, Singapore is the only maritime society.

The last major societal type is industrial. The inventions that mark the beginning of the modern technological revolution occurred in the eighteenth century. But it was not until early in the nineteenth that Britain, which pioneered in industrialization, reached the point where it could be classified as a truly industrial society. Since then, more than twenty others have followed Britain's lead.

*Earlier—sometime between 22,000 and 10,000 B.C.—the dog achieved the distinction of being the first animal domesticated by humans.[11]

Historical Eras

As Figure 4.2 makes clear, the types of human societies in the world system have changed greatly in the last 10,000 to 12,000 years. There was a time when every society was at the hunting and gathering level of development; today, we have everything from hunting and gathering to industrial societies.

To understand a given society, past or present, it is not enough to know what type of society it is or was. It is equally important to know when it existed, since this tells us a great deal about its *social* environment. For example, the situation of hunting and gathering societies in the last hundred years has been far more precarious than it was 10,000 years ago. Such groups have found themselves in the unenviable position of interacting with far more advanced and far more powerful societies. No matter where hunting and gathering societies have been located, members of industrial societies have penetrated, using vast resources in ways that have transformed the conditions of life for less advanced groups. This has often been done with the best of intentions—as in the establishment of medical, educational, or religious missions—but good intentions have made little difference. The ultimate effect has been to transform and eventually destroy the social and cultural systems of technologically primitive peoples.

In studying a society, therefore, it is important to specify the historical era involved. The various eras are named according to the type of society that was politically and militarily dominant at the time. Thus, the long period in which all human societies were hunting and gathering societies is designated as the hunting and gathering era, while the period in which we live today is the industrial era.

From the standpoint of ecological-evolutionary theory, the four major eras in human history have been:*

1. The hunting and gathering era: from human beginnings to about 8000 B.C.
2. The horticultural era: from about 8000 B.C. to about 3000 B.C. (Advanced horticultural from about 4000 B.C. to 3000 B.C.)
3. The agrarian era: from about 3000 B.C. to about 1800 A.D. (Advanced agrarian from about 1000 B.C. to about 1800 A.D.)
4. The industrial era: from about 1800 A.D. to the present.

The best way to understand what sociocultural evolution has meant is to examine in sequence the four types of societies whose dominance in successive eras has defined the upper limits of technological advance. In them we can trace all the basic trends in population, culture, the material products of culture, social organization, and social institutions.

The reason for these trends *is that the rise of technologically more advanced societies contributed directly to the decline of those less advanced.* For when horticultural societies appeared, the chances for survival of neighboring hunting and gathering societies were substantially reduced unless they too adopted the new technology. The same was true for both hunting and gathering and horticultural societies after agrarian societies appeared. The less advanced societies lacked both the numbers and the weapons needed to defend themselves against the more advanced societies that coveted their territories and other resources. Those that managed to survive did so only in remote and isolated areas protected by oceans or other geographical barriers, or in territories judged undesirable by members of the more advanced societies (e.g., deserts, tropical rain forests, mountainous areas). In recent times, the pattern of military conquest and expansion has greatly declined, but the pattern of cultural penetration by technologically more advanced nations has increased tremendously, as we will see in later chapters.

---

*These dates are for the world as a whole. In many parts of the world, the horticultural and agrarian eras began later. For example, the agrarian era did not begin in the New World until the sixteenth century A.D., after European colonization and settlement.

DIFFERENCES AMONG TYPES OF SOCIETIES

One of the most important propositions in ecological-evolutionary theory asserts that advances in subsistence technology are a necessary condition for any significant increase in the size and complexity of a society (see page 59). Beginning in Chapter 5, we will put this proposition to the test as we examine each of the major types of societies.

Before plunging into the detailed evidence that bears on this proposition, it may be helpful to consider a much more limited body of evidence that was assembled over a period of years by George Peter Murdock with the aid of his students and colleagues. Together they assembled and codified a tremendous amount of information on more than a thousand societies. These data enable us to classify most of these societies in terms of the taxonomy described earlier in this chapter and to compare the various types of societies in a number of important ways.[13] Since the societies differ considerably in their levels of technological advance, we will be able to see whether they also differ in some of the ways that ecological-evolutionary theory says they should.

Science and Measurement

Science requires the precise and accurate comparison of phenomena. In most cases, it is not enough simply to say, for example, that X is larger than Y, or that it is hotter, or faster, or growing more rapidly. For this reason, scientists in every field use quantitative tools to measure and describe things, and to analyze relationships among them.

Sociology is no exception. In comparing human societies, for example, it is not enough to say merely that one type of society is larger than another; this could mean that it is 1 percent larger or a thousand times larger. Such imprecise statements fail to clarify the nature of relationships that exist among phenomena and thus hamper the search for patterns and their explanation.

Sociologists and other social scientists make great use of a set of quantitative tools known as *statistics,* the most basic of which are called summary measures. A summary measure reduces a number of different measurements to a single measure that represents them all. The most widely used are *measures of central tendency*—or what are popularly known as "averages."

The most familiar measure of central tendency is the arithmetic mean. The *arithmetic mean* is determined by adding the measurements of the individual units and dividing the sum by the number of units. For example, if 5 hunting and gathering societies have 25, 32, 39, 48, and 56 members respectively, the sum of the individual measurements is 200; when this is divided by the number of societies—5—we obtain a mean of 40.

Another widely used measure of central tendency is the *median*. We determine the median by arranging the individual measurements in order and identifying the one that is in the middle. In the example above, the median is 39. The median is often a more meaningful measure of central tendency than the mean, because it minimizes the effect of a single, highly discrepant case. If the sizes of the 5 societies in the example above had been 25, 32, 39, 48, and 156 (instead of 56), we would have obtained a mean of 60, which would have been a poor "summary" of the situation. The median, however, would still have been 39, a truer reflection of the size of most of the societies.

TABLE 4.2 Median Size of Societies, by Type of Society

Type of Society	Median Size of Society	No. of Societies
Hunting and gathering	40	46
Simple horticultural	1,500	53
Advanced horticultural	5,250	69
Agrarian	Over 100,000	38
Industrial	18,000,000*	16
Fishing	90	16
Herding	5,750	19

Sources: See Appendix and World Bank, *World Development Indicators* Online Database (http://www.worldbank.org/data/onlinedatabases/onlinedatabases.html).
*The mean is 49 million.

Size of Societies

One of the most important consequences of technological advance, according to ecological-evolutionary theory, is an increase in the size of societies. Table 4.2 confirms this. Technologically more advanced types of societies have, on average, much larger populations. Thus, the median size (see "Science and Measurement" above) of industrial societies is larger than the median size of agrarian societies, which is larger than the median size of horticultural societies, which is larger than the median size of hunting and gathering societies. The median sizes of fishing and herding societies are also about what one would expect in view of their places in the taxonomy of societies (see Figure 4.1). Fishing societies are larger, on average, than hunting and gathering societies, but much smaller, on average, than horticultural societies. Herding societies are roughly the same size as advanced horticultural societies.

Permanence of Settlements

Ecological-evolutionary theory also predicts that technological advance leads societies to establish more permanent settlements.[14] Because the hunting of wild animals and the gathering of uncultivated vegetable products soon deplete the supply of foodstuffs in the immediate area surrounding human settlements, hunter-gatherers are forced to move about with considerable frequency. In contrast, societies that practice horticulture or agriculture should, according to our theory, be able to establish more permanent settlements.

Murdock's data confirm this. Of the 167 hunting and gathering societies for which data were available, *only 10 percent* were reported to have permanent settlements, and all of these enjoyed unusually favorable environmental conditions or partial reliance on horticulture, fishing, or other more advanced technologies. In contrast, *94 percent* of the 507 horticultural and agrarian societies had permanent settlements.

Societal Complexity

A third important prediction of ecological-evolutionary theory is that technological advance is linked to greater complexity of the social system. Murdock's data permit us to test this hypothesis in two ways. First, we can compare societies on the basis of *the amount of occupational specialization* found in them. Second, we can compare them on the basis of *the complexity of their status systems*. Thus, we can test the complexity of both the horizontal and the vertical dimensions of social organization.

Table 4.3 shows the frequency with which several kinds of occupational specialists are found in seven different types of societies. In hunting and gathering societies, technologically the least advanced, there are no specialists in the six areas indicated. Specialization in those areas occurs in a tiny minority of simple horticultural societies but becomes considerably more common in advanced horticultural and agrarian societies. In *every* industrial society, there are specialists in *all* of these fields. In fishing societies, the level of occupational specialization is comparable

TABLE 4.3 Frequency of Craft Specialization, by Type of Society (in Percentages)

Type of Society	Metal-working	Weaving	Leather Working	Pottery	Boat Building	House Building	Average
Hunting and gathering	0	0	0	0	0	0	0
Simple horticultural	0	1	1	0	8	4	2
Advanced horticultural	96	5	12	14	4	2	22
Agrarian	98	34	24	24	5	18	34
Industrial	100	100	100	100	100	100	100
Fishing	7	0	0	0	5	2	2
Herding	44	3	6	0	0	1	9

Source: See Appendix, pp. 372–374.

to that in hunting and gathering and simple horticultural societies, while herding societies occupy an intermediate position between simple and advanced horticultural societies.

Figure 4.3 shows the relationship between subsistence technology and the complexity of status systems.* Once again, as ecological-evolutionary theory would lead us to expect, there is a steady progression from hunting and gathering to industrial societies, with no complex status systems found in the former but universally present in the latter. The two environmentally specialized types of societies—fishing and herding societies—rarely had complex status systems, which is what ecological-evolutionary theory would lead us to expect. None of the fishing societies and only 3 percent of the herding societies had status systems that could be classified as complex.

Ideology

Finally, there are a number of reasons to suspect that advancing technology will change the way people view the world and their place in it (e.g., see Chapter 11). One important aspect of this is the structure of their religious beliefs. Do they believe in one god or many? Does that god, or do those gods, encourage moral behavior? Again Murdock's data allow us to explore this question.

As Figure 4.4 indicates, belief in a god who created the world and who is concerned with the moral conduct of humans has been found in only a small minority of technologically

FIGURE 4.3 *Percentage of societies having complex status systems, by type of society.*

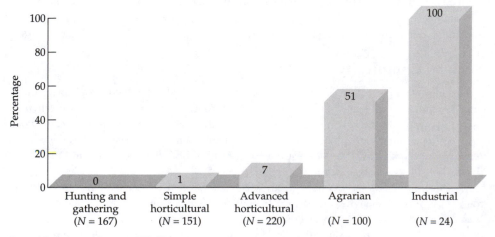

Source: See Appendix, pp. 372–374.

*Complex status systems are those which distinguish a large number of distinct levels or strata.

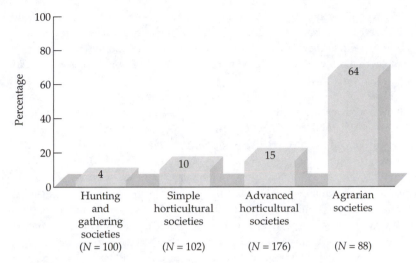

FIGURE 4.4 *Percentage of societies with belief in a creator god concerned with the moral conduct of humans, by type of society.*
Source: See Appendix, pp. 372–374.

less advanced societies—hunting and gathering, simple horticultural, and advanced horticultural—but it is found in the majority of agrarian and in almost all industrial societies.*[15]

SOCIETAL TYPES: WHAT THEY ARE AND WHAT THEY ARE NOT

By now it should be clear that the societal types with which we will be concerned throughout this volume are sets of societies in which individual societies resemble others of their type more than those of other types. The societies of one type are not identical, however. They differ from one another in many ways. Often, in fact, a number of societies of one type resemble some of the societies of another type *in certain respects* more than they resemble the majority of societies of their own type. For example, as Figure 4.4 indicates, the religious beliefs of a small minority of hunting and gathering societies (4 percent) resemble those of the majority of agrarian societies more than they resemble the beliefs of other hunting and gathering societies.

The differences between societal types are something like the differences between age categories within a population. Every society finds it useful—even necessary—to make distinctions between children and adults, and many societies go further and differentiate between infants, children, adolescents, young adults, the middle-aged, and the elderly. These distinctions reflect real and important differences within the population, but we recognize that the characteristics of all the individuals in a category are not identical. For example, a few elderly people will be in better physical condition than many middle-aged ones, and some adolescents may already be employed while some adults are still students in school. But these exceptions do not keep us from using age categories as tools that help us understand and anticipate the different ways individuals respond to various situations.

The reason we find age categories useful is because the physiological process of development and aging has such a profound impact on the daily lives of individuals. It sets limits on what is possible for individuals at various ages, and within those limits it makes some patterns of action more likely than others. Furthermore, the physiological process of development and aging has a similar impact on everyone who is at the same stage in the life cycle: this is why

*The clear exception is Japan, where Shintoism is the dominant belief.

the members of a given age category resemble one another more than they resemble the members of other age categories. This is also why the members of adjacent categories resemble one another more than they resemble members of more distant categories (e.g., why adolescents resemble children or young adults more than they resemble babies or the elderly).

Obviously, however, the physiological process of development and aging is not the only force that shapes our lives and personalities. This is why all the members of a given age category are not exactly alike and why there are always differences among them.

Societal types are much like age categories in all these ways. The reason they are so valuable is because subsistence technology has such a profound impact on the life of societies. It sets limits on what is possible for individual societies at every stage of development, and within those limits it makes certain social and cultural patterns more likely than others. Furthermore, it is a force that has a similar impact on all societies that share a common mode of subsistence: this is why societies of a given type tend to resemble one another more than they resemble societies of other types. This is also why societies of adjacent types (see Figure 4.1) resemble one another more than they resemble societies of more distant types (e.g., why simple horticultural societies resemble hunting and gathering societies more than they resemble industrial societies).

But subsistence technology is not the only force that influences the nature of societies, any more than the physiological process of development and aging is the only force that influences individual health, personality, and behavior. This is why there are differences among societies within a given societal type just as there are differences among individuals in the same age category.

In summary then, societal types are valuable analytical tools that help us to understand societies, both individually and collectively. They are sets of societies that share a single common characteristic, subsistence technology. But subsistence technology is not just any characteristic chosen at random from the almost endless list of societal characteristics. On the contrary, it appears to be *the single most powerful force responsible for the most important differences among human societies*.

Technological Determinism Rejected

Today, as in the past, efforts to understand the role of technology in human life are hindered by those who take extreme positions on the subject. Over the years, a few scholars have argued that technology explains almost every sociocultural pattern.[16] To combat this exaggerated view and to uphold the importance of ideological and organizational factors, other scholars have minimized or even denied the importance of technology.[17] Unfortunately, the unreasonableness of *both* positions has escaped many social scientists, with the result that sociology and anthropology have both been slow in coming to a realistic assessment of technology's role in the evolutionary process.

Much of the confusion results from a failure to think in *probabilistic* and *variable* terms. Few, if any, significant social patterns are determined by a single factor. Where human societies are concerned, one can rarely say that A and A alone causes B. Usually B is due to the combined effect of a number of factors, and, although A may be the most important, it is not likely to be strong enough to dictate the outcome. The most we can say, as a rule, is that if A is operative, B will occur with *some degree of probability*.

The problem is further complicated because so many of the B's we deal with are not *categorical* variables—things that are either present or absent, or true or false; they are *continuous* variables—things that vary by degree. For example, as we noted in Chapter 2, when we examine a society's population, we are not interested merely in noting that it exists; we are interested in its many graduated properties, such as its relative size, wealth, or military power.

A number of Third World societies today contain elements of advanced technology side by side with features of their traditional technologies: traditional and modern modes of transport in Cairo, Egypt.

The same is true of most of the other things we are concerned with—the *degree* of occupational specialization, the *frequency* of warfare, the *extent* of the authority exercised by leaders, and so forth. To think in categorical, either-or terms about such matters is bound to be misleading.

While ecological-evolutionary theory emphasizes the tremendous importance of technology and technological innovation in the life of human societies, it does not claim that technology can explain everything in sociocultural evolution. It recognizes that other forces have also played a part—often an important part. Its view of technology's role in human affairs can best be summarized in the following propositions:

1. Because subsistence technology sets limits on what is possible within a society, an advance in subsistence technology is a necessary precondition for substantial growth or development in terms of size, complexity, power, and wealth; this is true both for individual societies and for the world system.
2. Because subsistence technology sets limits on what is possible within a society and greatly influences the relative cost of each of the options within those limits, it is the single most important cause of the *totality of differences* among societies (but not of each individual difference).
3. Because societies that have grown substantially in size, complexity, wealth, and power enjoy a great advantage in intersocietal competition and are therefore more likely to transmit their social and cultural characteristics to future generations, the nature of the world system has been increasingly shaped by the process of technological advance and increasingly reflects the characteristics of those societies that are technologically the most advanced and most innovative.

If these propositions are correct, students of human societies can ill afford to ignore or neglect subsistence technology and the role it plays in human life. In fact, these propositions indicate that the first step in analyzing any society should be to identify its primary subsistence technology. This will ensure that we take into account from the outset the most powerful of the variables affecting it.

Our basic task for the rest of this volume will be to apply these principles in a broadly comparative study of human societies. We will examine each of the major societal types that have emerged in the course of history, seeing how technological advance has influenced its social institutions and how these institutions have, in turn, reacted to technology and influenced its development. We will, for obvious reasons, give special attention to the industrial and industrializing societies of our own day. Our ultimate goal is to achieve a better understanding of the forces that influence human societies, in the hope that this will help us understand and perhaps eventually control the process of change that is such a striking, and at times threatening, feature of the contemporary world.

PART TWO

PREINDUSTRIAL
SOCIETIES

5

Hunting and Gathering Societies

For the first 5 million years or more of hominid history, our ancestors all lived in hunting and gathering societies.* This was the only type of society in existence throughout this period. Only in the last 10,000 to 12,000 years—the last one-fourth or one-fifth of 1 percent of hominid history—have other types of societies evolved.

Despite their longevity, however, hunting and gathering societies may soon be extinct.** They simply have not been able to compete with technologically more advanced societies for territories and other vital resources. As a result, in recent centuries hunting and gathering societies have survived only in remote and isolated regions. And now, in the twenty-first century, with the development of new technologies and new resource needs, industrial societies have penetrated even into these areas. Thus, regrettably, few, if any, hunting and gathering societies are likely to survive far into the present century.

Fortunately, in recent centuries, anthropologists, explorers, missionaries, colonial administrators, and others have had opportunities to observe a large number of modern hunting and gathering societies and in some cases have provided detailed reports of their way of life. In addition, from their excavation and interpretation of bones and artifacts, archaeologists are developing a growing body of information about prehistoric hunting and gathering societies.

Taken individually, each of these sources of information has serious limitations. Since writing developed only after the advent of agriculture, written descriptions are available only for those hunting and gathering societies that were in contact with technologically more advanced societies, and in many cases these societies had already been pushed into marginal environments (e.g., deserts, rain forests, the Arctic) by horticulturalists and agriculturalists.*** Archaeologists, on the other hand, though they can tell us about societies in the era prior to the development of horticulture and agriculture, cannot directly observe behavior or interview the subjects of their study—they must make inferences from the physical traces left behind.

But the strengths of these sources are complementary, and, taken together, they can be quite informative. Therefore, we will first examine the archaeological and ethnographic evidence on hunting and gathering societies individually, and then consider the question of whether they provide consistent or contradictory images of hunting and gathering societies.

---

*Clearly, however, the importance of hunting changed dramatically in this era. Early hominids may merely have scavenged the carcasses of animals that had died or were killed by other predators, but they probably did not hunt, and large-game hunting is almost certainly a relatively recent innovation.

**Far less than 0.001 percent of the world's population relies on hunting and gathering for subsistence today.[1]

***The latter point may not be as important as it seems, since our present conception of "fertile" regions is based on their potential for farming. Yet many areas that are unsuited to farming have supported substantial populations of game animals (e.g., the Kalahari Desert, various polar regions), and thus supported populations of hunters and gatherers about as well as many areas that we think of today as much more fertile.

HUNTING AND GATHERING
SOCIETIES 100,000 B.C. TO 8000 B.C.

The best evidence currently available indicates that genetically modern humans evolved sometime between 100,000 and 200,000 years ago (see Excursus, pages 105–107). These first modern humans were more intelligent and probably better able to communicate among themselves than were their hominid forebears, but we should not ignore the fact that they inherited a number of valuable customs and technologies from them. Indeed, although the archaeological record shows that the rate of innovation was quite slow (see Table 5.1), hominids had accumulated a number of quite useful tools and effective practices in the nearly 5 million years that had elapsed between the time when our hominid ancestors diverged from the ancestors of the modern great apes and modern humans evolved. For example, they had developed a variety of tools capable of performing a number of crucial tasks (e.g., cutting, skinning, pounding), they had invented spears (see Figure 5.1) and had developed a number of techniques to make them more effective for hunting large game animals, and perhaps most important, they had domesticated fire.

Fire did far more than warm people and allow them to occupy very cold environments. In fact, mastery of it fostered something of a technological and social revolution. It set humans apart from all other animals,* giving them some control over the cycle of day and night, and giving them a little more freedom of movement. It was also important for protection, and it was a powerful weapon for driving predators away from camp or out of an attractive cave that humans wanted to use. Fire was also used to harden the points of wooden spears, and possibly to kill large animals by driving them over cliffs or into swamps.

Fire was probably also involved in the beginnings of religious experience, as a basis of ritual (e.g., in burnt sacrifices), even as an object of worship. But most important, fire strengthened the network of interrelationships within societies, drawing the group together at the end of a day to communicate, to remember, and to plan.[3]

Work in early hominid societies was quite probably divided between the sexes, and in the millennia just prior to the emergence of modern humans, men had learned to hunt large animals by working together in groups. There is also evidence that they began the practice of burying their dead, and the items left in the graves (e.g., food, implements, flowers) suggest that they may have believed in an afterlife.**[4]

FIGURE 5.1 *Two comparisons of the spear with the bow and arrow.*

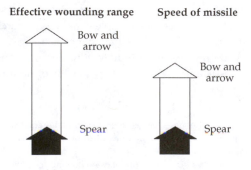

---

*As Goudsblom points out, *control* of fire is unique to humans (hominids). It is found in all human groups and in no nonhuman groups.[2]

**On the darker side, it should be noted that there is also evidence that hominids sometimes turned their weapons on one another, and there is even some suggestion that they may have occasionally practiced cannibalism.

TABLE 5.1 The Rising Rate of Technological Innovation: 4,000,000 B.C. to 8000 B.C.

Time Periods and Their Major Technological Innovations		No. of Major Innovations	Innovations per Thousand Years
4,000,000 to 100,000 B.C.		6	0.0015
Hand ax	Wooden spear		
Use of fire	Constructed shelters		
Fire-hardened spear point	Colored pigments		
100,000 to 40,000 B.C.		4	0.0667
Use of bone for tools	Skin clothing (probable)		
Built-in handles on tools	Harpoon heads		
40,000 to 10,000 B.C.		20	0.6667
Spear-thrower	Bow and arrow		
Lamps	Pins or awls		
Fish gorgets	Cord		
Needles with eyes	Antler hammers		
Shovels or scoops	Mattocks		
Stone saws	Graving tools		
Spoons	Stone ax with hafted handle		
Jewelry	Pestles and grinding slabs		
Separate handles	Musical instruments		
Boats			
Domestication of dog			
10,000 to 8000 B.C.		16	8.0
Beer	Fishhooks		
Fish traps	Fishnets		
Adzes	Sickles		
Plant cultivation	Domestication of sheep		
Basketry	Cloth		
Grinding equipment	Leather-working tools		
Paving	Sledge		
Ice picks	Combs		

Sources: This table is based on data in Grahame Clark and Stuart Piggott, *Prehistoric Societies* (New York: Knopf, 1965); S. A. Semenov, *Prehistoric Technology* (New York: Barnes and Noble, 1964); John Pfeiffer, *The Emergence of Man,* 3d ed. (New York: Harper & Row, 1978); Jacquetta Hawkes, *Prehistory, UNESCO History of Mankind,* vol. 1, part 1 (New York: Mentor, 1965); Alexander Marshak, *The Roots of Civilization* (New York: McGraw-Hill, 1972); P. S. Bellwood, "The Peopling of the Pacific," *Scientific American,* 243 (Nov. 1980), pp. 174–185; Bruce Bower, "When the Human Spirit Soared," *Science News,* vol. 130 (Dec. 13, 1986), pp. 376–379; and "Site Surrenders Fabric of Prehistoric Life," *Science News,* vol. 144 (July 24, 1993), p. 54; Robin Dennell, "Needles and Spear Throwers," *Natural History* (Oct. 1986), pp. 70–78; John Putnam, "In Search of Modern Hunters," *National Geographic,* vol. 174, no. 4 (Oct. 1988), p. 449; Paul Mellars, "Major Issues in the Emergence of Modern Humans," *Current Anthropology,* 30 (1989), pp. 349–385; and "The Dawn of Creativity," *U.S. News and World Report* (May 20, 1996).

Nonetheless, the emergence of genetically modern humans marks a critical juncture in our species' evolutionary history. For, at this point, *cultural evolution replaced biological evolution as the primary means of adaptation and change in human societies.* Even so, if we look for some dramatic change in societies immediately following the emergence of biologically modern humans, we are in for a disappointment. Though the archaeological record for this period is sparse, there is nothing to suggest that there were any major new developments until much later.* Living remained precarious, and life expectancy short. One authority who analyzed the remains of forty individuals who lived 50,000 to 100,000 years ago found that only one of them reached the age of fifty, and only 10 percent the age of forty. Half of them died before their twentieth year![6]

Few important innovations appeared until near the end of this period when the rate of innovation begins to increase at an accelerating rate. For example, the spear did not change

---

*Even newly discovered evidence of sophisticated tools (e.g., bone harpoon heads) in Africa in this period (about 90,000 B.C.) suggests that these innovations were highly localized and did not spread far.[5]

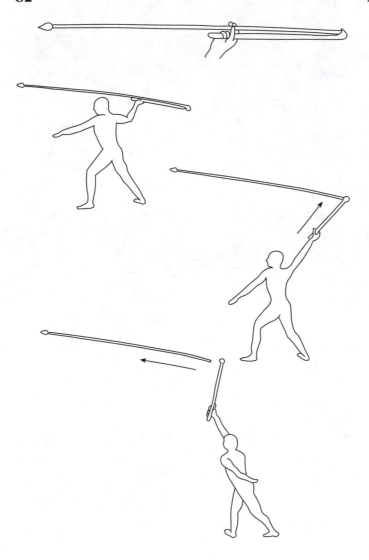

FIGURE 5.2 *The spear-thrower applies the principle of the lever and doubles the distance a spear can be hurled.*
Source: After John Purcell, *From Hand Ax to Laser: Man's Growing Mastery of Energy* (New York: Vanguard Press, 1982). Illustrated by Judy Skorpil.

very much until the period from 40,000 B.C. to 8000 B.C., when hunters made several major improvements. First, they developed the spear-thrower, which applies the principle of the lever and doubles the distance a spear can be hurled (see Figure 5.2).[7] Second, at the other end of the spear they began using sharpened bone points to increase the penetrating power. Finally, they added barbs to the spearhead to create a much more serious wound.[8]

It is also not until the latter half of this era that the bow and arrow was invented. Employing the principle of the concentration of energy, hunters in this period created a weapon of great usefulness and versatility (see Figure 5.1). Its effective wounding range is roughly four times that of the spear and twice that of the spear thrown with the aid of a spear-thrower.[9] Furthermore, an arrow travels two and a half to three times faster than a spear. This is important not only because of the time advantage it affords the hunter, but also because the force of the blow is a function of the missile's speed.* Finally, unlike the spear, the bow and arrow permit the hunter to sight the missile at eye level, which greatly increases the accuracy of his aim.

Other technological improvements, though less dramatic, were no less important. As one writer puts it, people toward the end of this era "began to make the tool fit the task with an altogether new precision."[10] Innovations included such diverse tools as pins or awls, needles with eyes, spoons, graving tools, axes, stone saws, antler hammers, shovels or scoops, pestles and grinding slabs (for grinding minerals to obtain coloring materials), and mattocks.

In colder regions, people usually lived in caves.** This was not always possible, however, as in the case of the mammoth hunters who ranged from the former Czechoslovakia to Siberia and whose way of life forced them to remain in caveless country even during the winter. The drawing on page 84 shows a modern reconstruction of one of their settlements. Some societies also built houses of earth and clay.[11]

The discovery of such settlements has provided us with information on the size of societies in the hunting and gathering era. In general, they were quite small, many with as few as six to thirty persons. The largest settlement of hunters and gatherers ever found was spread out along a two-mile stretch of river in France and may have housed as many as 400 to 600 persons,[12] but this was exceptional and may have been only a temporary gathering of a number of societies taking advantage of a salmon run or other special situation.

Some of the best known innovations from the latter half of this era occur in the arts (see page 84). The drawings on the walls of caves in France are world famous, but they are only

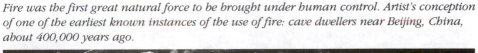

Fire was the first great natural force to be brought under human control. Artist's conception of one of the earliest known instances of the use of fire: cave dwellers near Beijing, China, about 400,000 years ago.

*These advantages are partly offset by the greater weight of the spear, which is why it continued to be used for some purposes.
**It should be noted, however, that this impression may be an artifact of the better preservation of human tools and traces left in caves.

Artist's conception of mammoth hunters' settlement in the former Czechoslovakia about 25,000 years ago, based on archaeological finds.

one of the new art forms developed at this time. There was sculpture of various kinds as well as bone and ivory carvings, often on the handles of weapons and tools.[13]

It would be hard to exaggerate the importance of these artistic remains, for they provide many insights into the evolution of human thought and the rapidly growing body of nontechnological information. Drawings of men dressed to resemble animals strongly suggest magical or religious practice and a belief in sympathetic magic. This belief—that anything

Lascaux cave painting (about 15,000 B.C.).

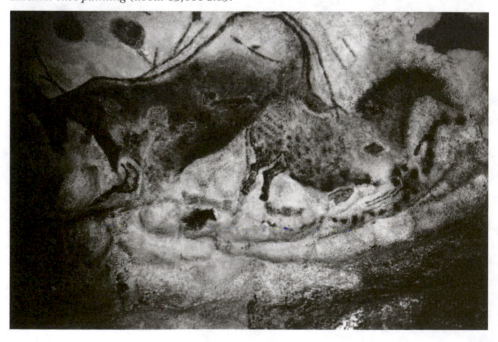

The Venus of Willendorf,
Germany (about 20,000 B.C.).

done to an image, or a part, of a person or animal will affect that person or animal—is further suggested by the fact that a great number of the drawings have spears or darts drawn or scratched into animals' flanks.[14] Sympathetic magic was apparently also used in an attempt to produce fertility, in both humans and animals. At least this is the most likely explanation for the numerous female figures with exaggerated evidences of pregnancy (see illustration above). Most scholars think it is no coincidence that the artist ignored the facial features and focused on the symbols of fertility.

Many examples of the art of this period indicate the development not only of new beliefs, but also of ceremony and ritual. This is suggested by the drawings of men dancing and by engravings of processions of men standing before animals, heads bowed and weapons resting on their shoulders in a nonthreatening position. It has been suggested that they are asking the forgiveness of the animals they plan to kill, as some modern hunters do.[15] In summary, the art of this era reveals the growth of human consciousness and the effort of people to understand and control their environment, and it attests to the growing gulf developing between them and the rest of the animal world.

By the close of the hunting and gathering era (about 8000 B.C.), human societies possessed a far greater store of cultural information than they possessed 30,000 years before. They had, in fact, acquired more in those last 30,000 years than in all the previous millions of years of hominid history.

Table 5.1 shows how dramatic the change was in the rate of technological innovation alone. It lists all the known technological innovations of importance from the beginnings of the hominid family to the end of the hunting and gathering era. The four time intervals involved correspond to the periods which archaeologists label the Lower Paleolithic, Middle Paleolithic, Upper Paleolithic, and Mesolithic, and it should be noted that they differ tremendously in duration (from 3,000 years to 3.9 million years). By dividing the number of innovations by the approximate time required to produce them, we arrive at the figures in the right-hand column, which are a rough measure of the relative rate of innovation during the successive periods.

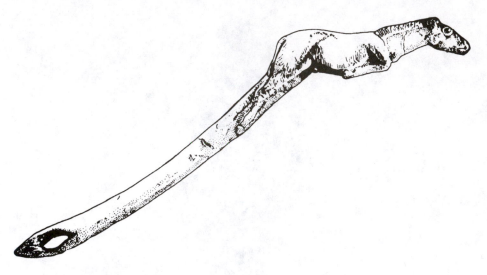

Handle of spear-thrower, France.

The rapid acceleration in the rate of change in the last 30,000 years of the hunting and gathering era cannot be explained by genetic change alone, since, as we noted earlier, our species had already evolved by 100,000 B.C. and was present for all but the earliest time period in Table 5.1.

What, then, was the cause?

In recent years, a growing number of scholars have concluded that the explosive growth in the rate of technological innovation in this period resulted from critical advances in language.[16] While symbol use almost certainly began much earlier than this, earlier symbol systems were probably much more primitive and much less effective as instruments for learning, remembering, and sharing information. According to proponents of this view, the relatively modest genetic changes that were involved in the transition to *Homo sapiens sapiens* (fully modern man) paved the way for the explosive growth of culture that occurred at the end of the Old Stone Age, and for all the revolutionary social and cultural changes that followed. In other words, there was a critical "threshold effect"* involved: until a certain point was reached in biological evolution, the development of full-fledged symbol systems was impossible. But once that point was reached, the development of language could proceed rapidly.

The striking advances in technology at the end of the hunting and gathering era coincided with, and were probably the cause of, an equally striking growth in the size of the human population. According to estimates based on recent archaeological research, the rate of growth of the human population increased substantially after 40,000 B.C. (see Table 5.2). This growth of population then would have increased the need for food and also increased the number of people looking for ways of providing it, thus contributing to the rising rate of innovation.

Despite the rapid increase in the rate of growth during this period, the human population at the end of the hunting and gathering era still numbered less than 10 million and its rate of growth was still less than 0.1 percent per year (compared with 1.5 percent per year today). The reason for this was the inability of societies to provide adequately for their members and to protect them against disease and other dangers. A recent study of more than 300 skeletons of adults from Europe and Africa during the hunting and gathering era indicates that the average age at death was just 33 years for men and 28 for women.[17] Thus, the reproductive years for women were far fewer than they are today. With the high rates of infant mortality

*See footnote on page 14.

TABLE 5.2 The Growth of Human Population during the Hunting and Gathering Era

Approximate Date	Estimated Human Population	Average Percentage Increase in Human Population Worldwide per Thousand Years*
1,800,000 B.C.	400,000	
150,000 B.C.	800,000	0.04
40,000 B.C.	1,200,000	0.40
8000 B.C.	8,500,000	6.10

*These figures are our own calculations.
Source: Adapted from Fekri Hassan, *Demographic Archaeology* (New York: Academic Press, 1981), table 12.3.

that also prevailed,[18] it is no wonder that the rate of growth of the human population was still extremely low at the end of the hunting and gathering era.

HUNTING AND GATHERING SOCIETIES OF THE RECENT PAST

Even after the emergence of more advanced types of societies, hunting and gathering societies continued to flourish in many parts of the world. A hundred years ago there were still large numbers of them in both the New World and Australia, and smaller numbers in southwest Africa, in parts of the rain forest in central Africa, in certain remote areas in southeast Asia and neighboring islands, and in Arctic Asia.[19] As recently as 1788 there were probably 5,000 hunting and gathering societies in Australia alone[20] and almost certainly as many in North America. Although the settlement of these areas by Europeans and the spreading influence of industrialization are now destroying the last of them, we have detailed descriptions of many of these groups.

There is considerable variation among the 174 societies in Murdock's data bank (see Appendix). For example, 12 percent of them relied on hunting and gathering for their *entire* subsistence, while 13 percent relied on these techniques for only about half. Most groups (81 percent) depended on fishing to some extent, and a few (15 percent) obtained nearly half their food from this source. A minority (28 percent) derived part from horticulture, and a few (less than 5 percent) almost half. In short, a few were pure hunting and gathering societies, but most of them incorporated limited elements of fishing or horticulture or both.

Population

Size and Density Despite these variations in subsistence technology, modern hunting and gathering societies* have a lot in common. For example, none supports a large or dense population: nearly 80 percent have less than one person per square mile.[21] Communities, therefore, are necessarily small. And, since communities are almost always autonomous, societies are equally small. The average size of those that survived into the modern era has been approximately 40.[22] As ecological-evolutionary theory would lead us to expect, the more completely societies depend for their subsistence on hunting and gathering, the smaller they tend to be, while those that incorporate fishing, horticulture, or herding as secondary means of subsistence are larger (see Table 5.3).

The rate of population growth in hunting societies is usually very low.** In many cases, the number of births is virtually matched by the number of deaths. In part, this is because of

---

*When referring to "modern" hunting and gathering societies, we mean those that survived into the modern era (i.e., the last several hundred years). In writing about these societies, the present tense is usually used for convenience even though most of the studies were conducted some years ago.
**Rapid population growth occurs in these societies only when they are able to expand into new (uninhabited) territories or gain access to new sources of food.

TABLE 5.3 Average Size of Hunting and Gathering Societies, by Percentage of Food Supply Obtained through Hunting and Gathering

Percentage of Food Supply Obtained through Hunting and Gathering	Median Size	Number of Societies
86–100*	29	34
50–85*	49	71

*These figures are estimates made by Murdock and his associates, based on nonquantitative statements in ethnographic sources.
Source: See Appendix, pp. 372–374.

high death rates from natural causes, such as accidents and disease.[23] But it is also the result of physiological responses to the diet and nomadic lifestyle of hunters and gatherers. For example, prolonged nursing of infants and low levels of body fat both reduce fertility, and high levels of maternal mobility increase the risks of miscarriage.[24] Furthermore, since the braking effects of these variables rise and fall with the availability of food, they help to promote a rough balance between population size and environmental resources.[25]

Nonetheless, the most important factors producing equilibrium between births and deaths are probably cultural. Delayed marriages and postpartum sex taboos reduce the number of children a woman will give birth to, and we cannot ignore the fact that infanticide and abortion are widespread in these societies. One study revealed that infanticide was practiced in 80 of 86 hunting and gathering societies examined, while another study found that abortion was practiced in 13 of 15 societies.[26] Some scholars estimate that between 15 and 50 percent of all live births end in infanticide in societies at this level of development.[27]

The members of hunting and gathering societies are not, of course, less loving than the members of other societies. Their norms and values, like those of every society, simply reflect the past experience of the group. And this has taught them that any other course of action can be disastrous. When a mother already has one child at the breast, and may have to keep it there for several years because there is no safe alternative source of nourishment,[28] another baby can mean death for both children. This is especially likely to be true if the food supply is variable, that is, if hunting and gathering provide a glut of food at some times and shortages at others. If, in addition, the mother must participate regularly in the search for food and watch over her children at the same time, and if she must carry all her possessions as well as her children to a new campsite every few weeks or months (see below), the logic of abortion and infanticide becomes obvious. They are simply measures that ensure the health and survival of mothers and children, and thus the survival of the society.

Nomadism   Modern hunting and gathering societies are usually nomadic. Some groups are reported to remain in an area for periods as short as a week.[29] In contrast, a few occupy permanent settlements, but all of these either rely on fishing or horticulture as important secondary sources of subsistence or are located in areas with unusually high concentrations of game and other food resources.[30]

The nomadic character of most hunting and gathering groups is an inevitable result of their subsistence technology. One anthropologist described the basic problem when he said of a group of African Pygmies with whom he had lived that "after a month, as a rule, the fruits of the forest have been gathered all around the vicinity of the camp, and the game has been scared away to a greater distance than is comfortable for daily hunting."[31] He went on to say that since "the economy relies on the day-to-day quest, the simplest thing is for the camp to move."

Hunters and gatherers may also change campsites for other reasons. A study of the Hadza in east Africa, for example, indicates that they often move to the place where a large animal has been killed simply to avoid carrying the meat.[32] Since their possessions are few, such a move requires little effort. The Hadza also move to a new site when someone dies, or even when a member becomes sick or has a bad dream, because these are all regarded as bad omens.

Many hunting and gathering groups disperse for a part of the year, with individual families striking out on their own. This pattern has been observed in such widely scattered groups as the !Kung San* of southwest Africa, the Eskimo, and the Australian aborigines. Sometimes seasonal changes in flora and fauna make it more advantageous for the group to split up and do their hunting and foraging in smaller groups. Sometimes the splitting up of the group seems to be a response to controversies and conflicts that require a cooling-off period—after which the desire for more social interaction serves to bring the group together again.[34]

Despite their nomadism, hunters and gatherers usually restrict their movements to a fairly well defined territory. When the society moves, it usually settles in or near some former campsite. There may even be a regular circuit of sites that the group uses year after year. A group is usually deterred from entering new territories because they are already occupied by others. Moreover, hunters and gatherers normally have a strong attachment to their traditional territory, which has often acquired a sacred character that is maintained through song and legend.

Kinship

Ties of **kinship** are vitally important in most hunting and gathering groups. It is hard for members of modern industrial societies to appreciate the tremendous significance of these ties, because so much of our own social interaction is organized independently of kinship, in terms of roles such as teacher and student, clerk and customer, or friend and friend.

In contrast, social interaction in hunting and gathering societies is usually organized around kinship roles. A student of the Australian aborigines reports that "in a typical Australian **tribe** it is found that a man can define his relations to every person with whom he has any social dealings whatever, whether of his own or of another tribe, by means of the terms of [kinship]."[35] Another writer says of these people that "every one with whom a person comes in contact is regarded as related to him, and the kind of relationship must be ascertained so that the two persons concerned will know what their mutual behavior should be."[36] He adds that kinship ties are the anatomy and physiology of aboriginal society and "must be understood if the behavior of the aborigines as social beings is to be understood." Though there are exceptions, kinship is usually the basic organizing principle in hunting and gathering societies.[37]

Viewed in evolutionary perspective, the family has often been described as the matrix, or womb, from which all other social institutions have evolved. This points to a basic truth: in hunting and gathering societies, kin groups perform many of the functions that are performed by schools, business firms, governmental agencies, and other specialized organizations in larger, more advanced, and more differentiated societies.

Kin groups in hunting and gathering societies are of two types, nuclear and extended families. A nuclear family includes a man, his wife or wives, and their unmarried children; an extended family contains multiple nuclear families linked by a parent-child relationship (e.g., parents of a married couple or their married children).[38] **Polygyny,** marriage of a man to two or more women, is widespread; only 10 percent of the hunting and gathering groups in Murdock's data set are classified as monogamous. It does not follow, of course, that 90 percent of the families in this kind of society are polygynous: this is impossible, given the roughly equal numbers of men and women. Usually only one or two of the most influential men have more than one wife, and they seldom have more than two or three. This limited polygyny is

*The '!' denotes a clicking sound in the language (Khoisan) spoken by these people.[33]

!Kung San mother carrying infant while digging roots.

possible because girls usually marry younger than boys, and some men are obliged to remain bachelors. Multiple wives appear to be an economic asset in these societies and, to some extent, a status symbol as well.

      Divorce is permitted in virtually all hunting and gathering societies and is fairly common in some.[39] In others, however, it is made relatively difficult. The most we can say is that there is great variability in this matter.

      The nuclear family is usually part of a larger and more inclusive kin group known as the extended family.[40] In the majority of modern hunting and gathering societies the extended family includes both maternal and paternal relatives—a pattern that is not found in the majority of horticultural, herding, and agrarian societies. Compared with extended family systems that emphasize ties with either maternal or paternal kin, this bilateral, or two-sided, system effectively doubles the number of people to whom an individual can turn for help in time of difficulty, an arrangement that appears to have considerable adaptive value in societies that are so small.[41]

      The extended family is also important because the ties of kinship among its members encourage the practice of sharing. When the daily acquisition of food is uncertain, as it is in many hunting and gathering societies, a nuclear family could easily starve if it had to depend exclusively on its own efforts. A family might be surfeited with food for a time and then suddenly have nothing. Or all the adult members of the family could become ill or injured at the same time. In either case the family would be dependent on the generosity of others. Although sharing can, and does, take place between unrelated persons, kinship ties strengthen the tendency. In this connection it is interesting to note that many hunting and gathering peoples create what we would call fictional ties of kinship when there is no "real" relationship by blood or marriage. These ties are just as meaningful to them as "true" kinship ties, and they serve to strengthen the bonds uniting the group—much like the role of godparent in some more developed societies.

Through marriages with people in nearby groups (a practice known as **exogamy**), a society gradually establishes a web of kinship ties with neighboring groups. According to one anthropologist, "One of the important functions of exogamy is that of opening up territories so that peaceful movements can take place among them, and particularly so that any large temporary variations in food resources can be taken advantage of by related groups."[42] This is also the explanation for the custom of wife lending, practiced by hunting and gathering peoples as diverse as the Eskimo and the Australian aborigines.[43] As in the case of exogamy, the purpose seems to be to strengthen, restore, or create bonds between the men involved. Thus, if two individuals or two groups have had a quarrel, they may settle it by lending one another their wives. The practice is predicated on the assumption that women are prized possessions that one does not share with everyone. It would be a mistake to suppose, however, that women are merely property in these societies; they often have considerable influence in the life of the group and are by no means mere chattels.

The Economy

Economic institutions are not very complex in hunting and gathering societies. One reason is that the combination of a simple technology and a nomadic way of life makes it impossible for most hunting and gathering peoples to accumulate many possessions (see photo on page 92). In describing the !Kung San of southwest Africa, one ethnographer explains, "It is not advantageous to multiply and accumulate in this society. Any man can make what he needs when he wants to. Most of the materials he uses are abundant and free for anyone to take. Furthermore, in their nomadic lives, without beasts of burden, the fact that the people themselves must carry everything puts a sharp limit on the quantity of objects they want to possess."[44] The minority of hunting and gathering groups that are able to establish permanent settlements may accumulate more possessions, but even they are severely limited by their simple technology.[45]

The quest for food is obviously a crucial activity in every hunting and gathering society. Since most of these societies have no way to store food for extended periods, the food quest must be fairly continuous. Moreover, unlike the situation in more advanced societies, every adult member of the group, except some of the elderly, participates and makes a contribution in this most basic part of the economy.

Prior to the last quarter century, most studies of hunting and gathering societies emphasized the uncertainty of the food supply and the difficulty of obtaining it.[46] A number of more recent studies, however, paint a brighter picture. Reports from the Pygmies of the Congo, the aborigines of Australia, and even the !Kung of the Kalahari Desert in southwestern Africa indicate that they all secure an ample supply of food without an undue expenditure of time or energy.[47] This has led some anthropologists to swing to the opposite extreme and refer to hunters and gatherers as "the most leisured people in the world" and to their way of life as "the original affluent society."[48]

Neither view does justice to the diversity and changeability of the situations reported by the numerous observers who have lived among these peoples. Conditions vary considerably from group to group, and within a group they may vary from season to season. For example, the Indians of northern California usually had an abundance of food, and yet even they occasionally encountered a shortage so severe that some of them starved.[49]

A very few societies do not practice hunting. For the rest, hunting usually provides less food, in terms of bulk, than gathering. According to one estimate, the gathering done by women accounts for 60 to 80 percent of the food supply of hunters and gatherers, except in

Home and possessions of Paiute family in southern Utah in the 1870s.

arctic regions.[50] Yet hunting is valued more highly than gathering in virtually all these groups
for several reasons. For one thing, meat is generally preferred to vegetables.[51] Whether this
reflects a genetically based need or preference, we do not know; certainly not everyone feels
this way. In some groups, preference for meat may simply reflect its scarcity. Hunting may
also be valued because it requires greater skill and involves more uncertainty regarding the
outcome. Added to all this is the fact that meat, unlike vegetables, is commonly shared beyond the immediate family, so success in hunting may be rewarded by widespread respect
and deference. One leading anthropologist even suggests that sharing meat "is basic to the
continued association of families in any human group that hunts."[52]

    Because of the primitive nature of its technology, the division of labor in a hunting and
gathering economy is largely limited to distinctions based on age and sex. Almost all hunting
and military activities fall to the males, as do most political, religious, ceremonial, and artistic
activities. The collection and preparation of vegetables and the care of children are women's
responsibilities.[53] Some activities, such as constructing a shelter, may be defined as either
men's or women's work, depending on the society.[54] Still other activities may be considered
appropriate for both sexes. Further division of labor results because both the very young and
the aged are limited in their capabilities.

    There are no full-time occupational specialties in hunting and gathering societies, al-
though there is usually some part-time specialization. For example, most groups have at least

Why Were Women Not the Hunters?

The revival of the women's movement in recent decades and its claim that biological differences between the sexes should be irrelevant in the division of labor invite the question of why men were the hunters and women the gatherers in hunting and gathering societies. Why not the reverse, or perhaps a sharing of responsibilities?

In recent years, a number of social scientists have reexamined these questions and concluded that the biological differences between the sexes made a role reversal, or even a sharing of responsibilities, impossible in technologically limited societies such as these. Hunting with bows and spears requires speed, agility, and upper-body strength, and women, *on average,* are biologically disadvantaged in all three respects.

These disadvantages are linked to the special role of women in the reproductive process. The later stages of pregnancy, for example, reduce the speed and agility of women in obvious ways. But the requirements of reproduction have other, more subtle consequences. Because of the physiological demands of pregnancy and lactation on a mother's body, women have a higher ratio of fat to muscle than men. On average, about 21 percent of their weight consists of fatty tissue compared to 15 percent for men. This provides women with nutritional reserves on which they can draw during food shortages, both for their own sustenance and for that of a fetus or nursing infant. But less muscle tissue means reduced upper-body strength. Tests by the U.S. Army indicate that, *on average,* women have 42 percent less upper-body strength than men and 30 percent less lower-body strength.

With training, women can obviously develop their muscles to a level that exceeds that of the average man. For example, when Candy Csencsits placed second in the 1983 Ms. Olympia Contest, she was down to 7 percent body fat (champion male bodybuilders have even less, 3 to 5 percent). But when women drop below 15 percent body fat, they often cease to ovulate and become infertile. Thus, muscular development in women appears to conflict with the role of childbearing. In other words, if there ever were societies that used women extensively in hunting, they probably did not survive because of low birthrates.

In addition to all this, women in most hunting and gathering societies must nurse their babies for at least two to four years, because of the lack of a safe and adequate substitute for mother's milk. And since nursing infants need to be fed often, mothers are not able to roam as widely or as fast as hunting requires. Finally, in most of these societies, women in the prime of their lives are usually either pregnant or lactating and thus have little opportunity to develop and maintain the many complex skills required in hunting. The end result, therefore, has been the classic division of labor in which men hunt and women gather.

Sources: Ernestine Friedel, *Women and Men* (New York: Holt, Rinehart, and Winston, 1975); Joan Huber and Glenna Spitze, *Sex Stratification* (New York: Academic Press, 1983); Janet Saltzman Chafetz, *Sex and Advantage* (Totowa, NJ: Rowman and Allanheld, 1984); Michael Levin, "Women as Soldiers—The Record So Far," *The Public Interest,* 76 (Summer 1984), pp. 31–44; Blythe Hamer, "Women Body Builders," *Science 86,* 7 (March 1986), pp. 74–75; and U.S. Army Research Institute of Environmental Medicine, Associated Press report, Jan. 31, 1996.

a **headman** and a **shaman** or medicine man. When their services are required, they function in these specialized capacities, but, as one writer says of the headmen of the Bergdama and the !Kung, "when not engaged on public business they follow the same occupations as all other people."[55] He adds that this is most of the time.

Within hunting and gathering societies, the family or kin group is normally the only significant form of economic organization. Sometimes, when the practice of sharing is widespread and hunting and gathering are carried on as communal activities, even the kin group ceases to be economically important.

With respect to subsistence, each society is virtually self-sufficient. Trade between societies often occurs, but except where contacts have been established with more advanced societies, the bartered items tend to be nonessentials—primarily objects with status or aesthetic value. Such exchanges usually involve things that are scarce or nonexistent in one group's territory but present in the other's (e.g., certain kinds of shells, stones, or feathers).

Trade with advanced societies is more likely to involve economically important items. For example, many groups obtain metal tools and weapons this way.[56] In the past, these imports were seldom on a scale sufficient to alter the basic character of hunting and gathering societies.[57] In the last century, however, as contacts with industrialized and industrializing societies have increased, the volume and importance of such items have often greatly distorted traditional patterns of economic life and done much to undermine the sociocultural system as a whole.

The Polity

The political institutions of modern hunting and gathering societies are very rudimentary. As we have seen, most local communities are autonomous and independent entities (i.e., they are societies as well as communities) even though they have populations of fewer than fifty people. Because they are so small, hunting and gathering societies have not developed political mechanisms of the kind required to control and coordinate large or diverse populations.

The primitive nature of the political systems of these societies can be seen clearly in their limited development of specialized political roles and in the equally limited authority given to people in those roles. In most cases there is simply a headman who provides minimal leadership for the group (see Figure 5.3).[58] Allan Holmberg, who lived among the Siriono of eastern Bolivia, wrote a description of their headmen that, except for details, is a portrait of the "typical" headman in a hunting and gathering society.

> Presiding over every band of Siriono is a headman, who is at least nominally the highest official of the group. Although his authority theoretically extends throughout the band, in actual practice its exercise depends almost entirely upon his personal qualities as a leader. In any case, there is no obligation to obey the orders of a headman, no punishment for nonfulfillment. Indeed, little attention is paid to what is said by a headman unless he is a member of one's immediate family. To maintain his prestige a headman must fulfill, in a superior fashion, those obligations required of everyone else.
>
> The prerogatives of a headman are few. . . . The principal privilege . . . if it could be called such, is that it is his right to occupy, with his immediate family, the center of the [communal] house. Like any other man he must make his bows and arrows, his tools; he must hunt, fish, collect, and [so forth]. He makes suggestions as to migrations, hunting trips, etc., but these are not always followed by his [people]. As a mark of status, however, a headman always possesses more than one wife.
>
> While headmen complain a great deal that other members of the band do not satisfy their obligations to them, little heed is paid to their requests. . . .
>
> In general, however, headmen fare better than other members of the band. Their requests more frequently bear fruit than those of others because headmen are the best hunters and are thus in a better position than most to reciprocate for any favors done them.[59]

There are similar reports on headmen in most other hunting and gathering societies.[60] In a number of instances it is said that the headman "held his place only so long as he gave satisfaction."

Occasionally the headman enjoys a bit more power and privilege. Among the Bergdama of southwest Africa, for example, the headman "is treated with universal respect, being speci-

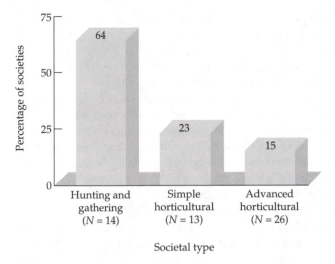

FIGURE 5.3 *Percentage of societies in which political leaders rely on persuasion (by societal type).*
Source: Appendix, pp. 372–374.

fied as a 'great man' by adults and 'grandfather' by children; he usually has the most wives (sometimes three or more); he has the pick of all wild animal skins for clothing himself and his family, and only his wives wear necklaces or girdles of ostrich eggshell beads; and he receives portions of all game killed in the chase, and tribute from men finding honey."[61]

At the opposite extreme are a number of hunting and gathering societies, including 12 percent of those in Murdock's data set, that do not even have a headman. In these societies, decisions that affect the entire group are arrived at through informal discussions among the more respected and influential members, typically the heads of families.[62]

The limited development of political institutions in hunting and gathering societies contrasts markedly with the situation in more advanced societies. The small size and relative

Indigenous hunters and gatherers of Australia enact a traditional ritual.

isolation of these societies make it possible for them to handle their political problems very informally. Consensus is achieved much more readily in a small, homogeneous group of a few dozen people (of whom only the adults, and often only the adult males, have a voice) than in larger, more heterogeneous communities with thousands of members. A headman is valuable to such a small group only if he contributes special knowledge, insight, or skills.

Even if the leader of a hunting and gathering band were ambitious and eager to increase his power, he would not get very far. Unlike leaders in technologically more advanced societies, he would find it impossible to build and maintain an organization of dependent retainers to do his bidding, or to obtain a monopoly on weapons. The materials for making weapons lie ready at hand, and every man is trained to make and use them. If a person becomes unhappy with the group, he or she can usually leave it and join another.[63] Thus, there are no opportunities for building political empires, even on a small scale.

Given the rudimentary nature of political institutions in hunting and gathering societies, one might suppose that there are few restrictions on people. In one sense this is true; there are few rules imposed by political authorities—no courts, no police, no prisons. Individuals are hardly free, however, to do as they wish. No society is indifferent to the actions of its members, and even in the absence of formal constraints, the group controls their conduct through informal norms and sanctions.

Though there are minor variations from one hunting and gathering society to another, similar patterns of social control have developed in groups as far apart as the Kaska Indians of the Canadian Northwest, the Andaman Islanders of southeast Asia, and the !Kung of southwest Africa.[64] First, there is the custom of blood revenge, whereby the injured party, aided, perhaps, by his kinsmen, punishes the offender himself. As one student of the !Kung put it, "when disputes arise between the members of the band . . . there is no appeal to any supreme authority [since] . . . there is no such authority. . . . The only remedy is self-help."[65] This mode of social control is usually invoked only when the victim of the offense is a single individual or a family. In contrast, when an entire band suffers because of a member's actions, group pressure is brought to bear on the individual. For example, if a man refuses to do his part in providing food, he is punished by losing the respect of others.[66] In the case of more serious offenses, the penalty may be ostracism or even banishment. The third method of control is a deterrent that applies primarily to violations of ritual proscriptions. In such cases, the group's fear of supernatural sanctions provides the needed restraint. The !Kung, for example, believe that girls who fail to observe the restrictions imposed on them at puberty turn into frogs.[67] All three methods of social control are very informal and would not work except in small, homogeneous groups in which ties among the members are intimate and continuous, and contradictory ideas are absent.

Stratification

The rudimentary nature of the political system and the primitive nature of the economic system contribute to yet another distinctive characteristic of modern hunting and gathering societies: minimal inequality in power and privilege. Differences between individuals are so slight, in fact, that a number of observers have spoken of a kind of "primitive communism." To some extent this is justified. As we have seen, political authority with the power to coerce is virtually nonexistent. Differences in influence exist, but only to the degree permitted by those who are influenced, and only as a result of their respect for another individual's skills or wisdom. When individuals lose this respect, they also lose their influence.

In most hunting and gathering societies, differences in wealth are very minor. Many factors are responsible for this. For one thing, as we have seen, the nomadic way of life prevents any substantial accumulation of possessions. In addition, the ready availability of

TABLE 5.4 Private Ownership of Land, by Societal Type

| | Percentage of Societies in Which Private Ownership of Land Is: | | |
Societal Type	Absent	Present	Number of Societies
Hunting and gathering	83	17	100
Simple horticultural	22	78	81
Advanced horticultural	7	93	204
Agrarian	3	97	86

Source: See Appendix, pp. 372–374.

most essential resources (e.g., wood for bows, flint for stone tools) precludes the need to amass things, while technological limitations greatly restrict what can be produced. Finally, there is the widespread practice of sharing in most of these groups.

As a general rule the concept of private property has only limited development among hunting and gathering peoples. Things that an individual uses constantly, such as tools and weapons, are always recognized as his own, but fields and forests are the common property of the entire society (see Table 5.4). These territorial rights are often taken quite seriously, and outsiders are frequently obliged to ask permission to enter another group's territory to seek food.[68] Animals and plants are normally considered common property until they are killed or gathered, at which time they become the property of those who killed or gathered them. Even then, however, use of them is hedged about by the rule of sharing.[69]

A successful hunter does not normally keep his kill for himself alone or even, in most cases, for his family.[70] The reason for this seems to be the same as that which underlies insurance systems in industrial societies: it is an effective method of spreading risks. As we have seen, poor hunting conditions, ill health, or just a streak of bad luck can render any individual or family incapable of providing for itself, and sharing food greatly enhances everyone's chances of survival.

Despite near equality in power and wealth, there is inequality in prestige in most hunting and gathering societies. The interesting thing about this, from the viewpoint of members of industrial societies, is the extent to which prestige depends on the personal qualities of an individual rather than on impersonal criteria, such as the offices or roles he occupies or the possessions he controls. This is, of course, a natural consequence of the limited development of specialized offices and roles and the limited opportunities for accumulating possessions and wealth. But it sharply differentiates these societies from more advanced ones.

The Andaman Islanders accord honor and respect to three kinds of people: (1) older people, (2) people endowed with supernatural powers, and (3) people with certain personal qualities, notably "skill in hunting and warfare, generosity and kindness, and freedom from bad temper."[71] Men are apparently more likely than women to become honored members of the group. Similar types of people are accorded honor and prestige in most other hunting and gathering societies, and skill in oratory is often honored as well.[72]

Because personal characteristics are so important, systems of stratification in these groups have an openness about them not often found in more advanced societies. Almost no organizational or institutional barriers block the rise of talented individuals. For example, even where the office of headman is inherited, as it is in approximately half the societies,[73] others may surpass him in achieving honor. The study of the Siriono Indians cited earlier tells of a headman who was a very poor hunter and whose status, as a result, was low. The importance attached to age also contributes to the openness of the system. Almost anyone who lives long enough usually ends up with a fair degree of honor and respect.

Religion

In almost every carefully studied hunting and gathering society of the modern era, there is evidence that its members have grappled with the problem of explaining the world around them, especially those aspects of it that influence their own lives. Up to a point, their explanations and their interpretations of reality are the same as ours: animals run when they are frightened, people become hungry when they do not have enough to eat, and serious illness can cause death.

Because their store of information is so much more limited than ours, however, members of these societies quickly reach the limits of their ability to explain things in naturalistic terms. Insufficient food causes hunger; but why is there insufficient food? Illness is the cause of a death; but what caused the illness? To answer questions such as these, members of hunting and gathering societies, like people in every society confronted with what they do not fully understand, have developed their own sets of explanations. These explanations form the basis of a type of religion known as animism.[74]

The central element in animism is the belief that spirits inhabit virtually everything in the world of nature: rocks, trees, lakes, clouds, and other inanimate things, as well as animals and humans. These spirits are constantly intervening in human affairs, sometimes helping, sometimes harming. They cause the arrow to strike the deer, or they warn the animal so it bolts; they enter the body to heal a wound, or they settle in the intestines to twist and burn them. Furthermore, these spirits can be influenced by humans who know the proper rituals, sacrifices, and magic charms. Some humans, however, are more skillful at this than others, and when people fail in their efforts to appease a spirit, as when a sick child fails to recover, they turn to the expert in such matters, the medicine man or shaman.

!Kung San shaman in trance, southwestern Africa.

Shamans are not specialists in the strict sense of the term, any more than headmen are specialists. They are individuals who spend most of their time doing the same things as others of their sex (most shamans are men, but some are women), serving in their more specialized role only when the need arises.

While a shaman uses his powers in various ways, one of the most common is in healing. He may also use them to ensure the success of hunting expeditions, to protect the group against evil spirits and other dangers, and generally to ensure the group's well-being. Shamans do not always use their special powers for the benefit of others, however. Sometimes they employ them to punish people who have offended them.[75]

Because of their role, shamans usually command respect and often are more influential than the headman.[76] Sometimes, as with the Northern Maidu in California, the headman "was chosen largely through the aid of the shaman, who was supposed to reveal to the older men the choice of the spirits."[77] The role of shaman also tends to be profitable, since others are usually happy to offer gifts in exchange for help or to maintain goodwill.[78]

Education

Socialization of the young in hunting and gathering societies is largely an informal process in which children learn both through their play and through observing and imitating their elders. At a relatively early age boys are allowed to join the men on the hunt, participating in any activities of which they are capable. Fathers commonly make miniature bows as soon as their sons can handle them, and encourage the boys to practice. Girls assist their mothers in their campsite duties and in gathering vegetables and fruits. Thus children prepare for their future roles.

This informal socialization is often supplemented by a formal process of initiation that marks the transition from childhood to manhood or womanhood.[79] Initiation rites vary considerably from one society to another, though girls' ceremonies are usually linked with their first menstruation. The rites for boys commonly involve painful experiences (e.g., circumcision, scarification, or knocking out a tooth), which prove their courage and thus their right to the privileges of manhood. As a rule, these rites are also the occasion for introducing young men to their group's most sacred lore, and this combination of experiences helps to impress on them its value and importance.

Compared with horticultural and agrarian societies, hunting and gathering societies put more stress on training the child to be independent and self-reliant, less on obedience (see Table 5.5). This is apparently a cultural response to a subsistence economy in which it is imperative to have venturesome, independent adults who take initiative in finding and securing food.[80] In contrast, venturesomeness and independence are less valuable and less often encouraged in technologically more advanced horticultural and agrarian societies. Rather, it is

TABLE 5.5 Emphases in Child-Rearing, by Societal Type (in Percentages)

Societal Type	Self-Reliance Stressed More than Obedience	Self-Reliance and Obedience Stressed Equally	Obedience Stressed More than Self-Reliance	N
Hunting and gathering	63	13	23	19
Simple horticultural	34	20	46	26
Advanced horticultural	24	13	63	39
Agrarian	12	7	82	15

Note: The values in this table are arithmetic averages of four separate sets of data for (1) young boys, (2) older boys, (3) young girls, and (4) older girls. Controlling for age, greater emphasis was placed on self-reliance for boys than for girls in all types of societies. Controlling for sex, greater emphasis was placed on self-reliance for older boys than for younger, but no consistent pattern was observed among girls.
Source: See Appendix, pp. 372–374.

important that children in those societies learn to conform to the established norms of plant-ing, cultivating, and harvesting, and the other proven routines of farming.

The Arts and Leisure

Modern hunting and gathering peoples have produced a variety of artistic works. Some are strikingly similar to the cave drawings and carvings of hunters and gatherers of prehistoric times. The motivation behind these efforts is not always clear, but in some cases it is plainly religious, in others, magical.*[81] And sometimes it appears to be purely aesthetic.

Music, too, plays a part in the lives of most, if not all, hunters and gatherers. In Pygmy hunter festivals, songs and the music of a primitive wooden trumpet are central.[83] These festivals have great religious significance and express the people's devotion to, and trust in, the forest in which they live and on which they depend. And, as with the visual arts, music may be used purely for aesthetic purposes, self-expression, and enjoyment.[84] Dancing is an-other valued feature of life in many of these societies, and, again, the motives for it are varied.

Another popular leisure activity is storytelling. Pygmies are said to be blessed with a lively imagination.[85] Stories range from accounts of the day's hunt (often embellished to hold the listeners' attention) to sacred myths and legends passed down over many generations. Legends commonly deal with the origins of the world and of the group. Stories about the exploits of great heroes of the past are popular and are often used to explain the group's customs. Sacred myths and legends, as we have seen, frequently enter into initiation rites, especially for boys, and they are sometimes accompanied by music and dance. This complex interweaving of art, religion, entertainment, and education provides a strong foundation for tradition and for sociocultural continuity.

Hunters and gatherers, like people everywhere, enjoy gossip, small talk, and other nones-sential activities. Games are played in virtually all of these societies, but it is interesting to note that games of strategy are absent, while games of chance are more common than in other types of societies (see Table 5.6). Since a society's games, like the rest of its culture, reflect its experi-ences, the absence of games of strategy suggests that hunters and gatherers feel less sense of control over the events in their lives than the members of more advanced societies feel.

Tribal Ties: Links between Societies

As we have noted a number of times, each band or local group of hunters and gatherers is usually autonomous. Rarely are even two of them brought together under a single leader, and when this does happen, it usually involves groups that are no longer completely dependent on hunting and gathering.

TABLE 5.6 Types of Games, by Societal Type

Type of Society	Percentage of Societies Having Games of:			No. of Societies
	Physical Skill	**Chance**	**Strategy**	
Hunting and gathering	97	81	0	129
Simple horticultural	78	34	10	67
Advanced horticultural	90	37	57	60
Agrarian	97	74	71	35
Fishing	97	61	3	33
Herding	92	39	54	13

Source: See Appendix, pp. 372–374.

*A key difference between religion and magic is that in the former the objects of attention are valued for their *intrinsic* worth, whereas in the latter they are valued only as a *means* toward some (material) end. That is, they can be manipulated for human purposes.[82]

Cave art by contemporary Australian hunters and gatherers: the water snake and turtle are important figures in the religion of these people.

Despite the virtual absence of formal political organizations encompassing different communities, there are often informal social and cultural ties. The most inclusive of these, and one that is nearly universal, is the tribe—a group of people who speak a distinctive language or dialect, share a culture that distinguishes them from other peoples, and know themselves, and are known, by a distinctive name.[86] Unlike a society, a tribe is not necessarily organized politically. On the contrary, among hunting and gathering peoples almost none are.

Most tribes appear to have been formed by the process of societal fission or division. When the population of a hunting and gathering band grows too large for the resources of the immediate area, it divides. Division may also occur because of conflict within a band.[87] In either case, although a new group is formed, its members will naturally continue to share the culture of the parent group. Normally the new group locates somewhere near the old one, if only because its technology and accumulated experience become less relevant the farther it moves and the more the environment differs from the one its members have been used to. If this process of fission is repeated a number of times, a cluster of autonomous bands with the same language and similar stores of information develops, and a tribe emerges.

As this suggests, among hunters and gatherers the tribe is more important as a cultural unit than as a social unit. One writer, describing the !Kung, reports that the tribe "has no social solidarity, and is of very little, if any, importance in regulating social life. There appears to be no tribal organization among the [people], nothing in the nature of a central authority whose decisions are binding on all the members of the tribe, nor is collective action ever taken in the interests of the tribe as a whole."[88] Sometimes, as in Australia, an entire tribe assembles periodically for rituals and ceremonies, but this is not typical.

From the organizational standpoint the chief significance of these tribal groupings lies in their evolutionary potential: with technological advance, they may become political units.

Even among societies still on the hunting and gathering level, there is some evidence of movement in this direction. In a few of the more favorably situated sedentary groups, for example, several villages have been brought together under the leadership of a single individual.[89] This development is greatly facilitated by their common cultural heritage.

HUNTING AND GATHERING SOCIETIES IN THEORETICAL PERSPECTIVE

Archaeological and Ethnographic Evidence Compared

Now that we have completed our review of both the archaeological and the ethnographic evidence, we can consider the relationship between prehistoric hunting and gathering groups and those of the modern era. Though indiscriminate comparisons of the two can be misleading, our evidence indicates that careful comparisons can be extremely valuable.[90] To begin with, we must recognize that we cannot equate hunters and gatherers of the modern era with early hominid hunters and gatherers of a million or more years ago—before the process of human biological evolution had produced *Homo sapiens sapiens* and before the basic tools and weapons of modern hunters and gatherers had been invented. We can, however, reasonably compare hunters and gatherers of the recent past with others who have lived during the last 15,000 years.

We can see why, now that we are familiar with both sets of evidence. The similarities between these two sets of hunters and gatherers are many and basic; the differences are fewer and less important. The societies of the two periods are similar in such crucial matters as subsistence technology, size, relative equality,* and minimal occupational specialization. In addition, similarities in art suggest similarities in religious belief and practice.

The differences are largely of three types. First, in many hunting and gathering societies of the modern era there are some elements that originated in more advanced societies (e.g., metal tools and some religious ideas). Second, modern hunters and gatherers have had no opportunity to move into new territories, which means that population growth has been impossible for them and the number of deaths has had to balance the number of births. Prehistoric hunters and gatherers were not always subject to this harsh restriction. Finally, technologically advanced societies have often forced modern hunters and gatherers out of territories that were suitable for farming and herding.**

As we have seen, the archaeological record is much less complete than the ethnographic, being silent on many subjects about which the latter provides a wealth of information. Therefore, when the ethnographic record shows patterns that are consistent for all or most modern groups and when these patterns do not depend on conditions peculiar to the industrial era, archaeologists now tend to regard them as applicable to most of the hunting and gathering societies of the last 15,000 years. This reflects the growing awareness of the limiting nature of a hunting and gathering technology,[91] and the realization that the range of variation in the basic characteristics of societies that depend on that technology will inevitably be small. In short, except where relevant conditions have changed significantly, we can probably assume substantial similarity between the advanced hunting and gathering societies of late prehistoric times and those of recent centuries.***

---

*This is indicated by the absence of differentiation in the burial remains of prehistoric hunters and gatherers. In contrast, in technologically more advanced societies of later eras one finds clear evidence of distinctions between rich and poor, the former having rare and costly objects buried with them.

**See footnote on page 79. Moreover, hunters and gatherers in both the New World and Australia still occupied good farming and herding lands until fairly recently, so we are not entirely without information on societies that existed under such conditions.

***Archaeological evidence indicates that the societies of !Kung hunters and gatherers were not fundamentally altered by their contact with technologically more advanced societies over the past 2,000 years or so. In fact, the tools and diet of the !Kung in the 1960s apparently were not much different from those of 40,000 years earlier.[92]

A Model of Limited Development

In Chapter 2 we saw that human societies are systems of interrelated parts. In Chapters 3 and 4 we identified subsistence technology as the single most powerful variable influencing the other characteristics of the system. Now that we have completed our analysis of the first of the major societal types, we are in a better position to appreciate both the systemic nature of societies and the critical role of technology.

Figure 5.4 portrays the systemic qualities of a hunting and gathering society, and the relationships among its most important characteristics. The key element is the subsistence technology on which members of these societies depend for their survival and well-being. Because of their dependence on hunting and gathering, most of these groups are destined to be nomadic and to have a low level of productivity and a limited store of other kinds of information.

These characteristics lead in turn to other, second-order effects. Nomadism and the low level of productivity combine to limit possibilities for the accumulation of possessions. The low level of productivity and the limited store of other technological information, especially information relevant to transportation and communication, combine to keep hunting and gathering societies small. The limited development of these technologies also limits contacts with other societies. These characteristics combine with the small size of these societies to keep the rate of technological innovation low. The limited store of information about natural phenomena also contributes to the development of animistic beliefs.

Finally, these second-order effects, individually and collectively, produce a series of third-order effects. These include the low level of inequality that is characteristic of hunting and gathering societies, their limited division of labor, the kinship basis of social organization, and their ideological conservatism and low rates of social and cultural change. The latter, through a process of feedback, reinforces the dependence of these societies on hunting and gathering as their basic mode of subsistence. Thus, the system tends to be self-perpetuating.

The causal linkages indicated in Figure 5.4 may actually understate the degree to which the various characteristics of a hunting and gathering society are interrelated: some arrows that should have been included may have been omitted. The important point, however, is not the completeness of the model but the way it illustrates the systemic nature of these societies

FIGURE 5.4 *Model of relationships among the characteristics of hunting and gathering societies.*

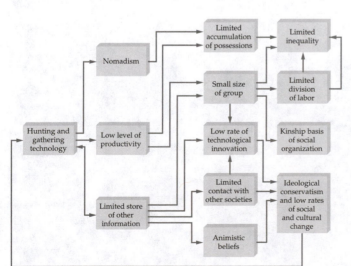

and shows the consequences of technology for every major component of the system, including basic beliefs and values.

Ecological-evolutionary theory, as we have seen, asserts that technology limits "the range of the possible" for a society, and in the case of hunting and gathering societies it is clear that that range is remarkably narrow. We do, of course, find differences among these societies, but not in their most basic characteristics. Many of these differences, as in modes of dress and housing, simply reflect variations in the environments to which these societies must adapt. Some differences, however, do not appear to be related to environmental conditions, and we have to assume that they reflect unknown and unknowable past experiences of the groups, experiences that led them to adopt dissimilar practices. We can see this, for example, in the case of marriage practices, which vary among societies at this level of development. It is clear that the limits set by a hunting and gathering technology are fairly broad with respect to this relationship. As a result, ideology—the information that helps people order societal life—comes into greater play.

But where the basic characteristics and development of hunting and gathering societies are concerned, technology sets strict and seemingly inviolable limits. These limits are less restrictive when the technology is applied to a particularly favorable environment. A society's biophysical environment, for example, may be especially rich in the resources on which the society depends, or its social environment may provide limited competition for those resources. But the only way the limits set by its technology can be expanded is for a hunting and gathering society to increase its store of technological information, as some of them have done by incorporating elements of fishing and horticulture.

The Last Hunting and Gathering Societies

In the summer of 1975, death came to the last full-blooded member of the Ona, a tribe of hunters and gatherers that had inhabited the southern tip of South America since at least the days of Ferdinand Magellan, the famed sixteenth-century explorer, and probably for centuries or even millennia before that.[93] It is estimated that in Magellan's day there were 2,000 Ona, divided into about thirty societies. The Ona survived the remoteness and harshness of their

One of the last photographs of the Ona of Tierra del Fuego, a tribe of hunters and gatherers that is now extinct.

homeland only to be destroyed by their contacts with technologically more advanced societies. Disease, loss of territory, and loss of members to other societies all took their toll. The last Ona society died years ago; now the last Ona is also dead.

The experience of the Ona has been the experience of tens of thousands of hunting and gathering societies during the 10,000 years since hunters and gatherers first began competing for territories and other resources with technologically more advanced societies. Hunters and gatherers have had only one defense: retreat to lands that other groups regarded as worthless or inaccessible.

Today, even this defense is crumbling and the last outposts of this ancient way of life are doomed. The speed of the process is demonstrated by the experience of an anthropologist who pioneered in the study of the !Kung of the Kalahari Desert in southwest Africa. She reports that to reach them in 1951 required an arduous trip across the desert by truck, lasting eight days from the final outposts of civilization until contact with the !Kung was made.[94] There was no road of any kind, not even a track across the sand and bush country. When she returned in 1962, only eleven years later, she reached them in one day over a well-cleared track. As they come more and more in contact with, and under the influence of, more advanced societies, their traditional way of life is doomed. Today, less than 5 percent of the 30,000 !Kung are still hunters and gatherers.[95]

In a few short years the last hunting and gathering society will probably have vanished—and with it an irreplaceable link to our past. For thousands of years these societies maintained a remarkably stable relationship with their environments and a highly satisfying way of life. Relying entirely on cultural information that they had accumulated over centuries, hunters and gatherers adapted to a wide variety of biophysical environments; and, until the advent of societies with larger populations and more sophisticated technologies, they also adapted successfully to their social environments. The process of change in each part of those sociocultural systems occurred so slowly that answering changes could occur in other parts without serious social unrest or upheaval. Today, this way of life, which served our species extremely well for so many years, is no longer possible, and is vanishing forever.

Excursus: Human Origins

Following the early work of Linnaeus (1707–1778), scientists classify living things into a set of categories based on biological similarities. The broader categories, such as "order" or "family," group together plants and animals that share broad similarities; successively narrower categories, such as "genus" or "species," group together those that are more and more alike. Modern humans are members of the order *Primates* and the family *Hominidae*—"hominids." Although there have been a number of animals classified as hominids on the basis of fossils (e.g., *Australopithecines**), humans are the only living members of this family. To be more precise we are members of the genus *Homo* ("human"), the species *sapiens* ("wise"), and the subspecies *sapiens* ("wise").** Despite superficial physical differences, modern humans constitute a single species.

How we came to be what and where we are today continues to be a fascinating area of study and,

in a number of cases, scholarly controversy. As we noted in the opening chapter, scientific evidence and explanations are always subject to revision and change in the light of new evidence. But given the fragmentary evidence—sometimes little more than a tooth, part of a skull or jawbone, a leg or finger bone, ashes from a fire, or a tool fashioned from rock—and the difficulty ascertaining the precise date and circumstances when it was left, it is hard to find more divergent interpretations of evidence than in the study of human origins.

While all of this makes it an exciting and stimulating area of science to work in, its findings and theories are difficult to summarize. There are areas of broad disagreement, and what is presented as conventional wisdom and consensus one day is the next day under assault by new evidence, new interpretations of evidence, and the theories and hypotheses offered to explain them. New species are proposed; fossils once assigned to one species are shifted to others; and estimates of what hominids were in what parts of the world at what times, and which are argued to be ancestral to

*Because the fossils were first found in southern Africa, the genus was named "southern apes."
**Literally, "very wise" person.

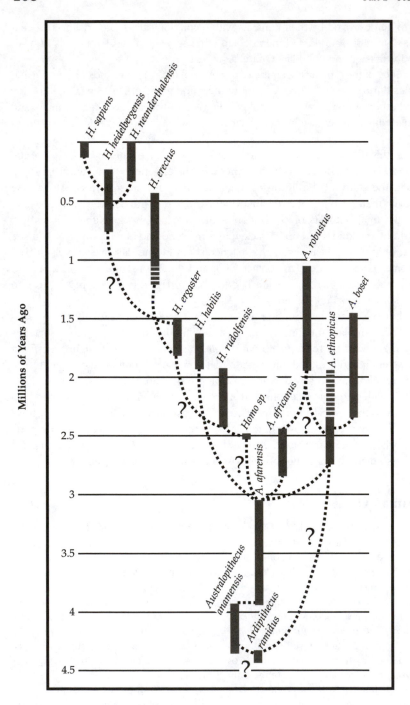

FIGURE 5.5 *A possible family tree.*
Source: Adapted from Donald Johanson and Blake Edgar, *From Lucy to Language* (New York: Simon and Schuster, 1996), p. 3.

which, constantly change as new fossils are found and old ones are reanalyzed.

There is general agreement that hominids originated in Africa between 5 and 6 million years ago, and that modern humans emerged sometime between 100,000 and 200,000 years ago. What happened in between, however, is the subject of much disagreement.

One of the best-known fossils, the 3.2-million-year-old remains of "Lucy," a 60-pound three-and-a-half-foot-tall female *Australopithecus afarensis* ("southern ape of the Afar"), has recently been pushed into the background by discoveries of the fossilized remains of even earlier hominids: the 4-million-year-old *Australopithecus anamensis* ("southern ape of the lake"), the 4.4-million-year-old *Ardipithecus ramidus* ("ground [base] root ape"), and the 5.2-million-year-old *Ardipithecus ramidus kadabba* ("ground [base] root ape basal family ancestor"). These fossils indicate that a bipedal, upright hominid with a brain about the size of a modern chimpanzee's (400 ml)* walked the earth more than 4 million years ago, and they push our knowledge ever closer to the theorized point of divergence between the ancestors of modern apes and those of modern humans.

Sometime during the next 2 million years, the first representatives of the genus *Homo* emerged, and *Australopithecines* and the genus *Homo* thereafter followed divergent evolutionary paths. The *Australopithecines* progressively moved into a more specialized vegetarian niche developing, along the way, jaws and teeth well suited to eating tough, gritty plants. The *Homo* moved into a more generalized niche developing a somewhat larger brain, an enhanced ability to make tools, and a much more differentiated diet.** The first path ended in the development of "robust," highly specialized vegetarians: *Australopithecus robustus* and *Australopithecus boisei.**** The second produced a se-

ries of ever-larger-brained omnivores who at some point migrated out of Africa and peopled the entire world.

Homo habilis ("handy man") is no longer considered the first representative of our genus. In fact, there is debate about how many species should be distinguished in the general time period and into which species existing fossils should be classified. *Homo erectus,* who was once thought to have been the first to leave Africa some 1 million years ago with his relatively large brain (850 to 1200 ml), mastery of fire, and stone tool kit, is now thought by some to have been a geographically isolated descendant of an earlier species, *Homo ergaster* ("working man"), who left Africa at a much earlier date. And Neanderthals, *Homo sapiens neanderthalensis,* grow even more enigmatic as we learn more about them.

How and where modern humans, *Homo sapiens sapiens,* enter the picture remains the center of an ongoing controversy. The "multiple origins" or "regional continuity" theory maintains that modern humans evolved independently in several regions of the world at about the same time among interbreeding populations of hominids who earlier migrated out of Africa. The "single origin" or "out of Africa" theory argues that the first modern humans emerged in Africa 100,000 to 200,000 years ago, migrated out, and quickly "replaced" other hominids throughout the world.

As we write, each theory can point to fairly compelling supporting evidence. For instance, the dating of fossils of modern humans throughout the world is roughly consistent with the "out of Africa" theory (e.g., the oldest are in Africa, and they get progressively more recent as you move farther away), and DNA studies have been argued to indicate an African origin. (Once thought to be definitive, the DNA studies are now highly controversial.) But there is also fossil evidence of regional differences that persist over hundreds of thousands of years, which favors the multiple origins theory.

Future finds and research will undoubtedly further complicate this ever changing picture, generating more excitement, more debate, and more controversy. But what could be a more fitting fate for this large-brained, symbol-using species than to eternally ponder and argue about its origins?[96]

---

*The brains of modern chimpanzees range in size from 300 to 480 ml. By comparison, the brains of modern humans are generally between 1100 and 1700 ml in volume (B. J. Williams, *Evolution and Human Origins: An Introduction to Physical Anthropology* [New York: Harper and Row, 1973], p. 173).

**While it was once generally believed that only *Homo* made and used tools, some researchers now argue that *Australopithecines* could have made tools previously attributed to *Homo.*

***Mary Leakey found the first fossil skull; and the species name, *boisei,* was chosen to honor Charles Boise, an early financial

supporter of her husband, Louis Leakey (Donald Johanson and Maitland Edey, *Lucy: The Beginnings of Humankind* [New York: Simon and Schuster, 1981], p. 93).

6

Horticultural Societies

Before the hunting and gathering era ended 10,000 to 12,000 years ago, human societies had accumulated substantial stores of information about plants and animals. People were as familiar with the behavior patterns of some animals as they were with their own, and probably understood them almost as well. They had also identified hundreds of varieties of edible plants and had become familiar with their processes of reproduction and growth. Some hunters and gatherers in the Middle East were even harvesting wild grains with stone sickles and hunting cattle, sheep, goats, and pigs.[1] Clearly the shift from hunting animals to herding them and from gathering plants to cultivating them was not as great or as difficult a step as one might imagine.

But what induced societies to take that step? Why, after hundreds of thousands of years of hunting and gathering, did the members of some societies abandon that ancient, time-hallowed way of life? Above all, why did they do it when the new mode of production meant more work and less freedom?

CAUSES OF THE SHIFT FROM HUNTING AND GATHERING TO HORTICULTURE

Until recent decades, scholars tended to assume that, because of human intelligence and unsatisfied human needs, technological innovation and societal development are normal and natural and require no special explanation. By shifting from hunting and gathering to horticulture, they reasoned, societies assured themselves of a greater and more stable supply of food, and the members of any society would naturally make such a shift once the principles of plant cultivation came to be understood. Furthermore, it was generally assumed that horticulture required less labor than hunting and gathering. Thus, by adopting horticulture—that is, farming without plows—societies traded a precarious and onerous way of life for a more secure and satisfying one. Or so it seemed.

More recently, however, doubts have been cast on these explanations. To begin with, a growing body of archaeological research indicates that the members of many hunting and gathering societies understood and occasionally applied the basic principles of plant cultivation thousands of years before horticulture became their primary mode of subsistence. In addition, ethnographic studies of modern hunting and gathering societies have made it clear that their members place a high value on their way of life: they cherish the challenge and excitement of the hunt, and the freedom and other benefits their way of life affords. Finally, it has also become clear that most societies have not shared the positive view of innovation and change that prevails in industrial societies today. On the contrary, they place a high value on tradition and continuity.

As a result, most scholars now doubt that hunters and gatherers abandoned hunting and gathering and adopted horticulture unless they were compelled to do so by circumstances beyond their control. Instead, they have come to believe that the gradual growth of human population over millions of years (see Table 5.2) and changing climate eventually created a situation in which it became imperative for societies to increase the supply and reliability of food resources. This was probably done gradually, with plant cultivation and animal domestication initially serving only as a minor means of supplementing the food resources obtained by hunting and gathering. But changing diet and a sedentary lifestyle led to still larger populations and greater dependence on domesticated plants and animals. Eventually, after hundreds or thousands of years the point would have been reached where horticulture replaced hunting and gathering as the dominant mode of subsistence. But the whole process would have been so gradual that the people involved may have been largely unaware of the significance and irreversibility of changes that were occurring.

Although their relative importance varied in different regions, three things are now generally thought to have contributed to the transition from hunting and gathering to plant and animal domestication: (1) environmental change, (2) population growth, and (3) growth in cultural information and technology.[2]

Global warming in the period between 15,000 and 8,000 years ago changed the climate greatly in many areas, raised ocean levels, and altered the habitat of a number of important animals and plants.* Shrinking habitats reduced the supply and changed the migration patterns of a number of large game animals. This forced societies either to follow surviving animal populations into new territories or to find substitute foods. It also permitted wild cereals to spread into areas where they became available first for gathering, and then for domestication.[3] In addition, the cumulative effects of population growth (see Table 5.2) meant that even though population densities were not high by modern standards, more people were competing for a shrinking resource base. Under these circumstances periodic food and resource shortages would have been especially acute.

The importance of the first two causes is attested to by the fact that domestication of a variety of species of plants occurred independently in the same approximate latitudes around the world—southwest Asia (barley, wild einkorn, and wild emmer wheat), India (fruits, herbs, and possibly rice), southeast Asia (various tubers), China (millet, rice, and soybeans), North and South America (maize, beans, squash, cocoa, and quinoa)—in the short period between 8000 and 3000 B.C.[4] It is also supported by the fact that many of the plants first domesticated, the ancestors of wheat, barley, millet, and rice, were "third choice" foods in the wild.[5] In all likelihood, then, they were domesticated not because people had a special appetite for them *per se,* but because they constituted a reliable and storable source of additional food.

During this same time period, a variety of animal species were also domesticated (see Figure 6.1). For example, sheep and goats were domesticated in southwest Asia and Greece, cattle in Turkey and China, pigs in southwest Asia, and llamas and guinea pigs in South America.[6]

Overall, domestication generally occurred gradually, but in some areas at least, the pressures to adopt horticulture may have been intensified by earlier advances in weapons technology that led to the rapid depletion and extinction of many species of big-game animals that previously had been important sources of food.

The shift from hunting and gathering to horticulture, though seemingly a change in only one aspect of technology, was destined to have profound and far-reaching consequences for human life as a whole. We will examine the more immediate consequences in the present chapter and the longer-term consequences in Chapters 7 through 16. Before doing this, however, we must first consider the new technology itself.

THE TECHNOLOGY OF HORTICULTURE

The practice of horticulture is referred to as *swidden cultivation,* and sometimes it is known as *slash-and-burn cultivation*. Both of these terms refer to the widespread practice of clearing new gardens by cutting and then burning existing vegetation, especially shrubs and small

---

*Later climatic shifts also affected developmental trends in horticultural and agrarian societies.

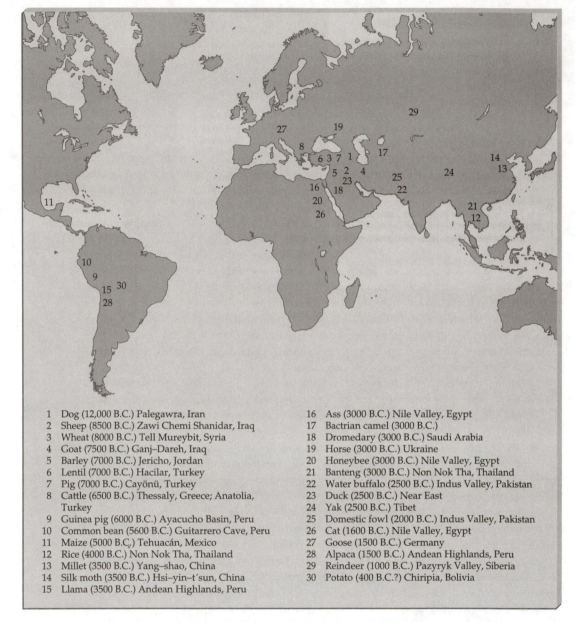

FIGURE 6.1 *Early evidence for domestication of selected plants and animals.*
Source: Adapted from Robert J. Wenke, *Patterns in Prehistory: Humankind's First Three Million Years*
(New York: Oxford University Press, 1990).

trees.* Larger trees are often left standing but are killed by girdling them, or cutting away a circular strip of bark all the way around the tree, thereby stopping the flow of nutrients from the roots to the branches.

  After existing vegetation has been burned away, the resulting layer of ash provides fertilizer for the crops that are planted. Good yields can be expected for a year or two, but after that, as the nutrients in the ash are consumed, yields decline. Also, because there are no

---

*This too appears to be an extension of, rather than a decisive break with, practices of the past. Archaeological and ethnographic evidence indicates that hunters and gatherers around the world used fire to clear trees and encourage the growth of plants (e.g., grasses and legumes) which would attract desired game animals.[7]

Women planting taro in a simple horticultural society in New Guinea. Note the tree stumps in the cultivated area: horticulturalists do not need to clear the land as thoroughly as agriculturalists, who use plows.

plows to dislodge them, weeds eventually take over. Thus, gardens must be abandoned and new plots cleared after only a few years.

The length of time a garden can be cultivated by horticulturalists varies considerably, depending on environmental conditions and on the length of time since the land was last cultivated. The longer the land remains uncultivated, the greater the amount of vegetation that grows on it and the thicker the layer of ash and nutrients when it is burned. Allowing the land to revert to jungle or forest is especially important because this destroys the weeds which spring up when land is cleared and which choke out cultivated plants.

Because of the need to allow the land periodically to revert to wilderness, horticulturalists are able to cultivate only a small fraction of the territory they occupy. Thus, horticultural societies seldom achieve the high levels of population density typical of agrarian societies. Nevertheless, their mode of subsistence is much more productive than hunting and gathering in terms of yield per acre, and their societies, as a result, almost always have larger and denser populations.

In the horticultural system of cultivation, men are usually responsible for clearing the land when new gardens are needed, while women are responsible for planting, tending, and harvesting the crops. This division of labor is almost certainly linked to the earlier division of labor in hunting and gathering societies, where women were responsible for providing the vegetable materials that people consumed. Men continue to hunt in many horticultural societies, but hunting is a much less productive activity since the ratio of game animals to humans is much lower (partly because of the growth of human population, partly because game animals tend to avoid areas of permanent human settlement). Overall, men's contribution to subsistence is often much less than that of women in horticultural societies and requires much less time. Thus, men in these societies often have substantial amounts of time at their disposal—a fact that has had important consequences, as we will see.

In our analysis of horticultural societies, we will use the same format we used in the last chapter. We will first examine the archaeological and ethnographic evidence on simple and advanced horticultural societies, and then, at the end of the chapter, we will return to ecological-evolutionary theory to help us formulate a coherent model of horticultural societies.

SIMPLE HORTICULTURAL SOCIETIES IN PREHISTORIC ASIA AND EUROPE

In Asia Minor, Palestine, Syria, and the hill country east of the Tigris River, archaeologists have found the remains of ancient settlements dating from about 8000 to 10,000 B.C., in which horticulture appears to have been the primary means of subsistence.[8] In traditional archaeological usage, the period in which simple horticultural societies were dominant in a region was called the Neolithic era, or New Stone Age. This name was chosen because in early research in Europe and the Middle East, excavated sites often yielded stone axes, adzes, and hammers that, unlike earlier stone tools, had been smoothed by grinding or polishing. Before radiocarbon dating, these tools were the best indicators of the relative age of excavated materials and of their place in evolutionary history.

As research progressed, however, and more and more sites were excavated, it became increasingly clear that these tools were not the most distinctive feature of Neolithic societies, and certainly not their greatest technological achievement. Rather, their most important innovations were in the area of subsistence technology. For the first time in history, groups of people were primarily dependent on horticulture, and hunting and gathering was relegated to a secondary role. In this connection, it is important to recognize that these early horticultural societies were not based on a single resource or activity. Horticulture was their basic means of subsistence, but it was supplemented by herding, fishing, hunting, and gathering in various combinations.[9] The presence of livestock in many of these early societies was especially important, as we will soon see.

The First Great Social Revolution

Although many scholars today describe the emergence of horticultural societies as the first great social revolution in human history, it would be wrong to assume that the rate of change seemed revolutionary to those involved. As far as we can judge, the process was so gradual that the changes occurring during a lifetime were neither very numerous nor overwhelming.

For example, hunters and gatherers in the Middle East had been using wild grains for a thousand years or more before the horticultural era began. Techniques of harvesting, storing, grinding, and cooking these grains were well known even before the techniques of cultivating them were adopted. Furthermore, as we have noted, hunting, and to some extent gathering, continued to play a part in the lives of early horticulturalists. There was almost certainly considerable continuity in other areas of life as well, especially in kinship, religion, and politics. The survival of fertility cults, indicated by the widespread presence of female figurines in Neolithic remains, is one evidence of this.[10] Our use of the term "revolutionary" in connection with the rise of horticultural societies, therefore, is based primarily on the *long-term consequences* of the change.

Permanence of Settlements   One immediate and very important consequence of the shift to horticulture was the greater permanence of settlements. No longer did a group of people have to move about constantly in quest of food; on the contrary, the practice of horticulture forced them to stay in one place for extended periods.* In the Middle East and in southeastern Europe, many truly permanent settlements seem to have been established. In most areas, however, simple horticulturalists usually have had to move their settlements every few years.[11] Why this was not necessary in the Middle East and southeastern Europe is still a mystery, since only continuing fertilization (by flooding or by human activity), the use of the plow, and crop rotation permit land to be kept under continuous cultivation,[12] and so far there is no evidence of any of these practices at that time. We do know, however, that these early horticulturalists kept livestock, and so it is possible that the value of manure as fertilizer was discovered at an early date.[13] This practice may not have spread because, in other areas, there was more arable land available.

In any case, the shift from hunting and gathering to horticulture substantially increased the permanence of human settlements, thereby enabling people to accumulate many more possessions than ever before. This is evident in the archaeological remains left by horticulturalists of the Neolithic era. Tools and weapons are much more numerous and varied than in older sites, and for the first time there are large, bulky objects such as stone cups and bowls and pottery.[14] Dwellings also became more substantial. Some buildings contained several rooms and a small courtyard and were made of materials like sun-dried clay blocks, capable of lasting for as long as two generations.[15] Even more noteworthy is the appearance of such things as religious shrines or ceremonial centers, village walls, and occasional paved or timbered (corduroy style) roadways or alleys; though none of these is typical of simple horticultural communities, they are not rare.[16]

The change from hunting and gathering to horticulture also resulted in larger settlements and denser populations (see Table 6.1). Jarmo, one of the oldest horticultural villages

*As we noted earlier, in extremely supportive environments some hunters and gatherers established relatively permanent settlements. Indeed, there is evidence that some of the hunters and gatherers in southwest Asia lived in permanent settlements in the millennium *before* they domesticated the cereal grains they were gathering and the animals they were hunting. Nonetheless, according to Murdock's data only about 10 percent of hunters and gatherers are sedentary, whereas more than 91 percent of simple horticulturalists and 95 percent of advanced horticulturalists are.

TABLE 6.1 Median Density of Population, by Type of Society

	Persons per Square Mile	No. of Societies
Hunting and gathering	0.6	27
Simple horticultural	13.8	35
Advanced horticultural	42.7	38
Agrarian	100.0+	27

Source: See Appendix, pp. 372–374.

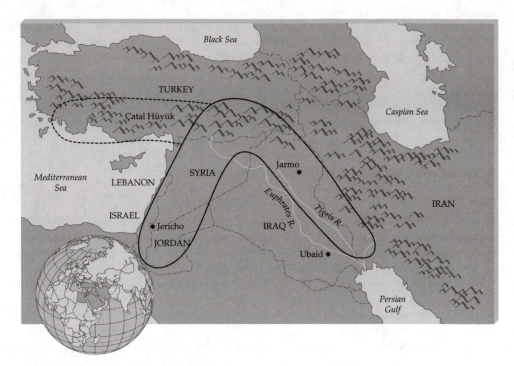

FIGURE 6.2 *Early horticultural societies in southwest Asia. The "fertile crescent" is outlined, and its extensions into Turkey is indicated by the dashed lines.*
Source: Adapted from Robert J. Wenke, *Patterns in Prehistory: Humankind's First 3 Million Years* (New York: Oxford University Press, 1990) and Luigi Luca Cavalli-Sforza and Francesco Covalli Sforza, *The Great Human Diasporas: The History of Diversity and Evolution* (New York: Addison-Wesley, 1995).

yet discovered, had about twenty-five houses and a population of 150,[17] nearly four times that of the average hunting and gathering band. Neolithic villages in Europe had from eight to fifty houses, suggesting populations ranging up to at least 200.[18] In several cases there were even more striking concentrations of population. One was a town located on the site of Jericho 5,000 years before the days of Joshua of biblical fame. Excavations there have uncovered a community that apparently housed 2,000 to 3,000 inhabitants.[19] More recent excavations of Çatal Hüyük,* in what is now Turkey, revealed a community occupying an even larger area with a population estimated between 4,000 and 6,000 in 6000 B.C.[21]

Growth of Trade and Commerce   These two communities, though obviously exceptional, illustrate another development associated with the rise of horticultural societies—the rapid expansion and growing importance of trade and commerce.[22] Modern scholars believe that the "great" size of Jericho and Çatal Hüyük was not due merely to the practice of horticulture. As one writer has put it, "It is . . . most unlikely that [horticulture] should have flourished more at Jericho, 200 metres below sea level, than elsewhere in Palestine. Some other resource must have existed, and this was probably trade."[23] As he points out, Jericho, because of its location on the Dead Sea, had easy access to salt, bitumen,** and sulfur, all of which were valuable materials in simple horticultural societies and not available everywhere. This view of Jericho as an early center of trade is supported by the discovery there of products such as obsidian from Asia Minor and cowrie shells from the Red Sea. In the case of Çatal Hüyük, obsidian***

*Pronounced "Chatal Huooyook."[20]
**Bitumen was used to fix blades in handles, mend pottery, etc.
***Obsidian, or volcanic glass, was much sought after for use in weapons and cutting tools.

Artist's conception of farmhouse in Denmark during the horticultural era there (about 2700 B.C.). Compare this with the dwelling of the family of the Paiute hunter on page 92.

seems to have been the key local resource responsible for its growth. Even in remote villages, there is evidence of trade. For example, shells from the Mediterranean have been found in the sites of horticultural villages and in graves in northern Europe, and obsidian from Çatal Hüyük has been found throughout the Middle East and in what is now Turkey and Cyprus.[24]

The growth in trade and commerce, combined with the increasing quantity of material products, may well have led to the beginnings of formal record keeping. Archaeologists have found a variety of clay tokens in horticultural sites from modern Turkey to Iran, but until recently no one could identify their use. Then it was discovered that the markings on many of the tokens were remarkably similar to symbols later used in early forms of writing for such words as "sheep," "wool," "cloth," "bread," "bed," and a variety of numerals.[25] This strongly suggests that the tokens were used to represent those same objects and numbers. Since these tokens were often stored in small clay jars, they were probably records of early business transactions, such as loans. But whatever their precise use in the societies of the time, these tokens tell us of a major breakthrough in the ability of human societies to store information.

Another probable consequence of the growth in trade and commerce was an increase in occupational specialization, at least in the chief commercial centers. Direct evidence of this has been found at several sites. For example, excavation of a community south of Jericho revealed a number of small workshops where specialized craftsmen, such as a butcher, a bead maker, and a maker of bone tools, worked.[26] This kind of specialization, however, was limited.[27] Most communities were still largely self-sufficient, and most families still produced nearly everything they used.[28] Innovations continued in the domestic arts, with the invention of pottery and weaving being especially important.[29]

Increase in Warfare   There is little evidence of warfare in early horticultural societies. Graves rarely contain weapons, and most communities had no walls or other defenses.[30] Some, it is true, had ditches and fences, but these were more suitable for protection against marauding animals than against human enemies. Later in the horticultural era the picture changed drastically and warfare became increasingly common. In this period, battle-axes, daggers, and other arms are found in the graves of all adult males, reflecting the impact of technological advance, specifically metallurgy. The causes of this increase in warfare are not clear, but some scholars think it was linked with the growth of population and the resulting scarcity of new land suitable for horticulture. It may also have been related to declining opportunities for hunting, a traditional male activity. Warfare, with its demands for bravery and skill in the use of arms, would be a natural substitute, and if women were doing much of the work of tending the gardens, as is the case in most horticultural societies of the modern era, men would have had plenty of time to spend in this activity.[31] Moreover, the frictions created by growing pressure for land would provide a ready-made justification. Finally, some experts suspect that the increase in warfare was linked with the increase in wealth, especially in the form of cattle, which could be easily stolen.[32]

One consequence of horticulture was that, as more and more societies adopted the new technology, it became increasingly difficult for other societies in the same area to continue hunting and gathering. As the population grew in a horticultural society, new settlements would form on the outer fringes. When they moved into territory occupied by hunters and gatherers, the horticulturalists would, by remaining in one place for a number of years, deplete the supply of game to the point that it could no longer support the hunters. If the hunters were tempted to fight for their "rights," they would usually find themselves badly outnumbered, if the population sizes of contemporary groups are any indication (see Table 4.2).[33]

SIMPLE HORTICULTURAL SOCIETIES IN THE MODERN ERA

In recent centuries simple horticultural societies have been confined almost entirely to the New World and the islands of the Pacific. All of these societies have practiced some version of slash-and-burn horticulture. In most matters where comparisons are possible these societies are strikingly similar to simple horticultural societies of prehistoric times.[34] As with hunting and gathering societies, ethnography provides a richer source of information than archaeology. It answers many questions that would remain unanswered if our knowledge of horticultural societies were limited to what can be gleaned from the archaeological record.

Population and Economy

As we saw in our brief introduction to the various types of societies in Chapter 4, horticultural societies of the modern era have been substantially larger than hunting and gathering societies. Where the average hunting and gathering society of the recent past has had a population of approximately 40 people (including children), the average simple horticultural society has had about 1,500 and the average advanced horticultural society more than 5,000. Their larger numbers have given horticultural societies a substantial advantage when they have competed with hunting and gathering societies for territory, and this was almost certainly a major factor in the considerable decline in the number of hunting and gathering societies during the horticultural era (see Figure 4.2).

The larger populations of horticultural societies are due primarily to their greater economic productivity. The clearest indication of this is the greater population density that horticultural societies have been able to sustain. As Table 6.1 indicates, simple horticultural econo-

The Chinese Experience

The horticultural societies of China are of special interest because the shift to the new mode of subsistence began late enough there, and writing developed early enough, that some memory of the horticultural era was preserved in legends that were eventually written down. For a long time scholars thought this material was entirely fictional, but modern archaeological research has substantiated enough of it that it is now regarded as a mingling of fact and fiction.[35]

According to the legends, China's earliest inhabitants were hunters but the growth of population eventually forced a shift to horticulture. As one source recounts, "The ancient people ate meat of animals and birds. At the time of Shen-nung [an early legendary ruler and cultural hero] there were so many people that the animals and birds became inadequate for people's wants and therefore Shen-nung taught the people to cultivate."[36] Other legends relate that Shen-nung introduced pottery and describe the era as a period of peace and self-sufficiency. "During the Age of Shen-nung people rested at ease and acted with vigor. They cared for their mothers, but not for their fathers. They lived among deer. They ate what they cultivated and wore what they wove. They did not think of harming one another." This preference for mothers is especially intriguing, because it is contrary to the later Chinese tradition and yet conforms to one of the distinctive features of contemporary horticultural societies (see page 119). Finally, there is a legend that describes the Age of Shen-nung as the last era in which people were free from coercive political authority. "People were administered without a criminal law and prestige was built without the use of force. After Shen-nung, however, the strong began to rule over the weak and the few over the many."

mies have been able to support more than twenty times as many people per square mile of territory as hunting and gathering economies, and advanced horticultural economies have supported even denser populations.

Increased productivity has not been the whole story, however. The larger populations of horticultural societies also reflect the emergence of *multicommunity* societies. Among hunters and gatherers, as we have seen, each community is usually politically independent, and thus a separate society in its own right. In horticultural societies, however, a number of communities are usually united under a single leader. The typical simple horticultural society consists of slightly more than ten communities, the average advanced horticultural society of seventeen.[37]

This widespread occurrence of multicommunity societies at the horticultural level and their virtual absence at the hunting and gathering level support the conclusion based on archaeological evidence (see page 113) that this shift in subsistence technology was the critical step that made possible the production of *a stable and dependable economic surplus*. Hunters and gatherers may produce surpluses for brief periods, but a complex institutional system cannot be built on such an uncertain foundation. Full-time occupational specialization involving priests, kings, craftsmen, and soldiers is possible only when an economy becomes productive enough so that some individuals regularly produce more of the necessities of life than they and their families require. In addition, they must be persuaded or forced to part with enough of this surplus to free others to perform tasks unrelated to basic subsistence. An economic surplus, therefore, is an essential precondition both for the emergence of full-time occupational specialization and for the development of complex social institutions.

TABLE 6.2 The Division of Labor between the Sexes in Horticultural and Agrarian Societies

	Percentage Distribution				
Type of Society	Cultivation Primarily a Female Responsibility	Both Sexes Share Equally	Cultivation Primarily a Male Responsibility	Total	No. of Societies
Horticultural	39	33	28	100	389
Agrarian	8	33	59	100	100

Source: See Appendix, pp. 372–374.

One other noteworthy feature of the economies of horticultural societies is *the importance of women's productive activities*. For those whose ideas about farming are based on agricultural practices, it usually comes as a surprise to discover that in many horticultural societies women—not men—do most of the work of plant cultivation (see Table 6.2). As we will see shortly, the relative freedom of men from time-consuming economic responsibilities in these societies has had interesting and important consequences.

The Continuing Importance of Kinship

As with hunting and gathering societies, the ethnographic record not only supports the view provided by archaeology but also broadens and extends it. For example, ethnographic studies show that kinship ties have been extremely important in simple horticultural societies of the modern era. In most instances, these ties provide the basic framework of the social system.[38] This is hardly surprising in view of the small size of these groups: almost everyone is related in some way to almost everyone else. Kinship obligations must constantly be considered in relations between individuals. The virtual absence of competing social organizations (e.g., craft guilds, political parties) further enhances the importance of kinship.

Kinship systems in these societies are sometimes very complex, with intricate systems of rules governing relations among numerous categories of kin. Extended kin groups, or *clans,* are common and usually very important, since they perform a number of essential functions for their members.[39] Above all, they function as *mutual aid associations,* providing individuals with protection against enemies and with economic support. Although both functions are important, the former is critical, for the political system is too limited in these societies to provide police services. Clans also perform important regulatory functions in the area of marriage, and they sometimes have important religious functions as well. Finally, the most powerful or respected clan often assumes leadership of an entire community, with its head serving as its headman, or even as tribal chief.

In horticultural societies, both simple and advanced, the concept of the kin group includes the dead as well as the living. This manifests itself in many ways, but especially in religious rituals designed to appease the spirits of dead ancestors. Nowhere is ancestor worship more common than in horticultural societies (see Figure 6.3).

The reason for such a high incidence of ancestor worship among horticulturalists, relative to hunters and gatherers, is probably tied to the greater permanence of their settlements. Because of this, the living remain in close physical proximity to their buried dead and carry on their daily activities in the very same settings in which their ancestors lived. Under such circumstances, ancestors are more likely to be remembered and honored. In agrarian societies, more awesome and more powerful polytheistic and monotheistic deities usually displaced ancestors from the central position they occupied in most horticultural societies, though ancestor worship continued to be important in many of them (e.g., China, Rome).

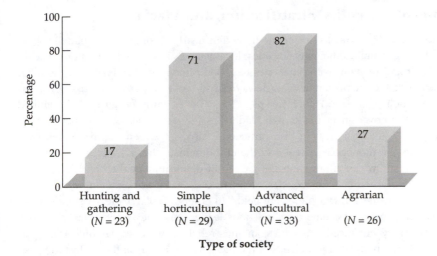

FIGURE 6.3 *Incidence of ancestor worship, by societal type.*
Source: Adapted from Dean Sheils, "Toward a Unified Theory of Ancestor Worship: A Cross-Cultural Study," *Social Forces,* 54(1975): 427–440, appendix, part B.

Another distinctive feature of kinship systems in horticultural societies is the importance many of them attach to ties with the mother's side of the family. This can be seen in Murdock's data, where the percentage of societies having *matrilineal* kin groups (i.e., descent traced through the maternal line) is as follows:[40]

Hunting and gathering societies	7 percent
Simple horticultural societies	24 percent
Advanced horticultural societies	12 percent
Agrarian societies	4 percent

This unusual pattern appears to be linked to the relative contributions men and women make to subsistence. For in those horticultural societies where men also make a substantial contribution, the matrilineal pattern is not as likely to develop (see Table 6.3). Nonetheless, two very different interpretations of this connection are possible. On the one hand, it may indicate recognition of the *importance* of women's economic contribution to these societies, while on the other, it may be a consequence of the long-term *absence of men* who are off hunting or fighting. In the latter case, matrilineal kinship would put control of the absent men's property in the hands of their *sisters*—members of their own kin group—rather than wives—who by the rules of exogamy are members of another kin group.[41]

TABLE 6.3 Matrilineality among Simple Horticultural Societies, by Percentage of Subsistence Obtained from Hunting and Herding

Percentage of Subsistence Obtained by Hunting and Herding	Percentage of Societies Matrilineal	No. of Societies
26 or more	14	29
16 to 25	24	54
15 or less	30	60

Source: See Appendix, pp. 372–374.

Developments in Polity, Stratification, and Warfare

The power of political leaders has been quite limited in nearly all simple horticultural societies. Even in the larger, multicommunity societies, local villages have virtual autonomy except
in matters of war and relations with other societies. Both the village headman and the tribal
chief (i.e., leader of the multicommunity society) depend more on persuasion than on coercion to achieve their goals (see Figure 5.3, page 95). This is partly because of the limited
development of the governmental system; a leader has few subordinates so dependent on
him that they are obliged to carry out his instructions. Also, since men still make their own
weapons, no one can monopolize them and thereby dominate the others. The absence of
weapons that only a few can afford limits the growth of political inequality.

In some simple horticultural societies, shamans also serve as headmen or chiefs because of the awe or respect in which they are held.[42] In others, secular leaders assume important religious functions and become quasi-religious leaders. As one writer notes, a "chief's
influence is definitely enhanced when he combines religious with secular functions."[43] In
short, in many simple horticultural societies of the modern era, just as in the prehistoric past,
"church" and "state" are closely linked and sometimes almost become one.

The only other important basis of political power in these societies is membership in a
large and prosperous kin group. As we noted earlier, the senior member and leader of the
largest, most powerful, or most respected clan often becomes the village headman or tribal
chief.[44] He can usually count on the support of his kinsmen, and that is a substantial political
resource in this kind of society.

Social inequality is generally rather limited in most simple horticultural societies of the
modern era. Although extremes of wealth and political power are absent, substantial differences in prestige are not uncommon. Political and religious leaders usually enjoy high status,
but this depends far more on personal achievements than on mere occupancy of an office.
Other bases of status include military prowess (which is highly honored in nearly all horticultural societies), skill in oratory, age, kinship ties, and in some cases wealth in the form of
wives, pigs, and ornaments.[45] Each society has its own distinctive combination of criteria.

The more advanced the technology and economy of one of these groups, the greater
social inequality tends to be. Societies that practice irrigation, own domesticated animals, or
practice metallurgy for ornamental and ceremonial purposes are usually less egalitarian than
groups without these characteristics. We see this clearly when we compare the villagers of
eastern Brazil and the Amazon River basin with their more advanced neighbors to the north
and west who, in pre-Spanish days, practiced irrigation and metallurgy. Hereditary class differences were absent in the former, but common in the latter, where a hereditary class of chiefs
and nobles was set apart from commoners.[46]

Ethnographers have found warfare to be more common among horticulturalists than
among hunters and gatherers (see Table 6.4). This finding parallels the findings of archaeology, where the evidence indicates that warfare increased substantially during the horticultural
era. Now, as in the past, combat appears to serve as a psychic substitute for the excitement,

TABLE 6.4 Incidence of Warfare, by Societal Type (in Percentages)

Type of Society	Perpetual	Common	Rare or Absent	Total	No. of Societies
Hunting and gathering	0	27	73	100	22
Simple horticultural	5	55	41	100	22
Advanced horticultural	34	48	17	100	29

Source: Adapted from data in Gregory Leavitt, "The Frequency of Warfare: An Evolutionary Perspective,"
Sociological Inquiry, 14 (January 1977), appendix B.

In horticultural societies, combat appears to provide a psychic substitute for the excitement, challenge, and rewards that hunting once provided. Yanamamö men intoxicated on ebene, a hallucinogenic drug, prepare for a "friendly" duel with men from a neighboring village. Such duels often turn violent and lead to war.

challenge, and rewards which hunting previously provided and which were so important in the lives of men in hunting and gathering societies.

Warfare may also function as an important mechanism of population control in these groups. In addition to the direct loss of life in combat, warfare is a stimulus for female infanticide, which provides an even greater check on population growth.[47] In societies in which warfare is the normal state of affairs, it is imperative that the group be able to field the largest possible number of warriors, and female infanticide seems to be a common method of accomplishing this. By reducing the number of girls, the group can devote its resources to the care and nurture of its boys. A survey of studies of 609 "primitive" societies found that the sex ratio among the young was most imbalanced in those societies in which warfare was current at the time of the study and most nearly normal in those societies in which warfare had not occurred for more than twenty-five years.[48] In the former, boys outnumbered girls by a ratio of seven to five on the average, indicating that nearly 30 percent of the females born in these societies had died as a result of female infanticide or neglect.

As warfare grows in importance in a society, several new patterns tend to develop. Above all, there is the cult of the warrior, which heaps honors on successful fighters. Record keeping and publicity are as important to these warrior heroes as to modern athletes, and, in the absence of statisticians and sportswriters, they devise techniques of their own—especially trophy taking. Trophies include such things as skulls and shrunken heads, which are preserved and displayed like modern athletic trophies (see page 123).[49]

The high incidence of warfare in simple horticultural societies helps to keep the channels of vertical mobility open. Almost every boy becomes a warrior and thus has a chance to win honor and influence. Nevertheless, the channels of vertical mobility are somewhat more

Ceremonial Cannibalism

Ceremonial cannibalism, a widespread practice in simple horticultural societies, may have developed as a by-product of trophy collecting. Utilitarian cannibalism, or the eating of other humans to avoid starvation, is an ancient practice, traceable to distant prehistoric times, but ceremonial cannibalism seems to be a more recent innovation. The basic idea underlying it is that one can appropriate the valued qualities of a conquered enemy by eating his body. Ceremonial cannibalism is usually surrounded by a complex, and often prolonged, set of rituals, as the following account from South America indicates.

> The prisoners taken by a Tupinamba war party were received with manifestations of anger, scorn, and derision, but after the first hostile outburst, they were not hampered in their movements nor were they unkindly treated. Their captors, whose quarters they shared, treated them as relatives. The prisoners generally married village girls, very often the sisters or daughters of their masters, or, in certain cases, the widow of a dead warrior whose hammock and ornaments they used. They received fields for their maintenance, they were free to hunt and fish, and they were reminded of their servile condition by few restrictions and humiliations.
>
> The period of captivity lasted from a few months to several years. When, finally, the date for the execution had been set by the village council, invitations were sent to nearby villages to join in the celebration. The ritual for the slaughter of a captive was worked out to the most minute detail. The club and cord which figured prominently in the ceremony were carefully painted and decorated in accordance with strict rules. For three days before the event, the village women danced, sang, and tormented the victim with descriptions of his impending fate. On the eve of his execution a mock repetition of his capture took place, during which the prisoner was allowed to escape but was immediately retaken; the man who overpowered him in a wrestling match adopted a new name, as did the ceremonial executioner.
>
> The prisoner spent his last night dancing, pelting his tormentors, and singing songs which foretold their ruin and proclaimed his pride at dying as a warrior. In the morning he was dragged to the plaza by old women amidst shouts, songs, and music. The ceremonial rope was removed from his neck and tied around his waist, and it was held at both ends by two or more men. The victim was once more permitted to give vent to his feelings by throwing fruit or potsherds at his enemies. The executioner, who appeared painted and dressed in a long feather cloak, derided the victim, who boasted of his past deeds and predicted that his relatives would avenge him.
>
> The actual execution was a cruel game. The prisoner was allowed sufficient freedom of movement to dodge the blows aimed at him; sometimes a club was put in his hands so that he could parry the blows without being able to strike back. When at last he fell, his skull shattered, everyone shouted and whistled. Old women rushed in to drink the warm blood, children were invited to dip their hands in it, and mothers smeared their nipples so that even infants could have a taste. While the quartered body was being roasted on a babracot the old women, who were the most eager to taste human flesh, licked the grease running from the sticks. Certain delicate or sacred portions, such as the fingers and the grease around the liver, were given to distinguished guests.[50]

restricted in horticultural societies than in hunting and gathering societies, because status advantages can more easily be passed from parent to child. This is partly due to the greater amount of private property in horticultural societies, and its increased importance. In addition, there are the beginnings of inequality among kin groups: it is a distinct advantage to be born into a large, powerful, and wealthy clan. Finally, the institutional structures of these societies frequently evolve to the point where they can, to some extent, supplement the personal

Record keeping and symbols of success are no less important to warriors in horticultural societies than they are to modern athletes. The Jivaro Indians of South America collected heads as trophies and developed a technique for shrinking and preserving them for purposes of display.

attributes of their leaders. No longer does a headman have to be the best man in the group; he need only be competent, because he now has assistants who will support and help him. As a consequence, the headmanship is more likely to be inherited than is the case in hunting and gathering societies. This growth in the heritability of status, though modest in scope and of limited importance in simple horticultural societies, marked the beginning of a trend that was destined to become tremendously important in more advanced societies.

ADVANCED HORTICULTURAL SOCIETIES IN PREHISTORIC ASIA AND EUROPE

Each of the inventions and discoveries of the horticultural era increased to some degree the ability of societies to utilize the resources in their environments. But none had such far-reaching effects as *the manufacture and use of metal weapons and tools*. This is why metallurgy is used as the criterion for differentiating between simple and advanced horticultural societies. Societies are classified as advanced horticultural only if the use of metal weapons and tools was widespread. Societies in which this was rare, or in which metals were used only for artistic and ceremonial artifacts (as in a number of pre-Columbian South and Central

American Indian societies where gold was the only metal known), are better classified as simple horticultural, since the impact of metallurgy on societal life was limited.

The Shift from Stone to Metals

To a person who is not technically inclined, the shift from stone to metal may suggest a radical break with the past and the introduction of something completely new. Actually, however, the use of metals evolved from the use of stone by a series of surprisingly small steps.

For thousands of years people had been aware of differences among rocks and stones. They knew that some were better for tools and weapons because they were harder and held a cutting edge longer. They were also aware of the colors in rocks and used the more unusual ones for beads and other ornaments, and as a source of pigments for paint.

This interest in unusual rocks undoubtedly attracted people to copper. In its native form, copper appears as a purplish green or greenish black nugget which, when scratched or rubbed, shows a yellowish kernel of pure unoxidized copper. At first, copper was simply hammered cold into small tools and ornaments such as awls, pins, and hooks. A few articles made by this method have been found in Middle Eastern sites dating from about 7000 B.C.[51] Later, between 5000 and 4000 B.C., the technique of annealing was discovered.[52] By alternately heating and hammering copper, it was made less brittle and thus could be used for a wide variety of purposes. The heat from a simple wood fire was sufficient. Later still, people discovered techniques for extracting copper from ore by means of smelting, and they also found ways to melt copper and cast it in molds.[53]

These discoveries illustrate again the cumulative nature of technological progress. Since both smelting and melting copper require higher temperatures than a simple wood fire can produce, these important discoveries must have come after the invention of pottery and the pottery kiln.[54] And these inventions in turn came after the establishment of permanent communities where heavy and bulky objects could be accumulated. Figure 6.4 summarizes the complex chain of causation involved and reminds us again of the systemic nature of human societies.

FIGURE 6.4 *Model of the chain of causes leading from the adoption of horticulture to the widespread use of copper in the manufacture of tools, weapons, and other artifacts.*

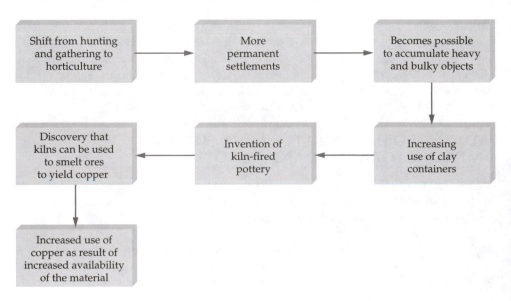

As far as we can judge, the use of copper tools and weapons increased rather slowly for a variety of reasons.[55] For one thing, until smelting was discovered, the supply of copper was extremely limited; even then, the ore often had to be carried some distance by primitive and costly methods of transportation. In addition, metalworking (particularly smelting and casting) was probably mastered by only a few specialists, who may have treated their skills as a kind of magic (as smiths in contemporary horticultural societies often do) to protect a lucrative monopoly. Finally, since any man could make his own tools and weapons out of stone, people were undoubtedly reluctant to switch to the costlier product.[56] Thus, though copper was discovered as early as 6000 to 7000 B.C., no truly advanced horticultural society (i.e., one in which metal tools and weapons were widespread) seems to have developed until about 4000 B.C.[57]

To see what the widespread adoption of metal tools and weapons meant for the life of a horticultural society, we will turn to China, where the archaeological record is unusually rich and informative.

Social Consequences of Metal Tools and Weapons

Advanced horticultural societies flourished in China from the middle of the second millennium B.C. to the middle of the first.[58] The plow, for reasons that are unclear, was slow to appear in China, thus delaying the emergence of agrarian societies. This prolonged horticultural era was undoubtedly a major reason why the overall level of technological development in China's advanced horticultural societies surpassed that in most others of that type.

One indication of this is the fact that the dominant metal in China during most of this era was not copper, as in the Middle East and Europe, but bronze. This is significant because bronze,* which represents an important advance in metallurgy, is much harder than copper and can be used for many purposes for which copper is unsuitable. In the Middle East the technique of making bronze was not really mastered until some time *after* the first agrarian societies had made their appearance.[60] Variations in the sequence of such major innovations as bronze and the plow warn us of the inadequacy of *unilinear* theories of evolution, which assume that all societies follow exactly the same evolutionary path. Some variation is the rule, not the exception.

When the advanced horticultural era in China is compared with the simple horticultural period, the differences are striking. During the earlier era northern China was covered with many small, mostly self-sufficient, autonomous villages. But in the later period the villages were no longer autonomous and a few had become urban centers of some size and substance.

The emergence of these urban centers was largely the result of the military success of villages that had one important advantage: *bronze weapons*. As one scholar described this period, "In the course of a few centuries the villages of the plain fell under the domination of walled cities on whose rulers the possession of bronze weapons, chariots, and slaves conferred a measure of superiority to which no [simple horticultural] community could aspire."[61]

The importance of this development can hardly be exaggerated. For the first time in Chinese history people found that the conquest of other people could be a profitable alternative to the conquest of nature. Much the same thing happened in other parts of the world at this same stage of societal development. Thus, beginning in advanced horticultural societies and continuing in agrarian, we find almost as much energy expended in war as in the more basic struggle for subsistence. One might say that *bronze was to the conquest of people what plant cultivation was to the conquest of nature: both were decisive turning points in sociocultural evolution.*

---

*Bronze involves the important technique of *alloying,* the combining of two or more metals—in this case, copper with tin.[59]

From the military standpoint China's advanced horticulturalists enjoyed a great advantage over simple horticulturalists. Recently excavated burial remains show that their warriors wore elaborate armor, including helmets. They also carried shields and were equipped with spears, dagger-axes, knives, hatchets, and reflex bows capable of a pull of 160 pounds.[62] In addition, they used horse-drawn chariots carrying teams of three men.

These societies also enjoyed substantial *numerical* superiority over simple horticultural societies and every victory brought more people under their control, enabling them to enlarge their armies still further.[63] This could not have been accomplished by a hunting and gathering society, whose simple technology would make it impossible for conquerors to incorporate a defeated people into the group. At that level of development, the *economic surplus* (i.e., production in excess of what is needed to keep the producers healthy and productive) was small and unpredictable. But with the introduction of horticulture the situation changed dramatically. *For the first time, the conquest, control, and exploitation of other societies had become possible—and profitable.* All that was needed to transform this possibility into a reality was an advance in military technology that would give one society a definite advantage over its neighbors. That advance was bronze. It tipped the balance of military power decisively in favor of advanced horticulturalists.

The earliest advanced horticultural society in China of which we have any knowledge was established around 1600 B.C., and its structure was basically feudalistic.[64] In most regions, especially those that were some distance from the capital, power was in the hands of a warrior nobility that ruled the people in their immediate area. They paid tribute to the king and supported him militarily, but otherwise were essentially independent.[65] They were so independent, in fact, that they often waged war among themselves.

Marked social inequality was the rule in these societies. There were two basic classes, a small warrior nobility and the great mass of common people.[66] The warrior nobility were the governing class and lived in walled cities that served as their fortresses. It was they who enjoyed most of the benefits of the new technology and the new social system. The chief use of bronze was to manufacture weapons and ceremonial objects for the benefit of this elite class. Almost none of this scarce material was made available to the common people for farm tools.[67] The situation was much the same in the Middle East and Europe for 2,000 years or more. As one writer put it, this was a world in which metals played a major role in the military, religious, and artistic spheres, but not in subsistence activities.[68]

Kinship was extremely important in the political systems of advanced horticultural China. Membership in the governing class was largely hereditary, and as far as possible leading officials assigned the major offices under their control to kinsmen.[69] The origins of these noble families are unknown, but they were probably descendants of early conquerors and their chief officers.

The walled towns where the aristocracy lived, though small by modern standards, were nonetheless an important innovation. One recently excavated town, probably the capital of an early state, covered slightly over one square mile, or twenty times the area of Çatal Hüyük.[70] The size of the walled areas, however, does not tell the full story of these towns, especially in the earlier period, for many of the common people had their homes and workshops outside the protected area and cultivated nearby fields.

The walled area, while basically a fortress and place of residence for the governing class, was also a political and religious center. Religious activities were quite important and were so closely tied to the political system that one writer describes the state as "a kind of theocracy."[71] Though this may be an overstatement, ancient inscriptions prove that the ruler performed major religious functions and was what we today would call the head of both church and state.

The physical structure of those early urban centers was impressive and reflected the evolution of the **state** (see Glossary) and its newly acquired ability to mobilize labor on a large

Chariots, together with bronze weapons, gave the advanced horticulturalists of China a great advantage over their simple horticultural neighbors. Burial remains of a warrior with his horses and chariot, eleventh century B.C.

The Great Wall of China: this 1,500-mile-long fortification, begun late in China's horticultural era, illustrates the growing power of political elites and their ability to mobilize labor on a massive scale.

scale. One scholar estimates, for example, that it required the labor of 10,000 men working eighteen years to build the wall around the capital of one early state. Such massive undertakings apparently utilized large numbers of captives taken in war, many of whom were used later as human sacrifices.[72]

Not much is known about the daily life of the common people, but their chief functions were obviously to produce the economic surplus on which the governing class depended and to provide workers and soldiers for various projects and military campaigns. Not all labor was of the brute, physical type, however. Some people were craft specialists who provided the new and unusual luxury goods that the governing class demanded for display and for ceremonial purposes; others produced military equipment.[73] Although many of these specialists were probably also part-time farmers, the increase in occupational specialization was undoubtedly accompanied by a significant growth in trade.

Despite their increasingly exploitative character, the advanced horticultural societies of China made important advances in a number of areas. The more important innovations included writing, money, the use of the horse, probably irrigation, and the manufacture of iron at the very end of the horticultural era. In addition, there were lesser innovations too numerous to mention, some of them Chinese inventions or discoveries, others products of diffusion. In most cases, it is impossible to determine which were which.

ADVANCED HORTICULTURAL SOCIETIES IN THE MODERN ERA

For several centuries advanced horticultural societies have been limited to two parts of the world, sub-Saharan Africa and southeast Asia. Until recently they occupied most of sub-Saharan Africa. In southeast Asia, on the other hand, agrarian societies have occupied most of the land, and horticulturalists have been confined to the hill country.

These advanced horticulturalists of modern times differ in one important respect from those of prehistoric times: the dominant metal in their societies has been iron rather than copper or bronze. This is important, because iron ore is so much more plentiful than copper and tin that it can be used for ordinary tools as well as weapons. However, because it is much more difficult to separate iron from the ore, the manufacture of iron was a later development.

The history of Africa proves once again that the evolutionary process does not compel all societies to follow exactly the same pattern of development. Bronze was never the dominant metal in most of Africa below the Sahara. During the period when bronze was dominant in the Middle East, cultural contacts between Egypt and the territories to the south were minimal. By the time there was sufficient contact to permit diffusion of specialized skills like metallurgy, iron had become dominant.[74] Thus, most of Africa seems to have moved directly from the Stone Age to the Iron Age.

Increased Size and Complexity

Compared with hunting and gathering or simple horticultural societies, advanced horticultural societies are usually larger and more complex. Table 4.2 (page 71) summarizes the evidence from Murdock's data set: on average, advanced horticultural societies are three and a half times the size of simple horticultural and 130 times the size of hunting and gathering societies. Table 4.3 (page 72) shows that craft specialization is much more common in advanced horticultural societies than in either simple horticultural or hunting and gathering societies. Murdock's data also show that social inequality increases markedly at this level of societal development. Slavery, for example, is found in 83 percent of advanced horticultural societies, but in only 15 percent of simple (see Figure 6.5). And finally, class systems are reported in 7 percent of advanced horticultural societies and in only 1 percent of simple (see Figure 4.3, page 72).

Trade and commerce are much more important in horticultural societies than in hunting and gathering societies: the marketplace in Ouagadougou, Burkina Faso.

One consequence of the more highly developed economy and stratification system in advanced horticultural societies is their increased emphasis on the economic aspect of marriage. In almost every one of these societies, marriageable daughters are viewed as a valuable property, and men who want to marry them must either pay for the privilege or render extended service to their prospective in-laws. Fortunately for young men with limited resources, extended kin groups usually view marriage as a sensible investment and are willing to loan suitors part of the bride price. This economic approach to marriage is much more common in advanced horticultural societies than in either hunting and gathering or simple horticultural societies.

Political Development

The growth in social inequality is closely linked with the growth of government. A generation ago, one of the pioneers in the study of African political systems argued that most traditional African societies fell into one of two basic categories: those "which have centralized authority, administrative machinery, and judicial institutions—in short, a government—and in which cleavages of wealth, privilege, and status correspond to the distribution of authority," and those which have none of these attributes.[75] Though recent studies suggest that this twofold division was an oversimplification, they confirm that African societies differ in the ways described and that there is a strong relationship between the development of the state and the growth of social inequality.[76]

African societies afford a valuable opportunity to study the early stages of political development. A leading student of east African political systems suggests that a critical step in the process occurs when the head of a strong clan begins to take on, as retainers, men who are not related to him, thereby overcoming one of the traditional constraints on power and its expansion.[77] These retainers are usually individuals who have been expelled from their own

In almost every politically advanced society of horticultural Africa there was a sharp cleavage between nobles and commoners: early bronze casting of Dahomean chief and his entourage of relatives and retainers. Note the fine workmanship.

kin group for misconduct or whose group has been destroyed in war or by some natural disaster, and they offer their allegiance and service in exchange for protection and a liveli-hood.

Since there is a natural tendency for men in this position to turn to the strongest ex-tended family in their society, power begins to accumulate. This is reinforced by the wealth of such a family, which permits it to buy more wives to produce more sons and warriors, and by the development of myths that attribute the group's success to the magical powers of its leader. The final link in this chain of state building is forged when less powerful families, and even whole communities, are brought under the control of the head of a strong kin group—either by conquest or by the decision of weaker groups to put themselves under the strong group's protection. When this happens, each of the subordinate groups is usually allowed to retain its land, and its leader his authority within his own group, but the group is compelled to pay tribute. The leader of the dominant group then uses these revenues to support his kins-men and retainers, thereby increasing their dependence on him and, he hopes, their loyalty as well.

Sometimes this state-building process is stimulated by feuds that get out of hand. Where strong political authority is lacking, feuds can be a serious matter. Individuals and families are forced to settle their own grievances, which often sets off a deadly cycle of action and reac-tion. More than one east African group has voluntarily put itself under the authority of a strong neighboring leader just to break such a cycle and reestablish peace among its members.

One might imagine that these processes, once set in motion, would continue until eventually all Africa came under a single authority. But powerful countervailing forces have prevented this. Technological limitations, especially in transportation and communication, were most important. Advanced horticulturalists in Africa, as in the New World, had no knowl-edge of the wheel and did not have draft animals until contact with Europeans. As a result, the farther a ruler's power was extended into outlying areas, the weaker it became. Not only were

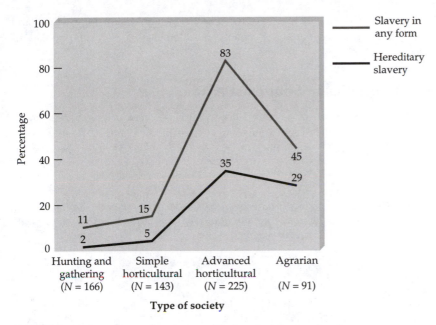

FIGURE 6.5 *Percentage of societies with slavery, by type of society.*
Source: Appendix, pp. 372–374.

these areas vulnerable to attack by other societies, but even more serious, they were likely to revolt. From the territorial standpoint, Songhay was probably the largest kingdom that ever developed in sub-Saharan Africa. In the early fourteenth century it controlled approximately 500,000 square miles in the western Sudan (i.e., twice the size of present-day France).[78] Most African kingdoms, however, were much smaller.

By the standards of modern industrial societies, the governments of Africa's advanced horticultural societies were extremely unstable. Revolts were a common occurrence, not only in outlying provinces but even in the capitals. These were seldom, if ever, popular uprisings. Rather, they were instigated by powerful members of the nobility, often the king's own brothers. This pattern was so common that the Zulus had a proverb that "the king should not eat with his brothers lest they poison him."[79]

In virtually every politically developed society of horticultural Africa there was a sharply defined cleavage between a hereditary nobility and the mass of commoners. Historically, this distinction grew out of the state-building process.[80] Nobles were usually descendants of past rulers and their chief officers, or hereditary leaders of subordinated groups. They comprised a warrior aristocracy supported by the labor of the common people. Below the commoners there was often a class of slaves, many of them captives taken in war, and, as in other horticultural societies, they were frequently slaughtered as human sacrifices (see Figure 6.5).

In horticultural Africa, as in the New World and elsewhere, religion and politics were intimately related. In many instances the king was viewed as divine or as having access to divine powers.[81] This served to make tyrannical and exploitative practices legitimate. It also helps explain why no efforts were made to establish other kinds of political systems: given their ideological heritage, any alternative was inconceivable. These beliefs did not protect a ruler against attacks from his kinsmen, however, because they shared his special religious status and thus were qualified to assume the duties and privileges of the royal office—if they could seize it.

A comparison of the politically complex societies of horticultural Africa with those which remained autonomous villages shows that the former were more developed in other ways as well. They were far more likely to have full-time craft specialization, for example, and they were also more likely to have urban or semiurban settlements—a few with populations of 20,000 or more.[82]

Horticultural Societies in Southeast Asia

Before concluding this discussion of advanced horticultural societies in the modern era, a brief comment on those in southeast Asia is necessary. The striking feature of these societies is their organizational simplicity, especially in terms of political development. In most in-

Mayan temple at Tikal, Guatemala. Several horticultural societies in the New World achieved a level of technological advance approaching that of ancient Egypt and Mesopotamia in the first centuries after they became agrarian societies.

stances, villages have been autonomous; and when multicommunity societies have developed, they have invariably been small.[83] Urban or semiurban settlements have been absent.

The reason appears to be ecological. Centuries ago, after this region came under the domination of more powerful agrarian societies, horticultural societies survived only in hill country where transportation was difficult and the land unsuited to the plow and permanent cultivation. This combination of more powerful neighbors and the deficiencies of their own territories apparently prevented all but the most limited development and caused these groups to be looked down upon, and often exploited, by their agrarian neighbors. Ecological factors of a different type had a similar effect in certain parts of Africa: political development was quite limited in the tropical rain forests. Apparently the dense vegetation and other hindrances to the movement of armies and goods made it impossible to build and maintain extensive kingdoms.[84]

HORTICULTURAL SOCIETIES IN THEORETICAL PERSPECTIVE

Few events in human history have been as important as the shift from hunting and gathering to horticulture. It is no exaggeration to say that *the adoption of horticulture in the realm of technology was comparable to the adoption of symbol use in the realm of communication: each was a decisive break with the mammal and primate world*. Hunting and gathering, like the use of signals, are adaptations our species inherited from its prehuman ancestors. In contrast, horticulture and symbols are more peculiarly human.*

Of all the changes in human life that resulted from the horticultural revolution, the most fundamental—the one with the most profound consequences—was the creation of a *stable economic surplus*. Hunting and gathering societies were rarely able to create such a surplus: food producers and their dependents usually consumed within days all they were able to provide. With nothing left over to support *non*producers of food, except children and the aged, only the most limited occupational specialization was possible. There could be no governmental or religious institutions staffed by full-time officials and priests, nor could there be full-time artisans and merchants. And this, in turn, ruled out the development of towns and cities, since these are based on populations that are freed from the necessity of producing their own food.

The shift from hunting and gathering to plant cultivation provided societies with the means of establishing an economic surplus, but only if the growth in productivity was not consumed by a corresponding growth in population. To translate the potential for a stable surplus into a *reality* required an ideology that would motivate the producers of food to turn over part of their harvest to an individual in authority who could dispense it as he saw fit.

Traditional religious beliefs often answered this need. In a number of societies people were already accustomed to offering sacrifices, and nothing was more natural than that they should continue this practice as they shifted to plant cultivation, giving part of their yield to priests. With greater productivity, rituals became more elaborate and more frequent and priestly activities became full-time, for one man at first and eventually for others. In this way, small proto-urban communities began to develop around important shrines—communities that could exist only if a stable economic surplus was maintained.

In other societies the development of a stable surplus appears to have evolved out of a tradition of turning over to the headman part of the fruits of the hunt to distribute to the families of unsuccessful hunters. Here too the increase in productivity that resulted from the

---

*It is worth noting that although symbols do appear to be uniquely human, plant cultivation and animal husbandry really are not. Ants, too, have accomplished these feats. In fact, a number of traits associated with humans and human societies have parallels in ant societies. In addition to plant and animal domestication, various species of ants have developed organized warfare, a division of labor, castelike stratification, slavery, and even drug addiction![93]

Horticulture in the New World: Testing Ground for Ecological-Evolutionary Theory

No one knows for certain when humans first settled the New World. There is convincing evidence that humans were in the Americas by 12,000 to 14,000 years ago, but some archaeologists believe they were here much earlier, perhaps as much as 50,000 years ago.[85] The original settlers appear to have been hunters and gatherers who migrated from Asia by means of the land bridge that once connected Siberia and Alaska.

When the last Ice Age ended and the waters locked in the glaciers melted, the level of the oceans rose and the land bridge was submerged. As a result, the inhabitants of the New World were cut off from the inhabitants of the Old World during the horticultural revolution. Thus, there was no way information about the techniques of plant cultivation could have spread from Asia to the Americas.[86]

Despite this, horticultural societies did develop in the New World, and some of them achieved a level of technological advance comparable to that of early agrarian Mesopotamia and Egypt. Space limitations prevent us from tracing these developments in detail, and much of the account would be repetitive if we did. But in the New World, as in the Old, the shift from hunting and gathering to horticulture was preceded by the growth of population and led to more permanent settlements, more substantial dwellings, increased wealth and possessions, greater inequality, the development of pottery and later of metallurgy, the beginnings of full-time craft specialization, the appearance of permanent markets and increased trade, the beginnings of urbanism, the establishment of permanent religious centers, the construction of massive temples and temple complexes (see page 132), and a marked increase in both militarism and imperialism.[87]

There were also some differences: New World horticulturalists were not as successful in domesticating animals, for example, nor was their metallurgy as advanced, although some evidence indicates that copper smelting was independently developed and practiced on an extensive scale in Peru about 500 A.D.[88] On the other hand, they developed a numerical system that included the concept of zero centuries before this was invented in the Old World. Overall, however, the similarities far outweigh the differences.

The fact that horticulture developed at all in the isolated New World is the important point, for it provides an independent test of some basic ideas. For a long time scholars debated whether the striking similarities in patterns of societal development in the Middle East, China, and Europe were due to the independent operation of the same basic laws of sociocultural evolution or were simply the result of the diffusion of ideas from a single source. Despite the fact that different species of plants and animals were involved, the issue was impossible to resolve as long as only Old World societies were involved, because the possibility of diffusion could never be ruled out. The New World, however, is a different matter. Its contacts with the Old World ended several thousand years before horticulture began, and contact was not resumed until about 1000 A.D., when Leif Ericson briefly visited Vinland, somewhere on the northeast coast of North America.*

---

*Though attempts have been made to prove other contacts, they have not been successful. Moreover, careful studies of the evolution of plant cultivation in the New World convince scholars that this was entirely an indigenous process. For example, the transformation of maize, or corn, from a wild plant to a cultivated plant took much longer than one would expect if the process had been guided by information on the techniques of plant cultivation brought from the Old World.[89]

In short, the New World has been a kind of "Second Earth," where ideas about sociocultural evolution suggested by studies of the Old World can be put to the test.[90] The remarkable parallels between developments in the New World and the Old strongly suggest that there are limits to the amount of variation that is possible in the sequence of basic technological innovations. People must know certain things about both fire and rocks, for example, before metallurgy is possible, and a society must be familiar with the hoe before it can invent the plow. In addition, major technological innovations have fairly predictable consequences for other aspects of sociocultural systems—especially for social organization, the demographic variables, and material production.[91]

This is not to say that sociocultural evolution compels societies to march in lockstep. But much is predictable about the critical early stages of societal development. Marvin Harris, a major contributor to ecological-evolutionary theory, put the matter as well as anyone: *"Similar technologies applied to similar environments tend to produce similar arrangements of labor in production and distribution, and these in turn call forth similar kinds of social groupings, which justify and coordinate their activities by means of similar systems of values and beliefs."*[92]

Kano, a city in northern Nigeria, has been an important commercial and political center for more than 500 years. The style of architecture remains much as it was centuries ago.

shift to plant cultivation made full-time employment possible, first for a headman, later for his aides. Thus, the foundation was laid for the emergence of the state as a specialized entity, distinct from the rest of society.

In either case, the outcome was the same: the potential for a stable, dependable economic surplus became a reality, opening up important new possibilities for the organization of societal life. The possibilities would not all be realized in horticultural societies, however. The most dramatic and the most revolutionary would be realized only in agrarian and industrial societies, where the economic surplus would be many times larger.

Technological Advance but Moral Regress?

For years, many anthropologists presented an idyllic view of life in simpler societies, making them seem like the last remnants of Eden. But as numerous scholars have noted, it is one of the great ironies of evolution that progress in technology and social organization has often been linked with ethical regress. Horticultural societies provide several striking examples. Some of the most shocking, by the standards of modern western societies, are the emergence and spread of head-hunting, human sacrifice, and cannibalism.

There is also evidence that rates of homicide rise to unprecedented levels. For example, a recent study of simple horticulturalists in New Guinea found that nearly a third of all deaths over a forty-year period were due to homicide. In fact, the rate of homicide in this society was *more than 50 times* that in the United States, which for many years has had the highest rate of any modern industrial society. Evidence from other simple horticultural societies indicates that this is not an isolated instance but reflects a relatively widespread tendency in societies at this level of development.

In addition, there is a precipitous decline in the practice of sharing, a marked increase in inequality, and a dramatic increase in the frequency and scale of warfare. As Figure 6.5 shows, more than eight out of ten of the advanced horticultural societies

Human sacrifice, from carving on Mayan temple, Chichén Itzá, Mexico.

in Murdock's data set practiced some form of slavery and in more than one third of these societies slavery was an inheritable condition. Warfare is also "perpetual" or "common" in more than 80 percent of advanced horticultural societies (Table 6.4). Since war captives constituted the great majority of slaves, the parallel increases in warfare and slavery are not unrelated. Trophy-taking, human sacrifice, and cannibalism are also linked to warfare; war captives apparently often faced the unenviable fates of either death or servitude. Horticulture and warfare are also associated with the development of female infanticide and the rise of patriarchal systems in which women are dominated and, in many cases, physically abused by men.

These startling developments and sobering patterns serve to remind us that technological advance does not necessarily imply or entail moral progress.

Sources: Margaret Mead, *Coming of Age in Samoa* (New York: Morrow, 1928); Bruce Knauft, "Reconsidering Violence in Simple Human Societies," *Current Anthropology,* 28 (Aug.-Oct. 1987), p. 462; Marvin Harris, *Cannibals and Kings: The Origins of Culture* (New York: Random House, 1987), chap. 6; Napoleon Chagnon, *Yanamamö: The Fierce People* (New York: Holt, Rinehart, Winston, 1977).

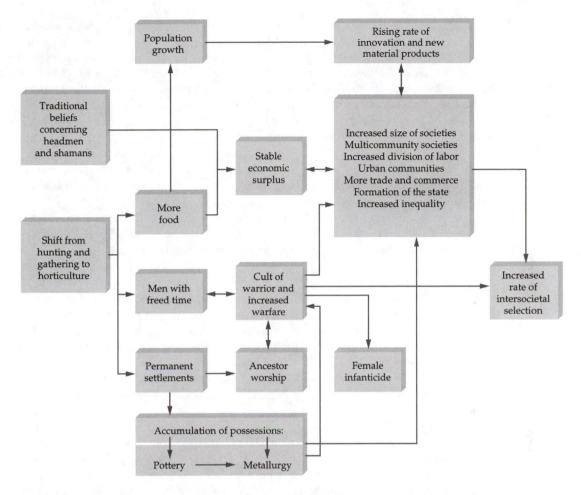

FIGURE 6.6 *Model of the potential effects of the shift from hunting and gathering to horticulture.*

It is important to note that in horticultural societies we see, for the first time, ideology playing a recognizable role in societal development. In hunting and gathering societies, the limits set by technology are so narrow that ideology's role in the developmental process is negligible.* But the picture changes with the shift to horticulture, where ideological differences sometimes give rise to significant differences in societal development.

Figure 6.6 summarizes the effects of the shift from hunting and gathering to horticulture. Not all of these consequences occurred in every horticultural society, but the model indicates *the possibilities* inherent in the new subsistence technology.

At a minimum, the shift to horticulture meant more food and more permanent settlements, and frequently more free time for men. More food meant population growth and, when combined with certain traditional beliefs concerning the role of headmen and shamans, created the possibility of a stable economic surplus. The increase in free time for men often led to increased warfare and the emergence of the cult of the warrior. More permanent settlements made it feasible for people to accumulate far more possessions than was possible when frequent moves were necessary. Also, more permanent settlements, in combination with the emergence of the cult of the warrior, frequently led to the practice of ancestor

---

*This is not to say that these societies do not have a rich cultural life, but simply that differences in cultural beliefs have minimal effects on their material life.

worship, and the greater frequency of warfare contributed to the practice of female infanticide.

The development of a stable economic surplus was especially important since it paved the way for growth in the size of societies, the formation of multicommunity societies, an increased division of labor, urban communities, increased trade and commerce, the formation of the state, and greatly increased inequality. Several of these developments, especially the formation of multicommunity societies, the formation of the state, and increased inequality, were also stimulated by the increase in warfare, the increasing accumulation of possessions, and the production of new material products of many kinds. Finally, all of these developments, but especially the increase in warfare and the increasing differences in the military might of societies (many of which remained at the hunting and gathering level), contributed to a substantial rise in the rate of intersocietal selection.

In several instances boxes in Figure 6.6 are connected by two-headed arrows. These indicate that a process of feedback was operating, with the paired developments mutually stimulating one another. The most important of these is the two-headed arrow linking a stable economic surplus with the important set of changes in social organization in the large box to the right. In other words, once the creation of a stable economic surplus had given rise to an increased division of labor, urban communities, multicommunity societies, the formation of the state, and so forth, these developments in social organization tended to stabilize and ensure the continued production of an economic surplus. New institutional arrangements ensured that priests, political and military leaders, merchants, craftsmen, and other specialists would get a share—and usually a disproportionate share—of the goods and services produced in the society. These specialists would have the first claim on food and other essentials. Thus, in order to survive, farmers were obliged to produce more than they and their families required.

The rise in the rate of intersocietal selection is another feature of Figure 6.6 that merits attention. It is a reminder that the horticultural revolution meant dramatic change not only for individual societies but also for the world system of societies. If Figure 6.6 is compared with Figure 3.5, the similarity in trends is striking. This is no coincidence, since the shift from hunting and gathering to horticulture was the first major step along the road that has led to the modern world system.

Excursus: Race, Environment, and Societal Development

After the first explorers returned to Europe from Africa, the Americas, and Asia, Europeans were intrigued by differences in the level of development of societies in various parts of the world. Interest in these differences led quite naturally to efforts to explain them.

The apparent association between differences in physical appearance and levels of technological development gave rise to a number of racialist explanations. Racialist explanations assert that societies differ in their level of development and in other ways because the members differ in their culture-building abilities.[94] Translated into modern scientific terminology, these theories assert that societies differ in their levels of development because of differences in the genetic heritages of their populations.

These theories have had great appeal because they seem to fit the evidence rather well. During the last several hundred years, societies dominated by Europeans have been technologically the most advanced and organizationally the most complex and powerful. Societies dominated by Asians have ranked next, while societies dominated by Africans have been the least developed technologically and organizationally. Since the level of societal development is obviously not responsible for the race of a population, racialist theorists have argued that the race must be responsible for the level of development.

Racialist theories can be quite compelling if one does not have an ecological and evolutionary perspective. If one adopts such a perspective, however, those theories prove to have a number of weaknesses.

To begin with, we find that the recent ranking of societies in terms of development has not always prevailed. For thousands of years Middle Eastern societies—not European societies—were the most highly developed.[95] Also, for many centuries China equaled or surpassed northwestern Europe. Finally, for several centuries before and after the start of the Christian era, the center of civilization was in the Mediterranean basin, and North African societies, such as Carthage and Egypt, were much more advanced than the barbarian societies of northwest Europe; also, there is some evidence that steel was being produced in Africa 1,900 years before this capability was developed in Europe.[96] While there have been some changes in the racial composition of some populations during this period (e.g., in ancient times the proportion of fair-haired and fair-skinned individuals in Greek and Roman societies seems to have been appreciably higher than today), they do not appear to have been great enough to cause the substantial changes that have occurred in the relative level of societal development.

If, then, the evolutionary record undermines the credibility of racialist theories, where do we look for an explanation? Here the ecological perspective comes to our aid. It suggests that environmental differences offer a promising alternative. Recent research has shown that many tropical and semitropical regions are poorly suited to plow agriculture.[97] Although the lushness of tropical rain forests suggests rich and fertile soils, modern research has found the opposite: the soils of tropical rain forests are among the poorest in the world. While it is possible to clear small and temporary gardens in these forests, as horticulturalists have done for centuries, it is not possible to clear permanent fields and cultivate them continuously as agriculturalists do. The fertility of these soils is quickly exhausted and, worse yet, some of the soils harden and become compacted to the point where cultivation of any kind is impossible. In addition, large-scale clearing of the rain forest appears to break the hydrological cycle and rainfall declines. In short, indigenous development beyond the level of horticultural societies seems to have been impossible in much of sub-Saharan Africa and much of Latin America.

In addition, research has shown that human populations in tropical regions are exposed to many more tiny predators than are populations in temperate regions.[98] In fact, the number, variety, and seriousness of the parasites (bacteria, viruses, worms, etc.) that prey on human populations seem to increase steadily as one moves from polar regions to the tropics. In the tropics, the problems created by these micropredators have often been overwhelming. Large portions of the population have been affected by debilitating diseases of one kind or another—diseases such as malaria, onchocerciasis (which causes blindness), and schistosomiasis (which causes people to become listless and lacking in energy).

Prior to the invention of the microscope, the causes of such diseases were not only unknown, but *unknowable*. Societies afflicted by them were badly handicapped, but they had no method of overcoming their handicap. Thus, the most serious challenges that confronted horticulturalists in the tropics were profoundly different from those that confronted horticulturalists in temperate areas such as Europe. In the latter, the basic challenge was to increase the food supply, and this could be achieved through the gradual improvement of tools of various kinds—in other words, through the exercise of ordinary human intelligence. In contrast, in tropical regions this was impossible. Because of environmental constraints that were beyond human control, the usual course of evolution, from horticulture to agriculture, was impossible in most tropical societies, and human health and vitality were constantly undermined by forces that would remain unknowable until the technological development elsewhere (in temperate regions) and in other societies of modern industrial technology—a late stage in an evolutionary process that presupposes an earlier agricultural stage.

Thus, the adoption of an ecological and evolutionary perspective provides quite a different explanation of the relationship of race and societal development than that provided by earlier racialist theories.

Moreover, because the former explanation fits more of the facts than the latter, it has greater scientific credibility. Although it would be premature to suggest that we now fully understand the causes of the complex relationship between race and societal development, it appears that ecological-evolutionary theory substantially advances our understanding of it.

7

Agrarian Societies

"The thousand years or so immediately preceding 3000 B.C. were perhaps more fertile in fruitful inventions and discoveries than any period in human history prior to the sixteenth century, A.D."[1] So wrote V. Gordon Childe, one of the most influential archaeologists of the twentieth century. The innovations of that period included the invention of the wheel and its application both to wagons and to the manufacture of pottery, the invention of the plow, the harnessing of animals to pull wagons and plows and their use as pack animals, the harnessing of wind power for sailboats, the invention of writing and numerical notation, and the invention of the calendar.[2]

Collectively, these innovations transformed the conditions of life for societies in the Middle East, and eventually for societies throughout the world. With these new cultural resources, societies expanded their populations, increased their material wealth, and developed social organizations far more complex than anything known before.

SIMPLE AGRARIAN SOCIETIES

Technology

Although all of the innovations mentioned above were important, the plow had the greatest potential for social and cultural change. To a modern city dweller, the plow may not sound very exciting, yet without it we would still be back in the horticultural era. To appreciate its importance, we need to recognize two basic problems that confront farmers everywhere: controlling weeds and maintaining the fertility of the soil.[3] With traditional horticultural tools and techniques, both problems become more severe the longer a plot of ground is cultivated. Weeds multiply faster than horticulturalists with hoes can root them out; and unless periodic flooding or fertilization replenishes them, the soil's nutrients seep deeper into the ground, below the reach of plants and too deep to be brought back to the surface with hoes and other simple tools. Within a few years the yield from such a garden usually becomes so small that the farmer is forced to abandon it and clear a new one.

The plow, if it did not eliminate these problems, at least reduced them to manageable proportions. Because it turns the soil over to a greater depth than the hoe, the plow buries weeds, not only killing them but also adding humus to the soil. Deeper cultivation also brings back to the surface the nutrients that have seeped below root level. Thus, the plow made more permanent cultivation possible in a greater variety of soils,* and thereby led to the widespread replacement of horticulture (from the Latin *horti cultura,* or the cultivation of a garden) by agriculture (from *agri cultura,* the cultivation of a field).

The invention of the plow also facilitated the harnessing of animal energy.[5] As long as the digging stick and hoe were the basic tools of cultivation, men and women supplied the

---

*Before the plow and systems of fertilization, permanent cultivation was only possible in a few very limited areas, such as alluvial flood plains.[4]

141

Hoeing the ground.

Plow drawn by men.

Plow drawn by oxen.
2242. Tools in the sculptures on a Theban tomb.

Intensification of cultivation in ancient Egypt from horticulture to agriculture. Note the humans pulling the plow in the middle panel.

energy. But a plow could be pulled, and it did not take long for people to discover that oxen could do the job better than people. The importance of this discovery can hardly be exaggerated, since it established a principle with broad applicability. In Childe's words, "The ox was the first step to the steam engine and the [gasoline] motor."[6]

More immediately, however, the harnessing of animal energy led to greatly increased productivity. With a plow and a pair of oxen, a farmer could cultivate a far larger area than was possible with a hoe.[7] In addition, the use of oxen led, in many societies, to feeding them in stalls, and this in turn led to the use of manure as fertilizer.[8] In short, the shift from hoe to plow not only meant permanently cultivated fields and larger crops; it also meant the potential for a larger economic surplus and new and more complex forms of social organization.

The earliest evidence of the plow comes from Mesopotamian cylinder seals and Egyptian paintings dating from a little before 3000 B.C.[9] Modern research indicates that the plow, like so many other innovations in the last 10,000 years, presupposed certain earlier inventions and discoveries—underlining again the cumulative nature of technological change. The first plows of the Mesopotamians and the Egyptians were, in fact, simply modified versions of the hoe, the basic farm implement of all advanced horticultural societies. In the earliest period, the plow was probably pulled by men, but before long, cattle and oxen were used. These plows, like all plows in simple agrarian societies, were made of wood, though sometimes the plowshare was made of bronze for greater strength.

The plow and related techniques of agriculture apparently spread by diffusion until agrarian societies were eventually established throughout most of Europe and much of North Africa and Asia. (See Figure 7.1.) The plow did not spread to sub-Saharan Africa until the period of European colonialism, and in the New World, too, it was unknown until introduced by Europeans.

The full impact of the new technology was not felt immediately in either Mesopotamia or Egypt. Even so, the shift to agriculture was followed quickly by further development of a

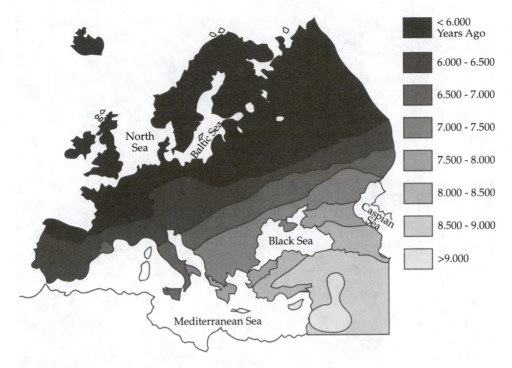

FIGURE 7.1 *The early diffusion of plant cultivation into Europe.*
Source: After Luigi Luca Cavalli-Sforza and Francesco Cavalli-Sforza, *The Great Human Diasporas: The History of Diversity and Evolution* (New York: Addison-Wesley, 1995), p. 135.

number of trends that started with plant and animal domestication. For example, the simple "tokens" that were used as early as 8,000 B.C. to record the quantities and types of commodities produced and exchanged evolved into systems of counting and writing,[10] urban communities increased in size and complexity and became recognizable as "cities," and empire building occurred on a greatly expanded scale (which in Egypt led to the unification of the entire country under a single ruler for the first time in history). This was the period that historians refer to as "the dawn of civilization."

Similar developments occurred (though at later dates) in horticultural societies in China and Mesoamerica, proving that the plow is not a necessary precondition for literacy, urbanism, and imperialism.* But the rarity of these developments in *horticultural* societies and their frequency in agrarian societies shows that the shift to agriculture, by increasing productivity, greatly increased the *probability* of their occurrence.

Religion and the Growth of the Economic Surplus

In the earliest agrarian societies, religion was an extremely powerful force. Mesopotamian societies believed that "man was . . . created for one purpose only: to serve the gods by supplying them with food, drink, and shelter so that they might have full leisure for their divine activities."[12] Each temple was believed to be, quite literally, the house of a particular god, and each community had its own special deity. Priests and other attendants constituted

---

*In the New World, empires based on horticulture developed in the Valley of Mexico, Central America, and along the coast of South America. With the exception of the Peruvian civilizations, which had an accounting system based on knots, all of them had written languages and numerical systems. Furthermore, the capital of the Aztec empire, Tenochtitlán, may have had a permanent population of more than 200,000 prior to contact with the Spanish.[11]

The temple of Luxor, Egypt, built about 1400 B.C.

the god's court or household, and their chief task was to minister to his needs. Another responsibility was to mediate between the god and the community, trying to discover his will and appease his anger. In order to perform these tasks, temples and their staffs had to be supported by a steady flow of goods. Over the years the temples were continually enlarged and became increasingly costly. In fact, they became, in many respects, substantial business enterprises, a development that apparently provided the stimulus for the *invention of true writing*, which was originally a means of recording the business activities of temples.[13] Many scholars have described the early Mesopotamian city-states as theocracies, since the local deity was regarded as the real ruler and the king merely as his "tenant farmer."[14]

Egypt was also a theocracy, but of a different type. The ruler was himself believed to be a god.[15] To his subjects he "was the incarnation, the living embodiment, of the god of any district he happened to be visiting; he was their actual God in living form, whom they could see, speak to, and adore."[16] Like the gods of the Mesopotamian city-states, he was the owner of all the land and entitled to a portion of all that was produced; as in Mesopotamia, these revenues supported a small army of specialists (e.g., officials, craftsmen, soldiers).

In later years there was a secularizing trend, especially in Mesopotamia.[17] By then, however, these societies had developed other institutional arrangements—notably political ones—to ensure the continued transfer of the economic surplus from the peasant producers to the governing class. Nevertheless, religion continued to play an important role as a legitimizing agency. It provided a rationale to justify the operation of the political system and its often harsh economic consequences.

The experience of Mesopotamia and Egypt thus supports the impression gained from horticultural societies concerning the importance of religion in the formation of an economic surplus. *Technological advance created the possibility of a surplus, but to transform that possibility into a reality required an ideology that motivated farmers to produce more than they needed to stay alive and productive, and persuaded them to turn that surplus over to someone else.* Although this has sometimes been accomplished by means of secular and political ideologies, a system of beliefs that defined people's obligations with reference to the supernatural worked best in most societies of the past.

Population: Growth in Size of Communities and Societies

In the first few centuries after the shift to agriculture, there was striking growth in the size of a number of communities, especially in Mesopotamian societies.[18] For example, the population of the city of Uruk, which was already an impressive 10,000 in 3800 B.C., increased to 50,000 by 3000 B.C.[19] The largest cities were the capitals of the most prosperous societies, and, although it is impossible to determine exactly the size of the cities and towns of 3000 and 2000 B.C., scholars believe that one or more of them had a population of at least 100,000.[20]

Egypt was the largest of the simple agrarian societies of ancient times and politically the most stable. It enjoyed the unique distinction of being a united and independent nation throughout most of the time it was a simple agrarian society. This achievement was due to its unique environmental situation: no other society had such excellent natural defenses (i.e., it was bounded by desert, mountains, and seas) and was so little threatened by other societies.

In the second half of the second millennium, Egypt embarked on a program of expansion that extended its boundaries to Syria and the Sudan. There were also other important empires in this era, especially those established by the Babylonians in the eighteenth century

A ceremonial slate palette of King Narmer, who first unified the two kingdoms of Egypt, shows him vanquishing an enemy and surveying the dead.

B.C. and the Hittites in the thirteenth century B.C. Babylonia succeeded briefly in uniting most of Mesopotamia, while the Hittites conquered much of what is now Turkey and Syria.

The Polity: Growth of the State

These conquests posed serious organizational problems for the rulers of early agrarian societies. Traditional modes of government based on kinship ties were no longer adequate for administering the affairs of societies whose populations now sometimes numbered in the millions. Though rulers continued to rely on relatives to help them govern, they were forced to turn increasingly to others. One solution was to incorporate a conquered group as a subdivision of the conquering society, leaving its former ruler in charge but in a subordinate capacity. Eventually all of the more successful rulers found it necessary to create new kinds of governmental structures that were no longer based on kinship ties alone.

We can see these newer patterns evolving in both military and civil affairs. For example, the first armies in agrarian societies, like those in horticultural, were simply militias made up of all the able-bodied men in the society.[21] During this period, wars did not last long and were fought only after the harvest was in. In fact, the period following the harvest came to be known as the "season when kings go forth to war." These limitations were necessary because, with the shift to agriculture, men's responsibilities in farming were much greater than they had been in horticultural societies.

As long as wars were brief and limited to skirmishes with neighboring peoples, militias were adequate. But once rulers became interested in empire building, a new system was necessary. As early as the middle of the third millennium, would-be empire builders in Mesopotamia established small but highly trained *professional armies*. For example, Sargon, the famous Akkadian king, had a standing army of 5,400 men.[22] As far as possible, recruits were sons of old soldiers, and thus a military caste was gradually created. The Egyptians followed a similar policy except that they relied chiefly on foreign mercenaries. These new armies were *royal,* rather than national, armies. Their expenses were paid by the king out of his enormous revenues, and the profits resulting from their activities were his also. Not only were these armies useful in dealing with foreign enemies, they also served as a defense against internal threats.[23]

In civil affairs, too, the casual and informal practices of simpler societies proved inadequate. As states expanded and the problems of administration multiplied, new kinds of governmental positions were created and governmental **bureaucracies** began to take shape.[24] In addition to the many officials who comprised the royal court and were responsible for administering the king's complex household affairs, there were officials scattered throughout the countryside to administer the affairs of units ranging from small districts to provinces with hundreds of villages and towns (see Figure 7.2). Each official had a staff of scribes and other lesser officials to assist him, and written records became increasingly important as administrative problems grew more complex.[25]

Throughout most of the history of the simple agrarian societies of antiquity, writing was a complex craft mastered by only a few individuals after long apprenticeships.[26] This is not surprising, considering the complex systems of writing then in use. Even after a 2,000-year process of simplification, Mesopotamian cuneiform script still had between 600 and 1,000 distinct characters. Before a person could learn to read or write, he had to memorize this formidable array of symbols and learn the complex rules for combining them. The Egyptian hieroglyphic and hieratic scripts were equally complicated. Thus, those who could write formed a specialized occupational group in society—the scribes—and their services were much in demand. For the most part, this occupation was filled by the sons of the rich and powerful, since only they could afford the necessary education.[27] Because of the political importance of their skill and the limited supply of qualified personnel, most scribes were at least members of the middle class.

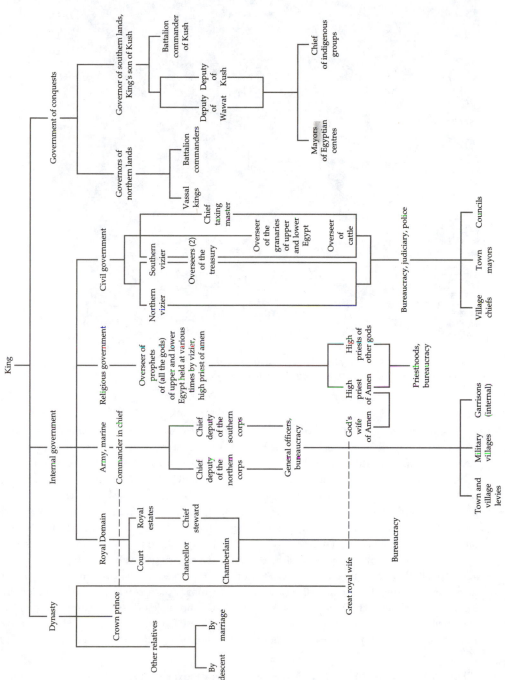

FIGURE 7.2 *This organizational chart of the government of Egypt illustrates the extent to which bureaucratic organization in agrarian empires replaced earlier systems of organization based on kinship.*
Source: David O'Connor, *Ancient Egypt: A Social History* (Cambridge: Cambridge University Press, 1983). Reproduced by permission of the publisher.

*Model of a royal granary, found in an Egyptian tomb (about 2000 B.C.). Note the
scribes sitting by the door recording the deliveries of grain.*

One consequence of the growth of empires and the development of bureaucracy was the
establishment of the first formal legal systems. Over the centuries every society had developed
certain concepts of justice, as well as informal techniques for implementing them. The most
common solution, as we saw in our survey of hunting and gathering societies, was to rely on
blood revenge by the injured party and his relatives. Because of the anarchic tendencies in such
a system, people began to seek settlement by arbitration, and to help them in this they would
turn to the most respected and powerful members of the community. In this way, headmen and
other political leaders gradually acquired judicial powers (i.e., the power to administer justice).
Later, as empires grew, peoples of diverse cultures were brought within the framework of a
single political system. In many instances the official appointed to rule over an area was not a
native and was therefore unfamiliar with local conceptions of justice (which varied considerably
from place to place). This generated pressure to clarify and standardize judicial practice, which
eventually led to the *first formal codes of law*. The most famous of these was the Code of
Hammurabi, the great Babylonian empire builder of the early second millennium.

The Economy: The First Monetary Systems
and the Growth of Trade

Money as we know it was absent in the first simple agrarian societies. There were, nevertheless, certain standardized media of exchange. Barley served this function in ancient Mesopotamia,
wheat in Egypt. Wages, rents, taxes, and various other obligations were paid in specified
quantities of these grains.[28]

As media of exchange, grains were less than ideal because they were both perishable and bulky. So, from a fairly early date, various metals, particularly silver and copper, were adopted as alternatives.[29] Initially, they were circulated in the form of crude bars of irregular size and weight, and their use was restricted to major transactions, since metal was still scarce. Later, as the production of metals increased, smaller units were introduced in local trade and sizes and weights were gradually standardized. As a final stage in the process, governments assumed the responsibility for manufacturing metallic currencies and full-fledged monetary systems took shape. This did not occur, however, until the very end of the simple agrarian era.

The growth of monetary systems had enormous implications for societal development. *Money has always facilitated the movement, the exchange, and ultimately the production of goods and services of every kind.* The establishment of a monetary system greatly expands the market for the things each individual produces, because products can then be sold even to people who produce nothing the producer wants in exchange. Thus the demand for goods and services is increased.

One immediate consequence of the emergence of a monetary system is the growth of opportunities for *merchants,* or middlemen, who purchase goods which they do not want for themselves but which they know are in demand by others. Once a class of merchants has come into being, it serves not only to satisfy existing demands but also to create new ones. By displaying new and unusual articles, merchants generate new needs and desires and thereby stimulate economic activity.

In the long run, a money economy subverts many of the values of simpler societies, especially the cooperative tendencies of extended kin systems. It fosters instead a more individualistic, rationalistic, and competitive approach to life, and lays a foundation for many of the attitudes and values that characterize modern industrial societies.

All of these tendencies were still quite limited, however, in the simple agrarian societies of the ancient Middle East. The newly emerging money economies barely penetrated the rural villages, where most people lived. Even in the cities and towns, the role of money was quite limited compared with what we are accustomed to. Fully developed cash economies still lay far in the future.

Stratification: Increasing Inequality

In most simple agrarian societies of the ancient world, newly emerging or expanding social and cultural differences created internal divisions within society, and sometimes conflict as well. Three cleavages were especially serious. First, there was one between the small governing class and the much larger mass of people who had no voice in political decisions and who had to hand over all or most of the surplus they produced to the governing class. Second, there was a division between the urban minority and the far more numerous rural population. Finally, there was a cleavage between the small literate minority and the illiterate masses.

Because these three lines of cleavage tended to converge, their impact was greatly magnified. The small and often literate urban governing class lived in a strikingly different world from that of the illiterate, rural, peasant majority—despite the fact that they were members of the same society. Each group had its own distinct subculture.[30]

The subculture of the common people was a mixture of primitive superstition and the practical information they needed in their daily lives. It was extremely parochial in outlook and knew little of the world beyond the village. The subculture of the governing class, in contrast, incorporated the refinements we identify with "civilization," such as philosophy, art, literature, history, and science. It also included a contempt for physical labor of any kind, and for those who engaged in it.

In many respects the differences within simple agrarian societies were greater than similarities between them. Apart from the problems of language, an Egyptian peasant could have adapted far more easily to the life of a Babylonian peasant than to the life of a member of the governing class of his own society. As this gulf widened, members of the governing class found it increasingly difficult to recognize the ignorant, downtrodden peasants as fellow human beings. The scribes of ancient Egypt were fond of saying that the lower classes lacked intelligence and had to be driven like cattle, with a stick.[31]

Slowdown in the Rate of Technological Innovation

Another significant development in these societies was a marked slowdown in the rate of technological innovation and progress, beginning within a few centuries after the shift from horticulture to agriculture. V. Gordon Childe described the change this way:

> Before the [agrarian] revolution comparatively poor and illiterate communities had made an impressive series of contributions to man's progress. The two millennia immediately preceding 3,000 B.C. had witnessed discoveries in applied science that directly or indirectly affected the prosperity of millions of [people] and demonstrably furthered the biological welfare of our species by facilitating its multiplication. We have mentioned the following applications of science: artificial irrigation using canals and ditches; the plow; the harnessing of animal motive-power; the sailboat; wheeled vehicles; orchard husbandry; fermentation; the production and use of copper; bricks; the arch; glazing; the seal; and—in the earliest stages of the revolution—a solar calendar, writing, numerical notation, and bronze.
>
> The two thousand years after the revolution—say from 2,600 to 600 B.C.—produced few contributions of anything like comparable importance to human progress. Perhaps only four achievements deserve to be put in the same category as the fifteen just enumerated. They are: the "decimal notation" of Babylonia (about 2,000 B.C.); an economical method for smelting iron on an industrial scale (1,400 B.C.); a truly alphabetic script (1,300 B.C.); aqueducts for supplying water to cities (700 B.C.).[32]

Childe went on to note that two of these four innovations, the smelting of iron and the development of the alphabet, "cannot be credited to the societies that had initiated and reaped the fruits of the [agrarian] revolution" but rather were the products of somewhat less advanced neighboring societies.[33]

At first glance this slowing of the rate of cultural innovation seems an unlikely development. Larger populations, increased intersocietal contacts, and the greater store of information available to potential innovators should have produced higher rates of innovation, especially in technology.* The fact that they did not poses an interesting problem.

To explain this unusual development, we need to return to the concept of feedback. This, as we have seen, is the effect produced when the impact of an initial force reverts back to, and influences, the initial force itself. Until now, however, we have only seen examples of *positive* feedback, in which the secondary effect enhances or strengthens the original force. This is the type of feedback that has been involved in all of the major social and cultural changes we have examined so far. Now we are seeing one of the rare instances in sociocultural evolution in which major technological advances generated *negative* feedback. In other words, this is a case in which the secondary effect diminished or weakened the original force.

As Figure 7.3 indicates, changes in social organization and ideology that were themselves consequences of technological advance had the effect of *slowing* the rate of technological innovation and advance. As the older system of a militia that included all of a society's able-bodied men was replaced by a professional army, there was a substantial increase in the power of the governing class, which controlled the new army. New beliefs and values emerged

*To avoid misunderstanding, it is worth emphasizing that we do not assume that innovation is necessary or automatic, only that *under these conditions* its rate should have increased, not decreased (e.g., see Chapter 3).

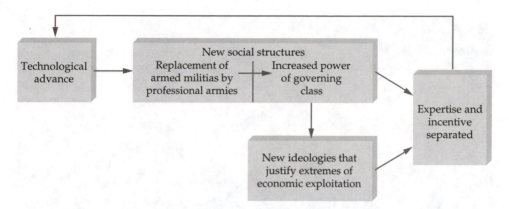

FIGURE 7.3 *Model of the causes of the decline in the rate of technological innovation during the first two millennia of the agrarian era. Negative feedback is indicated by the minus sign over the arrow to technological advance.*

that justified and legitimized the new system and thereby reinforced it and made it even worse. Thus, the governing class found it increasingly easy to extract most of the economic surplus from the peasants, so that peasants were left with little more than the bare necessities of life.[34]

As a result, the peasants lost the incentive for innovation, knowing that any benefits that resulted from their inventions and discoveries would simply be appropriated by the governing class, whereas losses—which could be devastating given the peasant's narrow margin of survival—would be borne by themselves.* At the same time, the governing class, though it had a vested interest in a more productive economy, no longer had the necessary knowledge of and experience with subsistence technology and thus was in no position to make creative innovations. In short, *expertise and incentive were inadvertently divorced,* with disastrous results for technological progress.

Under the circumstances it is hardly surprising that members of the governing class turned increasingly to warfare and conquest, practices that first became profitable with the advent of horticulture, as the best ways to increase their wealth. Warfare was something they understood; moreover, in their system of values, waging war was one of the few occupations considered appropriate for members of their class. More than ever before, the resources of societies were turned from the conquest of nature to the conquest of people.[35] And this, due to the new, more productive technology, could be a highly profitable enterprise. With vast numbers of peasants producing more than they needed to survive and remain productive, there was a large economic surplus that could be extracted by means of taxes, tribute, tithes, and rents and used to support the host of servants and artisans who catered to the whims of the governing class and the army of soldiers and officials who ensured the flow of revenues.

These developments help to explain the growing complexity of social organization during this period. Having cut themselves off from the sweaty world of work and having turned their efforts instead to conquest, members of the governing class found new challenges for their creative talents in the field of social organization. The exercise of power and the manipulation of others were activities in keeping with their dignity. Moreover, they were

---

*It is possible that the process was even more complicated and that the health and mental capacities of many peasants may have been impaired by protein-deficient diets, parasites, debilitating chronic diseases, and by environments not conducive to learning in early childhood. In short, the basic intelligence and creative potential of many peasants may have been permanently impaired.

One consequence of the growth of empires was an increase in the economic surplus extracted from conquered peoples in the form of tribute: Egyptian carving showing tribute bearers (about 2000 B.C.).

rewarding: the better organized an army or government, the greater its chances of success in struggles with other groups.[36]

By the end of the period when simple agrarian societies were dominant, substantial changes had occurred in societies that had adopted the new technology. The largest of them were substantially larger than any horticultural society had ever been, and substantially more complex. There was a much greater division of labor within them, and social inequality had also increased. But as impressive as they were, these changes were only a prelude to what was to come in the remainder of the agrarian era.

ADVANCED AGRARIAN SOCIETIES

Technology

During the period in which simple agrarian societies dominated the Middle East, the most important technological advance was the discovery of the technique of smelting iron. Prior to this, bronze had been the most important metal. But since the supply was limited* and the demands of the governing class always took precedence over the needs of peasants, bronze was used primarily for military, ornamental, and ceremonial purposes. It never really replaced stone and wood in ordinary tools, certainly not in agricultural tools, and so its impact on the economy was limited.

*This was because of the scarcity of tin, an essential component of bronze.

People knew of iron at least as early as the first half of the third millennium B.C., but apparently only in its meteoric form, which is very scarce.[37] Sometime during the second millennium, the Hittites of Asia Minor discovered iron ore and invented a technique for smelting it. For centuries they kept this a closely guarded secret, which gave them a virtual monopoly on a highly valued commodity. Then, about 1200 B.C., their nation was destroyed. This led to the rapid dispersal of both the Hittite people and the technology of smelting iron.

As one would expect, in view of the class structure of simple agrarian societies, the initial use of iron was limited largely to the governing class. Some of the earliest iron objects recovered from Egypt were a dagger, a bracelet, and a headrest found in the tomb of the pharaoh Tutankhamen. Prior to the military collapse of the Hittite empire, iron was five times more expensive than gold, forty times more than silver. It was not until about 800 B.C. that iron came into general use for *ordinary tools*. Thus, it is not until this period that we can speak of true advanced agrarian societies, although many Middle Eastern societies of the previous three or four centuries were certainly transitional types.

Throughout the agrarian era societies depended on humans and animals as their chief sources of energy: Indian peasants raising water from ditch to irrigate field. The man on the post moves back and forth on the crossbeam to raise the water and to lower the bucket again to the ditch below, where the other man refills it.

During this transitional period two further discoveries greatly enhanced the value of iron. First it was found that if the outer layers of the iron absorbed some carbon from the fire during the forging process, the metal became somewhat harder. Later it was discovered that this carburized iron could be hardened still further by quenching the hot metal in water, thus producing steel. With these developments, iron became not only more common than bronze but also more useful for both military and economic purposes. As one writer has said, "After the discovery of quench-hardening, iron gradually passed into the position from which it has never subsequently been ousted; it became the supremely useful material for making all the tools and weapons that are intended for cutting, chopping, piercing, or slashing."[38]

From its point of origin in the Middle East, iron making spread until eventually it was practiced in nearly all of the Old World, even in many horticultural societies. By the time of Christ, advanced agrarian societies were firmly established in the Middle East, throughout most of the Mediterranean world, and in much of India and China. Within the next thousand years, the advanced agrarian pattern spread over most of Europe and much of Southeast Asia, and expanded further in India and China. Still later it was transplanted to the European colonies in the New World.

Compared with simpler societies, advanced agrarian societies enjoyed a very productive technology. Unfortunately, the same conditions that slowed the rate of technological advance in simple agrarian societies continued to prevail. As a result, their progress was not nearly what one would expect on the basis of their size, the degree of contact among them, and, above all, their store of accumulated information.[39]

Nevertheless, over the centuries quite a number of important innovations were made. A partial list would include the catapult, the crossbow, gunpowder, horseshoes, a workable harness for horses, stirrups, the wood-turning lathe, the auger, the screw, the wheelbarrow, the rotary fan for ventilation, the clock, the spinning wheel, porcelain, printing, iron casting, the magnet, water-powered mills, windmills, and, in the period just preceding the emergence of the first industrial societies, the workable steam engine, the fly shuttle, the spinning jenny, the spinning machine, and various other power-driven tools. Because of these and other innovations, the most advanced agrarian societies of the eighteenth century A.D. were far superior, from the technological standpoint, to their predecessors of 2,500 years earlier.

The level of technological development was not uniform throughout the agrarian world, despite diffusion. Information spread slowly in most cases, and some areas were considerably ahead of others. During much of the advanced agrarian era, especially from 500 to 1500 A.D., the Middle East, China, and parts of India were technologically superior to Europe.[40] In part, this was simply a continuation of older patterns: the Middle East had been the center of innovation for more than 5,000 years following its shift to horticulture. An even more important factor in Europe's relative backwardness, however, was the collapse of the Roman Empire. For centuries afterward, Europe was divided into scores of petty kingdoms and principalities that had only enough resources to maintain the smallest urban settlements and the most limited occupational specialization. Therefore, Europeans were inactive on many of the most promising and challenging technological frontiers of the time. Though they made relative gains during the later Middle Ages—due largely to the diffusion of knowledge from the East— they did not really catch up until the sixteenth century and did not take the lead until even later.

Population: Continuing Trends

Size of Societies and Communities   The populations of advanced agrarian societies were substantially larger than those of any societies that preceded them. This was due partly to advances in agricultural technology that permitted greater population densities, and partly to advances in military technology that aided the process of empire building. The largest simple agrarian society, Egypt, probably had fewer than 15 million members.[41] In contrast, the largest advanced agrarian society, mid-nineteenth-century China, had approximately 400 million.*[42] While that was exceptional, India reached 175 million in the middle of the nineteenth century, and the Roman and the Russian empires each had at least 70 million people.[43]

Similar differences are found in communities. The largest cities in simple agrarian societies had populations of about 100,000. By comparison, the upper limit for cities in advanced agrarian societies was about a million.[44] Only the capitals of major empires ever attained this size, however, and they maintained it but briefly. Cities of 100,000, while much more numerous than in simple agrarian societies, were still quite rare by modern standards.

Fertility and Mortality   Birthrates in both simple and advanced agrarian societies have averaged 40 or more births per 1,000 population per year, triple that of most modern industrial societies.[45] In general, there seems to have been little interest in limiting the size of families, since large families, particularly ones with many sons, were valued for both economic and religious reasons. From the economic standpoint, children were viewed by peasants as an important asset, a valuable source of cheap labor.[46] Children were also important as the only form of "old-age insurance" available to peasants. Religion added yet another incentive for large families, either by encouraging ancestor worship, for which perpetuation of the family line was essential, or simply by declaring large families to be a sign of God's favor.[47]

One of the few constraints on the growth of families was the threat of severe deprivation. When crops failed and famine was imminent, families often resorted to infanticide, abandoning their newborn by the roadside or leaving them at the door of a church or monastery in the hope that someone who was able to provide for the baby might take pity and raise it.[48] If conditions became bad enough, even older children would be abandoned by their parents (see "Mother Goose Revisited," page 161).

There is also evidence that many women would have liked to avoid the burdens and risks of repeated pregnancies. Unfortunately for them, in societies in which men were dominant and in which an effective contraceptive technology did not yet exist, their wishes had little effect.

Despite their high birthrates, advanced agrarian societies generally grew slowly. Sometimes they failed to grow at all or even declined in size. The reason was that death rates were almost as high as birthrates, and sometimes higher. Wars, disease, accidents, and famine all took their toll. Infant mortality was especially high before the development of modern sanitation and medicine. Recent studies show that children born in Rome 2,000 years ago lived only 20 years on average.[49] Even as recently as the seventeenth century, the children of British queens and duchesses had a life expectancy of only 30 years, and nearly a third died before their fifth birthday.[50] For the common people, conditions were even worse. With death rates averaging nearly 40 per 1,000 per year, life expectancy at birth was barely 25 years, and even those who reached adulthood usually died young. (See Table 7.1.)

Large cities were notoriously unhealthy places, especially for the common people. The citizens of Rome, for example, had a shorter life expectancy than those in the provinces.[51] England in the early eighteenth century presented a similar situation. During the first half of that century, there were an estimated 500,000 more deaths than births in London.[52] The reasons for this become clear when we read descriptions of sanitary conditions in medieval cities:

> The streets of medieval towns were generally little more than narrow alleys, the overhanging
> upper stories of the houses nearly meeting, and thus effectually excluding all but a minimum of

---

*Growth in China's population *after* the middle of the nineteenth century was due increasingly to the beginnings of industrialization. The same was true in India.

TABLE 7.1   Average Age at Death of Those Who Reached Adulthood During Agrarian Era

	Males	Females
Early Bronze Age, 3000 B.C.	33.7	29.5
Middle Bronze Age, 2000 B.C.		
Commoners	36.3	30.8
Royalty	35.9	36.1
Late Bronze Age, 1500 B.C.	39.5	32.1
Early Iron Age, 1150 B.C.	38.6	31.3
Imperial Rome, 120 A.D.	40.2	34.6
Medieval Byzantium, 1400 A.D.	37.7	31.1

Sources: J. L. Angel, "Ecology and Population in the Eastern Mediterranean," *World Archaeology,* 4 (1972), pp. 88–105; and J. L. Angel, "Paleoecology, Paleodemography, and Health," in Steven Polgar, *Population, Ecology, and Social Evolution* (The Hague: Mouton, 1975), pp. 167–190.

light and air. . . . In most continental towns and some English ones, a high city wall further impeded the free circulation of air. . . . Rich citizens might possess a courtyard in which garbage was collected and occasionally removed to the suburbs, but the usual practice was to throw everything into the streets including the garbage of slaughter houses and other offensive trades. . . . Filth of every imaginable description accumulated indefinitely in the unpaved streets and in all available space and was trodden into the ground. The water supply would be obtained either from wells or springs, polluted by the gradual percolation through the soil of the accumulated filth, or else from an equally polluted river. In some towns, notably London, small streams running down a central gutter served at once as sewers and as water supply. . . . In seventeenth century London, which before the Fire largely remained a medieval city, the poorer class house had only a covering of weatherboards, a little black pitch forming the only

Sanitary standards were low in most agrarian societies: open-air butcher shop in the Middle East.

waterproofing, and these houses were generally built back to back. Thousands of Londoners dwelt in cellars or horribly overcrowded tenements. A small house in Dowgate accommodated 11 married couples and 15 single persons. . . . Another source of unhealthiness were the church vaults and graveyards, so filled with corpses that the level of the latter was generally raised above that of the surrounding ground. In years of pestilence, recourse had to be made to plague pits in order to dispose of the harvest of death.[53]

This account calls attention to one of the striking demographic characteristics of advanced agrarian societies: the disasters that periodically overtook them and produced sharp increases in the death rate.[54] The most devastating of all, the Black Plague that hit Europe in the middle of the fourteenth century, is said to have killed between a quarter and a half of the population in a four-year period.[55]

Crop failures and famines seldom affected such large areas, but they were more frequent and could be just as deadly. One Finnish province lost a third of its population during the famine of 1696–1697, and many parts of France suffered comparable losses a few years earlier.[56] Even allowing for a considerable margin of error in the reports of such disasters, it is clear from other kinds of evidence—for example, the severe labor shortages and the abandonment of farms that followed plagues and famines—that the number of deaths was huge. For these reasons, the growth of advanced agrarian populations was anything but continuous.

The Economy: Increasing Differentiation

Division of Labor   The growth in both territorial and population size that came with the shift from the simple to the advanced agrarian level brought with it an increase in the division of labor. For the first time, there was significant economic specialization both by regions and by communities, and this was accompanied by increased occupational specialization.

The Roman Empire provides a good illustration of both regional and local specialization. North Africa and Spain were noted as suppliers of dried figs and olive oil; Gaul, Dalmatia, Asia Minor, and Syria for their wine; Spain and Egypt for salted meats; Egypt, North Africa, Sicily, and the Black Sea region for grain; and the latter for salted fish as well.[57] The tendency toward specialization at the community level is illustrated by a passage from a manual for wealthy farmers, written in the second century B.C., which advised:

> Tunics, togas, blankets, smocks and shoes should be bought at Rome; caps, iron tools, scythes, spades, mattocks, axes, harnesses, ornaments and small chains at Cales and Minturnae; spades at Venafrum, carts and sledges at Suessa and in Lucania, jars and pots at Alba and at Rome; tiles at Venafrum, oil mills at Pompeii and at Rufrius's yard at Nola, nails and bars at Rome; pails, oil urns, water pitchers, wine urns, other copper vessels at Capua and at Nola; Campanian baskets, pulley-ropes and all sorts of cordage at Capua; Roman baskets at Suessa and Casium.[58]

Similar patterns are reported in other agrarian societies.[59] Even at the village level a measure of specialization was not uncommon. In the agricultural off-season, peasants often turned to handicrafts to make ends meet, and villages often developed a reputation for a particular commodity.

In the larger urban centers occupational specialization reached a level that surpassed anything achieved in simpler societies. For example, a tax roll for Paris from the year 1313 lists 157 different trades, and tax records from two sections of Barcelona in 1385 indicate a hundred occupations (see Table 7.2).[60] The clothing industry alone contained such specialized occupations as wool comber, wool spinner, silk spinner (two kinds), girdle maker, and headdress maker (seven kinds, including specialists in felt, fur, wool and cotton, flowers, peacock feathers, gold embroidery and pearls, and silk). Though such specialization was found only in the largest cities, smaller cities often had forty or fifty different kinds of craftsmen, and even small towns had ten or twenty.[61] In addition to craft specialists, urban centers also had special-

TABLE 7.2 Occupations of Householders in Two Sections of Barcelona in 1385 A.D.

Sailors	227	Longshoremen	50	Silversmiths	29
Merchants	151	Innkeepers	49	Curriers	29
Shoemakers	108	Brokers	45	Notaries	28
Tailors	96	Carpenters	43	Tavern-keepers	27
Fishermen	94	Bakers	40	Spicers	26
Seamen	73	Janitors	39	Bargemen	25
Wooldressers	70	Hucksters	36	76 other occupations	525
Weavers	63	Butchers	34		
Tanners	61	Scriveners	32	Total	2000

Source: Adapted from Josiah Cox Russell, *Medieval Regions and Their Cities* (Bloomington: Indiana University Press, 1972), p. 170.

ists in government, commerce, religion, education, the armed forces, and domestic service. There were also specialists in illegal occupations (e.g., thieves, prostitutes), which were a normal part of urban life in advanced agrarian societies.

Command Economies   Because politics and economics were always highly interdependent in advanced agrarian societies, the people who dominated the political system also dominated the economic system. The leading officeholders in government were usually the chief landholders as well, and in these societies land and control of those who worked it was the most important economic resource. As one economic historian has written, this was a time in which "true wealth consisted in being master."[62]

In these societies, the answers to basic economic questions—how resources should be used, what should be produced and in what quantities, and how those products should be distributed—were determined less by the forces of supply and demand than by arbitrary decisions of the political elite. These were command economies, not market economies.[63]

The economy of an advanced agrarian society consisted of two distinct parts: a rural agricultural sector and an urban manufacturing and commercial sector. These were not of equal economic importance, however. One historian has estimated that the Roman state derived approximately twenty times more tax revenue from agriculture than from trade and handicrafts. He went on to say that "this apportionment of the burden of taxation probably corresponded roughly to the economic structure of the empire. All the evidence goes to show that its wealth was derived almost entirely from agriculture, and to a very small extent from industry and trade."[64] The same could be said of every agrarian society. This does not mean, however, that the urban economy was of little interest to members of the governing class. On the contrary, it was of great interest because it provided the luxury goods they valued so highly. The urban economy, however, depended on the ability of the rural economy to produce a surplus that could support the urban population.

In many respects the economy of the typical agrarian society resembled a tree with roots spreading in every direction, constantly drawing in new resources. The pattern was similar to that shown in Figure 7.4. At the economic center of the society was the national capital, controlled by the king or emperor and the leading members of the governing class. Surrounding it were various provincial or regional capitals controlled by royal governors and other members of the governing class. Each of these in turn was surrounded by smaller county seats and market towns controlled by lesser members of the governing class. Finally, each of these towns was surrounded by scores of small villages.

In this system, there was a steady flow of goods from smaller units to larger, or from villages to county seats, and then on to regional and national capitals. Basically this flow was achieved by means of taxation, but it was supplemented by rents, interest on debts, tithes and other religious offerings, and profits, all of which helped to transfer the economic surplus

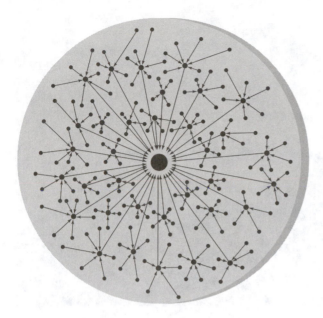

FIGURE 7.4 *As the arrows indicate, goods and resources extracted from villages flowed to regional centers and then on to the national capital, with each level keeping what it could.*

from the peasant producers to the urban-based governing class, its allies, and their dependents.

With what they retained of their surplus after paying taxes, rents, interest, and other obligations, peasants could go to the urban centers and trade for commodities that were not available in their villages (e.g., metal tools, salt, etc.). Many towns and cities were also religious centers, and the peasants often used these facilities. Finally, the peasants did benefit to some degree from the maintenance of law and order provided by urban-based governments, even though the law was used disproportionately to protect the rights of the governing class and keep the peasants in a subordinate position. The maintenance of order was extremely important in an agrarian society because so much depended on the success of each harvest, and each harvest depended on months of prior effort. Disruption at any point in the agricultural cycle could be disastrous for everyone.

The Rural Economy   In most advanced agrarian societies, the governing elite (which included religious leaders) owned a grossly disproportionate share of the land. Although there are no precise figures for earlier times, the traditional pattern could still be seen recently in many parts of Latin America, the Middle East, and Southeast Asia. Typically, a minority of 1 to 3 percent of the population has owned from one-third to two-thirds of the arable land in these societies.[65]

Not only did the governing class usually own most of the land, but it often owned most of the peasants who worked it. Slavery and serfdom were common in agrarian societies, with large landholdings and large numbers of slaves or serfs normally going hand in hand. Thus, one nineteenth-century Russian nobleman who owned 2 million acres of land also owned nearly 300,000 serfs. Rulers always had the largest holdings. Prior to the emancipation of the serfs in Russia, the czar owned 27.4 million of them.[66]

Even when the peasant owned his own land and was legally free, he usually found it difficult to make ends meet. A bad crop one year and he had to borrow money at rates as high

Peasant using traditional plow, Iran.

as 120 percent a year.[67] In any event, there were always taxes, and these usually fell more heavily on the peasant landowner than on his wealthier neighbor, either because of special exemptions granted the latter or simply because of his greater ability to evade such obligations.[68] If a peasant did not own his land, he had to pay rent, which was always high. In addition, he was often subject to compulsory labor service, tithes, fines, and obligatory "gifts" to the governing class.[69]

Because the number and variety of obligations were so great, it is difficult to determine just how large the total was, but in most societies it appears to have been at least half the total value of the goods the peasants produced.[70] The basic philosophy of the governing class seems to have been to tax peasants to the limit of their ability to pay.[71] A story is told of a leading Japanese official of the seventeenth century who, returning to one of his estates after an absence of ten years and finding the villagers in well-built houses instead of the hovels he remembered, exclaimed, "These people are too comfortable. They must be more heavily taxed."[72]

Living conditions for most peasants were primitive, and many were worse off than most hunters and gatherers had been thousands of years earlier. For example, the diet of the average peasant in medieval England consisted of little more than a hunk of bread and a mug of ale in the morning; a lump of cheese and bread with perhaps an onion or two to flavor it and more ale at noon; and a thick soup or pottage with bread and cheese in the evening. Meat was rare and the beer thin. Household furniture consisted of a few stools, a table, and a chest to hold the best clothes and any other treasured possessions.[73] Beds were uncommon; most peasants simply slept on earthen floors covered with straw.

Even later in France, toward the end of the agrarian era,

> Great masses of the people lived in a state of chronic malnutrition, subsisting mainly on porridge made of bread and water with some occasional, home-grown vegetables thrown in. They ate meat only a few times a year, on feast days or after autumn slaughtering if they did not have enough silage to feed the livestock over the winter. . . . For most peasants village life was a struggle for survival, and survival meant keeping above the line that divided the poor from the indigent.[74]

Mother Goose Revisited

Most of us think of Mother Goose rhymes and stories as charming survivals from a simpler, happier world of the past. Yet if we look at them closely, and at other older folk tales, a very different picture emerges. It is a picture of widespread poverty and despair, except for the fortunate few who lived in palaces.

Recall for a moment old Mother Hubbard who went to the cupboard to fetch her poor dog a bone, or the old woman who lived in a shoe and had so many children she didn't know what to do. We also learn something of life in agrarian societies from the story of Tom Thumb. In a late-seventeenth-century French version, the story begins, "Once upon a time there was a woodsman and his wife, who had seven children, all boys. . . . They were very poor, and their seven children were a great inconvenience, because none was old enough to support himself. . . . A very difficult year came, and the famine was so great that these poor folk resolved to get rid of their children." Shades of Hansel and Gretel! And in the French version of "The Sorcerer's Apprentice," a poor father sells his son to the devil in exchange for an ample supply of food for twelve years.

Though fairy tales often had happy endings, these endings usually depended on magic, trickery, or uncommon luck—not ordinary hard work. Cinderella had her fairy godmother; Jack (of beanstalk fame) combined a generous mix of magic, trickery, daring, and luck to win his fortune; and the miller's son in Puss 'n Boots, who inherited only a cat, inherited a most remarkable cat.

If Mother Goose has powers to charm, it is because we today overlook the poverty and despair that are portrayed, or we imagine that they are just part of the world of make-believe, like the fairy godmothers who provided the happy endings. But if we look closely at the conditions of life of ordinary people in agrarian societies, we find that there is at least as much truth as fiction in these old rhymes and tales.

But many did not survive and lost their farms. "Then they took to the road for good, drifting about with the flotsam and jetsam of France's *population flottante* ('floating population'), which included several million desperate souls by the 1780s." The same author concludes by saying that "The human condition has changed so much since then that we can hardly imagine the way it appeared to people whose lives really were nasty, brutish, and short."[75]

In China, conditions were so wretched that female infanticide was widely practiced. One nineteenth-century scholar indicated that in some districts as many as a quarter of the female infants were killed at birth.[76] Sometimes signs were posted near ponds, reading, "Girls may not be drowned here." In rural areas, the traditional greeting when peasants met was "Have you eaten today?" (the equivalent of "How are you today?").

To compound the misery created by their economic situation, peasants were often subjected to further cruelties. Families were sometimes split up if it served their master's economic interests.[77] Peasants often found it difficult to defend their wives and daughters from the amorous attentions of the governing class, and in some areas the lord of the manor maintained the notorious *jus primae noctis* (i.e., literally, the right of the first night, meaning the right to initial sexual relations with all brides on their wedding nights).[78] Finally, peasants were subject at all times to the whims and tempers of their superiors, who could invoke severe punishments even for minor offenses. Even petty thievery could be punished by death, often by cruel and frightful means.[79]

To the governing class, all this seemed only fitting and proper, since most of them, like their predecessors in simple agrarian societies, viewed peasants as subhuman. In legal documents in medieval England, a peasant's children were listed not as his *familia,* but as his *sequela,* meaning "brood" or "litter."[80] Estate records in Europe, Asia, and the Americas often listed peasants with the livestock.[81] Even so civilized a Roman as Cato the Elder argued that slaves, like livestock, should be disposed of when no longer productive.[82]

As shocking as these views seem today, they were clearly rooted in the experiences and interests of agrarian elites. In fact, the lives and experiences of the governing class and the peasantry were so divergent, and their contacts were so limited (normally a class of supervisory officials and retainers stood between them)[83] that it may be more surprising that some members of the privileged class recognized their common humanity than that the majority did not.

Despite the heavy burdens laid on them, not all peasants were reduced to the subsistence level. By various means, many contrived to hide part of their harvest and otherwise evade their obligations.[84] A small minority even managed, by rendering special services to the governing class or by other means, to rise a bit above their fellows, operating larger farms and generally living a bit more comfortably.[85]

For the majority, however, the one real hope for a substantial improvement in their lot lay, ironically, in the devastation wrought by plagues, famines, and wars. Only when death reduced their numbers to the point where good workers were scarce was the governing class forced to bid competitively for their services, thus raising incomes above the subsistence level.[86] Usually, however, high birthrates kept this from occurring, or, when it did, soon brought about a return to the former situation.

The Urban Economy   When we think of famous agrarian societies of the past, most of us conjure up images of cities: Rome, Constantinople, Alexandria, Jerusalem, Baghdad, Babylon, and others that loom large in the historical record. Thus it is with a sense of shock that we discover that rarely if ever did all of the urban communities of an advanced agrarian society contain as much as 10 percent of its total population, and in most cases they held even less.[87]

How can this be? Why are our impressions of these ancient societies wrong? The reason is that their histories were recorded by a literate minority—people who themselves usually lived in cities and towns and who regarded the life of the rural villages as unimportant and unworthy of their attention. Thus, the historical record is largely a record of city life, particularly the life of the governing class.

The most striking feature of the cities and towns of these societies was the great diversity of people who lived in them. City residents ranged from the most illustrious members of the governing class to beggars and other destitute people who barely managed to stay alive. Unlike most of the cities and towns in modern industrial societies, these were not primarily centers of economic production. Though some manufacturing was carried on in them, their political and commercial functions, and frequently their religious ones as well, were much more important.

Since cities and towns were the centers of government, and social and cultural centers as well, most members of the governing class preferred to live in them.[88] As a result, urban populations included not only civil and military officials, but the extensive households of the governing class as well. Servants were far more numerous in these societies than in ours, both because of the absence of laborsaving devices and because the governing class viewed manual work of any kind as degrading. Furthermore, one of their chief forms of status competition was to see who could maintain the most luxurious household. The household staff of the head of one small kingdom, Edward IV of England, numbered 400.[89] A more important ruler, such as the Roman emperor at the height of empire, had thousands. As one historian put it, one "is dumbfounded by the extraordinary degree of specialization [and] the insensate luxury" of the imperial household.[90] One group of servants was responsible for the emperor's palace clothes, another for his city clothes, another for those he wore to the theater, yet another for

LA VIA APPIA

Servants were far more numerous in advanced agrarian societies than in modern industrial societies, both because of the lack of laborsaving devices in homes and because the governing class considered it degrading to do any kind of manual work: slaves transporting a wealthy Roman matron.

his military uniforms. Other servants attended to eating vessels, a different group to those used for drinking, another to silver vessels, and still others to gold vessels and those set with jewels. For entertainment, the emperor had his own choristers, an orchestra, dancing women, clowns, and dwarfs. Lesser members of the Roman governing class obviously could not maintain household staffs as elaborate as this, but many had staffs of hundreds, and some had a thousand or more. *All this was made possible by the labors of the peasantry.*

Part of the peasants' surplus also went to support two important groups that were allied with the governing class yet separate from it. The first of these was the clergy, of whom more will be said shortly. The second was the merchant class. Merchants were a peculiar group in the structure of agrarian societies. Although some of them were extremely wealthy, they were rarely accepted as equals by members of the governing class—even by those who were much less wealthy. For merchants worked to obtain their wealth, and this, by the values of the governing class, was demeaning.[91] Nevertheless, the latter avidly sought the goods that merchants sold and coveted their wealth, acquiring it whenever they could by taxes, marriage, or outright confiscation.[92] The attitude of the merchants toward the governing class was equally ambivalent: they both feared and envied them, but, given the chance, they emulated their way of life and sought to be accepted by them.

Like modern merchants, the merchants of agrarian societies often created the demand for their goods, thereby spurring productivity. And like modern advertisers, they were primarily interested in creating a demand for luxuries. One reason for this was the high cost of moving goods from town to town. With the primitive transportation available,[93] only lightweight luxury items such as silks, spices, and fine swords could be moved far without costs becoming prohibitive.

A report on China shortly after World War II indicates what an enormous difference modern methods of transportation have made in the cost of moving goods. To ship a ton of goods one mile at that time, the costs were as follows (measured in United States cents at that time).[94]

Steamboat	2.4	Pack mule	17.0
Railroad	2.7	Wheelbarrow	20.0
Junk	12.0	Pack donkey	24.0
Animal-drawn cart	13.0	Carrying by pole	48.0

Figures from Europe are strikingly similar: in 1900, for example, it cost ten times more to move goods by horse-drawn wagon than by rail.[95] In short, modern methods of transportation have slashed this cost by 80 to 95 percent.

The prosperity of the merchant class was due in no small measure to the labors of another, humbler class with which merchants were closely affiliated—the artisans, who numbered approximately 3 to 5 percent of the total population.[96] Except for the peasantry, this class was the most productive element in the economy. Most artisans lived in urban centers and, like the rest of the urban population, were ultimately dependent on the surplus produced by the peasants. Craft specialization was rather highly developed in the larger urban centers, as we have seen.

The shops where artisans worked were small by modern standards and bore little resemblance to modern factories. In Rome in the first century B.C., a shop employing fifty men was considered very large.[97] A pewter business employing eighteen men was the largest mentioned in any of London's medieval craft records, and even this modest size was not attained until the middle of the fifteenth century.[98] Typically, the shop was also the residence of both the merchant and his workmen, and work was carried on either in the living quarters or in an adjoining room.[99]

The economic situation of the artisans, like that of the merchants, was variable. In Beijing at the time of World War I, wages ranged from $2.50 a month for members of the Incense and Cosmetic Workers Guild to $36 a month for members of the Gold Foil Beaters

The souk, or market, Fez, Morocco: compare with the market in Ouagadougou, page 129.

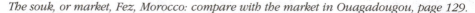

Guild.[100] Those in highly skilled trades and some of the self-employed fared moderately well by agrarian standards. Apprentices and journeymen in less skilled trades, however, worked long hours for bare subsistence wages. In Beijing, for example, a seven-day workweek and ten-hour workday were typical, and many artisans remained too poor ever to marry.

Merchants and artisans in the same trade were commonly organized into guilds. These organizations were an attempt to create, in an urban setting, a functional approximation of the extended kin groups of horticultural societies. Many guilds spoke of their members as brothers, for example, and functioned as mutual aid associations, restricting entry into the field, forbidding price cutting, and otherwise trying to protect the interests of their members.[101] But a guild included merchant employers as well as artisan employees, and the employers were naturally dominant, controlling key offices and formulating policies that benefited themselves more than the artisans.[102]

Beneath the artisans in the class structure of the cities were a variety of other kinds of people, including unskilled laborers who supplied much of the animal energy required by the system. The working conditions of these men were usually terrible, and accidents and injuries were common. As a result, their work life was short. For example, early in the present century, the average Beijing rickshaw man was able to work only five years, after which he was good for little except begging.[103]

The class of unskilled laborers shaded off into still more deprived groups—the unemployed, the beggars, and the criminals. The high birthrates of agrarian societies ensured a perennial oversupply of unskilled labor, and such people usually migrated to the cities, hoping to find some kind of employment. As long as men were young and healthy, they could usually get work as day laborers. But after they were injured or lost their youth and strength, they were quickly replaced by fresh labor and left to fend for themselves, usually as beggars or thieves. No agrarian society ever found a solution to this problem.* But then, the leading classes were not especially interested in finding one. The system served their needs quite well just as it was.

Many of the sisters of the men who made up the urban lower classes earned their livelihood as prostitutes. Moralists have often condemned these women as though they elected this career in preference to a more honorable one. The record indicates, however, that most of them had little choice: their only alternative was a life of unrelieved drudgery and poverty as servants or unskilled laborers, and many could not even hope for that.[104] The men they might have married were too poor to afford wives, and the system of prostitution was often, in effect, a substitute for marriage that was forced on these people by society. To be sure, the poor were not the only ones to avail themselves of the services of prostitutes, nor were all girls in that "profession" because of poverty. But economic factors were clearly the chief cause of its high incidence in agrarian societies.

The number of profitable working years for prostitutes was hardly longer than that for the rickshaw boys, porters, and others who sold their physical assets for a meager livelihood. As a result, the cities and towns in agrarian societies often swarmed with beggars of both sexes. Estimates by observers suggest that beggars comprised from a tenth to as high as a third of the total population of urban communities.[105] The proportion was not nearly so high for society as a whole, of course, since many of the rural poor migrated to the cities and towns in the hope of finding greater opportunities.

The Polity: Continuing Development of the State

In nearly all advanced agrarian societies, government was the basic integrating force. In any society created by conquest and run for the benefit of a tiny elite, coercion was necessary to

---

*Indeed, although the magnitude of this problem was much greater in many agrarian societies, the existence of a sizable "homeless" population in cities today indicates that it has not been solved by industrial societies either.

Working equipment for member of the governing class in sixteenth-century Europe.

hold things together. Not only did the natural antagonisms of the peasant masses have to be kept in check, but diverse groups of conquered people often had to be welded together politically. The scope of this problem is suggested by the size of some of these societies. Whereas the largest simple agrarian society, Egypt, controlled roughly 800,000 square miles (much of it desert and uninhabited), several advanced agrarian societies covered between 2 and 8 million square miles.

Nearly every advanced agrarian society was a monarchy headed by a king or emperor whose position was usually hereditary. Republican government, in which power was divided among a small ruling elite, was an infrequent exception limited almost entirely to the least powerful and least developed agrarian societies.[106] The prevalence of monarchical government seems to have been the result of the militaristic and exploitative character of societies at this level. Governments were constantly threatening, or being threatened by, their neighbors. At the same time, they were in danger from internal enemies—dissatisfied and ambitious members of the governing class, eager to seize control for themselves, and restless, hostile members of the far larger lower classes. Under such conditions republican government was nearly impossible.[107]

Because of the tendency to romanticize the past, many today are unaware of the frequency of both internal and external conflict in the great agrarian empires. In Rome, for example, 31 of the 79 emperors were murdered, 6 were driven to suicide, 4 were forcibly deposed, and several more met unknown fates at the hands of internal enemies.[108] Although Rome's record may have been worse than most, struggles for control were common in all advanced agrarian societies.[109]

Because of the absence of significant commercialization, most of the intrasocietal conflict in simple agrarian societies was *intra*class.[110] Members of the governing elite competed and fought one another for social position and control of territory, and, at the village level, individual peasants and peasant families competed for access to the best farmland. What did not happen was conflict *between* these classes. Even wars of conquest were conflicts among elites, not between elites and peasants, and replacement of one elite by another often had little effect on the lives of peasants. In many ways the classes lived in different worlds, and under these conditions the control and taxation by elites may have seemed as natural and inevitable to peasants as the seasons themselves.

Commercialization had the power to change this dramatically. Not only did a wealthy commercial class itself constitute a potential threat to the power of an aristocratic governing elite, but the introduction of commercial elements into the rural economy could trigger violence. If elites, in order to better meet their financial obligations, demanded higher rents,

One use of the economic surplus in an agrarian society: the Taj Mahal, a tomb erected by the Mogul emperor Shah Jahan in memory of his favorite wife.

greater shares of harvests, and more burdensome services from the peasants, they under-mined the traditional order on which their control rested, and this could spark peasant rebel-lions.* For instance, one authority on Russia reports that in the short period from 1801 to 1861, there were no less than 1,467 peasant uprisings in various parts of that country.[111] Most of these disturbances were confined to a limited area only because authorities acted swiftly and ruthlessly. Had they not, many would have spread as widely as the famous English revolt of 1381 or the German Peasants' War of 1524–1525.

External threats were no less frequent or serious, and warfare was a chronic condition. A survey of eleven European countries of the agrarian era found that, on average, these countries were involved in some kind of conflict with neighboring societies nearly every second year.[112] Such conditions encouraged the rise of authoritarian governments.

Most members of the governing class considered political power a prize to be sought for the rewards it offered rather than an opportunity for public service, and the office of king or emperor was the *supreme prize*. Efforts to raise the living standards of the common people were rare, efforts at self-aggrandizement commonplace.[113] In many societies, government offices were bought and sold like pieces of property, which the purchasers then used to obtain the greatest possible profit. Officeholders demanded payment before they would act, and justice was typically sold to the highest bidder. No wonder the common people of China developed the saying "To enter a court of justice is to enter a tiger's mouth."[114]

These practices reflected what is known as the *proprietary theory of the state,* which defines the state as a piece of property that its owners may use, within broad and ill-defined limits, for their personal advantage.[115] Guided by this theory, agrarian rulers and governing classes saw nothing immoral in the use of what we (not they) would call "public office" for private gain. To them, it was simply the legitimate use of what they regarded as their "patri-mony." It is said of the Ptolemies of Egypt, for example, that they showed the first emperors of Rome "how a country might be run on the lines of a profitable estate."[116] In the case of medieval Europe, we read:

> The proprietary conception of rulership created an inextricable confusion of public and private affairs. Rights of government were a form of private ownership. "Crown lands" and "the king's estate" were synonymous. There was no differentiation between the king in his private and public capacities. A kingdom, like any estate endowed with elements of governmental authority, was the private concern of its owner. Since *"state"* and *"estate"* were identical, "the State" was indistinguishable from the prince and his personal "patrimony."[117]

The proprietary theory of the state can be traced back to horticultural societies and, in a sense, even to hunting and gathering bands. In those simpler societies, no distinction was made between the private and public aspects of the lives and activities of leaders. When a surplus first began to be produced, at least part of it was turned over to the leader, who held it as trustee for the group. As long as the surplus was small and consisted of perishable commodities, there was little the leader could do with it except redistribute it, thereby win-ning respect for his generosity. Eventually, however, as we saw in Chapter 6, it grew large enough to permit him to create a staff of dependent retainers who could be used to enforce his wishes. At this point, the proprietary theory of the state was born. Later rulers merely applied it on an ever expanding scale, as productivity and the economic surplus steadily increased.

Recent research provides a good picture of the extremes to which rulers and governing classes have carried the proprietary principle. In late-nineteenth-century China, for example, the average income for families not in the governing class was approximately 20 to 25 taels per year. By contrast, the governing class averaged 450 taels per year, with some receiving as

---

*It is important to note that these peasant uprisings were not "revolutions." In fact, in most instances what the peasants wanted was a *return to the old order,* not its replacement with a new one.

much as 200,000.[118] The emperor's income, of course, was considerably larger even than this. To cite another example, the English nobility at the end of the twelfth century and early in the thirteenth had an average income roughly 200 times that of ordinary field hands, and the king's equaled that of 24,000 field hands.[119] Putting together the evidence from many sources, it appears that the combined income of the ruler and the governing class in most advanced agrarian societies equaled *not less than half of the total national income,* even though they numbered 2 percent or less of the population.[120]

Despite their many similarities, the polities of advanced agrarian societies varied in a number of ways, the most important being the *degree of political centralization.* In some societies the central government was very strong; in others its powers were severely limited. In the main, these differences reflected the current state of the perennial struggle between the ruler and the other members of the governing class. The king or emperor naturally wanted the greatest possible control over his subordinates, and the subordinates just as naturally wanted to minimize his control. Since land (including the peasants who worked it) and political office were the most valuable resources in agrarian systems of stratification, most of the struggles between rulers and the governing class were over them. In a few instances, very powerful rulers gained such great power that both land and political offices were held solely at their pleasure and were subject to instant confiscation if an individual's services were judged unsatisfactory.[121] A Dutch traveler of the early seventeenth century left a vivid picture of the situation in the Mogul empire in India:

> Immediately on the death of a lord who has enjoyed the King's [favor], be he great or small, without any exception—sometimes even before the breath is out of the body—the King's officers are ready on the spot and make an inventory of the entire estate, recording everything down to the value of a single piece, even to the dresses and jewels of the ladies, provided they have not concealed them. The King takes back the whole estate absolutely for himself, except in a case where the deceased has done good service in his lifetime, when the women and children are given enough to live on, but no more.[122]

In Turkey, specially trained slaves became high-ranking officials over whom the sultan held life-and-death power.[123]

At the other extreme, during much of the medieval period in Europe, the governing classes were very independent. Though their lands were typically royal grants given in exchange for pledges of service, their monarchs usually lacked the power to enforce these pledges.[124] Although examples of both extremes can be found, the usual pattern was something in between, and in most cases the powers of the ruler and the governing class were fairly evenly balanced.

Religion: The Emergence of Universal Faiths

During the era in which advanced agrarian societies were dominant, there were a number of important developments in the religious sphere. The most important by far was the emergence and spread of three new religions, Buddhism, Christianity, and Islam. Each proclaimed a *universal faith,* and each succeeded in creating a community of believers that transcended societal boundaries. In contrast, in older religions, people's beliefs and loyalties were thought of as local affairs. Where one lived determined the god or gods one worshiped, for the prevailing view was that there were many gods and that, like kings, each had his or her own people and territory.

The ancient Israelites were some of the first to reject this view and move toward a more universalistic outlook. Centuries before the birth of Christ, the prophets proclaimed that there was only one God and that He ruled over the entire world. For a time, Judaism was a missionary religion and won converts in many parts of the Roman world.[125] This ended, however,

(a)

(b)

Buddhism, Christianity, and Islam all have roots in the advanced agrarian era: (a) Muslims at a mosque complex in Mecca, (b) Christians in St. Peter's Square, Vatican City, and (c) Buddhist monks at Wat Bevornivet Temple in Thailand.

(c)

when early Christian missionaries won most of these Gentile converts to the new faith. From then on, implementation of the universalistic vision became the mission of Christians and Muslims, who eventually converted, at least nominally, most of the population of Europe, North Africa, and the Middle East, and some of the people of India, Central Asia, China, and Southeast Asia.

Buddhism, the other major universal faith, began in India as an offshoot of Hinduism and spread through most of Southeast Asia, China, Korea, and Japan, though it later died out in the land of its origin. Older ethnic faiths, such as Hinduism, Confucianism, and Shintoism, still survived in much of Asia, but even they eventually incorporated some elements of universalism in their thought.

The emergence and spread of universal faiths reflected the broader social and intellectual horizons that resulted from advances in transportation technology and the spreading web of trade relations. Empire building, by bringing diverse populations under a single government, also helped to weaken parochial or "tribal" views. As people's knowledge of other societies increased, and with it their awareness of the essential unity of all humanity, the basic postulate of the older ethnic faiths (i.e., the belief in tribal deities) was gradually undermined.

Another important development was the growing separation of religious and political institutions.[126] Compared with the situation in advanced horticultural and simple agrarian societies, the governments of advanced agrarian societies were much more secular. Kings and emperors were, it is true, still said to rule "by the grace of God"; the divine right of kings was still generally accepted; and occasionally a ruler even claimed to be a god. But few rulers functioned as high priests, and theocracies (i.e., states in which a priesthood rules in the name of a god) were almost unknown. This separation of church and state was part of the more general trend toward institutional specialization that has been so basic in the evolutionary process since the start of the horticultural era.

Despite the growing separation of politics and religion, leaders in the two spheres continued to work closely together. This was especially evident in struggles between the governing class and the common people. When rebellious voices challenged the right of the governing class to control the economic surplus, the clergy usually defended the elite, asserting that their power had been given them by God and any challenge to it was a challenge to His authority.[127] By legitimizing the actions of the governing class in this way, the clergy reduced the need for costly coercive measures against the lower classes.

In appreciation for this, and also because of their own religious beliefs, agrarian rulers were often extremely generous with religious groups, giving them large grants of land and special tax exemptions. In effect, a symbiotic relationship was established, with a religious organization legitimizing the actions of the governing class in return for generous financial support. Modern research indicates that religious groups frequently owned as much as a quarter or a third of a nation's land.[128]

Despite such profitable alliances, most religions of the agrarian era fostered some concern for distributive justice. This is especially evident in Judaism and Christianity.[129] One historian captured the contradictory nature of medieval Christianity in this discerning characterization: "Democratic, yet aristocratic; charitable, yet exploitative; generous, yet mercenary; humanitarian, yet cruel; indulgent, yet severely repressive of some things; progressive, yet reactionary; radical, yet conservative—all these are qualities of the Church in the Middle Ages."[130]

Magic and Fatalism   Two other aspects of the beliefs of agrarian societies deserve comment: (1) the widespread belief in magic and (2) the equally widespread attitude of fatalism.[131] Logically, these are contradictory. If magic really works, people do not need to be fatalistic, and if they are true fatalists, they should have no confidence in magic. But people are not always logical: they often hope for things they know are impossible. Considering the tremendous pressures operating on the common people in agrarian societies, and their limited sources of information, it is hardly surprising that many of them held these mutually contradictory views.

Fatalism and belief in magic both contributed to the slowdown in the rate of technological advance in agrarian societies. Magic encouraged people to depend on supernatural forces for the answers to their problems. Fatalism convinced them that control was out of their hands. Neither attitude motivated people to try to improve conditions themselves by building better tools or devising better techniques for satisfying their needs.

Kinship: Changing Significance in Society

For individuals, kinship ties remained of great importance throughout the agrarian era. For societies, however, they ceased to be the chief integrating force. In most horticultural societies, the largest and most powerful clan in a society, aided perhaps by dependent retainers, could still provide enough people to staff important political offices. But in advanced agrarian societies, this was no longer possible. Civil and military offices were so numerous that not even the largest of extended families could fill them all.

The fact that kinship ties were no longer the chief integrating force in societies did not mean, however, that they were no longer politically important. The royal office itself was inherited in most societies, as were numerous other political offices. Many of these, civil and military offices alike, were a family's patrimony, handed down like any other family possession from father to son (or, sometimes, daughter). Offices that were not actually owned might still be closed to anyone who was not a member of the nobility or who did not qualify as coming from one of the "right families."

Even in the allocation of offices to which such restrictions did not apply, families continued to play an important role. Family funds might be used to purchase an office, for example. And those who had it in their power to assign an office were naturally influenced by their own family's interests. Although nepotism still occurs in modern industrial societies, it is usually a violation of the law and lacks public approval. In advanced agrarian societies, however, it was an accepted part of life, and there was little criticism, and still less punishment, of those who practiced it.

During the agrarian era, the family remained very important in the economic sphere as well. In fact, it was usually *the basic unit of economic organization*. Businesses were almost always family enterprises; the corporate form of enterprise, owned jointly by unrelated persons, was virtually unheard of, even in the largest cities. And in rural areas the peasant family was the basic work unit.

The family's economic significance is evident in many ways. For instance, because of its economic implications, marriage was considered much too important to be decided by young people; even among the peasantry, marriages were usually arranged by parents, often with the aid of marriage brokers.[132] Sometimes the young couple did not even meet until the ceremony itself. In selecting spouses for their children, parents were primarily concerned with the economic and status implications of the match and only secondarily with other matters. Marriage arrangements often involved an outright economic transaction. The husband might make a payment for the bride, or her parents would provide her with a dowry.[133]

As one would suppose, marriages contracted in this way did not necessarily produce sexual or psychological compatibility between the spouses, but this was not seen as the primary purpose of marriage. Ties between man and wife usually endured because of the value that was placed on the relationship by society, and because the economic arrangement was usually of critical importance to the individuals involved. Within these families, male dominance was the rule and obedience was generally held to be the prime virtue in women and children.[134] In this, the family reflected the general authoritarian pattern of life in agrarian societies.

Leisure and the Arts

Although the life of the peasant was hard, even harsh, there were occasional opportunities for leisure and recreation.[135] Weddings and religious festivals, for example, were important occasions for people to get together for a good time. Singing and dancing were the chief forms of entertainment at such festivities and, in most societies, alcoholic beverages added to the merriment. People also amused themselves with games and contests, courtship and lovemaking, gossiping and storytelling, and a host of other activities.

Class distinctions were as evident in leisure activity as in any other, with falconry, jousting, and chess among the activities favored by the governing class. But some forms of entertainment, such as archery and dice, had a universal appeal. Gambling in particular was popular with every class.

The rise of professional entertainers was part of the general trend toward occupational specialization. Actors, minstrels, jesters, clowns, acrobats, jugglers, and geishas are some of the more familiar. In general, the status of such people was extremely low, probably because of their economic insecurity and their excessive dependence on the favor of others. Yet entertainers who had a powerful patron often found their work quite lucrative.

Recreation was frequently raucous and crude. It could also be brutal and violent, and in this the Romans were probably unsurpassed. In their so-called games, first in the Circus Maximus, later in the Colosseum, tens of thousands came to watch wild animals devour helpless victims, and armed gladiators maim and kill one another. When the Colosseum was first opened in 80 A.D., the emperor Titus promised the people of Rome 100 consecutive days of such games, with fights to the death between more than 10,000 prisoners and 5,000 wild animals (including lions, tigers, and elephants), and a naval battle between 3,000 men in an arena especially flooded for the occasion.[136]

In agrarian Europe, cockfights and dogfights were very popular, and public hangings often drew large and exuberant crowds. Wedding parties and other festivities frequently ended in drunken brawls. In fact, violence typically followed drinking. From what we know of life in agrarian societies, it would appear that alcohol simply removed a fragile overlay of inhibitions, revealing people's frustrations and bitterness.

But if the agrarian world at play was often unattractive, its artistic accomplishments were quite the opposite. In their sculpture, their painting, and their architecture, these societies left monuments of lasting beauty. Thousands of cathedrals, churches, mosques, pagodas, temples, and palaces, and the treasures within them, testify to an impressive development of the arts during that era. Achievements in literature were probably no less impressive, though language barriers make it difficult for us to appreciate them as fully.* Developments in music during most of the agrarian era seem to have been less spectacular than in the other arts. Toward the end of the era, however, the invention of new instruments and the genius of composers like Bach, Handel, Mozart, and Beethoven combined to produce an outburst of magnificent music that has transcended societal boundaries in unprecedented fashion.

Most artists were subsidized by the governing class or by the religious elite, drawing on the economic surplus extracted from the peasant masses. Thus, the remarkable artistic achievements of agrarian societies were a product of their harshly exploitative social system. Yet, if

---

*Robert Frost once said that "poetry is what gets lost in translation," and anyone who has ever seriously tried to translate a poem understands the complexity of the language problem.

As can be seen clearly in this fourth-century mosaic, "Fight of the Gladiators," recreation was frequently violent or brutal in agrarian societies. In the Roman "games," tens of thousands came to watch wild animals devour helpless victims, and armed gladiators maim and kill one another.

the peasants had been allowed to keep the surplus, the result would simply have been more poor people. Again, as with horticultural societies, this link between an exploitative class system and impressive cultural achievements reminds us of the difficulty we face in passing ethical judgments on complex sociocultural systems.

Stratification: Increasing Complexity

The basic cleavages in advanced agrarian societies were much the same as they had been in simple agrarian societies and, as a consequence, so were the basic patterns of inequality. The principal division in society was still the one between the governing class and the great mass of peasants and others over whom it exercised control both politically and economically. But the system of stratification had altered in one respect from that of simpler societal types: it had become more complex.

This growing complexity can be seen in two areas. First, in advanced agrarian societies there were more people in occupations whose status fell somewhere between the extremes. These people were either directly employed by the governing class (e.g., household servants, stewards, men-at-arms) or served them indirectly (e.g., merchants, artisans).

Second, advanced agrarian societies experienced a growing overlap in the rankings of different classes of people, especially in terms of wealth and property. Some merchants, for example, now had more wealth than some members of the governing class, and a tiny minority of peasants, by luck and hard work, actually amassed greater wealth than some impoverished members of the nobility. Although members of the governing class still had greater wealth, *on average,* than merchants or any other group, this was no longer true of every member of the class. Similarly, although merchants were, *on average,* wealthier than peasants, there were exceptions.

Figure 7.5 depicts the stratification system of advanced agrarian societies. The ruler was invariably the most powerful, prestigious, and wealthy individual in society: he was, in fact, literally in a class by himself. For example, the English kings Richard I and John, who ruled in the last decade of the twelfth century and the first decade of the thirteenth, had incomes thirty times that of the wealthiest nobleman of the day.[137] By the reign of Richard II, at the end of the fourteenth century, the king's income had risen to forty times that of the wealthiest member of the governing class. In late-fifteenth- and early-sixteenth-century Spain, the king was reputed to enjoy one-third of all the revenues of the land (meaning, apparently, one-third of the economic surplus). Similar patterns are reported in virtually every advanced agrarian society.

At the opposite extreme in the system of stratification was a wretched class of individuals for whose labor the society had no need. These were mostly peasant sons and daughters who were unable to inherit land or to marry someone who did, and thus were forced out on their own in a society that suffered a chronic labor surplus. As we have seen, these individuals could usually eke out a living while they were young and healthy, but most of them soon drifted into the ranks of the expendables (see Figure 7.5) and died at an early age.[138]

On the whole, the class divisions within advanced agrarian societies were greater than those in simple agrarian societies. And, as we noted earlier, pressures of commercialization were conducive to violence. Though most were local incidents involving small numbers of people, some spread to become large-scale insurrections. Furthermore, despite the fact that peasants generally revolted in order to *restore* traditional class relationships or to *defend* traditional religious beliefs from perceived corruption, their rebellions would later play a role in advancing the interests of the commercial classes.[139] Artisans and merchants also revolted on a number of occasions,[140] and these groups, unlike the peasants, sometimes emerged victorious. In Europe, the merchants were so successful in their challenges to the governing class that eventually *they* became the governing class in many cities and towns. From an evolutionary perspective, this proved to be a very important development indeed, as we will see.

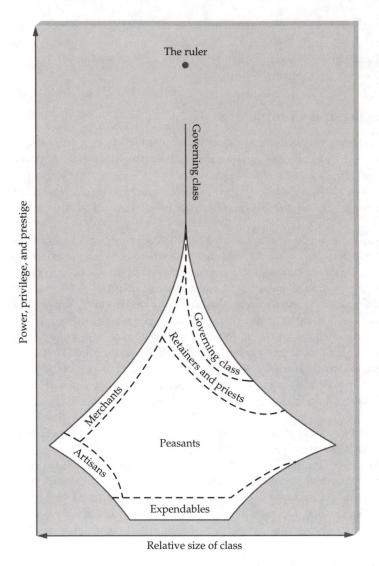

FIGURE 7.5 *Model of the class structure of advanced agrarian societies.*

VARIATIONS ON AGRARIAN THEMES

In surveying societies at the same level of development, it is natural to emphasize those characteristics which are found in all or most of them, and to slight the differences. This may give an impression of greater uniformity than really exists. Obviously there were variations in every area of life in advanced agrarian societies, and we have noted many of them, or at least hinted at them in qualifying phrases, saying that a particular pattern was found in "most" or "many" of these societies.

To begin with, advanced agrarian societies varied technologically. The first to emerge resembled their simple agrarian predecessors more than they resembled the advanced agrarian societies of northwest Europe on the eve of the Industrial Revolution. Furthermore, the size of advanced agrarian societies ranged all the way from tiny principalities and city-states to giant empires. Most were monarchies, but a few were republics. Some were governed by enormously powerful autocratic rulers; in others, power was diffused more widely among members of the governing class. Similar variations occurred in almost every area of life.

Clearly, then, there has been variation among societies at the advanced agrarian level—indeed, at every level of societal development. There is, however, one important difference. In the less advanced societal types (i.e., hunting and gathering, fishing, and simple horticultural), intratype variation is due primarily to differences in the *biophysical environment*. We see this clearly when we compare the Eskimo with the Australian aborigines, for example, or the !Kung San of the Kalahari Desert with the Pygmies of the rain forest. In advanced agrarian societies, on the other hand, differences in the biophysical environment have not been as important a cause of intratype variation. This is exactly what ecological-evolutionary theory would lead us to expect, since the further a society advances on the evolutionary scale, the greater is its ability to overcome the limitations imposed by the biotic and physical world and the more likely it is, because of geographical expansion, to include within its borders a variety of environments, thus making its overall environment less distinctive.

In studying advanced agrarian societies, historians have often focused attention on religion as the chief source of the differences among them. Thus, they have contrasted Christian societies with Islamic societies, for example, or Buddhist societies with Hindu societies.

There is, of course, no doubt that each of these religions was responsible for social and cultural variations among advanced agrarian societies. Christianity and Islam, like Judaism, had a special day of worship and rest each week, while the Oriental religions did not. Most of the religions encouraged monasticism, but Protestantism and Islam did not. Islam sanctioned the practice of polygyny, which Christianity forbade; Confucianism encouraged ancestor worship; Buddhism encouraged families to send their sons to live in monasteries for a year or two before assuming adult responsibilities; and Hinduism had a hereditary priestly caste. Theologically, there were tremendous differences among the various religions, and members of advanced agrarian societies often fought and died in order to extend or defend their faith.

Without denying the importance of these and other religious influences, we cannot fail to note that no faith was able to break the "agrarian mold" that shaped the basic patterns of life in these societies.* For regardless of its dominant religion, every advanced agrarian society was much like the rest with respect to its fundamental characteristics. Class structure, social inequality, the division of labor, the distinctive role of urban populations in the larger society, the cleavage between urban and rural subcultures, the disdain of the governing class for both work and workers, the widespread belief in magic and fatalism, the use of the economic surplus for the benefit of the governing class and for the construction of monumental edifices, high birth and death rates—all these and more were present in all advanced agrarian societies.

The greatest variations among advanced agrarian societies stemmed not from ideological differences but from differences in their *social environments*. These differences were of two kinds. One involved proximity to trade routes and the other the influence of frontier territories.

From the standpoint of trade, the most advantageous location for a society was at the point where several important trade routes intersected.[141] Having such a location ensured continuing contact with a large number of other societies and increased opportunities for acquiring useful information through diffusion. It also provided a valuable source of income and fostered economic growth and development. Societies that were not so well situated were handicapped and tended to be less developed, unless some compensating factor offset this handicap. Because of the importance of trade routes, societies in the Middle East, where routes from Europe, Asia, and Africa converged, remained at the forefront of social and cultural development for most of the agrarian era. Toward the end, however, as trade with the New World became important, the advantage shifted to western European societies.

*For a discussion of religion's role in the rise of industrial societies, see Chapter 9.

A very different kind of environmental influence made itself felt when agrarian populations expanded into territories that previously were uninhabited or were inhabited by smaller,
less advanced societies. Under the radically altered conditions that were encountered, traditional
patterns of life often broke down and a new and different kind of society—*a frontier society*—
emerged briefly.

The first known instance of this was the establishment of the new nation of Israel in the
largely uninhabited hill country in the eastern part of Palestine in the thirteenth century B.C.[142]
More recently, the process was repeated in the Norwegian-Irish settlement of Iceland; in the
settlement of North America by migrants from Britain, France, and other parts of northwestern
Europe; in the British settlement of Australia and New Zealand; in the Boer settlement of
South Africa; and in the Cossack settlement of the Russian steppes.[143] In each instance the
frontier region escaped for a time from the control of traditional authorities and land became
available for settlement by lower-status members of agrarian societies who were willing to
assume the risks and hardships of frontier life.

Frontier societies are of special interest from the standpoint of ecological-evolutionary
theory because they show the extent to which the agrarian way of life was shaped by an
oversupply of labor and an undersupply of land. When these conditions were eliminated even
temporarily, as happened in frontier regions, striking deviations from the usual patterns of
agrarian life developed.

To begin with, the settlers themselves tended to be the poor, the dispossessed, the
noninheriting sons and daughters, troublemakers, misfits, and even criminals deported by the
parent society. Frontier regions held little attraction for the rich and powerful, who preferred
to remain close to the traditional centers of power and influence. Thus, in frontier regions
established authority was usually weak or absent, and because societal life was not under the
control of the governing class, traditional agrarian patterns tended to break down and new
patterns emerged.[144]

One of the most significant changes that occurred was the breakdown of the traditional
class system. Except when elites created a plantation system and the native population was
enslaved or enserfed (as in much of Latin America) or when slaves were imported (as in the
Caribbean and the southern United States), a highly egalitarian system of family farms and
ranches was likely to develop.[145] This is what happened in Canada, the United States (except
in the South), Australia, New Zealand, and South Africa. In these areas there was a chronic
shortage of labor; workers were more highly valued than in the older, settled areas, where
there was usually a surplus of labor. On the frontier, there were neither enough farmers to
cultivate the newly opened land nor enough fighters to defend it. It is not surprising, then, that
frontier life generated a striking independence of spirit and a stubborn resistance to authority.
Having risked their lives to establish themselves in a new land, frontier settlers were not
prepared to hand over their surplus to anyone. Thus, frontier conditions usually broke
down the sharp inequalities and exploitative patterns that characterized traditional agrarian
societies.

This condition was usually temporary, however. As resistance from the native population came to an end and the population of settlers grew in number and density, as roads were
built and governmental authority was established, there was a waning of the spirit of independence and individualism and the traditional system began to reassert itself. To be sure, this did
not happen overnight. On the contrary, it usually took a century or more. But in the end, the
typical agrarian pattern usually prevailed.

Only one thing ever prevented this from happening—the onset of industrialization. In a
number of instances during the last century and a half, the Industrial Revolution generated a
new demand for labor before the frontier was fully absorbed into the old system. This happened in the United States, Canada, Australia, and New Zealand. These societies were thus

spared the agony of slowly sliding back into the classic agrarian pattern in which a massive, impoverished peasantry is dominated and exploited by a small, hereditary aristocracy.

In the United States this process had actually gotten well under way in much of the South with its system of slavery. But the Confederacy's defeat in the Civil War and the South's eventual industrialization halted the restoration of the old agrarian system. In other parts of the country, the process had barely begun before the forces of industrialization intervened.

Looking back, it seems clear that the frontier experience was excellent preparation for the Industrial Revolution. Above all, it established a tradition of individual initiative, innovation, and receptivity to change that was lacking in other agrarian societies. Also, by creating a more egalitarian class system, the frontier prepared the way for the more open and fluid class systems of modern industrial societies. These developments help explain the relative ease with which the overseas English-speaking democracies (e.g., the United States, Australia, and Canada) made the transition to the industrial era, and why they have so long been in the forefront with respect to productivity, standard of living, and political stability. It is interesting to speculate on what the situation in these societies might be today if they had been settled a thousand years earlier and a more typical agrarian social system had had time to take root.

AGRARIAN SOCIETIES IN THEORETICAL PERSPECTIVE

The initial effect of the shift from horticulture to agriculture, as we saw at the beginning of this chapter, was an increase in food production. Societies that adopted the plow were able to produce substantially more food in a given territory than those that relied on the hoe and digging stick.

This increase in productivity could be used, as Figure 7.6 indicates, either to expand the economic surplus of the society or to expand its population. Actually, the historical record shows that in most agrarian societies *both* of these things happened to some degree. The expansion of the economic surplus was more significant than population growth, however, since it was a necessary precondition for so many social and cultural changes. Figure 7.6 makes no attempt to portray all of them, or all of their interrelationships, since that would require an impossibly complex diagram. Instead, the figure focuses only on the most critical developments.

The single most important consequence of the greater economic surplus was *further growth of the state and of the power of the governing class* that controlled it. This contributed, directly or indirectly, to most of the other important social and cultural changes of the agrarian era. It lay behind the shift from militias to professional armies; the increase in inequality, and the development of ideologies justifying inequality and the power of elites; the rise of the merchant class and the increase in trade and commerce; the growth of urban populations; the increase in the division of labor; and the slowing of the rate of innovation.

Many of the changes in agrarian societies were a continuation of trends that began in horticultural societies. But the shift to agriculture magnified those trends dramatically. To cite a single example, the largest society ever constructed on a horticultural foundation appears to have been the Aztec empire in the years immediately preceding the Spanish conquest of Mexico. At the peak of its power it is estimated to have controlled a population of 15 million people.[146] In contrast, mid-nineteenth-century China, before it began to industrialize, had a population of approximately 400 million, and the Roman and Russian empires each had at least 70 million.[147]

As great as they are, these differences in population size are probably no greater in degree than differences in many other basic features of these two types of societies. Their numbers, in other words, are but a reflection of the vastly different potentials inherent in the subsistence technologies on which horticultural societies and agrarian societies were built.

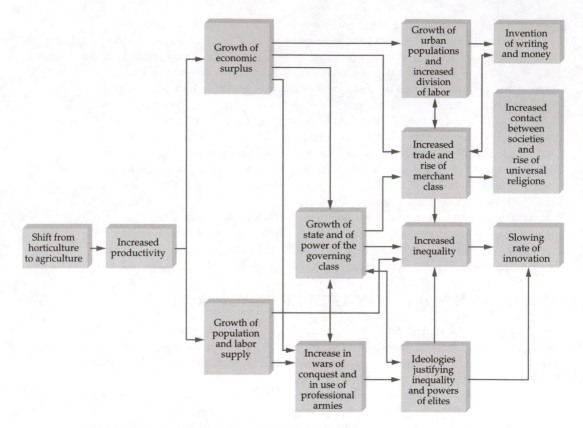

FIGURE 7.6 *Model of the effects of the shift from horticulture to agriculture.*

8

Some Evolutionary Bypaths and a Brief Review

ENVIRONMENTALLY SPECIALIZED SOCIETAL TYPES

Up to this point in our survey of human societies, we have concentrated on those types which have been in the mainstream of evolutionary history, the ones that developed their technologies around the resources of fields and forests. The types of societies to which we now turn have adapted to *less common environments*—two to aquatic environments and one to grasslands and arid environments. Though these specialized kinds of societies have contributed to sociocultural evolution in many important ways, their contributions have been more limited than those of the mainstream societies. This is because of the specialized nature of the problems with which they have dealt in their subsistence activities. For these reasons, we will not examine them in the same detail as the others.

Fishing Societies

To call any group a "fishing" society is something of a misnomer, for no society ever depended exclusively on fishing for its food supply.[1] Except in the Arctic, nearly all fishing peoples obtain fruits and vegetables by foraging or cultivation. Many of them also supplement their diet by hunting, and occasionally by raising livestock. To call a society a fishing society, then, merely indicates that fishing is its most important subsistence activity.

In recent centuries fishing societies have been found in many parts of the world, but the majority have been in the northwestern part of North America—Oregon, Washington, British Columbia, Alaska, and the arctic regions of Canada. There have also been some in northeastern Asia, among the islands of the Pacific (though most of the Pacific peoples have been simple horticulturalists), in scattered parts of Africa and South America, and elsewhere.

Historically, fishing societies are probably the second oldest type, emerging a few thousand years before the first horticultural societies. The practice of fishing is, of course, even older and more widespread and has provided a supplementary source of subsistence in many societies for thousands of years.

In some ways fishing societies might be regarded as hunting and gathering societies that have adapted to aquatic rather than terrestrial environments. One might argue that the chief difference is simply that fish rather than land animals are the object of the hunt and that the technology of the group is modified accordingly. But there is a reason why fishing societies should be considered a separate societal type: *a fishing economy has the potential for supporting a larger, more sedentary population than a hunting and gathering economy.*

This is because fishing peoples are much less likely to deplete the food resources of their environment than are hunters and gatherers. Fish have much higher reproductive rates

African fishing village, Benin.

than most land animals. In addition, fishing peoples usually work only a small part of their food-producing territory. Even if they catch all the fish in their immediate area, the supply is quickly replenished by the great surplus spawned in adjacent areas. This could not happen with land animals, at least not after hunting and gathering bands occupied most of the habitable territory.

Thus, although fishing societies are only a bit more advanced technologically than hunting and gathering societies, we would expect them to be somewhat larger, more sedentary, and more complex.[2] This is, in fact, precisely what we find. With respect to size, they are more than twice as large. Murdock's data set shows that the average size of modern fishing communities is approximately 90, the average size of hunting and gathering groups only 40.[3] With respect to settlement patterns, only 10 percent of the hunting and gathering societies live in permanent settlements, compared to 55 percent of the fishing societies.

Social inequality, too, is both more common and more pronounced. A system of hereditary nobility is found in 28 percent of fishing societies but in only 2 percent of hunting and gathering societies, while slavery occurs in slightly over 50 percent of fishing societies but in only 11 percent of hunting and gathering societies.

Unlike hunting and gathering societies, fishing societies seldom evolved into a more advanced type.* There are several reasons for this. To begin with, territories suited to a predominantly fishing economy are strung out along thin coastal strips, so that it has been virtually impossible to create large, defensible political entities.[4] Instead, when neighboring horticultural societies became powerful enough, fishing societies have usually been conquered and absorbed by them. Even though fishing continued in the area, it became only a minor part of the economy of the larger society, and the leaders of the fishing groups were

*It is possible that some evolved directly into maritime societies, but there is no real evidence of this. Maritime societies seem, instead, usually to have evolved out of advanced horticultural or agrarian societies.

The Shui-jen, or water people, of southern China are descended from fishing peoples of an earlier time. They still depend on fishing for their livelihood and remain largely separate from the mainland population.

reduced to the status of minor officials, too weak to defend the local surplus. As a result, fishing communities in *agrarian* societies have often been socially and culturally less advanced (except in subsistence technology) than the fishing communities of more primitive *fishing* societies. Typically, their situation was no better than that of peasant villages, and for the same reason—their surplus was confiscated by more powerful elements in the society.[5]

Herding Societies

Herding societies, like fishing societies, represent an adaptation to specialized environmental conditions. Other than that, the two have little in common. Their environments are radically different, and the technology of herding societies is usually more advanced.

Herding societies cover approximately the same range of technological development as horticultural and agrarian societies. Animals were first domesticated about the same time plants were first cultivated, and the two practices typically went hand in hand in the horticultural and agrarian societies of the Old World.* In some areas, however, crop cultivation was severely limited because of insufficient rainfall, too short a growing season (in northern latitudes), or mountainous terrain. This was true of much of central Asia, the Arabian peninsula, and North Africa, and also parts of Europe and sub-Saharan Africa. Because it was possible to raise livestock in many of these areas, however, a new and different type of society emerged.**

---

*This was not true in most of the New World, where there were almost no large animals suitable for domestication by the time plants were domesticated.
**Most of these societies have also had some secondary means of subsistence, usually horticulture or agriculture on a small scale.

A pastoral economy usually necessitates a nomadic or seminomadic way of life.[6] In fact, "nomad" comes from an early Greek word meaning a "herder of cattle."[7] In the sample of herding societies in Murdock's data set, nearly 90 percent are wholly or partially nomadic. In this respect they closely resemble hunters and gatherers.

Herders are also like hunters and gatherers in the size of their communities. On average, their communities are a bit smaller than fishing communities and much smaller than simple horticultural communities, as the following figures show:

Hunting and gathering communities	40
Herding communities	72
Fishing communities	90
Simple horticultural communities	138

The explanation for this is primarily environmental. Given the sparse resources of their territories, large and dense settlements are impossible.[8]

Despite the small size of their communities, herding societies are usually fairly large. Whereas the typical hunting and gathering or fishing society contains only a single community, and the typical simple horticultural society fewer than a dozen, the average herding society contains several dozen. Thus, the median population of herding societies far surpasses that of the other three types:

Hunting and gathering societies	40
Fishing societies	90
Simple horticultural societies	1,500
Herding societies	5,750

The greater size of herding societies reflects the combined influence of environment and technology. Open grasslands, where the majority of herders live, present few natural barriers to movement and, therefore, to political expansion. Furthermore, since about 2000 B.C., many herding peoples have ridden horses or camels, which made them a potent military force and greatly facilitated their political expansion.

The basic resource in these societies is livestock, and the size of the herd is the measure of a man. Large herds signify not only wealth but also power, for only a strong man or the head of a strong family can defend such vulnerable property against rivals and enemies. Thus, in most of these societies, and especially in the more advanced (i.e., those with horses or camels and herds of larger animals such as cattle), marked social inequality is the rule. Hereditary slavery, for example, is far more common in herding societies than in any other type.[9]

With respect to kinship, herding societies are noteworthy on at least two counts. First, they are more likely than any other type of society to require the payment of a bride price or bride service.[10] Second, they are the most likely to require newly married couples to live with the husband's kinsmen.[11]

These strong patriarchal tendencies have several sources. Above all, they reflect the often militant nature of pastoral life. Raiding and warfare are frequent activities, and as we have noted before, these activities stimulate the growth of political authority. In addition, the basic economic activity in these societies is men's work. In this respect they stand in sharp contrast to horticultural societies, where women often play the dominant role in subsistence activities.

One of the most important technological advances made by herding peoples was the utilization of horses, and later camels, for transportation. This practice originated about 1800 B.C., when certain herding groups in the Middle East began harnessing horses to chariots.[12] This gave them an important military advantage over their less mobile agrarian neighbors and enabled them to win control of much of the Middle East—at least until the new technology

Livestock is the basic resource in herding societies, and the size of his herd is the measure of a man. Large herds signify not only wealth but also power, for only a strong man or the head of a strong family can defend such vulnerable property: roundup time in Mongolia.

was adopted by the more numerous agrarian peoples. Herders later learned to *ride* their horses, which led to a new wave of conquests, beginning about 900 B.C.[13]

During the next 2,500 years, a succession of herding groups attacked agrarian societies from China to Europe, frequently conquering them. The empires and dynasties they established include some of the largest and most famous in history—the great Mongol empire, for example, founded by Genghis Khan early in the thirteenth century A.D. and expanded by his successors. At the peak of its power, the Mongol empire stretched from eastern Europe to the shores of the Pacific and launched attacks in places as distant as Austria and Japan. Other famous empires and dynasties founded by herding peoples include the Mogul empire, established in India by a branch of the Mongols; the Manchu dynasty in China; the Ottoman empire in the Middle East; and the early Islamic states established by followers of the prophet Muhammad.

Despite their many military victories, herding peoples were never able to destroy the agrarian social order. In the end, it was always they, not agrarian peoples, who changed their mode of life. There were a number of reasons for this, but it was primarily because the economic surplus that could be produced by agricultural activities was so much greater than what could be produced by converting the land to herding activities. After a few early conquerors tried to turn fields into pastures, they realized they were, in effect, killing the goose that laid the golden eggs, and abandoned their preferred way of life for economic reasons. Thus, despite impressive military victories, the limits of the herding world were never extended.

Although animal husbandry was, and continues to be, an important secondary source of subsistence in the agrarian world, it was the primary source only in areas unsuited to plant cultivation. In recent centuries, even these areas have, in most cases, been brought under the control of agrarian or industrial societies, and herding societies, like other preindustrial types, are vanishing.

Maritime Societies

Maritime societies have been the rarest of all the major societal types. Never have there been more than a few at any one time. Yet once they played a very important role in the civilized world.

Technologically, maritime societies were much like agrarian societies. What set them apart was the way they used this technology to take advantage of the special opportunities afforded by their environmental situation. Located on large bodies of water in an era when it was cheaper to move goods by water than by land (see page XXX), these peoples found trade and commerce far more profitable than either fishing or the cultivation of their limited land resources and gradually created societies in which overseas trade was the chief economic activity.

The first maritime society in history may have been that developed by the Minoans on the island of Crete, around 2000 B.C. We are told that the wealth and power of the Minoan rulers "depended more upon foreign trade and religious prerogative than upon the land rents and forced services."[14] The island location of Minoan society was important not only because it afforded ready access to the sea, but also because it provided protection against more powerful agrarian societies. In fact, most maritime societies developed on islands or peninsulas that were difficult to attack by land (see page XXX). Their only military advantage was in naval warfare.

During the next 1,500 years a number of other maritime societies were established in the Mediterranean world. These included the Mycenaeans, or pre-Hellenic Greeks, about 2000 B.C.; the Phoenicians; the Carthaginians; and possibly some of the later Greek city-states. The spread of the maritime pattern in this period was largely, perhaps wholly, the result of

Maritime societies usually developed on islands or peninsulas that were difficult to attack by land: aerial view of the Lebanese city of Sur (formerly Tyre), once a maritime society. In ancient times, when Tyre was an important Phoenician city-state, it was an island. The land-bridge that now connects the city to the mainland was formed when Alexander the Great laid siege to the city in 332 B.C. His soldiers built a causeway from the mainland that transformed the island into the peninsula that exists today.

A Venetian merchant's bedroom reveals the wealth that commercial activities brought to leading citizens of most maritime societies.

diffusion and the migration of maritime peoples. Eventually all of these societies were conquered by agrarian societies and either destroyed or absorbed as subunits. This was not the end of overseas trade and commerce, of course, since these were important activities in most advanced agrarian societies. It was, however, a temporary end to societies in which this was the dominant form of economic activity.

Then, more than a thousand years later, there was a revival of maritime societies during the Middle Ages. Venice and Genoa are the best known, but there were others (e.g., Danzig and Lübeck in northern Europe). Later, the Netherlands became an important maritime society and during the seventeenth and eighteenth centuries apparently derived the major part of its income from overseas trade.[15] Britain moved far in this direction in the seventeenth, eighteenth, nineteenth, and early twentieth centuries but probably never quite reached the point where it depended more on overseas commerce than on, first, agriculture and, later, industry. Nevertheless, because of the great growth of overseas commerce, Britain acquired a number of the characteristics of maritime societies. Finally, in the twentieth century, Danzig for a time and, more recently, Singapore emerged as maritime societies.

In many ways maritime societies resembled advanced agrarian societies, particularly their urban centers. But there were also important differences. To begin with, most maritime societies were much smaller, often containing only a single city and the area immediately around it. Only two maritime societies, Carthage and the Netherlands, ever developed empires worthy of the name and, significantly, both of these were *overseas* empires.[16] In each case the empire was created more as an adjunct to commercial activity than as a political venture.

This curious feature is linked with another, more basic peculiarity of maritime societies. In a largely agrarian world in which monarchy was the normal—almost universal—form of government, maritime societies were usually republics. There were some monarchies among them, but this pattern was most likely to occur early in a maritime society's history, suggesting a carryover from a premaritime past.[17]

The explanation for the republican tendency in maritime societies seems to be that commerce, rather than warfare and the exploitation of peasant masses, was the chief interest of the governing class. Being less concerned than the typical agrarian state with conquest and the control of large peasant populations, these nations had less need for a strong, centralized, hierarchical government. An oligarchy of wealthy merchants could do the job, since their primary responsibilities would be to regulate commercial competition and to provide naval forces to defend their access to foreign ports.

Another peculiarity of maritime societies was their unusual system of values and incentives. As we saw in the last chapter, the governing class in agrarian societies typically viewed work of any kind as degrading. Since this was the class that all others looked up to and emulated, its view of economic activity rubbed off on the rest. This was especially evident in the case of merchants, who, when they became wealthy, usually gave up their commercial activities. As we noted, this antiwork ethic undoubtedly contributed to the slowdown in the rate of technological innovation and progress.

In maritime societies, in contrast, merchants were the dominant class, and a very different view of economic activity prevailed. Though more research is needed on the subject, there is reason to believe that maritime societies made disproportionate technological and economic contributions to the emergence of modern industrial societies. It is also significant that the rate of technological advance in *agrarian* societies appears to have been correlated with the social and political strength of their merchant class.[18] In other words, *the greater the social status and political influence of its merchants, the higher the rate of technological and economic innovation in preindustrial societies tended to be*. This suggests one possible explanation of the striking differences in levels of development of societies in our own era.

A BRIEF REVIEW: SOCIOCULTURAL EVOLUTION TO THE EVE OF THE INDUSTRIAL REVOLUTION

Now that we have completed our survey of the various types of preindustrial societies, we need to pause and briefly review the ground we have covered. In particular, we should consider how well the evidence we have examined conforms to ecological-evolutionary theory.

As we saw in Chapter 3, the central thesis of this theory is that subsistence technology is the key to societal growth and development, both for individual societies and for the world system of societies. Technological advance expands the limits of what is possible for a society and thereby improves its chances in the process of intersocietal selection. As a consequence, technological advance has also been the basic determinant of the patterns of sociocultural evolution in the world system.

Figure 3.5 suggests that this evolutionary process has generated a number of fundamental trends in the world system. These trends provide us with an excellent test of the validity of ecological-evolutionary theory as it applies to the experience of human societies through the first 99.9 percent of human history.

What exactly *had* happened with respect to each of those trends by the time the agrarian era was coming to a close?

Growth of Human Population   In the opinion of the experts, there were between 3 and 10 million people at the end of the hunting and gathering era (8000 B.C.). By the end of the agrarian era (1800 A.D.), there were nearly a billion (see Figure 8.1).

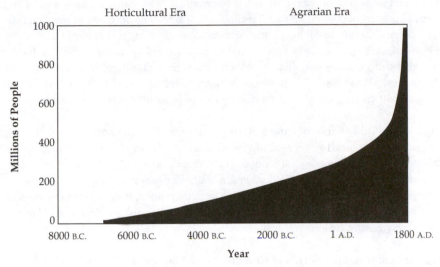

FIGURE 8.1 *World population 8000 B.C. to 1800 A.D.*

Growth in Average Size of Societies and Communities   At the end of the hunting and gathering era, the average size of both societies and communities appears to have been somewhere between 25 and 50. Although it is impossible to obtain reliable estimates of the average size of communities and societies for the entire world system at the end of the agrarian era, there is no doubt that both were substantially larger because by then there were so many horticultural, herding, maritime, and agrarian societies. We also know that, whereas the largest society prior to the horticultural era had no more than a few hundred members at most, by the end of the agrarian era there was one with 400 million, and a number with over 10 million.

Increased Permanence of Communities   Before the first fishing and horticultural societies appeared, nearly all human communities were nomadic. By the end of the agrarian era, only a small minority were nomadic.

Expansion of Societies into New Environments   Most of this trend occurred either before the end of the hunting and gathering era or during the industrial era. The horticultural and agrarian eras, however, did see greatly heightened activity in marine environments. By the end of the agrarian era, oceans, lakes, and rivers had become important both as sources of food and as trade routes.

Increasing Impact of Societies on the Biophysical Environment   Prior to the horticultural era, the most notable impact of human societies on the biophysical environment seems to have been their apparent extermination of numerous species of large mammals. Societies of the horticultural and agrarian eras had a far more profound effect on the physical landscape, clearing vast forests, damming rivers, irrigating arid areas, and mining an increasing variety of minerals.

Invention of New Symbol Systems   During the horticultural era, the first primitive record-keeping systems were invented. These were followed, during the agrarian era, by prealphabetic and eventually alphabetic systems of writing, numeral systems, measurement systems, systems of musical notation, and monetary systems.

Increasing Store of Technological Information   During the horticultural and agrarian eras, the store of technological information increased enormously, a fact amply attested to by the great growth of human population. Striking technological advances occurred in plant cultivation, animal domestication, metallurgy, construction, transportation, and communication. By the end of the agrarian era, societies knew how to produce enormous quantities of foods, fibers, and other things; move people and products over great distances; build monumental edifices of great durability; and inflict tremendous damage on one another, to cite but four of the more significant consequences of the expanded store of technological information.

Increasing Store of Other Kinds of Information   During the horticultural and agrarian eras, the store of nontechnological information increased dramatically. By the close of the agrarian era, many societies had amassed great amounts of political, economic, philosophical, ideological, historical, aesthetic, scientific, and other kinds of information. Much of this new information emerged as a by-product of the growing size and complexity of societies, a process that created new problems requiring new solutions and new information and that led to the emergence of new norms, beliefs, and values.

Growth in the Quantity, Diversity, and Complexity of Material Products   No brief summary can do justice to this trend, though there are many comparisons that provide dramatic illustrations. Compare, for example, the greatest structures created by advanced agrarian societies—cathedrals, temples, palaces—with the greatest created by the members of hunting and gathering societies—shelters made from rocks and branches as temporary protection for one or more families. More important, by the end of the agrarian era, human societies were providing the material necessities required to sustain 100 times more people than they had provided for at the end of the hunting and gathering era.

Increasing Complexity of Social Organization   In hunting and gathering societies, full-time occupational specialization was extremely rare, possibly nonexistent. The usual pattern was a division of labor by age and sex, with part-time specialization by a headman and/or a shaman. In agrarian and maritime societies, in contrast, occupational specialties numbered in the hundreds, and there was a complex division of labor that often involved specialization by communities and even regions. In hunting and gathering societies the only organized groups were families, whereas in agrarian societies there were separate communities, often organized into provinces, plus numerous specialized associations, especially religious, political, economic, and educational. Political and religious associations, in particular, were often extremely complex.

Increasing Inequality within and among Societies   In hunting and gathering societies, there were only minor status distinctions among individuals. The members of agrarian and maritime societies, however, were usually born into classes, which profoundly influenced their opportunities in life. Similarly, prior to the horticultural era, differences among societies were minimal; but by the end of the agrarian era, advanced agrarian and maritime societies were far wealthier and far more powerful than other societies in the world system.

Accelerating Rate of Social and Cultural Change   During the last 10,000 years of the hunting and gathering era, the rate of social and cultural change was greater than it had been prior to that time. But that could not compare with the increase in the rate of change in the next 10,000 years. Although there was a temporary slowing of the rate of technological innovation during the first part of the agrarian era, it accelerated again well before the end of the agrarian era, as shown in Figure 3.1 (page 54).

By 1800 A.D., near the close of the agrarian era, the patterns of human life had been dramatically altered for all but the few who still lived in hunting and gathering societies in remote areas. The vast majority of people were now living in either agrarian or advanced horticultural societies, with smaller numbers in simple horticultural, herding, maritime, and fishing societies. This was not, of course, a stable world system. The deadly process of intersocietal selection that had begun thousands of years earlier was still working to the disadvantage of the technologically less advanced. And every time advanced agrarian societies took another step forward, they tilted the balance a bit more in their favor and against the rest.

This was the human situation on the eve of the Industrial Revolution.

PART THREE

INDUSTRIAL SOCIETIES AND INDUSTRIALIZING SOCIETIES

9

The Industrial Revolution

Throughout much of the agrarian era, the rate of technological innovation was less than one would expect in view of the size of agrarian societies, the amount of information available to them, and the extent of contact among them. As we have seen, the cause of this lay in their highly exploitative social systems and in the ideologies that shaped their members' economic attitudes and activities. Not surprisingly, these had *negative feedback effects* on both technological innovation and economic development.

Late in the agrarian era, however, the rate of innovation in western Europe increased substantially within a relatively short period of time, and by the latter part of the eighteenth century the Industrial Revolution was well under way. Not long thereafter, England became the first truly industrial society—that is, the first society to derive more than half of its income from productive activities involving machines powered by inanimate energy sources. With this, a new era of far more rapid and pervasive social and cultural change was launched.

What was responsible for this important development? What happened to break the agrarian mold and produce this burst of technological innovation in societies that had been so resistant to change? What happened, in other words, to turn the system of negative feedback into a system of *positive* feedback?

CAUSES OF THE INDUSTRIAL REVOLUTION

The Accumulation of Information in the Agrarian Era

Probably the least heralded of the major causes of the Industrial Revolution was the gradual accumulation of technological information throughout the agrarian era. For despite the slowdown in the *rate* of innovation, discoveries and inventions did not cease. Evidence of significant advances can be found in agriculture, mining, metallurgy, transportation, construction, and various other fields.[1] Advances in construction and engineering, for example, can still be traced if one compares the churches and cathedrals built in western Europe in successive centuries. As a result of many such advances, the store of technological information available in the eighteenth century was far greater than in the thirteenth, just as it had been far greater in the thirteenth century than in the eighth. This enormous store of information held obvious potential for an increase in the rate of technological innovation when other conditions within societies became favorable.

Late in the sixteenth century, during the reign of Queen Elizabeth I, the noted English philosopher and statesman Francis Bacon wrote that three inventions "had changed the whole face and state of things throughout the world"—the mariner's compass, the printing press, and gunpowder.[2] He was right: the world, especially his part of it, had already changed significantly because of these inventions, and the pace of change in western Europe was quickening. Bacon was more insightful than most of his contemporaries in recognizing the importance of technological innovation. But even someone as observant as he could not conceive of the vastly greater changes yet to come, since the first modest stirrings of the Industrial Revolution still lay more than a century in the future.

Advances in Water Transportation and the Conquest of the New World

As Bacon perceived, some innovations of the late agrarian era were more important for societal change than others. Those with a potential for altering agrarian social structure and ideology were most important of all, and in this respect, improvements in ships and navigation proved to be some of the most critical.

Prior to the introduction of the compass in Europe, late in the twelfth century, navigation beyond the sight of land was so hazardous that it was undertaken only for short distances or in familiar areas, as in crossing the English Channel or the Mediterranean Sea. Acquisition of the compass was followed over the next several centuries by a series of important advances in the technology of shipbuilding. These included the invention of the stern rudder (which replaced steering oars attached to the sides of ships), the construction of larger ships with multiple masts, the substitution of several smaller sails for a single large sail on each mast, and a reduction in the width of ships relative to their length.[3] All of these innovations made ships more responsive and more manageable, and therefore safer on stormy seas.

With such ships at their command, and with the compass to guide them, western European sailors increasingly ventured out into open seas for extended periods. During the fifteenth century they began a series of voyages intended to find new trade routes to India and China that would enable Europeans to bypass the merchants of the Middle East. Instead, of course, they "discovered" the New World and quickly subdued it. Less than fifty years after Columbus first set foot in America, Spain had conquered the two most powerful societies in the New World, the Incan empire in Peru and the Aztec empire in Mexico.*

Almost immediately the conquerors began to ship vast quantities of gold and silver back to Europe. This had a number of consequences, one of which was a tremendous growth in the money economy and a decline in the older barter system.[4] Although money had been used for more than 2,000 years, the supply of precious metals remained so limited that many payments were still made in goods rather than in cash—especially in rural areas, but by no means only there. This situation seriously hindered economic and technological advance, because an economy that operates on the basis of barter is not flexible and the flow of resources from areas of oversupply to areas of short supply is sluggish. Furthermore, it is difficult to determine what is economically most advantageous in a barter system. When money is used, it is much easier for people to calculate their costs and incomes and thus determine which of the alternatives open to them is likely to yield the greatest profit.

Money is extremely important in breaking down barriers to technological innovation. In societies where technological progress has been halting and uncertain for centuries and where there is no efficient accounting system, people with money are reluctant to invest in new and unproven enterprises. Also, where money is scarce, people tend to state obligations (e.g., wages, rents, debts) in relatively inflexible and traditional terms, which makes the economy unresponsive to changing conditions and new opportunities. But all of this began to change in western Europe during the sixteenth and seventeenth centuries in response to the flow of precious metals from the New World.

---

*Despite the undeniable impact of gunpowder on world history, that invention, unlike the compass and printing press, was not a significant cause of the Industrial Revolution. In fact, in the conquest of the New World, the decimation of native populations by diseases brought from Europe (e.g., smallpox, measles), and to which these populations had never developed immunity, appears to have been of much greater importance than European arms.

This influx of gold and silver had a second important effect: it produced inflation.[5] This was a natural consequence of the greatly increased supply of money combined with a much more limited increase in the supply of goods. Prices doubled, tripled, even quadrupled within a century. As is always the case when this happens, some people prospered and some were hurt. In general, those with fixed incomes, especially the landed aristocracy, were hurt, while merchants and entrepreneurs tended to benefit. This meant a marked improvement in the position of merchants relative to the governing class. More of the economic resources of European societies wound up in the hands of people who were interested in, and knew something about, both economics and technology. More than that, *these were people oriented to rational profit making (not a typical orientation in agrarian societies) and therefore motivated to provide financial support for technological innovations that would increase the efficiency of people and machines.* The rise in prices in the sixteenth century was simultaneously a stimulant to feverish enterprise and an acid dissolving traditional relationships.[6]

The benefits to Europe from the discovery of the New World were even greater in the eighteenth and nineteenth centuries than they had been earlier. As the population of European colonists increased, so did opportunities for trade. The colonists provided a growing market for Europe's manufactured goods and paid for them with a swelling flood of cheap and abundant raw materials.[7] Between 1698 and 1775, Britain's trade with its colonies increased more than fivefold,[8] and that was only the beginning. As a result, *the center of world trade shifted for the first time in more than 5,000 years, as western Europe replaced the Middle East in the favored position.*

Looking backward, it is difficult to exaggerate the importance of the discovery and conquest of the New World, with respect both to the rise of European power in the world system of societies and to the subsequent occurrence of the Industrial Revolution. Suddenly, a handful of relatively small societies had access to an enormous treasure house of resources. In addition to the gold and silver, western European societies quickly gained control over vast territories whose forests were a source of great quantities of cheap lumber and, when cleared, provided seemingly endless acres of rich farmland. Contact with the native peoples of the Americas also provided Europeans with information about new plants—especially corn and potatoes—that became valuable new food resources. Never before in history had technologically advanced societies enjoyed such a favorable ratio of resources to population. It was almost as though a new Garden of Eden had been created, but for the benefit of a favored few.

The Printing Press and the Spread of Information

The printing press was another technological innovation that played an important role in helping western European societies break the traditional agrarian mold. Printing sped the dissemination of both new technological and new ideological information, and thus was a major factor in overcoming resistance to innovation and change.[9]

Printing apparently originated in China about the fifth century A.D.[10] This early method of printing was extremely expensive, however, because it required a highly skilled craftsman to engrave the contents of every page on a separate block of wood. As a result, printed materials remained a luxury until Johann Gutenberg, a goldsmith and engraver, invented a system of movable type in the middle of the fifteenth century.*[11] Thus, the expense of skilled engraving was eliminated from printing, except in the manufacture of the type (i.e., letters and other symbols), which could be combined in various ways and used over and over again.

---

*Gutenberg's key achievement was the development of a system for manufacturing, and printing with, interchangeable *letters*. Centuries earlier the Chinese had developed and used movable type, but it did not have the impact of Gutenberg's invention because written Chinese is based on ideograms rather than letters. Thus, it requires tens and even hundreds of thousands of unique characters to communicate what European languages, based on the Roman alphabet, can convey with various arrangements of twenty-six letters.[12]

Gutenberg's invention resulted in a tremendous increase in the quantity of printed materials in western Europe. In medieval monasteries, it took ten to fifteen years to produce a single copy of the Bible using traditional methods. It is not surprising, therefore, that before Gutenberg, books in Europe numbered in the *thousands*. In fact it is quite likely that more books were printed in the first fifty years after the invention of the printing press than all the scribes of Europe had produced in the previous thousand years, and by 1500 A.D. there were more than 10 *million* printed books.[13] Among the materials that achieved wider circulation were treatises on the new scientific theories of men like Copernicus and Galileo in the sixteenth and seventeenth centuries and books on farming that revolutionized English agriculture in the eighteenth. One of the most significant applications of the printing press, however, occurred less than a century after its invention, when it was used to spread the teachings of the Protestant reformers. Historians today regard the printing press as a major factor in the success of the Protestant movement.[14]

As many scholars have observed, a number of the new Protestant doctrines substantially altered the thinking of many members of agrarian societies in ways that were conducive to economic and other kinds of change.[15] In the first place, the reformers taught that work is an important form of service to God. Martin Luther, for example, insisted that all honest forms of work are as truly Christian callings as the ministry or priesthood. This challenged both the medieval Catholic view of work as a punishment for sin and the traditional aristocratic view of work as degrading and beneath the dignity of a gentleman. At the same time, it supported the efforts of merchants and craftsmen to upgrade their status. Second, the new Protestant faiths undermined fatalism and trust in magic and, in the long run, stimulated the spread of rationalism. Though the reformers dealt with these things only in the area of religion—and even there imperfectly—they strengthened a trend that ultimately had far-reaching consequences.[16] Some branches of Protestantism, for example, encouraged their adherents to plan their lives rather than merely live from day to day, as the name "Methodism" reminds us. Third, many of the newer Protestant faiths emphasized the value of denying the pleasures of this world and living frugally, a practice that enabled those who became economically successful to accumulate capital.

To the extent that people followed these teachings, they developed a new outlook on life: they worked harder, acted more rationally, and lived more thriftily. In short, the Reformation remolded the attitudes, beliefs, and values of countless people in ways that undermined the traditional agrarian economy and stimulated economic and technological innovation. Related to this, certain branches of Protestantism, notably Calvinism, elevated the activities of merchants and businessmen to a status they had not previously enjoyed in any agrarian society. As one scholar has noted, this was not surprising in a faith which had its headquarters in Geneva and its most influential adherents in other leading business centers, such as London, Antwerp, and Amsterdam.[17]

Protestantism was also important to economic development because of the insistence of the reformers that people should be able to read the Bible for themselves and thus have direct access to God's Word. This meant that literacy assumed a new significance in societies that became Protestant: it became a religious obligation for the masses rather than an option for elites. But while the initial motivation for the spread of literacy among the masses was religious, its most important long-term effects were broader. More literate populations proved to be more innovative and creative than their less literate competitors, and societies that encouraged literacy at an early date gained an important advantage over other societies in the developmental process.[18]

In summary, it seems more than coincidence that the Industrial Revolution had its beginnings in predominantly Protestant nations. The new Protestant ideology, like the conquest of the New World, undermined belief systems and social structures that had been formidable barriers to innovation and change. Above all, it encouraged a new respect for work and rational planning and discouraged both fatalism and reliance on magic. But it is important to recognize that the success of the Reformation movement and its influence on the subsequent course of European history were due in no small measure to prior changes in technology and economics and to the discovery and conquest of the New World with its vast treasure of natural resources. The latter development was especially important because it enabled many of those who adopted the Protestant work ethic to prosper to a degree that otherwise would not have been possible, thereby confirming the validity of the new ethic and reinforcing it. In short, the Protestant Reformation was an important link in the chain of causation that led to the Industrial Revolution, even if it was not the critical link that some have suggested.

Advances in Agriculture

Throughout the agrarian era, the chief restraint on societal growth and development was the state of agricultural technology. The rural elite, so long as it managed to extract a surplus sufficient to maintain its customary lifestyle, was content to preserve the status quo. And the peasants, so long as they managed simply to survive, were content to follow the practices inherited from their forebears—or if not content, at least not motivated to change them. Thus agriculture, which was the basis of the economic surplus, remained largely the same from one century to the next.

In the sixteenth century, however, the situation began to change in much of western Europe.[19] The growth of trade, the increased use of money, and, above all, inflation began to undermine the traditional agrarian system. On the one hand, a growing number of large landowners found that, as transportation costs declined in the wake of advances in shipping, markets for certain farm commodities (e.g., wool, grain) expanded. On the other hand, the effects of inflation were threatening the profitability of their farms, which depended on rents and other obligations that had been established long before the rise in prices. Many landowners realized that if they hoped to maintain their traditional standard of living under the new economic conditions, they had to try something new. Some of them therefore brought new land under cultivation by draining swamps, or by enclosing for their own private use what had previously been "common land," pastures available to both peasants and elites. Other landowners turned to raising sheep in an effort to benefit from the growing trade in wool. Still others eliminated traditional modes of payment by which tenants paid their landlords through customary services or with goods or produce, and began to require instead payments of money, which had become more important in economic relationships and which could more easily be adjusted to take account of inflation. Thus, during the sixteenth and seventeenth centuries, agriculture in Europe, and particularly in England, gradually became more profit-oriented and capitalistic and less governed by tradition and custom.

Then, in the eighteenth century, a new wave of inflation hit western Europe, and landowners were again faced with a choice between innovation and a declining standard of living.[20] In England, where the traditional system of agriculture had already been seriously weakened, a number of other important innovations were adopted. Early in the century, for example, one landowner devised a system of crop rotation that enabled farmers to keep all of their land continuously under cultivation; previously, farmers had to leave land fallow, or uncultivated, one year in four in order to restore its fertility. A little later another landowner discovered the principle of selective breeding, simultaneously making a fortune for himself from his stud farm and greatly improving the quality of British livestock. Other members of the rural elite invented a variety of simple machines that increased the efficiency of farm labor, while still others published books expounding the new techniques. The practice of enclosing common lands, meanwhile, continued.

By the end of the eighteenth century, the traditional system of agriculture had been replaced in most of England by a new system of larger, more efficient farms operated on rational and capitalistic principles. But the adoption of this new system meant the massive displacement of many poor rural families whose labor was no longer needed and whose right to common lands was no longer protected by tradition. Some of these people migrated to the new frontier societies overseas. Many others, however, migrated to the cities and towns, where they became a source of cheap labor in the mills and factories that were beginning to appear.

A Model of the Causes of the Industrial Revolution

Figure 9.1 summarizes the principal causes of the Industrial Revolution. As the model indicates, *the basic cause was the growing store of technological information in the latter part of the agrarian era*. Advances in navigation and shipbuilding were especially important because, without them, the societies of western Europe could not have won control of the resources of two vast continents. This revolutionary development, abetted by the success of the Protestant Reformation, led to changes in economics, social organization, and ideology which made it possible for these societies to break the historic agrarian mold. Because of this, the longtime agrarian pattern of negative feedback from social organization and ideology to technology was transformed into a positive one, thereby freeing creative forces that had been curbed for centuries.

It is interesting to note that England, the first society to become industrialized, experienced significant change in several of the factors that are primarily responsible for shaping a society's development. Its environment was drastically altered through the discovery and conquest of the New World, and its store of both technological and ideological information underwent substantial change in the sixteenth, seventeenth, and eighteenth centuries. These developments combined to produce major changes in the processes of innovation and selection. These developments will also provide us with useful clues when, in a later chapter, we ponder the question of why societies trying to industrialize today find it so much more difficult than did the societies that industrialized a hundred years or more earlier.

FIGURE 9.1 *Model of the causes of the Industrial Revolution in western Europe.*

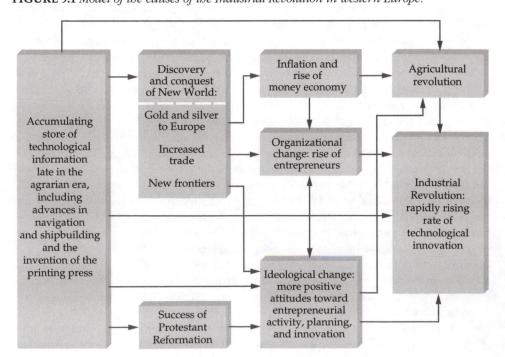

A BRIEF HISTORY OF THE INDUSTRIAL REVOLUTION

Before the end of the nineteenth century, economic historians were already beginning to use the term "Industrial Revolution" to refer to the series of dramatic technological and economic innovations that occurred in England during the period from about 1760 to 1830. In their view, the mechanization of the textile industry; the technical advances in, and expansion of, the iron industry; the harnessing of steam power, the establishment of the factory system; and other, related developments of that period had transformed English society. What was still essentially an agrarian society in the middle of the eighteenth century had become an industrial society by the middle of the nineteenth.

The time limits that early writers assigned to the Industrial Revolution are now widely questioned. Most scholars today believe it is a mistake to put a terminal date on a revolution that is still continuing.[21] Others argue that 1760 is too late a starting date, since the acceleration in industrial activity began not in the middle of the eighteenth century but in the middle of the sixteenth or earlier.[22]

There is some merit in both criticisms. The rate of technological advance did, in fact, begin to accelerate long before 1760, as we have seen. But it does not follow that we should treat those earlier developments as part of the Industrial Revolution. To be meaningful, this term should be limited to *the period during which the productive activities of societies were rapidly transformed by the invention of a succession of machines powered by newer, inanimate sources of energy, such as coal, electricity, petroleum, and natural gas.* Using this criterion, we cannot put the start of the Industrial Revolution much, if any, before the middle of the eighteenth century.

The other criticism of the dates is sounder: the Industrial Revolution definitely was not over by 1830. Only its first phase ended at that time. Subsequently, there have been three other phases, and each has contributed substantially to the importance of industrial activity in the societies involved, and to their transformation.

We cannot assign precise dates to these phases, since they are all rather arbitrary divisions in what has been essentially a continuous process of development. However, by organizing our review in terms of phases, we can see more clearly the progression of events. In the first phase, which began in mid-eighteenth-century England, the revolution was concentrated in the textile, iron, and coal industries, and the invention of the first true steam engine was the most important innovation. The second phase got its start in the middle of the nineteenth century and involved rapid growth in the railroad industry, the mass production of steel, the replacement of sailing ships by steamships, and use of the new technology in agriculture. Around the turn of the century, the Industrial Revolution entered a third phase, with rapid growth in the automobile, electrical, telephone, and petroleum industries. World War II marked the beginning of a fourth phase, distinguished by remarkable developments in aviation, aluminum, electronics, plastics, nuclear power, computers, and automation.

These four phases should not be thought of as stages that each society must pass through to become industrialized. On the contrary, many societies in recent decades have skipped over certain phases, or at least parts of them, and combined elements from different phases. For example, a Third World nation today often develops its railway, highway, and air transportation systems simultaneously. But a review of the way things happened *initially* enables us to see how one innovation often made further innovations possible, even imperative.

First Phase

The first phase of the Industrial Revolution, as we noted, began in the middle of the eighteenth century and lasted about a hundred years. Geographically, it was centered in England.

James Hargreave's spinning jenny.

Many of the best known innovations occurred in the textile industry and were of two kinds: machines that increased the efficiency of human labor, and machines that harnessed new sources of energy. The flying shuttle is a good example of the first—and a good example, too, of the way one invention stimulated others. Because it enabled one weaver to do the work formerly done by two, spinners could no longer keep up with the demand for yarn. This disruption of the traditional balance between spinning and weaving triggered a succession of further inventions. First, the traditional spinning wheel was replaced by the spinning jenny, which enabled a worker to spin 4 threads simultaneously and, after a number of modifications, 120 threads. But although the spinning jenny was a tremendous improvement from the standpoint of speed, its yarn was so coarse and loose that flax had to be mixed in with the cotton to produce a satisfactory fiber. This was remedied with the water frame, a machine that could satisfactorily spin pure cotton, and later with the spinning mule, whose cotton threads were stronger and finer. All of these advances in spinning reversed the earlier situation: now weaving was the bottleneck in the industry—until a new series of innovations in weaving machines helped restore the balance once again.

By the end of the eighteenth century, the new looms had become so large and heavy that they were almost impossible to operate. To work the treadle even at a slow speed required two powerful men—and they had to be relieved after a short time.[23] This led to a search for alternative sources of power. One possibility was waterpower, which had already been used for a variety of purposes for centuries.[24] But England was poorly supplied with suitable streams and rivers, and the wheels and troughs used in water systems were extremely inefficient.[25] Eventually, James Watt developed the first true steam engine,[26] a source of power that could be employed anywhere, and by the end of the century it had been adapted for use in the textile industry.

The net effect of these innovations was such a rapid expansion of the British textile industry that between 1770 and 1845 its contribution to the national income increased more than fivefold.[27] This was an extraordinary rate of growth by the standards of traditional agrarian societies. The actual increase in production was even larger, since per unit costs of production dropped considerably during this period.

One of the immediate consequences of advances in textile production was *the creation of the factory system*. Prior to the Industrial Revolution, and even during its early years, spinning and weaving were cottage industries. Entrepreneurs provided the raw materials, and poor families, working in their own homes and using their own spinning wheels and looms, provided the labor. But after heavier and more expensive machines came to be used, this arrangement was impossible: families could neither afford the new equipment nor power it. Businessmen were forced to buy their own machines, construct buildings to house them, and provide engines to run them, thereby creating the factory system that has become such a prominent feature of modern industrial societies.

Iron was another industry that expanded greatly during the first phase of the Industrial Revolution. Despite increasing demand for iron by both the textile industry and the military, technical difficulties greatly restricted its manufacture until late in the eighteenth century. One problem was England's growing shortage of wood, which was used to make charcoal for smelting and refining. This problem had been partially solved earlier in the century, when it was found that coke (derived from coal) could be substituted for charcoal, at least in the smelting process. But a serious bottleneck remained. Because it is hard and brittle, pig iron must be converted into wrought, or malleable, iron before it can be used for most purposes. This process required charcoal and was very time-consuming until the traditional forge was replaced by the newly invented coal-fired blast furnace. These innovations opened the way for rapid expansion: in 1788, England produced only 68,000 tons of iron; by 1845, it produced twenty-four times that.[28] The new blast furnaces also made it possible to perform all the processes of iron making in a single establishment. Thus, the factory system spread from the textile industry to the iron industry.

Between them, the iron industry and the steam engine substantially increased the demand for coal. At the same time, the steam engine helped alleviate the ancient problem of flooding in coal mines by providing a source of power to pump out the water that constantly seeped into shafts and tunnels. The growth of the coal industry, though not quite so dramatic as that of the iron industry, was still impressive: in 1760, Britain produced barely 5 million tons; by 1845, the figure had risen over ninefold.[29]

No discussion of developments in this period would be complete without mention of the machine-tool industry. Although never as large or financially important as the textile, iron, and coal industries, it was crucial for technological progress because it produced the increasingly complex industrial machinery. This industry, which began undramatically with the invention of the first practical lathe, was soon producing machines capable of precision work to the thousandth of an inch.[30] For many years a single tool was used for drilling, boring, grinding, and milling; but special tools were gradually designed for each operation.

Another striking advance in the eighteenth century was the production of machines with interchangeable parts. This greatly facilitated industrial growth, since damage to one part of a complex machine no longer meant that the entire machine had to be discarded or a new part specially made. Spare parts could now be kept on hand and replacements made on the spot by mechanics with limited skills and equipment.

During this initial phase of the Industrial Revolution, shortly after 1800, Britain became the first nation in which machine-based industry replaced agriculture as the most important economic activity, and thus the first industrial society.[31] The United States would not reach this point until about 1870.[32]

Second Phase

The second phase of the Industrial Revolution began in the middle decades of the nineteenth century. Expansion continued at a rapid pace in the textile, iron, and coal industries, but now there were breakthroughs in a number of others as well. By the end of the century industrialization had occurred in most segments of the British economy. Meanwhile, the Industrial Revolution began to make significant headway in several other countries of northwestern Europe and in the United States.

One of the most important developments during this phase was the application of the steam engine to transportation, something inventors had been trying to accomplish for decades. By 1850 most of England was linked together by a network of railroads.[33] The results were tremendous: the greatly reduced cost of moving goods by rail led to a significant reduction in the price of most heavy bulk commodities, and this in turn led to greater demand. In addition, railroads helped break down local monopolies and oligopolies (i.e., markets with only a few sellers), and this increased competition and further lowered prices. Thus, England gradually became a single giant market for a growing number of commodities, a development destined to have far-reaching consequences.

Even before the steam engine was adapted to land transportation, it had been used on water. For many years, however, steamships were limited to coastal and river shipping, both because inefficient engines made it impossible to bunker enough wood or coal for long voyages and because paddle wheels worked poorly in high seas. Then, in only a few decades, several things happened. More-efficient compound engines substantially reduced the amount of fuel required; iron and steel began to replace wood in ship construction, permitting longer and larger vessels with greater carrying capacity (the upper limit in length for wooden ships was only about 300 feet); and the screw propeller replaced the cumbersome and easily damaged paddle wheel.[34] After this, steamships increased so rapidly that by 1893 steam tonnage exceeded sailing tonnage worldwide.

In the iron industry, meanwhile, a way was finally found to produce steel cheaply and in large quantities, making it available for many new purposes.[35] Between 1845 and the early 1880s, Britain's production of iron and steel increased more than fivefold.[36] This meant that in less than a century, from 1788 to the early 1880s, the increase was a hundredfold, and the quality of the product was vastly improved.

The tremendous growth in railroads and steamships and the expansion of the iron industry all combined to increase the demand for coal. Though there were no spectacular breakthroughs in mining techniques, improvements in engines and in the quality of steel tools pushed production up fivefold.[37]

A number of new industries emerged in addition to the railroads, none as important at the time, but some destined to surpass them later on. The rubber industry developed after Charles Goodyear discovered the technique of vulcanization, which prevented rubber goods from becoming sticky in hot weather, stiff and brittle in cold. About the same time, Samuel Morse and several others invented the telegraph, and this quickly became the basis of another new industry. Then, in the 1860s, the electric dynamo was invented, and the door was opened to the use of electricity in industry. A second critical development in this field, the invention of the transformer, helped alleviate one of the greatest impediments to the use of electricity: the loss of energy during long-distance transmission. The petroleum industry also got its start in these years, chiefly by providing a substitute for whale oil in lighting homes.

The Industrial Revolution began to have an impact even on agriculture, through improved equipment (e.g., sturdier steel plows), new kinds of machines (e.g., threshing machines, mowers, reapers, steam plows), and synthetic fertilizers from the growing chemical industry. The result was a substantial increase in productivity. In Germany, for example, production per acre rose 50 percent in only twenty-five years. In the United States, the number of hours required to produce a given amount of corn and wheat was cut in half between 1840 and 1900.[38]

An important organizational innovation in this second phase of the Industrial Revolution was the *multidivisional enterprise with a hierarchy of salaried managers*.[39] This occurred first in the new railroad, steamship, and telegraph industries, all of which required workers in widely scattered locations. No longer was it possible for a single family to fill all or even most of the managerial positions needed to supervise employees and coordinate their activities: hired personnel had to assume this responsibility. This was an important step in the development of the modern corporation.

Another spur in this direction was the great quantity of new material products that had become available to the members of society. As further advances in production and transportation continued to lower the cost of goods and increase the demand for them, the sheer volume of sales made it impossible for the owners of some businesses to oversee all of the transactions. For example, around the turn of the century, Sears, Roebuck was processing 100,000 orders a day, more than any merchant of an earlier generation would have handled in a lifetime.[40] As sales increased, so did the number of retail outlets in a wide variety of businesses, each requiring a local manager at first, and eventually intermediate layers of management.

Throughout this period, industrialization was spreading rapidly in northwest Europe and North America. Before the century closed, Britain had lost its position of economic and technological dominance. The iron and steel industry illustrates the trend: although Britain nearly doubled its production of pig iron between 1865 and 1900, its share of the world market dropped from 54 to 23 percent.[41] Its chief rivals were the United States and Germany, whose respective shares rose from 9 to 35 percent and from 10 to 19 percent.

As these figures indicate, though industrialization was spreading, it was still largely limited to a few countries. The United States, Britain, Germany, and France, for example, produced 84 percent of the world's iron in 1900. A similar picture emerges when we look at national shares of all manufacturing activity. In 1888, the percentages are estimated to have been as follows:[42]

United States	32 percent
Britain	18 percent
Germany	13 percent
France	11 percent
All other countries	26 percent

The fact that "all other countries" contributed more to all types of manufacturing than to iron production indicates that the new technology spread faster in light industries, such as textiles, than in heavy industries. This was because light industries required less capital and because the rate of innovation in them had slowed considerably, thus reducing the need for highly skilled and innovative personnel.

The last factor points to a final characteristic of this phase of the Industrial Revolution: a growing dependence on science and engineering. Before 1850 most of the major advances were made by simple craftsmen or gentlemen amateurs. After that date, key inventions came primarily from people with formal technical or scientific training. This was especially true in the chemical industry, but it was evident in others as well.

Finally, near the end of the nineteenth century, the innovative process began to be institutionalized, and laboratories were built to enable teams of trained people to work together to solve technical problems.[43] The laboratories established by Thomas Edison exemplified the new trend, and the successes he and others achieved led many to emulate them, especially in Germany and the United States. These developments also contributed to the growth of scientific study in universities, to the training of engineers, and to increasing cooperation between innovative industries and institutions of higher education. Most of these developments did not come to full flower, however, until the third and fourth phases of the Industrial Revolution.

Third Phase

Early in the twentieth century, the Industrial Revolution entered a new phase that involved the rapid spread of important new technologies in the fields of transportation and communication as well as new technologies for harnessing energy and creating synthetic materials. These developments largely resulted from various inventions and discoveries of the late nineteenth century, especially the internal combustion engine, the telephone, the radio, moving pictures, the electrical generator, and plastics, each of which subsequently transformed the lives of hundreds of millions of people.

One of the most important developments was the enormous expansion of the automobile industry. In 1900, barely 20,000 cars were produced worldwide, but by midcentury, production totaled 8 million.[44]

The auto industry's rapid growth had a profound impact on a number of other industries as well. On the eve of World War II, for example, the manufacture of cars in the United States was consuming 20 percent of the nation's steel, 54 percent of its malleable iron, 73 percent of its plate glass, and 80 percent of its rubber.[45] More striking yet, 90 percent of the nation's gasoline was being consumed by automobiles, a development that was largely responsible for the thirteenfold increase in petroleum production between 1900 and 1940.[46]

In the field of communications, technological change transformed the economy and daily life in other ways. By midcentury, telephones and radios had become standard items in tens of millions of households in industrial societies, and movies had become a commonplace experience in the lives of most individuals. Once again, it is hard to exaggerate the impact of these technologies on industrial societies and, in the case of radio and movies, their impact on the beliefs and values of vast numbers of people.

These and other important developments were made possible by the rapid expansion of the electrical industry. Between 1900 and 1950, world capacity to produce electricity increased 100-fold.[47] With the availability of inexpensive electric power, electric lights replaced gaslights and candles in the vast majority of households, and electricity came increasingly to be used to power household appliances ranging from refrigerators and vacuum cleaners to radios and toasters. Industrial uses of electrical power also grew enormously.

During the third phase of the Industrial Revolution, technology came to play an increasingly important role in warfare. Tanks and other motorized vehicles replaced the cavalry, while aircraft added a radically new component to military operations. Meanwhile, newly developed weapons systems—such as poison gas, germ warfare, and nuclear weapons—although never employed to their full potential, added fearful and deadly new elements to the arsenals of many nations.

No previous war depended as heavily on industrial production as World War II, and all of the nations involved extended themselves to increase their output of military supplies. Because of the importance of aircraft, the aviation industry received a tremendous stimulus. In the United States, for example, the production of planes rose from 3,600 in 1938 to more than 96,000 in 1944.[48] Although the manufacture of aircraft dropped off substantially after the war ended, the air transport industry (both passenger and cargo) began an explosive growth that continues to the present day.

During the third phase of the Industrial Revolution, as during the second, industrial technology spread to new parts of the world, leading to changes in the relative ranking of nations in economic terms. While the United States continued to be the leader, producing a third of the world's industrial output, Britain, Germany, and France lost ground relatively (see Table 9.1) despite substantial growth in absolute terms. In contrast, important gains were registered by Japan and a number of other nations.

TABLE 9.1 Percentage Distribution of World Industrial Output (Excluding Handicrafts), in 1888 and 1937, by Society

Society	1888	1937
United States	32	34
United Kingdom	18	10
Germany	13	11
France	11	5
Russia	8	10
Japan	No data	4
All others	17	26

Source: Calculated from W. S. Woytinsky and E. S. Woytinsky, *World Population and Production: Trends and Outlook* (New York: Twentieth Century Fund, 1953), pp. 1003–1004.

Fourth Phase

The most recent phase in the Industrial Revolution is commonly referred to as "the information age," because it has revolutionized access to information in many forms. It began in the 1950s as the television industry began its explosive growth. By 1960, 87 percent of American homes had television sets, and some even had multiple sets.[49] Today, TV sets are standard equipment in nearly every household in industrial societies and in ever increasing numbers of industrializing Third World societies.

Television has revolutionized human experience to a degree that few other innovations have equaled. It has enabled hundreds of millions of ordinary people to see and vicariously experience in their homes all manner of things far outside the range of normal everyday experience. They can, for example, "travel" to remote parts of the globe and observe at close range and in complete safety and comfort the lives of jungle animals and undersea creatures, erupting volcanoes and other natural disasters, and close-up views of the surface of the moon and Mars. They can also watch their political leaders debate alternative policies or witness the ravages of wars in distant areas.

Unfortunately, television, like the movies, often provides a grossly distorted view of society by focusing on deviant and unrepresentative lifestyles and behavior. Violence in all its manifestations is portrayed with extraordinary frequency. For example, during a recent four-year period, in which the homicide rate in American society dropped 20 percent, coverage of murders on the major TV network evening news shows increased 721 percent.[50]

Television and the movies put enormous power in the hands of the tiny and largely invisible elite who control the content of what the public sees. It gives them the power to manipulate and transform the values, beliefs, and ultimately the actions of vast numbers of people.* In recent years, television has increasingly set the agenda for politicians in the United States and elsewhere. By supplying dramatic and heartrending visual images of suffering in remote regions, television newscasters have on several occasions successfully pressured western political leaders to intervene in military conflicts where their own nations' interests were minimally involved (e.g., Somalia, Bosnia, Liberia).

The second major invention of the information age has been the computer. The first computers were huge, bulky machines with only the most limited capabilities. It was not until tiny transistors loaded on silicon chips were substituted for vacuum tubes that computers began to be the extraordinarily useful machines we know today.**

Not only are transistors far smaller than vacuum tubes, but they have paved the way for a fantastic continuing process of miniaturization and power saving. As recently as 1971, the best silicon chip contained only 2,300 transistors; today, the Pentium 4 chip contains 42 million, and experts say that it is now possible to crowd billions onto a single chip.[52]

This amazing process of miniaturization began in large measure because of the American space program of the 1960s. New rocket engines had made it possible for the first time for

---

*Advertising provides the most obvious example of this, but more subtle instances can be found in the programs themselves and in movies where potentially dangerous or harmful activities are portrayed in a positive light and without any indication of the risks involved (e.g., smoking/lung cancer and emphysema, casual sex/sexually transmitted diseases and unwanted pregnancies, drug use/drug addiction and its consequences).

In recent years, the potential for media manipulation has increased greatly as computers have made it possible to create images of actual people saying and doing things they never said or did, and the images are so realistic that it is impossible for viewers to tell that they are merely creations of some unseen image-meister. In the movie *Contact,* for example, this new technology was used to create the appearance of President Clinton holding a press conference to discuss contact with aliens from outer space. The political dangers of misuse of this new technology are hard to exaggerate.

**The first general-purpose digital computer, *ENIAC* (electronic numerical integrator and computer), occupied 1,500 square feet, weighed 30 tons, had no storage memory, and could perform only 5 *thousand* additions per second. By contrast, a notebook computer with a Pentium 4 chip can be held in one's hands, weighs only a few pounds, stores millions of bytes of information, and can perform more than a billion additions per second.[51]

The first general purpose electronic digital computer (ENIAC) was a massive piece of equipment weighing thirty tons and occupying an entire room, had no storage memory, and could perform only 5 thousand additions per second. By contrast, a notebook computer with a Pentium 4 chip can be held in one's hands, weighs only a few pounds, stores millions of bytes of information, and can perform more than a billion additions per second.

engineers to build spacecraft capable of escaping Earth's gravitational pull, but even these powerful engines could carry only a small payload. Weight reduction was imperative, and the miniaturization of equipment of every kind, including computers, was one of the more obvious solutions.

Today, transistors are essential parts of everyday life. In addition to computers, they are the electronic brains in tens of millions of cars, jets, television sets, toys, cameras, wristwatches, faxes, cellular phones, radios, musical instruments, and countless other devices.

Computers have transformed the world of work, creating and storing the countless files and records on which businesses and governments depend. Even farming, that most traditional of occupations, is becoming computerized. Dairy farmers now monitor with electronic sensors linked to computers roughly half of the dairy cows in the United States. These systems make it possible for them to record and analyze data on the health, food intake, weight, and other vital signs of each and every cow.[53]

Recently, the Internet has vastly expanded the reach of the information age. By means of a single computer in one's home, one can gain direct and almost instant access to an incredible variety of information ranging from the entire contents of encyclopedias to the latest quotations from stock markets around the world, and one can communicate with people worldwide.

These new technologies of the information age are not the only developments of importance in recent decades. New materials technologies have made a wide range of useful and inexpensive new fabrics available (e.g., rayon, nylon, polyester) and an even wider range of materials made of plastic. The latter are especially important, since plastics have become the most versatile of modern materials: they can now be manufactured to almost any set of specifications and are used in everything from toys to heavy construction projects. The drug industry—both legal and illegal—is another area that has expanded enormously in recent decades as a result of major technological breakthroughs.

Finally, one of the most important developments of the current phase of the Industrial Revolution has been the rapid spread of industrial technology to societies outside northwestern Europe and North America. In 1888, 83 percent of the world's industrial output occurred in just five societies: the United States, Britain, Germany, France, and Russia (see Table 9.1). Even as recently as 1937, these five societies were responsible for 78 percent of the world's industrial output. Today, by comparison, these five are responsible for only 44 percent, and Japan now ranks second (see Table 9.2).

As Table 9.2 suggests, the fourth phase of the Industrial Revolution has been a period of extraordinary economic growth in most societies. Gross domestic product, or GDP, is a mea-

TABLE 9.2 Percentage Distribution of Gross World Product, by Society in 2001

Society	Gross Domestic Product*	Percentage Share of Gross World Product
United States	$9,013,861	26.1
Japan	5,647,678	16.4
Germany	2,701,606	7.8
France	1,804,853	5.2
United Kingdom	1,334,599	3.9
Italy	1,225,264	3.6
China	1,117,227	3.2
Brazil	798,745	2.3
Spain	723,472	2.1
Canada	717,386	2.1
Korea, Rep.	639,239	1.9
Netherlands	502,544	1.5
India	492,497	1.4
Australia	469,217	1.4
Russian Federation	377,613	1.1
Mexico	371,745	1.1
Switzerland	340,323	1.0
Belgium	321,108	0.9
Sweden	281,293	0.8
Argentina	279,978	0.8
Austria	269,758	0.8
Indonesia	216,179	0.6
Denmark	207,448	0.6
Turkey	190,294	0.6
South Africa	175,901	0.5
Thailand	174,570	0.5
Norway	172,838	0.5
Finland	166,646	0.5
Hong Kong	164,799	0.5
Total of the above	30,898,681	89.6
All others**	3,446,857	10.4

*In millions of 1995 U.S. dollars
**Each less than 0.5 percent of GWP
Source: Calculated from World Bank, *World Development Indicators* Online Database (www.worldbank.org/data/onlinedatabases/onlinedatabases.html).

sure of the value of all the goods and services produced in a society. Since 1950, the combined GDPs of the industrialized societies of Europe, North America, Japan, and Australia have risen about 600 percent, while the combined GDPs of the industrializing societies of the Third World have increased more than 800 percent![54] Such growth on a global scale is unprecedented.*

New Energy, New Machines, New Materials: The Key Innovations

In studying the Industrial Revolution, it is easy to become so immersed in the details of individual inventions and discoveries that we fail to see the larger picture. When we look for basic patterns, however, we find that the revolution in technology has involved three kinds of critical innovations.

First, the Industrial Revolution has greatly increased the amount of *energy* available to societies. New technologies have made accessible for the first time vast quantities of energy stored in coal, petroleum, natural gas, and certain radioactive materials. The importance of this development is difficult to exaggerate.

Second, the Industrial Revolution has produced thousands of *new machines* which use this energy to perform an enormous variety of tasks. These machines provide billions of people with countless goods and services—many of which were previously unavailable to even the most powerful kings and emperors.

Third, the Industrial Revolution has made available many *new materials* to use in the construction of new machines and new products. Plastic has probably been the most useful new material to date, for it is easily the most versatile material that humans have ever had to work with.

Collectively, these three sets of innovations—the vast new stores of energy, the new machines, and the new materials—have transformed the world. As we will see in the next several chapters, these advances in our species' ability to take resources from the biophysical environment and convert them into things we need or want have given rise to a social and cultural revolution unequaled in history, not only in its scope and speed, but in the enormity of its impact on human life.

CAUSES OF THE CONTINUING INDUSTRIAL REVOLUTION

As the twenty-first century opens, the technological revolution that began in the eighteenth century shows no signs of abating. On the contrary, the rate of innovation continues to accelerate. Thus, to understand the Industrial Revolution it is not enough merely to understand the forces that gave it its start several centuries ago. We also need to understand the forces that are responsible for its continuation today.

Greater Informational Resources and a Larger Population

Several of these forces are ones that we first identified in Chapter 3. For example, the existing store of useful information about the material world is far greater today than ever before. This means that the informational resources available to would-be innovators today are vastly greater than in the past (see Table 3.1 and the related discussion, pages 50–51). In addition,

---

*Although some argue that the gains in GDP have not benefited the majority of people in Third World societies, this view is challenged by data on trends in infant mortality, life expectancy, literacy, school enrollments, and other basic indicators of quality of life. While millions in the Third World are still mired in poverty, millions of others have experienced significant improvements in living standards. To appreciate the magnitude of the change, one need only compare current conditions in those societies with those of the agrarian era.

the human population is substantially larger today than it was over two centuries ago, and this means more minds at work on the problems confronting human societies.

Changing Attitudes toward Innovation

In preindustrial societies, traditions have always been held in high esteem and change has generally been viewed as undesirable, even dangerous. Innovators, far from being praised or admired for their efforts, have commonly been accused of abandoning the hallowed ways of the past and of their forebears. Because of this strong attachment to the past, social scientists often refer to preindustrial societies as "traditional" societies.

In contemporary industrial societies, in contrast, the attitude toward innovation and change is largely positive. Members of these societies are not just tolerant of innovation: *they actively promote and encourage it.* Many, in fact, are *neophiles,* people who love novelty for its own sake. In the arts, for example, innovation is often praised merely because of its novelty and without regard to aesthetic criteria (see "Neophilic Art"), with the result that on a number of occasions entries submitted to art exhibits as hoaxes have actually won prizes.

In the educational world, a strongly positive attitude toward innovation is also much in evidence. In preindustrial societies, the basic function of education was to transmit the cultural heritage of the past to successive generations, and great emphasis was placed on rote learning of materials. Today, most educators scorn memorization and argue that the chief aim of schools should be to train young people to think creatively. Universities, in turn, have increasingly become centers of research and innovation. Faculty members are often expected to devote more time and energy to research than to teaching.

The institutionalization of innovation is also evident in industry and government. Industrial enterprises and governmental agencies have created countless research centers within their own organizations, and they often subsidize research in universities as well. As a result, expenditures for research and development have risen enormously. In the United States, for example, even after adjustments for inflation, these expenditures have increased more than sixfold since 1953.[55] Industrial societies are the first in history to search systematically and continuously for new technological answers to human problems.

The reasons for the modern attitude toward innovation and change are not hard to find. For the most part, the changes that have already occurred have meant improvements in the

Neophilic Art

Some time ago, the Associated Press reported that two valuable pieces of modern sculpture stored in the yard outside an important art gallery—tangles of rusting metal—had been mistaken for junk and carted away by trash collectors.

More recently, a custodian at the Boulder Public Library inadvertently disposed of an exhibit made up of foul-smelling trash collected in a local park and carefully assembled by University of Colorado art students because he failed to recognize its artistic merit.

And experts are still debating whether or not a painting that a California woman purchased from a thrift shop for $5 is actually a very valuable work by abstract expressionist Jackson Pollack and, therefore, worth millions of dollars, or simply an "ugly splattering of paint" by some rank amateur.

As these examples suggest, even in innovative societies, not quite everyone is able to appreciate the artistic value of neophilic art, just as in the old fairy tale not quite everyone was able to appreciate the beauty of the emperor's "new clothes."

quality of life for the vast majority of people in industrial societies—greatly improved standards of living, improved health, and greater longevity. Under the circumstances, it would be much more surprising if people's attitudes toward change had *not* changed.

The Rise of Modern Science

The emergence of **science** as a major new institutional system is another development that has contributed greatly to the continuing revolution in technology. Although science is sometimes confused with technology, the two are not the same. Science is the search for general and abstract principles that explain the workings of the world we live in. Technology, in contrast, is information about specific ways in which the material world can be manipulated to satisfy human needs and desires. It is a much more practical and "down-to-earth" body of information.

Science and technology today are obviously interdependent. Almost all of modern science presupposes an advanced technology. Modern science is possible only because of technological advances which have enhanced the powers of our senses and of our brains, thus enabling us to learn things which would otherwise remain forever unknown. For example, modern molecular biology and modern medical science are possible only because of the invention of the microscope and the electron microscope, which revealed for the first time the previously invisible and unknowable world of cells and molecules, bacteria and viruses. Similarly, modern astronomy is possible only because of the invention of the telescope, the radio telescope, and space probes, which extend the range of our vision far beyond what was previously possible.

But if modern science is a product of the Industrial Revolution, it is also an important cause of its continuation. Today, technological advance depends increasingly upon the kind of abstract, theoretical knowledge that is the special concern of the sciences. More and more, fundamental discoveries and major inventions are the work of men and women with advanced scientific training, and less and less the work of untrained mechanics. Without the contributions of modern science, it is highly unlikely that the rate of technological innovation would still be accelerating.

The Threat of War

Prior to the Industrial Revolution, military technology changed slowly. As a result, military success among societies at the same level of development depended largely on the size of armies and the organizational and tactical skills of their commanders.

Today, in contrast, military technology becomes obsolete in a very short time and the size of armies and their commanders' skills are often less important than the productive capacity of a nation's economy and the skills of its engineers and scientists. To maintain its relative military preeminence, the United States has invested substantial sums in technological research of many kinds.[56] Although the aim of this research is to create new and improved weapons systems, the new technologies that result often have significant nonmilitary applications. A classic example of this is the silicon chip, which was developed in response to the need to reduce the size and weight of materials used in the space program, a program whose funding has depended greatly on its military relevance.

Environmental Feedback

For the first time in history, the most significant changes in the biophysical environments of most societies are not the result of spontaneous natural forces but, rather, of human actions (see, e.g., Chapters 15 and 16). The global ecosystem now has to support a much larger human population than ever before, and the standards of living for much of this population are steadily rising. As a result, natural resources of every kind are being consumed far more rapidly than in the past, and supplies of many of them are threatened with depletion. In addition, many new technologies have had unanticipated side effects, such as acid rain. The need to solve such problems leads to further research and the development of still newer technologies. Thus, technological advance has itself become one of the most important causes of the need for continued technological advance.

The Desire for Ever Higher Standards of Living

Finally, it is clear that one of the most important factors responsible for the continuing Industrial Revolution is the desire of most people for ever higher standards of living. One might suppose that the tremendous improvements in living standards in industrial societies during the last two hundred years would satisfy their members, but this has not been the case. The desire for goods and services seems insatiable: the more people have, the more they want.

This appears to be part of our genetic heritage—an element of human nature that results from our enormous capacity for learning, and especially from our powers of imagination. No matter what we have, or what we are able to do, we can always dream of more. And having dreamed, some are driven to make the dream a reality. Where this process will end— or if it will end—no one can say. For the present, however, it is a powerful force contributing to the continuing revolution in technology.

VARYING LEVELS OF INDUSTRIALIZATION IN THE WORLD SYSTEM OF SOCIETIES

Societies today differ enormously in the degree to which they have industrialized. Some rely almost entirely on the newer energy sources, such as coal, oil, natural gas, and nuclear energy, while others still depend primarily on human and animal power, wind, water, and wood. Some have become almost totally dependent on machine technology while others still rely primarily on hand tools. And some are now heavily dependent on new kinds of materials, while others still depend largely on traditional ones.

Unfortunately, there is no single measure of industrialization that enables us to gauge perfectly the degree to which contemporary societies have adopted the new industrial technology. Different measures reflect different aspects of industrialization and thus yield somewhat different rankings of societies. Whatever measure is used, however, it must be a *per capita* (i.e., per person) measure, to take account of differences in the population size of societies. For example, if we simply took the total production of societies as a measure (see Table 9.2), China would appear to be one of the most industrialized societies in the world system. But this is a distortion caused by China's huge size: its level of industrialization is actually rather low by contemporary standards (as Table 9.3 shows).

One of the better measures currently available is the GDP, or gross domestic product, per capita. It is the per capita value of all the goods and services produced in a society in a specified period of time. It is, thus, a measure of the productivity of an economy. According to this measure, Switzerland is the most industrialized society in the world.

Table 9.3 reveals several important patterns. First, there are enormous differences in the levels of industrialization of contemporary societies. Second, only a small minority of them can be considered full-fledged industrial societies. Third, with the exception of Japan, all of these are either in Europe or were settled primarily by European peoples. Fourth, most of the least industrialized societies are in Africa and Asia, while most of the intermediate cases are found in Latin America, the Middle East, and along the Pacific rim of Asia.

When we consider the distribution of these societies on a map of the world (see Figure 9.2), it becomes clear that all of the technologically most advanced societies are in temperate regions, while nearly all of the least advanced are located in tropical or semitropical regions. This is no coincidence. Rather, it is an indication of the tremendous importance of the *biophysical*

TABLE 9.3 Gross Domestic Product Per Capita 2001 for Selected Contemporary Societies

Society	GDP/Capita*	Society	GNP/Capita
Switzerland	$47,064	Latvia	$2,816
Japan	44,458	Russian Federation	2,609
Denmark	38,710	Tunisia	2,562
Norway	38,298	Peru	2,311
Austria	33,172	Lithuania	2,308
Germany	32,813	Colombia	2,277
Finland	32,121	Jamaica	2,171
Sweden	31,627	Dominican Republic	2,077
United States	31,592	El Salvador	1,757
Netherlands	31,333	Paraguay	1,703
Belgium	31,218	Jordan	1,639
France	30,492	Bulgaria	1,630
Ireland	29,401	Algeria	1,616
Singapore	27,118	Bosnia and Herzegovina	1,584
Hong Kong	24,505	Guatemala	1,554
Australia	24,203	Swaziland	1,529
Canada	23,081	Ecuador	1,478
United Kingdom	22,697	Morocco	1,436
Italy	21,144	Romania	1,393
New Zealand	18,425	Egypt	1,229
Spain	17,595	Philippines	1,165
Israel	16,576	Indonesia	1,034
Greece	13,669	Ukraine	986
South Korea	13,502	Bolivia	944
Kuwait	13,345	Papua New Guinea	897
Portugal	13,109	China	878
Slovenia	11,984	Syria	796
Barbados	8,610	Congo	792
Argentina	7,468	Honduras	711
Saudi Arabia	6,614	Cameroon	696
Uruguay	5,870	Senegal	629
Czech Republic	5,583	Zimbabwe	559
Trinidad and Tobago	5,553	Angola	525
Hungary	5,540	Pakistan	517
Chile	5,385	India	477
Croatia	5,355	Laos	465
Malaysia	4,708	Ghana	421
Brazil	4,633	Bangladesh	386
Slovak Republic	4,405	Uganda	355
Gabon	4,378	Haiti	354
Botswana	4,130	Kenya	325
South Africa	4,068	Cambodia	317
Costa Rica	3,900	Nigeria	257
Mexico	3,739	Rwanda	253
Poland	3,716	Nepal	248
Venezuela	3,326	Mozambique	213
Panama	3,243	Sierra Leone	158
Lebanon	2,890	Burundi	141
Turkey	2,873	Ethiopia	121
Thailand	2,853	Zaire	85

*In millions of 1995 U.S. dollars
Source: World Bank, *World Development Indicators* Online Database (*www.worldbank.org/data/ onlinedatabases/onlinedatabases.html*).

environment. As we have noted before, environmental variables, such as climate, the quality of soils, and the prevalence of disease, have had an enormous impact on societal development, not only in the distant past but also in the modern era. Although little attention has been paid to these variables by even the most eminent of scholars,[57] they have been a kind of "hidden" factor in the developmental process, greatly favoring some societies and badly handicapping others.[58]

FIGURE 9.2 *Industrial societies in the late twentieth century are darkened.*

In the remainder of this chapter and in those that immediately follow, we will be concerned with the small minority of societies that are highly industrialized. Our goal will be to see how the new technology they have created has transformed the conditions of life for the hundreds of millions of people living in them. Then, in Chapter 14, we will turn to the societies of the Third World, which retain far more of the elements of their preindustrial past.

CONSEQUENCES OF THE INDUSTRIAL REVOLUTION

From an early date it was clear that the Industrial Revolution involved more than just a change in the techniques of production: it was also producing far-reaching changes in virtually every aspect of human life. Though our chief concern in this volume is with the long-run consequences of the revolution, we cannot ignore its impact on the lives of those who were first exposed to it and the new social order to which it gave rise.

Initial Consequences

The first indication of serious change came with the invention of the new spinning and weaving machines in the late eighteenth century. Because of their greatly increased size and weight, they required specially constructed buildings and either steam engines or waterfalls to power them. In short, the new technology necessitated the creation of factories.

Factories, however, required a concentrated supply of dependable labor. A few of the early ones were built in open countryside, but their owners quickly found they could not hire enough workers unless they built adjoining tenements and thus, in effect, created new urban settlements. Most factories were built in or near existing towns, and the cry that went out from them for workers coincided with the declining need for labor on the farms.

During the early stages of the Industrial Revolution, numbers of children were employed in factories in both the United States and Britain: textile mill employees in North Carolina, 1908.

Although the ensuing migration to urban areas was not new, its *magnitude* was, and most communities were unable to cope with the sudden influx. The migrants themselves were badly prepared for their new way of life. Sanitary practices that had been tolerable in sparsely settled rural areas, for example, became a threat to health, even to life itself, in crowded urban communities.

Equally serious problems resulted from the abrupt disruption of social relationships. Long-standing ties of kinship and friendship were severed and could not easily be replaced, while local customs and institutions that had provided rural villagers with some measure of protection and support were lost for good. Thus, it was an uprooted, vulnerable mass of people who streamed into towns and cities and were thrown into situations utterly foreign to them, and into a way of life that often culminated in injury, illness, or unemployment. A multitude of social ills—poverty, alcoholism, crime, vice, mental and physical illness, personal demoralization—were endemic.

Local officials had neither the means nor the will to cope with rampant problems in housing, health, education, and crime. Cities and towns became more crowded, open space disappeared, and people accustomed to fields and woodlands found themselves trapped in a deteriorating environment of filthy, crowded streets and tenements, polluted air, and long workdays rarely relieved by experiences of either beauty or hope.[59]

The misery of the new urban dwellers was compounded by the harshness of the factory system, which often operated along quasi-penal lines.[60] Regardless of how hard life had been before, country folk had at least had some control over their own hour-to-hour movements; but now work was, if anything, longer, more arduous, and more restrictive. Women and children, though they had always worked extremely hard in homes and fields, now worked in factories with dangerous, noisy machinery and in dark and dangerous mines. Minor infractions of complex rules, such as whistling on the job or leaving a lamp lit a few minutes too

Children and the Factory System

The following testimony was given by Peter Smart to a parliamentary committee investigating working conditions in 1832. Similar testimony was provided by numerous others.

Q. Where do you reside?

A. At Dundee.

Q. Have you worked in a mill from your youth?

A. Yes, since I was 5 years of age.

Q. Had you a father and mother in the country at the time?

A. My mother stopped in Perth, about eleven miles from the mill, and my father was in the army.

Q. Were you hired for any length of time when you went?

A. Yes, my mother got 15 shillings for six years, I having my meat and clothes.

Q. What were your hours of labor, as you recollect, in the mill?

A. We began at 4 o'clock in the morning and worked till 10 or 11 at night; as long as we could stand on our feet.

Q. Were you kept on the premises constantly?

A. Constantly.

Q. Locked up?

A. Yes, locked up.

Q. Night and day?

A. Night and day; I never went home while I was at the mill.

Q. Do the children ever attempt to run away?

A. Very often.

Q. Were they pursued and brought back again?

A. Yes, the overseer pursued them and brought them back.

Q. Did you ever attempt to run away?

A. Yes, I ran away twice.

Q. And you were brought back?

A. Yes; and I was sent up to the master's loft, and thrashed with a whip for running away.

Q. Do you know whether the children were, in point of fact, compelled to stop during the whole time for which they were engaged?

A. Yes, they were.

Q. By law?

A. I cannot say by law; but they were compelled by the master; I never saw any law used there but the law of their own hands.

Source: Parliamentary Papers, 1831–1832, vol. XV.

long after sunrise, led to fines, more serious infractions to floggings. One observer of the period wrote poignantly of hearing children, whose families could not afford clocks, running through the streets in the dark, long before the mills opened, so fearful were they of being late.[61]

The immediate effects of industrialization have been traumatic for vast numbers of people in virtually every society that has made the transition from agrarianism. The details have varied, but the suffering has been no less acute in socialist societies than in capitalist. Whether life for the new urban working class was better or worse than it had been for the peasants and the urban lower classes of the old agrarian societies is still a matter of debate.[62] But one point is not debatable: the transition to an industrial economy has exacted a cruel price in terms of human suffering and demoralization for countless millions of people.

Long-Run Consequences: An Overview

In subsequent chapters we will examine in detail the new societies and the distinctive life patterns that have resulted from two centuries of industrialization. For the moment, however, we will note just a few of the most important and most striking consequences. Collectively, these changes in population, social organization, ideology, and language add up to a revolution without parallel in human history, from the standpoint of scope as well as speed.

1. World population has multiplied eightfold (from 725 million to more than six billion) just since 1750, a rate of growth more than fifteen times higher than the rate between the time of Christ and 1750.
2. The rural-urban balance within societies has been reversed: agrarian societies were approximately 90 percent rural, whereas several advanced industrial societies are more than 90 percent urban and most more than 70 percent.
3. The largest urban communities of the industrial era are more than twenty-six times the size of the largest of the agrarian era.
4. Women in industrial societies give birth to only a small fraction (e.g., one-quarter or one-fifth) of the number of children borne by women in preindustrial societies.
5. Life expectancy at birth is almost three times greater in advanced industrial societies than it was in agrarian.
6. The family, for the first time in history, is no longer a significant productive unit in the economy.
7. The role and status of women in the economy and in society at large have changed substantially.
8. The role and status of youth have also changed, and youth cultures have become a significant factor in the life of industrial societies.
9. The average per capita production and consumption of goods and services in advanced industrial societies is more than ten times greater than in advanced agrarian societies.
10. The division of labor is vastly more complex.
11. Hereditary monarchical government has disappeared in industrial societies, except occasionally as a ceremonial and symbolic survival, and the proprietary theory of the state has vanished entirely.
12. The functions and powers of government have been vastly enlarged.
13. Free public educational systems have been established and illiteracy has been largely eliminated in industrial societies.
14. New ideologies have spread widely (notably socialism, capitalism, nationalism, and pragmatism), while older ones inherited from the agrarian era have been substantially altered or have declined in influence, especially in industrial societies.
15. The speed of travel has increased a hundred times and the speed of communication 10 million times, rendering the entire planet, in effect, smaller than England in the agrarian era.
16. A global culture has begun to emerge, as evidenced in styles of dress, music, language, technology, and organizational patterns (e.g., factories, public schools).
17. Global political institutions (e.g., the United Nations, the World Court) have been established for the first time.
18. Several societies have acquired the capacity to obliterate much of the human population.

All this in only a little more than 200 years!

10

Industrial Societies: Technologies and Economies

There is no sharp line of demarcation separating industrial societies from other societies in the modern world. Levels of industrialization vary by degree, ranging from very high levels in societies such as Switzerland and Japan at one extreme to very low levels in Ethiopia and Zaire with most societies falling somewhere in between (see Table 9.3, page 214).

Based on the best available indicators, the most advanced industrial societies today are:

Australia	Denmark	Italy	Sweden
Austria	Finland	Japan	Switzerland
Belgium	France	Netherlands	United Kingdom
Canada	Germany	Norway	United States

These are the societies with which we will be primarily concerned in the next several chapters, since they provide the clearest picture of what industrialization means and how it transforms societies.*

THE TECHNOLOGICAL FOUNDATION OF INDUSTRIAL SOCIETIES

The best way to appreciate the dramatic difference between an agrarian society and an industrial one is to look at the measurable changes that have occurred as a result of the shift from the older technology to the new, and *agricultural productivity* is a good place to begin. As Table 10.1 shows, the application of industrial technology to agriculture has had a revolutionary impact on production, making it possible to produce a given quantity of grain, fiber, milk, or meat with only a tiny fraction of the labor required with the older agrarian technology.** The labor used to produce a given quantity of wheat, corn, cotton, and chicken has been cut more than an average 98 percent. In the case of milk and beef, the reductions have been somewhat less, but still dramatic. Because of these advances in agricultural technology, tens of millions of people who would otherwise be working on farms are able to be employed in other ways. As a result, the percentage of farmers and farmworkers in the American labor force dropped from 72 percent in 1820 to a little more than 2 percent today.[1]

The basic cause of this remarkable trend has been the harnessing of new energy sources. In agrarian societies, people and animals were the chief sources of the energy used in most

---

*Although Hong Kong and Singapore have very high per capita GDPs, for a number of reasons they are exceptional, not typical, examples of industrialization.

**In this discussion, we draw heavily on data from the United States because excellent statistical materials make it possible to trace trends well back into the nineteenth century.

219

Table 10.1 Productivity of American Agriculture, 1800–1997

	Number of Worker-Hours Required			
Production of:	**1800**	**1910–1917**	**1997**	**Percentage Reduction**
100 bushels of wheat	373	106	6	98
100 bushels of corn	344	135	3	99
1 bale of cotton	601	276	3	99
1,000 pounds of milk	n.a.*	38	2	95
1,000 pounds of beef	n.a.*	46	8	83
1,000 pounds of chicken	n.a.*	95	1	99

*Not ascertained.

Sources: U.S. Department of Commerce, *Historical Statistics of the United States: Colonial Times to 1970,* Series K 445–485; U.S. Department of Commerce, *Statistical Abstract of the United States 1997,* tables 1101 and 1103; and *Statistical Abstract of the United States, 2002,* table 801.

work activity, such as pushing, pulling, digging, lifting, and cutting. Their efforts were supplemented to some extent by wind power and waterpower. As recently as 1850 these four sources still supplied over 87 percent of the energy used in work activities in the United States. Today, they account for less than 1 percent.*[2] In their stead, industrial societies use coal, petroleum, natural gas, hydroelectric power, and nuclear power. Except for coal, these sources were still untapped in 1850, and even coal had not been used as a substitute for human and animal energy until the invention of the steam engine in the eighteenth century.

Not only have energy sources changed, but the quantities used have multiplied enormously. In 1850, all the prime movers in the United States (human bodies, work animals,

*Wind and falling water continue to be used to generate *electricity,* however, which is then harnessed to do work. In fact, with growing concern about pollution, they have been attracting greater attention in recent years (e.g, see Chapter 16).[3]

The application of industrial technology in farming has had a revolutionary impact on production, making it possible to reduce the labor required in many areas: shown here is corn harvesting.

steam engines in factories, sailing ships, etc.) generated less than 9 million horsepower; today, it is more than 35 *billion,* a more than 4,100-fold increase in only a century and a half and a more than 380-fold increase in per capita terms.[4] According to recent figures, when all energy sources are totaled, the United States consumed, in a single year, the equivalent of 9 *tons of oil for every man, woman, and child in the population!*[5]

This remarkable increase in the production and consumption of energy has been closely linked to enormous increases in the production and consumption of a wide variety of other things. In the case of iron and steel, for example, British production multiplied nearly 7,000-fold between 1750 and 1970,[6] while production in the United States increased 12,000-fold from 1820 to 1974.[7] And, although the amount and world share of iron and steel produced in the United States declined in recent years,* world production has continued to grow, increasing 14 percent since 1980.[8]

The production and consumption of raw materials in modern industrial societies are tremendous. In the most recent year for which figures are available, the United States consumed, on a per capita basis, 6.3 tons of stone; 4.4 tons of sand and gravel; 880 pounds of cement; 145 pounds of lime; 548 pounds of iron ore; 274 pounds of clay; and 418 pounds of salt, to cite but a few items.[9]

Change in a society's gross national product (GNP), corrected for the effects of inflation, is one of the best ways to measure the magnitude of the technological advance brought about by industrialization.** It tells us the extent to which the changes in technology have enhanced a society's ability to produce goods and services. When we compare British society's GNP in 1830 with current figures, we find that there has been a 27-fold increase.[10] As striking as this figure is, it is less than one-third of the American figure, which shows an *81-fold* increase since 1870.[11] As these figures indicate, the technologies of industrial societies are much more powerful and productive than the technologies of even the most advanced agrarian societies of the past. Small wonder that the advances in technology have been accompanied by revolutionary changes throughout society.

THE ECONOMIES OF INDUSTRIAL SOCIETIES

In modern industrial societies, the impact of technological innovation is usually registered first in their economies. The economy of a society is, in effect, an institutionalized set of answers to the basic questions of production and distribution: What kinds of goods and services will be produced? By whom and where? In what quantities? At what prices? And by what means will they be allocated to the various members of society?

The way in which these questions are answered reflects, to a large degree, constraints imposed by the environment, by the technology on which a society depends, and by the necessity of keeping the productive system functioning. But it also reflects the beliefs and values—the ideology—of those who control the society. Thus, until recently, there were fundamental differences between the economies of the communist societies of eastern Europe and the western industrial democracies (see Chapter 15). Still today, there are differences among industrial societies, though these differences are not nearly as great as those that existed just a decade ago.

Before we consider these differences, however, we need to consider the characteristics that are common to the economies of all industrial societies. These shared characteristics are a response to the new technology on which each of these societies depends.

---

*Iron and steel production has declined in a number of industrial societies in recent years largely because newer materials, such as aluminum and plastics, have come to replace iron and steel in the manufacture of many things.
**Although it is important to use per capita measures when comparing two or more societies of different sizes (as in Table 9.3, page 214), when we compare the same society at two different times, *total* GNP or *total* GDP is the preferred measure, since our goal is to identify the magnitude of the change that has occurred in a society's productive capacity.

The Urbanization of Production

Prior to the Industrial Revolution, agriculture was the chief form of economic activity, production was centered in rural areas, and farmers were a substantial majority of the labor force. In addition to farming, the rural population often engaged in a variety of crafts during the winter months, using this less demanding period as a time to earn additional income. Urban populations were small, and many urban residents were members of the governing class and not actively involved in the labor force. Moreover, many of the urban dwellers who were employed produced nonessential goods and services for the enjoyment of the upper class.

The Industrial Revolution changed all this. As we saw in Chapter 9, the new machines required the development of factories and large concentrations of industrial workers. At the same time that new urban industries were generating a growing demand for workers in cities and towns, technological advances in agriculture were reducing the need for workers on farms. As a result, industrialization led to a massive migration of people from rural areas to urban—a migration that only now seems to be nearing its end in the most advanced industrial societies.

The effect of these changes has been to shift the locus of production in societies from rural areas to urban. In most advanced industrial societies today, less than 4 percent of gross domestic product (GDP) comes from agricultural activity.[12] Equally important, the rural economy of industrial societies has been completely transformed. Many of the people who live in rural areas today commute to work in urban communities. In much of eastern Europe, for example, there is a segment of the population that has come to be known as worker-peasants: the men commute to cities and towns where they work in factories during the week, and on weekends they help the women on the farms. (Women generally continue to work on the farms during the week.) Similar patterns have also developed in western societies: by 1970 the majority of American "farmers" were already earning more from nonfarm activities (e.g., work in factories) than from the sale of farm products.[13]

Rise in Productivity and in the Standard of Living

The most striking characteristic of the economies of industrial societies is their remarkable productivity. As we noted earlier, Britain's gross national product has grown nearly *thirtyfold* since 1830, and that of the United States more than *eightyfold* just since 1870. Most other industrialized societies have experienced comparable growth. Because most of this increase in productivity has not been consumed by population growth, there has been an enormous increase in the size of the economic surplus in every industrial society.

In agrarian societies, the modest economic surplus was appropriated by a small minority of the population, and if the rich got richer, the poor generally got poorer. But because per capita incomes in Britain are *eleven times* and in the United States are *twelve times* what they were in 1830 and 1870, respectively, it has been possible for the incomes of elites and nonelites alike to increase.[14] How industrialization has affected the *relative shares* of income going to elites and nonelites is an issue we will return to in Chapter 12, but for now it should be noted that the growth in the economic surplus has greatly improved the standard of living for the vast majority of people in industrial societies.

The magnitude of the gains in the living standards of the masses is evident when we compare the lifestyle of the average member of most industrial societies today to that of the typical peasant in agrarian societies of the past, or to that of workers during the early phases of the Industrial Revolution. Most members of industrial societies today enjoy a food supply that is larger, more dependable (i.e., less subject to acute shortages), and of higher quality and greater variety than was available in any agrarian society of the past. Most live in superior housing, with an indoor water supply, plumbing, electricity, usually central heating, and sometimes even air conditioning in warmer climates. The majority of their homes and apartments are equipped with furnishings and appliances that are more than adequate for health and comfort, and some of them would have aroused envy in the elites of agrarian societies of the past. Widespread educational opportunities are available, and so is vastly improved health care. Modern transportation and communication systems broaden and enrich their lives and provide them with varied forms of entertainment. And countless other goods and services, unheard of in agrarian societies, are also available to the majority of people in most industrial societies, and to a large minority in the rest.

This is not to suggest that life in industrial societies is free of problems: obviously, it is not. But it is clear that industrialization has meant a remarkable improvement in the standard of living for the average individual compared with that of the average individual in preindustrial or early industrial societies. Relative to the peasant masses of the agrarian era, most members of industrial societies live lives of unbelievable affluence and abundance. And there are very few people in these societies whose standard of living approaches the degradation of the expendables of agrarian societies. Even those dependent on public welfare are much better off than that.

The Shift from Labor-Intensive to Capital-Intensive Industries

The basis of the enormous productivity and affluence of modern industrial societies is their fantastic store of technological information. But most of this information would be useless unless it were *converted into capital goods*. Without the complex machines, factories, transportation facilities, power plants, and other capital goods essential to production in an industrial society, the output of its workers would not be much greater than that of workers in agrarian societies.

We can see the importance of capital goods when we compare two contemporary industries, one capital-intensive and the other labor-intensive. The petroleum industry is a good example of the former: it has expensive, highly automated machinery and a small labor force. The fast-food industry, utilizing simpler and less expensive machines, is far more labor-intensive. Exxon, for example, recently reported annual sales of $1,934,151 *per employee,* while the sales of McDonald's hamburger chain were about $37,303 per employee per year.[15] These differences are also reflected by the fact that in 2001 every $100 of sales generated $7.40 of profits in the petroleum industry, but only $3.20 in the food industry.[16]

One of the chief reasons for the tremendous growth in per capita GNP in industrial societies has been the massive movement of workers away from small, capital-poor family farms and into capital-intensive industries during the last 150 years. As these farmers joined the urban labor force, their economic contribution increased substantially. Since about 80 percent of the population of the typical agrarian society were food producers, in contrast to a tiny minority—in some cases less than 3 percent—in industrial societies, the impact of that shift has been tremendous.

Today, however, that flow has largely ended, and with it a major boost to economic growth. The small, traditional family farm has been largely replaced by huge agribusinesses that are as capital-intensive as some urban-based industries. To appreciate the changes that have occurred in agriculture, one need only consider vertically integrated Smithfield Foods. Employing a "birth to bacon" approach to pork production that encompasses genetics, artificial insemination, automated feeding, and computer-regulated temperature and ventilation, it generates more than $5 billion in revenue a year. Its 973,000-square-foot meatpacking plant in Tar Heel, North Carolina, the world's largest, can process 32,000 hogs a day.[17]

Although agricultural operations on this scale are still unusual, small-scale farming with minimal capitalization is becoming a thing of the past in a growing number of industrial societies. According to the most recent figures available, the average farm in the United States is valued at $450,000, and in California its value is more than twice that.[18]

Changes in the Labor Force

The Shift from Primary Industries From the onset of industrialization there has been a movement of workers out of primary industries, the ones that produce raw materials (i.e., farming, fishing, mining, and forestry). In traditional agrarian societies these industries provided a livelihood for 80 percent or more of the labor force. With industrialization, most of these people, or their children, gradually moved either into secondary industries, the mills and factories that process the raw materials and turn them into finished products, or into tertiary industries, which provide the great variety of services found in industrial societies—education, health care, police and fire protection, social services, government, retail trade, and so on. As industrialization proceeds, the initial rapid growth in secondary industries slows down considerably, and tertiary industries become the chief area of growth in the economy.

Table 10.2 shows how striking this process has been in the United States, completely transforming the labor force in the last 150 years. From a nearly 70 percent concentration of workers in primary industries, more than 70 percent are now in tertiary industries, and growth in these industries continues at the expense of the other two. Similar trends are found in every industrial society, although growth in the tertiary industries has been much less pronounced in the societies of eastern Europe.

Growth of White-Collar Jobs Another striking change in the labor force has been the rapid expansion of white-collar, or nonmanual, jobs. This trend is especially evident in the United States. At the beginning of the twentieth century, only 17 percent of American workers were employed in white-collar jobs; today, 60 percent are in such jobs (see Table 12.2, page 264).[19]

The rapid growth of white-collar jobs has been associated with the growth of the tertiary, or service, industries. As opportunities for farm employment have declined, opportunities for employment in clerical and sales work, the professions, and management have increased. More recently, jobs in the secondary industries (i.e., manufacturing, construction) have also begun to decline, both in absolute and in relative terms, and this has meant a decline in blue-collar jobs. In 1960, for example, 30 percent of American workers were employed in secondary industries. Today, that figure is only about 21 percent (see Table 10.2).

Increased Employment of Women Outside of Households Until the twentieth century, most women worked only within households—as wives, mothers, sisters, or daughters in their own family's household, or as servants in someone else's. The Industrial Revolution and the new technology have changed all this. Today, the majority of women in industrial societies are also employed outside households, working for corporations, state enterprises, and other kinds of work organizations.

Table 10.2 Changing Patterns of Employment in the American Labor Force, 1840 to 2001; Percentages Employed in Primary, Secondary, and Tertiary Industries

Year	Primary Industries	Secondary Industries	Tertiary Industries	Total
1840	69	15	16	100
1870	55	21	21	100
1900	40	28	32	100
1930	23	29	48	100
1960	8	30	62	100
1990	3	25	72	100
2001	3	21	76	100

Sources: Calculations based on *Historical Statistics of the United States: Colonial Times to 1970,* Series D 152–166; and *Statistical Abstract of the United States 2002,* table 591.

In many work organizations, especially in the service sector, a majority of the workers are women. This is particularly true of a number of white-collar jobs that have come to be identified as women's jobs (e.g., nursing, social work, elementary school teaching, secretarial work, clerical work, retail sales work of most kinds). Despite efforts by feminists to discourage the sexual division of labor, it is remarkably persistent, at least partly because of the preference of many women, but also because of the demands of marriage and family life.

Growth in the Size of Work Organizations   Workers today find themselves increasingly in the employ of organizations of enormous size. Governments have become the largest employers of all, even in nonsocialist societies. The federal government of the United States, for example, currently employs 2.9 million people,* and state and local governments employ an additional 18 million.[21] The city of New York alone employs more than half a million people.[22] And despite recent "downsizing," many private corporations also employ large numbers of workers: IBM has 355,421; General Motors 350,000; and Sears 289,000, to name three of the largest.[23]

Increase in Occupational Specialization   Growth in the size of work organizations along with advances in technology have been responsible for yet another important trend: the substantial increase in the level of occupational specialization. Contemporary industrial societies have an astonishing number of highly specialized occupations. The U.S. Department of Labor lists more than 28,000 different kinds of jobs that are found in American society today.[24] The meat-packing industry illustrates the extremes to which occupational specialization is often carried. Forty-hour-a-week jobs in that industry include:

belly opener	gut sorter	rump sawyer
bladder trimmer	head boner	side splitter
brain picker	jowl trimmer	skull grinder
foot cutter	leg skinner	snout puller
gut puller	lung splitter	toe puller

Further increases in specialization seem unlikely in most blue-collar occupations, since extreme specialization appears to be counterproductive: workers quickly become bored and this often leads to carelessness, hostility, and even sabotage. In many industries, management has responded by diversifying work activities, thus reversing the historic trend toward greater specialization. Indiana Bell Telephone, for example, used to assemble its telephone books in twenty-one steps, each performed by a different clerk. Now, each clerk has responsibility for assembling an entire book, with the result that labor turnover (a sensitive measure of worker morale) was reduced as much as 50 percent.[25] Some years ago, Volvo, the Swedish automobile manufacturer, conducted two experiments to reduce boredom and improve morale. One was a system of job rotation involving work at a variety of highly specialized tasks; the other was a system of teamwork involving groups of three to nine workers who share a common set of responsibilities, choose their own leader, and are paid on the basis of group output.[26] These changes reduced Volvo's annual worker turnover from 40 to 10 percent. Other industries are responding to the problem of boredom by replacing workers with robots and other automated machines.

While the trend toward greater occupational specialization is apparently waning in blue-collar occupations, it is still growing in many kinds of white-collar jobs. This is especially evident in professional and managerial occupations, where many people seem to derive greater satisfaction from their work when their areas of responsibility and expertise are more

---

*If active military forces are added, this figure is nearly 4 million.[20]

narrowly defined. This is because professional and managerial occupations usually involve such complex bodies of information that no one can master them entirely; as a result, frustration is more likely to come from too little specialization than from too much. Thus, general practitioners in medicine have been largely replaced by a variety of medical specialists, just as general historians in the academic world have been replaced by specialists in such fields as medieval English history and nineteenth-century German history. In addition, some of the traditional components of professional and managerial jobs are now being performed by machines, and more efficiently. This is true, for example, of some kinds of teaching (e.g., foreign-language instruction, elementary math) and medical diagnosis (e.g., MRI, PET, and CAT scans, computerized laboratory tests).

Formation of Labor Unions   Since the beginnings of the Industrial Revolution, large numbers of workers have found themselves confronted with similar problems and grievances, including long working hours (70-hour workweeks were not uncommon in the past), inadequate pay, dangerous working conditions, abusive supervisors, and lack of job security. These conditions have led to the formation of labor unions designed to protect and promote the common interests of workers.

In some instances, unions have been organized along craft or trade lines, such as bricklayers and carpenters unions. Others have been organized on an industrywide basis, as in steelworkers and autoworkers unions. In several instances, unions have been organized on a national basis, with every worker in the entire nation eligible to join, as in the case of Solidarity in Poland.

Prior to the twentieth century, the membership of labor unions consisted almost entirely of blue-collar workers. Now, however, a substantial minority are employed in white-collar jobs. In the United States, for example, approximately one-quarter of labor union members are white-collar workers, with most of them public school teachers or other government employees.

The degree to which the labor forces of industrial societies are unionized varies greatly (see Table 10.3). More than 90 percent of the workers in Sweden are currently members of unions, whereas less than 10 percent are in France.

Table 10.3 Percentage of Wage and Salary Earners in Labor Unions in Industrial Societies, 1995, and Change, 1985–1995

Society	Percentage in Unions, 1995	Change in Percentage, 1985–1995
Sweden	91	9
Denmark	80	2
Finland	79	16
Italy	44	-7
Austria	41	-19
Canada	37	-2
Australia	35	-30
United Kingdom	33	-28
Germany	29	-18
Netherlands	26	-11
Japan	24	-17
Switzerland	23	-22
United States	14	-21
France	9	-37
Average	40.4	-13.2

Source: *World Labor Report 1997–98: Industrial Relations, Democracy and Social Stability* (Geneva: International Labour Office, 1997).

The record of the union movement has also varied greatly in many countries *over time*. In the United States, for example, 35 percent of workers were members of unions in 1945, but only about 14 percent are today.[27] In contrast, membership in unions in Belgium grew from 37 percent of the labor force in 1950 to 68 percent in 1990.[28] Canada offers yet a third pattern, one of relative stability: in 1950, 36 percent of Canadian workers were unionized, and 37 percent are today.[29]

As Table 10.3 shows, however, in recent years there has been a decline in union membership in most industrial societies. In several societies this decline has been quite substantial; the percentage of workers in unions fell 37 percent in France, 30 percent in Australia, 28 percent in the United Kingdom, and more than 20 percent in several other societies.

Command and Market Economies   In the prehistoric past, before societies were able to produce a sustained economic surplus, all economies were essentially *subsistence* economies in which each community provided for its own members' needs, and trade and exchange were limited to nonessentials (e.g., feathers, amber, and other objects valued for ceremonial and aesthetic reasons). With the shift from hunting and gathering to farming, conditions changed in a number of important ways. No longer was it necessary for all adults to be food producers. New and more specialized kinds of occupations began to emerge, trade and commerce increased, and political systems developed that were able to impose the will of small political elites on the other members of society.

With these developments, subsistence economies began to be supplemented either by command economies or by market economies. A *command economy* is elitist: basic choices among economic alternatives are made by a tiny political elite. Sometimes these decision makers claim to act on behalf of the population as a whole, but they are not willing to transfer their enormous decision-making power to the larger population on whose behalf they claim to act.

In a *market economy,* in contrast, producers freely exchange what they produce for goods and services produced by others. Prices are set by the forces of supply and demand, that is, by the relative quantity and quality of the various things that are available and by the relative eagerness of would-be consumers. As this suggests, decision making in a market system is considerably more dispersed than in a command economy.

The Rise of Market Economies

The origins of modern market systems can be traced back to the simple barter systems of prehistoric societies. But a full-fledged market economy (i.e., one in which market forces shape the majority of major economic decisions) was not possible until the use of money became widespread and most of the goods and services people valued had acquired a monetary value. In addition, the basic economic resources of land, labor, and capital had to be freed from traditional constraints on their use and transfer. People had to be free to sell ancestral lands when that was profitable; workers had to be free to leave their jobs and take new ones when they could get higher wages or better working conditions; and owners of businesses had to be free to use their capital however they wished. Restraints on economic activity based on family sentiments, religious taboos, social customs, or organizational restrictions (guild restrictions on output, for example, or legal restrictions on the movement of serfs and slaves) had to be substantially reduced or eliminated. In short, individual economic advantage, as measured in monetary terms, had to become the decisive determinant of economic action.

As we saw in Chapter 9, the discovery of the New World gave a powerful impetus to the first requirement: the great flow of gold and silver led to the emergence of a money economy in western Europe. At the same time, a series of ideological changes weakened traditional

In a market economy, prices are set by the forces of supply and demand: the New York Stock Exchange.

social bonds that had previously immobilized both people and property. These same factors also sparked the Industrial Revolution, and once that was under way and the economy had changed further, the effect became cumulative. Each change stimulated further change; the more resources that came under the control of western Europe's entrepreneurial class, the better able they were to promote other changes.

By the end of the nineteenth century it looked as if every industrial society would soon have a market economy. Industrial societies were coming increasingly under the control of political parties that were dominated by businessmen committed to the philosophy of laissez-faire capitalism, or free enterprise. Following the teachings of Adam Smith, this new governing class argued that the most productive economy, and the most beneficial, was one in which governmental restrictions were held to a minimum.

Moves toward Mixed Economies

It was not long, however, before it became evident that the new market economy was not the unmixed blessing its enthusiasts made it out to be. In their pursuit of profits, businessmen often adopted practices that were harmful to others. In an attempt to cut labor costs, many employers fired adult workers and replaced them with children, simultaneously creating adult unemployment and endangering the health and welfare of children. Efforts to reduce costs also led to dangerous working conditions and the production of shoddy, even unsafe, merchandise.

Protests soon began to be raised, sometimes by social reformers like Robert Owen, sometimes by poets and novelists like Thomas Hood and Upton Sinclair. Even before the middle of the nineteenth century, the British Parliament began enacting legislation to protect society against the extremes of free enterprise. The Factory Acts of 1833 and 1844, the Mines Act of 1842, and the Ten Hour Law of 1847 prohibited the employment of children under the age of 9 in textile factories, restricted children under 13 to six and a half hours of work per day in factories, forbade the employment of women or of boys under 10 in the mines, limited women and young people aged 13 to 18 to ten working hours per day, and provided for inspectors to enforce these laws.[30] By 1901 the minimum age for child labor in England was raised to 12, and in 1908 limitations were finally imposed on the working hours of men. Other legislation forced employers to provide for the safety of their employees in dangerous industries and established the first minimum wage.

None of these reforms would have come about, however, without the efforts of workers themselves. By the latter part of the eighteenth century, small groups of workers had already begun banding together to negotiate with their employers on wages, hours, and working conditions. During the nineteenth century, the labor movement had many ups and downs, but by 1900 there were 2 million members of labor unions in Britain and nearly a million each in the United States and Germany.[31]

Before that date, however, another major defect in the market system had become evident. There was a tendency for it to lose its competitive character and evolve in the direction of monopolies. This danger was greatest in older, established industries in which there was little technological innovation and in which *fixed costs* were a significant part of total costs.

Fixed costs are costs of production that do not increase in proportion to the quantity of goods produced. The costs of designing, tooling, and advertising a new-model car, for example, are all fixed costs: they remain essentially the same whether 5 million cars of that model are produced or only 1 million. As a result, the company that sells 5 million cars can usually either price its cars less than its competitors or offer a better car for the same money. Either way, the larger company tends, over time, to win an ever larger share of the market, which increases its advantage even more.*

Table 10.4 illustrates how, in an industry in which fixed costs are relatively great compared to variable costs, the company that has the highest volume of sales has a *growing competitive advantage*. Note that the amount that the three companies in the example spend on variable costs varies directly with the number of units each produces—$1 per unit. But fixed costs are the same for each company—$5,000—regardless of how many units it produces. Thus, the differences in "cost per unit" are due entirely to the influence of fixed costs. Note also that the initial pricing advantage enjoyed by Company A because of its initial high volume of sales enables that company to gain a growing share of the market, and, with it, an increasing ability to undersell its competitors. As this example illustrates, if pure market forces were allowed to operate with no restrictions, smaller competitors would eventually be forced out of business in any industry in which fixed costs are a significant part of total costs.

---

*General Motors enjoyed this kind of advantage in the American automobile market until the 1970s when sharp increases in the price of gasoline made fuel efficiency of prime importance to consumers and to the American government, which began to mandate more fuel-efficient vehicles. This created a unique opportunity for Japanese automakers, who had long been producing small, fuel-efficient cars. In addition, Japanese labor costs were substantially lower than those in the United States and by the 1970s the cost of transporting cars overseas had declined dramatically. The final straws that broke the camel's back and destroyed General Motors' longtime market advantage were: (1) the enormous and increasingly inefficient managerial bureaucracy that had been allowed to develop over the years, which left the company without the leadership it needed to adjust to rapidly and drastically changing conditions, and (2) a union that was equally slow to recognize the threat posed by Japanese automakers and which refused to make concessions when this became imperative. As a result, General Motors' share of the American market has steadily declined for twenty years despite the enormous advantage it enjoyed simply by virtue of its once huge market share.

Boys working in a British mine in the nineteenth century: after the Mines Act of 1842, boys under the age of 10 could no longer be employed in mines.

In an effort to prevent the growth of monopolies, the United States passed the Sherman Antitrust Act in 1890. Although it has not been vigorously enforced, this act has served as a deterrent. A number of industries might now be dominated by a single company had not the managers of the leading firms been fearful of the legal consequences. For example, economists and even industry leaders have testified before Congress that economies of scale made it possible for General Motors (GM) to undersell its American competitors by a substantial margin for years. But rather than face antitrust action, GM's managers chose to price their cars competitively, thereby increasing their profits while perhaps offering their customers a bit more car for the money.[32]

The situation in which an industry is dominated not by a single firm but by a very few of them is known as *oligopoly*. This has become common in capitalist societies. Table 10.5 gives some idea of the current situation in the United States. As a rough rule of thumb, economists consider an industry oligopolistic when as few as four companies control 50 percent or more of production.[33] This standard can be deceptive, however, because the degree of national concentration means different things in different industries, depending chiefly on whether the market is local, regional, or national. The newspaper industry in the United States, for example, might appear highly competitive since, according to Audit Bureau of

Table 10.4 Illustration of How Fixed Costs Contribute to the Growth of Monopoly in a Free Enterprise System

Time Period and Firm	Number of Units Sold	Variable Costs*	Fixed Costs*	Total Costs	Cost per Unit**
Time I:					
Company A	10,000	$10,000	$5,000	$15,000	$1.50
Company B	9,000	9,000	5,000	14,000	1.56
Company C	8,000	8,000	5,000	13,000	1.63
Time II:					
Company A	11,500	11,500	5,000	16,500	1.43
Company B	8,500	8,500	5,000	13,500	1.59
Company C	7,000	7,000	5,000	12,000	1.71
Time III:					
Company A	13,000	13,000	5,000	18,000	1.38
Company B	8,000	8,000	5,000	13,000	1.63
Company C	6,000	6,000	5,000	11,000	1.83

*Variable costs need not be exactly proportional to sales volume, and fixed costs need not be exactly identical for all firms, but they are shown this way to make the essential principles clearer.
**Cost per unit equals total cost divided by number of units sold.

Table 10.5 Percentage of Production by the Four Largest Companies in Selected Industries in the United States

Industry	Percentage	Industry	Percentage
Cigarettes	99	Dog and cat food	58
Tires	97	Broadcasting	48
Washing machines	96	Mobile homes	45
Breweries	90	Explosives	45
Light bulbs	89	Steel mills	33
Ammunition	89	Book printing	32
Aircraft	85	Pharmaceuticals	32
Breakfast cereals	83	Petroleum refining	29
Motor vehicles	82	Meatpacking	27
Turbines	78	Fur goods	23
Burial caskets	74	Fluid milk	21
Coffee and tea	58	Newspapers*	19

Source: Adapted from U.S. Department of Commerce, Bureau of the Census, *Census of Manufacturing, 1997, Subject Series, Concentration Ratios in Manufacturing* (Washington D.C., 2001), table 2.
*Share of circulation of largest 100 newspapers, according to the Audit Bureau of Circulation, August 19, 2003.

Circulation statistics, the four largest companies produce only about 19 percent of the papers. But a moment's reflection reminds us that most newspapers produce for a local market, and in most communities the paper or papers are owned by a single person or firm.[34] Since the same is true of a number of other industries as well, Table 10.5 actually *understates* the extent of oligopoly.

Where oligopoly prevails, the law of supply and demand often stops functioning, primarily because collusion between firms is so easy. Collusion can take various forms. A fairly common practice in the construction industry is *bid rigging,* whereby firms get together and decide among themselves who will take which job and then bid accordingly, with the "low" bid set as high as they dare. *Price leading,* a perfectly legal practice, appears to be standard procedure in several major industries: one firm, usually the largest, sets its prices at a level that ensures profits for all and maximizes profits for itself. In this situation, competition is largely restricted to secondary matters, such as design and advertising.

Another development which has weakened the role of market forces has been the increase in what is known as *vertical integration,* the process by which a company gains control of companies in other industries that either supply it with materials or buy its products.[35] A furniture manufacturer, for example, buys up a number of lumber companies and sawmills to provide its raw materials and then buys into retail establishments that sell the furniture it produces. In this way, it eliminates many of the uncertainties of the market situation. Another device with a similar purpose is the establishment of interlocking directorates, which bring the top officials or directors of a company on which one depends for some essential commodity onto the controlling board of one's own company. This device is widely used to bring officers of major banks onto the boards of firms that require ready access to large amounts of capital.[36]

Finally, the market system has been weakened by the nature of military technology. Modern warfare requires the mobilization of all of a nation's economic resources. Obviously this effort must be planned and implemented far in advance of the outbreak of hostilities. In societies that wish to maintain a strong military position, this inevitably leads to the development of a military-industrial complex from which most elements of the market system are eliminated. For one thing, there is only one buyer for the product, the government. In addition, there is frequently only one producer, and seldom more than a handful, for a particular weapons system. The situation is prejudicial to an open market in yet another way: the military is not inclined to shop around for bargains, because this increases security risks, and truly competitive bidding encourages companies to cut corners and turn out defective products. So long as the military has the taxing power of the government behind it, it has little motivation to economize. Thus, there is a natural tendency for market forces to be replaced by the principles of command in the vast and important area of military procurement, even in societies whose leaders are committed to the principles of free enterprise.

We can summarize most of the foregoing by saying that the experience of the last two hundred years has revealed *three basic flaws in market systems*. First, not only do they fail to protect the weaker and more vulnerable members of society, such as workers and consumers, but also they compel the strong to act ruthlessly if they wish to remain strong. Second, the market system has what might be called a built-in tendency to self-destruct, which causes most free competitive markets to evolve into oligopolistic or monopolistic markets unless checked by governmental intervention. Finally, the market system cannot respond adequately to many or most of the needs of society as a whole, as contrasted with the needs and desires of individuals.

This final flaw is particularly evident during societal crises, such as wars, depressions, or environmental crises. As long as individuals and organizations are free to act according to what they perceive as their own best interests, the more selfish ones tend to win out. A corporation that responds voluntarily to environmental problems by installing expensive anti-pollution devices, for example, may well find itself at a competitive disadvantage with firms that do not.

For a variety of reasons, then, even those societies that have remained ideologically most committed to the market system and to the principle of free enterprise now have what can only be described as *mixed market–command economies*.* The nature of the economic mix varies considerably from society to society, with governmental intervention in, and control of, the economy being greater in Scandinavia and western Europe and less in Japan, the United States, and Canada. But even where market elements are predominant, the role of government in the economic life of societies is enormous. Businesses are obliged to operate within well-defined limits set by an increasingly complex system of governmental regulations. Minimum wage laws must be observed, government-prescribed safety standards maintained, and compulsory social insurance payments for workers made, to name but three of the many controls that the governments of industrial societies now exercise.

A good measure of the greatly increased power of government in the economic life of all western industrial societies is the growth in the percentage of gross domestic product that governments control through taxes and use to support various activities. As Table 10.6 indicates, the governments of industrial societies, on average, spent less than 10 percent of their societies' GDPs in 1870, and now spend nearly half. Even the United States, which ranks fairly low among industrial societies in government spending, experienced a nearly ninefold increase since 1870.

Finally, it should be noted that in most of the societies of Europe, major industries, such as steel, telecommunications, automaking, airlines, and utilities, have, until recently, been operated as state enterprises. In a survey conducted more than a decade ago, it was found that the majority of the most basic industries in all but one of those societies were state owned.[37] During the last ten years or so, however, several of these societies have decided that a number of these industries could be operated more efficiently as private enterprises subject to governmental regulation and control rather than as purely state enterprises.

Viewed from a sociological perspective, the mixed economies that have evolved in industrial societies during the last hundred years reflect an effort by the members of these societies to achieve two goals that seem, to some degree at least, mutually contradictory. On

*Chapter 15 examines the pressures on the command economies of the former Soviet Union and eastern European societies to incorporate market elements.

Table 10.6 Government Spending as a Percentage of GDP, 1870–1996

Society	1870	1920	1960	1996
Sweden	5.7	8.1	31.0	64.7
France	12.6	27.6	34.6	54.5
Belgium	*	*	30.3	54.3
Italy	11.9	22.5	30.1	52.9
Austria	*	14.7	35.7	51.7
Netherlands	9.1	13.5	33.7	49.9
Germany	10.0	25.0	32.4	49.0
Norway	3.7	13.7	29.9	45.5
Canada	*	13.3	28.6	44.7
United Kingdom	9.4	26.2	32.2	41.9
Switzerland	*	4.6	17.2	37.6
Australia	*	*	21.2	36.6
Japan	8.8	14.8	17.5	36.2
United States	3.9	7.0	27.0	33.3
Average	8.3	15.9	28.7	46.6

*Missing data.
Source: The Economist, Sept. 20, 1997.

the one hand, they want the economic growth and higher standard of living that market systems seem better able to provide. On the other hand, they also want the economic security and attention to the needs of society that command economies seem better able to provide.

Small groups of ideologues continue to argue for a purer type of economic system, but the majority of citizens in industrial societies seem to prefer the more pragmatic approach represented by a mixed market-command economy. While people argue endlessly over details of the mix, there seems to be little popular support for abandoning or substantially reducing either of the two basic components of the mixed economy.

Evolution of the Modern Corporation

The origins of the modern corporation lie in the sixteenth century, when English and Dutch merchants, trading in remote areas, banded together in what came to be known as joint stock companies.[38] This form of organization had several advantages over family enterprises and partnerships. Above all, it permitted people to pool capital and thereby spread their risks. This was extremely important in ventures where risks were great and large investments essential. In addition, a joint stock company, unlike a family enterprise or a partnership, was not disrupted by the death of one of the owners.*

During the next several centuries, the joint stock company, or corporation, gradually spread to new fields of enterprise, and a series of changes made it safer and more attractive to investors. The most important change was the adoption of the principle of *limited liability*. Prior to the nineteenth century, stockholders in most corporations had unlimited liability: in case of bankruptcy they could lose not only their investment in the company but all their personal property as well. This naturally made investors extremely cautious; unless they had intimate knowledge of a business and those running it, they were taking an enormous risk. The passage of laws limiting the liability of stockholders to the investment itself greatly stimulated the flow of capital into this new form of enterprise.

In industrial societies today, nearly all of the largest and most powerful private enterprises are corporations. In the United States in recent years, for example, 87 percent of all business was done by corporations, and among larger concerns (i.e., those with annual receipts

---

*The law requires, for example, that a partnership be dissolved on the death of any of the partners. This was not required of joint stock companies.

of $1 million or more), they accounted for 90 percent of the total.[39] And the very largest concerns, those with annual profits in the hundreds of millions or billions of dollars, are all corporations.[40]

As corporations have grown, there has been a tremendous change in their character, especially with respect to their control. The largest ones are rarely controlled by the people who own them (i.e., the stockholders); they are controlled by employees who have been hired to manage them.[41] This shift is a consequence of the fragmentation of stock ownership which has accompanied the enormous growth in size of these organizations. In some corporations, no one owns even as much as 1 percent of the stock, and most stockholders own only a minute fraction of 1 percent. Furthermore, the stockholders are scattered around the world. Mobilizing a majority of the voting stock to wrest control from the managers is extraordinarily difficult and expensive.

The character of the corporation was also altered during the twentieth century by increasing government control. As we have seen, this intervention of government into the economy is a response to the inherent defects of an unregulated market system. Over the years, the scope of government involvement in corporations has steadily increased, creating some problems while alleviating others. Many economic questions that were once resolved by the forces of supply and demand are now decided by government officials, much as they are in socialist societies. As a result of such changes, the owners of the largest corporations have become, in most cases, merely investors: *real control of these organizations now lies in the hands of management and government.*

INCREASING ECONOMIC INTEGRATION OF THE WORLD SYSTEM

To be complete, our survey of the economies of modern industrial societies has to take note of one further development: the growing web of economic ties among societies, industrial and nonindustrial, throughout the world.

Human societies have exchanged goods with one another since prehistoric times, but the volume of trade was always small because of the limitations of technology. Since the cost of transporting goods was often greater than the cost of producing them, intersocietal trade was largely restricted, for thousands of years, to small items of substantial value, especially luxury goods produced for elites.

With advances in ship construction and navigational technology in the thirteenth, fourteenth, and fifteenth centuries, the volume of international trade began to increase. By 1850, the volume of goods exchanged was six times what it had been in 1750, and in 1950, it was twenty times what it was in 1850.[42] More recently, during the last forty years, the dollar value of international trade (corrected for inflation) has been growing at a rate that would be equivalent to a 400-fold increase if it lasted a century.[43]

The result of this trend has been a substantial increase in the division of labor among societies, and a growing economic integration of the world system. The other side of the coin, of course, is that societies are steadily declining in economic self-sufficiency. As Table 10.7 shows, the value of trade is now 60 percent or more of the gross domestic product in most advanced industrial societies.

The societies of western Europe have moved further in this direction than other industrial societies and have formed the European Union, whose goal is the complete integration of the economies of the member societies. This development could be the prelude to political unification and the formation of a new multinational society embracing much of western Europe.

In the world system as a whole, movement toward economic and political unification is far less advanced, but a number of international organizations—economic and political—have

Table 10.7 Trade as a Percentage of GDP, 1995

Society	Trade as a Percentage of GDP
Belgium	165.5
Netherlands	124.8
Austria	104.8
Sweden	87.0
Switzerland	86.6
Denmark	84.8
Canada	82.5
Norway	77.1
Finland	72.0
Germany	68.0
United Kingdom	56.4
Italy	54.9
France	54.3
Australia	45.6
United States	29.2
Japan	20.3
Average	75.9

Note: A percentage greater than 100 indicates that the sum of imports and exports combined was greater than all the goods and services produced within the society that year.
Source: World Bank, *World Development Indicators* Online Database (www.worldbank.org/data/onlinedatabases/onlinedatabases.html).

emerged, most of them in the last half-century. These include the International Monetary Fund, the Food and Agriculture Organization, the World Bank, the International Labor Organization, the World Health Organization, the International Court of Justice, and the United Nations.

One of the striking developments of the last century has been the transformation of an ever growing number of businesses into multinational corporations. Some now have a greater volume of sales outside their home countries than within them. Two-thirds of Coca-Cola's sales and nearly 60 percent of McDonald's 31,276 stores, for example, are now outside the United States.[44] Sony, a leading Japanese corporation, makes 72 percent of its sales abroad, and more than 90 percent of the sales of GlaxoSmithKline, a British-owned drug manufacturer, are outside the United Kingdom.[45]

Corporations not only increasingly sell their products or services abroad, but produce abroad as well. The opening of German and Japanese automobile plants in the United States is only one instance of what has become a common practice. In many cases, corporations based in industrial societies manufacture products in Third World societies to take advantage of cheaper labor.

Economic integration is further heightened through foreign-aid programs and foreign loans, the latter provided by private corporations as well as by governments and intergovernmental bodies like the World Bank. Banks in Europe, Japan, and North America have extended tens of billions of dollars of loans to Third World societies. Nor is borrowing limited to the Third World: the United States has become the world's largest debtor nation.

The future is not likely to see any significant reversal of the trend toward greater economic integration within the world system of societies. The technologies of communication and transportation have advanced to the point where economic ties between societies are almost as easy to create and sustain as ties within societies. Today, no nation—and few large corporations—can afford to be isolated from the expanding economic network of the world system.

11

Industrial Societies: Ideologies and Polities

As we saw in the last chapter, industrialization has increased the size of economic surpluses and fundamentally altered the nature of the labor forces and economies of industrial societies. In the process, it has greatly expanded the range of what people are able to do and, thereby, has greatly increased the potential impact of ideologies and collective decision making on social life. Knowledge of the key tenets of modern ideologies and of their relationship with political institutions is essential to an understanding of industrial societies and more especially the differences among them. Therefore, before we trace the development of modern industrial politics and consider the impact of the mass media on politics and life, we will first explore the origins and key elements of the dominant ideologies of the industrial era.

IDEOLOGIES IN INDUSTRIAL SOCIETIES

During the last five centuries the bounds of human knowledge have expanded enormously. The voyages of exploration that began in the fifteenth century gave humans their first accurate view of the earth as a whole. Astronomers of the sixteenth and seventeenth centuries did the same for the solar system. More recently, the natural sciences have given us a vision of a universe of incredible complexity, whose age is measured in billions of years and whose size must be expressed in billions of light-years. And, finally, in the last hundred years, the social sciences have begun the task of demythologizing the social order, challenging ancient beliefs about the nature of man and subjecting virtually every aspect of human life to systematic scrutiny.

Theistic Religions

Not surprisingly, this flood of new information about ourselves and the world we live in has shaken and unsettled many traditional beliefs, and the institutional systems based on them. This is especially evident in the case of theistic religions. The thought forms of the great historic faiths—Judaism, Christianity, Islam, Hinduism, and Buddhism—bear the imprint of the agrarian era during which they evolved. But beliefs about the natural world and the social order that were "self-evident" during the agrarian era often appear alien and antiquated to members of industrial societies. This has created an acute crisis for theistic faiths in industrial societies. Religious leaders have tried, in many cases, to translate the most important elements of their traditions into modern terms, while steering a course between irrelevant orthodoxy and heretical innovation. The turmoil and controversy within the Roman Catholic Church created by Vatican Council II was but one in a series of intellectual crises that began at the time of Copernicus and Galileo.

Although the majority of people in most industrial societies still profess a belief in God when questioned, a growing number say they are agnostics or atheists. In one international survey of religious beliefs, those identifying themselves as such ranged from 16 percent in Italy to 61 percent in Japan, with an average of 33 percent for the eight industrial societies in the survey.[1] Equally significant, many "believers" indicated varying degrees of doubt concerning a number of basic historic beliefs. For example, in western Europe, barely half of the population said they believed in a life after death, and fewer still believed in hell or the devil.[2] Moreover, when asked to choose from a list of possibilities those things that are especially important to encourage in children, less than 8 percent, on average, chose religion.[3]

These trends are less pronounced in Canada and the United States than in western Europe and Japan, but even in these societies change is clearly evident. In Canada, for example, people reporting church or synagogue attendance in the previous week dropped from 58 percent in 1955 to about 25 percent in 2002.[4] In the United States, although the percentage of people claiming to have attended church or synagogue in the previous week has remained basically unchanged at about 40 percent for more than 60 years, the number of people who say that religion is very important in their lives dropped from 75 percent in 1952 to 61 percent in 2003, and the number who believe that religion can answer today's problems dropped from 81 to 59 percent.[5] The latter is especially important, since it suggests that the members of industrial societies are placing increasing faith in new secular ideologies in their efforts to solve their own and their societies' problems.

New Secular Ideologies

Beginning in seventeenth- and eighteenth-century Europe, a number of new ideologies appeared in which the role of supernatural beliefs was substantially reduced or totally eliminated. While some of these new ideologies quickly died out, a number of them not only survived but have prospered in the industrial era. The most important of these new faiths have been democratic republicanism, capitalism, democratic socialism, revolutionary socialism (or communism), nationalism, pragmatism, and hedonism. It is these ideologies that guide the members of industrial societies in shaping their economies, politics, and their lives in general.

Democratic republicanism, as its name suggests, is a special form of the more general ideology known as *republicanism.* The basic doctrine of republicanism is its repudiation of hereditary monarchy—the type of government that prevailed in most agrarian societies of the past—and the proprietary theory of the state (see page 168).

Although republicanism has existed as an ideology for thousands of years, republican governments were rare in the agrarian era, except in maritime societies. Prior to the nineteenth century, most republicans rejected democratic republicanism, preferring instead *oligarchical republicanism.* In other words, they advocated a form of government in which power was concentrated in the hands of a few wealthy individuals, as it was in maritime societies. Oligarchical republicans have generally been distrustful of the masses of common people, afraid that they would misuse the powers of government if they ever gained political control.

The government of the United States in the first fifty years following the American Revolution provides a good example of oligarchical republicanism. Most members of the new political elite thought it wise to limit political power to a small minority of the population—men of property who, in their view, had the greatest stake in the welfare of society and also the greatest capacity to govern. In the new constitution adopted by the state of North Carolina in 1776, for example, the right to vote was limited to landowners, and the right to sit in the state senate was limited even more—to those who owned 300 acres. To be eligible to be governor of the state, a man had to have a net worth of £1,000, eight times the net worth of the average white adult male in the South at the time.[6] Similar provisions were present in the constitutions of virtually all of the other states in postrevolutionary America.

Luther nailing his famous 95 theses to door of the castle church, Wittenberg, Germany, 1517. Luther's doctrine of the priesthood of all believers had revolutionary social implications: though Luther was slow to see this, others soon did.

Not everyone in early America was satisfied with oligarchical republicanism, and even in the eighteenth century there were some who advocated *democratic republicanism,* or what Abraham Lincoln would later describe as "government of the people, by the people, and for the people." Not surprisingly, many of the most ardent advocates of democratic republicanism were people who lived on what was then the western frontier. As we saw in Chapter 7 (pages 178–179), frontier regions have long been noted for their egalitarianism and their resistance to established systems of authority. With strong support from this increasingly important part of the population, democratic republicanism won growing support in the early decades of the nineteenth century. With the election of Andrew Jackson in 1828, the fate of oligarchical republicanism in the United States was sealed. Property requirements for voting were gradually reduced, and soon eliminated altogether. By the late 1850s, nearly all white males were eligible to vote.*

*Later, the Fifteenth Amendment to the Constitution, adopted in 1870, extended the franchise to blacks, and the Nineteenth, adopted in 1920, extended it to women. The 1964 civil rights bill and 1965 voter's rights act were subsequently passed by Congress to enforce the Fifteenth Amendment.

The Founding Fathers of the United States created an oligarchical republic, not a democratic republic: the Constitutional Convention, Philadelphia, 1787.

Since that time, democratic republicanism has been the dominant political ideology in American society and has won the support of hundreds of millions of other people throughout the world. Nevertheless, only a small minority of societies are as yet governed by democratic principles, and these are largely confined to the industrial societies of western Europe, North America, Australia, and Japan. One reason for this has been the rise of a new, competing ideology, revolutionary socialism (see below, pages 240–242).

Capitalism is another important new ideology of the industrial era. Its intellectual father was Adam Smith, a Scottish professor of moral philosophy who combined an analytical mind with a crusading nature.[7] In his most influential work, *An Inquiry into the Nature and Causes of the Wealth of Nations,* published in 1776, Smith made a powerful case for the thesis that the intervention of government into the economic life of a society retards growth and development. The only useful function government can perform in the economic sphere, according to Smith, is to enforce contracts that individuals enter into freely. To do more than this is harmful. Smith backed up his argument with an impressive analysis designed to show that the law of supply and demand, operating in a truly free market,* would ensure that "the private interests and passions of men" are led in the direction "most agreeable to the interest of the whole society."[8] It would be a self-regulating system, but it would function, said Smith, as though an "invisible hand" were at work, ensuring the best possible outcome.

Smith's work laid the foundation for the emerging academic discipline of modern economics. More important, his basic beliefs about the harm done by governmental intervention in the economy became the basis of a powerful new ideology that for 200 years has exercised a profound influence on societies around the globe. This ideology has provided moral justification for policies that minimize governmental control of those in business and business enterprises. In societies where capitalism is the dominant ideology, the term "free enterprise"

---

*As we saw in the last chapter, no society has ever had a "truly free market" system overall. That is an abstract, theoretical construct—but some have had more free market elements than others.

has become a symbol that is often invoked with considerable success to influence public opinion. As we will see shortly, the realities of contemporary capitalism are strikingly different from its ideals, as has been true, of course, of every ideology from Christianity to socialism.

Another important new ideology of the industrial era is *socialism*. While its underlying principle has been applied in hunting and gathering societies for thousands of years, the modern concept dates from the nineteenth century and was an explicit response to, and reaction against, the realities of early capitalism. Socialists argued that the basic economic resources of a society should be the common property of all its members, and used for the benefit of all. Where proponents of capitalism praised free enterprise for the growth in productivity it generated, socialists attacked it for its harsh working conditions, its low wages and economic inequality, its unemployment, its child labor, its boom-and-bust cycles, and its alienating and exploitative character. Where capitalists advocated the private ownership of the means of production (i.e., mines, factories, railroads, utilities), socialists favored public ownership. Where capitalists argued that economic inequality is necessary to provide incentives for people to work productively, socialists insisted that a more egalitarian distribution would achieve a better result.

Since early in its history, the socialist movement has been split into a variety of warring sects that have often fought more with one another than with the advocates of capitalism and other ideologies.[9] The most important of the struggles has been between democratic socialism and revolutionary socialism.

Democratic socialism assumes that socialist principles have an inherent appeal to most people. Its proponents therefore maintain that, in democratic societies, socialists should seek power by democratic means and that, after coming to power, they should let other political parties compete freely for the support of the electorate and return to power anytime they can win a majority of the vote. Democratic socialists believe that any other policy defeats one of socialism's basic aims: to maximize the freedom of individuals. They argue that political democracy is as essential to socialism as public ownership of the means of production, and that failure to practice political democracy subverts the very nature of socialism.

During the twentieth century, parties adhering to these principles (e.g., the New Democratic Party in Canada, the Labour Party in Britain, the Social Democratic Party in Germany, the Socialist Party in France) developed large followings and won many elections. Because of the continuing appeal of capitalist principles in these societies, however, none of these parties has tried to abolish entirely private ownership of the means of production. Although they have taken some steps in that direction (i.e., they have nationalized some industries), the major thrust of their policies has been the creation of a *welfare state*. In other words, they have used the powers of government to tax the profits of privately owned enterprises to fund health, educational, and social service programs that benefit ordinary citizens who do not own any significant amount of property. This allows everyone to share in the benefits of the productive system without totally abolishing private ownership and control.

In contrast, the other major faction within the socialist movement has doubted the possibility of achieving socialism through peaceful, democratic means. *Revolutionary socialists* have maintained that this can be achieved only by force and by the expropriation of private property. The spiritual father of revolutionary socialism is Karl Marx, whose writings and political activities in the nineteenth century laid the foundation for the Communist parties of the twentieth century. In societies controlled by his followers, he occupied an honored status not unlike that accorded great religious figures of the past. His doctrines were taught to children in all the schools, his writings were cited by the party elite to justify their policies, and pictures and statues of him were placed in prominent locations.

Marx believed that the evils found in societies can all be traced to the influence of the institution of private property. This institution stimulates greed and selfishness, exploitation, injustice, and oppression. By destroying it, humans can free themselves forever from these

Karl Marx

evils and set human societies on a new course that will lead in time to the development of a world in which freedom, justice, and equality prevail and in which everyone's material and spiritual needs are met.

Marx based these beliefs on a complex and interesting theory of history in which he argued that capitalism contains the seeds of its own destruction and that socialist revolutions, led by members of the then new and growing army of industrial workers, are not only inevitable but will ultimately prevail. In short, after a brief but bloody period of revolution, human societies will advance to a stage of societal development in which everyone's legitimate needs and desires will be fulfilled. In an initial phase of this new stage of development, people will be rewarded according to the socialist principle "to each according to his *work*." In a later, higher phase of development, people will be rewarded according to the communist principle "to each according to his *need*."

Marxist socialism has been a far more comprehensive ideology than either capitalism or democratic socialism. Where these other ideologies allow people to make their own choices in most aspects of their lives, Marxism has traditionally imposed its own standards on everything from politics and economics to art and religion. In this respect, Marxism resembles traditional religions more than it does other modern ideologies.[10]

For much of the twentieth century, it seemed that revolutionary socialism was destined to become the most successful and the most powerful of the new secular ideologies. For several decades following World War II, Communist parties seized power in more than twenty societies ranging from China to Cuba and from Mozambique to the former Czechoslovakia. In France and Italy, Communist parties were able to enlist the support of millions of voters, while in other countries, such as Britain and the United States, growing numbers of intellectuals, journalists, media celebrities, and students were sympathetic to the ideals of revolutionary socialism and to the revolutionary movements around the world that endorsed those ideals.

This period of growth and expansion came to an end in the late 1980s with the collapse of the Soviet empire in eastern Europe and with the termination of its financial and other support of expansionist revolutionary socialist parties in Cuba, Vietnam, and elsewhere, and with China's increasingly rapid movement toward a mixed economy. During the 1970s and 1980s, the flaws and failures of the revolutionary socialist regimes in the Soviet Union, China, Cuba, and elsewhere gradually became more and more evident, first to the citizens of the countries involved, and later even to outsiders. Today, Marxism survives chiefly in scattered parts of the Third World. The reasons for the collapse of Marxism is a subject to which we return in Chapter 15.

The fifth of the major new secular ideologies is *nationalism*.[11] As with other ideologies, some of its elements have existed for thousands of years: group loyalty and tribalism, for example, are hardly new. During the agrarian era, however, the peasant masses, who made up 80 percent or more of the population, had little interest in politics beyond the village level.[12] The rise and fall of empires were of no concern to them—unless, of course, they were drawn into these struggles against their will. This lack of interest in politics at the national level was only natural in societies in which the dominant ideology defined the state as the private property of the ruler.

Nationalism has been a potent ideology in colonial territories ever since the American Revolution, and it is important today in many societies of the Third World that have only recently become free of colonial control. More importantly, it is also a potent—even a virulent—force among the various ethnic and religious minorities within both industrial and industrializing societies, as the recent history of the former Soviet Union and Yugoslavia demonstrates.

In many societies in recent decades, nationalism has been combined with other ideologies. The Nazi (literally, National Socialist in German) regime in Germany prior to World War II is one example. In American society, nationalism of a far milder variety is sometimes linked to Christianity and capitalism to form what some have called the nation's "civil religion."[13]

The next of the major new ideologies, *pragmatism,* differs from all the others in one essential respect: it offers no preconceived ideas as to how societies should be organized. Rather, it asserts that social institutions should be judged by their consequences and those that prove beneficial should be strengthened and preserved while those that are not should be eliminated.

Two American philosophers, Charles Peirce and William James, were the spiritual fathers of modern pragmatism. Like Adam Smith and Karl Marx, they developed, expanded, and systematized certain ideas that had existed for centuries. Although the teachings of Peirce and James have not given rise to any organized group of disciples, the basic principles of pragmatism have been adopted widely in the modern world. In fact, it is no exaggeration to say that many contemporary world leaders who profess to believe in other ideologies are also, to a greater or lesser degree, pragmatists. For example, Deng Xiaoping, China's recent Communist leader, once said, regarding his un-Marxist economic innovations, that he did not care if a cat was black or white as long as it caught mice. Such leaders have discovered that no ideology can provide a completely satisfactory blueprint for organizing and governing society. If they hope to be successful, or merely retain power, they have to improvise, and this means they have to adopt the pragmatic principle of judging policies and programs by their consequences.

The last of the new ideologies is *hedonism,* or the pursuit of pleasure. Unlike most of the other new secular ideologies, hedonism does not give rise to organized political movements. Rather, it has become a pervasive influence in the lives of hundreds of millions of individuals. Its more obvious manifestations can be seen in the enormous expansion in the last hundred years of industries that seek to satisfy hedonistic desires—movies, television, sports, tourism, vacationing, popular music and concerts, gambling, drugs, and all the rest that cater to the desires of individuals (see "Leisure and the Arts" in Chapter 13).

This desire for pleasure is nothing new, but the productivity and affluence of industrial societies have produced vastly greater opportunities for its satisfaction. The economic impact of this on industrial societies is obvious in the rapid expansion of the entertainment and leisure industries noted above. Its political impact, in contrast, is far more subtle but no less important: politicians are increasingly judged by their ability to "entertain," and when politics appears boring, as it often does, people lose interest and small groups with special interests (economic, religious, and so on) find it easier to advance those interests.

Surprising as it may seem, despite their many differences, the new secular ideologies all have one thing in common: *they are all based on the belief that human destiny is largely subject to human control*. This is in sharp contrast to ideologies that originated in the preindustrial past. Those ideologies asserted that events depended on forces beyond human control—fate, God, the gods—and taught that the way to appease those forces was through magic, ritual, and adherence to tradition.

Members of modern societies are not nearly so passive. New information in areas ranging from science to history has improved their understanding of human nature and of the world they inhabit, while new technological information has increased their capacity to alter and adapt to that world. The result has been a growing awareness of humanity's potential for shaping its own future. This awareness underlies all of the new secular ideologies of the industrial era, and the members of contemporary societies have come to rely increasingly on these ideologies, and less and less on traditional ones, in their efforts to control their lives and shape the life of society as a whole.

DIFFERENCES AMONG INDUSTRIAL SOCIETIES

Because of their similar technologies and their increasingly pragmatic ideologies, industrial societies are similar to one another in many ways, as is apparent to anyone who has traveled among them. There are also, of course, important differences, and these reflect differences in their biophysical environments, in their social environments, and in numerous features of the cultures they have inherited from the past (see Figure 1.2). The effects of such differences can be clearly seen when we compare traditionally Protestant Sweden in northern Europe with traditionally Catholic Italy in southern Europe, for example, or former frontier societies, such as Australia and the United States, with their motherland, England.

The most significant differences among industrial societies in the past hundred years, however, have been consequences of the new secular ideologies. As technology has expanded the limits of the possible for these societies and increased the range of their alternatives, *the ideologies that guide them in choosing among the alternatives and in using their enormous economic surpluses have become an important source of societal variation*. Industrial societies have many potentially significant options available to them that were not available to any society in the past, and they are guided in making their choices among these options by the beliefs and values contained in their ideologies.

The importance of ideology was never more evident than in the former revolutionary socialist industrial societies of eastern Europe—the Soviet Union, East Germany, Czechoslovakia, Poland, and Hungary—and in comparisons of these societies with the much more pragmatic democracies of western Europe, North America (Canada and the United States), Australia, and Japan. Prior to the 1990s, differences between these two sets of societies were strikingly evident in their politics, economics, education, mass media, stratification, religion, and even art. As we will show in Chapter 15, the rulers of those societies, guided by Marxist ideology, conducted some of the most important social experiments in human history, testing the "limits of the possible" in new and important ways. Students of human societies need to study these experiments and learn why they failed, since it is often possible to learn more from experiments that fail than from those that succeed.

Among the western democracies, the United States has enjoyed political, military, and economic preeminence since World War II. In matters of ideology, the democracies differ considerably in the degree to which they have adopted and institutionalized the principles of socialism or, conversely, of capitalism. Since the primary difference between socialists and capitalists concerns the issue of *how and by whom* basic economic decisions are made, the relative strength of the two ideologies in a society is reflected in *the extent to which its economy is regulated or controlled by government*.

One measure of this control is how much of a society's GDP (gross domestic product) is consumed by its government. As Table 10.6 (page 233) made clear, governments consume far more in the western European and Scandinavian democracies than in Australia, Japan, and the United States. This reflects the popularity of democratic socialism in western and northern Europe and the success of its Social Democratic parties in creating and expanding what has come to be called "the welfare state" or "welfare capitalism." In contrast, the much lower levels of governmental expenditure in Australia, Japan, and the United States reflect traditions that emphasize private or individual, as opposed to governmental, decision making in economic matters.*

THE POLITIES OF INDUSTRIAL SOCIETIES

A society's polity is an institutionalized set of answers to questions about how it should be governed. Who will have power to make what decisions, and under what conditions? How will those decision makers be chosen, and when and how will they be replaced? Above all, what limits or checks, if any, will there be on their powers?

The answers to these questions obviously reflect a society's dominant ideology, whether it involves belief in the divine right of kings, belief in democracy, or belief in the doctrines of Karl Marx or Adam Smith. The answers also say something about a society's level of technological development. For it is no coincidence that multiparty democracy is a product of the industrial era and is found most often in industrial societies. In fact, we cannot understand the polities of industrial societies unless we recognize the remarkable political transformation that has occurred in them as a by-product of industrialization.

The Democratic Trend

Prior to the Industrial Revolution, nearly all large and powerful nations were monarchies governed by hereditary kings and emperors. The power to govern was believed to be a God-given right and the state was viewed as the private property of the ruling family. The state and the ruler's estate were one and the same—and the heads of states were "rulers," not merely "leaders." In 1750, the republican idea that the powers of government are derived from the consent of the governed was still only a thesis for philosophers to debate, not a political reality.

Today, the older view of government has all but disappeared, especially in industrial societies. While a few of them still retain some of the trappings of monarchy, as in Britain, Sweden, and Japan, the western industrial societies are all democratic republics. Even in eastern Europe, where oligarchical republicanism recently held sway, the democratic form of republicanism appears to be taking hold.

---

*In recent years the magnitude of this difference has diminished. Western European governments have reduced their involvement in industrial production, while the American, Canadian, and Japanese governments have been expanding their scope of activity and their levels of expenditure.

People who are sensitive to the undemocratic elements that still exist in western industrial societies sometimes have difficulty appreciating the enormity of the changes that have occurred in almost all industrial societies. These include not just the introduction of contested elections and the formation of political parties that mobilize the masses of people in support of particular leaders and policies, but—most important of all—*the exercise of the powers of government to benefit the masses of ordinary people in countless ways*. This was unheard of in agrarian societies of the past, where the powers of government were used almost entirely for the benefit of the governing class.

The nature of the change may best be symbolized by the way ordinary people are referred to in legal codes. In agrarian societies of the recent past, they were called "subjects"; in industrial societies today, they are "citizens."

Democracy as a Variable

In discussing political systems, we should resist the temptation to think in categorical, either-or terms. To divide governments into those that are democratic and those that are not is to oversimplify. In the real world, governments differ by degree in their practice of democracy, and the degree of democracy in a given society often changes over time. Thus, we need to think of democracy as a variable like other societal characteristics, such as population size or economic productivity. Thinking of democracy in this way helps us recognize why large and complex societies can never be completely democratic. Full and equal participation by everyone in all political decisions would require that people abandon all of their other activities. Thus, not surprisingly, even the most democratic industrial society has never achieved more than a representative form of democracy.

Once we recognize the variable nature of democracy, we can better appreciate the magnitude of the change that has occurred in the polities of western industrial societies during the last 150 years. As recently as 1865, 76 percent of the members of the British Parliament were members of the aristocracy and gentry (i.e., the old governing class of preindustrial Britain) and nearly half of the seats were filled in uncontested elections.[14] One-quarter of the members of Parliament belonged to just thirty-one families, a fact that led one writer of the period to refer to Parliament as "one vast cousinhood."[15]

In the United States, as we noted in our discussion of ideologies, the government was originally an *oligarchical republic*. The right to vote was limited to men of property, as in Britain, and the great majority of people were denied this right. This was still true even half a century after the republic was established. In the presidential election of 1824, only 350,000 votes were cast, indicating that less than 10 percent of the adult population was entitled to vote.[16] Since then, the elimination of property requirements for the right to vote and to hold office, the abolition of slavery and the extension of the franchise (i.e., the right to vote) to blacks, women, and eighteen-year-olds, the passage of the civil rights acts, the direct election of senators, and the "one person, one vote" decision of the Supreme Court have greatly increased not only the percentage of Americans who are eligible to vote but, equally important, the effectiveness and importance of their votes. As a result, about half of all governmental expenditures in the United States today are for social programs that benefit the masses of ordinary people.[17] This is a tremendous change from the practices of governments during the agrarian era.

Similar trends can be observed in the recent history of the other western democratic societies, although nearly all of them lagged behind the United States in removing property requirements for the right to vote (see Figure 11.1). In Sweden and Britain, for example, these requirements were not finally removed until after World War I (see Table 11.1).[18] On the other hand, the democracies of western Europe now spend a higher percentage of their total income on social programs than the United States does (see Table 10.6, page 233).

Table 11.1 Percentage of the British Population Age Twenty-one and Over Eligible to Vote

Before First Reform Act, 1831	5.0
After First Reform Act, 1832	7.1
After Second Reform Act, 1867	16.4
After Third Reform Act, 1884	28.5
After World War I, 1919	74.0
After Equal Franchise Act, 1928	96.9

Source: Judith Ryder and Harold Silver, *Modern English Society: History and Structure, 1850–1970* (London: Methuen, 1970), p. 74.

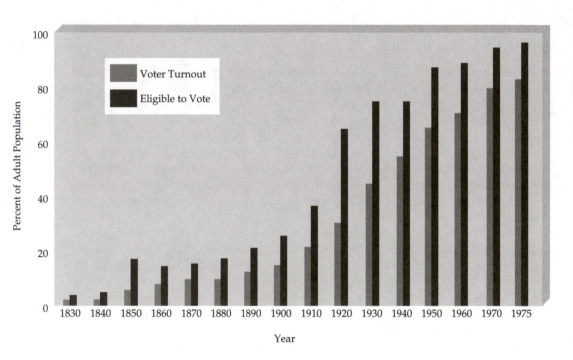

FIGURE 11.1 *Extension of the franchise in western Europe: 1830 to 1975.*
Source: Percentage of population age 20 and older eligible to vote, and turnout at elections, calculated from data on Austria, Belgium, Denmark, Finland, France, Germany, Italy, the Netherlands, Norway, and Sweden presented in Peter Flora (et al.) *State Economy and Society in Western Europe 1815–1975,* Volume 1, *The Growth of Mass Democracies and Welfare States* (Chicago: St. James Press, 1983).

Causes of the Democratic Trend

The tremendous strength and appeal of democratic ideology have been among the more remarkable characteristics of the industrial era. In the history of industrial societies, there has been only a single instance in which members of a democratic nation abandoned democracy in favor of another form of government, and that happened in a society (Germany in the 1930s) that was confronted by an exceptional set of circumstances, both economic and political. Thus, the record suggests that the democratic trend has been no accident, but rather a response to a powerful set of social forces.

For the most part, these seem to be the same forces that gave rise to *all* the major new ideologies of the industrial era—the Protestant Reformation, the conquest of the New World, and, most important of all, the Industrial Revolution. Protestantism appears to have been especially significant in the early rise and spread of democratic beliefs and values.[19] If it did nothing else, the Protestant Reformation proved that established authority *could* be challenged and overthrown. But even more important, the Protestant doctrine of the priesthood of all believers—the doctrine that all believers are equal in God's sight and can relate directly to him without the mediation of the clergy—had *political implications of a revolutionary nature*. Though the reformers, Luther and Calvin, did not recognize this, others soon did, and the bitter German Peasants' Revolt of 1524–1525 and the Leveler movement a century later in England were both stimulated by it.

This new doctrine also led to the adoption of democratic or semidemocratic forms of church government by the more radical Protestant groups, such as the Anabaptists, Mennonites, Baptists, Quakers, Puritans, and Presbyterians. It is no coincidence that democratization began in church governments some generations before it began in civil governments. Nor is it coincidence that when it did begin in civil government, its early successes were chiefly in countries where the democratization of church governments had already made considerable headway. The first major and enduring victory of the democratic movement was in the United States, a country which since colonial days had been a refuge for the more radical and more democratic Protestant groups.

The conquest of the New World was another important factor in the spread of democratic government. Conditions in the frontier regions of the United States, Canada, and Australia were far more favorable to democracy than conditions in the older, heavily settled societies of Europe. In fact, the Jacksonian movement, which did so much to broaden the base of political participation in American society, had its greatest strength in what was then the western frontier. The conquest of the New World was also important because, as we noted in Chapter 9 (see pages 196–197), it weakened the power of the traditional governing classes in European societies and strengthened the influence of the merchant class, which had long been noted for its republican tendencies.

As important as these influences were, however, the democratic movement would not have succeeded without the Industrial Revolution. Industrialization eliminated the need for large numbers of unskilled and uneducated workers living at or near the subsistence level, and as new sources of energy were tapped and new machines invented, societies had to produce more skilled and educated workers. But people with skills and education are much less likely to be politically apathetic and servile. On the contrary, they tend to be self-assertive, jealous of their rights, and politically demanding.[20] Such characteristics are essential in a democracy, for they hold in check the powerful oligarchical tendencies that are present in any large and complex social system.

Industrialization also made possible the remarkable development of the *mass media*. To a great extent this has been a response to the spread of literacy and to the increased demand for information generated by the rising level of education. Through newspapers, magazines, radio, and television, the average citizen of a modern industrial society is vastly more aware of political events than his or her counterpart in agrarian societies. Although much of the information received is superficial and distorted, it nevertheless generates interest and concern. Thus the media not only satisfy a need, they also help to create it.[21]

Finally, industrialization, by stimulating the growth of urban communities, further strengthened democratic tendencies. Isolated rural communities have long been noted for their lack of political sophistication and for their paternalistic political patterns. Urban populations, in contrast, have always been better informed and more apt to challenge established authority without waiting for conditions to become desperate. Thus, merely by increasing the size of urban populations, industrialization contributed to the democratic trend.

Mass Political Parties

The growth of democracy and the rise of industrial societies have produced a totally new kind of political organization, the mass political party, which serves to mobilize public opinion in support of political programs and candidates. Wherever there are more candidates than offices, there is a process of selection, and the candidates who are supported by parties usually win.

Party organizations differ in several respects. Some, such as the Republican and Democratic parties in the United States, are largely pragmatic, *brokerage-type parties*. They have no strong ideological commitments and no well-defined political programs. Their chief goal is to gain control of public offices in order to trade favors with special interest groups, offering preferential legislative treatment in exchange for electoral and financial support. In this type of party, discipline is weak, since each elected official is free to work out his or her own "deals." Some degree of party unity is maintained, however, because once an interest group establishes close ties with the officials of a certain party, it usually continues working with them. This is reinforced by the tendency of the more ideologically inclined to separate into opposing camps, liberals gravitating toward one party, conservatives toward the other. Sometimes the more ideologically inclined win control of the party machinery, but this is usually short-lived.

In contrast to brokerage-type parties, many of which were formed in the nineteenth century, political parties formed in the twentieth century have often had strong ideological commitments. Such parties, including both fascist parties of the right and socialist parties of the left, traditionally had well-developed programs designed to transform society, and their leaders were willing to be defeated again and again rather than compromise principles they held sacred. Since World War II, however, many of these parties have become less ideological and more pragmatic.

Nationalist ideologies have given rise to political parties in several industrial societies. The most famous was the German National Socialist (Nazi) Party organized by Adolf Hitler following Germany's defeat in World War I. Usually, however, nationalist ideologies are simply one element in the overall program of the major conservative parties in democratic societies. Thus, the Republicans in the United States, the Conservatives in Britain and Canada, and the conservatives in France usually place more emphasis on national defense and other policies relevant to nationalist ideals than their opponents do.

In ethnically divided societies, minorities sometimes form nationalist parties to protect or promote their own group's special interests. This has happened among the French in Canada, the Scottish and Welsh in Britain, and the Basques in Spain.

Finally, religious groups in western Europe and Japan have formed a number of political parties. The most successful of these have been the Christian-Democratic parties formed by Catholics in Italy, Germany, Austria, and several other countries. While the original aim of these parties was to defend the Catholic Church's position on such issues as birth control, abortion, divorce, and tax support for church schools, they have often become the chief conservative opposition to social democratic parties.

The more successful Communist parties in the democracies of western Europe have softened their stance on many issues over the years. The Italian Communist Party, for example, came to support the participation of Italy in the NATO alliance and pledged itself to support the principles of western-style democracy long before Gorbachev.

A more recent development in party organization in industrial societies has been the formation of so-called Green parties by environmentally concerned groups. Concerns with environmental issues have grown considerably in much of Europe in recent years in response to fear of nuclear war, the Chernobyl nuclear accident in the former Soviet Union, and Europe's dying forests and polluted air and bodies of water. Although the presence of Green parties in the European Parliament has risen and fallen over the past four elections, they hold 14.9 percent of its seats in the current parliament, more than they ever have.[22]

The explosion at the nuclear power plant at Chernobyl, which spread radioactive materials over much of Europe and rendered the surrounding area uninhabitable for years to come, gave powerful impetus to Green parties in western Europe.

Their success has been more limited and more volatile in the legislatures of their own countries, however. The percentage of seats Green parties currently hold ranges from a low of 0 percent in Great Britain, Canada, and Japan to a high of 9.2 percent in Germany, and their volatility is evidenced by their experience in Sweden.[23] The Green Ecology Party, the first new political party to emerge in Sweden in 70 years, won 20 legislative seats in 1988, lost them all in 1991 when it failed to get a necessary minimum of 4 percent of the popular vote, regained representation when it won 18 in 1994, and held 17 (4.9%) in 2002.[24]

The future of these parties is uncertain because they are still small and there are increasing signs that the established parties are adopting stronger policies on environmental issues to regain the support of voters who have shifted to the Green parties.[25] But modern technology could change things overnight: another Chernobyl explosion or comparable environmental disaster, especially one in western Europe itself, and the Green parties could become a major force.

Special Interest Groups

The industrial democracies are made up of a great variety of groups, each with its own special interests. Labor and management are two of the more familiar, but there are many others. In American society, for example, blacks, Hispanics, religious groups, the elderly, welfare mothers, veterans, professional groups, women, men, pro-choice groups, pro-life groups, environmentalists, pro-handgun advocates, anti-handgun advocates, homosexuals, groups representing individual industries, and dozens more are organized to promote their own interests. Each has interests that conflict, to a greater or lesser degree, with the interests of other groups, and often with the interests of society as a whole.

One of the more difficult problems facing democratic societies today is that of protecting the interests of society as a whole against the claims and demands of these special interests.* Paradoxically, it is far easier for politicians to rally support for programs that offer special favors to limited interest groups than for programs designed to promote the common good.** The reason is simple: since political success in a democratic society depends on voter support, politicians tend to respond most readily to the appeals of groups that are able to mobilize large numbers of voters. Some rationalize their actions by arguing that the interests of society are simply the sum of the interests of its parts, but that argument ignores the systemic nature of human societies.

Interest groups vary greatly in their ability to influence public policy, and their success is largely a function of their political and economic resources. The most important resource is the active support of large numbers of voters. Money is also essential in many societies, especially in those where the allegiance of voters to political parties is weak and where large campaign contributions can be used to influence voters through the mass media—especially television.

The Mass Media

One of the most important developments of the industrial era has been the emergence of the mass media as a major political force, not only in industrial societies, but in other societies as well. The rise of the media to their present position of influence and power is the result of a succession of technological breakthroughs.

The story of the mass media is generally thought to begin with the penny newspapers of New York in the 1830s. Because the price of these papers brought them within the reach of a substantial portion of the population, a tiny group of individuals—publishers and journalists—were able to transmit their views and opinions to large numbers of readers, most of whom had no opportunity to check the accuracy of most of what they read. Thus, publishers and journalists quickly found themselves in a position of considerable power in societies where public opinion was becoming increasingly important, thanks to the rise and spread of democratic institutions. The popularity, and hence the success and influence, of newspapers was greatly enhanced during this same period by the invention of the telegraph in 1837, which enabled them to provide information about important events in distant places much more quickly than was possible by any other means then available.

During the next hundred years or so, other inventions enhanced the power of the mass media still more by adding the enormously powerful elements of sound and visual imagery. The new technologies—especially radio and television—created an even greater concentration of power in the hands of a few since these media were able to reach national and even international audiences. Thus, in modern industrial societies the media elite—a few hundred individuals, or even a few thousand at most—are able to shape the flow of information and manipulate public opinion in ways that elected officials cannot afford to ignore.

---

*A clear majority of Americans—63 percent—believe that the United States government is run by a few big interests working for themselves rather than for the benefit of the people.[26]
**The construction of the interstate highway system in the United States, for example, was primarily a response to a massive lobbying effort by the trucking industry, the highway construction industry, the cement industry, and the automobile industry, and only secondarily a response to the public's desire for safer and faster highways.

The visual imagery that television provides has proven an especially potent force, since visual images stir emotions far more powerfully than the written or spoken word. The second plane strikes the World Trade Center's twin towers in New York City, as seen by millions of television viewers on September 11, 2001.

Although the media elite lack the power themselves to enact legislation, they are able, in large measure, to set the agenda for elected officials. In other words, they are able to make it all but impossible for elected officials to ignore those issues which they deem to be of primary concern. This is because journalists are "gatekeepers" who control the flow of information within a society. No television newscast can possibly report all of the day's political news that is of importance in the brief 23 minutes that are available (after time out for commercials) on the major networks' evening newscasts. Even *The New York Times,* whose motto is "All the News That's Fit to Print," provides no more than a highly abridged summary of the day's events. Editors and reporters are constantly forced to pick and choose which among them they will report and, equally important, which they will feature and which they will "bury" on an inside page, or, in the case of television news, mention only briefly and without visual imagery.

Because of this power, the media elite have considerable influence over the public's perception of what the problems confronting society, and requiring political action, actually are. When these elite "gatekeepers" act in concert in selecting the political stories they feature and the slant they give them, as they commonly do, elected officials can ignore them only at their own peril.

The visual imagery television provides has proved an especially potent force, since visual images stir the emotions far more powerfully than the written or spoken word. The power to choose among competing visual images, and to select the tiny handful that will be shown to tens of millions of people, is an awesome power in a democratic society, especially when it is in the hands of such a small group of individuals who are all but invisible and subject to only the most limited of controls by the public as a whole.

A study of the presidential election of 1976 in the United States provides a dramatic illustration of the power of the media elite to influence the political life of a democratic society.[27] That year Jimmy Carter won a very modest plurality in the first Democratic primary in the small state of New Hampshire. He received just 28 percent of the vote compared to 23 percent for the candidate who ran second and 49 percent for other candidates. Although Carter's victory at the polls was extremely modest, since he received only a little more than 10 percent of the total vote cast (counting the vote in the Republican primary), his victory in the media was overwhelming. Both *Time* and *Newsweek* featured him on their covers and devoted 90 percent of their reports on the primary to him! In the week that followed, both television and the daily press gave Carter four times the coverage of all his Democratic Party rivals combined. This proved to be decisive, because, as researchers found, 95 percent of the voters in subsequent primaries voted for the candidate they felt they knew best—and that, thanks to the media, was Jimmy Carter.

Media journalists strive to project an image of impartiality and objectivity, but in recent years a growing number of them have acknowledged the presence of intentional bias. Thus, a former president of CBS News said at one point that "our job is to give the people not what they want but what we decide they ought to have," and a president of ABC News asserted that while media journalists "can't decide *everything* that people should be allowed to see (emphasis in the original), they have the right and responsibility to impose their own judgments in presenting the news."[28] Regardless of how one judges the uses to which the media elite have put their power, one can only agree that the power they enjoy in modern democratic societies is impressive.

Political Conflict and Stability

Every social system generates internal conflict, and industrial societies are no exception. Nevertheless, their success in channeling such conflict into nonviolent forms is remarkable. Compared with agrarian societies in particular, they are much less prone to revolutions, coups, and other serious political upheavals. This is especially true of the democracies and other societies that are past the transitional or early phase of industrialization. One study of sixty-two societies found an extremely strong statistical correlation between their levels of political stability and their levels of economic development.[29]

There are a number of reasons for the political stability of the western industrial democracies. First, their greater productivity and their higher standards of living give the majority of the population a vested interest in political stability. Revolution and anarchy would be very costly for most members of advanced industrial societies. Second, a democratic ideology strengthens the allegiance of most segments of the population to their government and weakens support for revolutionary movements. Especially noteworthy in this connection is the loyalty shown by the military and the absence of military coups in advanced industrial societies. Finally, the very complexity of the structure of industrial societies seems to generate a readiness to compromise on most controversial issues. This is partly *because there are so many people in intermediate positions between the contending groups*. Most of the population, for example, has modest property holdings. Such people are likely to benefit from peaceful compromise and therefore reject extreme or violent proposals. Contrary to Marx's expectations, this is true of the great majority of blue-collar workers. Moreover, since the complexity of industrial societies means that each individual simultaneously fills a number of different roles and often belongs to a variety of groups, people who are opponents in one controversy are often allies in another. For example, middle-class whites and blacks who may be divided over racial issues often find themselves allied on economic issues. This, too, has a moderating effect.

Although political conflicts are restrained in industrial societies, they are still present in various forms and involve a wide range of issues. The most common type of conflict is between economic classes, and, in most democratic nations, this has become the basic framework for partisan politics. Typically, some parties appeal primarily to the working class and other less advantaged elements in the population, promising improved conditions if they are elected. Opposing parties rely for support on the more privileged elements in the population and campaign for office on a platform promising economic growth.

Sweden provides a good example of a strong relationship between economic class and party preference. As Table 11.2 shows, support for the Socialist and Communist parties is more than twice as strong in the working class as in the middle and upper classes. The strength of the relationship between party preference and economic class varies greatly in

Table 11.2 Party Preferences of the Swedish Population in Elections by Occupational Class, in Percentages

	Socialist and Communist	Other Parties	Total
Upper and middle classes	30	70	100
Working class	74	26	100

Source: Adapted from Walter Korpi, *The Democratic Class Struggle* (London: Routledge & Kegan Paul, 1983), figure 5.3.

Table 11.3 Strength of Relationship between Occupational Class and Party Preference in Eleven Industrial Societies

Society	Percentage Point Difference*
Finland (average of 3 surveys)	50
Norway (average of 3 surveys)	46
Denmark (1 survey)	44
Sweden (average of 8 surveys)	44
Italy (1 survey)	37
Britain (average of 14 surveys)	37
Australia (average of 7 surveys)	35
West Germany (average of 9 surveys)	22
France (average of 2 surveys)	22
United States (average of 10 surveys)	16
Canada (average of 10 surveys)	7

*Specifically, the figures are the difference between the percentage of urban upper- and middle-class people who support Labor, Socialist, Green, and Communist parties and the percentage of urban working-class people who do so. Canada's Liberal Party and the Democratic Party in the United States are also included, since there are no mass socialist parties in those societies.
Source: See note 30.

industrial societies, however, being strongest in Scandinavian societies and weakest in North American, as Table 11.3 shows. The limited relation between class and party preference in the United States and Canada is due in part to the absence of major working-class parties with strong ideological commitments. In both countries, the two major parties are pragmatic, brokerage types that tend to downplay class-related issues.

Another factor that influences the relation between economic class and party preference is the presence of serious ethnic and religious divisions within a population. It is probably no coincidence that the countries in Table 11.3 with the strongest relation between class and party preference are generally the most homogeneous both ethnically and religiously. In contrast, Canada has been divided for years by struggles between an English-speaking majority and a large French-speaking minority. In both Canada and the United States, religion and ethnicity have been important determinants of party preference.

Modern industrial democracies differ dramatically from traditional agrarian societies by virtue of their inclusion of ethnic and religious minorities and the economically disadvantaged in the political process. In agrarian societies, such groups had little or no political power. In industrial societies, in contrast, these groups have sometimes won control of the machinery of government, or at least a share in it, as the working class has done in Scandinavia, the French in Canada, and the Catholics in the Netherlands.

The Growth of Government

Apart from the rise of democracy, the most important political change associated with indus-trialization has been the growth of government. The range of activities and the diversity of functions performed by government are far greater in modern industrial societies than in any other type of society. In a traditional agrarian society, the government's chief functions were defense, taxation, the maintenance of law and order, and the support of religion. In modern industrial societies, the last of these has usually been dropped, but dozens of new functions have been added.

Many of the new functions of government arise because they are required by an indus-trial system. For example, with industrialization, machines increasingly do the work that was once done by illiterate, unskilled workers, but the economy requires more educated workers. To ensure continuing economic growth, public educational systems must be created, first at the elementary level, then at the secondary, and finally at the university level. Only governments have the power to raise the money needed to finance such expen-sive systems.

A better-educated populace quickly becomes a more demanding populace. Educated people want or require things that uneducated peasants in agrarian societies of the past never dreamed of: health care, pensions for their later years, dependable systems of transportation and communication, adequate housing, and much more.[31] While private businesses can sup-ply many of these things, there are some they cannot supply and others they cannot supply profitably for the entire population.

Highways are an example of the former, housing of the latter. A modern highway system is both too complex (requiring land-condemnation powers, for example) and too unprofitable to be constructed with private resources. Housing, on the other hand, can be profitably supplied by private businesses for most of the population in most industrial societ-ies, but governments must step in to provide housing for those who cannot afford what is offered by private enterprise.

In the western industrial democracies, much of the growth of government reflects the influence of two important developments we noted earlier: (1) the rise of democracy and (2) the movement away from pure laissez-faire capitalism toward a mixed economy. In the first instance, a democratic system of government provides the masses of ordinary citizens with a powerful instrument for pressuring elites to satisfy their needs and desires. In the second, a mixed economy is, by definition, one in which government plays a greatly expanded role.

In the revolutionary socialist societies of eastern Europe, the absence, until recently, of a democratic system of government made it far more difficult for ordinary citizens to express their wishes and to pressure political elites into using the society's resources for things they wanted. Despite this, a vast expansion of the scope of governmental activity occurred, simply because socialism led to the virtual abolition of private enterprise. Thus, while the mecha-nisms involved in eastern Europe and in the western democracies were different, the end result in both cases has been a vast expansion in the scope and power of government.

Governmental Bureaucracies: Their Expansion and Transformation

One of the best measures of the growth of government is the size of the governmental bureaucracy. In the United States, as Figure 11.2 shows, the number of civilian employees of the federal government rose steadily for more than a century and a half.

The number of federal employees per 1,000 population increased an astonishing 2,800 percent between 1816 and 1970. Although the number of federal employees has declined since 1970, this was more than offset by the rapid growth in state and local governments. In

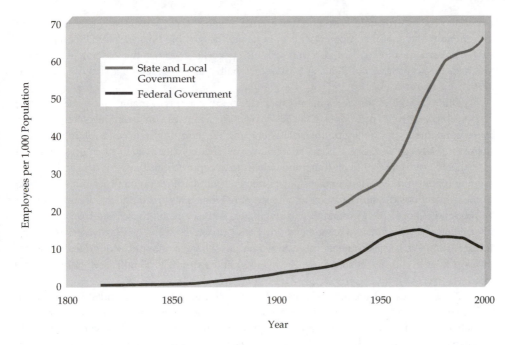

FIGURE 11.2 *United States federal and local government employment: 1816 to 2000.*
Source: U.S. Bureau of the Census, *Historical Statistics of the United States: Colonial Times to 1970,* Series
A1–15, Y241–250, Y332–334; and *Statistical Abstract of the U.S. 1997,* table 1 and table 506; and *Statistical Abstract of the U.S., 2002,* tables 2 and 441.

fact, taken together, federal, state, and local governments now employ nearly 21 million people, or more than 15 percent of the civilian labor force.[32]

The great growth in the powers of governments and in the size of their bureaucracies has made top administrative officials extremely powerful figures in industrial societies. Although this might be interpreted as simply a perpetuation of the old agrarian pattern with its dominance by a hereditary governing class, it is not. Government offices are no longer private property to be bought and sold and inherited by one's children. Rather, they tend to be assigned competitively on the basis of education and experience. Furthermore, in the exercise of the office, officials are expected to act on the basis of the public interest rather than of private advantage. Although reality falls far short of these ideals, there is a marked contrast between the practices of officials in most modern industrial societies and the practices of those in traditional agrarian societies. Members of industrial societies have discovered this repeatedly in their dealings with the officials of many of the governments of less industrialized societies of the Third World, where bureaucratic corruption is a customary way of life.

In large measure, the explanation for the change lies in the newer ideologies, which assert that the powers of government are derived from the people and should therefore be used for their benefit. This is in sharp contrast to the traditional ideology of agrarian societies, which defined the state as the property of the ruler. When modern officials use public office for private advantage, they are subject to a variety of official sanctions, including criminal prosecution. Such constraints were rare in agrarian societies of the past.

Despite the less venal behavior of public officials in industrial societies, the growing size and power of government bureaucracies have become matters of concern. A series of Gallup polls taken since 1967 shows that far more Americans fear big government than fear big business or big labor. Even before September 11, 2001, and the ensuing legislation that expanded the investigative powers of government agencies, 64 percent saw big government as a threat to the nation compared with 24 percent who saw big business, and 9 percent who saw big labor as threats.[33] More ominously, 87 percent said that the federal government violated their constitutional rights at least occasionally, and 70 percent expected it would do so in the future.[34]

One of the chief problems of bureaucracies everywhere is to maintain a sense of public responsibility in their personnel. Officials in welfare agencies, for example, often become more concerned with enlarging their staffs and raising their own rank and salary than with delivering services to those whom the agency was created to serve. In most governmental bureaucracies it is also difficult to get individuals to accept responsibility for decisions. Buck-passing, paper-shuffling, and endless delays become standard operating procedures. Because of the tremendous division of labor, and hence of responsibility, within these organizations, it is frequently impossible to establish accountability, and as a result these patterns persist year after year, and generation after generation. These problems were especially serious in the former Communist governments of eastern Europe, where command economies put enormous power in the hands of a greatly expanded and extremely complex set of bureaucracies.[35]

So far, critics of bureaucratic power have not come up with any workable alternative. The sheer size and complexity of government in a modern industrial society make mass participation in decision making impossible. A substantial delegation of power, therefore, is inevitable, and those to whom the power is delegated generally do what they deem appropriate. This is one of the most serious limitations to the application of democratic principles in any large-scale organization.

12

Industrial Societies: Social Stratification

STRATIFICATION IN INDUSTRIAL SOCIETIES

As the technologies of societies have advanced, their systems of stratification have grown more complex. Wealth, income, and other differences were minimal in hunting and gathering societies, but they grew ever larger with the emergence of horticulture and then agriculture. Following the Industrial Revolution, the complexity of stratification systems has increased at an accelerating rate, but in some respects, the trend toward ever increasing inequality appears to have reversed itself.

The increased productivity of industrial technology has greatly expanded the range of possibilities for inequality, and refinements in the division of labor have created numerous occupational positions between the highest paid and most respected, and the lowest paid and least respected. There has also been an increase in the degree to which different dimensions of inequality are independent of one another—people high or low on one dimension are not necessarily high or low on all, or even most, others. Furthermore, as we noted in Chapter 10, increasing productivity has also raised the standard of living of the average person in industrial societies.

As a result, it is no longer possible to characterize stratification as a simple matter of a few "haves" and a huge majority of "have nots," as was the case in the typical advanced agrarian society. Also, because the size of the economic "pie" in industrial societies has grown so much over time, it is not possible to make statements about whether the wealth or income of different segments of the population has gone up or down simply on the basis of whether their proportionate "slice of the pie" is growing or declining. For, if the pie is growing, the competition for wealth and income is not a zero-sum "game." In fact, the *wealth* or *income* of the rich or the poor may actually be growing in periods when their wealth or income *share* is shrinking.

All of this means that we must examine different dimensions of stratification separately, and that we must distinguish between the degree of inequality on a given dimension and the amounts of that social good held by different segments of the population. We will also want to look at long-term trends in inequality in industrial societies, and to compare the extent of inequality in industrial societies to that found in contemporary and past preindustrial societies.

POLITICAL STRATIFICATION

Despite the differences in the political systems of industrial societies, one thing is true of them all: their political elites have the greatest influence in choosing among the wide range of options available to industrial societies and in influencing the way their huge economic surpluses will be apportioned. Therefore, in examining the patterns of inequality in industrial societies, we begin with these elites and with the system of political stratification.

In agrarian societies, the governing elite was generally a small, homogeneous, and well-defined group, and top positions were often hereditary. In industrial societies, there is a greater openness of the political system that allows a somewhat more diverse set or group to enter the ranks of the political elite through multiple channels, and multiparty electoral systems produce and sustain competing groups of elites. To complicate matters further, constitutional principles in the democracies often provide a variety of checks on executive authority, while federal systems divide political power between national officials and regional officials.

In the United States, for example, political power is divided among officials at federal, state, and local levels, and among executive, legislative, and judicial branches of government. Moreover, these people have achieved office in a variety of ways. Some have been appointed, others elected. Of the latter, some have been elected as Republicans, others as Democrats, and still others have run as third-party candidates or in nonpartisan elections. Political power also lies in the hands of many people who hold no governmental office and exercise no governmental responsibilities. These are people who command substantial economic resources (e.g., heads of large corporations, heads of large private foundations, wealthy individuals) or who are able to deliver large blocs of votes (e.g., heads of labor unions, leaders of some ethnic and religious groups). Last, but hardly least, those who control the flow of information in American society—newspaper editors, television newscasters, and others—help define the nation's political agenda and influence the decision-making process (see "The Mass Media," pages 250–252).

The composition of the political elites of other industrial societies varies somewhat from society to society, depending on the relative strength of the various ideologies and interest groups within them. Also, it tends to change over time in response to technological advances, international developments, and other events. But most of the groups mentioned above are influential in most of the western democracies and compete with one another for control of the economic surplus and for a voice in shaping the policies of their societies on issues.

In a number of industrial societies, there is a strong symbiotic relation between politicians and economic elites. This is especially evident in societies with brokerage-type political parties. In these societies, politicians constantly need money to finance expensive election campaigns, while economic elites seek legislative favors (e.g., lower taxes, larger governmental subsidies, less restrictive regulation) that only politicians can provide. Although this kind of symbiotic relationship is strongest where brokerage-type parties are dominant, leaders of some of the more ideologically oriented parties (e.g., the French Socialists) have discovered that electoral success can depend on economic conditions, and this often forces them to work more closely with economic elites than they might otherwise choose to do.

Control of the economic surplus in industrial societies is not simply a matter of elites versus the masses, as it is sometimes made to appear. Different sets of elites often come into conflict with one another. For example, President Ronald Reagan's tax proposals in 1985 led to conflicts between the heads of older "rust-belt" industries of the Midwest and executives in the newer high-tech industries in other parts of the United States. President George W. Bush's proposals regarding use of national forests and other wilderness areas has led to sharp conflicts between the timber industry and its employees on the one hand and environmentalists on the other.

Another significant feature of the relation between elites and the masses in western industrial societies is the amount of power that has been acquired by organizations representing large blocs of ordinary citizens. The growth in power of labor organizations in the twentieth century is a good example of this. By organizing politically and economically, union members were able to share significantly in the benefits of the rapidly expanding economy. Traditional elites resisted less vigorously than they might have been expected to, because the rapid expansion of the surplus made it possible for them to avoid costly conflicts while still

Nine of the most powerful individuals in American society: members of the Supreme Court of the United States (from left) Antonin Scalia, Ruth Bader Ginsburg, John Paul Stevens, David Souter, Chief Justice J. William Rehnquist, Clarence Thomas, Sandra Day O'Connor, Stephen Breyer, and Anthony Kennedy.

obtaining greater benefits for themselves. In other words, the great expansion of the economic surplus changed the nature of the conflict from the near **zero-sum game** (see Glossary) it had been throughout most of the agrarian era to a strongly **positive-sum game** from which almost everyone could benefit.

More recently, organizations have been formed to promote a variety of different viewpoints (e.g., anti-war groups, pro- and anti-abortion groups) and the interests of a variety of nonelite groups (e.g., racial minorities, women, retired people, the handicapped). While such groups have never gotten all they wanted, they have often won important concessions, including a larger share of the economic surplus.

Today, because of the enormous productivity of industrial societies and because of their democratic polities, almost all parts of the population share to some degree both in the control of the economic surplus and in its benefits. To be sure, they do not share equally in either, but they do share in them. As a result, the vast majority of the members of these societies enjoy a standard of living far above the subsistence level. Even people who are classified as living in poverty in these societies usually live considerably above the subsistence level—which is why so many people in industrializing societies are eager to migrate to the western democracies (see "Prison Proves 'Best Home'," page 260).

Because so many different groups have a voice in modern democratic societies, no year passes without efforts to redistribute wealth and income or effect other changes. Although elected officials make most of the final decisions, they know that they can be replaced if a majority of the electorate becomes dissatisfied with their actions—or inaction. This makes it impossible for them to ignore the more pressing concerns of the masses of ordinary citizens.

Prison Proves "Best Home"

Ramchandra Gnanu Malekar, Maryland Correctional Training Center inmate 130755, leaned back in his chair and raised both feet to display his shoes. "Look here," he said in wonder. "I have never seen shoes like this kind."

They were fairly ordinary two-tone shoes, but Malekar, who grew up in a village outside Bombay where sandals were considered something of a luxury, found them astonishing. "And I have undershirts," he said, unbuttoning far enough to show off a small patch of silky blue material. "Nylon, poplin, cotton. I have never in my whole life had such clothes in my house."

For Malekar, "my house" is now a large Maryland jail facility, where the young Indian citizen is serving a six-year sentence for manslaughter. He was convicted of strangling Lalita Khambadkone, the woman who brought him from Bombay to Maryland to work as a servant.

Last Friday, almost two years to the day after the slaying, Malekar sat in the brightly lit visiting center of the jail and described it as the finest home he has ever known. He has a bed for the first time in his life, he said, and eats off plates. Though he had been "so emaciated that a child could have pushed him," he has now developed into a robust young man with muscular upper arms that he boasts are 13 inches around.

"Fried chicken," he said delightedly, when asked what foods were new to him. "French toast, scrambled egg, pancake, Spanish rice, Chinese rice, chicken stew, macaroni, sweet potato, mashed potato."

It is all very different from the poverty-ridden village where Malekar grew up. Prison in the United States is far better than the life he knew in India.

Source: The Washington Post

The Distribution of Income

In industrial societies, incomes vary enormously. In the United States, for example, there are many families whose annual incomes total less than $10,000 per year, even when the value of welfare payments, food stamps, housing subsidies, medical aid, unemployment compensation, social security, and other benefits is included. At the other end of the income scale, there are some athletes, entertainers, and business executives with incomes of $1 million or more per year. Beyond them, there is a tiny group of entrepreneurs and CEOs who make $10 million or more in a single year, and there are several families with enormous fortunes that should, at normal interest rates, provide them with incomes in excess of $100 million per year. Thus, the ratio of the highest to the lowest family incomes in the United States appears to be more than 10,000 to 1.

In fact, the United States has the most unequal distribution of income of any of the advanced industrial societies (see Table 12.1). The highest-earning 20 percent of households receive 3.0 times the share of the lowest-earning 40 percent. Canada's income distribution is substantially more equal—the ratio is about 1.9—falling near the average for advanced industrial societies.

Nonetheless, incomes in industrial societies, including the United States, are much more equally distributed than they are in contemporary nonindustrial societies. As the bottom two rows of Table 12.1 show, in industrial societies the shares of income going to the lowest-earning 40 percent are generally higher (20.5 versus 19.9), and the shares going to the highest-

TABLE 12.1 Percentage Shares of Income Received by Highest-Earning 20 Percent and Lowest-Earning 40 Percent of Households in Industrial Societies

Society	Highest-Earning 20 Percent	Lowest-Earning 40 Percent	Ratio of Highest 20 to Lowest 40
Finland	35.0	24.8	1.4
Japan	35.7	24.8	1.4
Sweden	34.5	23.7	1.5
Norway	35.8	24.1	1.5
Denmark	35.8	23.1	1.6
Belgium	37.3	22.3	1.7
Austria	37.9	20.1	1.9
Canada	39.3	20.2	1.9
Netherlands	40.1	19.9	2.0
France	40.2	19.8	2.0
Switzerland	40.3	19.6	2.1
Australia	41.3	17.9	2.3
Italy	42.6	18.0	2.4
United Kingdom	43.2	17.8	2.4
Germany	44.7	16.2	2.8
United States	46.4	15.6	3.0
Industrial average	**39.4**	**20.5**	**2.0**
Nonindustrial average*	**48.7**	**15.9**	**3.7**

*Average for 105 other societies.
Source: World Bank, *World Development Indicators* Online Database (www.worldbank.org/data/onlinedatabases/onlinedatabases.html). Note: Latest figure is reported, years vary.

earning 20 percent are generally lower (39.4 versus 48.7) than in nonindustrial societies. Consequently the ratio of the highest to lowest income shares is only 2.0 for the industrial societies compared to 3.7 for nonindustrial societies.

The relatively more unequal distribution of income in the United States does not mean that low-income households earn less than those in other societies. In fact, because the economy of the United States is more productive than many others (see Tables 9.2 and 9.3, pages 209 and 214) the incomes of the lowest-earning households are actually relatively high. For example, by our estimate, the lowest-earning households in the United States earn from 7 to 29 times what their counterparts in industrializing societies earn.[1]

It also does not mean that over the long term income inequality has been increasing in the United States. In fact, over the past sixty years income inequality has generally decreased (see Figure 12.1). Income inequality dropped dramatically after the stock market crash of 1929 and continued to fall into the 1950s. During the 1960s it remained relatively steady and then it began to rise quite steeply in the late 1970s and 1980s, but it has not reached its 1929 level.

It would be a mistake, however, to conclude that as the *share* of the top-earning 20 percent declined from 1929 through 1950 their *income* declined. In fact, over this period the *incomes* of all groups increased, but since the income of the lowest-earning 40 percent grew *faster* than that of the top 20 percent, the income gap between them shrank somewhat. Similarly, the more recent decline in the proportionate share of the lowest-earning 40 percent of families does not imply that their incomes declined. Although the share of income received by the lowest-earning 40 percent of families declined from 16.9 percent in 1980 to 14.1 percent in 2000, because per capita personal income increased more than 44 percent, net of inflation, their incomes actually increased substantially.[2]

Median household incomes also increased in this period, especially in per capita terms. In constant (2000) dollars, household incomes went from $35,238 in 1980 to $42,151 in 2000, an increase of nearly 20 percent.[3] But because households in 2000 were smaller than households in 1980, *per capita* household incomes rose from $12,767 to $16,088, an increase of 26 percent.[4] As we will see in the next chapter, however, these increases in household income

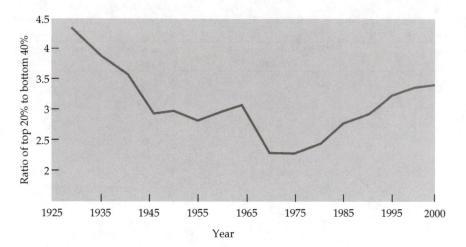

FIGURE 12.1 *United States income inequality from 1925 to 2000, ratio of top 20 percent to bottom 40 percent.*
Sources: U.S. Bureau of the Census, *Historical Statistics of the United States: Colonial Times to 1970,* series G319–336; *Statistical Abstract of the U.S. 1997,* table 725; and *Statistical Abstract of the U.S., 2002,* table 659.
Note: The latest ratio for the United States differs slightly from that in Table 12.1 because it is for a later date and has been taken from a different source.

have largely been a result of the fact that more household members, especially married women, have entered the paid labor force.

Finally, as large as the current ratio of top to bottom incomes is, income inequality in industrial societies is not nearly as great as it was in agrarian societies of the not-so-distant past. As we saw in Chapter 7, the top 1 or 2 percent of the families in those societies generally received not less than *half* of the total income. In contrast, the top 5 percent of American households currently receives only about 21 percent of the total income.[5] And, unlike the situation in the typical agrarian or early industrial society, relatively few individuals remain persistently in the lowest income categories year after year. According to a Treasury Department study, almost 40 percent of households that were in the lowest income category in the United States in 1979 moved to a higher income category one year later, and after ten years 85 percent had done so, including more than 14 percent that had moved into the *very highest income category.*[6] Similarly, another study found that only about 30 percent of the individuals living in poverty in the United States in one year were still living in poverty a year later, and only about 2 percent remain in poverty eight years or longer.[7]

The Distribution of Wealth

Wealth has long been more unequally distributed than income in industrial societies. For instance, not long ago, figures for the United States showed that the highest-paid 5 percent received only 21 percent of total income, whereas the richest 1 percent owned 38 percent of total wealth, and the top 5 percent, more than half.[8]

These figures exaggerate the difference, however, because inequalities in wealth are much more closely linked to age than are inequalities in income. As individuals grow older, most accumulate household furnishings and other possessions, pay off mortgages on their homes, and build up equity in pension funds. For example, a recent study of asset ownership in the United States showed that the youngest families (under age 35) had a median net worth of $11,600, middle-aged families (ages 55 to 64) had a net worth of $181,500, and the oldest families (over 75) had a net worth of about $151,400.[9]

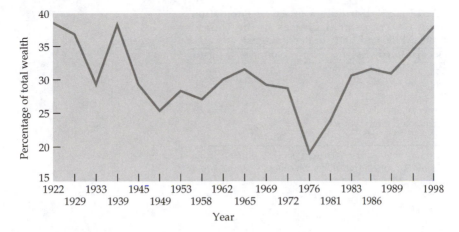

FIGURE 12.2 *Wealth owned by top 1 percent, United States households from 1922 to 1998.*
Sources: Edward N. Wolff, "Changing Inequality of Wealth," *American Economic Review,* 82 (May 1992);
and Edward Wolff, quoted in "The Wealth Divide: The Growing Gap in the United States between the Rich
and the Rest," *Multinational Monitor,* May 2003.

Turning to *trends,* there is no clear evidence that ownership of wealth has consistently
grown either more concentrated or more dispersed. As Figure 12.2 shows, the percentage of
wealth owned by the richest 1 percent of households has risen and fallen several times over
the last seventy years. First measured at 38 percent in 1922, its share of societal wealth
declined dramatically during the Great Depression, rose abruptly just before World War II, fell
below 30 percent and remained there in the two decades following the war, increased slightly
in the 1960s, plummeted to a low of about 19 percent in the mid-1970s, and then increased
again in the 1980s and 1990s.* Although the long-term trend between 1922 and 1981 was
generally downward, wealth inequality has increased substantially in recent years, and is now
again as high today as it was in the 1920s.[11]

These cycles of concentration and dispersion are apparently consequences of changes
in the relative levels of income inequality and of rising or falling prices of stocks and real
estate.[12] The overall shape of the trend in wealth concentration—a long-term decline and
recent increase—is similar to that seen earlier for income inequality (see Figure 12.1), and the
dramatic dips in inequality follow steep declines in stock market prices (e.g., 1929, 1973–
1975).

Occupational Stratification

For most members of industrial societies, their occupations are the chief determinant of their
income and wealth. About 72 percent of the national income of the United States today, for
example, is distributed in the form of wages, salaries, and fringe benefits of employment, such
as health insurance and employers' contributions to social security.[13]

As we noted earlier, the range of benefits received by people in different kinds of
occupations varies greatly in the United States, with the top 10 percent enjoying incomes that
are 10, 15, or more times larger on average than the incomes of those in the bottom 10
percent—the unemployed, part-time workers, and the unskilled. A handful of people at the
very top of the occupational ladder in the western democracies—business leaders, entertainers,

*There is some evidence that wealth may have been more equally distributed in the United States prior to
industrialization, but it is important to note that it was then a "frontier," not a typical agrarian society.[10]

TABLE 12.2 Distribution of Adult Population among Occupational Classes in the United States, 1900 and 2001 (in Percentages)

Occupational Class	1900	2001
Upper white-collar	10	31
Upper blue-collar	11	11
Lower white-collar	7	29
Lower blue-collar	34	27
Farmer and farm laborer	38	2
	100	100

Sources: Figures based on data in U.S. Bureau of the Census, *Historical Statistics of the United States: Colonial Times to 1970,* series D182–232, and U.S. Bureau of the Census, *Statistical Abstract of the U.S., 2002,* table 588.

and athletes—are paid about 1,000 times more than full-time workers who receive the minimum wage.

Prior to World War II, lower white-collar workers enjoyed, on average, higher incomes than skilled blue-collar workers in the United States.[14] Since then, however, the relative rankings of these two classes have gradually been reversed, creating the present pattern, which favors skilled manual workers in many countries. An even more important change in the occupational system in industrial societies has been the substantial growth in the relative number of high- and middle-status occupations. As Table 12.2 indicates, the percentage of upper and lower white-collar jobs in the American labor force has more than tripled since the beginning of the last century. The percentage of upper blue-collar workers has remained steady, the percentage of lower blue-collar workers has declined slightly, and, as we saw in Chapter 10, farm employment has plummeted. These developments have brought about an important change in the class structure of American society and, to a lesser extent, other industrial societies. No longer are the majority of people concentrated in the lower class, as in agrarian societies of the past (see Figure 7.5, page 176). Today, most of the people in most industrial societies are members of the middle class. This is yet another consequence of the technological innovations that have so transformed the conditions of life for members of these societies since the beginnings of industrialization.

Educational Stratification

One of the great achievements of industrial societies has been the tremendous expansion of educational opportunities. Formal education is no longer a privilege limited to children of a small affluent minority. Today, all children are allowed to attend school for ten years or more at public expense.*

Despite the great increase in educational opportunities, inequalities in their utilization persist. Some young people drop out of school as soon as possible, while others go on to receive advanced degrees. The amount of education an individual receives is a function of many things—intelligence, motivation, health, peer influence, family tradition, family resources.[15]

Differences in educational achievement, whatever the cause, have substantial consequences for subsequent achievement in the occupational system of stratification. Most jobs in modern industrial societies have educational prerequisites, and insufficient years of education

---

*As we noted in Chapter 9, this is largely a legacy of the Protestant Reformation and its encouragement of mass literacy.

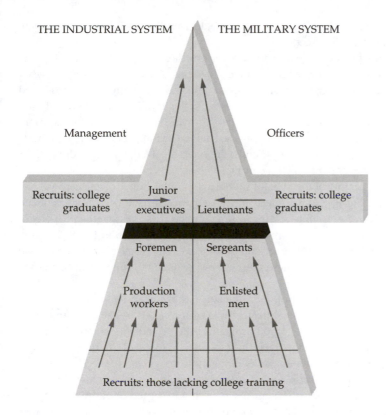

THE INDUSTRIAL SYSTEM   THE MILITARY SYSTEM

Management   Officers

Recruits: college   Junior   Recruits: college
graduates   executives Lieutenants   graduates

Foremen   Sergeants

Production   Enlisted
workers   men

Recruits: those lacking college training

FIGURE 12.3 *Model of recruitment and promotion in modern industry compared with recruitment and promotion in the military.*

or lack of an appropriate diploma can bar otherwise qualified individuals from careers in many fields. In effect, modern personnel practices have created a civilian counterpart to the traditional military caste system, with its sharp distinction between officers and enlisted personnel. Just as the ceiling on promotion for enlisted troops is normally the rank of sergeant, so the ceiling on promotion for less educated workers in industry tends to be the rank of foreman, or possibly plant superintendent. Higher positions in industry and government are usually reserved for people with a college or university degree who are recruited directly from outside the organization. Figure 12.3 illustrates the pattern.

The importance of educational stratification today is clearly evident in data on the relationship between education and income. The most highly educated Americans, for example, receive about six times more income than their least educated counterparts.[16] Because of the great economic value of education in modern industrial societies, many economists and sociologists have begun to refer to it as "human" capital. Like the more traditional forms of capital, it has the power to produce income.

Racial and Ethnic Stratification

Many industrial societies have racial or ethnic divisions within them. Canada, for example, has a serious cleavage between its French- and English-speaking populations, Belgium between Flemings and Walloons, and the United States between African-Americans and European-Americans—to cite but three of the more prominent instances. When membership in an ethnic or racial group has an appreciable influence on an individual's access to the benefits a society offers, the group has become, in effect, a class.

Classes of this kind, however, are different from most others in several respects. For one thing, the resource that is involved in ethnic and racial systems of stratification is an *ascribed* characteristic: racial or ethnic background, unlike occupation and education, cannot be altered by individual effort. In addition, racial and ethnic classes usually have a greater degree of class consciousness than most others; more, say, than people with high school diplomas, more even than manual workers. Finally, because physical traits (i.e., appearance) and primary relationships (i.e., ties with family and close friends) are often involved, it is more difficult for an individual to move into or out of an ethnic or racial class.

The most striking example of this type of stratification in the United States involves the two major racial groups. Since colonial times, African-Americans have been a subordinate group. Before the Civil War, the majority of African-Americans were slaves and the property of members of the white group. Even before the Emancipation Proclamation in 1862, a few African-Americans had established businesses and become wealthy (some even became slave owners themselves); but despite their achievements, they continued to suffer from handicaps imposed because of race.

Today, most of the more obvious of these limitations have been removed. Civil rights legislation ensures African-Americans equal treatment in stores, hotels, restaurants, and other business establishments, and affirmative action programs even provide preferential treatment in college admissions, hiring, and promotions. But more subtle forms of discrimination continue in housing, club membership, mortgage lending, and some other areas.

Yet, in some respects it would appear that little or no progress has been made in recent decades. For example, in 2001 African-Americans households earned about 69 percent of what white households earned, only slightly more than they did 30 years earlier.[17] In other respects it would appear that conditions may actually have deteriorated. More than 50 percent of African-American families with children under the age of 18 are headed by women, and 69 percent of African-American births today are to unmarried women (up from 38 percent in 1970).*[19] Children in these families are deprived not only of a father's contribution to socialization but of an important source of income as well. Black female-headed households earn less than half of what black married-couple households earn, and black female-headed households contain the vast majority of the black children who live in poverty.[20] Many of these youngsters enter school lacking a strong foundation for learning and later leave school poorly equipped to compete in the demanding occupational system of a modern industrial society. Whatever the underlying causes of the high proportion of female-headed families among African-Americans (a subject of controversy), its impact on children is undeniable.**

However, this is only part of the picture. There is also evidence of substantial economic progress. After years of virtually no change, the percentage of black children in poverty has dropped from 41.5 percent to 30.4 percent, and today, black married-couple families earn 84 percent of what comparable white families earn.[22] Moreover, whereas in 1940 black men made only about 41 percent of what white men earned, today they earn more than 70 percent, and, in recent years, young black men entering the labor force have earned more than 80 percent of what their white cohorts earn.[23] And, whereas black women earned only 36 percent of what white women earned in 1940, today they earn 99 percent of what white women earn .[24]

Perhaps more significant, the percentage of African-Americans in middle-class occupations has grown from less than 10 percent in 1940 to about 52 percent today (see Figure 12.4). Black homeownership is now at a record 48 percent, double what it was in 1940—24.[25]

*The comparable figures for whites are: percentage of white children under 18 who live in female-headed families, 17.3; percentage of white births to unmarried women, 27.[18]
**For example by some estimates, children from a fatherless home are 9 times more likely to drop out of high school, 5 times more likely to commit suicide, and 20 times more likely to end up in prison.[21]

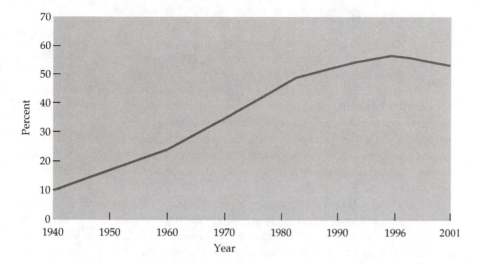

FIGURE 12.4 *The percentage of African-Americans in middle-class occupations, 1940 to 2001.* *Sources:* William Julius Wilson, *The Declining Significance of Race: Blacks and Changing American Institutions,* 2d ed. (Chicago: University of Chicago Press, 1980), Chapter 6; and U.S. Census Bureau, *Statistical Abstract of the U.S., 2002,* table 588.

These figures reveal a basic division within the African-American population. The removal of legal and social barriers opened a wide range of opportunities for those with the family and educational resources to pursue them, but it also led to a growing rift between them and others lacking such resources. Furthermore, since the effects of these social, economic, and educational deprivations persist and are passed on across generations, movement out of this disadvantaged class may be becoming more difficult. For example, while the median income of the highest-earning 5 percent of African-Americans families rose more than $27,000, net of inflation, between 1975 and 1992, the income of the lowest-earning 20 percent actually *declined* by more than $2,000.[26]

Although the white population is also sometimes thought of as a homogeneous unit, it too is divided. People of British extraction enjoy the highest status, followed by those of other northwestern European ancestry, and then by those of southern and eastern European ancestry.[27] This reflects the historic dominance of those who first settled the United States. Until about 1830, most of the white population was of British extraction and they occupied most of the dominant positions in the major institutions. Since most of the later immigrants were poor, had little education, and were unable to speak English, they tended to fill the more menial positions at first. The more they had in common with the older stock, the more readily they were accepted in marriage and in the better jobs and neighborhoods. Northwestern European Protestants were thus accepted more readily than southern and eastern European Catholics and Jews.

In Canada, the most serious cleavage is along ethnic lines and divides French-speaking Canadians from English-speaking ones. Although the French settled the country first, they were later conquered by the British, who dominated the political system from the eighteenth century on. The problem was further aggravated because the English industrialized the country while the French clung to an agrarian way of life. As a result, the English also dominated the economy, even in Quebec, the home province of the French.[28] In recent years the French have succeeded in eliminating most discriminatory practices through political action, but a substantial minority desires political independence.[29]

Age and Sex Stratification

Inequalities based on age and sex have been a part of every human society, past as well as present. To some extent, these inequalities reflect genetic differences among the members. On average, men have been stronger than women, and they have not been burdened biologically by the responsibility for bearing and nursing children. Adults have been larger, stronger, and more knowledgeable than children, though aged adults have become disadvantaged whenever their health, vitality, and mental abilities have declined.*

These biologically based differences have been reinforced and extended in most societies by cultural norms. Thus, the fact that the average woman is not as strong as the average man has often led to norms that exclude *all* women from activities for which *some* women would be physically qualified.

With respect to age and sex stratification, modern industrial societies resemble preindustrial societies in many ways. Continuity can be seen most clearly in the frequency with which older men still control the more powerful organizations. Most members of the United States Senate, for example, are men, and their average age in recent years has been 57 (the more powerful members of the Senate have been even older because of the seniority system that is used to select committee chairmen).[30] Most business leaders are also men, and although the CEOs of top corporations are three years younger than their counterparts twenty years ago, their average age is 56.[31] Finally, an earlier study of American military leaders, all of whom were male, found that their average age was 54.[32]

In virtually all of the industrial societies for which data are available, the income of women is substantially lower than that of men. On average, women earn about 74 percent of what men earn, but the ratio varies from a low of 59 percent in Japan to 91 percent in Switzerland.**[33]

*The social status of older people is also affected by the prevailing rate of social change. In societies where social change is slow or imperceptible, the value of their experience is high, because their knowledge continues to be relevant. On the other hand, where the rate of social change is high, especially technological and economic change, the value of their experience is low because much of their knowledge is often obsolete.

**According to one study, the ratio of women's to men's incomes in the United States is relatively low, not because of greater discrimination against women, but because of the greater disparity between the incomes of high- and low-paying jobs in the United States (e.g., see Table 12.1). The concentration of women in lower-paying jobs thus depresses women's incomes more relative to men's than it does in societies where the occupational income disparity is lower.[34]

The United Kingdom's first woman prime minister, Margaret Thatcher.

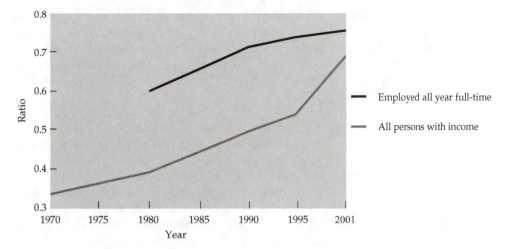

FIGURE 12.5 *Ratios of women's to men's income for all persons with income and for full-time, full-year employees, 1970 to 2001.*
Source: U.S. Census Bureau, *Statistical Abstract of the U.S., 1997,* tables 731 and 725; *Historical Statistics,* tables 5a and 5b.

There are a variety of reasons for this income disparity, but the most important appears to be the persistence of the division of labor between the sexes. In all industrial societies there are certain occupations that are filled primarily by men and others that are filled primarily by women (in addition, there are some in which there is a more balanced representation of the sexes) and women have greater household and child care responsibilities than men. The occupations filled primarily by women usually have lower wages or salaries than those filled primarily by men. They also tend to be occupations that offer fewer opportunities for promotion to more responsible positions.

The concentration of women in these lower-paying jobs is partly a heritage of the past when women seldom worked for long outside the home (see Figure 13.2, page 283) and when those who did were assumed (sometimes incorrectly) to be supplementing their husband's or father's income and, therefore, less in need of high wages than men, who were expected to be the primary providers for families.* Once established, this pattern has persisted because it tends to shape the expectations and aspirations of men and women. Thus, the pattern of women's employment has become, in part, a matter of choice, with some women viewing marriage as a more attractive alternative than the job market and a commitment to family as more rewarding and more important than a commitment to career.

But it is also rooted in the present. Married women in the paid labor force find that they must constantly balance the demands of their jobs and careers against those of their families and children. And, although there is some evidence that husbands with working wives are today performing more household and child care functions than they did in the past, the majority of these responsibilities still accrue to wives.[36]

Nevertheless, the wage gap between men and women has generally closed with advancing industrialization. In the United States, for example, employed women's wages as a percentage of men's rose from less than 50 in 1890 to nearly 65 in 1950, but then dropped a bit and hovered around 60 between 1950 and 1980.[37] They began to rise steeply in the 1980s and by 2001 had reached 76 (see Figure 12.5).[38] In fact, between 1979 and 2001, after adjusting for inflation, white women's incomes rose by nearly 26 percent, black women's rose by 17

---

*According to one study, there was a clear "marriage penalty" in the United States in 1900. It estimates that married women, on average, were paid 30 percent less than their unmarried cohorts.[35]

percent, while white men's incomes rose by only 2 percent and black men's income was stationary.[39] Furthermore, women between the ages of 20 and 24 today earn about 92 percent of what their male cohorts earn, and there is every reason to expect this gap will continue to shrink, as women's skills and labor experience continue to grow, and as larger numbers of women move into high-paid "traditionally male" occupations (e.g., see "The Changing Role of Women," in Chapter 13, page 282).[40]

The legal and political standing of women has also greatly improved as a result of industrialization. Laws that once restricted their right to own property have been eliminated, and women now own much of the wealth in all western societies. For instance, an analysis of tax returns in the United States for 1986 showed that 40 percent of the people with a net worth of $5 million or more were women.[41] Barriers to higher education have also been largely eliminated. In fact in the United States today, women earn the majority of bachelor's degrees and nearly half of all doctorates (see Table 13.4, page 285).[42] Even in the political arena, women have made substantial gains. In 1900, women were permitted to vote only in New Zealand and in four American states.[43] Today, they enjoy this right in every industrial society. Women are a growing presence in the parliaments of industrial societies (see Table 13.5, page 286), the percentage of parliamentary seats held by women has more than doubled in the past 20 years, and women have served as prime ministers in Britain, Canada, France, and Norway.[44]

VERTICAL MOBILITY

Compared with agrarian societies, industrial societies offer many more opportunities for individuals to improve their status. In agrarian societies, high birthrates ensured an oversupply of labor in almost every generation. At every level in society, a substantial percentage of the children were obliged to work in occupations of lower status than their parents or to join the ranks of beggars, outlaws, prostitutes, and vagabonds. Although a few improved their situation, far more were downwardly mobile.

In industrial societies, conditions are strikingly different. Falling birthrates have reduced the oversupply of labor, while technological advances have greatly increased the proportion of high-status, high-income jobs. Furthermore, because the upper classes have smaller families than the lower classes, opportunities are created for many children of the latter to become upwardly mobile. Finally, flawed though they are, the systems of free public education in industrial societies give talented and disciplined children from the lower classes an opportunity to acquire skills that can help them move up the social ladder.

As a result of these developments, there is no industrial society in which the rate of downward mobility greatly exceeds the rate of upward mobility. At worst, downward mobility may be slightly greater in a few of them.[45] In most industrial societies, however, there appears to be more upward mobility than downward, a remarkable change from the recent preindustrial past.

This development has undoubtedly been a factor in reducing the threat of the working-class revolution predicted by Marx and his followers. If, in every generation, a quarter or more of the children of workers are able to rise into the ranks of the middle class, resentment against the system is almost certain to be less than if only a few move up the ladder, the pattern Marx expected. Furthermore, since those who rise tend to be the more talented and ambitious members of the working class, much of its potential leadership for protest movements is lost.

SOCIAL INEQUALITY: TWO BASIC TRENDS

In agrarian societies of the past, systems of inequality were often built into the legal codes. There was no pretense that people were equal. Some were legally classified as members of a privileged nobility, some as commoners, others as slaves or serfs, and their legal rights and privileges varied accordingly. Democracy as we understand it was unknown in these societies. Political decisions were the God-given prerogative of a tiny elite; the rest of the population had no voice in decision making. The only thing that limited the power of the governing elite was the knowledge that if conditions became too oppressive the masses might revolt. Because of their enormous power, the ruler and the rest of the governing class together usually enjoyed not less than half of the national income and sometimes as much as two-thirds.[46]

In advanced industrial societies, legally based hereditary status has been virtually eliminated. In Britain and a few other societies, titles of nobility remain, but nearly all of the special rights and privileges that were once attached to them no longer exist. Equally important, the disadvantaged legal statuses of serf and slave have been completely abolished. Although social inequalities remain, they are no longer based solely on the accident of birth.

In addition, opportunities for participation in political decision making have substantially broadened in industrial societies. The franchise has been extended ever more widely until virtually the entire adult population is now able to vote in all of them. Although the system falls far short of equal influence for all, it is, by democratic standards, a tremendous advance over the situation that prevailed in agrarian societies not long ago.

Finally, income inequality has been greatly reduced in industrial societies. Though substantial inequalities still exist, the change has been tremendous. As we have seen (e.g., Table 12.1), the top 20 percent of the population in industrial societies appears to receive only about 40 percent of the national income, compared to the 50 percent or more that was received by the top 1 or 2 percent of the population in agrarian societies.

Thus, *the overall level of inequality in industrial societies is considerably less than that in agrarian societies of the past, or in most nonindustrial societies in the world today*. The best explanation for this egalitarian trend seems to be the enormous growth in productivity unleashed by the Industrial Revolution, together with the demographic transition (see Figure 13.1).[47] With per capita national incomes increasing rapidly, the dominant classes found it was no longer in their interest to fight all the claims of other classes to a larger share of the economic surplus.

Periodic concessions to the lower and middle classes could help elites preserve much of their power and privilege. By giving ground in relative terms (i.e., by conceding a larger share of total income to nonelites), they could even improve their economic position in absolute terms (i.e., their total income and wealth actually increased). This was possible because technological advances had transformed the old zero-sum game that prevailed in most preindustrial societies into a positive-sum game. Elites apparently concluded that it was better to settle for a smaller share of a much larger pie than to fight to preserve their historic share and, in the process, risk an end to economic growth and the loss of all the benefits it afforded.

An important consequence of this is the rising standard of living and the improved life chances of the average member of industrial societies. For the past few years, the United Nations has tried to develop an objective measure of the quality of life afforded by different societies in the world system today. Table 12.3 shows the results of their most recent effort. Industrial societies are all clustered near the top of this scale with an average score of 0.93 out of a possible 1. In contrast, industrializing societies lagged far behind this achievement with an average score of only 0.53.

This gap between the rich and poor nations of the world reveals the other side of the development coin: while on the one hand the advancing technology of industrialization has helped reduce the level of inequality *within* industrial societies, on the other it has increased inequality *among* societies in the world system. The gap has been widening ever since the start of the industrial era. For instance, in 1860, the wealthiest quarter of the world's population controlled 58 percent of world income, but by 2001 the 16 most advanced industrial societies, which comprise less than 13 percent of the world's population, controlled about 73 percent, and the share of the bottom quarter fell from 12.5 to less than 2 percent.[48] With the new technology gradually eroding the barriers between societies, the social impact of this trend is bound to increase. We will return to this subject in Chapter 14, when we examine the complex problems of the Third World as it struggles to develop economically in the shadow of far wealthier and more powerful societies.

TABLE 12.3 Quality of Life in Industrial Societies

Society	HDI*
Canada	0.96
France	0.95
Norway	0.94
United States	0.94
Japan	0.94
Finland	0.94
Netherlands	0.94
Sweden	0.94
Belgium	0.93
Austria	0.93
Australia	0.93
United Kingdom	0.93
Switzerland	0.93
Denmark	0.93
Germany	0.92
Italy	0.92
Industrial median	0.93
Nonindustrial median**	0.53

*Human Development Index, an index of well-being based on measures of life expectancy, literacy, education, and income.

**Median for 70 nonindustrial societies (see Table 14.7, page 310).

Source: United Nations, *Human Development Report, 1997* (Cary, N.C.: Oxford University Press, 1997).

13

Industrial Societies: Population, the Family, and Leisure

Industrialization has dramatically altered the size, rates of growth, and spatial distribution of the populations of industrial societies. These changes, in turn, have had a major impact on the size, composition, and functioning of families in these societies and how people spend their time. In this chapter, we will first examine the long-term trends in population, and then trace some of their most important effects on families, age and sex roles, and leisure in industrial societies.

POPULATION

Growth in Size of Societies

The populations of industrial societies have grown substantially over the past two centuries, though not nearly as much as their technological advances and gains in productivity would lead one to expect. For example, England and Wales had a population of approximately 9 million at the start of the nineteenth century, and their current population is about 53 million.[1] While this five- to sixfold increase is impressive when compared to rates of population growth in the preindustrial past, it falls far short of the more than twentyfold increase in Britain's gross national product during that same period (see Chapter 10). The same thing is true of other societies that have industrialized, with the exception of the United States, Canada, Australia, and other former frontier societies that entered the industrial era with populations that were abnormally small for their geographical size.

To better understand the reasons for this pattern of growth in population, we must consider the three factors that together determine the rate of population change: mortality, fertility, and migration.

Trends in Health and Longevity

Throughout the agrarian era, sickness and disease were a pervasive feature of human life. Prior to the invention of the microscope, it was impossible for anyone even to know of the existence of bacteria or viruses, much less to devise effective means of combating them. Medical knowledge was not advanced much beyond what had existed at the end of the hunting and gathering era and, for most illnesses, people were forced to rely on faith healing, magic, or medical practices of dubious value (e.g., the use of leeches and bloodletting) when they became ill.* As we have seen (Table 7.1, page 156), average life expectancy at birth in

---

*Some recent research has found leeches very helpful in preventing blood-clotting when reattaching severed fingers and other parts. This, of course, was not the use to which leeches were put in the preindustrial era.

TABLE 13.1 Death Rates for Communicable Diseases, 1860–2000

Cause of Death	Deaths per 100,000 Population per Year		
	Mass., 1860*	U.S., 1900	U.S., 2000
Influenza and pneumonia	***	202	24.3
Tuberculosis	365	194	0.3
Gastritis, enteritis, etc.	***	143	0**
Typhoid fever	76	31	0
Diphtheria	68	40	0
Smallpox	27	***	0
Measles	18	13	0
Scarlet fever	***	10	0

*Massachusetts was the first state to keep reliable statewide records on the causes of death; reliable national data are not available before 1900.
**A zero indicates that the rate is less than 0.1 per 100,000 population.
***Not reported.
Source: *Historical Statistics of the United States: Colonial Times to 1970,* pp. 58 and 63; *Statistical Abstract of the United States, 2002,* tables 100 and 101.

even the most advanced agrarian societies was as low as twenty to twenty-five years, and even the children of royalty and the upper classes did not have a much greater life expectancy.

During the industrial era, however, there has been an explosive growth in the store of information concerning the prevention and cure of disease—especially most communicable diseases, such as influenza, tuberculosis, diphtheria, and smallpox, which once killed large numbers of people and afflicted many more.*

As a result, the death rate from communicable diseases has dropped tremendously (see Table 13.1) and life expectancy at birth has more than tripled in industrial societies.

Moreover, whereas half or more of the babies born in hunting and gathering and horticultural societies, and a quarter or more of those born into relatively prosperous agrarian villages *died before they reached their fifteenth birthday,* in industrial societies, *99 percent survive.*[2] In fact, children born today in industrial societies can expect, on average, to live seventy-five years or longer. Equally important, they will live far healthier lives than was possible for most in preindustrial societies.

Declining Birthrates and Increasing Immigration

As health conditions improved and death rates declined, industrial societies experienced a period of rapid population growth. This was because birthrates remained at traditional levels, which created a widening gap between birthrates and death rates (see Figure 13.1).

Within a few decades, however, birthrates also began to decline. During the last 150 years, technological advances on various fronts (e.g., the vulcanization of rubber, the development of the contraceptive pill, safe methods of abortion and sterilization) have made it possible for members of industrial societies to control the number of their offspring by safe and effective means. At the same time, technological advances in other areas, together with various social changes (e.g., the creation of social security programs, prohibitions against child labor), have virtually eliminated the historic economic incentive for having children. In addition, the increasing employment of women outside the home has made child-rearing more difficult and more expensive. As a result, birthrates have dropped greatly in all industrial societies.

*Several new diseases, such as AIDS and West Nile virus, have emerged in recent decades, and methods for controlling them still leave much to be desired, though advances seem likely.

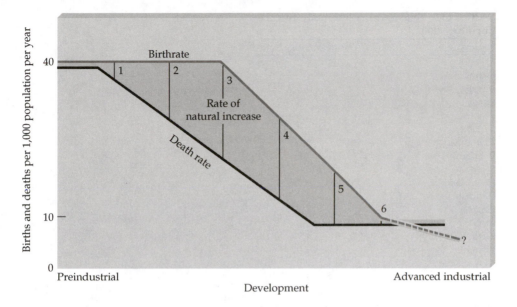

FIGURE 13.1 *Generalized long-term trends in fertility, mortality, and natural increase in industrialized societies. The vertical lines measure the rate of natural increase at six different periods of time; rates of population growth increased (time 1–3) and then declined (time 4–6) with advancing industrial development.*

In most industrial societies, in fact, birthrates have dropped substantially below the level required to keep populations at their present size. To maintain stable populations, women in industrial societies today must have, on average, about 2.11 children each.* As Table 13.2 makes clear, the fertility rate in every industrial society is below this figure. If these rates were to continue, industrial societies as a group would experience a 29 percent decline in population over the next seventy-five years, and Italy, which has the lowest fertility rate, would experience a 40 percent decline. Even the United States, which has the highest rate of fertility among industrial societies, would decline by about 5 percent.**

Declines of these magnitudes are unlikely, however, because of the great influx of immigrants from the developing world. The economic opportunities and high standards of living in the industrial democracies, together with the growth of the welfare state and its many benefits, are a powerful magnet for people whose own societies are suffering the throes of early industrialization.

Although the overwhelming majority of emigrants from developing societies remain within the developing world, there is a substantial flow of people out of developing societies and into the advanced societies. Every year, on average, between 1996 and 2001 there was a net outflow of about 3.6 million people primarily from developing societies.[3] China contributed 508,000 to this flow; Mexico 284,000; Pakistan 213,000; the Congo 180,000.[4] The United States was the most popular destination, absorbing 27 percent of the emigrants; Germany was the second most popular, absorbing 9 percent; and Canada was third at 5 percent.[5] Europe collectively took in about 21 percent.[6] As a result, more than 23 percent of Australia's population

*Because some girls die before reaching the age of reproduction, and because some couples are infertile, those women capable of bearing children have to have slightly more than two apiece.
**Note that with an average total fertility rate of 3.1, the nonindustrial societies could experience a nearly 50 percent *increase* in population over this same time period.

TABLE 13.2 Total Fertility Rate in Industrial Societies, 2002

Society	Total Fertility Rate*
Italy	1.2
Germany	1.3
Austria	1.3
Japan	1.3
Switzerland	1.4
Canada	1.5
United Kingdom	1.6
Belgium	1.6
Sweden	1.6
Netherlands	1.7
Denmark	1.7
Finland	1.7
Norway	1.7
Australia	1.7
France	1.9
United States	2.0
Industrial average	1.5
Nonindustrial average	3.1**

*The total fertility rate is an estimate of the number of children the average woman will have in her lifetime.
** The average is 3.5 if China is excluded.
Source: Population Reference Bureau, *World Population Data Sheet 2003*.

is foreign-born, 20 percent of Canada's, 19 percent of Switzerland's, 10 percent of the United States's, 9 percent of Germany's, and 6 percent of France's.[7] And in England, there are some schools in which not a single English child is enrolled.[8]

Immigration of this magnitude would create problems in any society, but it is especially serious when substantial cultural differences are introduced into populations that have been culturally homogeneous for centuries. It is difficult to exaggerate, for example, the cultural gulf that separates devout Muslims from Pakistan, Turkey, and Algeria from the nominally Christian but largely secularist native populations of England, Germany, and France.* Even when the migrants are Christians from southern Europe, as with Slavic immigrants in Germany or the Portuguese in Luxembourg, the effect can be unsettling.

But when high levels of immigration are combined with global economic recession and high rates of unemployment, the situation can become explosive. The rising rates of ethnic violence and the resurgence of xenophobia in western Europe are obviously a result of this volatile mixture of ethnicity and economics.[9] But even if their economies recover and their unemployment rates drop substantially, industrial societies will still confront serious ethnic, racial, and religious strains. As the continuing conflict in India, the Philippines, South Africa, Northern Ireland, and the recent explosions of violence in the former Soviet Union and Yugoslavia attest, ethnic, racial, and religious conflicts are some of the most enduring and intractable problems faced by societies.

---

*One indication of the magnitude of this gulf emerged in the late 1980s when Muslim immigrants in England—a nation that prides itself on freedom of expression—threatened to assassinate the author of a book they found offensive, while burning his book in public rallies and threatening stores that sold it. More recently, problems have emerged in France, where Muslim immigrants have challenged traditional dress codes in the schools and engaged in anti-Semitic activities of various kinds, and in Germany and England where young Muslim men have been recruited by al Qaeda to engage in terrorist activities in the United States and elsewhere.

Emigration from the Third World to advanced industrial societies has become so great that immigrants often outnumber the native population in large sections of major cities: Turkish shops in the Kreuzberg district of West Berlin.

Population Distribution: The Growth of Urban Populations

Another revolutionary demographic change has been the massive shift of population from rural areas to cities and towns. Even in the most advanced agrarian societies, the limitations of agricultural technology required that 90 to 95 percent of the population live in rural areas, where the basic raw materials were produced. Since urban communities were dependent on the surplus that could be extracted from the peasantry, they could never grow beyond 5 to 10 percent of the population.

Advances in agriculture in the last two hundred years removed this constraint on urban growth. Thanks to the new technology, farms required far fewer workers (see Table 10.2, page 224). Simultaneously, the new system of factory production, with its need for large concentrations of workers, stimulated the growth of cities and towns. As a result, nearly 80 percent of the populations of industrial societies now live in urban areas.

Nowhere are the consequences of the Industrial Revolution more clearly evident than in the major cities of the industrial world. Vast concentrations of people live and work in organizational systems of extraordinary complexity. Most of the time these systems function so smoothly that we forget the complex infrastructure of water and sewer systems, power systems, communications systems, and transportation systems on which they depend. It is only when we experience such disasters as earthquakes, hurricanes, or war, and these systems break down for a time, that we are reminded of the technological foundation on which industrial societies are built and on which they depend.

THE FAMILY

The impact of industrialization on kinship has been no less dramatic than its impact on population, the economy, the polity, and stratification. The consequences for kinship, the oldest institutional system in human societies, can be seen in its changing functions, in the smaller size and altered composition of nuclear families, and in the changing roles of women and young people.

Changing Functions of the Family

In the simplest human societies, the basic integrative force in societal life was the kin group, an all-purpose organization that provided for the physical, political, economic, educational, religious, and psychic needs of all its members. As societies grew in size and complexity, this had to change. No longer could an individual's relationships with other people always be defined in terms of kinship. New roles and organizations began to emerge and, as a result, the functions of the kin group were gradually eroded.

Although this process began thousands of years ago, kin groups remained of great importance throughout the agrarian era. Above all, the nuclear family (i.e., mother, father, and children) was still the basic productive unit in the economy. The peasant family was almost invariably a work unit, and this was also true of many other families. Place of work and place of residence were normally the same, and all of the members of a family, including the children, shared in the work.

Government, too, was still a family affair. Members of the political elite usually inherited their status, while the royal family considered the state its personal property. Education remained primarily a family responsibility: boys usually learned the male role and productive skills from their fathers; girls learned theirs from mothers and aunts. With the growth of urban communities, the kinship system was not always as strong or pervasive as it had been in simpler societies. But family ties remained central in the lives of most people and provided the basic framework for societal life.

In industrial societies, many of the family's traditional functions have been eliminated or greatly altered. The family is now an economic unit only in terms of consumption, not of production. Families no longer control the political system; nepotism (preferential treatment of relatives in the workplace) may still occur, but it is not accepted as normal or legitimate. Schools, religious groups, and other organizations have assumed much of the responsibility for the education, socialization, and supervision of children, and a wide variety of organizations, from youth groups to summer camps and from beauty colleges to universities, have taken over the task of providing young people with the skills they will need in their adult lives.

But the family has not been stripped of all its historic functions. Some of the most critical functions, including reproduction and the early socialization of children, still fall to the nuclear family. And as the larger kin system, or extended family, has diminished in importance, and as societal life has become increasingly complex and depersonalized, the nuclear family's responsibilities have in some ways become more important. For example, it usually bears the primary responsibility for fulfilling the psychic and emotional needs of its members. With respect to children, the nuclear family is still expected to be the major factor in personality development, instilling basic values, providing affection, offering guidance and encouragement in school and career decisions, training in the use of money, and much more. And all of this must be accomplished in a social environment that is culturally far less homogeneous, and therefore far more difficult, than the one in which most agrarian families raised their children.

Marriage today is undertaken for more personal reasons than in the past. Because most horticultural and agrarian societies viewed marriage largely in economic terms, marriages were usually arranged by parents with economic considerations in mind. The individuals most intimately involved were often denied even veto power. Sexual attraction and affection were not considered of primary importance: everyone knew that these might grow or wane, but the family's need for a firm economic base would persist.

In industrial societies, in contrast, marriage has become an arrangement that is undertaken primarily to enhance personal happiness and to permit individuals to fulfill personal goals, such as establishing a home or having children. Most people today view marriage as the union of a man and a woman who are attracted to one another both physically and emotionally and who hope to find pleasure, comfort, convenience, and companionship by sharing their lives.

In short, marriage and the family are becoming more a matter of choice than of necessity. One indication of this is the growing number of people who live apart from any family group. One reason for this is the decision of many young adults to postpone marriage. Since 1960, the average age of women at marriage has risen from 20 to 25 and of men from 23 to 27.[10] The number who have divorced and not remarried has increased by nearly 50 percent.[11] Unlike previous generations, however, many unmarried or divorced people today share living accommodations with another person. Currently, about 10 percent of younger women, aged 20 to 34, report that they are living with someone to whom they are not related by blood ties or marriage, and unmarried partners now comprise more than 5 percent of U.S. households.[12]

Causes of Change in the Family

Change in the family is essentially the result of technological advance and the organizational and ideological changes that have followed in its wake. One of the most important of these has been the enormous increase in specialization. Specialized organizations of various kinds have steadily removed from home and family much of the responsibility for a wide range of services. These include not only educating and caring for the young, but also caring for the ill and the aged, processing food and preparing meals, making and caring for wearing apparel, and much more. As a result, the nuclear family itself has become a much more specialized institution.

Specific elements of the new technology have also had a great impact on the nuclear family, especially those that have given people control over fertility. Because of advances in methods of limiting family size, couples today have a much wider range of options available to them in almost every area of their lives than couples had in societies of the past. Nothing better illustrates how technological advance expands the "limits of the possible," for individuals and families as well as for societies, than these advances.

Industrialization has also served to undermine the traditional authority structure of the family. The father is no longer the head of the family in the way he was in agrarian societies, and parents do not have nearly as much control over their children's conduct as they had in agrarian societies or earlier in the industrial era. Peer group influence and the mass media have become much more powerful than family influences for many teenagers, and serious family conflict often results.

In large measure, the drastic decline in parental authority is an inevitable result of the technological and other changes that have destroyed the family's role as a productive unit that had to work together for the mutual benefit, even the survival, of its members. Related to this, industrialization has had the effect of drawing families apart both physically and psychologically. Most fathers and many mothers are away from home all day because of work, while schools

During the nineteenth and early twentieth centuries, large families were the rule: the Dudleys of Richmond, Virginia, 1903.

and other organizations draw children out of the family for other purposes. Today, children in the lower grades may spend more time with their teachers than with their mothers, and teenagers often spend more time with friends than with parents or siblings. Similarly, husbands and wives see less of one another or of their children than of their coworkers.

Another important cause of the decline of authority within the home has been the new democratic ideology which has permeated industrial societies, and which carries with it an individualistic bias that puts more emphasis on the rights of individuals than on their responsibilities to the groups to which they belong. Just as the democratic trend has altered roles within political, economic, and educational institutions, so, too, has it altered roles within the family.

A final factor contributing to the weakening of family ties is the greater number of options available to individuals who wish to sever those ties. Divorce is easier, and so is economic independence for women, even women with children (see page 281). As a result of all of these factors—increased specialization, new ideologies, and new technologies—the nuclear family today is far less cohesive than its agrarian predecessor.

Finally, the extended family has been substantially weakened by technological advances that make the populations of industrial societies highly mobile. Although the lower cost and greater ease of transportation and communication make it possible for individuals to stay in contact with relatives across greater distances, the relationships are not as intimate as when relatives live within the same community.

The Nuclear Family in Industrial Societies

One of the most drastic changes in the nuclear family is in the number of children, as Table 13.3 indicates. British marriages contracted around 1860 produced a median of six children. Barely two generations later, the median had dropped to two. Families with eight or more

TABLE 13.3   Number of Children Born to British Couples Married around 1860 and around 1925

Number of Children Born	Percentage of Marriages	
	Marriages around 1860	Marriages around 1925
None	9	17
One	5	24
Two	6	25
Three	8	14
Four	9	8
Five	10	5
Six	10	3
Seven	10	2
Eight	9	1
Nine	8	0.6
Ten	6	0.4
Over ten	10	0.3
Total	100	100

Source: Royal Commission on Population, *Report* (London: H. M. Stationery Office, 1949), p. 26.

children declined from 33 percent of the total to only 2 percent. Although the decline was more rapid in Britain than in most industrial societies, the general pattern has been quite similar.[13]

Comparisons like the one in Table 13.3 are somewhat misleading if we assume that they also reflect the degree of change in the number of children actually living within a family at the same time. In the earlier period, the death rate among children was so much higher than it is today that there were often considerably fewer children living in an agrarian family than were born into it. Another factor that reduced the number of children living with their parents at any given time was the long duration of the childbearing period. Women who had eight, ten, or more children often bore them over a period of twenty years or more. Typically, by the time the youngest children were five or ten, many of their older siblings would have left home or died. Thus, although the nuclear family was larger in agrarian societies, the number of its members who actually lived together at any one time was not as different as the change in birthrates suggests.

Perhaps more significant than the shrinking size of the nuclear family is the change that occurred in its composition due to increases in divorce and in the number of people raising children outside of marriage. During the last hundred years, the divorce rate in virtually every industrial society has risen substantially. In the United States in 1890 it was only 0.5 per 1,000 population per year; today it is 4.0.*[14] In large measure, this trend is a result of the altered functions of the family, the changed perception of marriage which accompanied it, the new options available to women, and the newer attitudes of society toward divorce. Half or more of all divorced people eventually remarry, however, which indicates that marriage is still considered a meaningful and valuable institution.[16]

Despite the great increase in divorce, its impact on the nuclear family has not been as dramatic as one might suppose. This is because marriages during the agrarian era, and early in the industrial era, were disrupted about as often as they are today, though for a different reason: the death of one or both parents. In eighteenth-century Sweden, approximately 50 percent of nuclear families were broken by parental death before all the children had reached adulthood; in late-eighteenth-century France, the figure was 60 percent; and in early-twentieth-

*It has declined rather steadily, however, from its peak of 5.3 reached in 1979 and 1981.[15]

century India it was 70 percent.[17] Thus, despite the rising divorce rate, the percentage of ever-married women between the ages of 45 and 64 who were still living with their first husband remained virtually unchanged in the United States during most of the twentieth century.

More recently, however, as the divorce rate has continued to rise, and as more women have opted to raise children outside of marriage, there has been a rapid increase in one-parent families. This trend has been particularly pronounced in the United States, where 27 percent of all children under the age of 18 live in single-parent homes.[18] Eighty-four percent of these are headed by women.[19] In fact, the proportion of families that are single-parent has increased 76 percent since 1970.

This kind of family arrangement has not worked out at all well for large numbers of the people involved. Thirty-nine percent of all female-headed families in the United States have incomes below the poverty level, compared with less than 8 percent of families with both parents present.[20] In addition, many of the children in these families do poorly in school and become involved in crime or with drugs. In short, these families contribute disproportionately to several of the major problems confronting modern industrial societies.

The nuclear family today also has fewer extended kin living with it. Its household less frequently accommodates aged grandparents or unmarried aunts and uncles. This is no longer necessary in most cases because modern urban communities provide so many alternative facilities for single individuals—apartments, nursing homes, restaurants, laundries, and so on. Moreover, as these facilities have developed, changes have occurred in societal values: most members of industrial societies are jealous of their privacy and value it more highly than the benefits they might enjoy as members of larger and more inclusive households.

The Changing Role of Women

Nowhere are the effects of industrialization on society's norms, values, and sanctions seen more clearly than in the changing role of women.[21] Throughout history most women spent their prime years bearing children, nursing them, caring for them when they were sick or dying, and rearing them when they survived; doing domestic chores; tending gardens; and often helping in the fields. It is hardly surprising, therefore, that women seldom played significant roles outside the home or made outstanding contributions to the arts.

The first signs of change came in the nineteenth century when the economic benefits of large families began to be outweighed by their costs. Efforts to limit fertility were soon aided by innovations in the area of birth control. During the nineteenth and early twentieth centuries, however, the average woman still produced a large family, still had babies for whom there was no alternative but prolonged breastfeeding, still carried the full burden of child care and housework, and sometimes was also obliged to work outside the home.

Because women were usually supplementary wage earners for their families, they were not trained for skilled jobs and were relegated to those that paid the least. Their availability for work at low wages posed a threat to the emerging labor movement and, as a consequence, women were virtually excluded from it. It was, in effect, a working*men's* movement, and its goal was to wrest a greater share of the growing economic surplus from the upper classes.

In contrast, the early women's movements in western societies were dominated by the better educated, more leisured, and economically secure women of the upper classes, and their goals were primarily to obtain for women some of the legal and civil rights that already belonged to upper- and middle-class men: the right to vote, to hold public office, to own property, and to attend universities. Late in the nineteenth century, they also became concerned with the situation of working mothers and sought to have their hours of employment shortened and night work eliminated entirely.

By the 1920s, the original goals of the women's movements in western industrial societies had been largely achieved and these movements declined. Changes continued to occur

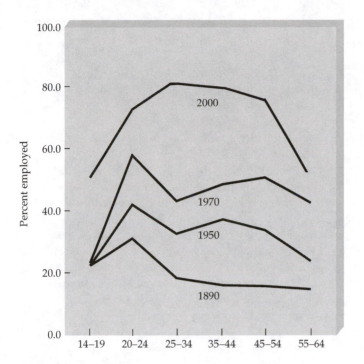

FIGURE 13.2 *Female labor force participation by age from 1890 to 2000.*
Sources: James P. Smith and Michael P. Ward, *Women's Wages and Work in the Twentieth Century* (Santa Monica, Calif.: Rand, 1984), Table 1; *Statistical Abstract of the U.S., 1997,* table 620, and *Statistical Abstract of the U.S., 2002,* table 561.

in the role of women, but chiefly as a result of technological innovations—not because of organized political efforts. These innovations included many laborsaving devices for the home, such as refrigerators, freezers, automatic washing machines and dryers, vacuum cleaners, electric irons, and frozen foods, all of which, taken together, greatly reduced the time and energy consumed by housekeeping. The development of a safe alternative to breastfeeding and more effective methods of birth control were especially important in freeing married women from historic constraints on their lives and in enabling substantial numbers of them to seek employment and engage in other activities outside the home for the first time.

During the twentieth century, there was a rapid increase in women's participation in the labor force in most industrial societies. Figure 13.2 shows the percentage of women in various age categories who were in the paid labor force in 1890, 1950, 1970, and 2000. As the plotted percentages clearly show, in each succeeding period a larger percentage of women at every age have been employed. Today 60 percent of all American women are employed outside the home, including more than 70 percent of those between the ages of 20 and 54.[22] Increasing numbers of married women, and married women with children, have entered and remained in the labor force. Figure 13.3 shows one of the important reasons why. Although the incomes of married-couple families have increased on average in recent decades, this is primarily because more married women are now working for pay. The incomes of families where the wife is not in the paid labor force increased quite modestly in this period.

The tremendous increase in women's participation in the labor force in recent decades has been the foundation for the new women's movement that began in the 1960s. This newer movement has had a diversity of goals, but one underlying objective: to break the restrictive molds in which societies have cast women. This is based on the premise that with a single exception—women's capacity for childbearing—the differences between the sexes no longer

"I Never Meant to Leave Ambition at the Altar"

The following poem was written around 1920 by Hettie Barlow Dudley, who is shown seventeen years earlier in the photograph on page 280 with the other members of her family. In addition to the nine children shown, two others died in infancy of whooping cough. Soon after the picture was taken, her husband fell seriously ill and for more than a year she was the sole support of her large family. To provide for them, she made candy on a commercial scale, and the older boys in the family sold and delivered it to families and stores throughout Richmond. When her husband recovered, he announced that he would now take over the management, but she was unwilling to accept this and opted instead to terminate the business, thus bringing a promising entrepreneurial career to an abrupt end.

This poem, which she titled "The Living Poem," captures in a wry and moving manner the ways in which family responsibilities constrained and frustrated most ambitious and talented women in the era before modern technology provided effective means of birth control and laborsaving devices for the home. But the poem also reflects an indomitable spirit that enabled this woman to take pride and find happiness in what she was able to achieve within the constraints imposed on her.

Weary of my ceaseless tasks
    Of baking and of broiling,
I sought to cultivate my soul
    And end my labored toiling.
I set the mop and broom aside,
    Determined not to falter.
I surely never meant to leave
    Ambition at the altar.
I planned to write some poems rare
    To reach the Hall of Fame.
I yearned to win great honors
    To decorate my name.
And so I sought my pad and pen
    And sat me down to think.
Then, just as I began to write
    The baby spilled the ink.
So then I found a pencil
    And sharpened it quite fine.
But, goodness me! my muse had fled!
    I could not write a line.
I thought of birds and flowers,
    Of meadows and of brooks.
But ere I could arrange my thoughts
    I heard, "Ma, where'r my books?"

I waited till the kids were off
    At school another day,
I put the baby in the yard,
    And there I bade her stay.
Then, just as I had shaped my wits,
    And a fine rhyme was turning,
A neighbor rushed in calling loud,
    "Hettie, your pies are burning."
I am afraid I ne'er will rank
    With Hemans nor with Browning.*
I am afraid that laurel wreath
    Will ne'er my brow be crowning.
No matter when or where I try
    To put my thoughts on paper,
That Imp called "Interruption"
    Starts cutting up some caper.
So now I've laid them all aside,
    My glowing aspirations.
But as I cook and sweep and sew
    I have my compensations.
The world may watch—my friends may wait:
    My home is what I show 'em.
My happiness, my laurel wreath.
    I live, not write, my poems.

*The poets referred to are Felicia Hemans, whose work was much admired by Wordsworth, and Elizabeth Barrett Browning.

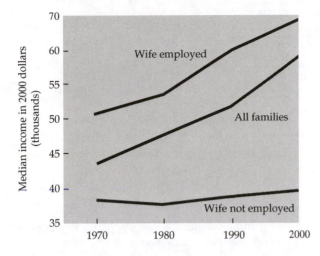

FIGURE 13.3 *Median incomes of married-couple families from 1970 to 2000.*
Source: Statistical Abstract of the U.S. 1997, table 730; and Statistical Abstract of the U.S., 2002, table 662.

provide a valid basis for the division of labor. Modern technology is able to compensate to a large degree for differences that are purely physical (e.g., strength, lactation), while differences with psychological components (e.g., emotional responses, competitiveness) are to some as yet undetermined degree the result of socialization rather than genetics and therefore modifiable.

The changes that have occurred in the labor force in recent decades are striking. The percentage of managers, executives, and physicians who are women has more than tripled in the last thirty years; and for architects and engineers it has quintupled.[23] These changes have been matched by equally striking changes in women's access to higher education, especially postgraduate education, in recent decades (see Table 13.4).

The patterns of change vary somewhat among industrial societies. Thus, the proportion of women who hold managerial positions is higher in the United States than in most other industrial societies (see Table 13.5). On the other hand, the proportion of women in Congress tends to be lower than their counterparts in other societies.

The women's movement also emphasizes that power and prestige in modern societies derive from activities outside the family and that if women are to have equal access to these rewards and share equally in shaping society's institutions, they must participate fully in both the economy and the polity. But women cannot have equal access to the more interesting and demanding jobs and to promotions, higher pay, political offices, and other opportunities

TABLE 13.4 Proportion of Degrees Awarded to Women in the United States, 1960 and 2000

Type of Degree	1960	2000
Bachelor's degree	38.5	57.3
Doctor of Philosophy	10.5	44.9
Master of Business Administration	3.6	40.7
Law	2.5	47.3
Engineering	0.3	19.0

Source: U.S. National Center for Educational Statistics, *Digest of Educational Statistics, 2002,* Chapter 3 (http://nces.ed.gov/pubs2003/digest02/).

TABLE 13.5 Proportion of Elite Positions Held by Women in Selected Industrial Societies

Society	Managerial Workers	Congress or Parliament
United States	46.0	14.3
United Kingdom	30.0	17.9
Germany	26.9	32.2
Sweden	30.5	45.3
Japan	8.9	7.3

Source: The Cabinet Office of Japan, International Labour Organization, and Inter-Parliamentary Union, as reported in the *New York Times,* July 25, 2003.

outside the home as long as the burden of responsibilities within the home is divided so unequally.* Thus, the women's movement seeks both to increase men's participation in household responsibilities and child care and to spread the burden of child care by tax rebates for working parents and by the creation of tax-supported child care centers.

Studies have shown that although men and women in industrial societies spend approximately equal amounts of time working (on average, 47 hours per week for men and 49.5 hours per week for women), men spend a much higher percentage of their time working for pay, while women spend proportionately more on family responsibilities.[25] The greater burden of household and child care responsibilities is, of course, one reason for both the differences in earnings between the sexes and the lower proportion of women who rise to supervisory and managerial positions (see "Organizational Discrimination or Individual Preference?"). The Family and Medical Leave Act in the United States—requiring employers to allow unpaid leave for those caring for children or sick parents—may help families to cope better with births and the medical needs of other family members, but it is unlikely to alter the imbalance in family responsibilities between the sexes. Industrial societies in Europe, especially the Scandinavian societies, have tried to do more in this regard. For instance, in Sweden the parents of a newborn child are given nine months of paid leave, and they decide how to divide the leave between them.[26]

Despite efforts such as these to deal with the changing role of women, numerous problems remain. Many individuals find it difficult to combine the role of employee with the roles of parent and spouse and to meet all of their responsibilities. More often than not, the demands of the job take precedence and marital and parental obligations are sacrificed (e.g., many children are left alone and unsupervised).

Efforts to expand nursery schools and other child care facilities have only partly met the need, even in eastern Europe, where women's involvement in the labor force has been greatest. Communist East Germany, for example, was reputed to have had the most extensive and the best child care system of any industrial society, but even it provided for only 60 percent of children under 3 years of age.[27]

For women themselves, the consequences of changes in their role are becoming increasingly evident. Not surprisingly, there has been considerable erosion of many traditional differences between the sexes in areas beyond employment and family life. It is evident in everything from clothing to mental and physical health, and from tobacco and alcohol consumption to frequency of crime, automobile accidents, and suicide.[28] Betty Friedan has argued that middle-aged women suffer less from depression and insomnia today than they did previously, and others report a decline in the use of tranquilizers by women. On the other hand,

*For example, the wage gap between men and women virtually disappears when you compare the incomes of single childless women to those of their male peers.[24]

Organizational Discrimination or Individual Preference?

Some time ago, a large American corporation was sued by several of its female employees for discriminating against women in promotions. In support of their claim they showed that while 82 percent of the entry-level clerical jobs in the company were filled by women, only 74 percent of the promotions had gone to women. This, they charged, was clear evidence of discrimination.

Management in this company had long prided itself on its policy of promoting on the basis of merit and was greatly distressed by the suit and by the allegation that it had failed in this regard. To find out whether it had, in fact, failed and, if so, how, the company hired sociologists to study the matter.

Interviews with 850 employees of the firm demonstrated that women in entry-level clerical positions were much less likely than their male counterparts to seek, or even to desire, promotions (e.g., 39 percent of the women reported that they had no desire for a higher-level position compared to 21 percent of the men). Also, male employees in these positions were twice as likely as female employees to have requested promotion during the previous year (28 percent versus 14 percent). Females, however, were more likely to report that they had received encouragement from management when they sought promotion (70 percent versus 55 percent). These and other findings indicated that the lower rate of promotion for women in this company was the result of choices made by the women themselves rather than sex discrimination by the company. These findings raised the obvious question of why women were less inclined to seek promotion than men. Further research indicated that both men and women saw promotions as requiring longer working hours and a greater burden of responsibility. This was a price that fewer women were willing or able to pay, especially married women. Whether by choice or necessity, they and their spouses had apparently developed a division of labor within the family that assigned primary responsibility for providing income to the husband and primary responsibility for child care and care of the home to the wife. Thus, the job was a secondary responsibility for the majority of married women in these entry-level positions and this led, not surprisingly, to lower rates of promotion.

This study also found, however, that among individuals already in supervisory positions, the rates of promotion were the same for both sexes. The authors of this study concluded that this was because the selective process operating in the entry-level positions weeded out those individuals of both sexes who were unwilling or unable to make the sacrifices required by supervisory responsibilities. This further supported the conclusion that it was a mistake to infer from the simple statistics on rates of promotion that the company was guilty of sex discrimination.

One cannot infer from this one study that all differences in rank and income between the sexes in industrial societies are the result of women's preferences, but it serves as a caution against the common assumption that sex discrimination is the sole explanation, or even the chief explanation, for the underrepresentation of women in managerial positions.

Source: Adapted from Carl Hoffman and John Shelton Reed, "Sex Discrimination?—The XYZ Affair," *The Public Interest*, no. 62, Winter 1981, pp. 21–39.

the once-large differences between the sexes in smoking habits has all but vanished, and among teenagers, more girls than boys now smoke. Similarly, differences in the incidence of heart disease between men and women are declining, and one recent study found that heart disease among middle-aged mothers employed in clerical and sales jobs was twice as common as among housewives.[29] And, finally, in the last half century, the percentage of arrests involving women has more than doubled.[30]

The Changing Role of Youth

In preindustrial societies, children were typically given chores to do while they were still quite young, and their responsibilities increased with every year. By their middle teens, sometimes earlier, they were doing much the same work as their parents and other adults. Reminders of this older pattern still survive in the rites of passage of some religious groups (e.g., confirmation rites and bar mitzvahs), which occur around the age of 13. In an earlier era, these signaled the end of childhood and the beginning of adulthood, a period in which the individual was obliged to earn his or her own way and contribute to the support of others.

With the rise of industrialization, the need for human labor was reduced to such an extent that children came to be viewed as a threat to adults in the job market, and labor unions fought to make child labor illegal. Their efforts were reinforced by the passage of legislation to make school attendance compulsory. Young people were thus gradually edged out of the labor force or into marginal, part-time jobs. In the home, there were fewer siblings for older children to care for, and fewer chores to perform. As opportunities for participation in the adult world were curtailed, a new age role gradually emerged. Whereas most people in their teens, and certainly those in their early twenties, had previously been viewed as young adults, they came increasingly to be seen as occupying an intermediate role, a role of neither adult nor child.

Most individuals in this new age role are students. In 1900 only about 8 percent of Americans aged 14 to 17 attended high school; today more than 96 percent do.[31] Moreover, 34 percent of those aged 20 to 24 are enrolled in school.[32] Such high levels of enrollment suggest that industrial societies may have expanded their educational institutions well beyond what is actually needed to equip people for their roles in the economy, or even for their roles as citizens in a democratic society.[33] In addition, these societies have failed to take account of the fact that some individuals are not disposed to be students for such a long period. Many young people have little interest in the intellectual aspect of education, or even in its vocational relevance, but would rather move quickly into adult roles. They frequently discover, however, that there are no viable alternatives. Many who drop out of the educational system have trouble finding employment and getting established in the world of work.

As always happens when one segment of a population is cut off for an extended period from full participation in the life of the larger society, young people in industrial societies have developed their own subculture. Many of its more distinctive features (e.g., music, sports, experimentation with sex and drugs) are a natural consequence of the distinctive attributes of youth, such as vitality, curiosity, the desire for fun and excitement, and resistance to adult authority. The innovative nature of youth culture in areas such as music, language, and dance is at least partly the result of deliberate efforts to establish a barrier between youth and adults. The faster youth culture changes, the harder it is for adults to keep up with it, thereby keeping them at a distance and preventing them from moving in and dominating the youth scene.

At a more fundamental level, however, youth culture simply reflects many of the distinctive characteristics of industrial societies themselves: their high rate of innovation, their affluence, their leisure, their emphasis on hedonism, their emphasis on individuality, and their tendency to specialize. The preoccupation of young people with changing fads and fashions, for example, can be viewed as simply another expression of their society's enormous economic surplus and its love of novelty.

The differences between the norms and values of the youth culture and those of the larger society can cause serious problems, however, especially when they involve decisions with long-term implications. Teenage pregnancy is a compelling example of this. Despite the fact that rates have been falling in recent years, every year in the United States, more than 900,000 unmarried girls in their teens become pregnant,[34] usually because they begin sexual activity while they are still emotionally immature and have inadequate information on reproduction and contraception. These individuals are thus forced to make decisions that neither their own experience nor the norms and values of the youth culture have equipped them to make. Should the girl have an abortion or have the child? Marry the father or remain single? Put the child up for adoption or struggle to raise it alone?

Even when the decision to marry is made without the complications of an unplanned pregnancy, teenage marriages are high-risk ventures, largely because the qualities that the youth culture values most highly in the opposite sex have little to do with the qualities that adults value in a marriage partner. Similarly, because their peer group values success in sports more highly than success in academics, many boys make a heavy investment in athletics at the expense of their studies, only to find their skills no longer in demand once they are through high school or college. Barely one high school varsity athlete in a thousand can expect to make it into the top ranks of the professionals.

In most industrial societies, great numbers of specialized youth groups have developed, each with its own distinct subculture. In the democracies these have included religious cults, counterculture groups, ghetto gangs, motorcycle gangs, homosexual groups, communes, and political groups of various persuasions.

Crimes of violence are associated with youth in all industrial societies. In the United States, for example, 63 percent of those arrested for robbery, the legal definition of which involves the threat or use of violence, are under 25, as are 55 percent of those arrested for all serious crimes.[35] Political violence is also largely the work of younger people, though older adults often guide such activity.

Many attempts have been made to explain the tendency toward violence among younger people, especially younger males, in industrial societies. In American society, scholarly explanations usually place the blame on society (e.g., widespread unemployment among youth, racism).[36] But in trying to understand this phenomenon, it is important to keep in mind what many experts seem not to realize: young men were often involved in crimes of violence in agrarian societies, and most hunting and gathering and horticultural societies provided frequent, socially approved opportunities for violence in hunting or warfare. While there is yet no definitive explanation of violence in younger men, it is certain that the causes are complex and most certainly include the biological influences of age and sex as well as distinctive characteristics of the individual, his family and friends, and the larger society. Without waiting for more precise explanations, however, industrial societies would do well to provide more socially acceptable (even socially useful) activities and programs that offer the kind of emotional and physical outlets most young men clearly require.

LEISURE AND THE ARTS

No preindustrial society ever offered such rich and varied opportunities for recreation as modern industrial societies provide. With the aid of electronic devices, one can now "command" performances by the world's greatest symphony orchestras, artists, and actors (even many now dead), all in the comfort of one's own home. With other elements of modern technology, individuals can travel quickly and comfortably to distant lands or, alternatively, bring the sights and sounds of those places into their own living rooms via television or video recorders. For those who prefer physical activity, there are scores of opportunities, from miniature golf to hang gliding.

TABLE 13.6 Average Hours per Week Spent on Leisure and Personal Care in Selected Industrial Societies

Society	Year	Sex	Personal Care and Leisure
Australia	1987	Men	117.1
		Women	118.1
Canada	1986	Men	121.6
		Women	121.6
Finland	1979	Men	126.3
		Women	120.7
Netherlands	1980	Men	135.2
		Women	127.5
Norway	1981	Men	124.7
		Women	121.0
United Kingdom	1989	Men	129.8
		Women	123.9
United States	1986	Men	108.5
		Women	111.6
Average		Men	123.3
		Women	120.6

Source: United Nations, *The World's Women 1970–1990: Trends and Statistics* (New York: United Nations, 1991), table 7A.

Industrial societies are also unique in the extent to which they have commercialized recreation. Entertainment and the manufacture of equipment for leisure activities are important industries. Ironically, even when members of industrial societies go camping to get "back to nature," they usually take numerous products of modern technology with them.

One of the attractive features of leisure in industrial societies is its relative democracy. Most members of these societies enjoy substantial amounts of leisure (see Table 13.6) and most can afford a wide variety of recreational activities. Members of agrarian societies of the recent past would find the opportunities available to the average member of modern industrial societies unbelievable.

Although technology's influence on the growth of leisure and on the creation of new recreational activities is obvious, its impact on the fine arts may not be. Yet the modern symphony orchestra is a triumph of modern technology, while recent trends in sculpture and painting reflect at least in part the influence of new materials and new processes that were not available to artists of an earlier era. It is also significant to note that modern art, with its movement away from realism and toward impressionism, expressionism, and abstractionism, began in the latter half of the nineteenth century as the new technology of photography was coming into its own. One cannot help but wonder if the new approach to painting and sculpture would have evolved if technology had not provided the camera as a substitute means of depicting reality and capturing images of people, places, and events for posterity. In any event, one of the most important consequences of the new technology for the arts has been an indirect one: traditional standards have given way to the belief that "newer is better" (see "Neophilic Art," page 211). This could not occur except in societies that have benefited greatly from change in other areas.

But it is television that has most altered modern life and leisure. According to one expert, "By the time the average American graduates from high school [he or she] has spent more hours watching the television screen than [he or she] has spent in school, or in any other activity except sleeping."[37] And despite a decline in network television viewing in recent years, television continues to occupy a major portion of people's leisure time in industrial societies. Every week in the United States, children ages 2 to 11 watch an average of 20.5 hours, and adults watch more than 30 hours of television.[38]

There are a number of reasons for television's great appeal. It combines the most attractive features of the other media: like printed matter and the radio, it can be enjoyed in the comfort of one's home, and, like movies, it presents things vividly. In addition, it informs and entertains while requiring almost no mental or physical effort on the viewer's part. This makes it especially attractive for people who are tired at the end of a day's work or who are simply unwilling or unable to engage in more demanding activities.

Because the images created by television are so vivid, they impress themselves on our consciousness in ways not unlike personal experience. Celebrities seen repeatedly on the screen become to many people a very real part of their lives; countless viewers have written expressions of love, even proposals of marriage, to actors and actresses whom they have never met. More important, events witnessed on television have the power to affect millions of people emotionally. Images of events such as the assassination of President Kennedy, the first moon landing, and more recently the collapse of the twin towers of the World Trade Center in New York on 9/11, and a variety of natural disasters have been indelibly etched in the memories of millions because their images were captured and broadcast over television.

Despite their seeming objectivity, television images have the potential to greatly distort and bias perceptions of social reality. Visually stunning events captured on film or videotape are likely to be seen over and over again by large audiences while unrecorded events, however significant, are not. The heart-rending images of starving Somali children made relief efforts all but inevitable, but millions starve and die every year in relative oblivion because their plight is not captured on videotape. Thus, rather than being the product of objective analysis and reasoned judgment, public opinion, public policies, and collective social action may lurch and careen haphazardly in response to such erratic contingencies as the availability of videotaped images of an event or problem, the time constraints of network news broadcasts, and the viewing habits of television audiences.

Soap operas and network prime time shows also create unrealistic and biased images. For example, one monthlong analysis of network prime time shows found a grossly distorted image of the American labor force: there were twelve prostitutes shown for every machinist, two butlers for every government worker, and twelve times more detectives than production workers.[39] Also, the effortlessly attained affluence of the average sitcom family may fuel the resentment of the economically less prosperous, and, when broadcast around the world, it provides a grossly distorted image of life in industrial societies.

It is not surprising, therefore, that, despite its popularity, people have mixed feelings about television. Although more than half of those recently polled named television "as the most enjoyable way to spend an evening," an almost equal number complained that "they spent too much time watching television."[40] A number of social critics also contend that television has exacerbated many of the most serious problems confronting modern industrial societies—crime, violence, teenage pregnancy.

PROBLEMS AND PROGRESS

The members of contemporary industrial societies are in a paradoxical situation. They are, on average, far healthier, wealthier, and freer to choose among alternative lifestyles than were the vast majority of people during the last 5,000 years, and they are probably happier as well (see pages 340–342). *Yet they are far more vocal concerning the shortcomings and problems of their societies.*

Like so many other changes, this is basically a consequence of industrialization. The mass media and multiparty political systems combine to keep social problems before the attention of the general public. Better education and new ideologies, meanwhile, provide people with an enhanced capacity for envisioning and expecting improvements in their living conditions and in other areas, and if improvements do not occur, they often become critical of both their leaders and the social system. Finally, affluence gives people the means and leisure to voice their opinions, and democratic polities give them the opportunity. As a result, social problems receive far more attention and are far more salient in democratic industrial societies than in any other kind of society.

There are, of course, good grounds for the concerns expressed by members of industrial societies. Their new high-information, high-energy technologies have a potential for creating problems more serious than those that confronted societies of the past. The threat of nuclear war and the pollution of the environment are the most obvious, but they are not the only ones. Others include the rapid consumption of nonrenewable resources, the weakening of family ties, drug and alcohol abuse, rising crime rates, urban decay, and the use of terrorist tactics as a means of achieving political goals. In addition, many older problems persist, even though progress has been made in dealing with some of them.

Although there is considerable controversy concerning the amount of progress industrial societies have actually achieved in dealing with humanity's problems, there is general agreement on several points. First, despite the presence of many continuing problems from the past, the most serious problems facing industrial societies today are either new problems or old problems with major new dimensions. Second, these problems are largely by-products, or consequences, of technological advance. Third, although many of these problems are distressingly complex, most could be alleviated by rational human effort—though in many cases not without great cost to many people. Finally, a completely problem-free society is not likely ever to be achieved, partly because of our species' genetic heritage, partly because of the constraints of the environment, partly because of the extraordinary complexity of modern social systems, and partly because the very process of problem solving itself so often creates new needs and new problems.

Because the problems that remain unsolved by one generation define the agenda for the next generation, we will postpone our analysis of social problems until the final chapter. In that chapter we will be concerned primarily with the future and what can, and cannot, be said about it.

INDUSTRIAL SOCIETIES IN THEORETICAL PERSPECTIVE

When we compare modern industrial societies with societies of the past, it is clear that they are a radically new type of sociocultural system. This is evident in everything from the family to the polity, and from ideology to technology. The foundation for these societies is, of course, their rich store of information, especially the technological information that enables them to harness vast amounts of energy to drive enormously productive machines.

If human societies had never created this technology, we would all still be in the agrarian era. The vast majority of people would still be illiterate peasant farmers eking out a marginal existence, women's lives would still be dominated by the cycle of reproduction and child care, and authoritarian elites who knew little and cared less about the lives of the masses would still regard the economic surplus as their rightful property. If we imagine a different sequence of events—one in which industrial societies had evolved but were subsequently forced to return to the technology of the agrarian era—*75 percent or more of the world's current population would die.* For an agrarian technology could not sustain more than a fourth or a fifth of the world's present population.

We will not try to trace here all of the consequences of the shift from an agrarian to an industrial technology or detail all of the causal linkages, as we did at the end of earlier chapters. These consequences are so numerous, and the linkages so complex, that a single diagram could not do justice to them. Instead, we will simply restate some of the basic points that have emerged from our analysis.

First, in industrial societies as in their predecessors, *technological innovation continues to be the most basic underlying force responsible for societal change and development*. Although other kinds of innovations also influence the course of social and cultural change, they tend to be dependent on prior technological change. We have seen numerous examples of this, especially in the new beliefs and values which shape these societies' institutions—beliefs and values which had little or no impact prior to industrialization.

Second, *many of the trends of the industrial era are continuations of trends that began in earlier eras*. Although industrialization intensified them, each of the following was initiated by technological advance in the more distant past:

The growing store of information
The increasing ability to produce and harness energy
The growing productivity of societies
The expanding economic surplus
The growth of world population
The growth in size of societies and communities
The increasing diversity of material products
The growth of capital goods
The increasing division of labor *within* societies
The increasing division of labor *among* societies
The increasing economic interdependence of societies
The growing complexity of associations and communities
The relative decline in importance of kinship systems
The increasing number and variety of symbol systems
The increasing impact of human activities on the biophysical environment
The increasingly destructive potential of military technology

Third, *some of the trends in industrial societies are new and represent a break with trends of the past*. The most significant of these involves inequality. During the long period between the close of the hunting and gathering era and the early stages of the industrial era, technological advance was accompanied by a steady decline in both political and economic equality. As a result, either advanced agrarian or early industrial societies achieved the dubious distinction of having the greatest degree of inequality of any type of society in history. Advanced industrial societies have appreciably reversed this trend. Other new trends include democratization, greatly improved opportunities for education, more upward mobility, declining birth and death rates, the institutionalization of science, research, and innovation, and changes in the family and related roles, especially in those of women and youth.

Fourth, *industrial societies are the first in human history in which the greatest threats posed by the biophysical environment are products of prior human activity*. Before the Industrial Revolution, famine and disease were two of the greatest threats to societies. Technology and science have succeeded in eliminating the first of these scourges in industrial societies, and they have brought the second largely under control: the members of industrial societies now die primarily from degenerative diseases that reflect the natural limits of our species' life span. Now, however, societies are threatened by feedback effects of their own technology on the biophysical environment.

14

Industrializing Societies

Despite the rapid growth and spread of industrialization during the last two centuries, less than a quarter of the world's population today lives in societies that can be considered fully industrialized.* Almost everyone, however, lives in a society that has been impacted by the technologies and economies of industrial societies. In some cases industrial technologies and economic practices have been grafted onto traditional technological and economic systems. These societies, thus, are best thought of not as traditional societies untouched by modern technologies, but as "hybrids" containing various admixtures of the old and the new.

Although it is sometimes convenient to refer to all nonindustrial societies today as "less developed countries" (LDCs), "developing nations," or simply as "the Third World," this practice should not obscure the many important differences among them. Some, such as South Korea, Taiwan, and, in recent years, China, are experiencing extremely rapid economic growth and rising standards of living, while others, such as Liberia, Haiti, and Somalia, are experiencing the opposite. Some, such as Iraq, Iran, and Vietnam, have fought long and costly wars with other nations; some, such as Afghanistan, Rwanda, Burundi, Cambodia, Somalia, and Liberia, have been convulsed by bloody civil wars; and others, such as Thailand and Botswana, have generally managed to avoid both kinds of conflicts.

TYPES OF INDUSTRIALIZING SOCIETIES

Much of the diversity among these societies results from circumstances that are unique to individual societies. *But some of their most important differences reflect a single underlying variable: their traditional subsistence technology.* For some of them were agrarian societies while others were horticultural at the start of the industrial era. This fundamental distinction has had enormous consequences, for both their current situations and their future prospects.[1] This is, of course, what ecological-evolutionary theory leads us to expect, since the social and cultural characteristics of a society in one period are major determinants of its characteristics in a later period (see Figure 1.2, page 18), and because the prospects of less technologically advanced societies are progressively lowered by the emergence of more technologically advanced societies. We would expect *industrializing agrarian* societies to have considerable difficulty coping with and adjusting to the impact of industrial societies, but we would expect *industrializing horticultural* societies to experience even greater difficulties and problems.

Before examining these issues in more detail, however, we should first note that, although quite a number of hunting and gathering and fishing societies also survived into the modern era in remote and isolated areas, advances in transportation and communication have opened up their territories to members of more advanced societies and thus destroyed their

---

*The sixteen highly industrialized societies, which were the focus of Chapters 10 through 13, collectively hold about 13 percent of the world's population.

only real defense. As a result, most of these groups have either been absorbed into more advanced societies or herded onto reservations where they live as wards of their conquerors, usually under conditions that make the preservation of their traditional ways of life virtually impossible. Even the few groups that still enjoy some degree of autonomy have usually adopted many cultural elements from more advanced societies and thus are no longer pure types. But this does not make them industrializing societies; that implies something utterly beyond their adaptive capacities. Groups with such limited social and cultural resources cannot possibly evolve into anything so advanced in the little time available to them. Unhappily, they are simply unusual hybrids with a very limited future.*

Industrializing Agrarian Societies

Industrializing agrarian societies comprise most of Latin America, southern and eastern Asia, the Middle East, and North Africa, and are also found in parts of southern and eastern Europe (see Figure 14.1). When we discuss industrializing agrarian societies, we are talking about China, India, the Philippines, Egypt, Brazil, Mexico, and several dozen other societies.** Naturally, these societies differ from one another in many ways, reflecting differences in their histories, in the social and biophysical environments to which they must adapt, and in their levels of technological advance. Yet despite their differences, they share a number of important characteristics because they all combine elements of both the agrarian past and the industrial present. Recognition of this fact can be enormously helpful as we try to understand them and their problems.

By at least one criterion, industrializing agrarian societies are the most important type in the world today: *most of the world's population lives in these societies.* In fact, nearly 40 percent of the world's population lives in just two industrializing agrarian societies, China and India. But this is not the only reason for us to be concerned with them. Industrializing agrarian societies have, for decades, been struggling with problems that often threaten to overwhelm them. Despite partial industrialization, many of their citizens are as poor as the common people ever were in traditional agrarian societies. At the same time, improved education and the exposure to western mass media have raised their hopes and expectations and given them an awareness of the possibility of a better life. This contradiction has created a situation that affects not only these societies but the entire world.

Industrializing Horticultural Societies

Industrializing horticultural societies, with a median size of 10 million, are much smaller than industrializing agrarian societies, with a median size of 21 million, and they are much more concentrated geographically (see Figure 14.1). Less than 10 percent of the world's population lives in industrializing horticultural societies today. These societies are found in only three places: Africa south of the Sahara, Papua New Guinea in the South Pacific, and Haiti in the

---

*Apart from agrarian and advanced horticultural societies, the only other hybrids that have a chance of surviving in the twenty-first century are maritime and herding societies. Because of limitations of space, however, we will not examine these two types of societies.

**Forty societies are classified as industrializing agrarian in the analyses that follow. They are (in alphabetical order): Afghanistan, Argentina, Bolivia, Brazil, Cambodia, Chile, China, Colombia, Costa Rica, Dominican Republic, Ecuador, Egypt, El Salvador, Guatemala, Guyana, Honduras, India, Indonesia, Jamaica, (North) Korea, (South) Korea, Laos, Malaysia, Mexico, Morocco, Nepal, Nicaragua, Pakistan, Panama, Paraguay, Peru, Philippines, Sri Lanka, Syria, Thailand, Trinidad and Tobago, Tunisia, Turkey, Uruguay, and Venezuela.[2] Because data are not available on many social characteristics for a number of these societies, however, the number of industrializing agrarian societies in the tables below will sometimes be smaller.

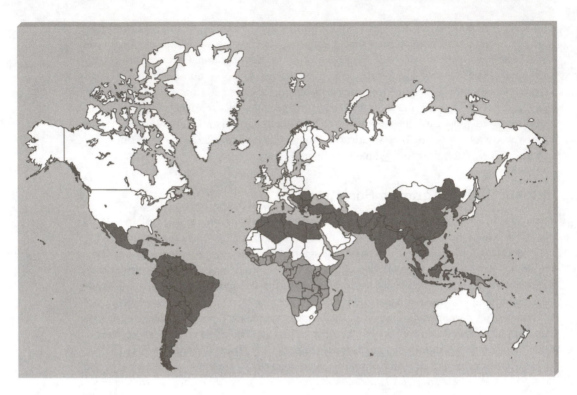

FIGURE 14.1 *Currently industrializing agrarian societies are shown in dark gray and industrializing horticultural societies are shown in light gray.*

Caribbean.* Horticultural societies also flourished until recently in Latin America and some of the less accessible parts of southeast Asia, but all of them have been either conquered or peacefully assimilated by larger and more powerful industrializing agrarian societies.[4] In sub-Saharan Africa, New Guinea, and Haiti, however, things are different: horticulture, rather than agriculture, continues to be the dominant mode of subsistence, and many social and cultural patterns from the preindustrial past survive and even flourish.

Industrializing horticultural societies, like industrializing agrarian societies, are confronted by a rapidly changing social environment dominated by industrial societies. They, too, are forced to adapt to the new industrial technology and to all of the changes and challenges that follow in its wake. And they, too, find many of the new cultural elements disruptive of their social institutions and traditional way of life.

There are, however, important differences between these two kinds of industrializing societies that stem from their dissimilar histories. Compared to societies with an agrarian heritage, those with a horticultural heritage are badly handicapped in the industrial era.[5] Their social and cultural heritages have not equipped them and their people to cope with the modern world as effectively as the heritages of agrarian societies. Many of the cultural ele-

---

*Thirty-two societies are classified as industrializing horticultural in the analyses that follow. They are (in alphabetical order): Angola, Benin, Burkina Faso, Burundi, Cameroon, Central African Republic, Chad, Congo, Cote d'Ivoire, Gabon, Ghana, Guinea, Haiti, Kenya, Madagascar, Malawi, Mali, Mauritania, Mozambique, Niger, Nigeria, Papua New Guinea, Republic of the Congo (Zaire), Rwanda, Senegal, Sierra Leone, Somalia, Tanzania, Togo, Uganda, Zambia, and Zimbabwe. Because data are not available on many social characteristics for a number of these societies, however, the number of industrializing horticultural societies in the tables below will sometimes be smaller.[3]

ments that are essential in the industrial era—such as urbanism, governmental bureaucracy, standardized monetary systems, and literacy—were either absent in horticultural societies or were far less developed than in agrarian societies. Thus, horticultural societies have been poorly prepared for the highly complex and highly competitive world system created by the Industrial Revolution, and for its formidable challenges.

TECHNOLOGY AND PRODUCTIVITY

Two of the best measures of a society's level of development are its energy consumption and its gross national product. Energy consumption, since it measures the extent to which inanimate sources of energy are harnessed by a society (see Table 14.1), reflects a society's *technological* power; GDP, the sum of all the goods and services produced in the society, reflects its *economic* power. Dividing these figures by the number of people, or amount of land, that was used to produce them, provides measures of technological and economic *efficiency*.

As Table 14.1 shows, industrializing societies lag far behind the advanced industrial societies on all of these measures. The per capita GDP of advanced industrial societies is about *eleven times* that of industrializing agrarian societies, and more than *sixty times* that of industrializing horticultural societies. Even more pronounced differences exist with regard to economic productivity per unit of land. For example, the advanced industrial societies produce *thirteen times* the GDP per 1,000 square kilometers of area of industrializing agrarian societies, and nearly *two hundred forty* times that of industrializing horticultural societies.* Similar patterns, though smaller in magnitude, are found with respect to the harnessing of energy. Industrializing agrarian societies use much more energy than do industrializing horticultural societies, but they harness only about *one-fourth* of the amount used by the advanced industrial societies.

Among the causes of these disparities are differences among these societies with respect to the institutional resources. For instance, differences in rates of literacy, secondary school enrollments, and the distribution of information (e.g., availability of newspapers and scientific journals) mirror these differences in productivity.[7]

It would be a mistake to suppose, however, that these societies are not growing economically. As the top row of Table 14.2 shows, between 1961 and 2001 the economies of industrializing agrarian societies grew at an average annual rate of 4.3 percent, a full percentage point more than industrial societies rate of 3.2 percent, and the economies of industrializing horticultural societies grew at a rate of 3.2 percent, about the same as industrial societies.

*It is worth noting that if the lesser industrialized societies, such as Greece, Portugal, or Spain, were grouped with the advanced industrial or with the industrializing agrarian societies, it would mute these differences somewhat, but it would not alter the basic pattern of results.[6]

TABLE 14.1 Technological and Economic Development, by Societal Type

	Advanced Industrial	Industrializing Agrarian	Industrializing Horticultural
GDP/population	$32,127	$3,056	$500
GDP/area	$5,022	$380	$21
Energy cons./population	5,031	1,176	501*
Energy cons./area	661	181	19*
Number of societies	16	37	31

Note: Energy consumption/area is measured in kilograms of oil per 1,000 square kilometers, and GNP/area is in 1995 U.S. millions of dollars per 1,000 square kilometers.
*N = 17.
Source: World Bank, *World Development Indicators* Online Database (www.worldbank.org/data/onlinedatabases/onlinedatabases.html).

TABLE 14.2 Average Annual Percentage Rates of Economic Growth 1961 to 2001, by Societal Type

	Advanced Industrial	Industrializing Agrarian	Industrializing Horticultural
GDP 1961 to 2001	3.2	4.3	3.0
GDP per capita 1961 to 2001	2.6	2.1	0.4
Number of societies	16	40	32

Source: World Bank, *World Development Indicators* Online Database (http://www.worldbank.org/data/onlinedatabases/onlinedatabases.html).

These rates suggest that the economies of all three types of societies were growing substantially, that industrializing horticultural societies were basically keeping up with industrial societies, and that industrializing agrarian societies were closing the economic gap between them and the industrial societies.

This would be a mistaken impression, however, as the second row of Table 14.2 shows. In *per capita* terms, the economies of industrializing agrarian societies grew at the much more modest rate of 2.1 percent, which is actually slower than the 2.6 percent growth rate of industrial societies, and, with a 0.4 growth rate, industrializing horticultural societies were losing ground rapidly. Thus despite the substantial growth of their economies, both types of industrializing societies fell further behind industrial societies in per capita terms.

What explains these discrepancies between the rates of growth in GDP and per capita GDP? Why are the industrializing societies losing ground in relation to the advanced industrial societies? The answer is found in the *differences in the rates of population growth in these different types of societies*. As Table 14.3 shows, in both periods, the populations of the industrializing societies grew much more rapidly than the populations of industrial societies. And while the rates of growth in GDP reflect only the rate of change in the amount of goods and services produced in a society, per capita rates measure the rate of economic growth *in relation to the rate of population growth*. Since the populations of advanced industrial societies are growing so slowly, a 3.2 percent rate of growth translates into a 2.6 percent rate of growth in per capita GDP. In contrast, the much higher rates of population growth in the industrializing societies reduce their net economic gains substantially. The 4.3 percent rate of growth in industrializing agrarian societies is cut in half, and the healthy 3 percent rate of growth in industrializing horticultural societies is reduced to an anemic 0.4 percent. Even more striking is the fact that for the period 1970 to 1995 per capita growth was actually *negative* in industrializing horticultural societies (-0.1), which meant that population *actually grew even faster* than the economy in this time period.[8]

Thus, because of their very high rates of population growth, most industrializing horticultural societies have been unable to raise the standard of living of their people. In contrast,

TABLE 14.3 Average Annual Percentage Rates of Population Growth 1961 to 2001, by Societal Type

	Advanced Industrial	Industrializing Agrarian	Industrializing Horticultural
1961 to 2001	0.6	2.1	2.6
Number of societies	16	40	32

Source: World Bank, *World Development Indicators* Online Database (http://www.worldbank.org/data/onlinedatabases/onlinedatabases.html).

The old and the new: Indian farmer plowing with oxen under high-power electrical transmission lines.

industrializing agrarian societies have done much better, especially those that have reduced their rates of population growth substantially (e.g., South Korea, China, Taiwan). Despite the many obstacles it faces, China, in part because of its success in slowing population growth, has one of the fastest-growing economies in the world today; its per capita gross domestic product has been growing at an average rate of more than 8 percent per year for the past two decades![9]

But while the rates of population growth generally declined in industrializing agrarian societies—dropping from 2.6 to 1.6 percent—they rose from 2.3 to more than 3, as death rates fell, and then dropped back to 2.3 in recent years as mortality rates rose in industrializing horticultural societies We will have more to say about population processes in the next section, but it is worth noting now that if this rate of growth were to continue, the economies of industrializing horticultural societies—the poorest societies with the fewest institutional resources—would have to grow at a rate of 2.3 percent per year just to keep pace with population; they would achieve no net economic gain and would generate no new resources for investment in their future.

Before leaving the subject of technology and productivity, it should be noted that much of the economic growth experienced by industrializing societies was due to the application of technology and capital supplied by corporations based in industrial societies. Without this transfer, growth in the economies of most of these societies would have been much less.

POPULATION GROWTH AND ITS CONSEQUENCES

The demographic transition that accompanied industrialization in the developed world was gradual. Death rates declined slowly as sanitation improved and as developments in transportation made food supplies more reliable. At first, birthrates remained high and the rate of population growth increased. But after a time, birthrates too began to decline and population growth slowed (see Figure 13.1, page 275). The process took more than a century to complete, and rates of European population growth, though unprecedented historically, were generally around 1 percent. There was also a sparsely settled "New World" to which large numbers of the growing "surplus population" migrated and found land and work to support themselves.

Developing societies today are in a different situation. Although the outline of the process is very similar, its pace has been greatly accelerated—the time scale has been drastically reduced, and there is no longer a "New World" to which excess population can easily migrate, though some emigrate to industrial societies, as we have seen. Death rates in currently developing societies plummeted following the rapid introduction of western technologies of medicine, sanitation, and public health protections (e.g., spraying ponds to kill mosquitoes that spread malaria).

Figure 14.2 shows the changes in economic development and vital rates that have occurred over the past three decades in industrial and industrializing societies. Connecting the points reveals a pattern very similar to that of the idealized "demographic transition" depicted in Figure 13.1 (page 275). The least developed industrializing horticultural societies are at an early phase of this transition, and for the past several decades their death rates have dropped at a much faster rate than their birth rates, producing an accelerating rate of population growth. HIV/AIDS has raised the death rates substantially in a number of industrializing horticultural societies, and may decline by as much as 22 percent by 2050, but, overall, the populations of industrializing horticultural societies are still projected to grow substantially in the near future.[10] In fact, more than 98 percent of the growth in world population expected by mid-century will occur in industrializing societies.[11]

The more developed industrializing agrarian societies are at a later phase; their birthrates are dropping faster than their death rates, and their rates of population growth are declining. Industrial societies are in a "post transition" phase; their birth and death rates have

FIGURE 14.2 *Recent trends in vital rates in advanced industrial and industrializing societies (compare with Figure 13.1).*
Source: World Bank, *World Development Indicators* Online Database (www.worldbank.org/data/onlinedatabases/onlinedatabases.html).

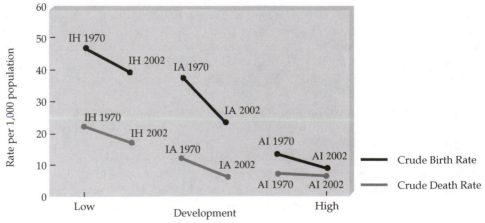

According to a United Nations study, one-fourth to two-thirds of the populations of the cities of most industrializing societies live in squatter settlements and shantytowns, such as this one in Lima, Peru.

stabilized. In fact, as we saw in the last chapter, if there were no migration into them, their populations would decline substantially in the coming decades.

The consequences of these demographic patterns are difficult to exaggerate. Despite the devastating impact of AIDS in sub-Saharan Africa, industrializing horticultural societies are growing today at a rate of 2.3 percent per year, and industrializing agrarian societies at a rate of 1.6 percent per year. Growth rates of 1.6 or 2.3 percent per year may not sound high, but they are *fifteen to twenty times higher* than the average rate of growth of world population during the agrarian era (compare Figures 13.1 and 14.2). A society growing at a rate of 1.6 percent a year will *double in size in just 44 years,* and one growing at a rate of 2.3 percent will *double in about 30 years!*

When societies grow this fast, it is extraordinarily difficult for them to find the resources needed to satisfy even the most basic needs of all their members. For example, although agricultural productivity increased in industrializing agrarian and industrializing horticultural societies in past decades, neither society gained ground in per capita terms because their populations grew as fast, or faster. Agricultural productivity merely kept pace with population growth in industrializing agrarian societies, and it actually fell nearly 6 percent behind population growth in industrializing horticultural societies. It is also difficult to create enough new jobs to provide employment for the growing numbers of people looking for work.* Moreover, since the technologies needed to successfully compete in the world economy in most industries

---

*Some Americans have used the history of their own country during the eighteenth and nineteenth centuries to argue that rapid population growth actually speeds economic growth and raises the standard of living in societies. They forget, however, that prior to the twentieth century the United States had a very small population in relation to its size and the wealth of its resources, and because of this the country suffered from labor *shortages.* This is not the situation in which industrializing nations find themselves today. On the contrary, most of them suffer from a *surplus* of labor.

are capital-intensive (see Chapter 10), they will not absorb large numbers of people, and, thus, the problem will probably get worse, not better, in coming decades.

Rapid population growth also impacts negatively on other critical aspects of the development process. For example, high birthrates make universal public education prohibitively expensive in these nations, yet without it the population is not equipped for many jobs in modern industry. This forces large numbers of people to find employment in traditional occupations, especially farming, and this in turn leads to the subdividing of already small farms to the point where they become hopelessly inefficient and the introduction of modern machinery is impossible. For example, in Egypt in 1950, 70 percent of farm owners were already trying to make a living with less than half an acre.[12] As one observer remarked, "Most of those who are working the land work not because the land requires their labor but because they require the work."[13] As early as 1939, it was estimated that 10 percent of Egypt's farmers could have supplied all the necessary labor if Egypt's farms had been even half as mechanized as America's. The story is much the same in other industrializing agrarian societies.

Another factor retarding economic development is the poverty of the excess population. Because these people cannot afford to buy anything but the basic necessities, they fail to generate a demand for the kinds of products that are essential components of the economy of every industrial society. Finally, this surplus population compounds all the other problems by its own productive achievements: an abundance of children. The society is thus trapped in a vicious circle.

ECONOMIES

The economies of industrializing societies consist of two very different components. The traditional component is very similar to the economy of the typical agrarian or horticultural society of the past. The tools, techniques, and division of labor are much the same, and so is the level of productivity. The modern—or at least modernizing—component has tools, techniques, and patterns of economic organization that have, for the most part, been borrowed from industrial societies or introduced by corporations based in those societies.

The industrial sector of the economy of these societies is not simply a scaled-down version of the economy of a typical industrial society, however. In other words, it is not likely to contain a representative sample of industries—some small steel mills, a small automobile plant or two, some textile mills, a variety of wholesale and retail distributors, and so on. Instead, this sector of the economy is often very one-sided in its development, with one or two key industries heavily overrepresented.

To understand why this is so, we have to bear in mind the tremendous difference between the circumstances under which these nations are industrializing and those under which the fully industrial societies industrialized. Today's developing societies are industrializing in a world that is dominated politically and economically by already industrialized societies with which they are interdependent. Producers in the already industrialized societies have easy access to their own large and affluent home markets and thus are now able to spread their fixed costs (see Table 10.4, page 230) over a large volume of goods. This gives them a great competitive advantage in most industries. Add to this the low cost of moving goods today, thanks to advances in transportation technology (see page 164, in Chapter 7), and it is easy to see why producers in industrializing societies are often in a poor competitive position even in their own home markets. Thus, European, American, and Japanese firms have come to dominate world markets for most manufactured products.

As a result, many of the industrializing societies have been forced into a distinctive and precarious ecological niche: they have become the producers of raw materials and cheap labor for the world economy. Furthermore, because of pressures generated by world markets

In recent years, the People's Republic of China has moved vigorously to check population growth: billboard promoting the one-child family, Chengdu.

and by their own desire to maximize income, they often become dangerously overspecialized (see Table 14.4).

A society that depends heavily on just a single commodity is highly vulnerable to any shift in the world economy that affects its specialty. Technological innovations (e.g., fiber optics that replace copper wiring in communications, synthetic fibers that replace cotton, sugar substitutes) and changing consumer preferences (e.g., reduced coffee or chocolate consumption) may permanently reduce, or even wipe out, demand for the product. Overproduction of the commodity (e.g., petroleum, coffee) can produce temporary "gluts" in the world market that drive the price of the commodity down, and, if lower prices spur societies to increase production to compensate for lost income, prices can spiral even lower. This volatility creates an unstable "boom or bust" atmosphere that is not conducive to rational economic planning and development by either business or government. Instead, it encourages a speculative approach with the goal of making a quick profit and then transferring capital to safer investments elsewhere.

Industrializing horticultural societies face especially serious obstacles to industrialization. Because the urban sector of their economies has historically been so much less developed than in agrarian societies, urban populations in industrializing horticultural societies have had less experience with such fundamentals of modern life as money, occupational specialization, literacy, and bureaucracy (see "Traditional Values and Norms Regarding Work" on page 306). This makes it very difficult for modernizing governments and businesses to find skilled personnel to staff their organizations. The problem is especially serious in societies in which national pride often demands that businesses and government be staffed with native personnel, regardless of the cost in organizational efficiency.[14]

There is tremendous economic and social variation within industrializing societies. In some societies a few remote villages are still largely untouched by the influences of

TABLE 14.4 Dependence on Leading Exports for Selected Industrializing Societies (in Percentages)

Society	Commodity	Dependence*
Industrializing Agrarian Societies		
Venezuela	Petroleum	76
Nepal	Textiles	55
Pakistan	Textiles	52
Trinidad and Tobago	Petroleum	46
Ecuador	Petroleum	34
El Salvador	Coffee	33
Paraguay	Textiles	30
Chile	Copper	30
Indonesia	Mineral fuels	25
Nicaragua	Coffee	24
Colombia	Coffee	19
Honduras	Bananas	18
Industrializing Horticultural Societies		
Nigeria	Mineral fuels	97
Angola	Petroleum	93
Gabon	Petroleum	87
Zambia	Copper	87
Congo	Petroleum	83
Niger	Metal ores	75
Uganda	Coffee	74
Ethiopia	Coffee	64
Burkina Faso	Cotton	63
Burundi	Coffee	63
Benin	Cotton	60
Mozambique	Shellfish	42

*Value of trade in this commodity as a percentage of all commodities traded.
Source: United Nations, *International Trade Statistics Yearbook 1995* (New York: United Nations, 1996), table 5.

industrialization, while in others the older patterns have been largely destroyed.[15] In addition, there is every conceivable combination of the old and the new—such as the woman in Nairobi, Kenya, who practiced witchcraft in order to earn the down payment on a truck so she could go into the trucking business, or in La Paz, Bolivia, where one can still shop for spells, amulets, and herbs at the Mercado de Brujas ("Witches Market").[16]

POLITIES

In Chapter 11 we discussed the historical role that industrialization played in promoting democratic forms of government in the already developed societies. As industrialization progressed, economic resources and political power shifted from agrarian elites to commercial classes and better-educated labor forces began to demand greater political rights. In recent years, industrializing horticultural societies have increasingly adopted multiparty political systems. In fact, over the past decade they have virtually closed the gap with industrializing agrarian societies. Nonetheless, multiparty systems are still less likely in industrializing societies than in industrial societies, where they have been universal for some time, and it may prove more difficult for developing societies to live by these more democratic constitutions than it was to adopt them.

There are also striking differences in the levels of political freedom and civil liberties enjoyed by citizens in these different types of societies, despite the similarities in the outward forms of their polities. These differences are clearly indicated by the data in Table 14.5.

Many industrializing societies have been forced into a specialized ecological niche as producers of raw materials for industrial societies. For years, much of Ghana's foreign exchange has come from the sale of cocoa, which is shown being collected at a cooperative marketing society.

Although advanced industrial societies all achieve nearly perfect scores on this scale, industrializing agrarian and industrializing horticultural societies rate much lower. Despite the fact that some of the most repressive societies are industrializing agrarian (e.g., North Korea, Syria, and China), industrializing horticultural societies actually accord less freedom, on average.

In industrializing agrarian societies, one of the greatest hindrances to the development of democracy has been the kind of governing class they inherited from the past. This class enjoyed a privileged status for centuries, and its members have seldom shown any desire to change things. Their ideal has been the kind of society that flourished before intellectuals, students, and the common people ever heard of liberty, equality, democracy, socialism, or communism. From their perspective, change is something to be resisted or, when possible, exploited for their own personal benefit.

In contrast, because of their newness and their cultural heritage, one of the most serious barriers to democratic institutions in industrializing horticultural societies has been the internal divisions rooted in traditional tribal loyalties, some of which are partly a legacy of colonial rule. Colonial powers seldom destroyed the older tribal groups. On the contrary, they usually preserved these groups in order to use them as instruments of administrative control, allowing tribal rulers to serve as lower-echelon officials. Colonial governments often pretended that these tribal groups were autonomous, because this enabled them to put the burden, and the onus, of political control on the groups' leaders. They even encouraged tribal rivalries, applying the ancient principle "Divide and rule." As a result, after independence was won, there was a fundamental tension between tribal loyalties and national loyalties in most industrializing

TABLE 14.5 Average Level of Freedom 2001–2002, by Societal Type

	Advanced Industrial	Industrializing Agrarian	Industrializing Horticultural
Mean level of freedom*	1.0	3.0	4.5
Median level of freedom*	1.2	3.5	4.6
Number of societies**	16	39	32

*The freedom score is the average for political rights and civil liberties; it ranges from 1.0, most free, to 7.0, not free.

**Afghanistan, with a score of 7 under the Taliban, was omitted from this table; if included, the mean for industrial agrarian would rise to 3.6.

Source: Our calculations from data reported by Freedom House, *Freedom in the World Country Ratings 1972–1973 to 2001–2002* (Freedom House, 2002; www.freedomhouse.org/research/freeworld/FHSCORES.xls).

Traditional Values and Norms Regarding Work

Industrializing horticultural societies face formidable barriers to industrialization that are largely a result of their centuries of reliance on horticulture. Among them are their distinctive values and norms regarding work. Some years ago, the Inter-African Labour Institute characterized the work traditions of horticultural Africa this way:

1. Work is viewed in its relation to the basic institution of family or clan; within the family, it is divided on the basis of age and sex.
2. Work is linked with religious rites.
3. Work activities are evaluated in the light of a subsistence economy rather than a profit economy (i.e., they are oriented more to the production of the necessities of life than to the production of an economic surplus).
4. Work requires neither foresight nor planning.
5. Time is largely irrelevant in work activities; no time limits are set for most tasks.
6. There is little specialization.
7. For men, work is episodic; when a task has to be done, men often do it without a break, but intervals of inactivity are long and frequent.
8. Men hardly ever work alone; work activities (e.g., hunting parties and work parties) often resemble a collective leisure activity in modern industrial society.

These traditions did little to prepare the members of these societies, especially the men, for work in a modern industrial economy. A parallel list of the characteristics of work in industrial societies would, in fact, be almost the opposite.

One of the biggest problems is suggested by item 7. As we saw in Chapter 6, cultivation is often primarily women's work. Men's responsibilities tend to be limited to the occasional clearing of new gardens. While women do the sustained, tedious chores—planting, cultivating, and harvesting crops—men are free to do more interesting and exciting things—hunting, fighting, politicking, socializing, and participating in ceremonial activities. The disciplined, routinized patterns of work that are typical of an industrial economy are seldom experienced by men in these societies. In this respect, the peasant farmers of agrarian societies are far better prepared for industrialization. Yet even they find the transition difficult.

Source: This list is based on a report from the Inter-African Labour Institute, *The Human Factors of Productivity in Africa,* as summarized in William H. Lewis (ed.), *French-Speaking Africa: The Search for Identity* (New York: Walker, 1965), p. 168. Many of these propositions were also supported in papers presented to a subsequent conference on competing demands for labor in traditional African societies, cosponsored by the Joint Committee on African Studies of the Social Science Research Council, the American Council of Learned Societies, and the Agricultural Development Council. See William O. Jones, "Labor and Leisure in Traditional African Societies," *Social Science Research Council Items,* 22 (March 1968), pp. 1–6.

horticultural societies. This is a problem that few industrializing agrarian societies have had to contend with.*

During the cold war, the superpowers often exploited these rivalries and supported opposing groups in conflicts for their own advantage. Civil wars within, and conflicts between, industrializing nations often served as "proxies" for wars between the superpowers.[17] Following the collapse of communism and the end of the cold war many of these conflicts subsided and the push for more representative forms of government gained momentum. As a result there has been a dramatic increase in the number of industrializing horticultural societies with multiparty democratic government. In just two years, 1990 and 1991, 22 formerly one-party states in sub-Saharan Africa legalized political opposition![18] But, given the weakness of the democratic "infrastructures" upon which most of these political systems rest, their future is far from secure. As the history of developing societies has shown all too often, internal conflicts and an ambitious military can easily topple a weakly rooted democratic government.

It is also impossible to ignore the numerous problems the governments of many industrializing horticultural societies have had with corruption. In Zaire (now the Republic of the Congo), for example, an international grant of $1.8 million to repair Kinshasa's broken-down city buses was reportedly "swindled down" to $200,000 by the time it reached the Transportation Ministry, while in Gabon the president built himself a $650 million marble palace with revolving rooms and walls that disappear at the touch of a button. For a number of years, oil-producing Arab nations were generous providers of foreign aid to sub-Saharan African societies, but they soon cut back on it after a series of bad experiences. A leading Arab publication reported, "In some cases now coming to light, for every $1 million of aid, less than $100,000 finds effective applications in African countries like Zambia and Zaire."[19]

SOCIAL STRATIFICATION

Systems of stratification in industrializing agrarian societies are as varied as the polities and economies to which they are linked. In a number of them, the class structure is still much as it was in the past, though modified to some degree by industrialization. The upper class is still basically an aristocracy of long-established, wealthy, landowning families that dominate the government, the army, the religious establishment, and other social institutions. The middle class is small and made up of merchants, lesser officials, lesser members of the clergy, and a few prosperous peasants. In addition, it includes a growing number of business and professional people with modern education and skills, members of the civil service with modern educational qualifications, and teachers trained in such new disciplines as science and engineering. As industrialization and modernization progress, some members of the new middle class may penetrate into the upper class by virtue of their wealth or political success. In effect, however, there tend to be two separate systems of stratification in these societies. One is dominant in rural areas and reflects the old order; the other is dominant in urban areas and reflects the new. With the passage of time, the newer system of stratification, which is based on the industrial economy, tends to become dominant throughout the country as a whole.

The major variations in the composition of the lower classes in industrializing agrarian societies are the result of differences in levels of economic development. The less developed the society, the larger the peasant class and the smaller the urban class, especially people who

*One of the striking features of industrializing horticultural societies is how new most of them are: almost without exception, they were established in the late nineteenth or the twentieth century. Most of them are products of European colonialism, and their boundaries are largely the result of the rivalries of colonial governments or missions, the outcomes of battles, the location of rivers, and other things that had little to do with the boundaries of the older societies they replaced. Actually, the process was not too different from the one that produced most other contemporary societies, though it occurred so long ago in the latter that its effects are currently minimal in most cases.

Satahu Sahni: Rickshaw Man

Satahu Sahni, one of Calcutta's poorer citizens, pulls a rickshaw for a living. He works from 6 a.m. to midnight, earning $3 a day. He lives in a one-room hut with his wife and two children. They spend about $2.50 a day for food alone, which provides tea and cookies for breakfast, a wheat cake for lunch, and rice and dried peas for supper. Satahu says of his work, "This job shouldn't be done by any human being, but I couldn't find any other thing to do."

Up and down hills, through broiling molten tar, across rough cobblestones, hauling heavy carts often loaded with more than one passenger as well as freight, Satahu and his fellow rickshaw men run day after day. In high humidity and with summer temperatures often above 100, a few of these men simply slip from between the shafts of their carts and drop dead every day. "It's really quite awful lately," said a British-educated Calcuttan, who has his own air-conditioned Mercedes and never rides in a rickshaw. "Not only do the poor runners die, but many passengers are injured when the rickshaws tip over backwards. Quite awful." But Satahu is fortunate compared to the hundreds of thousands of jobless persons and beggars in Calcutta who have no home at all and are forced to sleep on the open sidewalks at night and beg their food.

Source: Adapted from a copyrighted story by Myron Belkind of the Associated Press, by permission.

work in factories and other modern industries. At one extreme, nearly 80 percent of the labor force in Nepal are still in agriculture and 6 percent in industry.[20] At the opposite extreme, in South Korea only 11 percent work in agriculture, and 28 percent in manufacturing.[21]

As Table 14.6 shows, there is substantially more income inequality in industrializing societies than there is in the advanced industrial societies. The highest-earning 20 percent of households get a *much larger* share of total income, and the lowest-earning 20 percent of households get a *somewhat smaller share* than in industrial societies.

Because of the dramatic differences in the productivity of their economies, however, it is impossible to infer the *incomes* of these population segments from their proportionate share of total income. For example, the much smaller average share of income received by the

TABLE 14.6 Mean Income Share and Standardized Income, by Societal Type

Income Measure	Advanced Industrial	Industrializing Agrarian	Industrializing Horticultural
Highest-Earning 20 percent			
Percentage share	39.4	50.3	51.2
Standardized income*	$52,418.00	$13,432.00	$3,264.00
Lowest-Earning 20 Percent			
Percentage share	7.5	5.4	3.9
Standardized income	$9,954.00	$1,338.00	$343.00
Number of cases	16	34	20

*Standardized incomes are calculated as the proportionate share of income by the population quintiles (Actual Share/20) multiplied by the per capita GDP of the society (at Purchasing Power Parity). They are, thus, indicators of the per capita incomes of these population segments that can be compared across societies. For the use of a similar measure and its general rationale, see Patrick D. Nolan, "A Standardized Cross-National Comparison of Incomes," *The Sociological Quarterly,* vol. 34, no. 4 (Winter 1992).
Source: World Bank, *World Development Indicators* Online Database (www.worldbank.org/data/onlinedatabases/onlinedatabases.html).

Although it has long been legally abolished in advanced industrial societies, child labor continues to be quite common in many industrializing societies: a young girl at work in a match factory in southern India.

highest-earning households in industrial societies actually represents a much higher income—nearly 4 times that of similarly situated households in industrializing agrarian societies, and more than 15 times that of the top-earning households in industrializing horticultural societies. The relatively similar shares received by the lowest-earning households in all types of societies also mask striking differences in incomes. The lowest-earning households in industrial societies have more than 7 times the income of similarly situated households in industrializing agrarian societies, and nearly 30 times the income of the lowest-earning households in industrializing horticultural societies.

It is true, of course, that the need for cash income grows with increasing industrialization, but these comparisons caution against drawing conclusions about relative levels of poverty directly from data on income *shares* in societies that vary in terms of their levels of development. One conclusion that is clear from these data, though, is that *industrial societies have the richest rich and the richest poor in the world, and that industrializing horticultural societies have the poorest rich and the poorest poor in the world.*

This conclusion is reinforced by data on the quality of life in these types of societies. The United Nations has computed a "Human Development Index," based on measures of life expectancy, literacy, education, and income in different societies. We saw in Chapter 12 that the advanced industrial societies are all clustered in the highest category of the development scale with an average score of 0.93 (see Table 12.3, page 272). Table 14.7 shows the index scores and medians for industrializing agrarian and industrializing horticultural societies. The differences are quite dramatic; the median for industrializing agrarian societies is 0.72 and for industrializing horticultural it is 0.36. Furthermore, the vast majority of the industrializing

TABLE 14.7 Quality of Life Index for Industrializing Societies

Industrializing Agrarian Societies		Industrializing Horticultural Societies	
Society	**HDI***	**Society**	**HDI**
South Korea	0.89	Gabon	0.56
Costa Rica	0.89	Papua New Guinea	0.53
Argentina	0.89	Zimbabwe	0.51
Uruguay	0.88	Congo	0.50
Trinidad and Tobago	0.88	Ghana	0.47
Panama	0.86	Cameroon	0.47
Chile	0.86	Kenya	0.46
Venezuela	0.86	Nigeria	0.39
Mexico	0.85	Zaire	0.38
Colombia	0.85	Zambia	0.37
Thailand	0.83	Benin	0.37
Malaysia	0.83	Cote d'Ivoire	0.37
Brazil	0.78	Togo	0.37
Ecuador	0.78	Tanzania	0.36
Turkey	0.77	Mauritania	0.36
North Korea	0.77	Central African Rep.	0.36
Syria	0.76	Madagascar	0.35
Tunisia	0.75	Haiti	0.34
Jamaica	0.74	Angola	0.34
Dominican Republic	0.72	Uganda	0.33
Peru	0.72	Senegal	0.33
Sri Lanka	0.71	Malawi	0.32
Paraguay	0.71	Chad	0.29
Philippines	0.67	Mozambique	0.28
Indonesia	0.67	Guinea	0.27
Guyana	0.65	Burundi	0.25
China	0.63	Mali	0.23
Egypt	0.61	Burkina Faso	0.22
El Salvador	0.59	Niger	0.21
Bolivia	0.59	Rwanda	0.19
Honduras	0.58	Sierra Leone	0.18
Guatemala	0.57	**Industrializing horticultural median**	**0.36**
Morocco	0.57		
Nicaragua	0.53		
Laos	0.46		
India	0.45		
Pakistan	0.45		
Cambodia	0.35		
Nepal	0.35		
Industrializing agrarian median	**0.72**		

*Human Development Index, an index of well-being based on measures of life expectancy, literacy, education, and income.
Source: United Nations, *Human Development Report 1997* (Cary, N.C.: Oxford University Press, 1997).

horticultural societies have index scores below 0.50, putting them in the lowest category of human development. Small petroleum-rich Gabon (see Table 14.4) is a clear exception with a score of 0.56, putting it over the threshold of the middle category. In contrast, almost 90 percent of the industrializing agrarian societies had index scores of 0.50 or above, and 12 of them scored above 0.80, putting them in the highest category of human development.

Finally, although slavery has long since disappeared in Europe and North America, it still persists in a number of industrializing societies in Asia, Africa and the Middle East. Sadly the world seems to be little concerned (see "Slavery Is Still Alive and Well in Some Societies," page 311). In addition to Mauritania and the Sudan, there have been credible reports of slavery, debt-slavery, or forced prostitution in Saudi Arabia, Kuwait, South Africa, Nigeria,

Pakistan, India, Thailand, Myanmar (i.e., Burma), the Dominican Republic, and Haiti.[22] By some estimates, there may be tens of millions of slaves in industrializing societies today.[23]

CLEAVAGES AND CONFLICTS

Few societies in history have had such serious internal divisions as the majority of those now undergoing industrialization. Most of them are torn not only by ancient cleavages inherited from the preindustrial past, but also by others that are peculiar to societies trying to industrialize today.

The most basic of the older cleavages in *industrializing agrarian societies* is the one that separates the few who control the nation's resources from the vast majority who supply the labor and get little more than the barest necessities in return. The traditional antagonisms between urban and rural populations, and between the literate minority and the illiterate majority, are also present, though they tend to become less pronounced as advances in transportation and communication reduce the isolation, and hence the ignorance, of rural residents and the illiterate.

As we have already seen, the struggle to industrialize and modernize creates its own animosities and conflicts. There is a split within the more favored classes, for example, between

---

Slavery Is Still Alive and Well in Some Societies

Chattel slavery—the buying, selling, and ownership of human beings—ended in Europe and North America more than a hundred years ago and many imagine that that was the end of it. But such was not the case.

In the Arab-dominated nations of Sudan and Mauritania, slavery still flourishes. In Mauritania, slavery was not outlawed until 1980 and there is still no punishment for those who violate the law and no effort was made to notify those being held as slaves of the change in the law. As a result, Africa Watch estimates that there are still as many as 100,000 slaves in the country. In Sudan, the director of the American Anti-Slavery Group, Dr. Charles Jacobs, reports, "You can buy a black woman as a slave for as little as $15 in [the capital] Khartoum."

Sometimes slaves are sold to local owners, sometimes to buyers from Chad, Libya, and Arab states of the Persian Gulf. Slaves are often branded like cattle, forcibly converted to Islam, lashed if they resist, and tortured if they try to escape. They are put to work as household servants or made to perform hard labor in the fields. Girls are routinely raped.

Despite these horrors, civil rights leaders in the United States remain surprisingly indifferent. One of Jesse Jackson's aides, for example, told Jacobs that Jackson cannot get involved because "he is busy with affirmative action." The chairman of the Black Congressional Caucus recently dismissed the slave trade as a "sub, sub issue," and neither the NAACP nor Transafrica has taken action. The mass media, too, have remained surprisingly quiet, though a few black journalists outside the mainstream media have recently taken up the cause.

Perhaps the twenty-first century will finally see the end of this age-old practice.

Sources: Jeff Jacoby, *Boston Globe,* April 7, 1996; Tom Maland, Rod Norland, Melinda Liu, and Joseph Conterras, "Slavery," *Newsweek,* May 4, 1992, pp. 30–39; the Associated Press, April 5, 1992; Charles Wallace, "Slavery, Twentieth Century Style," *Los Angeles Times,* Aug. 6, 1991.

those educated along traditional lines and those with modern scientific and technical training. These groups often have difficulty understanding one another and tend to be mutually prejudiced against each other. Another new cleavage separates the powerful old landowning aristocracy and the new industrial entrepreneurs, who often have greater wealth.

As the monarchical political system in agrarian societies has broken down, many new groups have become politically active and many new issues have become politically relevant. For example, the political unrest and other changes associated with industrialization often intensify old tensions between religious and ethnic groups. This has occurred in such widely scattered countries as Vietnam, Indonesia, Sri Lanka, India, Lebanon, Iraq, Algeria, Egypt, Guyana, and others. In addition, the breakdown of the older political system and efforts to establish a modern regime can produce serious tensions between civilian leaders and the military. Struggles between these groups have caused countless crises in Latin American, Middle Eastern, and Asian nations. In democratic countries, mass political parties have introduced yet another cleavage. Although support for the various parties tends to follow other lines of cleavage, it is seldom a perfect reflection of them. Thus, it can create further divisions within an already badly divided population.[24]

Finally, the rapid rate of change characteristic of industrializing societies invariably creates a cleavage between the generations. This appears to be more serious than the generational gap in societies that have already industrialized, as indicated by the frequency and the bitterness of conflicts between students and political authorities in these nations and by the frequency of revolutionary activity in the younger generation. This is hardly surprising, of course, in societies that are changing so rapidly. The experiences of the different generations are so dissimilar that conflict is almost inevitable. Universities tend to be the centers of discontent, because they bring together large numbers of people who have maximum exposure to new ideas but little power to implement them. The result is often explosive.

Authoritarian governments of both the right and the left often manage to suppress these conflicts, so they are not always visible to the outside world. Yet as the Chinese experience indicates, suppressing them is not the same as eliminating them: any relaxation of control by the authorities results in new struggles for power. The fact of the matter is that industrialization and modernization are extremely stressful processes, and when the cleavages they generate are added to the historic cleavages inherent in an agrarian social order, the choice is often between harsh repression and chronic conflict.

The consequences of tribalism have been most serious in *industrializing horticultural societies*. Civil wars based on tribal divisions wrecked havoc in the Republic of the Congo, Angola, Rwanda, Burundi, Nigeria, Uganda, Zimbabwe, Liberia, and Sierra Leone among others. In most sub-Sharan African countries, in fact, tribalism remains a divisive force, often with the potential for civil war. When they were fighting for independence, many African leaders (as well as their friends in industrial societies) ignored or minimized the importance of these tribal loyalties, believing that their compatriots valued them as little as they did and that the old ties were rapidly losing their vitality. Although this may have been true in a few countries, it proved a serious misjudgment in most.[25] Even in cities and towns, tribal loyalties are still meaningful.[26] In view of the ethnic and linguistic diversity in these societies* and considering the virtual absence of truly national institutions in these societies until recently, this is hardly surprising. With increasing urbanization, with the establishment of schools that cultivate national loyalties, and with the growth of the mass media to reinforce these early lessons, tribal loyalties will probably disappear in time. But this will take decades or even generations, and in the meantime these allegiances often produce bitter and costly conflicts. Such conflicts often lie behind African famines, where food is used as a political or military weapon (see, for

---

*For example, Cameroon's 16 million citizens belong to 200 tribes and speak 24 languages; the Republic of the Congo and Papua New Guinea each have 700 languages and dialects.[27]

example, the experience of Somalia and Zimbabwe). Although nature has played some role in these food crises, politics and war have been decisive.[28]

EDUCATION

The importance of education for economic growth is abundantly clear: the most prosperous nations are those that have invested heavily in education. In the United States and Japan—two of the more striking examples of economic growth—high levels of national expenditure on education preceded industrialization.[29] In Japan, half the male population was literate by the 1870s, and in the United States, almost 90 percent of white adults were literate by this time.

The relation between education and economic growth is borne out by studies that indicate that expansion of primary and secondary school enrollments, especially the latter, has been linked to increases in per capita GNP since World War II.[30] However, these same studies found that this relation did not exist in the case of expanded enrollments in higher education. The reasons for this are not clear, but it may reflect the fact that many industrializing societies have overemphasized training in the humanities and neglected training in fields required by industrialization. In Europe, for example, from one-third to one-half of university students study science or engineering, compared to only 23 percent of those in Asia and 16 percent in Latin America.[31]

These figures are important not only because industrializing societies so urgently need technical and engineering skills, but also because those societies have so much trouble absorbing the nontechnical professionals their universities turn out. Not long ago,, for example, 58 percent of the students in India were enrolled in the humanities, fine arts, and law.[32] Most graduates simply cannot find jobs that utilize these skills. Unwilling to accept lesser employment, these graduates become a kind of intellectual proletariat with deep-seated hostilities toward the existing social order. Because such people are easily attracted to revolutionary movements, this leads to more political instability, and this, in turn, hampers economic progress. In short, far from aiding economic growth, an oversupply of nontechnically trained students in a society actually hinders it.*

IDEOLOGIES OLD AND NEW

Most leaders of modernizing movements are aware that social and economic progress requires more than increased capital and improved techniques of production. New creeds and new gods are needed to arouse and mobilize the common people who, after centuries of frustration, are often apathetic and fatalistic. Ironically, even a dedicated Marxist like Mao Zedong came to place the struggle for people's hearts and minds ahead of the struggle to transform the economy.

Today, in all but the most backward parts of the industrializing agrarian world, there is an intellectual ferment and a clash of ideas between the advocates of traditional belief systems and the proponents of newer ones. The situation is often extremely complicated, because both traditionalists and modernizers differ among themselves on many points, while others favor various blends of the old and the new.

A lot of the intellectual and ideological resistance to modernization has come from leaders of the traditional faiths. In southern and eastern Asia, these have been Buddhism,

---

*One may ask why the leaders of these societies allow this kind of educational imbalance to develop. There are two main reasons. First, in allowing the humanities to dominate their educational systems, they are following the example of the oldest and most prestigious educational institutions in the world—Oxford, Cambridge, and the famous Continental universities—as well as their own native traditions. Second, it costs much more to provide technical education, and these nations have very limited resources.

Osama bin Laden, leader of al-Qaeda and advocate of the Islamic fundamentalist view that all things modern and western should be rejected.

Hinduism, and Islam; in the Middle East, Islam.* In all these areas, religious leaders have often been the leaders of conservative and traditionalist movements. This is hardly surprising considering the historic role of these ideologies in agrarian societies and the nature of their beliefs. In general, they assert that the quest for truth is essentially complete: what people need to know has already been revealed—in the Vedas, or in the Koran, or to the Sangha. True wisdom, in their opinion, lies in turning to religious authorities for guidance and following their directions. In describing the traditionalist approach to education in the Middle East, one writer has said, "Education, as far as it is under the control of the ulema [the spiritual leaders of the Muslim community], is still bound up with authoritarianism, rote learning, and a rigid devotion to ancient authorities—providing only already known solutions to already formulated problems."[33] This approach sees little need for change, unless it is to root out whatever modernizing influences have crept in.

In the late nineteenth and early twentieth centuries, many western intellectuals thought these older faiths would simply die out as their adherents came to recognize the "obvious" superiority of western creeds such as Protestantism, humanism, and socialism. These newer faiths were then winning converts, especially among the better educated, and it looked as if it were only a matter of time until the older faiths would vanish altogether.

Since World War I, however, and even more since World War II, the situation has changed drastically in many areas. With the development of nationalist movements and a growing resistance to western ideas and influences, some of the traditional faiths have experienced a remarkable reinvigoration. After Sri Lanka won its independence, for example, a significant number of Christian converts there reconverted to Buddhism. In India, Hindu traditionalists became strong enough to pass laws forbidding the entry of foreign missionaries. In Egypt, most of the leaders of the Communist Party were imprisoned or executed. In Iran, the Ayatollah Khomeini led an Islamic revolution that overthrew the shah and ended his program of modernization. More recently, Osama bin Laden and hundreds of religious leaders throughout the Muslim world have promoted a militant brand of Islamic fundamentalism that has proven extraordinarily attractive to large numbers of young people.

---

*Roman Catholicism plays a similar role in Latin America in one respect: its opposition to all forms of birth control. Until a decade or two ago, the Catholic Church was also a very conservative force politically and economically, but that has changed considerably in more recent years.

Although religious leaders have often been among the most conspicuous proponents of traditionalism, they have usually had strong support from the old governing class, especially the large landowners.[34] In fact, the rural population as a whole, emotionally involved in its traditional religion and unfamiliar with alternatives, has generally supported them. Members of such old "professions" as herbalists and practitioners of traditional medicine have also been strong supporters of traditionalist ideologies and belief systems, because they recognize that their skills would become obsolete in a modern industrial society.

Ranged against the traditionalists are individuals and groups who, by virtue of educational, occupational, or other experience, have been converted to the newer faiths. Early in a modernization movement, a disproportionate number of the leaders are people who were won over to the new outlook during visits to industrial societies, either as students or as workers. This was true, for example, of India's Nehru and of Vietnam's Ho Chi Minh.[35] Later, however, most of the leaders are people who have been converted by experiences in their own countries. Frequently they are children of the old governing class who rise to positions of leadership because of their superior training and other resources.

As we have noted earlier, there are usually competing groups of modernizers, some advocating western-style democracy, others Marxism, still others some kind of hybrid system. The liberal democratic model was the first to be tried in most industrializing agrarian nations, as we noted. It has had its greatest support from the more prosperous segments of the new middle class—professional people, managers in new industries, and others with modern education. Socialism was usually tried next. Its support has been greatest among intellectuals, students, and the economically insecure—landless peasants and unemployed urban workers.

A more recent approach to modernization is nationalism, which reflects the dissatisfaction of many of the current generation of leaders with both of the older models. Nationalists often advocate a synthesis not only of capitalism and socialism but of modernism and traditionalism as well. Nationalism has often been a reaction against colonialism, especially in countries that were under foreign control until recently. It is also a reaction against the continued technological and economic dependence of industrializing societies on the more advanced industrial societies.

There is more to modern nationalism than this, however. It is also an effort to reaffirm the importance of a society's own cultural traditions. Sometimes this helps to heal the breach between traditionalists and modernists by providing a position that is acceptable to both. Moreover, it gives dignity to a nation's leaders in their relations with technologically more advanced societies.

Unfortunately, the cultivation of nationalist sentiments can easily lead to hatred of other nations and groups. If this does not happen spontaneously, leaders may even encourage it to divert criticism from themselves and their policies. It can be very useful politically to blame foreigners for all the defects and shortcomings, inevitable and otherwise, of one's own policies.

The traditional religions of *horticultural* societies were relatively undeveloped, both organizationally and intellectually, compared to those of agrarian Europe and Asia. There were no complex organizations of priests or monks, no body of sacred writings to serve as the core of a common faith, no tradition of philosophical speculation, and, most important of all, no universal faith to provide a bond between members of different societies. As a result, these faiths could not easily defend themselves against the inroads of Islam and Christianity, especially when the latter were introduced by peoples who were politically and economically dominant and whose way of life, therefore, seemed so obviously worthy of emulation.

People who still cling to the older tribal faiths in industrializing horticultural societies are usually residents of the more isolated rural areas or the less educated residents of the towns. Since this describes the majority of people in these societies, adherents of the older faiths are obviously still numerous. Not long ago in Benin and Togo, for example, only 30 percent of the people were even nominally Christian or Muslim; in Gabon and Zaire, less than 40 percent were.[36] In the cities, however, the picture was very different. In Dar es Salaam, the capital of Tanzania, 99.8 percent of the population claimed to be either Muslim or Christian thirty years ago, at a time when 40 percent of the society as a whole were non-Muslim and non-Christian.[37] Similarly, in Monrovia, Liberia's capital, 72 percent were either Christian or Muslim at a time when only 25 percent of the nation as a whole were Christian or Muslim.[38]

Conversion to Islam or Christianity is often for nonreligious reasons. For many people it is a status symbol, an effort to identify with modern ways and avoid being regarded as ignorant, backward country folk. In Dar es Salaam, for example, many pagan tribesmen "on arrival in town call themselves Muslims—some few call themselves Christians—in order to conform, not to be conspicuous in a [community] where Islam is supreme and where to 'have no religion,' as people put it, is the mark of the uncivilized. Some go so far as to be circumcised and to be formally admitted to Islam: most merely use a Muslim name instead of a tribal one; some have two names, a Christian and a Muslim, to cover all eventualities."[39] Under the circumstances, it is hardly surprising to find that "the outward observances of religion are strikingly absent in Dar es Salaam: it is rare to see an African Muslim praying his daily prayers [and] in Ramadhan [the Muslim month of fasting] people may be seen anywhere eating and drinking publicly during the daily hours [a forbidden practice]," and the consumption of alcohol, also forbidden, is almost universal.[40] In Monrovia, where Christianity is dominant, the pattern is not quite so pronounced, but even here "the professing of Christianity remains a basic requirement of 'civilized' status," and "for a great many of the civilized, church membership has become largely a question of social status."[41] In many areas, both urban and rural, those who have adopted Christianity or Islam often continue to practice traditional tribal religions as well.[42]

In the early years of colonial rule, Christian missions were an important force for modernization. This was primarily due to the mission schools, which introduced literacy and elements of western culture and, most important of all, opened up channels of communication with the larger world. As a result, the areas that came under Christian influence advanced more rapidly than those where paganism or Islam prevailed. In discussing Tanzania, one writer asserts:

> Mission schools and mission hospitals have been very important factors in changing tribal society, although their influence has been felt much more strongly in some areas than others. Very nearly a one-to-one correlation exists between mission influence, the cash-crop economy, fertile land, education, and the general desire for progress.[43]

Similarly, many people have commented on the singular economic success of the Christian Ibo of southeastern Nigeria compared with the Muslim and pagan tribes to the north.

With the rise of the independence movement after World War II, identification with Christianity became a somewhat ambiguous social attribute. Christianity was linked with colonialism, and colonialism was considered bad. Missionaries came under heavy attack for dominating the churches and refusing to let native Christians assume positions of leadership. Furthermore, in an era of great social change and uncertainty, mission-brand Christianity often seemed too tame and too western. In many areas, new sects were founded, some basically Christian, others largely pagan, many a mixture of both.[44] These sects have their greatest appeal for individuals who are in mid-passage in the difficult transition from traditional culture to modern. Such people are subject to great insecurity, both economically and intellectually, and the sects often provide a link to the past. They also are popular because they permit polygyny and other traditional practices condemned by the missionaries.

KINSHIP

In horticultural societies of the past, kin groups were extremely important. As one writer put it, "the [kin group] was the basic building block of [horticultural] society."[45] More than that, it was psychologically the center of the individual's world, establishing a person's identity and defining most of his or her basic rights and responsibilities.

Now the historic bases of power of the kin group are being undermined in these societies. In the modern sector of the economy, the kin group no longer controls its members' access to the means of livelihood, which it traditionally did through its control of the land. Similarly, the family plays a smaller role in the political system. And the once-important cult of the ancestors, centered in the kin group, has declined in importance as Christianity and Islam have expanded.

In the past, most of the advantages of the kin group were enjoyed by the older generation, while the disadvantages fell disproportionately on the younger. Before the growth of cities and towns, young people had no choice but to accept the burdens and patiently await the day when they would become the privileged elders. The growth of cities and towns has changed all this: by migrating to these urban centers, young people can largely escape the control of their elders.[46] Although ties to the extended family are not entirely eliminated, they are greatly weakened, and this has become a cause of social instability in most industrializing horticultural societies.[47]

These changes in the kinship system also appear to have contributed to the runaway growth of population in these societies.[48] For example, the traditional stigma attached to unmarried mothers is no longer as powerful as it used to be when family controls over young people were stronger. In addition, the decline of polygynous households (a result of the influence of Christian missions) has apparently contributed to higher birthrates. As some Africans point out, although a few older, wealthy men could afford many wives and have large numbers of children, the wives in polygynous households usually had, on average, fewer children than women in monogamous households. Thus, a pattern of marriage that might seem to increase the birthrate actually had the opposite effect.

THE STATUS OF WOMEN

For people accustomed to the status of women in advanced industrial societies today, the status of women in most industrializing societies is both surprising and shocking. In the developed world, as we have seen, industrialization has been a powerful force that has greatly reduced the impact of gender differences on people's lives.

The same cannot be said for most industrializing societies. This is especially true of Muslim societies, where women's lives are greatly restricted by interpretations of the Koran by Muslim clerics. In many cases, women are required, when in public, to wear clothing that covers their bodies from head to toe except for their hands, feet, and all or part of their face. In some cases (as in Saudi Arabia) women are forbidden to drive cars, and in others places (as in Afghanistan recently) they are forbidden to attend school. In most of these societies, most occupations are closed to women, and within marriages, husbands have far more power, both legal and informal, than their wives. For example, under traditional Islamic practice, husbands can divorce their wives simply by stating on several successive days, "I divorce you," but wives have no comparable right.

In non-Muslim industrializing societies the status of women is generally better, though rarely as good as in the more industrialized societies of Europe and North America. A good marriage is the best that most women can hope for, even if their lives are dominated by the wishes of their husbands and severely restricted by the demands of childbirth and child-rearing. Even worse, in many industrializing horticultural societies of sub-Saharan Africa, the notorious practice of genital mutilation persists, especially in rural areas.

Slowly, however, changes are beginning to occur. In Morocco, for example, the king recently decreed that a minority of seats in the parliament would be reserved for women. In Argentina, India, Pakistan, and the Philippines, a woman has even served as prime minister. This, however, it should be noted, has not greatly improved the lives of the vast majority of women in those societies.[49]

INDUSTRIALIZING SOCIETIES IN THEORETICAL PERSPECTIVE

Not many years ago, the prospects for industrializing societies looked bright. All they had to do, it appeared, was to follow the path blazed by the societies that had already industrialized. In fact, some people believed that because developing societies had the experience of others to draw on, they would be able to avoid many of the pitfalls of modernization and speed up the process.

Today, that prediction seems hopelessly naive. In much of the Third World, development has been distressingly slow. Improvements in the standard of living for the masses of their citizens have been especially disappointing. Hundreds of millions of people continue to live in poverty, with little prospect of any significant improvement in their situation.

Why were earlier predictions so wrong? Why have the majority of industrializing societies been unable to take greater advantage of the vastly expanded store of technological information that is now available?

One answer, originally developed by a group of Latin American scholars in the 1960s and known as dependency theory, is that the difficulties of the less developed societies are due to their social environment, or more specifically to the actions of industrial societies.[50] The backwardness and problems of the less developed societies, they argue, are the result of exploitation and oppression by the more developed societies. Dependency theory is, in effect, an extension to the global level of Marx's theory that the impoverishment of some is an inevitable consequence of the growing wealth of others.

There are currently a number of versions of dependency theory, each providing a somewhat different explanation of the problems confronting industrializing societies, but all of them locate the source outside the industrializing societies themselves.[51] Some blame multinational corporations, some blame the governments of industrial societies, and others blame the capitalist world economy that has caused so many developing nations to concentrate on the production of raw materials and on low-technology industries. Whatever the explanation, dependency theorists blame the difficulties of the industrializing societies on western industrial societies.

Another group of scholars, employing modernization theory, has developed a very different explanation of the problems confronting industrializing societies. They find the source of these problems within the industrializing societies themselves.[52] As with dependency theory, there are a number of versions of modernization theory, but most of them focus on the attitudes and values of the members of industrializing societies as the chief deterrent to industrialization. The difficulties of these societies, in their view, are due to the persistence of ideologies and institutional systems which were inherited from the preindustrial past and are incompatible with the needs and requirements of industrialization. They point out, for example, the persistence of fatalism, trust in magic, resistance to innovation and change, and the conflict between traditional patterns of work (see page 306, "Traditional Values and Norms Regarding Work") and the requirements of modern industrial enterprises. They emphasize the consequences of illiteracy and the lack of the information, training, and skills that are essential in the modern world. In short, modernization theory locates the causes of lagging development within the less developed societies themselves, rather than in their social environments.

In any attempt to evaluate the relative merits of dependency theory and modernization theory, it is important to keep two things in mind. First, there is little evidence to support the claim of many dependency theorists that life was better in most industrializing societies before the industrial era. Such a view cannot be supported by the historical record of the last 5,000 years. It is a mistake, therefore, to ask, What has caused these societies to regress? Rather, the question must be, Why have the conditions in so many of them improved so slowly?

The second point to remember is that there is no reason to assume that the source of problems in the industrializing societies is primarily internal or primarily external. On the contrary, ecological-evolutionary theory asserts that the characteristics of human societies—including the degree of their development—are the product of both internal and external forces (see Figure 1.2, page 18), and that the emergence of technologically more advanced societies reduces the prospects and competitiveness of less advanced societies. To ignore or neglect either aspect is to misunderstand and misinterpret the complex process of societal development.

One indication of the danger of neglecting either set of forces is provided by the results of the foreign aid programs created by western industrial societies in recent decades. Because of the tremendous success of the Marshall Plan in rebuilding West Germany following the massive destruction of World War II, many western leaders assumed that large transfers of capital to the less developed societies of Asia, Africa, and Latin America would produce similar results. Unfortunately, however, the results of such aid to most of these societies have been extremely disappointing. As noted earlier, much of the money was wasted on ill-conceived projects or simply vanished into the pockets of corrupt officials. It has gradually become clear that the success of foreign aid programs depends as much on the characteristics of the recipient society as on the generosity of the donors. Effective use of large amounts of capital presupposes supportive institutions and ideologies in the recipient society, plus large numbers of people with administrative and technical skills and honest elites capable of organizing vast and complex programs.

The greatest deficiency of both modernization theory and dependency theory, however, is their failure to focus more closely on the distinctive demographic situation of industrializing societies. For the fact is that no society, except for newly settled frontier societies (e.g., the United States and Canada), has ever successfully industrialized while burdened with anything approaching the rate of population growth existing in most of these societies today. As we have seen, even impressive economic gains can be completely consumed by rapid population growth.

From the perspective of ecological-evolutionary theory, it is clear that the demographic peculiarities of industrializing societies, as well as those characteristics of ideology and social structure that work against the resolution of their problems, all stem from a more basic underlying source. In most societies throughout human history, all of the basic components of their sociocultural systems—population, technology, ideology, social structure, and material products—evolved more or less in concert with one another. In contrast, in societies industrializing today, selected elements of an enormously powerful industrial technology have been introduced into sociocultural systems that are still geared to much less potent agrarian or advanced horticultural technologies.

Not surprisingly, these societies have had enormous difficulty in coordinating technological advance with changes in other areas of life. Even the western industrial democracies, in which the new technology evolved largely in concert with changes in population, ideology, social structure, and material products, have encountered difficulties in adjusting to the new industrial technology. In fact, most of their major problems reflect the failure of political ideologies, religious beliefs and values, legal norms, organization principles, and other cultural and structural elements to respond quickly enough to the new conditions created by ongoing changes in technology.

Considering the problems it can create even in those societies in which it evolved, it is hardly surprising that an industrial technology creates far greater ones when it is introduced as an alien force in societies still geared to simpler technologies. And when only selected elements of the new technology are introduced, the results can be disastrous.

India provides a good example of this. Over the last hundred years, improvements in transportation (especially railroads) and food production reduced the number of deaths from famine, and programs of mass immunization and other health measures reduced deaths from disease. While this drastic reduction in the death rate was occurring, the vast majority of Indians, unlike the members of earlier industrializing societies, were not really involved in the industrialization process as a whole. Most of them continued to live as peasant farmers, eking out a marginal existence on tiny farms, using traditional tools and techniques. As a result, their beliefs, values, and customs remained much as they had been for centuries, with large families highly valued and change viewed with profound skepticism. India's population is now expected to surpass China's by midcentury.

In the past, such imbalances in a sociocultural system would have been corrected through the play of natural forces. We saw earlier (in Chapter 6) how population pressures during the late hunting and gathering era led to the overkilling of large game animals and, eventually, to the emergence of a more advanced technology and a new way of life. And we have seen how plagues and famines of the past periodically decimated the populations of agrarian societies, restoring their demographic equilibrium. In the case of India and other societies industrializing today, however, more advanced societies have repeatedly averted this resolution of the problem by shipping in large amounts of food. In doing so, they have created the likelihood of more serious crises and greater problems in the future.

As Malthus warned two centuries ago, if fertility is not curbed by the forgoing of children, forces such as war, civil strife, famine, drought, and disease will stop population growth. The longer it takes for industrializing societies to devise cultural solutions and technological solutions to high rates of fertility, the greater the chance that these negative forces will play a major role in checking population growth. They are, in fact, already playing a significant role in much of the developing world, especially in sub-Saharan Africa.[53]

Of one thing we can be sure: the problems of industrializing societies are not going to be solved quickly. Because of the failure of most of these societies to control population growth in the past, they have large numbers of young people who are only now entering the reproductive years. Of every hundred Africans alive today, forty-two are under 15 years of age; in contrast, of every hundred Europeans, only seventeen are that young.[54] Because of the disproportionately large number of children and teenagers in industrializing societies, most of their populations will increase 50 percent in the next several decades even if every couple from now on limits itself to only two children.

In summary, industrializing societies provide a fascinating test of ecological-evolutionary theory, and other sociological theories as well. Their problems are so complex that they compel us to consider all of the components of sociocultural systems—population, culture, material products, social organization, and social institutions—as well as the relations among them. They also compel us to consider the relation of these sociocultural systems to the larger world system—which is good preparation for an analysis of the future, our primary concern in the final chapter.

15

Major Social Experiments of the Twentieth Century: Testing the Limits of the Possible

Before the Industrial Revolution, the nature and fate of human societies always seemed to be subject to forces beyond the control of mere mortals. Societies were as they were, and life was as it was, because of the will of God or the gods or the working of fate or natural law. Monarchical government, the patriarchal family system, widespread poverty and suffering, huge inequalities in power and privilege, and all the other basic features of life in agrarian societies seemed fixed and immutable features of an established order of things, much like famines, floods, earthquakes, and other natural disasters.

The Industrial Revolution drastically changed conditions and people's perception of things. Because of the enormous increases in productivity that resulted from advances in technology, the economic surplus expanded rapidly, and this, in turn, extended the limits of the possible and made numerous important social changes feasible. They also persuaded millions of people that things did not have to be the way they were, or the way they had always been: people have it in their power to change society and to improve social conditions. All that was needed was the will, the imagination, and a plan.

As we saw in Chapter 11, this view is present in all of the new secular ideologies of the industrial era. Reformers and revolutionaries alike have shared the conviction that social conditions can be improved. They have differed, however, in their goals and the means by which they have sought to achieve them: revolutionaries have been far more ambitious in their goals and much more willing to adopt ruthless means to attain them. Reformers have been more modest in their goals and more willing to work to attain them by democratic means.

There is much that can be learned from these efforts. Both have advocated and, when they had the power to do it, conducted massive social experiments that test the limits of what is possible in human societies. Some of these experiments have been successful; some have failed; and many have had mixed results. We can and should learn from all of them, though in some ways there is more to be learned from the failures, since they remind us that even in modern industrial societies there are limits to what is possible and they help us discover what those limits are and how costly overly ambitious efforts to transform societies can be.

SOME SUCCESSFUL EXPERIMENTS

Before turning to these failed experiments, however, we need to consider several of the more important successes to see what can be learned from them.

Among successful social experiments, the most important has almost certainly been the establishment of the democratic form of government (see Chapter 11). For those who live in modern democratic societies today, it is far too easy to forget that this form of government, which exists today in every industrial society and in many industrializing societies as well, is a modern phenomenon, the product of a series of social experiments.

Sometimes today it is difficult to appreciate just how successful the democratic experiment has been. The mass media constantly bombard us with stories about political scandals of various kinds, and it is easy to become cynical. Before becoming too critical, however, we need to recall the many achievements of this form of government and, more importantly, we need to consider it in comparison to the other possibilities. As Winston Churchill once put it, democracy seems a very poor form of government until we consider the alternatives.

Largely because of their democratic systems of government, western industrial societies have undertaken a succession of further social experiments that have, on the whole, been remarkably successful. One of the first, and one of the most successful, was the nineteenth-century American experiment with mass public education. In its day, this effort to provide, at public expense, a basic education for every child was a radical innovation, and it quickly proved a great success. In fact, it was so successful that free public education is now available, at least at the elementary level, in most societies around the world, and public subsidies are often provided even for college and university students. Although mass public education, like democracy itself, often falls short of what one might wish for it, it is a vast improvement over what went before, and it is now all but impossible to conceive of its absence.*

Another important set of experiments by democratic governments has been the effort to assure every citizen the basic necessities of life. These experiments began in the late nineteenth century when the German government created the first social insurance programs. These proved so successful that other industrial societies have created their own massive social welfare programs—old-age pensions, unemployment compensation, disability benefits for the handicapped, aid for dependent children, food stamps, and more. Once again, these programs have often been flawed and debates rage over their details and levels of funding, but the basic principle of a publicly funded safety net is now almost universally accepted in industrial societies.

One can easily cite other examples of successful social experiments undertaken by democratic governments in western industrial societies (e.g., national park systems, public health programs, programs to protect the public against dangerous products such as spoiled meat, programs to encourage economic development in backward regions, programs to protect the safety of workers, and special programs for the handicapped). Some of these programs have been tremendously successful, others less so.

In addition to the many experiments undertaken by governments, others have been carried out by private groups and individuals. The most successful and most important of these has probably been the creation of the modern corporation (see Chapter 10) with its principle of limited liability, which has facilitated the formation of the vast pools of capital required to finance many of the forms of modern industry.

Looking back over the many social experiments of the industrial era, it seems safe to say that societies in which leaders have been guided by pragmatic principles have fared better than those whose leaders have been committed to some dogmatic ideology. In fact, most of the worst disasters in industrial societies in the twentieth century were attributable to the

---

*Even when public schools have come under attack and efforts have been made to find alternatives (e.g., charter schools), critics of public schools have assumed that government would provide all or much of the funding for the alternative schools. Moreover, even when people argue over the amount that should be spent for public education, the basic principle of public support for education remains unchallenged.

action of leaders committed to revolutionary ideologies of one kind or another. One need only recall the disaster that befell Germany in the 1930s and 1940s as a result of Hitler's National Socialist (Nazi) regime, or the disasters that overtook the Soviet Union and its eastern European satellites (see below).

It is also noteworthy that the more successful social experiments of modern times have generally been associated with less ambitious programs and policies and with gradual, evolutionary processes of change, while the worst failures, those that cost tens of millions of people their lives, were associated with far more ambitious programs and policies.

Finally, one also has to conclude that it is a mistake to expect any significant social experiment to be problem-free. To hold social experiments to the standard of perfection is to doom them to failure before they even get under way. All we have a right to expect is that their benefits justify the costs entailed, not only the monetary costs but also the costs in terms of individual freedom, justice, and happiness.

A TRAGICALLY FLAWED EXPERIMENT

One of the great ironies of modern life is that as the conditions for the masses of people in industrial societies have improved, the level of dissatisfaction with existing social arrangements has tended to increase. Social arrangements that people had accepted more or less stoically for centuries are now seen as intolerable. With hindsight, one might say that this was all but inevitable. With the new powers of industrial technology at their command, people expect more from life and are increasingly intolerant of society's flaws.

During the last two hundred years, no one has articulated this sense of dissatisfaction with existing social arrangements more powerfully or more persuasively than Karl Marx, the founder of the Communist Party. In writings and speeches, Marx not only denounced the evils of the industrial societies of his day, he also laid out a vision of a radically new social order in which highly affluent societies would enjoy not only freedom and justice but social equality as well. This new social order, which Marx referred to as communism, would be governed by the principle "From each according to his ability, to each according to his need." This would be a system in which the exploitative institution of private property would be abolished, and the means of production would become the common property of all.

Marx realized that such radical change could not take place overnight. People who had grown up before the revolution would almost certainly cling to many of their old beliefs and values (e.g., selfishness) until the successes and benefits of the new social order led them to change. Thus, he wrote that there would have to be a short transitional period of socialism during which those who worked harder, and those who brought greater skills to the workplace, would still receive higher wages than those with lesser skills and those who did not work as hard. During this transitional period the governing principle would be "From each according to his ability, to each according to his work." In other words, some limited inequality would persist, but it would be nothing like the kind of inequality that existed before the revolution.

Another important element in Marx's vision was his belief that the institution of the state would gradually wither away after the revolution. This would occur because he saw government as an institution by which the rich and powerful oppressed and controlled others. In the new postrevolutionary society, there would be less and less need for such an institution. As people came to recognize the nature of the new society, it would no longer be necessary to have an institution to force them to do the things that were needed: people would *spontaneously* and *voluntarily* do what was right.

People's attitude toward work would also undergo a radical change after the revolution. Once private ownership of the means of production was abolished and people realized that they were no longer working for someone else but were themselves the owners and managers of society's wealth, they would work for the sheer joy and pleasure of it. In short, in response to the new social order that would prevail after the revolution, a radically new kind of human being with a radically new set of beliefs and values would emerge—*the new socialist man.*

Not surprisingly, Marx's vision has been enormously attractive to many people, especially to idealistic young people and intellectuals who, through their studies, have been sensitized to the shortcomings and defects of their own societies. It has also been attractive to many of the poor and powerless who have hoped to benefit from a revolution of the kind Marx advocated.

In 1917, thirty-four years after Marx's death, his followers had their first opportunity to put his ideas into action. In the wake of Russia's defeat by Germany, the czarist government collapsed and was replaced by a new reform-minded, democratically elected government. Within months, however, the small Russian Communist Party, under Lenin's leadership, seized power. For the next several years, the party's control was contested by its opponents and a bitter civil war was waged. By 1922, the Communists emerged victorious and were able to consolidate their position. Thus, from this time until shortly before the collapse of Communist rule in 1991, the leaders of the party were in complete control of Soviet society with a virtual monopoly of political power. Other political parties were banned and individuals who dared to question the actions of Communist Party leaders put their freedom, and even their lives, in jeopardy.

In the years following World War II, Marx's followers seized power throughout the rest of eastern Europe, in North Korea, China, Vietnam, Laos, Cambodia, Cuba, South Yemen, Ethiopia, Mozambique, Angola, and elsewhere. In most of these societies, too, Marxists were able to destroy their opponents and win almost total control over all of the major institutions of society. By the mid-1970s, one-third of the world's population lived in societies in which Marxists were in almost total control.

Thus, the stage was set for a series of tests of Marx's theories about human societies and how they might be transformed. These societies became, in effect, vast laboratories in which a series of daring social experiments were undertaken—experiments designed to transform the values, beliefs, and personalities of hundreds of millions of people.

Some argue that we cannot use the experience of these societies to judge the validity of Marx's ideas, because conditions for the conduct of the experiments were never perfect. There was always some internal resistance to Communist Party rule, and there was opposition from the western industrial democracies. Also, none of these societies was yet a wealthy or affluent society at the time the Communists seized power.

But if conditions for these experiments in social change were less than ideal, they were as close to ideal as any important social experiments are ever likely to be. Except in the earliest years of their existence, most Marxist elites never encountered any truly effective *organized* opposition within their own societies. The same cannot be said of other important social experiments of the twentieth century, such as the civil rights movement or the feminist movement.

What, then, can we learn from Marxist experiments? To what extent and in what ways have they been successful? In what ways have they failed? And, most important of all, *why* have they succeeded where they succeeded and *why* have they failed where they failed?

Some Successes and Partial Successes

Despite a dismal record overall, Marxist experiments have enjoyed a few successes—or, at least, partial successes. The one most often cited by western observers—even by critics of Marxist regimes—has been the virtual elimination of the scourge of unemployment. Marxist societies have never had large numbers of unemployed people.

In the Soviet Constitution of 1936, work was defined not merely as a right guaranteed to all citizens, but also as a *duty* for all who were able-bodied.[1] The right to work was never interpreted to mean, however, that one had a right to the kind of job one might wish, or even to work in the region of the country in which one was raised. Furthermore, this broad constitutional guarantee was never backed up by more specific laws and institutional arrangements to ensure its implementation, and thus some, such as teenagers who left school early and were thought to be poor workers, found it difficult to obtain employment.[2] More seriously, millions of innocent people were compelled to work as virtual slave laborers in prison camps in harsh and remote regions of Siberia.[3] Despite these and other failures that have made the record in the Soviet Union and other Marxist societies much less attractive than proponents have sought to make it, Communist regimes were notable for their success in minimizing unemployment. This achievement was not without cost, however, as we will see shortly.

Communist regimes also claimed great success in reducing the level of economic inequality among their citizens, and if one looked only at official statistics, that claim seemed amply justified. These statistics showed that most people in these societies had only modest incomes and that variations in wages and salaries were much smaller than in other societies. No one in these societies owned property valued at hundreds of millions, or billions, of dollars. In fact, the only kinds of property anyone was usually allowed to own were personal possessions, such as clothes, household furnishings, automobiles, savings accounts, and, in some cases, living quarters (e.g., apartments). In addition, no one in these societies ever had an income measured in millions of dollars per year, as is the case with leading business executives, athletes, and entertainers in many other societies.

Income distribution in these societies, however, never was quite as simple or obvious a matter as official government statistics made it seem. For example, these statistics always ignored the millions of political prisoners who usually lived (if they were so fortunate) under the most wretched conditions imaginable and had no income at all. This qualification is extremely important, since political prisoners in the Soviet Union, China, Cuba, Vietnam,

Despite the Communist Party's claim to govern in the interest of the working class, Soviet workers were denied the right to strike until 1989, when this right was granted, but only in nonessential industries: despite this, Soviet miners struck illegally in July 1989 for better food, a ban on special privileges for party officials, and a new national constitution.

Shortages of consumer goods were a characteristic feature of stores in many revolutionary socialist societies: empty shelves in a yard-goods store in Katowice, Poland, during the Communist era.

North Korea, and elsewhere once numbered as many as 70 million, and their living conditions were hardly better than slavery.

Another important aspect of economic inequality that has been repeatedly overlooked by most observers of Communist societies is the fact that wages, salaries, and property ownership never had the same meaning in these societies as in others. In Communist societies, more highly valued goods and services were, in effect, rationed and access was denied to all except a favored few—chiefly Communist Party officials. Special stores and other facilities (e.g., hospitals, schools, resorts) were maintained where these goods and services could be obtained by members of the political elite at very nominal cost, while the general public was rigorously excluded. Thus, party leaders whose official incomes were hardly greater than those of ordinary workers always had ready access to all kinds of attractive goods and services that were denied to others.[4] Because of this, official government statistics on wages and salaries were virtually meaningless.

In a number of cases, Communist leaders used their enormous political power to amass substantial fortunes. To cite but three examples: (1) after the overthrow of Todor Zhikov, Bulgarians learned that he had acquired no fewer than thirty separate homes for his personal use and had accumulated millions of dollars in secret foreign bank accounts;[5] (2) Nicolae Ceausescu of Romania amassed forty villas and twenty palaces for himself and his family and accumulated several million dollars in Swiss bank accounts at a time when the bulk of the population was often living without heat or light;[6] and (3) the East German Communist Party leader, Erich Honecker, accumulated millions in Swiss bank accounts by skimming profits from the sale of arms to Third World nations, while sharing with other top party leaders exclusive hunting preserves and other luxuries. Although it had long been clear that top party leaders enjoyed many privileges denied to others,[7] the *extent* of these privileges was not discovered until after the collapse of Communist power when previously secret arrangements became public knowledge.

The fact that factories and other large business enterprises were public property in Communist societies also never meant quite what it has seemed to mean to those of us who live in non-Communist societies. Public "ownership" never meant that everyone shared equally either in the control of these enterprises or in the benefits they produced. On the contrary, control was always in the hands of Communist Party leaders, and that control was used to ensure that these leaders were its chief beneficiaries. Thus, public ownership of the means of production was like a magician's sleight of hand; it created an illusion of far greater equality than ever existed.

What then is to be said about the claims that Communism promotes economic equality? Have these claims been totally without merit, or has there been an element of truth in them?

Looking back, it appears that the income policies of Communist regimes and their abolition of private ownership of the means of production may have reduced *economic* inequality in these societies to some degree, but it is important not to forget that most Communist societies usually had a large class of political prisoners at the bottom of the social ladder that was compelled to live under extraordinarily harsh and repressive conditions. If one compares the economic situation and living conditions of these people with that of the party elite, it is difficult to say that this was any more egalitarian than the conditions that have prevailed in the western industrial democracies.

Finally, there are some who believe that even if Communism has little or nothing to offer to advanced industrial societies in the modern world, it has at least enabled a number of less developed societies to industrialize more rapidly and more successfully than would have been possible otherwise. Thus, the argument goes, Communism helped the Soviet Union, Poland, Yugoslavia, China, North Korea, Vietnam and other less developed countries expand their industrial base more rapidly than would have been possible under some other form of government. Proponents of this view argue that the totalitarian nature of Communism enabled leaders to mobilize their country's resources more quickly and more effectively than other forms of government that allow, or are unable to prevent, internal conflicts over policy issues.

This argument seemed to have considerable merit back in the 1930s when Stalin carried out a crash program of industrialization in the Soviet Union and in the late 1950s when Mao imposed his Great Leap Forward program on China. With hindsight, however, it is now clear that the costs of these programs (including the deaths of tens of millions of innocent people) were enormous and their benefits meager by comparison.* The modest accomplishments of these programs, long concealed by inflated official statistics, seem even less impressive when they are compared to the striking accomplishments of programs undertaken in other societies that were industrializing during the same period, societies such as Italy, Spain, Japan, Taiwan, and South Korea.

The Failures

Despite some limited successes in the areas noted, Marxist experiments, as a whole, have proved a tragic failure, and not merely in the Soviet Union or in China, but in Cuba, North Korea, Vietnam, Ethiopia, and everywhere that Marx's followers seized power. This fact is important because it indicates that the failures have not been due to localized conditions or difficulties. Rather, it suggests that the failures stem from defects inherent in the Marxist system, since that is the one thing that all of these otherwise very different societies had in common.

To appreciate the magnitude of the failure of the Marxist system, one has to compare the realities of life in these societies with the promises Marx and his followers made. One also

*More recently reported evidence of the failures of the East German and North Korean regimes—once praised as examples of the striking achievements of Communist governments—is equally relevant here.

has to compare these societies to other societies that have followed other courses of development.

Economic Abundance and Affluence   Marx's harshest criticisms of the capitalist societies of his day were directed at their failure to provide satisfactorily for the material needs of ordinary working men and women. Looking at Britain, France, and Germany, the societies he knew best, Marx believed that while wealth was increasing, it was becoming concentrated more and more in the hands of an ever smaller class of wealthy individuals. In short, under capitalism, the rich were growing richer and the poor poorer, and this would continue until finally the working class revolted.

This is not what happened, of course. In the capitalist societies of western Europe and North America, the standard of living for members of the working class has risen enormously. In fact, the standard of living in the so-called capitalist societies of the west became so much higher than that in Communist societies that the leaders of those societies had to take harsh measures to prevent workers from emigrating. The most notorious instance of this was the Berlin Wall, erected by the leaders of the former Communist East German government in an effort to prevent workers from escaping to "capitalist" West Germany. Wherever and whenever the leaders of Marxist societies relaxed their control (e.g., China, Cuba, Vietnam), tens of thousands of ordinary workers left their native lands to take their chances abroad in nonsocialist societies. In part, these migrations were motivated by political concerns (see the discussion of freedom below), but in part they were motivated by economic concerns, that is, by the desire for better living conditions.

Social Equality   One of the great appeals of Marxism has long been its promise of social equality. After the revolution, the institutional bases of economic and political inequality would disappear. When Communists seized power, they would abolish private ownership of the means of production (i.e., private ownership of land, machinery, and businesses). For a time, there would still be a certain amount of inequality in wages so as to ensure that workers who had grown up under capitalism and had been conditioned to respond to material incentives would be properly motivated. But as a new generation of workers was raised under socialism, such incentives would no longer be required and moral incentives (i.e., praise and honor) would suffice and everyone's wages would be essentially the same. After the revolution, the state would also wither away and, with its demise, the basis for political inequality would be destroyed and a new egalitarian era begin.

Unfortunately, the abolition of private property and the reduction of wage differences failed to produce the happy transformation in human nature that Marx anticipated. On the contrary, when workers were freed from the fear of unemployment and lacking adequate material incentives, their performance deteriorated and production stagnated or declined in Marxist societies everywhere.[8]

For example, when authorities in Czechoslovakia in the early 1960s reduced wage differences to the point where engineers and highly skilled workers were being paid only 5 percent more than unskilled workers, they set off a chain reaction of negative social and economic effects. Morale problems developed among skilled workers, engineers, and other professionals. Large numbers of talented young people dropped out of school, feeling that it was not worth the effort required and the income that would be sacrificed to continue their education. These problems became so acute that within a few years authorities were forced to reverse themselves and increase rewards for better-educated and more highly skilled workers.

Despite a number of attempts by Communist authorities to eliminate inequalities in wages, the costs to society proved unacceptably high and the authorities always were forced to back down. It is also noteworthy that the authorities themselves were never willing to give up the many economic perquisites and privileges that they enjoyed and to which they felt entitled.

If the achievement of greater *economic* equality proved difficult, greater *political* equality proved impossible. Contrary to Marx's predictions, the state stubbornly refused to wither away. Instead, under Communism, governments grew steadily larger, more complex, and more powerful, and the gulf between Communist rulers and ordinary people steadily widened. In other words, contrary to Marx's promises, political inequality increased greatly in every society in which the Communists came to power. In fact, under Communism, the concentration of power and the degree of political inequality were greater than in most agrarian societies of the past.

Freedom and Justice   The greatest failure of Communist societies almost certainly was their failure to provide anything remotely resembling the great freedom that Marx promised—or even the more modest freedom found in most other societies. Far from providing a greater degree of freedom for ordinary people, Marxist societies became synonymous with political repression. All of the important political decisions in these societies were made by a tiny elite of top Communist Party officials. In some cases, as in the Soviet Union in Stalin's day, in China under Mao, in North Korea under Kim Il-Sung, and in Cuba under Castro, a single individual controlled the political process almost single-handedly.

Making matters worse, Marxist governments sought to dominate and control every aspect of human life and created what came to be known as *totalitarian societies*. Not content with dominating and controlling politics and economics, Marxist leaders sought to control virtually every aspect of life—everything from the arts and sciences to religion and even family life.

In the case of the arts, Marxist regimes transformed them into instruments of propaganda. Writers and artists who were willing to produce the kinds of materials that Communist leaders wanted were rewarded highly; those who refused usually found it all but impossible to get their writings published or their art exhibited or performed.

The sciences fared only a little better. Sociology, for example, was outlawed at an early date both in the Soviet Union and in Communist China, and when, after decades, it was finally legalized it was made into yet another instrument of propaganda. University teaching appointments were limited to trusted party members and the courses taught were little more than indoctrination into Marxist ideology. The same was true in most other Marxist societies, though in Poland and Hungary sociologists eventually managed to break out of the usual pattern. The natural sciences enjoyed a somewhat greater freedom because their potential usefulness to the Party was recognized from the outset, but even in those fields party leaders exercised continuing oversight and control, sometimes with disastrous results.*

Marxists even sought to control religion and family life. Efforts to control religion reflected not merely the usual kinds of activities of political leaders who hope to win the support of religious groups within their jurisdiction. Rather, the efforts of Marxist elites were a response to the fact that Marxism competed with traditional religions in a way that no other political system except Nazism ever did. In many ways, Marxism is itself a religion, since it claims to provide answers to nearly all of the same fundamental questions that traditional

---

*The most notorious case of this occurred in the Soviet Union when Stalin threw his enormous power and prestige behind a biologist named Lysenko, who rejected orthodox genetics and made all kinds of fantastic claims regarding the power of the environment to transform plants and animals (e.g., he claimed at one point that wheat plants, raised under the right environmental conditions, could produce rye seeds, which is equivalent to saying that dogs living under the right conditions can produce fox pups).[9] Because of Stalin and Lysenko, the important new science of genetics was outlawed in Soviet biology for many years, much to the detriment of Soviet society.

Until the mid-1980s, Soviet children were taught to admire Pavlik Morozov, a boy who denounced his father to the authorities and later was killed by outraged neighbors because of this: adult leader of the Young Pioneers recounting the story of Morozov's "heroism" to children soon to be inducted into this children's affiliate of the Communist Party, Moscow, 1985.

religions have sought to answer. Maurice Duverger, a distinguished French social scientist, called attention to this aspect of Marxism many years ago when he wrote:

> Marxism is not only a political doctrine, it is a complete philosophy, a way of thinking, a spiritual cosmogony. . . . It explains . . . the structure and evolution of the state, the changes in living creatures, the appearance of man on earth, religious feelings, sexual behavior, [even] the development of the arts and sciences.[10]

Because it competed with theistic faiths for the hearts and minds of people, and because its adherents were so sure of the truth of their doctrines, Marxists felt amply justified in their efforts to suppress competing faiths of every kind. And when they could not totally suppress them, they sought to control them by imprisoning or executing their leaders and by making life as difficult as possible for ordinary believers. For example, practicing believers usually were denied opportunities to enroll in universities or to fill the more responsible and reward-ing positions in Marxist societies, and children were even separated from their parents simply because the parents tried to teach them elements of their faith.

This is not the only way in which Marxists attempted to regulate and control family life, however. Children in Marxist societies were often encouraged to spy on their parents and to report less-than-enthusiastic support for Marxist ideals or for the regime in power. This effort—which passed largely unnoticed or unreported in the West—was fostered in the Soviet Union by promotion of the cult of Pavlik Morozov. Until the mid-1980s, Morozov was held up as a role model for Soviet children. This was a boy who had denounced his father to the authorities and was killed for this by outraged neighbors. As the photograph on page 330 indicates, efforts to promote political correctness within the family circle became an institutionalized element in the life of the Young Pioneers, an organization run by the Communist Party which virtually all children were expected to join.

Finally, in the most extreme cases, as we have noted, the denial of freedom within Marxist societies took the form of imprisonment and even execution. Aleksandr Solzhenitsyn and Roy Medvedev[11] were among the first to bring the magnitude of these actions by the Soviet government to the attention of western scholars. Tens of millions were imprisoned and as many as 55 million were executed or died in prison in the Soviet Union between 1917 and 1987.[12] In Communist China 30 to 40 million people were imprisoned for political reasons, and as many as 36 million people were killed by the government between 1949 and 1987.[13] Millions more were unjustly imprisoned and executed in Czechoslovakia, East Germany, Hungary, Albania, Cuba, Vietnam, Cambodia, North Korea, and other Communist countries.*

Environmental Disasters   No discussion of the failures of Communist regimes would be complete that ignored their record in the environmental area. The nuclear explosion and fire at the power plant at Chernobyl in 1986 was merely one in a series of disasters that resulted from the indifference of Communist leaders to environmental issues. Earlier, for example, there was another disastrous nuclear explosion at a nuclear weapons facility in the Ural Mountains that the Soviet government kept hidden from the outside world until the collapse of the Soviet Union. In addition to the immediate deaths of thousands and the shortened lifespans of tens of thousands more, these disasters made large areas unsafe for human habitation for centuries to come.

By now it is clear that countless other environmental catastrophes, both large and small, occurred under Communist regimes from East Germany to China. One of the more notorious, but also one of the more instructive, of these was the Soviet government's virtual destruction of the Aral Sea, a huge body of water in a vast desert region of central Asia. As recently as 1960 it was larger than any of the Great Lakes in the United States except for Lake Superior, but today it is barely half the size it was thirty years ago.[15] This is because of the Soviet government's desire for the income that could be earned from the export of cotton grown by means of irrigation using water from the rivers that fed the Aral Sea. But to produce cotton in the quantities demanded by the central authorities, water had to be diverted in such quantities that the rivers feeding the Aral no longer brought more than a trickle and the sea began to dry up. Thanks to the policies that created this disaster, 60,000 jobs in what was once a flourishing fishing industry were destroyed and widespread health problems developed (e.g., throat cancer and respiratory and eye diseases caused by salty materials that blow off the vast now dry portions of what was once the sea bed).[16]

The enormity of these disasters is directly attributable to the Communist system of governing. Because of the Communist Party's longstanding policies of controlling the flow of information within the society and of suppressing even the mildest expressions of political dissent, no effective challenge to the policies responsible could ever be mounted until the final years of Gorbachev's rule. Making matters worse, Marxist-Leninist theory, which served

---

*The Khmer Rouge may have killed as much as one-third of the population of Cambodia between 1975 and 1979.[14]

as the foundation for Communist Party policy, failed to offer even the slightest clue to the tremendous importance of the environment for human societies and their welfare.

Western industrial societies have also been responsible for their share of environmental disasters, but there has been one important difference: in the western democracies, leaders have not been able to remain indifferent to the environmental consequences of their policies. Democratic institutions, for all their defects, have provided at least some restraint on leaders who would like to ignore the problems their policies create. Thus, while the environmental record of western democratic governments has often left much to be desired, these governments have acted far more responsibly than their Communist counterparts.

Summing Up

Looking back at the many and massive social experiments undertaken by Karl Marx's disciples in the twentieth century, it is impossible not to view them as failures. But they have not been merely failures: they have been extraordinarily costly failures, tragedies that have exacted an enormous toll in terms of human suffering.

Not only have Communist societies failed to provide the wonderful benefits that Marx predicted, they have not even come close to providing the level of benefits that the western industrial societies, of which Marx was so critical, have provided. Marxists today often blame the failures of Communism on the backwardness of the societies that came under Communist control. But this ignores the fact that several societies were split, following World War II, into Communist and non-Communist "halves": East Germany and West Germany; North Korea and South Korea; North Vietnam and South Vietnam; and the People's Republic of China (mainland China) and the Republic of China (Taiwan). For all of their flaws and defects, few today would deny that West Germany, South Korea, South Vietnam, and Taiwan came far closer than their Communist counterparts to providing basic human rights and a reasonable standard of living to the masses of their citizens. If the latter succeeded in providing a somewhat greater degree of economic equality (and this is debatable), the price in terms of human suffering and lowered standards of living was far higher than most people would judge acceptable.

But these are not the only relevant comparisons. Prior to the Communist seizure of power in Cuba, for example, Cubans enjoyed the highest living standards in Latin America. Today, after thirty-five years of Communist rule, Cuba's economy is in ruins and its human rights record is among the worst in the hemisphere. One can also legitimately compare the record of the east European countries, such as Czechoslovakia, Hungary, and Poland, under Communism, with that of the non-Communist countries of southern Europe, such as Italy, Spain, and Greece during the period from 1945 to 1990: conditions at the outset were roughly similar in the two sets of societies, but in the years that followed, the latter, with the exception of Greece, fared far better both in economic terms and in terms of basic human rights such as freedom and justice.

LESSONS TO BE LEARNED

What, then, should we conclude from the experience of the many societies that came under Communist control? Should we just write them off as unfortunate blunders that are now best forgotten? Or, are there valuable insights that can be gleaned from their experience and that can, at the least, help us avoid repeating similar mistakes in the future?

One obvious lesson to be learned is that *people should distrust social theorists and politicians who promise too much*. If the experience of Russia, China, Cuba, and more than a dozen other Communist or once Communist societies teaches us anything at all, it is that good intentions and noble ideals are not enough. Utopian visions and efforts to implement them by force are much too likely to produce disastrous consequences. As has often been remarked, in politics the perfect is the enemy of the good (i.e., striving for perfection is likely to prevent the attainment of more modest, but reachable, goals).* This does not mean that nothing can be done to improve social conditions or that we have to accept the status quo, but it does mean that we seem destined to live in imperfect societies and that efforts to create a perfect society are likely to do much more harm than good.

If that is true, it raises a further question: Why is it impossible to create a perfect society? What is wrong with the Marxist vision of a highly affluent, egalitarian society in which perfect freedom and justice flourish?

Based on the experience of societies that Marxists have controlled, the basic flaw in their theory is the assumption they make concerning human nature. They assume that people are inherently good and only become greedy and selfish when the means of production (land, factories, machines, and other tools) are privately owned. Thus, they believe that if only the institution of private property were abolished, human beings would all become hardworking, socially responsible individuals who share the costs and benefits of society equally.

In Marx's day, this was still a plausible idea, and Marx did not live to see his ideas put to the test. But that day eventually came, and one of the first things his followers did wherever they came to power was to abolish private property. In addition, they also made Marx's ideas and ideals central elements in school curricula and reinforced them through the mass media and by the fine arts.

Unfortunately, however, these actions never produced the promised results. "The new socialist man" who loved his work and who had a highly developed social consciousness never emerged except briefly among some young people. But even these youthful idealists soon lost their enthusiasm when exposed to the vicissitudes of adult life. Worse yet, the Communist Party came to be an organization made up increasingly of socially ambitious individuals, and party leaders, as we have seen, often became notorious for their greed and self-serving actions.

Today, thanks to the rise of the new science of genetics, we also have a far better understanding of the causes of human behavior than was possible in Marx's day. We know, for example, that environment is not the sole determinant of our actions; our genetic heritage also has a profound effect. Thus, while manipulations of the social environment, such as the elimination of the institution of private property, may change the ways in which people go about promoting and protecting their individual interests, it is not nearly enough to eradicate something that is so basic a part of our species' genetic heritage.**

But the motivational problems of workers and the corruption of managers and officials in Marxist societies were due not only to faulty assumptions about human nature. They were also due to defective organizational arrangements spawned by the *command economies* of

---

*It is no coincidence that the Communist Party has usually been extremely hostile toward pragmatic liberal and leftist parties, such as the Social Democrats in Europe—parties whose goal has been the gradual amelioration of conditions through a democratic process, rather than the seizure of power by revolution and the total transformation of society.

**The importance of this aspect of our genetic heritage is best understood if we compare ourselves and other primates with the social insects (ants, termites, etc.). Primates are genetically programmed to be dependent on learning as their basic adaptive mechanism, and this, as we saw in Chapter 2, makes each of us highly aware of self and self-interest. In these respects we and other primates are profoundly different from the social insects and other species for which learning plays a much more limited role in shaping behavior and for which concern for the group and its interests is genetically programmed to take precedence. In fact, one might even say that Marxism is already operative in the world of social insects and other species that are genetically programmed to put the interests of society ahead of individual interests. But this is true because of genetics, not because of environment.

those societies. Lacking the system of automatic controls that are an inherent part of a market economy, economic planners were forced to devise elaborate plans and assign production quotas for the managers of every enterprise. To ensure fulfillment of these quotas, managers were awarded bonuses for meeting or exceeding them and were penalized for any shortfall. One unanticipated consequence of this seemingly rational procedure was that managers acquired a strong incentive to stockpile essential resources of every kind—*including labor*.[17] Thus, labor resources in these societies were used very inefficiently with the result that workers became cynical about the value of skilled work and honest effort.

Managers also developed a variety of other unfortunate responses to the system of central planning. They learned, for example, that quantity, not quality, was what their bosses, the central planners, cared about.*[18] They also learned that production figures could be inflated without much risk of discovery or penalty since their bosses were also being rewarded for good statistics and no one had a vested interest in seeing if actual performance matched reported performance.[19]

Finally, they learned that there were only minimal rewards for reinvestment in plant and for technological innovation. Lacking pressures from direct economic competition, party leaders and planners failed to appreciate the importance of continuous modernization of their society's industrial plant. According to one account, Soviet managers received bonuses of 33 percent for fulfilling production quotas, but only 8 percent for fulfilling the plan for new technology.[20] Thus, capital investment and technological advance were badly neglected, with the result that the command economies of Marxist societies became less and less competitive in world markets.

Today we also know that abolishing private ownership of the means of production does not lead to equal control by all of these important resources. In societies with populations numbering in the millions, and sometimes in the hundreds of millions, it is simply not possible for everyone to have an equal voice in decision making. Were everyone actively involved in every decision, nothing would ever get done: societies would become one great debating forum. Thus, after the abolition of private ownership of business enterprises and land in Communist societies, decision making concerning their use always remained in the hands of a tiny minority within the population, and this minority (the leadership of the Communist Party) used all the immense powers at its command to intimidate and, when necessary, to eliminate critics or potential critics. And because of the extreme centralization of power in Communist societies, the new political elite enjoyed far greater control than businesspeople in democratic societies have ever enjoyed. The latter have always had to share power and influence with their societies' own political elites.

There is, perhaps, a lesson here even for those of us who will never live in a Communist society. Many of us still look to government to solve all of society's ills. But that is a solution that leads to a concentration of power, and as Lord Acton, an insightful British writer of the nineteenth century, once observed, "Power tends to corrupt, and absolute power corrupts absolutely."[21]

---

*Quality controls are most likely to develop when producers are obliged to compete for the support of consumers, and *consumers* can penalize the producers of shoddy products by turning to their competitors. The massive loss of market share by American automobile manufacturers during the 1970s and 1980s is a good example of this. When people are using their own money to purchase goods and services, they are not nearly so willing to accept inferior products as when they are using other people's money (i.e., public funds).

Excursus: Is Free Market Capitalism the Cure?

A number of prominent politicians and economists in the United States and elsewhere have interpreted the collapse of Communism as vindication of their faith in free market capitalism. Market economies such as we have in western Europe, North America, Japan, and Australia, they argue, have proved far more productive, far more efficient, and far better able to satisfy the needs of people than command economies such as Communist societies have had.

This is a serious misreading of the record, however. As we noted in Chapter 10, the western industrial democracies abandoned true free market (laissez-faire) capitalism long ago. What these societies have had for decades are *mixed market-command economies* in which basic economic decisions are made partly in response to market forces, but also partly in response to democratic political actions. It is also important to keep in mind that these are economies that have developed *pragmatically* in response to experience. Thus, if there is any conclusion to be drawn from the experience of the twentieth century it is that a pragmatic approach that combines elements of market action and political action in economic decision making works far better than either the doctrinaire approach of the Marxists or the equally doctrinaire approach of their free market capitalist opponents.*

*It is no coincidence that the economic reforms undertaken in recent years in Russia, on advice of American economists and in response to pressures from western politicians, have created a wide range of new ills and social problems and have even led some non-Communist Russians to long for "the good old days."

16

Retrospect and Prospect

When studying something as complex as the evolution of human societies, it is easy to become so immersed in details that we lose sight of the larger picture. For this reason, we begin this final chapter with a brief look back over the long sweep of human history. Then we go on to consider an important question that we could not address until this point: What has sociocultural evolution really meant for humanity? More specifically, how has technological advance affected the quality of human life? Has it brought greater freedom, justice, and happiness? Or has the quality of life declined?

After considering these questions, we will turn our attention to *the future*. What lies ahead for human societies? Can ecological-evolutionary theory help us anticipate the problems and prospects of the next few decades? This is an important question, and a practical one as well. For most of us will live in that world, and it could be very different from the world we live in today.

LOOKING BACK

When we look back over the long course of hominid history, we see that we and our societies are an integral part of the global ecosystem and that our species' development has always been part of the same grand process of biological evolution that shapes all life on this planet. Yet it is equally clear that our species' development has been different from that of the rest of the biological world in some fundamental ways. If we understand where and how our path diverged, we can better understand our problems and those of our societies, and perhaps be able to create a better, happier future.

The Divergent Path

For millions of years there was little to suggest that our early ancestors were destined to become anything more than just another variety of primate. But genetic changes eventually provided them with the ability to create symbol systems, a trait that is as much a product of natural selection as wings, gills, social instincts, and other adaptive mechanisms of the biotic world.

With the aid of symbol systems, hominids were able to use their primate capacity for learning to far greater advantage. They could now create and share vast amounts of information that had been gleaned from individual experience. Eventually, hominid societies came to depend far more on new cultural information than on new genetic information in their adaptive efforts, and *human evolution came to be shaped primarily by the processes of cultural innovation and selection, rather than by the processes of biological evolution*.

The explanation of the tremendous adaptive capacity of cultural information is its potential for creating diversity. In this respect, it is like genetic information, which is responsible for the striking diversity in the biotic world. In the case of cultural information, however, *all of*

336

the diversity is concentrated within a single species. As a result, despite a common genetic heritage, human individuals become, with culture, far more varied than the members of any other species. Human societies are also extremely varied—again, unlike the situation in other social species. Though such diversity enhances our species' survival potential, it is a major source of problems, both within and among societies.

Another manifestation of culture's capacity for creating diversity is the great variety of needs and desires that humans have developed, *needs and desires not even remotely related to our survival as individuals or as a species*. To satisfy these culturally generated or intensified needs, societies have depended primarily on the kind of information—technological—that helps people utilize environmental resources in new ways and for new purposes. As technology advanced, however, it altered the conditions of life, and as that happened, further needs emerged. Efforts to satisfy these needs created further change, which led in turn to new needs, a process of positive feedback that has continued at an accelerating pace for at least 10,000 years.

Through this process, *humans established a new and unique relationship with the biophysical environment*. Since every other species of plant or animal uses the resources of its environment to satisfy only a limited set of genetically programmed needs, this characteristic is perhaps the most fundamental divergence of all.

The Question of Progress

Despite the problems that have attended our species' reliance on culture, one thing is clear: *culture has been a highly successful adaptive mechanism*. Humanity has not only survived, it has flourished by biological standards: there are far more of us alive today than at any time in the past, and our numbers are growing rapidly. Moreover, humans have spread into an enormous variety of environments—another important measure of biological success.

But numbers and dispersion are not enough on which to base an assessment of *human* evolution. We must also ask whether the process of sociocultural evolution has meant progress in terms of more uniquely human criteria and goals, such as freedom, justice, and happiness.

It is not easy to assess progress in terms such as these. For one thing, these concepts are so broad that they apply to countless aspects of human life. For another, the way we define them is the product of past experience, and this, as we have seen, varies greatly among individuals, groups, and societies. Nevertheless, because the subject is too important to ignore, we must at least make the effort to evaluate human progress in terms of these goals and try to determine whether our species' growing store of cultural information has had the effect of advancing or hindering them.

Freedom   The high value that the members of modern industrial societies attach to freedom is revealed in the growing challenge to all forms of authority, not only in the liberal democracies of the West but in the formerly authoritarian nations of eastern Europe and Asia as well. Even those who are not in the forefront of the libertarian movement are likely to consider the degree of freedom accorded individuals one of the basic measures of the attractiveness, and hence the progress, of a society, and they would deny that a technologically advanced, politically repressive society is truly progressive.

But human freedom is more than the absence of repressive social controls; it is also freedom from restraints imposed by nature. People who must spend most of their waking hours in an exhausting struggle to produce the necessities of life are not truly "free"—even if there are few social restraints on their actions. A woman whose life is a long succession of unwanted pregnancies is not "free"—regardless of the kind of society she lives in. Disease, physical and mental handicaps, geographical barriers, and all the laws of nature restrict people and deny them freedom. For freedom does not exist where there are no alternatives; and freedom can be measured only by the range of choices that are available. The fewer the viable choices, the less freedom there is—and it matters little whether the constraints are imposed by nature or by other people.

Once we recognize this, it becomes clear that humanity's long struggle to advance technologically is not irrelevant to the desire for freedom. Every technological innovation reflects the desire to overcome natural limitations on human action. Thanks to this struggle, some of us are now free to talk across oceans, free to travel faster than sound, free to live longer lives in better health while enjoying a range of experiences that far surpass in richness and variety what was available to the greatest kings and emperors of the past.

There has been a price to pay, of course: technological progress has necessitated larger and more complex social systems. If we want the option of flying to another part of the country instead of walking there, or of watching the day's events on a screen in our home instead of hearing about them weeks later, we have to accept certain social controls. The goods and services essential for those options can be produced only where there are organizations with rules and with sanctions to enforce the rules, and individuals with authority to exercise the sanctions. And these organizations can function efficiently only within a society that has rules to govern the relationships among them, and an authority system to enforce those rules. The only alternative is anarchy—and the loss of all the freedoms that modern technology affords.

Critics of modern society often say that the price has been too high, that the increased social restrictions outweigh the gains in freedom we derive from modern technology.[1] This is a matter all of us must decide for ourselves. In doing so, however, we need to beware of romanticizing the past. Before deciding that people are less free than they used to be, we must read accounts of peasant life in agrarian societies and of the life of horticultural and hunting and gathering peoples. In doing this, we must resist the temptation to abstract the attractive features and ignore the appalling ones. We must remember that slavery and serfdom were not accidental characteristics of agrarian societies, but reflections of basic, inescapable conditions of that way of life, as were the high mortality rate and short life span of many hunting and gathering peoples.

Once we recognize the danger of comparing some rosy version of life in less advanced societies with the negative side of life in industrial societies, we are in a better position to consider whether freedom is a correlate of technological advance. We can say, first of all, that technological progress has clearly raised the *upper* limit of freedom in human societies. Individuals with the greatest measure of freedom in contemporary societies—that is, members of the upper classes—enjoy a far wider range of choice than individuals with the greatest measure of freedom in agrarian societies, and the elites of agrarian societies had far more freedom than the elites of less advanced societies. This has been true with respect to everything from the use of a leisure hour to the use of a lifetime. In this sense, then, there is a high positive correlation between technological advance and gains in human freedom.

The relation between technological advance and freedom for the *average* member of society is more complicated. If we compare the typical peasant in an agrarian society with a typical hunter and gatherer, it is not at all clear that there were gains. In fact, the peasant had to live with a lot of new social controls while gaining very little freedom from natural controls. Thus, during much of the course of history—especially after the formation of the state—the average individual probably experienced a *decline* in freedom. With industrialization, however, the pattern changes. Once the difficult period of transition is past, technological progress and freedom for the average person are positively related, as Figure 16.1 illustrates. Whether people in industrial societies have more freedom than hunters and gatherers is less certain. Clearly they have more social restraints, but far fewer physical and biological ones.

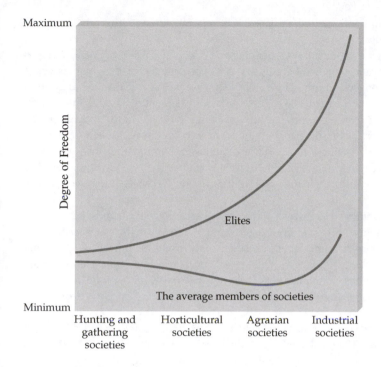

FIGURE 16.1 *Trends in freedom for elites and for the average members of societies.*

Before leaving the subject of freedom, we should take note of the popular misconception that governmental activity necessarily results in a loss of freedom for the members of society. This is at best a half-truth. Laws do, of course, place restrictions on people, but in democratic societies this is often done in order to increase freedom, not reduce it. The Pure Food and Drug Act in the United States, for example, was designed to restrict the freedom of businesspeople who were willing to sell spoiled food and dangerous drugs for profit, but it increased the freedom of the millions of people who used their products. Sometimes, of course, laws restrict everyone's freedom in one area—the freedom to proceed at will through a busy intersection, for example—in order to preserve it in others. In short, most legal norms *redistribute* freedom.

Justice Justice has to do with the *fairness* of a society in its treatment of its members. Although no one would quarrel with the idea that a society should be "fair," we run into trouble when we try to define what this means. Is a society fair when it rewards people on the basis of their contributions to the common good, or is it more equitable to allocate rewards on the basis of individual needs? Should handicapped individuals, for example, be paid the same as those who are able to outproduce them with less effort? And how does one arrive at a fair evaluation of the relative contributions of people in dissimilar activities—a symphony conductor, a bricklayer, a housewife, a garbage collector, a student?

And what about punishments? Does a "fair" society punish its members strictly in accordance with the letter of the law, or is it fairer to take circumstances and intent into account? What of a parent's theft to feed a hungry child, for example, or a mercy killing? And should a society deal less severely with those in positions of power than with lesser members of society when they commit crimes, or should everyone be treated equally? Questions like these point up the difficulty of measuring progress with respect to justice. Since an adequate treatment of the subject would require volumes, all we can do here is call attention to basic trends and offer tentative conclusions.

To begin with, as we observed in earlier chapters, social inequality became more pronounced as societies advanced technologically and status became increasingly dependent on the family into which one was born. The result was a weakening of the link between a person's *efforts* and a person's rewards. Whereas every normal, healthy boy in a hunting and gathering group had a chance of becoming the best hunter (and hence the most important man) in his society, a peasant's son had little hope of advancing even a notch above his father's social level, no matter how hard he tried. Increasingly rigid stratification systems locked people into roles and situations where they could neither develop nor use their talents, while those with little talent might occupy positions for which they were grossly unsuited.

The trend in punishment, meanwhile, was toward increasingly harsh and discriminatory treatment. In most agrarian societies, the privileged were free to abuse members of the lower class without fear of reproof; if the latter retaliated, they would be punished swiftly and severely. A master involved in a conflict with his slaves or serfs was often both prosecutor and judge; he could beat them with impunity and, in many societies, kill them if he wished. Nor were there legal sanctions against the beating of children by parents, employers, or schoolmasters.

Courts of law were equally harsh. In eighteenth-century England, the death penalty could be invoked for 222 different offenses, including such minor infractions as the theft of a handkerchief, the shooting of a rabbit, or the forgery of a birth certificate.[2] Nor was execution always a humane process: we are told that the hangman in Elizabethan England was "an artist, and the knife was his chief instrument; the art consisting in tossing his man off the ladder, hanging him, but cutting him down before he breaks his neck, so that he may be dismembered and disemboweled while still alive."[3]

In general, societies seem to have become less fair and less just as they advanced technologically. With industrialization, however, there are clear signs of a reversal. With respect to material rewards, industrialization has resulted in some decline in the level of social inequality among the members of a society. Public education now provides at least some chance for almost all children to develop their abilities, and women and minorities have gained numerous legal and economic opportunities long denied them. Industrial societies are also more solicitous of their poor and their handicapped, and provide a far broader range of legal rights and protections for their members, whatever their social status. Criminal justice is far less harsh. Industrial societies today rarely execute their members, and never for minor infractions, nor do they maim them, as was common in the agrarian era. In short, after a long period of declining justice with respect to both rewards and punishments, there is finally movement in the other direction.

Happiness   Of all the possible measures of progress, happiness is the most elusive, for it depends so much—perhaps primarily—on the quality of interpersonal relations: whether there is love, mutual respect, cooperation, and so forth. And these things do not depend on the level of technological development. Studies of modern hunting and gathering groups indicate that the most primitive peoples develop these qualities as surely as members of modern industrial societies do.[4]

There are several ways, however, in which technological progress is relevant to this kind of happiness. To begin with, some of life's greatest tragedies involve the premature death of a loved one—a cherished child, a parent, or a partner in a happy marriage. We saw how common this was in most societies prior to the Industrial Revolution and can therefore appreciate how the recently increased life span has contributed to human happiness.

Health, too, contributes to happiness. When we are seriously ill, life may not seem worth living. Disease was very poorly understood through most of human history, and technological advance prior to the Industrial Revolution had minimal impact in this area. More recently, however, advances in sanitation and medicine have dramatically improved the physical well-being of the members of many societies. Unfortunately, modern medical technology has also had a negative effect: it has been used to keep alive individuals who, in simpler societies, would mercifully be allowed to die. On balance, however, the result has undeniably been positive.

Hunger, another cause of enormous human misery over the centuries, has been drastically reduced in many societies as a result of industrialization. As recently as the eighteenth century, local crop failures in much of Europe could still result in starvation because of an inadequate transportation network. Today, thanks to advances in technology, food supplies can be safely stored for long periods, and moved to areas of scarcity, in every industrial society and in an increasing number of industrializing ones.

The industrialization of agriculture has also meant a substantially improved food supply, with respect to quality, quantity, and diversity, for most members of industrial societies. During the winter, for example, people can now enjoy fresh fruits and vegetables shipped in from areas with different growing seasons. Nor do the members of industrial societies have to subsist on short rations in the months prior to harvest, as members of traditional agrarian societies had to do. As with improvements in health, it is easy to take such benefits for granted and to lose sight of the numerous links between technological advance and human happiness.

The increased production of other kinds of goods and services, especially nonessential ones, has probably had much less effect on happiness. The absolute quantity of luxuries we enjoy is often not as important in this regard as how they compare with what people around us have. Thus the headman in a simple horticultural society may be quite content with his few special possessions, because they are more than his neighbors own and as good as anything he knows about, while middle-class Americans and Canadians, surrounded with goods and services the headman never dreamed of, may feel terribly deprived when they compare themselves with more prosperous neighbors. In other words, insofar as happiness depends on material possessions, *the relative degree of inequality* may be more important than anything else.

When we take into account the advances in health, the greater abundance and improved quality of food, and the drastic reduction in premature deaths, to say nothing of the improvements in freedom and justice, it is clear that industrialization has eliminated the source of much of the misery of earlier eras. Putting it all together, we are again led to the tentative conclusion that the long-term trend for the average individual has been curvilinear, as shown in Figure 16.1. Conditions seem to have been more conducive to human happiness for the average individual in hunting and gathering societies than in horticultural societies, and better in horticultural than in agrarian or even early industrial. But with further advances in industrialization, the situation of the average individual seems to have improved considerably, reversing the long-term trend.

Some years ago, in a study of almost seventy nations containing two-thirds of the world's population, the Gallup Poll and its associates abroad found a striking relation between the level of happiness expressed by the people they interviewed and the level of technological advance of the societies in which they lived (see Table 16.1).* The same relation was found between societal development and people's satisfaction with specific aspects of their lives (e.g., family life, health, housing, work). The results of this survey led George Gallup to comment: "For centuries, romantics and philosophers have beguiled us with tales of societies that were 'poor but happy.' If any such exist, the survey failed to discover them."

---

*A large number of studies since then have reconfirmed Gallup's original findings (see Ruut Veerhoven, *Happiness in Nations: Subjective Appreciation of Life in 56 Nations, 1946–1992* [Rotterdam, Netherlands: Risbo, 1993]).

TABLE 16.1 Degree of Happiness and Satisfaction with Life Expressed by Members of Societies around the World

	Percentage Very Happy or Fairly Happy	Percentage Highly Satisfied with Their Lives*
North America	89	76
Western Europe	82	67
Latin America	70	63
Africa	68	25
Far East**	68	24

*The values shown in this column are the arithmetic means of responses to questions about satisfaction with ten specific areas of life (see table 6 of Gallup's article).

**The Far East includes both Japan and India, and Gallup notes that "the differences between Japan [an advanced industrial society] and India [an industrializing agrarian society] with respect to personal happiness are very large."

Source: Adapted from George H. Gallup, "Human Needs and Satisfactions: A Global Survey," *Public Opinion Quarterly,* 40 (Winter 1976–1977), tables 2 and 6, pp. 465 and 467; and Ruut Veerhoven, *Happiness in Nations: Subjective Appreciation of Life in 56 Nations, 1946–1992,* (Rotterdam, Netherlands: Risbo, 1993), Tables 1.1.1a and 1.2.2b.

Concluding Thoughts   It should be clear by now that there is no simple one-to-one correspondence between technological advance and progress in terms of freedom, justice, and happiness. In fact, one may well ask whether technological advance has not lured societies into evolutionary paths where the costs often outweigh the benefits.

Had human history come to an end several hundred years ago, one would have been forced to answer affirmatively. During the last hundred years, however, technological advance has begun to make a strong positive contribution to the attainment of humanity's higher goals. Whether or not this will continue in the future is another question. We can say this, however: technology has at last brought into the realm of *the possible* a social order with greater freedom, justice, and happiness than any society has yet known.

Whatever our judgment about the wisdom of our species' pursuit of technological advance, one thing is clear: *for the evolution of human societies as a whole, technological advance can be equated with progress only in the limited sense of growth in the store of cultural information.*

LOOKING AHEAD

A noted scholar once wrote, "The past is not dead history; it is living material out of which man makes the present and builds the future."[5] Humanity has indeed created the present world from materials of the past and just as surely is now laying the foundation for the future. But what kind of future will it be? And what kinds of changes are we likely to encounter in the next several decades?

Trying to foresee the future has always been a risky business. A hundred years ago, for example, some very knowledgeable people proclaimed that warfare had developed to the point where no further advances in weaponry could be expected![6] Despite the difficulties, it is important to try to anticipate what lies ahead because the sooner we recognize problems and begin to address them, the better our chances of finding solutions.

There are several things to keep in mind as we try to see across the years. First, we need to be aware that there are some potential developments which cannot be anticipated but which could alter the picture substantially—the emergence of some new and virulent pestilence or plague, for example, or a shift in climate that is unrelated to human activity. Second, the subject we can speak about with the greatest confidence when discussing the future, especially the next quarter of a century or so, concerns the *problems* societies will face. For the serious, unresolved problems of societies today will almost surely continue to be problems in the years ahead.

Third, and finally, the more thoroughly a prediction is *grounded in a tested analysis of the past and present,* the better its chances of success. Our predictions will thus be based on our analysis of societal evolution up to the present, with special attention to anticipated changes in population, the biophysical environment, technology, ideology, political and economic institutions, the world system of societies, and the higher human goals.

We will not attempt to make flat, unqualified predictions, but rather frame statements which say that certain outcomes are likely under given circumstances. This puts the assumptions on which our predictions are based out in the open where others can examine them and challenge or modify them as new information or insights become available. In time, this should lead to more useful and more accurate predictions.

Population

One of the greatest challenges human societies face in the years ahead is that of slowing the rapid growth of population that has occurred in the last 250 years. In 1750, on the eve of the Industrial Revolution, the human population numbered only about 750 million. Since then, it has increased *eightfold* and is now growing at a rate of more than 70 million every year.

Few today realize how unprecedented this pattern of growth is. During the 10,000 years between the end of the hunting and gathering era and the beginning of the Industrial Revolution, it took from 1,400 to 3,000 years for world population to double.*[7]

Were numbers to continue to grow at the present rate, world population would increase to 20 billion by the end of the century. Obviously this will not happen; the resources of this planet—food, water, energy, minerals—cannot support anything like this number, and it is doubtful that people could tolerate the psychological stresses of the crowding such numbers imply. Long before the population reached 20 billion, food and water shortages, water and air pollution, disease and epidemics, and wars waged for control of increasingly scarce resources would all drive up the death rate.

The question, therefore, is not whether the rate of growth of the human population will decline—that is inevitable. The real question is how this decline will come about. Will brutal natural forces, such as famine and plague, take control and do the job, or will people have the wisdom and foresight to take the steps that are necessary before those forces take over?

At present, there are grounds for both optimism and pessimism. On the darker side, there is the inescapable fact that the present rate of growth—a net increase of nearly 80 million people per year, or the addition of more than two Canadas crowded onto an already crowded planet—is far beyond our planet's capacity to sustain for long. In addition, because of the extraordinary rate of growth in recent decades, a disproportionate share of the world's population has yet to enter the childbearing years. And finally, there are a number of powerful

*Had the population grown at its present rate of 1.2 percent per year, and had there been just a single man and woman at the end of the last Ice Age 12,000 years ago, world population today would number 8.4×10^{61} (i.e., the number 84 followed by 60 zeros).[8]

YOU HAVE TO ADMIT, THEY GOT THE PART RIGHT ABOUT BEING FRUITFUL AND MULTIPLYING.

THAVES 1-11

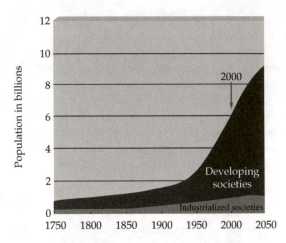

FIGURE 16.2 *Past trends and future estimates of world population.*
Source: Adapted from *Population Today,* 25, no. 9 (September 1997), p. 5, and *World Population Data 2003,* Population Reference Bureau.

and well-organized groups that strongly oppose any attempt at population control. Muslims and Catholics have been at the forefront of the fight in the United Nations to withhold funding for family planning efforts, and they have enjoyed the support of many Orthodox Jews and fundamentalist Protestants.

Fortunately, there is also a brighter side to the picture. Birthrates have been dropping in many of the industrializing societies of the Third World, where nearly all of the population growth has been concentrated in recent decades (see Figure 16.2).* In South Korea, for example, women now have only 1.3 children on average, and in Thailand and China, 1.7.[9] Even when you exclude China, women in the world's developing countries now average fewer than four children apiece, down substantially from six a generation ago.[10] Although this is still nearly twice replacement level, the trend is encouraging.

Another encouraging fact is the growth in the number of people who have come to understand that the success of a society is measured by the *quality of life* of its members, not by their numbers. Twice as many people crowding streets and highways does nothing to improve the quality of life; on the contrary, it lowers it. And creating babies faster than jobs are created, as in many of the poorest Third World societies today, only enlarges the pool of desperate people who are ready recruits for warlords and revolutionaries and invites crime and violence.

On balance, prospects for continuing decline in the rate of population growth are encouraging, but it is equally clear that world population will not be stabilized before it becomes substantially larger than it already is. One of the best recent estimates predicts that world population will reach 9 billion by 2050 (see Figure 16.2).

In the decades ahead, an ever growing proportion of the world's population will be crowded into cities. The percentage of the world's population that lives in cities has increased from 29 in 1950 to nearly 50 today.[11] Much of this urbanization has been concentrated in developing societies; in fact, the number of people living in cities in developing societies surpassed that of advanced industrial societies in about 1970, and the gap has been widening at an accelerating rate ever since. Some of the largest, most densely populated cities are now in the developing societies, and they continue to grow. For example, both Mexico City and

---

*As noted earlier (see Table 13.2) birthrates in industrial societies are now well below the level needed to sustain these societies at their present size. Were it not for immigration from Third World societies, these societies, as a group, would now have declining populations.

Calcutta already have population densities of more than 30,000 persons per square mile, and both continue to grow in size and crowding.*[12]

One other demographic trend that we can anticipate is continuing, and probably increasing, migration from industrializing societies to industrial societies. This trend, as we have seen (Chapter 13), is already well under way. It is even becoming possible to envision the day when the indigenous populations of some industrial societies will become minorities in their own homelands, a development that would almost certainly have explosive political consequences. In fact, this has already happened in the Baltic republic of Latvia, where Russian immigrants now outnumber native Latvians.

Natural Resources and the Biophysical Environment

As the human population grows in size, the demand for natural resources of every kind—food, water, forest products, minerals—is bound to increase. While increasing demand for these resources is nothing new—and has often been the impetus for technological advance in the past—*the rate of this increase in the years ahead will be unprecedented.* This is unavoidable given the impact of the exceptionally high rate of population growth acting in concert with the growing demand throughout the world for better standards of living—a demand that has been stimulated by the new technologies of transportation and communication that have brought awareness of western standards to peoples throughout the world and greatly raised their expectations.

Several false alarms in recent years have created a mood of complacency in some quarters.** During the 1970s, for example, there were claims that the supply of *petroleum* would soon be exhausted and that the future of industrial societies was in jeopardy. Now, however, it appears that the supply is ample to carry us well into the twenty-first century. More important, it has become clear that there are abundant alternative sources of energy available (see "Technology, Content of Change," pages 348–351), though none is yet as cheap as petroleum.

While energy shortages are no longer a threat hanging over industrial societies, they are already a harsh reality in some parts of the Third World, especially sub-Saharan Africa where wood is often the only fuel available for the preparation of food. Because of the demands of rapidly growing populations, forests are disappearing and growing numbers of people are forced to spend increasing numbers of hours walking long distances to obtain this vital daily necessity.

Food is another critical resource whose supply is threatened by population growth. Although world production of grain, the most basic source of food, has more than doubled since 1961 thanks to technological advances, this rate of growth has not kept pace with human population. As a result, per capita production is lower today than it was in 1967 and substantially lower (11 percent less) than it was in 1985. This has led to a sharp reduction in the supply of grain in private and government storehouses, which is now at the lowest level since record keeping began 40 years ago.[14]

Currently, there are more than 800 million "chronically hungry" people in the world according to estimates by the UN Food and Agriculture Organization,[15] and this number may well increase in the years ahead if population growth continues to outrun growth in the food supply. As the Chinese have discovered, it is impossible to halt population growth in less than a quarter of a century, even when unusually rigorous population control policies are adopted

---

*By comparison, New York City has a density of less than 15,000 per square mile.
**This complacency may spread as an increasing number of "doomsday" scenarios recklessly trumpeted by some environmental activists are shown to be exaggerations or "myths."[13] Unfortunately, this may distract attention from the very real challenges posed by environmental feedback from population growth and industrialization.

and enforced—and no other Third World nation has even dared to undertake anything comparable to the Chinese population control program. Thus, many societies—especially those in sub-Saharan Africa, which have already grown to a point where they are no longer able to feed themselves—face the possibility of widespread hunger and starvation in the years ahead.*

Arable land may well be the most critical of all the resources on which humans depend. Unfortunately, a number of developments are combining to cause a reduction in the supply available. For example, approximately 2.5 million acres of arable land is paved over every year in the United States alone as cities and towns expand.[16] Currently, it is estimated that 10 to 20 percent of the world's arable land has been degraded or made unusable by this and other practices, such as overgrazing, inappropriate land use (e.g., cultivation on steep hillsides, causing erosion), and salinization of irrigated land.[17] In the years ahead, technological fixes may not be enough to offset the combined impact of population growth and loss of arable land.

Water is another resource whose supply is threatened in many areas by population growth. This is especially acute in arid regions, such as the Middle East, where water shortages sometimes even threaten to lead to war.[18] The threat of water shortage is not limited to the Third World, however. Industrial societies, too, are finding that as their populations increase, and as industrial and agricultural demands for water rise, resources that once seemed ample are now stretched to the limit and conflicts over their control are becoming increasingly common (see, for example, the growing conflict in California).[19] Recently, the World Health Organization predicted that by 2025, 5 billion people will face shortages of fresh water and 2.7 billion will face severe shortages; since irrigation consumes over 70 percent of the water supply, this will mean less food.[20]

Finally, *biological diversity* is a resource that is increasingly threatened by the growth of human populations. Unlike food, water, and energy, the importance of this resource was unappreciated until quite recently. Now, however, we are beginning to recognize that the diversity of plants and animals on this planet may well prove vital to human health and well-being in the twenty-first century. We are only now beginning to recognize the enormous value of the information stored in the genes of obscure species of plants and animals, information that can be used by medical science in a variety of ways. In addition, modern developments in agriculture have made us dependent on a dangerously small number of varieties of grains, all of which are vulnerable to new, mutant species of insect pests and plant diseases.[21] Last, but not least, some are even beginning to appreciate that biological diversity is an essential aspect of the physical beauty of this planet.

As societies have sought to meet the demands of their growing populations with their rising expectations, they have been compelled to adopt increasingly powerful technologies of various kinds, many of which introduce new and hazardous materials into the environment. The problem of pollution now affects both the air we breathe and the rivers, streams, and other bodies of water on which we depend. Factories and automobiles generate enormous quantities of pollutants of many kinds. Farms, too, have become a serious source of pollution as efforts to increase production have led to a growing dependence on toxic pesticides and powerful chemical fertilizers that enter the food chain and contaminate water supplies. Even families and individuals contribute to the problem as they make increasing use of plastics, chemicals of various kinds, and other man-made materials that are difficult and expensive to dispose of and that accumulate into mountains of waste in landfills.

Some of the most dangerous pollutants are the radioactive materials that accumulate as by-products of the activities of military organizations, nuclear power plants, and medical

---

*While donations of food from abroad may provide a solution in the short run, it is not likely to prove an effective solution to overpopulation in the longer run, especially if the societies involved are unwilling to address the cause of the problem.

centers. These materials pollute the environment for hundreds, and sometimes even thousands, of years and no completely safe and economical method of disposing of them has yet been found. As these materials continue to accumulate in the environment, the impact on human health and welfare can only increase.

For many, the most alarming threat to the environment has come from predictions of imminent change in climate as a result of the buildup in the atmosphere of heat-trapping "greenhouse gases" produced by fossil-fuel-burning industrial plants. Studies by NASA indicate that the average temperature on the earth's surface has risen by about 0.7 degrees Fahrenheit since 1865.[22] Other studies indicate that the sea level rose four to eight inches during the twentieth century.[23] In addition, intense rainstorms and snowstorms have become more frequent in many areas. Many predict that all of these trends will continue in the twenty-first century and may even accelerate, with devastating results.[24]

Not all scientists, however, are convinced by claims that the changes of the past century are entirely, or even largely, the result of human activity. Skeptics point out that the geological record indicates that changeability has been the rule, not the exception, throughout our planet's history, and that the computer simulations on which predictions of future change are based leave much to be desired. In addition, they note that the evidence concerning global warming is not altogether unambiguous. For example, satellite-derived measures of temperature in the lower atmosphere during the last decade failed to reveal any increase, suggesting to some that land-based measures may be flawed by proximity to heat sources (e.g., cities).[25]

The inability of the experts to agree on the nature and causes of recent changes, or the seriousness of the problem (estimates of temperature change in the present century vary all the way from zero to seven degrees), creates a dilemma for policy makers, as even the experts themselves acknowledge: Precipitate action would be extremely costly and might prove unnecessary, thus diverting resources from other serious problems, but inaction could also be extremely costly if the threat is real. As a result, one climatologist concluded that it would be crazy to do nothing, but "we shouldn't do everything either; we don't want to squander resources on something that might turn out to be a nonproblem."[26]

Technology

Technological advance has been the most important factor in shaping the evolution of the world system in the past, and there is little reason to doubt that it will continue to be of major, perhaps paramount, importance in coming decades. Many of the most pressing problems of societies today are stimulating searches for technological solutions, and the new technologies that result will almost certainly give rise to social and cultural changes of many kinds.

Rate of Change   Benjamin Franklin once said that nothing is certain in this world but death and taxes. Were he alive today, he might add technological advance. A prediction of continuing advance at an accelerating rate does not depend simply on an extrapolation of the current trend. The basic factors responsible for the trend—the magnitude of the existing store of information, the great size of societal populations, and the amount of communication among societies (see pages 50–54)—are still operative and give every indication of providing even stronger impetus to innovation in the future than they do today. Furthermore, for the first time in history advanced industrial societies are engaging in a systematic, large-scale pursuit of new information. Investments in scientific and technological research and development have grown tremendously, while computers and other devices that increase our ability to acquire, analyze, and process information add their own impetus to the rate of change.

The only things that might conceivably slow the rate of technological innovation in the next several decades are nuclear war, collapse of the world economy, or an environmental catastrophe. Fortunately, none of these appears likely in that time frame.

Content of Change   Up to this point, industrial societies have relied primarily on coal, petroleum, and natural gas as the principal sources of the vast quantities of energy on which their way of life depends. Both coal and petroleum, however, are major sources of atmospheric pollution, and supplies of inexpensive and easily obtained petroleum are likely to be exhausted within the next few decades. Nuclear power, which once seemed so promising, is now being abandoned not only because of the hazards nuclear power plants pose but also because there is still no safe and inexpensive method of disposing of nuclear waste and of shutting down the power plants after their relatively brief period of use. Thus, there is growing pressure to find alternative energy sources for the years ahead.

Natural gas is a relatively clean, abundant, and inexpensive source of energy that is already widely used for industrial purposes and for heating of homes and its use will almost certainly increase in the decades ahead. Efforts have been under way for some time to adapt it for use in automobiles and, while some experimental vehicles powered by natural gas are already on the road, major problems remain.

Wind has become the fastest-growing source of energy in recent years (see Table 16.2), with growth especially rapid in Denmark and Germany.[27] In just a twenty-year period, from 1982 to 2002, the production of energy by windmills increased approximately 1,000-fold in the United States.[28] Although wind power still provides less than 1 percent of the country's energy needs, the American Wind Energy Association predicts this will increase to 6 percent by 2020.[29] While wind provides a clean, renewable, and cost-competitive alternative to fossil fuels, its chief drawback is the visual pollution that the new giant windmills create and the absence of strong, sustained winds in many areas.

The *sun* is another energy source that will almost certainly be more fully exploited in the years ahead. Although solar panels are an exceptionally clean source of energy, the cost of electricity produced by them is several times greater than the cost of conventional means; it can, however, be competitive at times of peak use.[30] In recent years, the production of electricity by means of solar panels has surged in western Europe and Japan, thanks in part to governmental subsidies (see Table 16.2 on page 359).[31]

Finally, efforts are currently under way to find the means of exploiting *hydrogen* and *nuclear fusion* as energy sources. Both hold the promise of providing clean, safe, and almost limitless supplies of energy, but the technical problems of fulfilling that promise have been enormous. Recently, however, Japanese automakers have found a way to combine gasoline- and hydrogen-powered engines in a way that seems promising for the future.

Of more immediate concern, successful efforts are under way on many fronts to improve the *end-use efficiency* of the various machines now in use in societies. In 1980, the average end-use efficiency of the machines in the most advanced industrial societies was estimated to be only 10 percent.[32] In other words, 90 percent of the energy consumed by them was wasted (e.g., by the generation of heat by equipment intended to provide light) or consumed in the production and transmission of energy to the ultimate consumer. While anything approaching 100 percent efficiency is impossible, there is some evidence of improvement in this regard. For example, one measure of energy efficiency, the dollars of gross world product produced per kilogram of carbon emitted into the atmosphere, has increased worldwide more than 35 percent since 1950.[33] But energy use in developing societies is increasing quite rapidly, and these are the least developed technologically and the least efficient utilizers of energy resources.[34] The history of modern technology provides ample grounds for optimism about the prospect for further increasing the energy efficiency of many existing technologies. Figure 16.3 shows the steady improvement that has been achieved in the efficiency of both steam engines and forms of lighting, and the same could be demonstrated for other technologies as well.

On another front, numerous organizations are trying to develop more economical ways of recycling the refuse of societies. Industrial societies in particular produce enormous quantities of solid waste. The United States alone creates more than 232 million tons of it a year, more than

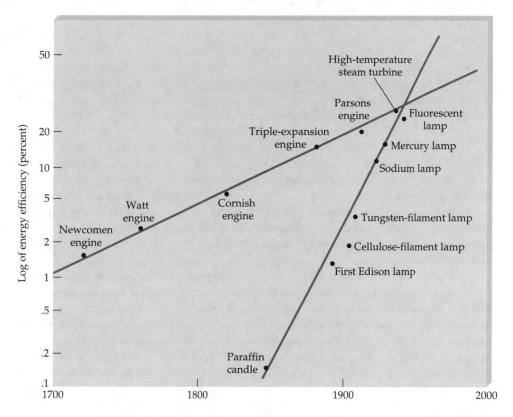

FIGURE 16.3 *Increasing energy efficiency in two areas of modern technology: steam engines and illumination. Note the logarithmic scale that is used to plot energy efficiency; if an ordinary linear scale had been used, the trend lines would be even steeper.*

twice the amount it produced just thirty-five years ago.[35] Disposal of these mountains of refuse has become an increasingly expensive problem, and recycling is the obvious solution, since it converts some of the waste into useful materials. Unfortunately, there is still no technology for converting most of it; and even where appropriate technology exists, the costs of conversion are often greater than the market value of the recycled materials.[36] With the seriousness of the waste disposal problem increasingly obvious, however, investment in research is growing and prospects are good for advances in recycling technology in the decades just ahead.[37]

Safer disposal of toxic substances will be another focus of research. Untold amounts of radioactive water, nerve gas, industrial waste, and other lethal materials are currently buried or stored in perishable containers. Scientists have recently made a number of breakthroughs with respect to some of these problems. For instance, they have found bacteria, weeds, and clay that can be used to extract plutonium—an extremely hazardous waste product of nuclear reactors that remains radioactive for thousands of years—from the wastewater in which it is stored, rendering it far more compact and thus much easier to dispose of.[38] Similar techniques are now being perfected to clean contaminated water and to render other toxic wastes harmless.[39] As the costs and dangers of toxic contaminants mount, there will undoubtedly be further advances in the development and application of these technologies.

Population control is another area in which there will probably be technological innovations in the next quarter century. Although technologies for limiting population growth already exist, many Third World societies have been slow to accept them, as we have seen.

Ideological and economic changes will have to occur before this problem is overcome, but the development of cheaper, safer, simpler, and more reliable methods of contraception, sterilization, and abortion will speed the process. For example, one new technique currently being tested is the administration of ovulation-controlling hormones by injection. Some women in Third World nations appear to be much more receptive to shots administered by medical personnel than to pills or devices they use at home. The "morning after" pill is another innovation that will almost surely be used more widely in the next several decades.

The current effort to find technological solutions for hunger, which is so widespread in the Third World, will certainly continue in the years ahead. Although this problem, as we have seen, is primarily the result of rapid population growth in these societies, it is aggravated by certain dietary patterns, such as the eating of meat. Since the meat of a grain-fed animal delivers only about one-eleventh to one-seventeenth of the calories of the grain consumed by the animal eaten, it dramatically increases the amount of grain consumed by a population.[40] Therefore, primarily as a result of rising demand in advanced industrial societies, the total amount of grain produced for animal feed increased from 289 million tons in 1960 to approximately 760 million tons in 2002.[41]

Thus, the fact that meat consumption has been declining in the more advanced industrial societies in recent years, because of health concerns, bodes well for future world grain supplies. The consumption of red meat in the United States fell from 132 pounds per person in 1970 to 85 in 2002.[42] But the future is clouded by the fact that meat consumption has been increasing in a number of societies with rapidly growing economies and rising standards of living (e.g., South Korea, Taiwan, China). Because of China's enormous population, improvements in the Chinese economy are having substantial impact on world meat production and consumption.[43]

At present there are a number of new technologies at various stages of development that promise to increase the world's food supply, though not without problems or risks. One of these, fish farming, is already in operation in a number of societies and promises to provide an increased supply of high-quality protein at relatively low cost.[44] World production has increased more than fivefold since 1984, reaching 36 million tons in 2000; in fact, one out of three fish consumed in the world today was raised on a farm.[45] Fish farming, or aquaculture as it is also known, is not without its problems. When huge numbers of fish are raised in a small, confined area, disease often takes a heavy toll. In addition, as fish farms grow in number and size, they consume ever increasing quantities of small fish, such as herring and menhaden, that become feedstock for the larger fish being farmed, thus depleting the supply of these fish that are so important in the food chain that sustains populations of larger fish in the wild.

Another promising innovation is soilless cultivation, which involves a recycled mixture of water and nutrients that is sprayed on the roots of plants suspended in frames. Developed in Israel, this technique should greatly increase food production in arid and semiarid areas. In addition, the new technology of recombinant DNA, a discussion of which follows, is providing new and modified strains of plants and animals. Once again, however, this new technology is not without problems and potential risks.

Electronics is another area in which significant advances can be expected in the years ahead. Despite the enormous progress already achieved in miniaturizing transistors, one expert estimated that the process had gone only "a little past half way" toward the point where shrinking would have to end because of the laws of physics. Others, however, suggest that when that point is reached, scientists and engineers will find ways to circumvent those limits with new materials and methods.[46]

The most exciting new area in electronics in recent years—one whose impact is expected to rival that of transistors—is the development of micro-electro-mechanical systems, popularly known as MEMS. MEMS sensors, built on silicon chips, translate physical actions into computational data. Tiny motors, called actuators, then translate computational commands back into physical responses. Air bags used in automobiles to protect riders in the event of a crash provide a familiar example of the application of these devices. The sensor, which consists of a whisker of silicon, can detect a car's sudden deceleration when it hits an object and instantly instructs the air bag to inflate. This device costs less than half the price of the mechanical sensors it replaced, but it has proved much more reliable.[47] MEMS have a wide variety of possible uses, and engineers are already at work on MEMS that do everything from protecting buildings and bridges against earthquakes to ones that conduct medical tests and enhance medical procedures of various kinds.

Yet another fundamental innovation with revolutionary potential for human societies in the next quarter century is the new technology of *recombinant DNA*. In recent years geneticists have learned how to remove a bit of genetic material from the cell of one kind of organism and implant it in the cell of another species. This new technology is particularly fascinating from the perspective of ecological-evolutionary theory, for it marks *a new stage in our species' capacity for handling information*. Until recently, the only information we could manipulate and recombine was cultural information. Now we can use the genetic alphabet in the same way (but only to a very limited extent so far) to create combinations of genetic information which do not exist in nature and which can serve as tools for accomplishing human purposes.

So far, most applications of recombinant DNA technology involve the transplantation of genes that govern the production of rare proteins from the cells of slower-breeding animals, including humans, into the cells of plants and bacteria. Bacteria grow and divide so rapidly that a single one can produce 100 trillion identical cells in 24 hours, each one containing at least 100 molecules of the desired protein.[48] In this way, large quantities of rare and valuable chemicals (e.g., insulin) can be produced at minimal cost.

By inserting human genes into plants, scientists have created tobacco plants that produce antibodies, potatoes that produce serum albumin, and rape plants that produce enkephalin, a painkiller normally produced in the human brain.[49] A biotechnology company in California is planning to market a new protective sun screen containing human skin pigment (melanin) grown in tobacco. These are just the beginning of what promises to become a flood of important innovations employing recombinant DNA.

Many other kinds of technological innovations can also be expected during the next few decades. Substantial resources are being invested in medical research of various kinds, including organ transplants and genetic diseases. Striking advances have recently been made in communications, data processing, and office automation, and further advances in these areas should be only a matter of time. In addition, it is very possible that some unanticipated breakthrough or breakthroughs, comparable to the silicon chip or recombinant DNA, will lay the foundation, as all fundamental innovations do, for a host of new applications.

Ideology

The most striking change in political ideology in the past fifty years has been the collapse of Marxism in eastern Europe, and its decline in China and other nations. While this development has been accompanied by some increase in support for democratic socialism and capitalism, it is *pragmatism* that has made the greatest gains and will probably continue to do so. Deng Xiaoping, the late Chinese leader, said it best: when some complained that his program of economic reform was a reintroduction of capitalism, he responded that it does not matter whether a cat is black or white as long as it catches mice.

If, as it appears, human societies are nearing a critical, or at least dangerous, point with respect to their impact on the biophysical environment, it seems safe to predict that ideology will play an even larger role in shaping societal change and development than it has played in the past. The beliefs, values, norms, and hence the institutions of a number of societies are certain to alter in some important ways. It will be surprising, for example, if industrial societies do not begin to perceive themselves less as rivals or even potential enemies and more as allies that must join forces to confront the "real" enemy—much as, in science fiction, the nations of planet Earth forget their quarrels and band together to defeat the "aliens from outer space." In this case, of course, the threats they must confront will be global overpopulation and environmental deterioration.

During the next several decades, the most advanced and wealthy nations will almost surely begin to try to persuade some of the less developed to alter the norms of their members with respect to family size. This may be done through the offer of incentives, such as loans and aid programs that are linked to population control, or by introducing new technologies. Industrial societies will also begin to provide their own populations with greater incentives and stronger sanctions aimed at protecting the environment (e.g., incentives to encourage recycling and taxes on unnecessary waste products). And one can also be fairly certain that the next quarter century will find growing numbers of scientists and others uniting in international efforts to devise ways of alleviating these increasingly urgent problems.

The chief exceptions to the trend toward increasing pragmatism will probably be found in parts of the Third World. In societies where Muslims are numerous, Islamic fundamentalism is spreading. This ideology is essentially a rejection of most of the social and cultural changes that have developed in response to industrialization. The goal of Islamic fundamentalists is to return to life as it was in the past, before industrialization and modernization began to make themselves felt. Because of the great numbers of Muslims in areas where much of the world's oil reserves are located, the spread of this antimodern ideology cannot be lightly dismissed.

In Latin America, revolutionary socialism still has some appeal, especially for students, intellectuals, and many members of the Catholic clergy. For the latter, the appeal is based on a modified version of Marxism known as "liberation theology," an ideology that emphasizes the similarities in some of the ideals of Marxism and Christianity while ignoring or minimizing the many differences in both ideals and methods. Like orthodox Marxism, liberation theology combines a harsh critique of the existing social order with an idealized vision of a new socialist society created by revolutionary means. Unfortunately, this utopian vision ignores the lessons learned at such great cost by the peoples of eastern Europe, China, and elsewhere. In addition, it is certain that the process of industrialization in any society will only be made more difficult by an ideology that ignores the imperative of population control.

In politically stable, fully industrialized societies, the ideologies most likely to create problems during the coming decades are hedonistic philosophies, encouraged by excessive affluence, that lead people to focus on their personal concerns and pleasures to the neglect of societal problems. If, however, an industrial society should become destabilized by some economic, political, or environmental crisis, then the greatest ideological threat will probably lie in nationalistic or other emotionally charged ideologies that promise simple solutions to complex societal problems.

For some decades now, the increasingly dominant hedonistic values have been challenged to some degree by concerns for the welfare of the biophysical environment. This has even given rise, as we have seen, to so-called Green parties in various industrial societies. It needs to be noted, however, that these parties have failed to attract large followings and that the dominant parties give little more than lip service to environmentalist programs. Thus, it seems unlikely that hedonism, with its seductive focus on instant gratification, will be displaced any time soon by the future-oriented, self-denying ethic of environmentalism. That is not likely to happen unless the point is reached when the costs of environmental neglect become too painful to tolerate.

Polity

The most important political trend in the twentieth century was the spread of democracy. This has involved both the increasing democratization of societies in which the process began prior to the start of the century and the beginnings of democracy in others.

The General Assembly of the United Nations: every nation, regardless of size, has an equal vote.

The year 1989 saw the beginning of a remarkable series of political changes in most of the societies of eastern Europe, when the Communist Party was forced to renounce its monopoly of power and compete with other parties in free elections. Although results have been far from ideal, a return to the old system is very unlikely. Even leaders of the old Communist Party in these societies have lost faith in the former system. Thus, we are likely to see further democratization in these societies during the next quarter century, though occasional pauses and even short-term reversals would not be surprising.

In the Third World, prospects for increasing democracy are mixed. They appear to be good in those societies that are industrializing most rapidly and whose better-educated populations insist on a greater voice in the formulation of governmental policies that affect their daily lives. In much of the Third World, however, especially in industrializing horticultural societies and most Muslim societies of the Middle East and North Africa, prospects for greater democracy are not nearly as promising. Faced with the staggering problems created by runaway population growth, and with a social and cultural heritage that equips them poorly for competition in the modern world economy, most of these societies will probably find democratic government a luxury they cannot afford.

A second important political trend that appears likely in the decades just ahead is the growth of nationalist movements. This trend is strikingly evident in the republics of the former Soviet Union and what was Yugoslavia. But the trend is not limited to those societies. Nationalist movements by ethnic minorities are also active in Canada, Northern Ireland, Spain, Bulgaria, Romania, Turkey, Iraq, Israel, India, Sri Lanka, Indonesia, Sudan, Ethiopia, Somalia, and much of sub-Saharan Africa, and there is the potential for such movements in a number of other societies as well.

Intrasocietal violence organized by the Communist Party is likely to decline in the decades ahead. In the recent past, much of this depended on the economic and military support of the Soviet Union, East Germany, Czechoslovakia, and China. On the other hand, fundamentalist Islamic movements and governments can be expected to support terrorism and violence wherever possible.

Economy

Barring a major collapse of the world economy, there will probably be continuing economic growth for the world system as a whole during the next quarter century. The wider application of techniques that are already known should so improve energy efficiency that increased productivity will be ensured, even when energy costs increase. In addition, there will almost certainly be advances in energy technology that boost world production higher still.

Whether living standards also rise will depend on the number of people who must share the fruits of the increased productivity. Population growth could well offset the effects of the rise in the gross world product (GWP), and thus prevent significant improvement in living standards for the world as a whole. And even if per capita GWP rises, it does not necessarily follow that per capita GNPs (gross national products) will rise in every society. Improvements are unlikely in many African societies, where runaway population growth continues to threaten economic disaster and even starvation. Although the situation may be alleviated temporarily by international aid programs, the basic problems in these societies will persist until their leaders face up to the problems confronting them. Unfortunately, there are few signs of this so far.

In contrast, a number of industrializing agrarian societies will probably join the ranks of industrial societies in the next quarter century. Based on current levels of development and current rates of economic growth, South Korea, Taiwan, Spain, and Ireland are the most likely candidates. Other possibilities include Israel, Slovenia, Argentina, Brazil, Portugal, Romania, Bulgaria, and Chile, though most of these societies have serious political problems that must be overcome before substantial economic development can be achieved.

Although oil exports have generated tremendous revenues in a number of developing societies, the future of these societies in the world economy will be determined by how well they use their oil profits to build more diversified modern economies: camels graze in front of an oil refinery in Iran.

During the 1980s, capitalism gained substantially at the expense of socialism, not only in eastern Europe but also in western Europe and much of the Third World. This gain was the result of a desire for more rapid economic growth and a growing recognition that market economies and private enterprise are more conducive to such growth than centrally planned economies and state enterprises. In western Europe, this trend may not continue much longer and may even be reversed, since these societies now have economies that are complex mixtures of both capitalism and socialism. Future changes in their economies will probably be more a matter of "fine-tuning" than of major overhauling.

In eastern Europe and much of the Third World, on the other hand, large-scale private enterprise was almost nonexistent until recently, and their command economies were dominated by bloated, inefficient, and sometimes corrupt governmental bureaucracies and state enterprises. Movement toward mixed economies is still in the early stages in most of these societies and will have to continue for years if a balance between market forces and governmental control is to be achieved. In view of the tremendous pressures for better living standards in these societies, it seems likely that the trend will persist for some time.

In Japan, the United States, and Canada, in contrast, the economies, though mixed, are even more market-oriented than those of western Europe. Long-term changes in these societies, therefore, are likely to be in the direction of greater governmental control of the economy. But, as in western Europe, the change is not likely to be drastic.

Another economic trend that is almost certain to continue is the increasing division of labor in the world system. Since 1750, the volume of international trade has increased well over 2,000-fold, which is, in part, a reflection of the growth of societal economic specialization during that time. This trend, a consequence of technological advances that have drastically reduced the cost of moving goods, has been highly beneficial for the most part. Societies now export things that they can produce more cheaply than other societies and import what they find more costly to produce.

The world economy, which is essentially a *capitalist* economy, has not been without its disadvantages, especially for societies that specialize in products whose value on the world market is low or fluctuates sharply. Yet even these societies have found this system more rewarding than trying to produce for themselves everything they need. For a few societies, the oil producers in particular, the system has worked enormously to their advantage, greatly enhancing their position in the world system of societies. In the long run, however, they will not be able to rely exclusively on this one highly profitable product, and their future in the world economy will come to depend on the extent to which they use their oil profits to build more diversified modern economies.

During the next quarter century, economic ties among societies are likely to grow even stronger than they are today. As this happens, societies will gradually lose more and more of their economic independence. At some point many societies, perhaps most, will find that these economic ties have become so vital that they cannot afford to remain vulnerable to disruption by international disputes or war. When that point is reached, it will provide an enormous impetus to develop some form of world government. Although it seems unlikely that a world government will be established in the next several decades, it could occur later in this century (see "The World System," page 356).

Finally, there is one glaring defect in the economies of virtually every contemporary society that will almost surely become more apparent during coming decades. This is the failure to attach realistic "price tags" to things. The costs of *disposing of* waste materials, for example, are not currently included in the price of most commodities. When those costs are routinely added to the price of plastic, glass, and aluminum containers, packaging materials, disposable diapers, and other materials accumulating in trash dumps today, buying patterns will alter, recycling will gain impetus, and new materials will be developed. Similarly, societies must eventually begin to assess the true—but usually delayed—costs of such things as inadequate systems of health care, child care, and education. A more realistic approach to assessing costs is long overdue and, when it is adopted, it will almost surely be accompanied by widespread changes in virtually every area of societal life, but the next few decades will probably see only the beginnings of such change.

The World System

As the world system of societies becomes increasingly integrated economically and in other ways, societies will become more dependent on one another. The growing interdependence of societies in the European Union is one of the most important developments in this respect, but almost certainly not the last. As the volume and importance of international trade increases, societies in other parts of the world may well initiate similar programs.

With increasing economic integration, individual societies will be ever more vulnerable to anything that threatens the functioning of the system as a whole. Above all, they will be vulnerable to war, regardless of where it occurs or which nations are involved.

There is no need to recount here estimates of the number of deaths and the magnitude of destruction that a nuclear war would produce. Suffice it to say that virtually all who have studied the matter carefully, including people of very different ideological persuasions, agree that such a war would be a catastrophe. For not only would the combatants be damaged beyond imagination, but neutral societies and noncombatants would also suffer enormously from radioactive fallout and from the disruption of the world economy that would inevitably follow.

During the next quarter century, the threat of nuclear war will no longer lie exclusively with the NATO powers and Russia, as it did in the recent past. The technology of nuclear weapons is now more widespread, and several Third World nations already have small nuclear arsenals. The greatest danger, therefore, is likely to come from the use of these weapon systems by irrational or fanatical leaders or from a process in which some limited conflict escalates out of control (e.g., between India and Pakistan). Another threat is the possibility that nuclear weapons may fall into the hands of a terrorist organization.

The potential for such conflicts in the next several decades is not inconsiderable. Even if relations among the major powers continue to improve, resource shortages and population pressures could lead to deteriorating relations among many other societies. For example, in an era of growing water shortages, it is worth noting that 200 of the world's major river basins are shared by at least two different societies.

Another cause for concern at present is the possibility of spreading ethnic conflicts within present or former multiethnic states, such as the Soviet Union and Yugoslavia. Struggles among their constituent groups (e.g., between Azerbaijanis and Armenians, or Ukrainians and Russians, or tribal groups in various African nations) could easily involve other societies in an escalating process similar to that in which the struggles within the multiethnic Austro-Hungarian Empire in the twentieth century contributed to the outbreak of World War I.

Faced with such threats, one obvious solution would seem to be the formation of a world government that would not interfere with the internal affairs of societies but which would have the authority, the mechanisms, and the power necessary to monitor the production of weapons and control their use. Although it would be exceedingly difficult to develop such a polity, it would be possible if the leaders of most societies wanted it badly enough.

One of the most difficult problems in such an endeavor stems from the great discrepancies in economic development and in standards of living between industrial and industrializing societies. The sixteen most advanced industrial societies, for example, currently have an average per capita GDP of $32,127, more than *eight times* that of the rest of the world, $3,861.*[50] Inclusion of industrializing societies in a world polity would almost certainly lead to

---

*The median is even lower—$1,529. Figures are for 2001, expressed in 1995 U.S. dollars.[51]

The city of Hiroshima shortly after the explosion of the first atomic bomb used in warfare, 1945. Advances in weapons technology since then have led to bombs that have 4,000 times the explosive force of the Hiroshima bomb.

demands for a substantial redistribution of world wealth and income. In exchange for permission to monitor their military installations, industrializing societies would probably insist upon major economic concessions. But this could easily kill enthusiasm for world government by members of industrial societies. For if world income were distributed equally among the world's societies, per capita income would be reduced by nearly 80 percent in many industrial societies, causing a decline in living standards to about *one-quarter* their current level.

Although this is hardly an attractive prospect, some less extreme version of income redistribution (e.g., very gradual) may eventually occur. Even if it still seemed harsh to advanced societies, they might consider it preferable to the continuing threat of war and disruption of the world economy. If there is to be a viable compromise in this century, however, governments should begin soon to narrow the economic gap between societies. Strong incentives should be provided to industrializing societies to bring population growth to an end, so that their standards of living can be improved, and industrial societies should be prepared to sacrifice some of their own potential growth to provide these incentives and to reduce the gap between haves and have-nots.

Somewhat more likely in the next few decades is a gradual strengthening of the United Nations, the closest thing to a world polity that now exists. The greatest obstacle to the effectiveness of that organization is probably the system of representation in the General Assembly, which provides an equal vote for the People's Republic of China, with its population of 1.3 *billion,* and for the Republic of Palau, with its population of 19 *thousand.* The special powers vested in the Security Council—the veto power in particular—partly compensate for this, but the present organizational structure of the United Nations as a whole does not generate much confidence on the part of many of the larger and more powerful nations.

Substantial changes will have to occur if the United Nations is ever to become the basis of a future world polity. Until such a polity is established, the world system of societies will remain vulnerable to massive disruption of the increasingly important and valuable network of ties among societies.

The Higher Goals

Early in this chapter we reached the conclusion that sociocultural evolution has, more often than not, been accompanied by declining levels of freedom, justice, and happiness for the majority of people, but that technological advances in the past 200 years have reversed this trend, at least for the vast majority of members of industrial societies. It would be gratifying to be able to predict that the increasing industrialization of the world system during the next quarter century will have a similar impact on the world as a whole. As our examination of population trends, the environment, and other matters has made clear, however, the prospects for greater attainment of humanity's higher goals in the decades immediately ahead are uncertain.

In many industrializing societies, we may well see a decline in individual freedom accompanied by an increase in the number of authoritarian regimes. This could have the effect of alleviating some human misery, however, since such regimes would be better able to control birthrates and thus perhaps lower the number of severely malnourished individuals in these societies. But even if this happens, there is not likely to be any great gain in either happiness or justice, since many will still be doomed to lives of abject poverty in crowded slums and shantytowns. What is more, population growth and shortages of vital resources will probably retard the pace of industrialization in many societies during the next few decades, greatly delaying the day when advances in productivity begin to provide appreciable benefits for the majority of their members.

Whatever difficulties human societies experience during the next few decades, however, they may suffer even more later in the present century. Levels of freedom, justice, and happiness are almost certain to decline seriously for the world system as a whole during that period—unless humanity begins *soon* to address its most basic problems. Our potential for shaping a better world is still, at this point, good—as good, in fact, as it has ever been. But this situation will not last: *the range of attractive options will decline with every year we fail to act.* Thus, the larger the human population becomes before growth is halted, the more likely it is that future political regimes will be harshly authoritarian and individual freedoms severely limited. The more the biophysical environment is damaged before that trend is reversed, the less likely it is that the human population *as a whole* will ever enjoy the enormous potential benefits of an industrial economy. And the longer sociocultural evolution continues to be shaped primarily by the blind forces of conflict and intersocietal selection, the more likely it is that our future will be shaped by convulsive changes that are forced upon us by developments beyond our control.

The latter, in fact, is precisely the outcome predicted for human societies by some who have considered the problem. For example, Robert Heilbroner, an economic historian long noted for his insightful analyses, wrote a book entitled *An Inquiry into the Human Prospect* in which he forecast such developments as nuclear wars among societies that are experiencing severe population and environmental crises.[52] He predicted, in effect, a future in which the forces of nature—including the irrational forces that are part of our genetic heritage—determine the outcomes of problems that *humanity failed to resolve with cultural resources.*

Heilbroner was not unaware of our species' remarkable adaptive capabilities. In fact, he believed that, in principle, we are capable of solving our problems through social and cultural mechanisms. What he doubted is our ability to do it *in time to avoid catastrophe.* He felt that it will require too long to alter certain dangerous behavior patterns—patterns that reflect our genetically based tendencies toward individualism, self-centeredness, and expansiveness of needs, and which are reflected in our lack of cooperation, our lack of concern for future generations and for members of other societies, and our disinclination to deny ourselves. Heilbroner pointed out the futility of pinning our hopes on what we believe it possible for humanity eventually to *become.* Rather, he said, we must consider what people are likely *to be* during the period in question, and he noted that the socialization process tends to produce individuals who are a generation or more behind the times, people who, tomorrow, will finally be prepared to respond to yesterday's problems.[53]

Even if one does not entirely agree with Heilbroner's pessimistic assessment, it is impossible to deny that certain aspects of our genetic heritage seriously handicap us in our efforts to solve our most urgent problems, or that the socialization process and other social and cultural mechanisms are often inadequate in helping societies adapt to the conditions created by a rapidly changing technology. But while there is nothing we can do to alter our genetic mechanisms, at least in the near future, *we can alter our social and cultural mechanisms.*

Of all the species on this planet, ours is the only one not doomed to have its evolutionary course shaped entirely by forces beyond its control. Thanks to symbol systems and culture, we can not only comprehend the evolutionary process, *we may also be able to chart for ourselves an evolutionary course within the limits set by our genetic heritage on the one hand and the constraints of the biophysical environment on the other*—a course that can provide for most people a reasonable degree of freedom, justice, and happiness.

But we also have the option to ignore this possibility until it is too late.

TABLE 16.2 Energy Production by Solar Panels and Wind, 1971-2001
(Production in Megawatts)

Year	Solar Panels	Wind
1971	0.1	1?
1981	8	25
1991	55	2,170
2001	391	24,930

Source: Adapted from Worldwatch Institute, *Vital Signs, 2002,* p. 45, and *Vital Signs, 2003,* p. 39.

Glossary

A.D. A system of dating (chronology) that locates events in terms of years since the estimated birth of Christ. The initials are from the Latin, *anno Domini,* "year of the Lord." (See B.C. and B.P.)

Adaptation The process of adjusting to, or changing, environmental conditions; hence, broadly, problem solving.

Adaptive Something that helps a system or organism survive in its environment.

Agrarian era The period in history when agrarian societies were the technologically most advanced (about 3000 B.C. to 1800 A.D.).

Agrarian society A society that depends primarily on plow agriculture for subsistence. Advanced agrarian societies have iron tools and weapons; simple agrarian societies do not.

Agriculture The cultivation of fields using the plow.

Anthropoids An order of primates that includes monkeys, apes and humans.

Archaeology The study of societies and cultures of the past, based on analysis of their physical remains.

Arithmetic mean An "average" or measure of central tendency that is computed by dividing the sum of a set of items by the number of items in the set.

Artisan A craftsperson. The term is usually applied to a worker who, unlike a modern factory worker, uses hand tools and produces a complete product.

Autocracy Rule by one person (compare with *Democracy, Oligarchy,* and *Theocracy*).

Autonomous Self-directing; free from outside political control.

Band A nomadic community at the hunting and gathering level; most bands are also societies.

B.C. A system of dating (chronology) that locates events in terms of years "before (the birth of) Christ." (See *A.D.* and *B.P.*)

Biological drive A genetically programmed predisposition to respond in a general way to a stimulus (compare with *Instinct*).

Biological evolution The process of genetic change by which existing species of plants and animals have developed out of preexisting species.

Biophysical environment The biological and physical aspects of the environment.

Body language Symbolic communication system involving physical movements and gestures (e.g., winking, nodding).

B.P. A system of dating (chronology) that locates events in terms of years "before the present." (Compare with *A.D.* and *B.C.*)

Bureaucracy (1) The administrative component of a government or formal organization; (2) an administrative system that is characterized by a highly formalized division of labor, a hierarchical system of authority, and action guided by a complex and formalized system of rules.

Capital goods Things that are necessary for the production of other things (e.g., plow, land, and draft animals for grain cultivation, or investment assets for making money in a capitalist society).

Capital-intensive industry   An industry which depends on expensive machinery to produce its products (compare with *Labor-intensive industry*).

Capitalism   An economic system in which the means of production are privately owned and the basic problems of production and distribution are settled within a market system, with minimal governmental regulation or control (see *Market economy*, and contrast with *Socialism*).

Carnivore   A meat eater.

Civilization   An advanced sociocultural system. The term is usually reserved for the cultures of societies with urban communities and writing.

Clan   A kin group whose members claim descent from a common ancestor.

Class   (1) An aggregation or group of people whose overall status is similar; (2) an aggregation or group of people who share some important resource that affects their access to power, privilege, or prestige.

Command economy   An economy in which the basic questions of production and distribution are decided by political elites (contrast with *Market economy*).

Communication   The exchange of information by means of signals or symbols.

Communism   A future state of society hypothesized by Marx in which the distribution of goods and services would be based on individual need; a society in which there is no inequality.

Community   An informally organized group whose members are united by a common place of residence or by a common subculture.

Comparative   A method of study that develops knowledge through systematic comparisons (see *Science*).

Constant   Something that is the same everywhere or cannot change (compare with *Variable*).

Continuity   The persistence of cultural elements in a society.

Cooperation   Interaction by two or more individuals for their mutual benefit.

Culture   Symbol systems and the information they convey.

Customs   Informal norms that define acceptable behavior in a society or in a subgroup within a society.

Democracy   A political system in which sovereignty is vested in the people (contrast with *Autocracy, Oligarchy,* and *Theocracy*).

Demography   The study of populations, especially their size, composition, and change.

Determinism   The belief that a specific set of identifiable factors is sufficient to explain completely a given phenomenon.

Development, societal   A process of change in which technological advance causes greater organizational complexity within a society or set of societies (compare with *Growth*).

Diffusion   Transmission of cultural elements from one society to another, or from one group to another within a society.

Discovery   New cultural information acquired by means other than diffusion (compare with *Invention*).

Distributive justice   Ideas about what is a fair or just distribution of valued items in a society.

DNA   Deoxyribonucleic acid; the chemical molecule that embodies genetic information.

Drive   See *Biological drive*.

Ecological-evolutionary theory   Theory concerning (1) the relationships within and among human societies, (2) the relationships between societies and their biophysical environments, and (3) the processes of sociocultural change and development.

Ecology   The science of the interrelationships of living things to one another and to their environments.

Economic surplus   Production that exceeds what is needed to keep the producers of essential goods and services alive and productive.

Economy   The economic system of a group, especially a society; in effect, an institutionalized set of answers to basic questions concerning the production and distribution of goods and services.

Egalitarian   Characterized by relative equality.

Elites   The most powerful and privileged members of a society or institutional system.

Empirical   Derived from the senses, observable.

Energy   The capacity for performing work.

Environment   Everything external to an entity (organism, population, society, etc.) that affects it, or is affected by it, in any way.

Era   A period of time during which a particular type of society is the most advanced in existence (e.g., the agrarian era).

Ethnography   The description of sociocultural systems based on direct observation.

Evolution   Long-term directional patterns of change that result from the interplay of three forces: (1) forces of continuity, (2) forces of innovation and change, and (3) forces of selection (see *Biological evolution* and *Sociocultural evolution*).

Extended family   A group of related individuals that is more inclusive than the nuclear family and less inclusive than the clan.

Falsifiable   A proposition, theory or hypothesis that can be shown to be false, and which therefore can be tested.

Family   A group organized around ties of kinship (see also *Nuclear family* and *Extended family*).

Feedback   A special type of causal relationship in which part of the effect produced by an initial cause or event reverts back to its source, modifying or reinforcing it (i.e., the influence that B exerts on A as a result of A's earlier influence on B).

Feudalism   A system in which elites pledge loyalty and military service to a sovereign in return for power over local political and economic affairs.

Fishing society   A society dependent primarily on fishing, or fishing and gathering, for subsistence.

Fixed costs   Costs of production that remain more or less constant regardless of the number of units produced (contrast with *Variable costs*).

Frontier society   An agrarian society that is expanding into territories which are uninhabited, or inhabited by much less advanced societies.

Function   (1) A characteristic activity of a person, thing, or institution; or (2) a consequence of, or purpose served by, that activity.

Fundamental innovation   An invention or discovery that either (1) opens the way for many other innovations or (2) alters the conditions of human life so that many other changes become either possible or necessary.

Gathering   Foraging for wild fruits and vegetables.

Gene   The basic unit of heredity; a conveyer of genetic information.

Genetic constants   Genetic attributes that are the same in every population of a species.

Genetic variables   Genetic attributes that vary among the populations within a species.

Governing class   A class, often hereditary, from which the political leaders of a society are recruited.

Gross domestic product (GDP)   The monetary value of the goods and services produced within a society during a specified period (usually a year).

Gross national product (GNP)   Gross domestic product plus net income from other nations.

Gross world product (GWP)   The total value of goods and services produced in all societies.

Group   Generally an aggregation whose members (1) cooperate to satisfy common, or complementary, needs; (2) have shared norms; and (3) have a sense of common identity. The term is applicable to a society and also to intersocietal and intrasocietal aggregations.

Growth   An increase in size. For societies, the term may refer either to population size or to territorial size (compare with *Development, societal*).

Guild   A mutual aid association of merchants and artisans in the same trade (found in agrarian and maritime societies).

Haplodiploidy   System of reproduction and sex determination in which haploid males develop from unfertilized eggs and have half of a complement of genes, and diploid females develop from fertilized eggs and have a full complement of genes.

Headman   The leader of a local community in a preliterate society.

Herbivore   A plant eater.

Herding society   A society dependent primarily on herding for subsistence.

Hominid   A member of the genus *Homo*, which includes our own species as well as an undetermined number of humanlike species that preceded us but are now extinct.

Homo sapiens   Our species. Some scientists would include Neanderthals with *Homo sapiens sapiens*.

Homo sapiens sapiens   Our subspecies; biologically modern humans.

Horticultural era   The period in history when there were no societies technologically more advanced than horticultural societies (about 8000 to 3000 B.C.).

Horticultural society   A society that depends primarily on gardening for subsistence. Advanced horticultural societies are differentiated from simple by the manufacture of metal tools and weapons.

Horticulture   The cultivation of small gardens using a hoe or digging stick as the chief tool. Horticulture is differentiated from agriculture by the absence of the plow.

Hunting and gathering era   The period in history when there were no societies more advanced than hunting and gathering (to about 8000 B.C.).

Hunting and gathering society   A society that depends primarily on hunting and gathering for subsistence.

Hybrid society   A society that relies about equally on two or more of the basic modes of subsistence.

Hypothesis   An educated guess, often derived from a theory, that is tested with evidence.

Ideology   Cultural information used to interpret human experience and order societal life. An ideology consists of a system of beliefs and related norms and values.

Insight   Learning or discovery through reflection.

Industrial era   The period in history when industrial societies have been dominant (from about 1800 A.D. to the present).

Industrialization   A process of increasing reliance on inanimate sources of energy and the machines powered by them (compare with *Modernization*).

Industrial Revolution   The revolution in technology that began in England in the eighteenth century and has since spread through most of the world system.

Industrial society   A society that derives most of its wealth and income from productive activities dependent on machines powered by inanimate energy sources (e.g., coal, petroleum, natural gas, hydroelectric power, nuclear power).

Information   A record of experience that is stored in the memory system of a plant, animal, or machine.

Innovation   The process of introducing new cultural elements into a society (e.g., inventions, discoveries); the new cultural element itself (see *Variations*).

Instinct   A genetically programmed predisposition to react in a specific, ritualized way to a stimulus (compare with *Biological drive*).

Institution   A system of social relationships and cultural elements that develops in a society in response to some set of basic and persistent needs (e.g., raising children).

Institutional system   A system of interrelated institutions.

Intersocietal selection   The process of selection whereby some societies survive while others become extinct.

Intrasocietal selection   The process of selection within a society whereby some of its cultural elements survive while others are eliminated.

Invention   An innovation that results from a useful new combination of information already possessed by a society (compare with *Discovery*).

Labor-intensive industry   An industry which depends on large numbers of workers to produce its products (compare with *Capital-intensive industry*).

Language   A system of symbols.

Laws   Written norms enforced by a government.

Learning   The process by which an organism acquires, through experience, information with the potential for changing its behavior.

Legitimate   That which is morally or legally justified by the norms or laws of a group.

Legitimize   To make legitimate; to provide an ideological or moral justification for a practice that might otherwise be regarded as objectionable.

Macrosociology   The branch of sociology that studies large social systems, especially human societies and the world system of societies.

Maritime society   A society in which overseas commercial activity is the primary source of wealth and income.

Market economy   An economy in which the basic problems of production and distribution are resolved by the forces of supply and demand (see *Capitalism,* and contrast with *Command economy*).

Mass media   Communications media that influence the masses (e.g., television, radio, newspapers, magazines, and movies).

Mean, arithmetic   See *Arithmetic mean*.

Median   An "average" or measure of central tendency that is the middle number in a series of numbers arranged in order from lowest to highest.

Millennium   A period of one thousand years.

Mixed economy   An economy that combines two or more basic principles of economic decision making, especially one that combines market and command principles.

Mobility, vertical   See *Vertical mobility*.

Modernization   All of the long-term social and cultural changes associated with industrialization (compare with *Industrialization*).

Monogamy   Marriage with but one person at a time (compare with *Polygamy*).

Monopoly   A commodity market with only a single seller.

Nationalism   An ideology that emphasizes the importance of a nation or an ethnic group.

Neophilia   The love of novelty or change for its own sake.

Nomad   A member of a group that has no fixed settlement and moves about periodically (usually in a well-defined territory) to obtain food and other necessities.

Norms   Rules of behavior to which sanctions—rewards and punishments—are attached. Norms may be formal and sanctions specific (e.g., laws) or informal and diffuse (e.g., customs).

Nuclear family   A married couple and their unmarried children living with them.

Oligarchy   The rule of the few (contrast with *Autocracy, Democracy,* and *Theocracy*).

Oligopoly   A commodity market dominated by a few sellers.

Omnivore   A plant and animal eater.

Organism   A living entity; a plant or animal.

Peasant   An agricultural worker in an agrarian society.

Per capita income   National income divided by population size.

Polity   The political system of a group, especially of a society; in effect, an institutionalized set of answers to basic questions concerning the governance of a society.

Polyandry   A (rare) form of marriage in which a woman may have two or more husbands at the same time (compare with *Polygyny*)

Polygamy   The general term for any form of marriage which permits multiple spouses (see *Polyandry* and *Polygyny*)

Polygyny   A form of marriage in which a man may have two or more wives at the same time (compare with *Polyandry*).

Population   (1) Organisms of the same species that tend to interbreed because of geographical proximity; (2) the members of a society, or a subgroup within a society, considered collectively.

Positive-sum game   A contest in which the sum of gains and losses is a positive number; the gains of one participant are not necessarily at the expense of others (contrast with *Zero-sum game*).

Pragmatism   The belief that social arrangements should be judged on the basis of their consequences rather than on the basis of preconceived ideas.

Prejudice   A preconceived opinion or feeling regarding a group.

Primary group   A small group in which face-to-face relations of at least a fairly intimate and personal nature are maintained; a family or clique.

Primary industries   Industries that produce or extract raw materials (especially farming, mining, forestry, and fishing).

Primates   An order of mammals that includes the anthropoids and prosimians.

Process   A series of related events with a definable outcome.

Race   A breeding population in which certain traits occur with a frequency that is appreciably different from that of other breeding populations within the same species; among humans, races have been differentiated on the basis of skin, hair, and eye color, hair type, body build, and shape of face and head.

Rate of natural increase   The difference between annual births and deaths in a society; the rate at which a population would grow if there were no migration into or out of it.

Religion   The basic beliefs of a group of people and the practices associated with those beliefs. The term can refer to nontheistic ideologies, such as communism and humanism, but is more often applied to ideologies that involve theistic beliefs.

Republic   A government based on representation.

Revolution   Change that is unusually sudden, rapid, violent, or far-reaching.

Revolutionary socialism   A socialist ideology developed by Marx and Engels and extended by Lenin that advocates the seizure of power by adherents and denial of power to others, sometimes called "Marxism" or "Marxism-Leninism"; a totalitarian or semitotalitarian system of government.

Role   Behavioral expectations and obligations of the occupant of a social position. The term may also be used to refer to the part a group, institution, or other social unit plays in the life of a society.

Sanction   A reward or punishment; also, the act of rewarding or punishing.

Science   A method of developing a cumulative body of empirically verified knowledge through systematic comparisons and the testing of hypotheses and theories.

Secondary group   Any group that is larger and more impersonal than a primary group.

Secondary industries   Industries that process raw materials and turn out finished products.

Selection   The process that determines the fate of the variations (1) in a gene pool, (2) in a sociocultural system, or (3) in the world system of societies (see *Intersocietal selection, Intrasocietal selection,* and *Variations*).

Serf   A peasant farmer who is bound to the land and subject to the owner of the land.

Shaman   A person believed to enjoy special powers because of a relationship he or she has established with the spirit world; a medicine man.

Signal   An information conveyer whose form and related meaning are both determined genetically (contrast with *Symbol*).

Slavery   A system in which some people are the legal property of others.

Social   Having to do with relationships among the members of societies.

Social controls   Mechanisms that order societal life by regulating people's actions and relationships; norms and their related sanctions.

Social environment   The other social systems with which a given social system has contact.

Social institution   See *Institution*.

Socialism   An economic system in which there is little or no private ownership of the means of production (compare with *Capitalism*).

Socialization   The lifelong process through which individuals learn to become functional members of their society.

Social movement   A loose-knit group that seeks to change society.

Social organization   The network of relationships among the members of a society or group.

Social structure   See *Social organization* and *Structure*.

Social system   A generic term that may be applied to all kinds of human groups, from primary groups to the world system of societies.

Societal   Of or pertaining to a society or societies.

Society, human   A human population is considered a society to the degree that it is politically autonomous and its members engage in a broad range of cooperative activities.

Sociocultural   A combination of social and cultural elements.

Sociocultural evolution   Long-term trends in the world system of societies that result from the interplay of the forces of continuity, innovation, and selection.

Sociocultural system   A system composed of a human population and its social organization, culture, material products, and social institutions; a human society.

Sociology   The branch of science that specializes in the study of human societies.

Species   A distinct population of organisms that is reproductively isolated (i.e., cannot reproduce with populations of other organisms).

State   The government of a society by full-time officials.

Status   The relative rank of a person, role, or group, according to culturally defined standards.

Stereotyping   Applying a simplified and standardized image to an entire group.

Stratification   Class or status differentiation within a population; hence, inequality.

Structure   The organization of the parts of a system.

Subculture   The distinctive culture of a group within a society.

Subsistence   The material necessities of life; also, the process by which they are obtained.

Subsistence technology   The technology that is used by the members of a society to obtain the basic necessities of life.

Surplus   See *Economic surplus*.

Symbol   An information conveyer whose form and meaning are determined by those who use it (contrast with *Signal*).

System   An entity made up of interrelated parts.

Systemic   A feature inherent in a particular system, or having the qualities of a system.

Tabula rasa   Literally "blank slate"; the notion that children are infinitely malleable through education and socialization.

Technology   Cultural information about the ways in which the material resources of the environment may be used to satisfy human needs and desires.

Tertiary industries   Industries that perform services (e.g., retail trade, government, the professions).

Theocracy   A society ruled by a priesthood in the name of some deity, or by a ruler believed to be divine.

Theory   A logically connected set of propositions that provide an empirically confirmed explanation of some aspect of the natural world, or a coherent set of principles that form the basic frame of reference for a field of inquiry.

Third World   Industrializing societies or less developed societies in the world today.

Tribe   A general term for a people whose members speak a common language or dialect, possess a common culture that distinguishes them from other peoples, and know themselves, or are known, by a distinctive name.

Urban community   A community whose inhabitants are wholly or largely freed from the necessity of producing their own food, fibers, and other raw materials.

Values   Cultural judgments about what is good (valuable) and what is not; moral beliefs to which the members of a group subscribe.

Variable   Any characteristic that can differ across observations; something that can vary or change (compare with *Constant*).

Variable costs   Costs of production that tend to vary in proportion to the number of units produced (contrast with *Fixed costs*).

Variations   Products of the process of innovation; new or alternative elements in a sociocultural system (see *Innovation* and *Selection*).

Vertebrates   Animals with backbones.

Vertical mobility   Change of status, either upward or downward.

Working class   Members of modern industrial societies belonging to families headed by manual workers.

World system   The totality of human societies and their interrelationships.

Zero-sum game   A contest in which gains and losses must sum to zero; the gains of any participant are necessarily at the expense of other participants (compare with *Positive-sum game*).

Web Pages of Interest

Agriculture

http://www.fedstats.gov/programs/agriculture.html Federal Information—U.S. Agriculture statistics.

Anthropology/Sociology

http://www.massey.ac.nz/~ALock/hbook/frontis.htm A book online with chapter reprints of: fossil skull evidence, human phylogeny, evolution of tree apes and humans from DNA sequences, evolution of the human brain, and hand and bipedal evolutionary issues—eventually goes into social relations, human ecology and evolution of culture, social relations, language and systems in evolutionary perspective, tempo and mode of change in society.

http://www.umsl.edu/~rkeel/280/Struchag.html Basic brief intro level definitions of culture, social structure, technology and change with basic concepts and approaches—includes associated theories.

http://www.aber.ac.uk/~dgc/tdet10.html Techno-evolution as progress.

http://www.socioweb.com/~markbl/socioweb/ The socioweb description of sociology, sociology resources, and many department home pages including courses, areas of specialization, faculty, etc.

http://www.ameranthassn.org/anthbroc.htm General description of anthropology as a discipline with excellent intro level definitions for "evolutionary perspective," "cultural perspective," "linguistic perspective," "biological perspective." Operated by the American Anthropological Association.

Australian Aborigines

http://www.lonelyplanet.com.au/dest/abor.htm Australian aborigines—description historical to present groups, photos of art, rituals—links to other sites.

Demography

http://www.census.gov/cgi-bin/ipc/popclockw World POPClock, an up-to-the-second estimate of world population.

http://www.prb.org Population Reference Bureau—Informing people about population since 1929, information on world population and population trends.

http://www.popnet.org/ Popnet Home, gateway to world population data.

http://www.dezines.com/web/quizes/population/index.html A world and U.S. population quiz—answers provided.

http://www.kaiwan.com/~mcivr/population15.html World population density facts.

http://www.pbs.org/kqed/population_bomb/worldp.html Shows world population distribution, growth, historical and current change, resource consumption, environmental impact in a quiz format (answers provided at bottom).

Environmental Issues

http://www.iis.u-tokyo.ac.ip/~utsuno/a1.html Accesses many pages regarding Human Society and Environmental Concerns—operated by Coordination Board for a Scientific Approach toward Globalism; Human Society in Harmony with Earth: The Man System.

http://www.nhes.com/ *World Climate Report,* Dissenting views on global climate change.

http://www.csuchico.edu/~pmaslin/fbiol/EcoEvltn.html Ecosystem evolution—coexistence processes of living organisms and social groups. General Darwinian notions are covered here.

Family Issues

http://www.trinity.edu/~mkearl/fam-type.html Kearl's Guide to the Sociology of the Family: Differences across Cultures and Time.

http://www.divorcereform.org/econ.html Effects on Divorced People—Divorce Statistics Collection.

General Data Sources

http://www.odci.gov/cia/publications/factbook/index.html *CIA World Fact Book* with data on all countries plus reference maps.

http://www.rand.org/ Information about publications and research by this research organization.

http://www.ilo.org/ilosearch/public/at-equery.htm Search the International Labour Organization public website in English.

http://www.albany.edu/sourcebook/ Source book of criminal justice statistics.

http://www.statcan.ca/ Welcome to Statistics Canada, gateway to Canadian census data.

http://coba.shsu.edu/EconFAQ/node71.html World and non-U.S. data, gateway to a wide variety of international economic data.

http://www.kaiwan.com/~mcivr/popula.html U.S. cities by African-American population figures.

http://www.ntis.gov/ National Technical Information Service (NTIS), information on government publications (e.g., *Statistical Abstract of the U.S.*) and how to purchase them.

http://www.census.gov/ U.S. Census Bureau home page.

http://www.medaccess.com/census/census_s.htm# Table of contents *Statistical Abstract of the United States.* All tables shown by clicking on desired subject.

http://www.iTools.com/research-it/research-it.html *Research-It!*—One-stop reference desk, gateway to a number of on-line research tools.

http://icg.fas.harvard.edu/~hist1651/census/ Historical Demographic, Economic and Social Data of the U.S., link to ICPSR historical and social statistics on the U.S.

http://www.eia.doe.gov/emeu/aer/ep/overview.html Energy Data and Analysis.

http://www.fedstats.gov/ Fedstats: One-stop shopping for federal statistics.

Great Apes

http://www.selu.com/~bio/gorilla/text/nh.html Excellent description of the mountain Gorilla—social behavior, physical description, locomotion, diet, and the relation to *H. sapiens*—also contains links to Gorilla genetics pages.

www.brown.edu/Departments/Anthropology/apelang.html Chimpanzee and Great Ape Language Resource Center—links to primate research centers, Chimpanzee and Gorilla home page links and guide to books on human intelligence emergence in Ice Age.

www.gsh.org/gsn/gsn/proj/jgi/jgi.chimp.sanct.html Covers general work and findings of Jane Goodall with lists and links to current chimp sanctuaries.

http://www.wcsu.ctstateu.edu/cyberchimp/chimp.html Chimpanzee resource home page—chimp links, information, institutes, primate networks, ecology links, anthropology links, primatology links.

http://jinrui.zool.kyoto-u.ac.jp/ChimpHome/chimpanzeeE.html Excellent information on chimps—"The World of Chimpanzees"—Details long-term studies, national parks with chimp troops, feeding and ranging patterns, phylogenic position, development, social structure, tool use, hunting, and meat-eating patterns—includes links to PanAfrica News, etc.

http://www.grungyape.com/orangutan/grungy.html Links to orang resources, research etc.—very nice concise description and pictures of orangs.

Human Origins

http://users.hol.gr/%7Edilos/prehis.html Human Prehistory: An Exhibition—Virtual tour through an exhibition of Charles Darwin's theory, the evolution of human society, prehistoric art with images from Lascaux, Venus figurines, tour covers first villages (includes Neolithic villages).

http://riceinfo.rice.edu/armadillo/Sciacademy/essay/poblo.html Human Evolution—excellent overview of human evolution for sociology introductory level.

http://www.talkorigins.org/faqs/homs/links.html Links to origins of mankind.

http://www.talkorigins.org/faqs/homs/gibbon.html Was Java Man (*Pithecanthropus*) a gibbon?—A debate with basic information regarding anthropoids.

http://www.talkorigins.org/faqs/homos/15000.html "Turkana Boy" (*H. Erectus*)—Photographs of skeleton and skullcap, discovered in 1984 by K. Kimeu.

http://www.talkorigins.org/ The Talkorigins Archive—Explores the creation/evolution debate. Includes access to a variety of photos including *H. erectus,* and *A. afarensis.*

http://www.bcvideo.com/bcvideo/ "The mysterious origins of man."

http://www.forerunner.com/forerunner/X0714_Lucy_fails_test.html "Lucy fails test as missing link."

http://www.ecsd.com/~rhhedgz1/primate.html Our primate family tree—briefly traces primate development from 45 million years to present day—Shows the "Johanson" style tree from *A. ramidus* to *H. sapiens.*

http://www.lookup.com/Homepages/92314/home.html "Paleoanthropology the Stone Way"—excellent reports on current paleoanthropological studies, important people currently in the field, well-known excavation areas, prehuman and early-hominid fossils, apes (in section titled "Our Closest Brothers") and other links to human origins and primate pages.

http://www.ants-inc.com/three_hs.html "Leaky Ancestors—the hominids"—shows skulls of hominid line with the skull structural changes of each successive generation identified.

Human Rights

http://www.channel1.com/aasg/ American Anti-Slavery Group, Statistics and press releases concerning slavery in the world today.

http://www.ippu.purdue.edu/info/gsp/governance/weshr.htm The Women's Economic and Social Human Rights Index.

http://www.freedomhouse.org/survey.htm Freedom House surveys.

http://www.un.org/Depts/unsd/gender/intro.htm United Nations statistics and indicators of the world's women.

Odds and Ends

http://aflcio.paywatch.org/ceopay/ceoyou/index.html Executive PayWatch—The CEO and You. A union-sponsored web page that gives you access to the compensation of the CEO of Fortune 500 corporations and its comparison to workers in that corporation.

http://www.culturalbridge.com/cnadd.htm Artifacts from Mao Zedong's "Cultural Revolution" in China.

http://pspmc1.vub.ac.be/Einmag_Abstr/AWRaifu.html An article, "The evolution of complexity: Globalisation and the Evolution of Human Society," by Adesina Wasiu Raifu–Technical University of Budapest.

Technology/History

http://www.supernet.ab.ca/~dfournel/tech2.html Technology time line with links to ancestors/hunting gathering societies, tools, etc.

Various Home Pages

http://www.un.org/ United Nations home page—databases included.

http://chs.ida.org/general/general.shtml Home page of the Central Intelligence Agency—*CIA World Fact Book* link.

http://www.nsf.gov/ The National Science Foundation

http://www.fbi.gov/ FBI Home Page

http://www.sciencemag.org/ Welcome to Science Online, online access to *Science,* the publication of the American Association for the Advancement of Science.

Appendix

Many of the figures and tables for preindustrial societies are based on data from a machine-readable version of George Peter Murdock's *Ethnographic Atlas* (1,267 cases), which originally appeared in installments of *Ethnology* (1962–1971), and a number of original data sets for a standard sample of societies (186 cases) made available by their authors in machine-readable form through the "electronic journal" *World Cultures*.

In most of the tables and figures we report results from analyses of the *Ethnographic Atlas* data because they depict the experience and characteristics of the largest, most extensive "sample" of human societies. To guard against the possibility that the total data set gives a distorted or lopsided picture of human societies, however, all the analyses were recomputed for a subset (734 cases) of the *Ethnographic Atlas* argued to be more "representative" of human societies. In all instances results for this "world sample" were substantially the same as those for the complete *Atlas*.

In those cases where the standard sample data sets contain information not available in the *Atlas*, we report results using them. The "standard sample" was carefully constructed to "represent" the regional, cultural, and developmental diversity of human societies, and as new variables are added, the volume and diversity of data on it continue to grow. This growing body of data greatly extends cross-cultural research possibilities, and strongly complements the *Atlas*. The original sources of data and the variables we used are identified below.

Dominant mode of subsistence was coded according to information on the society's percent dependence on each of five basic modes of subsistence (V1–V5 in the *Atlas*, V203–V207 in the standard sample): (1) hunting, (2) gathering, (3) fishing, (4) animal husbandry, and (5) agriculture; together with information on the presence or absence of metals (V44, V55 in the *Atlas*, V248, V249 in the standard sample), and the presence or absence of the plow (V39 in the *Atlas*, V243 in the standard sample).

After summing the scores for hunting and gathering to produce a composite measure of societal dependence on these two modes of subsistence, we classified societies on the basis of the following criteria:

1. If dependence on hunting and gathering, fishing, or animal husbandry was 6 or greater (more than 56% reliance), that mode was coded as dominant (i.e., the society was coded "hunting and gathering," "fishing," or "herding," respectively).
2. If agriculture was 6 or greater, the plow ABSENT, and metals ABSENT, the society was coded "simple horticultural."
3. If agriculture was 6 or greater, the plow ABSENT, and metals PRESENT, the society was coded "advanced horticultural."
4. If agriculture was 6 or greater, and the plow PRESENT, the society was coded "agrarian."
5. If a dependence score was 4 (36–45%), or 5 (46–55%), and NO OTHER MODE WAS SCORED AS HIGH OR HIGHER, that mode was classified dominant.
6. If no score was 4 or greater, two modes were scored equally high, or if relevant data were missing, the society was coded "other."

372

7. Also, because of their anomalous and hybrid nature, "mounted hunters" (those in which hunting and gathering was dominant, and in which V40 in the *Atlas* or V244 in the standard sample indicated horses were present) were coded "other."

These coding rules produced the following distributions of societal types:

Distribution of Societal Types in Different Data Sets

Societal Type	Ethnographic Atlas		World Sample		Standard Sample	
	N	**%**	**N**	**%**	**N**	**%**
Hunting and gathering	174	21	84	16	27	17
Simple horticultural	155	19	146	27	35	22
Advanced horticultural	246	30	140	26	38	24
Agrarian	103	13	90	17	32	20
Fishing	60	7	38	7	11	7
Herding	78	10	37	7	16	10
Totals	816	100	535	100	159	100

Note: 451 cases from the *Ethnographic Atlas,* 199 from the world sample, and 27 from the standard sample were missing relevant data, or were otherwise not classifiable according to the criteria. It should also be noted that the numerical base for particular tables and figures in the text varies because of missing data on the traits in question.

Data Sources for Tables and Figures

Table 4.2 Median Size: *Ethnographic Atlas,* Political Integration [*World Cultures,* V89].

Table 4.3 Craft Specialization: *Ethnographic Atlas,* Craft Specialization [*World Cultures,* V55–V60].

Figure 4.3 Complex Status Systems: *Ethnographic Atlas,* Class Stratification [*World Cultures,* V65].

Figure 4.4 Belief in a Supreme Creator: *Ethnographic Atlas,* High Gods [*World Cultures,* V34].

Figure 5.3 Leaders' Exercise of Authority, Marc H. Ross, "Political Decision Making and Conflict: Additional Cross-Cultural Codes," *Ethnology* 22 (1983), pp. 169–192 [*World Cultures,* STDS30: V763].

Table 5.3 Community Size: *Ethnographic Atlas,* Mean Size of Local Communities [*World Cultures,* V31].

Table 5.4 Private Ownership of Land: *Ethnographic Atlas,* Inheritance Rule for Real Property [*World Cultures,* V73].

Table 5.5 Emphases in Child-Rearing: Herbert Barry III, Lili Josephson, Edith Lauer, and Catherine Marshall, "Traits Inculcated in Childhood: Cross Cultural Codes 5," *Ethnology,* 15 (1976), pp. 83–114 [*World Cultures,* STDS13: V306–V309, V322–V325].

Table 5.6 Types of Games: *Ethnographic Atlas,* Games [*World Cultures,* V35].

Table 6.1 Population Density: George Peter Murdock and Caterina Provost, "Measurement of Cultural Complexity," *Ethnology,* 12 (1971), pp. 379–392 [World Cultures: STDS06: V156].

Table 6.2 Division of Labor: *Ethnographic Atlas,* Sex Differences in Agriculture [*World Cultures,* V54].

Table 6.3 Matrilineality: *Ethnographic Atlas,* Descent [*World Cultures,* V43].

Figure 6.5 Slavery: *Ethnographic Atlas,* Type of Slavery [*World Cultures,* V69].

Further information on tables and analyses is available from the authors.

Notes

Chapter 1

1 For the importance of an "ecosystem" approach for sociology, see William R. Catton, Jr., "Foundations of Human Ecology," *Sociological Perspectives*, 37 (1994), 75–95, and William R. Catton, Jr., *From Animistic to Naturalistic Sociology* (New York: McGraw-Hill, 1966).

2 Kingsley Davis, *Human Society* (New York: Macmillan, 1949), p. 27. See also Alfred E. Emerson, "Human Cultural Evolution and Its Relation to Organic Evolution of Insect Societies," in Herbert Barringer et al. (eds.), *Social Change in Developing Areas: A Reinterpretation of Evolutionary Theory* (Cambridge, Mass.: Schenkman, 1965), pp. 50–51.

3 Edward O. Wilson, *Sociobiology: The New Synthesis* (Cambridge, Mass.: Belknap, 1975), part III.

4 See, for example, Elizabeth Cashdan, "Hunters and Gatherers: Economic Behavior in Bands," in Stuart Plattner (ed.), *Economic Anthropology* (Stanford, Calif.: Stanford University Press, 1989), pp. 21–48, and *World Almanac and Book of Facts 2002* (New York: World Almanac Books, 2002), pp. 780–781.

5 Wilson, chap. 27; Ian Tattersall, *The Human Odyssey: Four Million Years of Human Evolution* (New York: Prentice-Hall, 1993), chap. 4; Monroe Strickberger, *Evolution* (Boston: Jones and Bartlett, 1990), chap. 19; Donald Johanson and James Shreeve, *Lucy's Child: The Discovery of a Human Ancestor* (New York: Morrow, 1989), chap. 9; Alexandra Maryanski and Jonathan H. Turner, *The Social Cage: Human Nature and the Evolution of Society* (Stanford, Calif.: Stanford University Press, 1992).

6 This definition is a slightly modified version of that provided by W. H. Thorpe, *Learning and Instinct in Animals,* 2d ed. (Cambridge, Mass.: Harvard University Press, 1963), p. 55. See also Zick Rubin, Letitia Anne Peplau, and Peter Salovey, *Psychology* (Boston: Houghton-Mifflin, 1993), pp. 109–110.

7 Wilson, pp. 151–152.

8 Sherwood L. Washburn and David A. Hamburg, "The Implications of Primate Research," in Irven DeVore (ed.), *Primate Behavior: Field Studies of Monkeys and Apes* (New York: Holt, 1965), p. 613.

9 Nicholas Wade, "Insight into Human-Chimp Differences," *New York Times,* April 12, 2002; Nicholas Wade, "Researchers Say Gene Is Linked to Language," *New York Times,* October 5, 2001; Tattersall, chap. 4; Sherwood Washburn, "The Evolution of Man," *Scientific American,* 239 (September 1978), p. 204; Dorothy Miller, "Evolution of the Primate Chromosomes," *Science,* 198 (Dec. 16, 1977), pp. 1116–1124. See also Mary-Claire King and A. C. Wilson, "Evolution at Two Levels in Humans and Chimpanzees," *Science,* 188 (April 11, 1975), pp. 107–116.

10 This paragraph is based on Wilson, pp. 176–185. See also Steven Pinker, *The Language Instinct: How the Mind Creates Language* (New York: William Morrow, 1994), chap. 11.

11 Karl von Frisch, "Dialect in the Language of the Bees," *Scientific American,* 167 (August 1962), pp. 3–7.

12 Masukazu Konishi, "The Role of Auditory Feedback in the Control of Vocalization in the White-Crowned Sparrow," *Journal of Comparative Ethology,* 22 (1965), pp. 770–783.

13 See, for example, Francine Patterson, "Conversations with a Gorilla," *National Geographic,* 154 (October 1978), pp. 438–466; or Steven Roger Fischer, *A History of Language* (London: Reaktion Books, 1999). For a more skeptical view of the ability of apes to use symbols, see Roger Brown, "Why Are Signal Languages Easier to Learn Than Spoken Languages? Part Two,"

Bulletin of the American Academy of Arts and Sciences, 32 (December 1978), pp. 38–39; Martin Gardner, *Science: Good, Bad, and Bogus* (Buffalo, N.Y.: Prometheus, 1981), pp. 391–408; Joel Wallman, *Aping Language* (Cambridge: Cambridge University Press, 1992). Pinker, op. cit., and James Trefil, *Are We Unique? A Scientist Explores the Unparalleled Intelligence of the Human Mind* (New York: Wiley, 1997), chaps. 3 and 4.

14 Ian Tattersall, *The Monkey in the Mirror: Essays in the Science of What Makes Us Human* (New York: Harcourt, 2002); John E. Pfeiffer, *The Emergence of Man,* 2d ed. (New York: Harper & Row, 1972), p. 381, citing Jane van Lawick-Goodall as authority; see also Robbins Burling, "Primate Calls, Human Language, and Nonverbal Communication," *Current Anthropology,* 34 (February 1993), pp. 25–33.

15 C. M. Matthews, *Words Words Words* (London: Lutterford, 1979), p. 138.

16 Helen Keller, *The Story of My Life* (New York: Doubleday, 1903).

17 Robert Lord, *Comparative Linguistics,* 2d ed. (London: English Universities Press, 1974), pp. 288–289.

18 For a good summary of these developments, see Marvin Harris, *The Rise of Anthropological Theory* (New York: Crowell, 1968), chap. 2.

19 For a good review of the early history of social research, see Bernard Lecuyer and Anthony Oberschall, "Sociology: The Early History of Social Research," in *International Encyclopedia of the Social Sciences* (New York: Macmillan and Free Press, 1968), vol. 15, pp. 36–53.

20 For pioneering statements of the new ecological-evolutionary approach, see O. D. Duncan, "Social Organization and the Ecosystem," in R. E. L. Faris (ed.), *Handbook of Modern Sociology* (Chicago: Rand McNally, 1964), pp. 39–45; and Walter Goldschmidt, *Man's Way: A Preface to the Understanding of Human Society* (New York: Holt, 1959). See also Marvin Harris, *Cultural Materialism: The Struggle for a Science of Culture* (New York: Random House, 1979) for a more recent statement.

Chapter 2

1 Anatol Rapaport, "Systems Analysis: General Systems Theory," *International Encyclopedia of the Social Sciences* (New York: Macmillan and Free Press, 1968), vol. 15, p. 454.

2 Francis Thompson, "The Mistress of Vision," *Selected Poems of Francis Thompson* (London: Burns Oates & Washbourne and Jonathan Cape, 1908).

3 Chandler Burr, "Homosexuality and Biology," *The Atlantic Monthly* (March 1993), pp. 47–65; Bruce Bower, "The Birth of Schizophrenia: A Debilitating Mental Disorder May Take Root in the Fetal Brain," *Science News,* 143 (May 29, 1993), pp. 346–347; and for a critique of some oversimplifications and errors, see John Horgan, "Eugenics Revisited," *Scientific American,* 268 (June 1993), pp. 122–131.

4 John Locke, *An Essay Concerning Human Understanding* (New York: Dover, 1959, first published 1690).

5 Steven Pinker, *The Blank Slate: The Modern Denial of Human Nature* (New York: Viking, 2002); Reinhold Niebuhr, *The Nature and Destiny of Man* (New York: Scribner, 1943), vol. 1; Robert Heilbroner, *An Inquiry into the Human Prospect* (New York: Norton, 1991), chap. 4; and Jan Szczepański, *Polish Society* (New York: Random House, 1970), p. 100 and chap. 9.

6 Stephen Jay Gould, "Human Babies as Embryos," *Natural History,* 85 (February 1976), p. 22ff.

7 Stephen Jay Gould, *Ever Since Darwin* (New York: Norton, 1977), pp. 63–69.

8 Theodosius Dobzhansky, *Mankind Evolving* (New York: Bantam, 1962), pp. 224–225; and John E. Pfeiffer, *The Emergence of Man,* 2d ed. (New York: Harper & Row, 1972), chap. 18.

9 Rene A. Spitz, "Hospitalism," *The Psychoanalytic Study of the Child,* 1 (1945), pp. 53–72, and "Hospitalism: A Follow-up Report," *The Psychoanalytic Study of the Child,* 2 (1946), pp. 113–117; and Boris Cyrulnik, *The Dawn of Meaning* (New York: McGraw-Hill, 1993), pp. 82–86 and pp. 95–96.

10 Pfeiffer, pp. 429–430, and Carl Sagan, *The Dragons of Eden* (New York: Ballantine Books, 1977), pp. 47–48.

11 George Kingsley Zipf, *Human Behavior and the Principle of Least Effort: An Introduction to Human Ecology* (New York: Hafner, 1965, first published 1949).

12 Helena Curtis, *Biology,* 2d ed. (New York: Worth, 1975), pp. 717–720; and Pinker, *The Language Instinct.*

13 Noam Chomsky, *Syntactic Structures* (The Hague: Mouton, 1957); *Aspects of the Theory of Syntax* (Cambridge, Mass.: MIT Press, 1965); and *Cartesian Linguistics* (New York: Harper & Row, 1966); Pinker, *The Language Instinct*; and Nicholas Wade, "Researchers Say Gene Is Linked to Language," *New York Times,* October 5, 2001.

14 Melvin Konner, *The Tangled Wing: Biological Constraints on the Human Spirit* (New York: Holt, Rinehart and Winston, 1982), pp. 147–151.

15 For a more detailed discussion of this subject, see Gerhard Lenski, *Power and Privilege* (New York: McGraw-Hill, 1966), pp. 25–32.

16 William Graham Sumner, *Folkways* (New York: Mentor, 1960, first published 1906), p. 32.

17 J. S. Weiner, *The Natural History of Man* (Garden City, N.Y.: Doubleday Anchor, 1973), p. 170.

18 Theodosius Dobzhansky, Francisco Ayala, G. Ledyard Stebbins, and James Valentine, *Evolution* (San Francisco: Freeman, 1977), chap. 5.

19 For discussions of the relation between human physique and climate, see Theodosius Dobzhansky, *Mankind Evolving* (New York: Bantam, 1962), p. 287ff; Weiner, p. 160ff.; E. Adamson Hoebel, *Anthropology: The Study of Man,* 3d ed. (New York: McGraw-Hill, 1966), p. 214ff; and B. J. Williams, *Evolution and Human Origins: An Introduction to Physical Anthropology* (New York: Harper & Row, 1973), chap. 13.

20 Weiner, pp. 153 and 167; and L. Luca Cavalli-Sforza, Paolo Menozzi, and Alberto Piazza, *The History and Geography of Human Genes* (Princeton, N.J.: Princeton University Press, 1994).

21 Dobzhansky, Ayala, et al., p. 148. Randolph Nesse, "When Bad Genes Happen to Good People," *Technology Review* (May/June 1995), pp. 30–40.

22 Dobzhansky, p. 158ff.

23 Paul R. Ehrlich and Richard W. Holm, *The Process of Evolution* (New York: McGraw-Hill, 1963), fig. 11.1, p. 253.

24 Cavalli-Sforza et al., op. cit.

25 Fred Blumenthal, "The Man in the Middle of the Peace Talks," *Washington Post,* July 14, 1968.

26 Richard Lederer, *Anguished English: An Anthology of Accidental Assaults upon Our Language* (New York: Dell, 1987), p. 138.

27 Curtis, p. 159.

28 Hoebel, p. 35.

29 Laura Martin, "'Eskimo Words for Snow': A Case Study in the Genesis and Decay of an Anthropological Example," *American Anthropologist,* 88 (1986), pp. 418–423.

30 Karl G. Heider, *The Dugum Dani: A Papuan Culture in the Highlands of West New Guinea* (New York: Wenner-Gren Foundation, 1970), pp. 32–33.

31 Hoebel, p. 35.

32 Robert Lord, *Comparative Linguistics,* 2d ed. (London: English Universities Press, 1974), p. 316. For other interesting examples of changes in the meanings of words, see Charlton Laird, *The Miracle of Language* (Greenwich, Conn.: Premier Books, 1953), p. 54ff.

33 For an excellent discussion of the differences between human communication with signals and symbols, see Robbins Burling, "Primate Calls, Human Language, and Nonverbal Communication," *Current Anthropology,* 34 (February 1993), pp. 25–53; and Terrence W. Deacon, *The Symbolic Species: The Co-Evolution of Language and the Brain* (New York: Norton, 1997).

34 V. Gordon Childe, *Man Makes Himself* (New York: Mentor, 1951), p. 144ff; Joannie M. Schrof, "From Tax Audits to Poetry," *U.S. News & World Report* (Nov. 5, 1990), p. 70; and Denise Schmandt-Besserat, *Before Writing: From Counting to Cuneiform* (Austin, Texas: University of Texas Press, 1992), p. 1.

35 This view of ideology borrows from Talcott Parsons's thesis that the prime function of religion is making sense out of the totality of human experience. If the term "religion" is defined to include nontheistic faiths (as we do in this volume), religion in the historic western sense becomes one form of ideology. See Parsons, *The Structure of Social Action* (New York: Free Press, 1968), vol. 2, pp. 566–567, 667–668, and 717.

36 See, for example, Robert S. Merrill, "Technology: The Study of Technology," *International Encyclopedia of the Social Sciences,* vol. 15, p. 576.

37 Ralph H. Turner, "Role: Sociological Analysis," *International Encyclopedia of the Social Sciences,* vol. 13, pp. 552–557.

38 For example, see Donald J. Treiman, *Occupational Prestige in Comparative Perspective* (New York: Academic Press, 1977).

39 For a more extended discussion of strata and classes, see Lenski, pp. 73–82.

40 James K. Feibleman, *The Institutions of Society* (London: G. Allen, 1956), p. 52.

Chapter 3

1 For an early statement of this distinction, see F. Stuart Chapin, *Cultural Change* (New York: Century, 1928), p. 345.

2 A. L. Kroeber, *Anthropology* (New York: Harcourt, Brace, 1948), pp. 353–355. For other examples, see Howard A. Rush, "Right Time and Place: Many Medical Discoveries Found to Result from Series of Accidents," *New York Times,* June 8, 1969; Irving Page, "A Sense of the History of Discovery," *Science,* Dec. 27, 1974, p. 1161; and Vern Riportella, "Fifty Years of Radio Astronomy," *Science News,* 123 (Apr. 30, 1983), p. 283.

3 Glynn Isaac, "The Food-Sharing Behavior of Protohuman Hominids," *Scientific American,* 238 (April 1978), pp. 90–108.

4 For an early statement of this principle, see William F. Ogburn, *Social Change* (New York: Viking, 1922), chap. 6.

5 William F. Ogburn and Dorothy S. Thomas, "Are Inventions Inevitable? A Note on Social Evolution," *Political Science Quarterly,* 37 (March 1922), pp. 83–98.

6 Ogburn mentioned this factor briefly, but did not stress it. (1950 edition, p. 110).

7 Basil Davidson with F. K. Buah, *A History of West Africa* (Garden City, N.Y.: Doubleday Anchor, 1966), pp. 8–9; William H. McNeill, *Plagues and Peoples* (Garden City, N.Y.: Doubleday Anchor, 1976).

8 Ralph Linton, *The Study of Man* (New York: Appleton-Century, 1936), pp. 326–327. Reprinted by permission of Prentice-Hall, Inc.

9 For example, see Richard Wilkinson, *Poverty and Progress: An Ecological Perspective on Economic Development* (New York: Praeger, 1973); and Marvin Harris, *Cannibals and Kings: The Origins of Cultures* (New York: Vintage Books, 1977).

10 Ogburn, 1950 edition, p. 107.

11 Rudolf Braun, "Zur Einwirkung soziokulturelle Umweltbedingungen auf das Unternehmverhalten," in Wolfram Fischer (ed.), *Wirtschafts und sozialgeschichtliche Probleme der frnhen Industrialisierung* (Berlin: Colloquium, 1968), p. 257.

12 Hans Zinsser, *Rats, Lice and History* (New York:Little Brown, 1934).

13 Robert Carneiro, "Political Expansion as an Expression of the Principle of Competitive Exclusion," in Ronald Cohen and Elman Service (eds.), *Origins of the State* (Philadelphia: Institute for the Study of Human Issues, 1978), pp. 205–223.

14 F. G. Bailey, *Tribe, Caste, and Nation* (Manchester: Manchester University Press, 1960).

15 O. D. Duncan, "Social Organization and the Ecosystem," in R. E. L. Faris (ed.), *Handbook of Modern Sociology* (Chicago: Rand McNally, 1964), pp. 37–39. See also Leslie White, *The Science of Culture* (New York: Grove, 1949), pp. 363–393.

16 See William F. Cottrell, *Energy and Society* (New York: McGraw-Hill, 1955), p. 2, for a somewhat similar assertion concerning energy's impact on human life.

17 Robert Carneiro, "On the Relationship between Size of Population and Complexity of Social Organization," *Southwestern Journal of Anthropology,* 23 (1967), pp. 234–243.

18 Ernest Gellner, *Plow, Sword and Book: The Structure of Human History* (Chicago: University of Chicago Press, 1989).

19 Robert S. Gottfried, *The Black Death: Natural and Human Disaster in Medieval Europe* (New York: Free Press, 1983), chap. 7.

20 Donald T. Campbell, "On the Conflicts between Biological and Social Evolution and between Psychology and Moral Tradition," *American Psychologist,* 30 (December 1975), pp. 1103–1126.

21 See, for example, Ernst Mayr, *The Growth of Biological Thought: Diversity, Evolution, and Inheritance* (Cambridge, Mass.: Belknap, 1982), chap. 8.

22 Thorstein Veblen, *Imperial Germany and the Industrial Revolution* (New York: Macmillan, 1915); Elman Service, "The Law of Evolutionary Potential," in Marshall Sahlins and Elman Service (eds.), *Evolution and Culture* (Ann Arbor: University of Michigan Press, 1960), pp. 93–122; see also Patrick D. Nolan, and Gerhard Lenski, "Techno-Economic Heritage, Patterns of Development, and the Advantage of Backwardness," *Social Forces,* 64 (1985), pp. 341–358.

Chapter 4

1 See Marvin Harris, *The Rise of Anthropological Theory* (New York: Thomas Y. Crowell, 1968), chap. 2; and Robert Nisbet, *Social Change and History* (New York: Oxford, 1969), chap. 4.

2 This method of classification is an expansion and modification of one developed earlier by Walter Goldschmidt in *Man's Way: A Preface to the Understanding of Human Society* (New York: Holt, 1959), chap. 6, and also reflects the influence of V. Gordon Childe, *Man Makes Himself* (New York: Mentor Books, 1951).

3 See, for example, R. F. Watters, "The Nature of Shifting Cultivation: A Review of Recent Research," *Pacific Viewpoint,* 1 (1960), pp. 59–99.

4 See Jacquetta Hawkes, *Prehistory: UNESCO History of Mankind* (New York: Mentor Books, 1965), chap. 6, for a good summary of archaeological finds relating to fishing. See also Grahame Clark and Stuart Piggott, *Prehistoric Societies* (New York: Knopf, 1965), chap. 7.

5 Bernadette Arnaud, "First Farmers," *Archaeology,* November/December 2000, pp. 56–59; Robert J. Wenke, *Patterns in Prehistory: Humankind's First Three Million Years* (New York: Oxford University Press, 1990), chap. 6; Robert Braidwood, "The Earliest Village Communities of Southwest Asia Reconsidered," and Karl Butzer, "Agricultural Origins in the Near East as a Geographical Problem," in Stuart Struever (ed.), *Prehistoric Agriculture* (Garden City, N.Y.: Natural History Press, 1971), pp. 222 and 249.

6 James Mellaart, *Earliest Civilizations in the Near East* (London: Thames and Hudson, 1965), p. 105; and R. J. Forbes, *Studies in Ancient Technology* (Leiden: Brill, 1971–1972), vols. 8 and 9.

7 See, for example, Leslie Aitchison, *A History of Metals* (London: MacDonald, 1960), vol. 1, p. 41; and Forbes, op. cit.

8 E. Cecil Curwen and Gudmund Hatt, *Plough and Pasture: The Early History of Farming* (New York: Collier Books, 1961), p. 64.

9 Aitchison, pp. 102 and 111–113; and Forbes, vol. 9, chap. 3.

10 Mellaart, p. 20; and Wenke, chap. 6.

11 Wenke, p. 240.

12   William H. McNeill, *The Rise of the West: A History of the Human Community* (New York: Mentor Books, 1965), p. 150.

13   See Appendix, pp. 372–374, for details concerning our use of these data.

14   Goldschmidt, p. 115.

15   This method of classifying religious beliefs is based on work by G. E. Swanson in *The Birth of the Gods: The Origin of Primitive Beliefs* (Ann Arbor: University of Michigan Press, 1960), chap. 3. For some proposed explanations of why such beliefs would vary across societies, see Emile Durkheim, *The Elementary Forms of the Religious Life* (New York: Free Press, 1965); Swanson, op. cit.; and John Simpson, "Sovereign Groups, Subsistence Technology, and the Presence of a High God in Primitive Societies," in R. Wuthnow (ed.), *The Religious Dimension in Quantitative Research* (New York: Academic Press, 1979), pp. 299–310.

16   Leslie White was the leading proponent of this point of view for many years. See, for example, his stimulating but extreme essay, "Energy and the Evolution of Culture," in *The Science of Culture* (New York: Grove Press, 1949), pp. 363–393.

17   Talcott Parsons is one of many who have consistently minimized the role of technology in the process of social change. Though not as extreme as some in his views, he was very influential. See *Societies: Evolutionary and Comparative Perspectives* (Englewood Cliffs, N.J.: Prentice-Hall, 1966), especially pp. 113–114, for his views.

Chapter 5

1   John A. J. Gowlett, *Ascent to Civilization: The Archaeology of Early Man* (New York: Knopf, 1984), p. 11.

2   Johan Goudsblom, *Fire and Civilization* (New York: Penguin, 1992), p. 1.

3   Goudsblom, chap. 2.

4   Marvin Harris, *Culture, People, Nature,* 3d ed. (New York: Harper & Row, 1980), p. 128; and Pfeiffer, p. 150ff.

5   John Noble Wilford, "When Humans Became Human," *New York Times,* February 26, 2002; *U.S. News & World Report,* "The Dawn of Creativity," May 20, 1996.

6   H. V. Vallois, "The Social Life of Early Man: The Evidence of Skeletons," in Sherwood Washburn (ed.), *Social Life of Early Man* (Chicago: Aldine, 1961), pp. 214–235.

7   S. A. Semenov, *Prehistoric Technology,* trans. M. W. Thompson (New York: Barnes & Noble, 1964), pp. 202–203.

8   E. Adamson Hoebel, *Anthropology,* 3d ed. (New York: McGraw-Hill, 1966), pp. 176–177; and Jacquetta Hawkes, *Prehistory: UNESCO History of Mankind,* vol. 1, part 1 (New York: Mentor Books, 1965), pp. 212–213.

9   This and the following statements concerning the bow and arrow are based on Semenov, pp. 202–204.

10   Hawkes, p. 212.

11   J. G. D. Clark, *Prehistoric Europe: The Economic Basis* (London: Methuen, 1952), pp. 132–133.

12   Hawkes, pp. 184–188; and John L. Pfeiffer, *The Emergence of Man,* 3d ed., p. 192.

13   Peter Ucko and Andrée Rosenfeld, *Paleolithic Cave Art* (New York: McGraw-Hill, 1967); or Grahame Clark, *The Stone Age Hunters,* chap. 4.

14   Grahame Clark and Stuart Piggott, *Prehistoric Societies* (New York: Knopf, 1965), pp. 93–95.

15   Hawkes, pp. 293–294, including fig. 35b.

16   Sherwood Washburn, "The Evolution of Man," *Scientific American,* 239 (September 1978), p. 206.

17   L. J. Angel, "Paleoecology, Paleodemography and Health," in Steven Polgar (ed.), *Population, Ecology and Social Evolution* (The Hague: Mouton, 1975), table 1, pp. 182–183.

18   Fekri Hassan, *Demographic Archaeology* (New York: Academic Press, 1981), chap. 12.

19 For summaries of work on hunters and gatherers, see Richard Lee and Irven DeVore (eds.), *Man the Hunter* (Chicago: Aldine, 1968); Carleton S. Coon, *The Hunting Peoples* (Boston: Little, Brown, 1971); and Elman Service, *The Hunters* (Englewood Cliffs, N.J.: Prentice-Hall, 1966).

20 This figure is based on Elkin's estimate that there were approximately 300,000 aborigines in Australia at the time of the first white settlement. This estimate was divided by 60, a very generous estimate for the average size of these societies. See A. P. Elkin, *The Australian Aborigines,* 3d ed. (Sydney: Angus and Robertson, 1954), p. 10.

21 Our calculations are based on twenty-seven societies in Murdock's data set.

22 See Table 4.2 of this volume.

23 Gertrude E. Dole, "The Development of Patterns of Kinship Nomenclature" (Ph.D. dissertation, University of Michigan, 1957), p. 26, found an average life expectancy at birth in very primitive societies of only 22 years and also found that individuals who live to age 50 are rare. Allan Holmberg, *Nomads of the Long Bow: The Siriono of Eastern Bolivia,* Smithsonian Institution, Institute of Social Anthropology, 10 (Washington, D.C., 1950), p. 85, reported that the average life span among the Siriono was only 35 to 40 years even among those who survived infancy.

24 Gina Bara Kolata, "!Kung Hunter-Gatherers: Feminism, Diet, and Birth Control," *Science,* 185 (Sept. 13, 1974), p. 934.

25 Nancy Howell, "Feedback and Buffers in Relation to Scarcity and Abundance: Studies of Hunter-Gatherer Populations," in David Coleman and Roger Schofield (eds.), *The State of Population* (New York: Basil Blackwell, 1986), pp. 156–187.

26 William Divale, "Systemic Population Control in the Middle and Upper Paleolithic: Inferences Based on Contemporary Hunters and Gatherers," *World Archaeology,* 4 (1972), fig. 11, p. 230; and John Whiting, "Effects of Climate on Certain Cultural Practices," in Ward Goodenough (ed.), *Explorations in Cultural Anthropology: Essays in Honor of George Peter Murdock* (New York: McGraw-Hill, 1964), table 9, pp. 528–533.

27 Don Dumond, "The Limitations of Human Population: A Natural History," *Science,* 187 (Feb. 28, 1975), p. 715.

28 Kolata, op. cit.

29 See, for example, John Garvan, *The Negritos of the Philippines* (Vienna: Ferdinand Berger, 1964), p. 27; or Edwin Loeb, *Sumatra: Its History and People* (Vienna: Institut für Volkerkunde, 1935), p. 283, on the Kubu.

30 Only one of the seventeen nonnomadic hunting and gathering societies in Murdock's data set depended on hunting and gathering for more than three-quarters of its subsistence, whereas three-quarters of the 150 nomadic hunting and gathering societies were in this category. The one exception among the nonnomadic societies (the Nomlaki) was located in the Sacramento Valley of northern California, a territory as favorable for a hunting and gathering people as any in the world (see Baumhoff, pp. 205–231).

31 Colin Turnbull, "The Mbuti Pygmies of the Congo," in James Gibbs (ed.), *Peoples of Africa* (New York: Holt, 1965), pp. 286–287.

32 James Woodburn, "Ecology, Nomadic Movement and the Composition of the Local Group among Hunters and Gatherers: An East African Example and Its Implications," in Peter J. Ucko, Ruth Tringham, and G. W. Dimbleby (eds.), *Man, Settlement and Urbanism* (London: Duckworth, 1972), p. 201ff.

33 Lorna Marshall, "The !Kung Bushmen of the Kalahari Desert," in James Gibbs (ed.), *Peoples of Africa* (New York: Holt, 1965), pp. 243–278.

34 Richard B. Lee, "Work Effort, Group Structure and Land-Use in Contemporary Hunter-Gatherers," in Ucko et al., pp. 181–184.

35 A. R. Radcliffe-Brown, "The Social Organization of Australian Tribes," *Oceania,* 1 (1930), pp. 44–46.

36   Elkin, p. 56 (Doubleday Anchor edition).

37   Service, *The Hunters,* p. 32ff. For some exceptions, see Colin Turnbull, *Wayward Servants, The Two Worlds of the African Pygmies* (Garden City, N.Y.: Natural History Press, 1965), pp. 109–112.

38   George Peter Murdock, *Social Structure* (New York: Free Press, 1949), chap. 1.

39   See, for example, Elkin, p. 50; Ivor Evans, *The Negritos of Malaya* (London: Cambridge, 1937), p. 254; and Garvan, p. 82.

40   Service, p. 42.

41   David Aberle, "Matrilineal Descent in Cross-Cultural Perspective," in D. Schneider and K. Gough (eds.), *Matrilineal Kinship* (Berkeley: University of California Press, 1961), p. 677; or Burton Pasternak, *Introduction to Kinship and Social Organization* (Englewood Cliffs, N.J.: Prentice-Hall, 1976), pp. 111–112.

42   Elman Service, *Primitive Social Organization: An Evolutionary Perspective* (New York: Random House, 1962), chap. 3, especially p. 61.

43   See, for example, Elkin, pp. 134–137.

44   Lorna Marshall, in Gibbs, pp. 257–258. Quoted by permission of Holt, Rinehart and Winston, Inc. See also Charles Hose and William McDougall, *The Pagan Tribes of Borneo* (London: Macmillan, 1912), pp. 190–191; Holmberg, p. 11; or Loeb, p. 300.

45   See, for example, Walter Goldschmidt, *Nomlaki Ethnography,* University of California Publications in American Archaeology and Ethnology, 42 (Berkeley, 1951), pp. 333–335 and 417–428.

46   See, for example, Loeb, p. 294, or Holmberg, pp. 30 and 91.

47   Turnbull, pp. 287 and 297; Frederick McCarthy and Margaret McArthur, "The Food Quest and the Time Factor in Aboriginal Economic Life," in Charles Mountford (ed.), *Records of the American-Australian Expedition to Arnhem Land* (Melbourne: Melbourne University Press, 1960), pp. 190–191; Kenneth MacLeish, "The Tasadays: Stone Age Cavemen of Mindanao," *National Geographic,* 142 (August 1972), pp. 243–245; Richard B. Lee, "What Hunters Do for a Living, or How to Make Out on Scarce Resources," in Lee and DeVore, pp. 36–37.

48   See Marshall Sahlins, "Notes on the Original Affluent Society," in Lee and DeVore, pp. 85–89.

49   Goldschmidt, p. 417. See also Asen Balicki, "The Netsilik Eskimos: Adaptive Responses," and the comments of Lorna Marshall and Colin Turnbull, in Lee and DeVore, pp. 78–82, 94, and 341, for challenges to the effort to portray life in hunting and gathering societies as idyllic and trouble-free.

50   Lee and DeVore, op. cit.

51   See, for example, Lee, p. 40.

52   Coon, *The Hunting Peoples,* p. 176.

53   In the hunting and gathering societies in Murdock's data set, hunting was entirely a male activity in 96 percent of the cases and predominantly a male activity in the rest. On the other hand, gathering was wholly or largely a female activity in 87 percent of the societies and predominantly a male activity in only 4 percent (in the remainder the activity was shared by both sexes).

54   Of the hunting and gathering societies in Murdock's data set, 53 percent defined this as a male responsibility, 26 percent as a female responsibility, and 21 percent as appropriate to both sexes.

55   I. Schapera, *Government and Politics in Tribal Societies* (London: Watts, 1956), p. 93. See also Holmberg's description of the Siriono headman quoted on p. 94 of this volume, and Hose and McDougall, p. 190, on the Punan shaman. Other specialists, much less common, may include part-time workers in certain arts and crafts and occasionally an assistant to the headman. Such individuals are most likely to be found in settled communities that depend less than totally on hunting and gathering or in those with especially favorable environments. See, for example, Goldschmidt, pp. 331–332, and Elkin, p. 254ff.

56 See, for example, Turnbull, pp. 287–288; Evans, pp. 57 and 112–113; Garvan, p. 66; or Hose and McDougall, p. 191. Turnbull warns, however, that many scholars exaggerate the dependence of the Pygmies on the neighboring horticultural villagers. He maintains that they turn to the villagers only for luxuries and diversion. See *Wayward Servants,* pp. 33–37.

57 Gerhard Lenski, *Power and Privilege* (New York: McGraw-Hill, 1966), pp. 95–96.

58 Occasionally there might be a second official. See, for example, Kaj Birket-Smith, *The Eskimos,* rev. ed. (London: Methuen, 1959), p. 145; Goldschmidt, pp. 324–325; and Frank Speck, *Penobscot Man* (Philadelphia: University of Pennsylvania Press, 1940), pp. 239–240.

59 Holmberg, pp. 59–60. Quoted by permission of the Smithsonian Institution Press. Following an older usage, Holmberg referred to the leaders of Siriono bands as "chiefs." In current usage, such persons are usually referred to as "headmen," and the term "chief" is reserved for the leaders of multicommunity societies. For this reason, the term "headman" has been substituted.

60 See, for example, John Cooper, "The Ona," in Julian Steward (ed.), *Handbook of South American Indians,* Smithsonian Institution, Bureau of American Ethnology, Bulletin 143 (Washington, D.C., 1946), vol. 1, p. 117; A. R. Radcliffe-Brown, *The Andaman Islanders* (Glencoe, Ill.: Free Press, 1948), p. 47; Hose and McDougall, p. 182, on the Punan of Borneo; Speck, p. 239, on the Penobscot of Maine; I. Schapera, *The Khoisan Peoples of South Africa* (London: Routledge, 1930), p. 151; and Roland Dixon, "The Northern Maidu," in Carleton S. Coon (ed.), *A Reader in General Anthropology* (New York: Holt, 1948), p. 272.

61 I. Schapera, *Government and Politics,* p. 117. Quoted by permission of C. A. Watts & Co., Ltd. See also A. H. Gayton, *Yokuts-Mono Chiefs and Shamans,* University of California Publications in American Archaeology and Ethnology, 24 (Berkeley, 1930), pp. 374–376.

62 See, for example, Colin Turnbull, *Wayward Servants,* chaps. 11 and 12, or *The Forest People* (New York: Simon & Schuster, 1961), on the Mbuti Pygmies. As he indicates, the office of headman is sometimes found among these people, but it has been more or less forced on them by the Bantu villagers and is of little significance except in their contacts with these villagers.

63 See, for example, Schapera, *Government and Politics,* p. 193, or Turnbull, *Wayward Servants,* pp. 100–109.

64 See John Honigmann, *The Kaska Indians: An Ethnographic Reconstruction,* Yale University Publications in Anthropology, 51 (1954), pp. 90–92 and 96–97; Radcliffe-Brown, *The Andaman Islanders,* pp. 48–52; and Schapera, *The Khoisan Peoples,* pp. 151–155.

65 Schapera, *The Khoisan Peoples,* p. 152.

66 Radcliffe-Brown, *The Andaman Islanders,* p. 50.

67 Schapera, *The Khoisan Peoples,* p. 152.

68 See, for example, Evans, p. 21; Marshall, "!Kung Bushmen," p. 248; or Radcliffe-Brown, p. 29. For an exception, see Birket-Smith, pp. 145–146. For intermediate cases, see Honigmann, pp. 84, 88, and 96; Elkin, p. 45; and H. Ling Roth, *The Aborigines of Tasmania* (London: Kegan Paul, Trench, Trubner, 1890), p. 71.

69 Sometimes certain trees become the private property of an individual who stakes a special claim to them, but this is uncommon and the number of trees involved is generally small. See, for example, Radcliffe-Brown, *The Andaman Islanders,* p. 41, or Goldschmidt, p. 333.

70 See, for example, McCarthy and McArthur, "The Food Quest and the Time Factor in Aboriginal Economic Life," pp. 179–180; Schapera, *The Khoisan Peoples,* pp. 100–101; Radcliffe-Brown, *The Andaman Islanders,* p. 43; Hose and McDougall, p. 187; or Speck, p. 47.

71 Radcliffe-Brown, *The Andaman Islanders,* pp. 44–48.

72 See, for example, Goldschmidt, pp. 324–326.

73 Among the sample of hunting and gathering societies in Murdock's data set, 53 percent had provision for the hereditary transmission of the office, usually to a son of the previous headman.

74 William D. Davis, *Societal Complexity and the Sources of Primitive Man's Conception of the Supernatural* (unpublished Ph.D. dissertation, University of North Carolina, Chapel Hill, 1971), chap. 5. Davis reports such beliefs in all but one of the eleven hunting and gathering societies he studied. See also Service, *The Hunters,* pp. 68–70.

75 For descriptions of shamans and their practices, see Evans, chaps. 19–20; Coon, *The Hunting Peoples,* chap. 16; Honigmann, pp. 104–108; Schapera, *The Khoisan Peoples,* pp. 195–201; Radcliffe-Brown, *The Andaman Islanders,* pp. 175–179; Elkin, chap. 11; or Gayton, pp. 392–398.

76 See, for example, Dixon, p. 282.

77 Dixon, p. 272.

78 Jacob Baegert, S. J., "Account of the Aboriginal Inhabitants of the California Peninsula," in Coon (ed.), *A Reader in General Anthropology,* p. 79. See also Radcliffe-Brown, *The Andaman Islanders,* p. 177.

79 See, for example, Elkin, chap. 7; Marshall, "!Kung Bushmen," pp. 264–267; Turnbull, "The Mbuti Pygmies," pp. 306–307; or Coon, *The Hunting Peoples,* chap. 14.

80 Herbert Barry III, Irving L. Child, and Margaret K. Bacon, "Relation of Child Training to Subsistence Economy," *American Anthropologist,* 61 (1959), p. 263. See also Michael R. Welch, "Subsistence Economy and Sociological Patterns: An Examination of Selected Aspects of Child Training Processes in Preindustrial Societies" (Ph.D. dissertation, University of North Carolina, Chapel Hill, 1980).

81 Some of the best evidence of religious motivation comes from Australia (see Elkin, pp. 191–192, or 232–234). For an example of art employed as an instrument of sympathetic magic, see Evans, p. 130ff.

82 For example see Keith A. Roberts, *Religion in Sociological Perspective* (Homewood, Ill.: Dorsey Press, 1984), pp. 67–72.

83 Turnbull, "The Mbuti Pygmies," pp. 308–312, *The Forest People,* chap. 4; and *Wayward Servants,* pp. 259–267.

84 See, for example, Hose and McDougall, p. 192, and Speck, p. 270ff.

85 Turnbull, *The Forest People,* p. 135.

86 This definition is based on Hoebel, *Anthropology,* p. 572; and Elkin, *The Australian Aborigines,* p. 25.

87 Examples are provided by the Punan of Borneo (Hose and McDougall, p. 183) and the Mbuti Pygmies of Africa (Turnbull, *Wayward Servants,* pp. 100–109).

88 Schapera, *The Khoisan Peoples,* p. 76. Quoted by permission of Routledge & Kegan Paul, Ltd.

89 See, for example, Goldschmidt, p. 324.

90 For similar comparisons, see Grahame Clark, *The Stone Age Hunters,* chap. 4; and Pfeiffer, *The Emergence of Man.*

91 See, for example, Clark and Piggott, *Prehistoric Societies,* p. 130ff; or Hole and Heizer, *An Introduction to Prehistoric Archeology* (New York: Holt, 1965), pp. 225–226.

92 See "Kalahari Conservatives," *Science News,* 140 (Dec. 14, 1991), p. 398.

93 Orlando Lizama, "Death of Woman Marked Tribe's End: First Seen by Magellan," *Washington Post,* Aug. 17, 1975.

94 Marshall, p. 273.

95 Kolata, p. 932.

96 Sources used in this excursus include: Donald Johanson and Blake Edgar, *From Lucy to Language* (New York: Simon and Schuster, 1996); Ian Tattersall, "Out of Africa Again . . . and Again?" *Scientific American* (April 1997); Ian Tattersall, *The Human Odyssey: Four Million Years of Human Evolution* (New York: Prentice-Hall, 1993); Maeve Leakey and Alan Walker, "Early Hominid Fossils from Africa," *Scientific American* (June 1997); Alan Thorne and Milford Wolpoff, "The Multiregional Evolution of Humans," *Scientific American* (April 1992); Allan

Wilson and Rebecca Cann, "The Recent African Genesis of Humans," *Scientific American* (April 1992); "Spanish Fossils Enter Human Ancestry Fray," *Science News* (May 31, 1997); "African Fossil Pushes Back Human Ancestry," *Science News* (Nov. 30, 1996); "Kenyan Fossils Unveil New Hominid Species," *Science News* (Aug. 19, 1995); "Team Unearths Oldest Known Human Ancestor," *Science News* (Oct. 1, 1994); "Homo Erectus Shows Staying Power on Java," *Science News* (Dec. 14, 1996); Robert Kunzig, "Atapuerca: The Face of an Ancestral Child," *Discover* (December 1997); John Noble Wilford "In Ancient Skulls from Ethiopia, Familiar Faces," *New York Times,* June 12, 2003; John Noble Wilford, "Fossils May Be Earliest Human Link," *New York Times,* July 12, 2001; Nicholas Wade, "Dating of Australian Remains Backs Theory of Early Migration of Humans," *New York Times,* Feb. 19, 2003; Nicholas Wade, "DNA Tests Cast Doubt on Link between Neanderthals and Modern Man," *New York Times,* March 29, 2000; Reuters, "New Weight for View Africa Was Human Cradle," *New York Times,* Dec. 7, 2000.

Chapter 6

1 Robert J. Wenke, *Patterns in Prehistory: Humankind's First Three Million Years* (New York: Oxford University Press, 1990), chap. 6.

2 Wenke, pp. 261–269; for example, see Marvin Harris, *Cannibals and Kings: The Origins of Cultures* (New York: Vintage Books, 1978); Brian Hayden, "Research and Development in the Stone Age: Technological Transitions among Hunters-Gatherers", *Current Anthropology,* 22 (1981), pp. 519–548; Mark Cohen, *The Food Crisis in Prehistory* (New Haven: Yale University Press, 1977).

3 H. E. Wright, "The Environmental Setting for Plant Domestication in the Near East," *Science,* 194 (1976), pp. 385–89; cited in Wenke, p. 235.

4 Wenke, chap. 6, and John Wilford, "The Seeds of History: A Find in Mexico," *The New York Times,* May 9, 1997.

5 Kent Flannery, "The Origins of Agriculture," *Annual Review of Anthropology,* 2 (1973), pp. 271–310, p. 307; cited in Wenke, p. 234; Jared Diamond, *Guns, Germs, and Steel* (New York: Norton, 1997), chap. 7.

6 Wenke, chap. 6.

7 Johan Goudsblom, *Fire and Civilization* (New York: Penguin, 1992), pp. 28–33.

8 See Bernadette Arnaud, "First Farmers," *Archaeology,* November/December 2000, pp. 56–59, on recent discoveries in northern Syria dating back to 9600 B.C. For earlier work, see Robert Braidwood and Bruce Howe, "Southwestern Asia beyond the Lands of the Mediterranean Littoral," in Robert Braidwood and Gordon Willey (eds.), *Courses toward Urban Life: Archeological Considerations of Some Cultural Alternatives* (Chicago: Aldine, 1962), pp. 137, 152–153, and 346; James Mellaart, *Earliest Civilizations of the Near East* (London: Thames and Hudson, 1965), pp. 12, 32–38, 47–50, and 81; or Barbara Bender, *Farming in Prehistory* (London: John Baker, 1975), chap. 6; Wenke, pp. 246–249.

9 Braidwood and Howe, p. 140; Mellaart, chap. 3ff.; V. Gordon Childe, "The New Stone Age," in Harry Shapiro (ed.), *Man, Culture, and Society* (New York: Oxford Galaxy, 1960), p. 103; E. Cecil Curwen and Gudmund Hatt, *Plough and Pasture: The Early History of Farming* (New York: Collier Books, 1961), p. 33.

10 Jacquetta Hawkes, *Prehistory: UNESCO History of Mankind,* vol. 1, part 1 (New York: Mentor Books, 1965), pp. 442–452; Mellaart, p. 42; Childe, "The New Stone Age," p. 107.

11 Childe, "The New Stone Age," pp. 100–101.

12 See, for example, Farmer, pp. 204–205; or Curwen and Hatt, p. 68 and chap. 16.

13 V. Gordon Childe, *What Happened in History,* rev. ed. (Baltimore: Penguin, 1964), pp. 64–65.

14 Mellaart, pp. 50–51, or Jean Perrot, "Palestine-Syria-Cilicia," in Braidwood and Willey, pp. 156–157.

15 Hawkes, pp. 384–395; Childe, "The New Stone Age," pp. 104–105; or Perrot, pp. 154–155.

16 Hawkes, pp. 395–401; and Mellaart, pp. 40–42.

17 Mellaart, p. 47; and Bender, pp. 148–149.

18 Childe, "The New Stone Age," p. 105. Elsewhere Childe speaks of twenty-five to thirty-five households as "a not uncommon number" in central Europe and southern Russia. See *What Happened in History,* p. 66.

19 Mellaart, p. 36; or Hawkes, p. 310.

20 Wenke, p. 326.

21 Mellaart, pp. 81–101; W. K. Stevens, "Prehistoric Society: A New Picture Emerges," *New York Times,* Dec. 16, 1986; Wenke, p. 326.

22 See, for example, Childe, "The New Stone Age," p. 106, or *What Happened in History,* pp. 67–68. See also Braidwood and Howe, p. 138.

23 Mellaart, p. 36. See also p. 84 for his views on Çatal Hüyük.

24 Childe, "The New Stone Age," p. 106; Wenke, p. 327.

25 Denise Schmandt-Bessert, "The Earliest Precursor of Writing," *Scientific American,* 238 (January 1978), pp. 50–59.

26 Mellaart, pp. 43–44.

27 See Childe, *What Happened in History,* p. 67.

28 Childe, "The New Stone Age," p. 106, *What Happened in History,* p. 67; and Wenke, chap. 6.

29 For a good review of these developments, see Hawkes, pp. 401–410 and 414–417; or V. Gordon Childe, *Man Makes Himself* (New York: Mentor, 1953), pp. 76–80.

30 Childe, "The New Stone Age," p. 107, or *What Happened in History,* p. 74; and Wenke, pp. 360–361.

31 Karl Heider, *The Dugum Dani: A Papuan Culture in the Highlands of West New Guinea* (New York: Wenner-Gren Foundation, 1970). See also the film *Dead Birds,* based on the same society.

32 Childe, "The New Stone Age," p. 107.

33 For the ethnographic evidence, see Table 4.2, p. 87.

34 A careful comparison of societies in the two eras suggests that modern simple horticulturalists may be a bit less advanced than their prehistoric predecessors. For example, 40 percent of those in Murdock's sample did not make pottery and 60 percent did not engage in weaving, both common practices in simple horticultural societies of prehistoric times.

35 See Kwang-chih Chang, *The Archaeology of Ancient China* (New Haven: Yale University Press, 1963), pp. 130–131. See also Curwen and Hatt, pp. 16–18, on truths contained in ancient traditions.

36 The quotations in this paragraph are all from Chang, pp. 131–133, and are used by permission of the Yale University Press.

37 Our calculation is based on Murdock's data set.

38 See, for example, Julian Steward and Louis Faron, *Native Peoples of South America* (New York: McGraw-Hill, 1959), p. 300, with reference to villagers who occupied most of the northern half of South America, that "kinship was the basis of society throughout most of this area." Many similar statements could be cited.

39 See E. Adamson Hoebel, *Anthropology,* 3d ed. (New York: McGraw-Hill, 1966), pp. 374–376, for a good, brief summary of these functions.

40 For similar findings based on Murdock's earlier sample of 565 societies, see David Aberle, "Matrilineal Descent in Cross-cultural Perspective," in David Schneider and Kathleen Gough (eds.), *Matrilineal Kinship* (Berkeley: University of California Press, 1961), table 17.4, p. 677.

41 The first interpretation is suggested by Aberle, p. 725; he states that "in general, matriliny is associated with horticulture, in the absence of major activities carried on and coordinated by males." See also Janet Saltzman Chafetz, *Sex and Advantage* (Totowa, N.J.: Rowman & Allenheld, 1984), pp. 42–43. The latter interpretation is suggested by Harris, *Cannibals and Kings,* chap. 6; and Charles S. Green, personal communication.

42 This dual role seems to have been quite common in South America. See Julian Steward and Louis Faron, *Native Peoples of South America* (New York: McGraw-Hill, 1959), p. 301, on the Indians of eastern Brazil and the Amazon Basin; or Julian Steward, "The Tribes of the Montaña and Bolivian East Andes," in Julian Steward (ed.), *Handbook of South American Indians,* Smithsonian Institution, Bureau of American Ethnology, Bulletin 143 (Washington, 1948), vol. III, p. 528. For a slightly different pattern in North America, see Irving Goldman, "The Zuni Indians of New Mexico," in Margaret Mead (ed.), *Cooperation and Competition among Primitive Peoples,* rev. ed. (Boston: Beacon Press, 1961), p. 313.

43 Robert Lowie, "Social and Political Organization," in Steward, *Handbook,* vol. V, p. 345. For examples of this, see Steward, *Handbook,* vol. III, pp. 85, 355, 419, and 478. See also Steward and Faron, p. 244.

44 See, for example, Alfred Métraux, *Native Tribes of Eastern Bolivia and Western Matto Grosso,* Smithsonian Institution, Bureau of American Ethnology, Bulletin 134 (Washington, 1942), p. 39, on the Araona; or Leopold Pospisil, "Kaupauku Papuan Political Structure," in F. Ray (ed.), *Systems of Political Control and Bureaucracy in Human Societies,* Proceedings of the 1958 Meetings of the American Ethnological Society (Seattle), p. 18.

45 For a more detailed discussion of these bases of status, see Gerhard Lenski, *Power and Privilege* (Chapel Hill: University of North Carolina Press, 1984, originally published 1966), pp. 126–131.

46 See Steward and Faron, pp. 302–303, on the former, and pp. 213–214, 243, and 248–249, on the latter.

47 Marvin Harris, *Cows, Pigs, Wars, and Witches: The Riddles of Culture* (New York: Random House, 1974), pp. 75–80.

48 William Divale, "Systemic Population Control in the Middle and Upper Paleolithic," *World Archaeology,* 4 (1972), fig. 9, p. 228.

49 Data provided by Leo Simmons, *The Role of the Aged in Primitive Society* (New Haven: Yale University Press, 1945), show that scalp taking or headhunting was a frequent practice in only one of five hunting and gathering societies but in thirteen of fourteen horticultural societies.

50 Alfred Métraux, "Warfare-Cannibalism-Trophies," in Steward, *Handbook,* vol. V, pp. 400–401. Quoted by permission of the Bureau of American Ethnology.

51 Colin Renfrew, *Before Civilization* (Cambridge: Cambridge University Press, 1979), p. 167; and Renfrew and Bahn, p. 296.

52 R. J. Forbes, *Studies in Ancient Technology,* 2d ed. (Leiden, Netherlands: Brill, 1972), vol. 9, p. 30; or Leslie Aitchison, *A History of Metals* (London: MacDonald, 1960), vol. 1, p. 21.

53 Forbes, pp. 32–34; or Aitchison, p. 40.

54 Aitchison, p. 40; Forbes, vol. 8, p. 26; or Ronald Wallace, *Those Who Vanished* (Homewood, Ill.: Dorsey, 1983), pp. 294–295.

55 Childe, *Man Makes Himself,* p. 99.

56 V. Gordon Childe, *The Bronze Age* (London: Cambridge, 1930), p. 11.

57 See, for example, Childe, *New Light,* p. 116. There is still some uncertainty about this point.

58 William Watson, *The Chinese Exhibition* (a guide to the exhibition of archaeological finds of the People's Republic of China, exhibited in Toronto, 1974), p. 14.

59 Renfrew and Bahn, p. 296.

60 Some bronze seems to have been manufactured accidentally a few centuries earlier as a result of using copper derived from ores containing tin, but the deliberate and conscious alloying of metals did not begin in the Middle East until after 3000 B.C. See Forbes, vol. 9, pp.

151–152. Recent research by scholars at the University of Pennsylvania suggests that the invention of bronze may have occurred in Thailand prior to 3600 B.C., which would explain why bronze was an integral part of advanced horticultural societies in China, but not in the Middle East.

61   William Watson, *China: Before the Han Dynasty* (New York: Praeger, 1961), p. 57.

62   Te-k'un Cheng, *Archaeology in China: Shang China* (Cambridge, England: Heffer, 1960), pp. 206–207.

63   Shang kings, for example, mounted "many military expeditions with an army of between 3,000 and 5,000 men." Cheng, p. 210; and Cho-yun Hsu, *Ancient China in Transition* (Stanford, Calif.: Stanford University Press, 1965), p. 67.

64   See note 58 above.

65   Cheng, pp. 200–206.

66   Cheng, pp. 200–215 and 248. For a more detailed picture of the system of stratification in the Chou era, see Hsu, *Ancient China in Transition*. In reading this book one must keep in mind that the Chan Kuo period, the "period of the warring states," is included, and by then, north-central China seems to have reached the agrarian level of development.

67   Watson, *China: Before the Han Dynasty,* p. 141, and Chang, p. 195ff.

68   Aitchison, p. 97.

69   Hsu, pp. 3–7 and chap. 4.

70   Chang, p. 150.

71   Watson, *China: Before the Han Dynasty,* p. 106. See also Hsu, p. 15ff., on the interrelations between religion and politics in Chou China.

72   Chang, pp. 150 and 159.

73   Ibid., p. 171.

74   Sonia Cole, *The Prehistory of East Africa* (New York: Mentor, 1965), pp. 46 and 299–301.

75   Meyer Fortes, in Meyer Fortes and E. E. Pritchard (eds.), *African Political Systems* (London: Oxford, 1940) p. 5.

76   In one study of twenty-two African horticultural societies, a correlation of 0.67 (Kendall's tau) was found between level of political development and level of social inequality (see Lenski, p. 163). See also Basil Davidson with F. K. Buah, *A History of West Africa: To the Nineteenth Century* (Garden City, N.Y.: Doubleday Anchor, 1966), p. 174.

77   See Lucy Mair, *Primitive Government* (Baltimore: Penguin, 1962), especially chap. 4. The discussion that follows is based largely on her work. See also Lenski, chaps. 6 and 7; Morton Fried, *The Evolution of Political Society* (New York: Random House, 1967); and Elman Service, *Origins of the State and Civilizations: The Process of Cultural Evolution* (New York: Norton, 1975).

78   Estimated from the map in Davidson, p. 68.

79   I. Schapera, *Government and Politics in Tribal Societies* (London: Watts, 1956), p. 169. See also the Swazi proverb that "nobles are the chief's murderers."

80   See, for example, Davidson, chap. 14.

81   See, for example, George Peter Murdock, *Africa: Its Peoples and Their Culture History* (New York: McGraw-Hill, 1959), p. 37.

82   See, for example, P. C. Lloyd, "The Yoruba of Nigeria," in James Gibbs (ed.), *Peoples of Africa* (New York: Holt, 1965), pp. 554–556.

83   For an example of a multicommunity society, see P. R. T. Gurdon, *The Khasis* (London: Macmillan, 1914). This author reports that these people were divided into fifteen small states averaging 15,000 in population and controlling about 400 square miles apiece (pp. 1 and 66).

84   Lenski, pp. 160–162. See also Davidson, pp. 76–77.

85   Paul Ricon, "Date Limit Set on First Americans," *BBC Science,* Aug. 5, 2003; John Noble Wilford, "New Answers to an Old Question: Who Got Here First?" *New York Times,* Nov. 9, 1999; Brian Fagan, *The Journey From Eden: The Peopling of Our World* (New York: Thames and Hudson, 1990), chap. 15.

86   This view is reinforced by recent archaeological finds revealing the progressive evolution of maize, beans, and other crops from wild, uncultivated forms to the cultivated forms found today. See Marvin Harris, *People, Culture, Nature,* 3d ed. (New York: Harper & Row, 1980), p. 165; Wallace, p. 218ff; or Wenke, pp. 251–259.

87   For a valuable survey of these developments, see Harris, chap. 10; for an extended survey of the three most highly developed cultures of the New World, the Aztecs, Mayas, and Incas, see Victor von Hagen, *The Ancient Sun Kingdoms of the Americas* (Cleveland: World, 1961). See also William Sanders and David Webster, "The Mesoamerican Urban Tradition," *American Anthropologist,* 90 (1988), pp. 521–546; and Norman Hammond, *Ancient Maya Civilization* (New Brunswick, N.J.: Rutgers University Press, 1982).

88   Renfrew and Bahn, pp. 300–301.

89   See Stephen Williams, *Fantastic Archaeology: The Wild Side of North American Prehistory* (Philadelphia: University of Pennsylvania Press, 1991), but for an alternative view, see Stephen C. Jett, "Precolumbian Transoceanic Contact," in Jesse D. Jennings (ed.), *Ancient North Americans* (San Francisco: W. H. Freeman, 1983), pp. 593–650.

90   Marvin Harris, *The Rise of Anthropological Theory* (New York: Crowell, 1968), p. 4.

91   Wenke, pp. 279, 477, 519–520.

92   Harris, p. 4. Emphasis added.

93   Remy Chauvin, *The World of Ants: A Science Fiction Universe* (New York: Hill and Wang, 1970); Erich Hoyt, *The Earth Dwellers: Advenures in the Land of Ants* (New York: Simon and Schuster, 1996); Caryl P. Haskins, *Of Ants and Men* (London: Allen and Unwin, 1943); Edward O. Wilson, *Sociobiology: The New Synthesis* (Cambridge, Mass.: Harvard University Press, 1975); and George Oster and Edward O. Wilson, *Caste and Ecology in the Social Insects* (Princeton, N.J.: Princeton University Press, 1978).

94   See, for example, the writings of Count Joseph A. deGobineau or Houston Stewart Chamberlain.

95   See, for example, Charles Singer, "Epilogue: East and West," in Charles Singer (ed.), *A History of Technology* (Oxford: Clarendon Press, 1956), vol. II, pp. 754–772; or William H. McNeill, *The Rise of the West* (Chicago: University of Chicago Press, 1963), parts I and II.

96   Renfrew and Bahn, p. 305.

97   Robert W. Steel, "Africa: Natural Resources," in *Encyclopaedia Britannica,* vol. 1, p. 258; Philip L. Wagner, "Tropical Agriculture," *Encylopaedia Britannica,* vol. 22, p. 255; Andrew Kamark, "The Resources of Tropical Africa," *Daedalus,* III (Spring 1982), p. 159; Andrew Kamark, *The Tropics and Economic Development* (Baltimore: Johns Hopkins University Press, 1976); and Frederic Pryor, "The Invention of the Plow," *Comparative Studies in Society and History,* 27 (1985), pp. 727–743.

98   William H. McNeill, *Plagues and Peoples* (Garden City, N.Y.: Doubleday Anchor, 1976); Kamark, "Resources," pp. 159–160; Matt Clark, "Blight of the Tropics," *Newsweek,* June 26, 1978, pp. 83–84; Paul Harrison, *Inside the Third World* (Harmondsworth, England: Penguin, 1982), chap. 16; and Erik Eckholm, "River Blindness," *The New York Times Magazine,* Jan. 8, 1989, p. 20ff.

Chapter 7

1   V. Gordon Childe, *What Happened in History* (Baltimore: Penguin, 1964), p. 77.

2   Childe, *What Happened in History,* chap. 4.

3   This paragraph and the one that follows are based on B. H. Farmer, "Agriculture: Comparative Technology," in *International Encyclopedia of the Social Sciences* (New York: Macmillan and Free Press, 1968), vol. 1, pp. 204–205.

4   Robert J. Wenke, *Patterns in Prehistory: Humankind's First Three Million Years* (New York: Oxford University Press, 1990), p. 373.

5   See Gudmund Hatt, "Farming of Non-European Peoples," in E. Cecil Curwen and Gudmund Hatt, *Plough and Pasture: The Early History of Farming* (New York: Collier Books, 1961), pp. 217–218.

6   Childe, *What Happened in History,* p. 89.

7   V. Gordon Childe, *Man Makes Himself* (New York: Mentor Books, 1951), p. 100.

8   Farmer, p. 205.

9   E. Cecil Curwen, "Prehistoric Farming of Europe and the Near East," in Curwen and Hatt, pp. 64–65; or C. W. Bishop, "The Origin and Early Diffusion of the Traction Plow," *Antiquity,* 10 (1936), p. 261.

10   Denise Schmandt-Besserat, *Before Writing: From Counting to Cuneiform* (Austin, Tex.: University of Texas Press, 1992), especially pp. 1–34, and pp. 195–199.

11   Wenke, chaps. 13 and 14.

12   Samuel Noah Kramer, *The Sumerians* (Chicago: University of Chicago Press, 1963), p. 123.

13   Childe, *Man Makes Himself,* pp. 143–144.

14   See, for example, Sir Leonard Woolley, *The Beginnings of Civilization, UNESCO History of Mankind,* vol. 1, part 2 (New York: Mentor Books, 1965), pp. 116, 119, 198, and 449ff.

15   Sir Leonard Woolley, *Prehistory* (New York: Harper & Row, 1963), vol. 1, part 2, p. 127.

16   Margaret Murray, *The Splendour That Was Egypt* (London: Sidgwick & Jackson, 1949), p. 174.

17   On Mesopotamia, see Woolley, *Beginnings,* p. 356; or A. Leo Oppenheim, *Ancient Mesopotamia: Portrait of a Dead Civilization* (Chicago: University of Chicago Press, 1964), pp. 84–85. On Egypt, see Ralph Turner, *The Great Cultural Traditions: The Foundations of Civilization* (New York: McGraw-Hill, 1941), vol. 1, p. 187; or George Steindorff and Keith Seele, *When Egypt Ruled the East,* rev. ed. (Chicago: Phoenix Books, 1963), p. 83.

18   Robert Adams, "Factors Influencing the Rise of Civilization in the Alluvium: Illustrated by Mesopotamia," in Carl Kraeling and Robert Adams (eds.), *City Invincible: A Symposium on Urbanization and Cultural Development in the Ancient Near East* (Chicago: University of Chicago Press, 1960), p. 33.

19   Wenke, pp. 338–345.

20   See, for example, Kramer, pp. 88–89; Woolley, p. 125; or Kingsley Davis, "The Origin and Growth of World Urbanism," *American Journal of Sociology,* 60 (1955), p. 431. See also Oppenheim, p. 140, who, though declining to estimate size, reports Nineveh to have been larger than Ur (generally thought to have been over 100,000) and Uruk nearly as large; or Mason Hammond, *The City in the Ancient World* (Cambridge, Mass.: Harvard, 1972).

21   Woolley, *Beginnings,* p. 185ff; or Steindorf and Seele, pp. 89–90.

22   Woolley, *Beginnings,* p. 188. Later armies were even larger.

23   Turner, p. 312.

24   McNeill, p. 68; Turner, pp. 310–311; Steindorff and Seele, chap. 9; Pierre Montet, *Everyday Life in Egypt: In the Days of Ramesses the Great,* trans. A. R. Maxwell-Hyslop and Margaret Drower (London: E. Arnold, 1958), chap. 10; Oppenheim, pp. 70ff., 230ff., and 276–277.

25   Oppenheim, p. 276. As one writer reports, "Sumerian bureaucracy has left us a staggering number of texts; we are unable to venture a guess as to how many tablets beyond the far more than 100,000 now in museums may be buried in southern Mesopotamia."

26   Childe, *Man Makes Himself,* pp. 148–149, or Childe, *What Happened in History,* p. 144.

27   See especially Kramer, p. 231, or Samuel Noah Kramer, *It Happened at Sumer* (Garden City, N.Y.: Doubleday, 1959), p. 3.

28   See Turner, p. 263, or Childe, *What Happened in History,* p. 118.

29   Childe, *What Happened in History,* pp. 118–119.

30   See Turner's excellent treatment of this topic, pp. 317–323.

31   Adolf Erman, *Life in Ancient Egypt,* trans. H. M. Tirard (London: Macmillan, 1894), p. 128.

32   Childe, *Man Makes Himself*, p. 180, quoted by permission of C. A. Watts & Co. See also McNeill, p. 53, or Childe, *What Happened in History*, p. 183ff.

33   *Man Makes Himself*, p. 181. Elsewhere, Childe adds a third innovation (or a fifth to the total list), the invention of glass in Egypt. See *What Happened in History*, p. 183.

34   See Childe, *Man Makes Himself*, chap. 9, for a classic discussion of this subject. The analysis that follows is heavily indebted to Childe's provocative discussion but varies in some details and emphasis.

35   See Childe, *What Happened in History*, p. 184.

36   For a classic statement of this principle, see Gaetano Mosca, *The Ruling Class*, translated by Hannah Kahn (New York: McGraw-Hill, 1939), p. 53.

37   For a good summary of the early history of iron, see Leslie Aitchison, *A History of Metals* (London: MacDonald, 1960), vol. 1, pp. 97–110. The discussion that follows is based largely on Aitchison.

38   Aitchison, p. 113.

39   See, for example, Charles Singer's comparison of the level of technology in the ancient empires of Egypt and Mesopotamia prior to 1000 B.C. and later in Greece and Rome, in "Epilogue: East and West in Retrospect," in Charles Singer (ed.), *A History of Technology* (Oxford: Clarendon Press, 1956), vol. II, pp. 754–755.

40   Singer, pp. 754–772.

41   This estimate was based on the known boundaries of these societies and on the fact that the Roman Empire, which was much larger and contained a much smaller percentage of uninhabitable land, had a maximum population of only about 70 million. See *The Cambridge Ancient History* (London: Cambridge, 1939), vol. XII, pp. 267–268. It is also noteworthy that in Roman times Egypt had a population of only 6 to 7 million. Even if allowance is made for the greater size of the Egyptian empire in the days of Egypt's independence, it is difficult to imagine a total population much in excess of 15 million. See Charles Issawi, *Egypt in Revolution: An Economic Analysis* (New York: Oxford, 1963), p. 20.

42   Chung-li Chang, *The Chinese Gentry: Studies on Their Role in Nineteenth-Century Chinese Society* (Seattle: University of Washington Press, 1955), p. 102.

43   On India, see Kingsley Davis, *The Population of India and Pakistan* (Princeton, N.J.: Princeton University Press, 1951), pp. 24–25; on Rome, see *The Cambridge Ancient History*, pp. 267–268, or *UNESCO, History of World Population Growth*, p. 15; on Russia, see Blum, p. 278.

44   See, for example, Tertius Chandler and Gerald Fox, *3000 Years of Urban Growth* (New York: Academic Press, 1974).

45   Warren Thompson and David Lewis, *Population Problems*, 5th ed. (New York: McGraw-Hill, 1965), p. 386; O. Andrew Collver, *Birth Rates in Latin America: New Estimates of Historical Trends and Fluctuations* (Berkeley, Calif.: Institute of International Studies, 1965), pp. 26–30; D. V. Glass and D. E. C. Eversley, *Population in History* (Chicago: Aldine, 1965), pp. 467, 532, 555, and 614. One of the lowest rates for an agrarian society prior to the twentieth century was for eighteenth-century Sweden, and it was nearly 36 per 1,000 (Glass and Eversley, p. 532).

46   See, for example, Horace Miner, *St. Denis: A French-Canadian Parish* (Chicago: Phoenix Books, University of Chicago Press, 1963), p. 65; G. G. Coulton, *The Medieval Village* (Cambridge: Cambridge University Press, 1926), p. 322; Manning Nash, *The Golden Road to Modernity: Village Life in Contemporary Burma* (New York: Wiley, 1965), pp. 265–266.

47   See, for example, John Noss, *Man's Religions*, rev. ed. (New York: Macmillan, 1956), pp. 227, 304ff., and 420–421; and *Miner*, pp. 65–66.

48   John Boswell, *The Kindness of Strangers: The Abandonment of Children in Western Europe from Late Antiquity to the Renaissance* (New York: Pantheon, 1989).

49   Harrison Brown, *The Challenge of Man's Future* (New York: Viking Compass, 1956), p. 75.

50   H. Hollingsworth, "A Demographic Study of the British Ducal Families," in Glass and Eversley, tables 2 and 5, pp. 358 and 360.

51   Brown, p. 75.

52   Warren Thompson, *Population Problems,* 3d ed. (New York: McGraw-Hill, 1942), p. 73.

53   M. C. Buer, *Health, Wealth, and Population in the Early Days of the Industrial Revolution, 1760–1815* (London: Routledge, 1926), pp. 77–78. Quoted by permission of Routledge & Kegan Paul, Ltd.

54   D. E. C. Eversley, "Population, Economy, and Society," in Glass and Eversley, p. 52; and William H. McNeill, *Plagues and Peoples* (Garden City, N.Y.: Doubleday Anchor, 1976).

55   Robert S. Gottfried, *The Black Death* (New York: Free Press, 1983), p. xiii.

56   K. F. Helleiner, "The Vital Revolution Reconsidered," in Glass and Eversley, p. 79.

57   Turner, p. 911.

58   F. R. Cowell, *Cicero and the Roman Republic* (London: Penguin, 1956), p. 79. Quoted by permission of Penguin Books.

59   See, for example, Jerome Blum, *Lord and Peasant in Russia from the Ninth to the Nineteenth Century* (Princeton, N.J.: Princeton University Press, 1961), pp. 126 and 394–395, on Russia; or Ralph Linton, *The Tree of Culture* (New York: Vintage Books, 1959), p. 231, on China.

60   S. B. Clough and C. W. Cole, *Economic History of Europe* (Boston: Heath, 1941), p. 25.

61   Ibid. See also Blum, pp. 16 and 126.

62   Marc Bloch, *Feudal Society,* trans. L. A. Manyon (Chicago: University of Chicago Press, 1962), p. 192. See also Robert Heilbroner, *The Making of Economic Society* (Englewood Cliffs, N.J.: Prentice-Hall, 1962), p. 27; H. R. Trevor-Roper, "The Gentry 1540–1640," *The Economic History Review Supplements,* no. 1 (n.d.).

63   Heilbroner, pp. 9–44.

64   A. H. M. Jones, *The Later Roman Empire 284–602: A Social, Economic and Administrative Survey* (Oxford: Blackwell, 1964), vol. 1, p. 465.

65   Gerhard Lenski and Jean Lenski, *Human Societies,* 4th ed. (New York: McGraw-Hill, 1982), table 7.2, p. 190.

66   Blum, pp. 356–357.

67   Gideon Sjoberg, *The Preindustrial City* (New York: Free Press, 1960), p. 215.

68   See, for example, Chung-li Chang, *Income of the Chinese Gentry* (Seattle: University of Washington Press, 1962), pp. 37–51.

69   For a survey of these obligations, see Gerhard Lenski, *Power and Privilege* (New York: McGraw-Hill, 1966), pp. 267–270.

70   Ibid., p. 228.

71   See, for example, Blum, p. 232, or W. H. Moreland, *The Agrarian System of Moslem India* (Allahabad, India: Central Book Depot, n.d.), p. 207.

72   George Sansom, *A History of Japan* (Stanford, Calif.: Stanford Press, 1963), vol. III, p. 29.

73   H. S. Bennett, *Life on the English Manor: A Study of Peasant Conditions, 1150–1400* (London: Cambridge, 1960), pp. 232–236.

74   Robert Darnton, *The Great Cat Massacre and Other Episodes in French Cultural History* (New York: Basic Books, 1984), p. 24. Quoted by permission of the publisher.

75   Ibid., p. 29.

76   Robert K. Douglas, *Society in China* (London: Innes, 1894), p. 354.

77   Blum, pp. 424 and 428, on Russia; and Gunnar Myrdal, *An American Dilemma* (New York: McGraw-Hill, 1964), p. 931, on the American South.

78   See Coulton, pp. 80 and 464–469; Blum, pp. 426–427; G. M. Carstairs, "A Village in Rajasthan," in M. N. Srnivas (ed.), *India's Villages* (Calcutta: West Bengal Government Press, 1955), pp. 37–38.

79   Bennett, p. 196; Coulton, pp. 190–191, 248–250, and 437–440.

80 G. G. Coulton, *Medieval Panorama* (New York: Meridian Books, 1955), p. 77, or Thompson, p. 708.

81 William Stubbs, *The Constitutional History of England* (Oxford: Clarendon Press, 1891), vol. 1, p. 454n.; Wolfram Eberhard, *A History of China,* 2d ed. (Berkeley: University of California Press, 1960), p. 32; and Yosoburo Takekoshi, *The Economic Aspects of the History of the Civilization of Japan* (New York: Macmillan, 1930), vol. 1, pp. 60–63.

82 See A. E. R. Boak, *A History of Rome to 565 A.D.,* 3d ed. (New York: MacMillan, 1943), p. 127, or Cowell, *Cicero and the Roman Republic,* p. 64. For an example of the application of Cato's principle in medieval Europe, see Bennett, p. 283.

83 See, for example, Bloch, p. 337; or George Homans, *English Villagers of the Thirteenth Century* (Cambridge, Mass.: Harvard, 1942), p. 229.

84 See, for example, Morton Fried, *The Fabric of Chinese Society: Study of the Social Life of a Chinese County Seat* (New York: Praeger, 1953), pp. 104–105; Moreland, pp. 168 and 207; and Bennett, pp. 100–101, 112–113, and 131ff.

85 See, for example, the franklins in thirteenth-century England (Homans, pp. 248–250).

86 May McKisack, *The Fourteenth Century* (Oxford: Clarendon Press, 1959), pp. 331–340; Philip Lindsay and Reg Groves, *The Peasants' Revolt, 1381* (London: Hutchinson, n.d.), pp. 30, 34, and 63; Charles Langlois, "History," in Arthur Tilley (ed.), *Medieval France* (London: Cambridge, 1922), pp. 150–151; and Paul Murray Kendall, *The Yorkist Age* (Garden City, N.Y.: Doubleday, 1962), p. 171ff.

87 Sjoberg, p. 83; Lynn White, *Medieval Technology and Social Change* (Oxford: Clarendon Press, 1962), p. 39; Henri Pirenne, *Economic and Social History of Medieval Europe* (New York: Harvest Books, n.d., first published 1933), p. 58; J. C. Russell, *British Medieval Population* (Albuquerque: University of New Mexico Press, 1948), p. 305; Blum, pp. 268 and 281.

88 See Sjoberg, pp. 108–116; or Samuel G. Stoney, *Plantations of the Carolina Low Country* (Charleston: Carolina Art Association, 1938), p. 36.

89 Kendall, p. 157.

90 Jerome Carcopino, *Daily Life in Ancient Rome* (New Haven: Yale University Press, 1940, p. 70).

91 See, for example, Sjoberg, p. 183ff. For an interesting example of the persistence of this pattern into the latter part of the nineteenth century in England, see W. Somerset Maugham, *Cakes and Ale* (New York: Pocket Books, 1944), p. 29.

92 On acquisition by marriage, see Elinor Barber, *The Bourgeoisie in Eighteenth Century France* (Princeton, N.J.: Princeton University Press, 1955), p. 89; or Sansom, vol. III, pp. 128–129. On confiscation, see B. B. Misra, *The Indian Middle Classes* (London: Oxford, 1961), pp. 25–27; Takekoshi, vol. II, p. 251ff.; Kendall, p. 181; or Sir James Ramsay, *A History of the Revenues of the Kings of England: 1066–1399* (Oxford: Clarendon Press, 1925), vol. I. p. 58.

93 Clough and Cole, p. 442.

94 John Lossing Buck, *Secretariat Paper, No. 1, Tenth Conference of the Institute of Pacific Relations* (Stratford on Avon, 1947), reprinted in Irwin T. Sanders et al., *Societies around the World* (New York: Dryden Press, 1953), p. 65.

95 Clough and Cole, p. 445. See also R. J. Unstead, *The Rise of Great Britain: 1688–1837* (London: A. & C. Black, 1978), pp. 97, 81, and 92.

96 See, for example, John Nef, *The Conquest of the Material World* (Chicago: University of Chicago Press, 1964), p. 69.

97 Cowell, p. 80. See also William Woodruff, *Impact of Western Man: A Study of Europe's Role in the World Economy* (New York: St. Martin's, 1966), p. 254.

98 Sylvia Thrupp, *The Merchant Class of Medieval London* (Ann Arbor: Ann Arbor Paperbacks, University of Michigan Press, 1962), p. 9.

99 See, for example, Nef, p. 78.

100 Sidney Gamble, *Peking: A Social Survey* (New York: Doran, 1921), pp. 183–185.

101 Thrupp, pp. 19, 30.

102 Thrupp, pp. 23 and 29–31; James Westfall Thompson, *Economic and Social History of Europe in the Later Middle Ages, 1300–1530* (New York: Century, 1931), p. 398.

103 Gamble, p. 283.

104 In Asia many were sold into prostitution by their parents. See Gamble, p. 253. Many more, in every part of the world, were ignorant country girls seeking work in the city who were trapped by hired procurers, while still others were driven into prostitution by unemployment and lack of funds. See M. Dorothy George, *London Life in the Eighteenth Century* (London: Kegan Paul, Trench, Trubner, 1925), pp. 112–113.

105 See, for example, Frederick Nussbaum, *A History of the Economic Institutions of Modern Europe* (New York: Crofts, 1933); Frank Aydelotte, *Elizabethan Rogues and Vagabonds* (Oxford: Clarendon Press, 1913), p. 4; or A. L. Beier, *Masterless Men: The Vagrancy Problem in England 1560–1640* (London: Methuen, 1985), chap. 2.

106 Lenski, pp. 197–198.

107 For the effect of war on the forms of government, see Herbert Spencer, *The Principles of Sociology* (New York: Appleton, 1897), vol. II, part 5, chap. 17; Pitirim Sorokin, *Social and Cultural Dynamics* (New York: Bedminster Press, 1962), vol. III, pp. 196–198; or Stanislaw Andrzejewski, *Military Organization and Society* (London: Routledge, 1954), pp. 92–95.

108 These figures were calculated from A. E. R. Boak, *A History of Rome* using the list of emperors from Harold Mattingly, *Roman Imperial Civilization* (New York: Doubleday Anchor, 1959), pp. 351–355.

109 For figures on several other societies, see Lenski, p. 235.

110 The discussion of conflict in agrarian societies and the importance of commercialization is based on Lenski, chaps. 8–9; and John H. Kautsky, *The Politics of Aristocratic Empires* (Chapel Hill, N.C.: University of North Carolina Press, 1982), especially chaps. 12 and 13.

111 Wolfram Eberhard, *Conquerors and Rulers: Social Forces in Medieval China* (Leiden, Netherlands: Brill, 1952), p. 52; and Blum, p. 558.

112 Sorokin, vol. II, chap. 10, especially p. 352. Quincy Wright, *A Study of War* (Chicago: University of Chicago Press, 1965), p. 653, reports wars on average in nearly two-thirds of the years from 1500 to 1699 for five European powers and Turkey.

113 See, among others, Lenski, pp. 210–242 and 266–284, for more detailed documentation.

114 Douglas, p. 104.

115 See Max Weber, *The Theory of Social and Economic Organization,* trans. A. M. Henderson and Talcott Parsons (New York: Free Press, 1947), pp. 341–348; and Max Weber, *Wirtschaft und Gesellschaft,* 2d ed. (Tübingen: Mohr, 1925), vol. II, pp. 679–723.

116 Mattingly, p. 137. See also Turner, vol. II, p. 620, or Michael Rostovtzeff, *The Social and Economic History of the Roman Empire,* rev. ed. (Oxford: Clarendon Press, 1957), p. 54.

117 Hans Rosenberg, *Bureaucracy, Aristocracy, and Autocracy: The Prussian Experience 1660–1815* (Cambridge, Mass.: Harvard University Press, 1958), pp. 5–6. Quoted by permission of Harvard University Press.

118 Chang, *The Income of the Chinese Gentry,* Summary Remarks, supplement 2, and chap. 1.

119 On the king's income, see Ramsay, vol. I, pp. 227 and 261. For the income of the nobility, see Sidney Painter, *Studies in the History of the English Feudal Barony* (Baltimore: Johns Hopkins University Press, 1943), pp. 170–171. For the income of field hands, see Bennett, p. 121.

120 Lenski, pp. 219 and 228.

121 See, for example, Albert Lybyer, *The Government of the Ottoman Empire in the Time of Suleiman the Magnificent* (Cambridge, Mass.: Harvard, 1913); or Moreland, *Agrarian System of Moslem India.*

122 F. Pelsaert, *Jahangir's India,* trans. W. H. Moreland and P. Geyl and quoted by Misra, p. 47. Quoted by permission of W. Heffer & Sons, Ltd.

123 Lybyer, pp. 47–58, and 115–117.

124 See, for example, James Westfall Thompson's statement that "the medieval state was a loose agglomeration of territories with rights of property and sovereignty everywhere shading into one another," in *Economic and Social History of the Middle Ages* (New York: Appleton-Century-Crofts, 1928), p. 699. See also Bloch, especially chaps. 14–24; Blum, chap. 2; or Sidney Painter, *The Rise of the Feudal Monarchies* (Ithaca, N.Y.: Cornell, 1951), and *Studies in the History of the English Feudal Barony.*

125 See Kenneth Scott Latourette, *A History of Christianity* (New York: Harper, 1953), pp. 15–16.

126 See Robert Bellah, "Religious Evolution," *American Sociological Review,* 29 (1964), pp. 367–368.

127 See, for example, Lenski, pp. 7–9. See also Kendall, p. 232ff.

128 Lenski, pp. 257–258.

129 Ibid., pp. 262–266, gives a more detailed treatment of this aspect of religion.

130 J. W. Thompson, *Economic and Social History of the Middle Ages,* p. 684.

131 See, for example, Carlo Levi, *Christ Stopped at Eboli* (New York: Farrar, Straus, 1947), chap. 11ff., for a good description of the role of magic in one agrarian community. On fatalism, see, for example, Edward Banfield, *The Moral Basis of a Backward Society* (New York: Free Press, 1967), pp. 36–37, 41, and 107ff.

132 Sjoberg, p. 146ff.

133 Ibid., p. 155.

134 Ibid., p. 163ff.; Henry Orenstein, *Gaon: Conflict and Cohesion in an Indian Village* (Princeton, N.J.: Princeton University Press, 1965), pp. 53–57; Kendall, chaps. 11 and 12; L. F. Salzman, *English Life in the Middle Ages* (London: Oxford University Press, 1927), pp. 254–256.

135 Bennett, p. 260. For other descriptions of the uses of leisure in agrarian societies, see Margaret Wade Labarge, *A Baronial Household of the Thirteenth Century* (New York: Barnes & Noble, 1966), chap. 10; Bennett, chap. 10; or G. G. Coulton, *Medieval Panorama* (New York: Meridian Books, 1955), chaps. 8 and 44.

136 F. R. Cowell, *Everyday Life in Ancient Rome* (New York: Putnam, 1961), p. 173.

137 The data in this paragraph are drawn from Lenski, p. 212.

138 For further details on the expendables, see Lenski, pp. 281–284.

139 For example, see Barrington Moore, Jr., *Social Origins of Dictatorship and Democracy: Lord and Peasant in the Making of the Modern World* (New York: Beacon Press, 1966); Theda Skocpol, *States and Social Revolutions: A Comparative Analysis of France, Russia, and China* (New York: Cambridge University Press, 1979); Jack Goldstone, *Revolution and Rebellion in the Early Modern World* (Berkeley, Calif.: University of California Press, 1991); and Kautsky.

140 See, for example, H. van Werveke, "The Rise of the Towns," in *The Cambridge Economic History of Europe* (London: Cambridge Press, 1963), vol. 3, pp. 34–37; L. Halphen, "Industry and Commerce," in Tilley, pp. 190–192; or Pirenne, *Economic and Social History of Medieval Europe,* pp. 187–206.

141 Amos H. Hawley, *Human Ecology* (New York: Ronald, 1950), pp. 242 and 387.

142 For important new analyses of the origins of ancient Israel, see Marvin Chaney, "Ancient Palestinian Peasant Movements and the Formation of Premonarchic Israel," in David Freedman and David Grof (eds.), *Palestine in Transition: The Emergence of Ancient Israel* (Sheffield: Almond Press, 1983), pp. 39–90; Norman K. Gottwald, "Two Models for the Origin of Ancient Israel: Social Revolution or Frontier Development," in E. B. Huffmon et al. (eds.), *The Quest for the Kingdom of God: Studies in Honor of G. E. Mendenhall* (Winona Lake, Ind.: Eisenbrauns, 1983), pp. 5–24; and Volkmar Fritz, "Conquest or Settlement? The Early Iron Age in Palestine," *Biblical Archaeologist,* 50 (June 1987), pp. 84–100.

143 See, for example, Richard Tomasson, *Iceland: The First New Society* (Minneapolis: University of Minnesota Press, 1980), chaps. 1 and 8; and Philip Longworth, *The Cossacks* (New York: Holt, Rinehart, 1970).

144   For the classic statement of the effect of frontier life, see Frederick Jackson Turner, *The Frontier in American History* (New York: Holt, 1920).

145   See James G. Leyburn, *Frontier Folkways* (New Haven, Conn.: Yale Press, 1936).

146   Holly Peters-Golden, "The Aztec," *in Culture Sketches: Case Studies in Cultural Anthropology,* 3d ed. (Boston: McGraw-Hill, 2002).

147   Chung-li Chang, *The Chinese Gentry* (Seattle: University of Washington Press, 1955), p. 102; *The Cambridge Ancient History,* pp. 267–268; and Blum, p. 278.

Chapter 8

1   According to Murdock's data, the Manus of New Guinea come as close to full dependence on fishing as any people in the world. See *Ethnology,* vol. 6, no. 2 (April 1967), pp. 170–230. Yet, as Margaret Mead indicates in her report, these people also depend heavily for their subsistence on garden products that they obtain through trade from neighboring peoples and to a lesser degree on pigs that they raise or obtain through trade. See Margaret Mead, *Growing up in New Guinea* (New York: Mentor Books, 1953, first published 1930), especially pp. 173–174.

2   For an earlier discussion of this point, see Gordon Hewes's excellent paper, "The Rubric 'Fishing and Fisheries,'" *American Anthropologist,* 50 (1948), pp. 241–242.

3   Our calculation from Murdock data, see appendix pages 419–421.

4   See Hewes, pp. 240–241.

5   For an interesting account of one such group, see Wilmond Menard, "The Sea Gypsies of China," *Natural History,* 64 (January 1965), pp. 13–21.

6   See, for example, Lawrence Krader, "Pastoralism," in *International Encyclopedia of the Social Sciences* (New York: Macmillan and Free Press, 1968), vol. II, pp. 456–457; or Carleton Coon, "The Nomads," in Sydney Fisher (ed.), *Social Forces in the Middle East* (Ithaca, N.Y.: Cornell University Press, 1955), pp. 23–42.

7   John L. Myres, "Nomadism," *Journal of the Royal Anthropological Institute,* 71 (1941), p. 20.

8   Krader reports that the average density of population in Mongolia was less than 1 per square mile, and among the Tuareg of Africa it was even lower ("Pastoralism," pp. 458–459).

9   It is found in 61 percent of these societies compared to 2 to 35 percent of other types.

10   This is found in 88 percent of these societies, compared to 37 to 82 percent of other types.

11   This requirement occurs in 97 percent of herding societies, compared to 72 to 87 percent of other types.

12   See William McNeill, *The Rise of the West: A History of the Human Community* (New York: Mentor Books, 1965), p. 126ff.; or Ralph Turner, *The Great Cultural Traditions* (New York: McGraw-Hill, 1941), p. 259.

13   For a good discussion of this important subject, see McNeill, p. 256ff.

14   McNeill, p. 111.

15   Charles Boxer, *The Dutch Seaborne Empire, 1600–1800* (London: Hutchison, 1965); and Peter Burke, *Venice and Amsterdam: A Study of Seventeenth Century Elites* (London: Temple Smith, 1974).

16   On the less familiar Carthaginian empire, see Donald Harden, *The Phoenicians* (New York: Praeger, 1963), chaps. 5 and 6. The British empire, it might be noted, was also an overseas empire.

17   The Netherlands changed from a republic to a monarchy in the nineteenth century because of decisions made by foreign powers at the Congress of Vienna, not because of internal Dutch preference (Wout Ultee, personal communication, Dec. 2, 1988).

18 Compare, for example, the status of merchants and the rate of innovation for Europe during the sixteenth, seventeenth, and eighteenth centuries with the situation in India. Both were higher in Europe. Although this could have been coincidence, the evidence suggests a causal link.

Chapter 9

1 Charles Singer et al. (eds.), *A History of Technology* (Oxford: Clarendon Press, 1954–1956), vols. 1 and 2. See also Terry S. Reynolds, "Medieval Roots of the Industrial Revolution," *Scientific American,* 251 (July 1984), pp. 123–130.

2 Michael Mann, *The Sources of Social Power* (Cambridge: Cambridge University Press, 1986), vol. I, p. 445.

3 William H. McNeill, *The Rise of the West* (Chicago: University of Chicago Press, 1963), pp. 570–571.

4 S. B. Clough and C. W. Cole, *Economic History of Europe* (Boston: Heath, 1941), pp. 127–128.

5 Ibid.

6 R. H. Tawney, *Religion and the Rise of the West* (New York: Mentor Books, 1947), p. 117.

7 Immanuel Wallerstein, *The Modern World-System* (New York: Academic Press, 1974), especially chap. 2.

8 Tawney, p. 257.

9 Elizabeth Eisenstein, *The Printing Press as an Agent of Change* (Cambridge: Cambridge University Press, 1979), vols. I and II.

10 James M. Wells, "The History of Printing," *Encyclopaedia Britannica,* vol. 18, p. 541.

11 Wells, pp. 541–542; and N. F. Blake, *Caxton: England's First Publisher* (New York: Barnes & Noble, 1976), chap. 1.

12 Daniel J. Boorstin, *The Discoverers* (New York: Random House, 1983), chaps. 62–63.

13 Ann Stanford, "A Link with the Past," *Endeavors,* vol. 2, no. 2 (Spring 1985), p. 8; Michael Clapham, "Printing," in Singer, op. cit., vol. II, p. 27; and Boorstin, pp. 533–534.

14 See, for example, Arthur G. Dickens, *Reformation and Society in Sixteenth Century Europe* (New York: Harcourt, Brace, 1966).

15 See, especially, Max Weber, *The Protestant Ethic and the Spirit of Capitalism,* trans. Talcott Parsons (New York: Scribner, 1958); or Reinhard Bendix, *Max Weber: An Intellectual Portrait* (Garden City, N.Y.: Doubleday, 1960), chaps. 3–8.

16 Ernest Gellner, *Plow, Sword and Book: The Structure of Human History* (Chicago: University of Chicago Press, 1989), chaps. 4 and 5.

17 Tawney, pp. 92–93.

18 Neil Smelser and S. M. Lipset (eds.), *Social Structure and Mobility in Economic Development* (Chicago: University of Chicago Press, 1967), p. 29ff.

19 Clough and Cole, pp. 185–194.

20 Clough and Cole, pp. 308–315.

21 See, for example, Robert Heilbroner, *The Making of Economic Society* (Englewood Cliffs, N.J.: Prentice-Hall, 1962), pp. 101–102.

22 See, for example, John Nef, *The Conquest of the Material World* (Chicago: University of Chicago Press, 1965), especially part 2.

23 Paul Mantoux, *The Industrial Revolution in the Eighteenth Century,* rev. ed. (London: Cape, 1961), pp. 243–244.

24 Reynolds, "Medieval Roots."

25 Mantoux, p. 312.

26 Earlier in the century, Thomas Savery and Thomas Newcomen invented the atmospheric engine, which laid the foundation for Watt's work. Its only practical use, however, was to pump water out of mines.

27   Phyllis Deane and W. A. Cole, *British Growth 1688–1959: Trends and Structure* (London: Cambridge, 1962), p. 212.

28   For 1788, see Clive Day, *Economic Development in Europe* (New York: Macmillan, 1942), p. 134; for 1845, see Deane and Cole, p. 225.

29   Deane and Cole, pp. 55 and 216.

30   S. Woytinsky and E. S. Woytinsky, *World Population and Production: Trends and Outlook* (New York: Twentieth Century Fund, 1953), p. 1147.

31   *British Historical Statistics* (Cambridge: Cambridge University Press, 1988), p. 822.

32   U.S. Department of Commerce, Bureau of the Census, *Historical Statistics of the United States, Colonial Times to 1970,* series F238–239.

33   J. H. Clapham, *An Economic History of Modern Britain,* 2d ed. (London: Cambridge, 1930), vol. 1, pp. 391–392.

34   Clough and Cole, pp. 594–595.

35   Ibid., pp. 535–537.

36   Deane and Cole, p. 225.

37   Ibid., p. 216.

38   *Historical Statistics of the U.S., Colonial Times to 1970,* p. 500.

39   Alfred D. Chandler, Jr., *The Visible Hand: The Managerial Revolution in America* (Cambridge, Mass.: Belknap Press, 1977), part II.

40   Ibid., p. 232.

41   Clough and Cole, p. 538.

42   Calculated from Woytinsky and Woytinsky, p. 1003.

43   Alfred D. Chandler, "Industrial Revolutions and Institutional Arrangements," *Bulletin of the American Academy of Arts and Sciences,* 33 (May 1980), pp. 40–45.

44   The first figure is an estimate based on Clough and Cole's report of French production in 1902 (p. 773) and Woytinsky and Woytinsky's report of American production in 1900 and 1902 (p. 1168). See also James M. Laux, *In First Gear: The French Automobile Industry to 1914* (Liverpool: Liverpool University Press, 1976), fig. 5. The second is from Lester Brown, Nicholas Lenssen, and Hal Kane, *Vital Signs 1995: The Trends that are Shaping our Future* (New York: Norton, 1995), p. 83.

45   Woytinsky and Woytinsky, p. 1164.

46   The 1900 figure is estimated from information provided by Woytinsky and Woytinsky, pp. 897–900; the 1940 figure is from fig. 257, p. 897.

47   Woytinsky and Woytinsky, p. 966.

48   Woytinsky and Woytinsky, p. 1171.

49   Calculated from *Historical Statistics of the U.S.,* Series R 93–105 and Series A 288–319.

50   *The Washington Post,* August 13, 1997.

51   *U.S. News & World Report,* February 19, 1996.

52   William Broad, "Incredible Shrinking Transistor," *New York Times,* February 4, 1996; "Intel Announces Transistor Breakthrough," *Associated Press,* June 11, 2001. According to one commentator, Frederic E. Davis, "Electrons or Photons?" *Wired,* March/April 1993, a decade ago: "Had automobile technology advanced at a similar pace over the past 20 years, your car would travel 500,000 miles an hour, get a million miles to the gallon, and cost a measly $1,000."

53   *New York Times,* July 21, 1997.

54   Calculations based on data in World Bank, *World Tables,* 3d. ed., vol. I (Baltimore: Johns Hopkins University Press, 1983), Table 1; World Bank, *World Development Report, 1982* (New York: Oxford University Press, 1982), table 2.0; *World Development Indicators 1997; and* World Bank, *World Development Indicators* Online Database (www.worldbank.org/data/onlinedatabases/onlinedatabases.html).

55 *Historical Statistics of the U.S.,* series W–109; *Statistical Abstract of the U.S., 1997,* table 963; and *Statistical Abstract of the U.S., 2002,* tables 752 and 680.

56 See the high percentage of all research and development expenditures coming from the U.S. Department of Defense, *Statistical Abstract of the U.S., 1997,* table 967.

57 See, for example, Max Weber and Karl Marx.

58 See, for example, William H. McNeill, *Plagues and Peoples* (Garden City, N.Y.: Doubleday Anchor, 1976).

59 J. L. Hammond and Barbara Hammond, *The Town Labourer: 1760–1830* (London: Guild Books, 1949, first published 1917), vol. I, chap. 3.

60 Hammond and Hammond, chaps. 2 and 6–9; or J. T. Ward (ed.), *The Factory System* (New York: Barnes & Noble, 1970), vols. I and II.

61 Hammond and Hammond, vol. I, pp. 32–33.

62 Compare and contrast the work of Hammond and Hammond, The Town Labourer, or Eric Hobsbawm, "The British Standard of Living, 1790–1850," *Economic History Review,* 2d series, 10 (1957), pp. 46–61, with Thomas Ashton, "The Standard of Life of the Workers in England, 1790–1830," *Journal of Economic History,* 9 (1949), supplement, pp. 19–38.

Chapter 10

1 Our calculations from U.S. Department of Commerce, Bureau of the Census, *Historical Statistics of the United States: Colonial Times to 1970,* series D-152–153; and U.S. Department of Commerce, Bureau of the Census, *Statistical Abstract of the United States, 2002,* table 588.

2 J. Frederic Dewhurst and associates, *America's Needs and Resources* (New York: Twentieth Century Fund, 1955), p. 1116; and *Statistical Abstract of the U.S., 1967,* table 752.

3 Lester Brown, Hal Kane, and Ed Ayres, *Vital Signs 1993: The Trends That Are Shaping Our Future* (New York: W. W. Norton, 1993), p. 58; and Lester Brown, Christopher Flavin, and Hal Kane, *Vital Signs 1996* (New York: Norton, 1996), pp. 56–57.

4 *Historical Statistics of the U.S.,* series S-1; *Statistical Abstract of the U.S., 2002,* table 1; and L. W. Nicholson 1996, "Work is Becoming Obsolete," *The Northwest Technocrat,* no. 342. Since the most recent figure is for 1995, this estimate of increase is conservative.

5 World Bank, *World Development Indicators* Online Database (www.worldbank.org/data/onlinedatabases/onlinedatabases.html).

6 The 1750 figure is from W. S. Woytinsky and E. S. Woytinsky, *World Population and Production: Trends and Outlooks* (New York: Twentieth Century Fund, 1953), p. 1100; the 1970 figure is from United Nations, *Statistical Yearbook, 1971,* tables 121 and 122, and is converted to short tons.

7 The 1820 figure is from Woytinsky and Woytinsky, p. 1101; the 1974 figure is from *Statistical Abstract of the U.S., 1989,* table 1182.

8 *Statistical Abstract of the U.S., 2002,* table 858.

9 Consumption figures are from the *Statistical Abstract of the U.S., 2002,* tables 855 and 856. Per capita calculations are our own.

10 *British Historical Statistics* (Cambridge: Cambridge University Press, 1988), pp. 837–841; *World Development Report 1982,* table 1; *World Development Indicators 1997 CD-ROM* (Washington: World Bank, 1997); and *World Development Indicators 2001 CD-ROM* (Washington: World Bank, 2001).

11 *Historical Statistics of the U.S.,* series F-3; *World Development Indicators 1997;* and *World Development Indicators 2001.*

12 *World Development Indicators Online Database.*

13 Associated Press, Aug. 7, 1972.

14 See notes 10 and 11.

15 Calculated from information at *Hoover's Online* (Hoovers Inc., http://Hoovers.com).

16 *Statistical Abstract of the U.S., 2002,* table 746.

17 David Barboza, "Goliath of the Hog World," *New York Times,* April 7, 2000.

18 Our calculations from *Statistical Abstract of the U.S., 2002,* table 787.

19 *Historical Statistics of the U.S.,* series D-182–232; and *Statistical Abstract of the U.S.,* 2002, table 588.

20 *Statistical Abstract of the U.S., 2002,* tables 441 and 491.

21 *Statistical Abstract of the U.S., 2002,* table 441.

22 *Statistical Abstract of the U.S., 2002,* table 445.

23 *Hoover's Online.*

24 U.S. Department of Labor, *Dictionary of Occupational Titles* (Washington: Government Printing Office, 1977, 1981); and DOT Online Index (www.immigration-usa.com/dot_index.html).

25 *Newsweek,* Mar. 26, 1973, p. 79.

26 Pehr Gyllenhammar, "Volvo's Solution to Blue Collar Blues," *Business and Society* (Autumn, 1973).

27 *Statistical Abstract of the U.S., 2002,* table 629.

28 Bruce Western, "Postwar Unionization in Eighteen Advanced Capitalist Countries," *American Sociological Review* 58 (April 1993), table 1.

29 International Labour Office, *World Labour Report 1997–1998, Industrial Relations, Democracy and Social Stability* (Geneva, International Labour Office, 1997).

30 S. B. Clough and C. W. Cole, *Economic History of Europe* (Boston: Heath, 1941), pp. 693–698.

31 G. D. H. Cole, *A Short History of the British Working Class Movement* (New York: Macmillan, 1927), vol. II, p. 202; and Carroll P. Daugherty, *Labor Problems in American Industry* (Boston: Houghton Mifflin, 1941), p. 405.

32 See, for example, "Chrysler Says GM Sets U.S. Car Prices," *Raleigh News and Observer,* Sept. 13, 1979, a report of testimony at a congressional hearing by the chairman of the Chrysler Corporation.

33 G. Warren Nutter, "Industrial Concentration," *International Encyclopedia of the Social Sciences* (New York: Macmillan and Free Press, 1968), vol. 7, p. 221.

34 Ben Bagdikian, "Why Newspapers Keep Dying," *Washington Post,* July 23, 1972; and Audit Bureau of Circulation, August 19, 2003.

35 John Kenneth Galbraith, *The New Industrial State* (New York: Signet, 1968), pp. 38–39.

36 Michael P. Allen, "The Structure of Interorganizational Elite Cooptation: Interlocking Corporate Directorates," *American Sociological Review,* 39 (1974), pp. 393–406.

37 *The Economist,* Dec. 30, 1978.

38 Clough and Cole, p. 148ff.; or Edward S. Mason, "Corporation," in *International Encyclopedia of the Social Sciences,* vol. 3, pp. 396–403.

39 Calculations based on data in *Statistical Abstract of the U.S., 2002,* table 700.

40 *Forbes,* May 12, 1980, pp. 214 and 236.

41 See Robert A. Gordon, *Business Leadership in the Large Corporation* (Berkeley: University of California Press, 1961); or Edward S. Mason (ed.), *The Corporation and Modern Society* (Cambridge: Harvard University Press, 1959), on American corporations; and P. Sargant Florence, *Ownership, Control, and Success of Large Companies* (London: Street and Maxwell, 1961); or David Granick, *The European Executive* (Garden City, N.Y.: Doubleday Anchor, 1964), on European corporations.

42 Richard Easterlin, "Economic Growth," in *Encyclopedia of the Social Sciences,* vol. 4, p. 405.

43 Calculations based on United Nations, *Statistical Yearbook, 1965,* table 148; and *Statistical Abstract of the U.S., 1979,* table 1539.

44 Based on recent company reports.

45 Based on recent company reports.

Chapter 11

1 *Index to International Public Opinion, 1982–83* (Westport, Conn.: Greenwood), p. 533.

2 *Index to International Public Opinion, 1980–81* (Westport, Conn.: Greenwood), pp. 526–537.

3 *Index to International Public Opinion, 1990–91,* (Westport, Conn.: Greenwood), p. 594.

4 *The Gallup Poll: Public Opinion 1991* (Wilmington, Del., 1992), p. 238; and John G. Stackhouse, Jr., "The Renaissance of Religion in Canada," *Books & Culture,* November/December 2002 (www.christianitytoday.com/bc/2002/006/5.20.html).

5 Ibid., p. 238, and *The Gallup Poll: Public Opinion 1996,* p. 218, 172; the PEW Research Center (*people-press.org/reports/print.php3?PageID=728*); and Eric Reed, "How Others See Us,"*LeadershipJournal.Net,* Spring 2003 (www.christianitytoday.com/le/2003/002/17.7.html).

6 Hugh Lefler, *North Carolina History* (Chapel Hill: University of North Carolina Press, 1934), pp. 108–109. For the net worth of free southerners in 1774, see *Historical Statistics of the U.S.,* p. 1175. The median would almost certainly be lower than the average reported here.

7 Robert Heilbroner, *The Worldly Philosophers,* rev. ed. (New York: Time Books, 1961), chap. 3; and Jacob Viner, "Adam Smith," in *International Encyclopedia of the Social Sciences,* vol. 14, pp. 322–329.

8 Heilbroner, p. 47.

9 See, for example, Daniel Bell, "Socialism," in *International Encyclopedia of the Social Sciences,* vol. 14, pp. 506–532.

10 Maurice Duverger, *Political Parties: Their Organization and Activity in the Modern State,* translated by Barbara North and Robert North (London: Methuen, 1959), pp. 118–119.

11 Hans Kohn, "Nationalism," *International Encyclopedia of the Social Sciences,* vol. 2, pp. 63–70.

12 John H. Kautsky, *The Politics of Aristocratic Empires* (Chapel Hill: University of North Carolina Press, 1982), part IV.

13 Robert Bellah, "Civil Religion in America," *Daedalus,* 96 (Winter 1967), pp. 1–21. See also Will Herberg, *Protestant-Catholic-Jew* (Garden City, N.Y.: Doubleday, 1955).

14 W. L. Guttsman, *The British Political Elite* (London: Macgibbon & Kee, 1963), pp. 18 and 41.

15 A. Todd, *On Parliamentary Government* (London: Longmans, 1887), p. 622; and W. L. Guttsman (ed.), *The English Ruling Class* (London: Weidenfeld and Nicolson, 1969), p. 154.

16 U.S. Department of Commerce, Bureau of the Census, *Historical Statistics of the U.S.: Colonial Times to 1970,* series Y–83.

17 U.S. Department of Commerce, Bureau of the Census, *Statistical Abstract of the U.S., 1997,* Table 577.

18 Judith Ryder and Harold Silver, *Modern English Society* (London: Methuen, 1970), p. 74; Dankwort Rustow, *The Politics of Compromise: A Study of Parties and Cabinet Government in Sweden* (Princeton, N.J.: Princeton University Press, 1955), pp. 84–85.

19 Kenneth A. Bollen, "Political Democracy and the Timing of Development," *American Sociological Review,* 44 (August 1979), pp. 572–587.

20 Many studies have documented the relationship between high rates of literacy and education on the one hand and democratic government on the other. See, for example, Daniel Lerner, *The Passing of Traditional Society: Modernizing the Middle East* (New York: Free Press, 1958), especially pp. 63–64 and 86–89; or S. M. Lipset, *Political Man* (Garden City, N.Y.: Doubleday, 1960), pp. 53–58.

21 On the relationship between democracy and the development of the mass media, see Lerner, *Passing of Traditional Society,* and Lipset, pp. 51–52.

22 *Wikipedia: The Free Encyclopedia* (*http://www.wikipedia.org/wiki/European_Parliament*); and A.S. Banks, Alan J. Day and Thomas C. Muller (eds.) *Political Handbook of the World 1997* (Binghamton, N.Y.: CSA Publications, 1997).

23   See Banks, Day and Muller, *The Political Handbook of the World 1997*; Swedish Parliament website: www.riksdagen.se/english/members/; German Parliament website: www.bundestag.de/htdocs_e/index.html; Canadian Parliament website: www.parl.gc.ca/information/about/people/house/standingsHofC.asp? lang=E; Diet of Japan website: www.shugiin.go.jp/index.nsf/html/index_e_strength.htm; the United Kingdom Parliament website: www.publications.parliament.uk/pa/cm200001/cmwib/wb010512/state.htm.

24   Banks, Day and Muller, *The Political Handbook of the World 1997*; and Swedish Parliament website.

25   James Markham, "Greening of European Politicians Spreads . . . ," *New York Times*, Apr. 12, 1989.

26   *The Gallup Poll: Public Opinion 1996,* p. 212.

27   Thomas E. Patterson, *The Mass Media Election: How Americans Choose Their President* (New York: Praeger, 1980).

28   Harry Waters, "Brave New Documentary," *Newsweek,* June 10, 1985, p. 71.

29   Ivo Feierabend and Rosalind Feierabend, "Aggressive Behaviors within Polities, 1948–1962: A Cross-National Study," *Journal of Conflict Resolution,* 10 (1966), table 3. Results of this study suggest that rates of political instability are greatest in societies making the transition from agrarian to industrial, though results were not statistically significant. See also Douglas Hibbs, *Mass Political Violence: A Cross-National Causal Analysis* (New York: Wiley, 1973), chap. 3.

30   The figures shown in Table 11.3 are based on our own calculations, using the following sources: Robert Alford, *Party and Society* (Chicago: Rand McNally, 1963), pp. 136, 202–203, 234–235, and 274–275; Richard Rose (ed.), *Electoral Behavior: A Comparative Handbook* (New York: Free Press, 1974), pp. 147, 294, 334, and 398; Hannu Uusitalo, "Class Structure and Party Choice: A Scandinavian Comparison," *Research Report No. 10* (1975), Research Group for Comparative Sociology, University of Helsinki, p. 21; Roy Pierce, *French Politics and Political Institutions* (New York: Harper & Row, 1968), table 10; Richard Rose, "Class and Party Divisions: Britain as a Test Case," *Sociology,* 2 (1968), pp. 129–162; Erik Allardt and Yrjo Littunen (eds.), *Cleavages, Ideologies and Party Systems: Contributions to Comparative Political Sociology,* in a series entitled Transactions of the Westermarck Society (Helsinki: The Academic Bookstore, 1964), vol. 10, pp. 102 and 212; S. M. Lipset, *Political Man* (Garden City, N.Y.: Doubleday, 1960), pp. 225 and 227; *Gallup Political Index,* Report No. 17 (October 1966), p. 15 and inside back cover; S. M. Lipset, "Industrial Proletariat in Comparative Perspective," in Jan Triska and C. Gati (eds.), *Blue Collar Workers in Eastern Europe* (London: Allen & Unwin, 1981), figure 1.1; Walter Korpi, *The Democratic Class Struggle* (London: Routledge & Kegan Paul, 1983), figure 5.3; and *Index to International Public Opinion 1985–86,* pp. 410, 411, and 4.

31   See, for example, Lipset, chaps. 2 and 4.

32   *Statistical Abstract of the U.S., 2002,* tables 441, and 560.

33   *Gallup Poll 1995,* and *Gallup Poll: Public Opinion 1991.*

34   Slightly smaller percentages believed that state and local governments had violated their constitutional rights also (i.e., state, 83 percent; local, 75 percent), the *Gallup Poll: Public Opinion 1995* (Wilmington, Del: Greenwood, 1996), p. 252.

35   Urii Davydov, "Technology and Bureaucracy," *Sotsiologicheskie Issledovaniia,* 5 (1988), pp. 116–127; and "The Weberian Renaissance," *Sotsiologicheskie Issledovaniia,* 3 (1986), pp. 56–68.

Chapter 12

1   These are the ratios to industrializing agrarian and industrializing horticultural societies, respectively (see Chapter 14); see also, Patrick D. Nolan, "A Standardized Cross-National Comparison of Incomes," *Sociological Quarterly,* 33 (1992), table 1.

2   *Statistical Abstract of the U.S., 2002,* tables 659, and 644.

3   Ibid., table 653.

4   Ibid., our computations from tables 51 and 653.

5   *Statistical Abstract of the U.S., 2002,* table 659.

6   Robert S. Stein, "Who Are the Rich and the Poor? Surprisingly They Change Almost Year to Year," *Investor's Business Daily,* Oct. 28, 1993.

7   Findings of the Panel Study of Income Dynamics conducted by the University of Michigan Institute for Social Research, reported in Claudia Smith Brinson, "Study Debunks Poverty Myths," *The State,* Mar. 29, 1992. William P. O'Hare, "A New Look at Poverty in America," *Population Bulletin,* vol. 51, No. 8 (September, 1996) Population Reference Bureau.

8   *Statistical Abstract of the U.S., 2002,* table 659; and Edward Wolff, quoted in "The Wealth Divide: The Growing Gap in the United States between the Rich and the Rest," *Multinational Monitor,* May 2003.

9   In 2001 dollars from Ana M. Aizcorbe, Arthur B. Kennickell, and Kevin B. Moore, "Recent Changes in U.S. Family Finances: Evidence From the 1998 and 2001 Survey of Consumer Finances," *Federal Reserve Bulletin,* January 2003.

10   Sylvia Nasar, "The Rich Get Richer, but Never the Same Way Twice," *New York Times,* Aug. 16, 1992.

11   Ibid.; and Edward Wolff, quoted in "The Wealth Divide: The Growing Gap in the United States between the Rich and the Rest," *Multinational Monitor,* May 2003.

12   Edward N. Wolff, "Changing Inequality of Wealth," *American Economic Review,* 82 (May 1992), p. 553.

13   *World Almanac, 2002,* p. 106.

14   See *Historical Statistics of the U.S.: Colonial Times to 1957* (1960), Series G-169–190.

15   See, for example, Christopher Jencks et al., "The Wisconsin Model of Status Attainment," *Sociology of Education,* 56 (1983), pp. 3–19.

16   *Statistical Abstract of the U.S., 2002,* 664.

17   *Statistical Abstract of the U.S., 1997,* table 718, and *Statistical Abstract of the U.S., 2002,* table 653.

18   *Statistical Abstract of the U.S., 2002,* tables 75, and 54.

19   *Statistical Abstract of the U.S., 2002,* tables 75, and 54.

20   Our calculations from U.S. Bureau of the Census, *Poverty in the United States: 2001,* September 2002; and U.S. Bureau of the Census, "Income 2001," September, 2002; see also *Statistical Abstract of the U.S., 1992,* tables 706 and 719.

21   Reported by M. Dart from: *Principal's Association Report on High Schools,* U.S. Bureau of the Census, D.H.H.S., and *Fulton County Georgia Jail Populations* and Texas Department of Corrections, 1992; see also, Sara McLanahan and Gary Sandefur, *Growing Up with a Single Parent: What Hurts, What Helps* (Cambridge, Mass.: Harvard University Press, 1994).

22   *Statistical Abstract of the U.S., 1997,* table 727; and *Statistical Abstract of the U.S., 2002,* tables 669 and 655.

23   Findings of a Rand Corporation Study reported in *New York Times,* Mar. 2, 1986, and *New York Times,* Nov. 16, 1997.

24   Stephan Thernstrom and Abigail Thernstrom, *America in Black and White: One Nation Indivisible* (New York: Simon and Schuster, 1997) p. 195; and *Statistical Abstract of the U.S., 2002,* table 665.

25   William Julius Wilson, *When Work Disappears* (New York: Knopf, 1996), U.S. Bureau of the Census, *Housing Vacancies and Home Ownership* (January, 1998); and Robert A. Callis and Linda B. Cavanaugh, "Residential Vacancies and Ownership," U.S Bureau of the Census, July 24, 2003.

26   Wilson, *When Work Disappears,* p. 195.

27   Members of minority groups usually adopt the dominant group's prestige evaluations for groups other than their own. Sometimes they even adopt its evaluation of their own group.

See, for example, Emory Bogardus, *Social Distance* (Yellow Springs, Ohio: Antioch Press, 1959), pp. 26–29.

28 See, for example, Everett C. Hughes, *French Canada in Transition* (Chicago: University of Chicago Press, 1943), especially chap. 7. See also John Porter, *The Vertical Mosaic: An Analysis of Social Class and Power in Canada* (Toronto: University of Toronto Press, 1965), chap. 3.

29 John Burns, "Separatists Vying for Quebec Power," *New York Times,* Sept. 24, 1989.

30 Remarks by Oregon secretary of state, Bill Bradbury, April 2001 (www.sos.state.or.us/executive/speeches/041301.htm).

31 Judy Olian, dean of Pennsylvania State University Smeal College of Business, "Gray Is Good," March, 2003 (www.smeal.psu.edu/news/releases/mar03/gray.html); and Catherine Fredman, "Route to the Top: White-Collar Climb," *Chief Executive,* March 2003 (www.chiefexecutive.net/depts/routetotop2003/186.htm).

32 Calculated from Morris Janowitz, *The Professional Soldier* (New York: Free Press, 1960), p. 63.

33 Women's average wages in manufacturing as a percentage of men's, reported in United Nations, *World's Women 2000: Trends and Statistics,* table 5g (unstats.un.org/unsd/demographic/ww2000/table5g.htm).

34 Francine D. Blau and Lawrence M. Kahn, "The Gender Earnings Gap: Learning from International Comparisons," *American Economic Review,* 82 (May 1992), pp. 533–538.

35 James P. Smith and Michael P. Ward, *Women's Wages and Work in the Twentieth Century* (Santa Monica, Calif.: Rand, 1984).

36 Douglas Martin, "For Many Fathers, Roles Are Shifting," *New York Times,* June 20, 1993; Maida Odom, "Women Doing Double Duty, Research Finds," *The State,* Sept. 18, 1993; and Carol Kleiman, "Housework Said to Impede Women's Careers," *Chicago Tribune,* reported in *The State,* Feb. 13, 1992, Martin O'Connell "Where's Papa! Father's Role in Child Care," *Population Trends and Public Policy,* no. 20 (September 1993).

37 Sylvia Nasar, "Women's Progress Stalled? Just Not So," *New York Times,* Oct. 18, 1992.

38 Bureau of Labor Statistics, "Highlights of Women's Earnings 2001"; and *Statistical Abstract of the U.S, 1997,* table 731.

39 *Statistical Abstract of the U.S., 1997.*

40 *Statistical Abstract of the U.S., 1997,* table 1.

41 *Statistical Abstract of the U.S., 1992,* table 736.

42 See also Suzanne M. Bianchi and Daphne Spain "Women, Work, and Family in America," *Population Bulletin,* vol. 51, no. 3 (December 1996), Population Reference Bureau.

43 William J. Goode, *World Revolution and Family Patterns* (New York: Free Press, 1963), p. 55.

44 United Nations, *World's Women 1970–1990: Trends and Statistics* (New York: United Nations, 1991), table 3; and Inter-Parliamentary Union, *Men and Women in Politics: Democracy Still in the Making—A World Comparative Study* (Geneva: United Nations, 1997).

45 Gerhard Lenski, *Power and Privilege: A Theory of Social Stratification* (Chapel Hill: University of North Carolina Press, 1984, originally published 1966), p. 412.

46 Ibid., p. 228.

47 Ibid., pp. 313–318, for a more thorough discussion of this subject.

48 L. J. Zimmerman, *Poor Lands, Rich Lands: The Widening Gap* (New York: Random House, 1965), table 2.8, p. 38; and our calculations based on *World Development Indicators* Online Database (www.worldbank.org/data/onlinedatabases/onlinedatabases.html).

Chapter 13

1 Thomas McKeown, *The Modern Rise of Population* (New York: Academic Press, 1976), p. 2; and *The World Almanac and Book of Facts 2002* (New York: World Almanac Books, 2002), pp. 859–861.

2   Monroe Strickberger, *Evolution* (Boston: Jones and Bartlett, 1990), p. 501; Rebecca Storey, "An Estimate of Mortality in a Pre-Columbian Urban Population," *American Anthropologist,* 87 (1985), pp. 519–535; and *Statistical Abstract of the U.S., 2002,* table 95.

3   U.S. Census Bureau figures reported in Roger Doyle, "Assembling the Future: How International Migrants Are Shaping the Twenty-first Century," *Scientific American* (February 2002).

4   Ibid.

5   Ibid.

6   Ibid.

7   *Statistical Abstract of the U.S., 2002,* table 1310; and *Statistical Abstract of the U.S., 1997,* table 1340.

8   Craig Whitney, "For Asia's Children, Hard Knocks," *New York Times,* Sept. 19, 1989.

9   For example, see Tyler Marshall, "Persistent Xenophobia Raises Urgent Questions in Germany," *Los Angeles Times,* June 6, 1993; "Anti-foreigner Attacks Up in Germany," *The State,* July 31, 1993; and Alexander Stille, "No Blacks Need Apply: A Nation of Emigrants Faces the Challenge of Immigration," *Atlantic Monthly,* February 1992.

10   *The World Almanac, 2002,* p. 882.

11   *Statistical Abstract of the U.S., 1999,* table 66.

12   *Statistical Abstract of the U.S., 1999,* table 66; and *Statistical Abstract of the U.S., 2002,* tables 49 and 59.

13   See, for example, U.S. Department of Commerce, Bureau of the Census, *Historical Statistics of the United States: Colonial Times to 1970,* p. 53.

14   *Statistical Abstract of the U.S., 2002,* table 66.

15   *Statistical Abstract of U.S., 2002,* table 66.

16   Edward L. Kain, *The Myth of Family Decline: Understanding Families in a World of Rapid Social Change* (Lexington, Mass.: Lexington Books, 1990).

17   Calculations based on Warren Thompson and David Lewis, *Population Problems,* 5th ed. (New York: McGraw-Hill, 1965), p. 374; J. Bourgeois-Pichat, "The General Development of the Population of France since the Eighteenth Century," in D. V. Glass and D. E. C. Eversley (eds.), *Population in History* (Chicago: Aldine, 1965), p. 498; and W. S. Woytinsky and E. S. Woytinsky, *World Population and Production: Trends and Outlooks* (New York: Twentieth Century Fund, 1953), p. 181.

18   *World Almanac, 2002,* p. 69.

19   Ibid.

20   *Current Population Survey,* March 1998.

21   In this section we have drawn heavily on suggestions provided by Joan Huber in two of her papers, "Toward a Socio-Technological Theory of the Women's Movement," *Social Problems,* 23 (1976), and "The Future of Parenthood: Implications of Declining Fertility," in Dana Hiller and Robin Sheets (eds.), *Women and Men* (Cincinnati: University of Cincinnati Press, 1976), pp. 333–351.

22   *Statistical Abstract of the U.S., 2002,* table 561.

23   *Statistical Abstract of the U.S. 1972,* table 366; *Statistical Abstract of the U.S., 2002,* table 588; Bureau of Labor Statistics, "Highlights of Women's Earnings in 2001," table 3; and Diana Furchtgott-Roth and Christine Stolba, *Women's Figures: An Illustrated Guide to the Economic Progress of Women in America* (Washington, D.C.: American Enterprise Institute Press, 1999).

24   Jane Waldfogel, "Working Mothers Then and Now: The Effects of Maternity Leave on Women's Pay," in Francine Blau and Ronald Ehrenberg (eds.), *Gender and Family Issues in the Workplace* (New York: Russell Sage, 1997); and *Kiplinger's Personal Finance Magazine,* "Watch the Wage Gap Disappear," July 1996.

25   United Nations, *The World's Women 1970–1990: Trends and Statistics* (New York: United Nations, 1991), table 7A.

26   United Press International news release, June 1, 1980.

27   Michael Getler, "Emancipation for E. German Women," *Washington Post,* April 24, 1979.

28 Joann Lublin, "As Women's Roles Grow More Like Men's, So Do Their Problems," *Wall Street Journal,* Jan. 14, 1980. See also *New York Times* series of articles, "Women's Lives: A Scorecard of Change," Aug. 20–22, 1989; and United Nations, *The World's Women 1970–1990,* pp. 56–57.

29 U.N., *World's Women..*

30 *Historical Statistics of the U.S.: Colonial Times to 1970,* series H-1004 and H-1005; and *Statistical Abstract of the U.S., 1989,* table 292.

31 U.S. National Center for Educational Statistics, *Digest of Educational Statistics, 2002,* chapter 2 (nces.ed.gov/pubs2003/digest02/); and Cynthia Crossen, "In 1860, America Had 40 Public High Schools; Teachers Chopped Wood," *Wall Street Journal,* Sept. 3, 2003.

32 U.S. National Center for Educational Statistics, *Digest of Educational Statistics, 2002,* chap. 2.

33 See, for example, Randall Collins, "Functional and Conflict Theories of Educational Stratification," *American Sociological Review,* 36 (1971), pp. 1002–1019.

34 *Statistical Abstract of the U.S., 2002,* table 83.

35 Federal Bureau of Investigation, *Crimes in the United States 2000,* Section IV (www.fbi.gov/ucr/00cius.htm).

36 See, for example, Richard Quinney, *The Social Reality of Crime* (Boston: Little, Brown, 1970).

37 Urie Bronfenbrenner, "The Disturbing Changes in the American Family," *Search* (Fall 1976), pp. 11–14.

38 *The World Almanac and Book of Facts 2002* (New York: World Almanac Books, 2002), p. 280; and David Bouder, "Viewers Tuning Out Network's New shows," Associated Press, Oct. 6, 1997.

39 Robert Kalaski, "TV's Unreal World of Work," *American Federationist,* December 1980.

40 *Gallup Poll 1991,* p. 49.

Chapter 14

1 See Gerhard Lenski and Patrick Nolan, "Trajectories of Development: A Test of Ecological-Evolutionary Theory," *Social Forces,* 63 (September 1984), pp. 1–23.

2 See Lenski and Nolan, "A Test," for the initial classification, and Gerhard Lenski and Patrick Nolan, "Trajectories of Development: A Further Test," *Social Forces,* 64 (March 1986), pp. 794–795; and Patrick Nolan, "World System Status, Techno-Economic Heritage, and Fertility," *Sociological Focus,* 21 (January 1988), pp. 9–33 for revisions in it.

3 Nolan, "World System Status."

4 See, for example, F. G. Bailey, *Tribe, Caste, and Nation* (Manchester: Manchester University Press, 1960), on the assimilation of hill tribes in India.

5 For a more detailed discussion of this subject, see Lenski and Nolan, "A Test."

6 For example, see William Breedlove and Patrick Nolan, "International Stratification and Inequality 1960–1980," *International Journal of Contemporary Sociology,* 25 (July–October 1988), pp. 105–123.

7 For example, see Lenski and Nolan, "A Test," tables 1 and 2.

8 See Patrick Nolan and Gerhard Lenski, *Human Societies,* 8th ed. (New York: McGraw-Hill, 1999), table 14.3.

9 *World Development Indicators,* Online Database (www.worldbank.org/data/onlinedatabases.html).

10 Population Reference Bureau, *World Population Data Sheet 2002, 2003;* United Nations, *World Population Prospects, the 2002 Revision.*

11 Ibid.

12 Manfred Halpern, *The Politics of Social Change in the Middle East and North Africa* (Princeton, N.J.: Princeton, 1963), p. 80.

13 Ibid.

14   See, for example, Gwendolen Carter (ed.), *African One-Party States* (Ithaca, N.Y.: Cornell, 1962), pp. 371ff, and 461ff; Guy Hunter, *The New Societies of Africa* (New York: Oxford University Press, 1964), chap. 9, especially p. 223ff; International Bank for Reconstruction and Development, *The Economic Development of Uganda* (Baltimore: Johns Hopkins University Press, 1962), pp. 23–24; or Ken Post, *The New States of West Africa* (Baltimore: Penguin, 1964), chap. 6.

15   On the latter, see, for example, J. A. K. Leslie's fascinating study, *A Survey of Dar es Salaam* (New York: Oxford University Press, 1963).

16   See Hunter, *New Societies,* p. 85; and "Bolivia's Witches Sell from Otherworldly Mall," *Chicago Tribune,* Feb. 29, 1992.

17   Gamini Weerakoon, "Africa: No Longer Proxy for the Superpowers," *World Press,* August 1991, pp. 9–10; and Reymer Kluver, "The Roots of a Continent's Civil Wars," *World Press,* p. 10.

18   "A Continent of Change," *Chicago Tribune,* Jan. 19, 1992.

19   David Lamb, "Africans Find Independence a Hard Road," *Los Angeles Times,* Feb. 15, 1979; see also Ray Vicker, "Arab Nations Growing More Cautious about Dispensing Aid to Third World," *Wall Street Journal,* Sept. 4, 1980.

20   Latest figure reported in *World Development Report* Online Database.

21   Ibid.

22   "Slavery Still Curses Humanity," *Denver Post,* July 13, 2003; Tommy Calvert, "U.S. Must Address Modern Slave Trade," *Chicago Sun-Times,* July 21, 2003; Andrew Bushell, "Pakistan's Slave Trade," Phoeniz.com, Feb. 14–21, 2002; Masland et al., op. cit.; and Charles Wallace, "Slavery, 20th Century Style," *The Los Angeles Times,* Aug. 6, 1991, and "Africa's Child-Slave Trade Comes to Light with Arrests," *New York Times,* Aug. 10, 1997.

23   Tom Masland, Rod Norland, Melinda Liu, and Joseph Conterras, "Slavery," *Newsweek,* May 4, 1992, pp. 30–39, reported 100 million; Dr. Charles Jacobs, president of the American Anti-Slavery Group, estimated there are 27 million slaves in the world today in a speech to the Unitarian Universalist Association, General Assembly 2003 (www.uua.org/ga/ga03/2051.html).

24   See, for example, Myron Weiner, *Party Building in a New Nation: The Indian National Congress* (Chicago: University of Chicago Press, 1967).

25   See, for example, June Kronholz, "In Africa Tribal Power Wanes, But Still Rivals Governments'," *Wall Street Journal,* June 15, 1981.

26   See Leslie, op. cit., p. 32; or Merran Fraenkel, *Tribe and Class in Monrovia* (London: Oxford University Press, 1964), especially chap. 3.

27   Kronholz, op. cit.

28   Sylvia Nasar, "It's Never Fair to Just Blame the Weather," *New York Times,* Jan. 17, 1993.

29   Neil Smelser and S. M. Lipset (eds.), *Social Structure and Mobility in Economic Development* (Chicago: Aldine, 1966), p. 29ff. Other statistics cited in this paragraph are from the same source. See also Herbert Passin, *Society and Education in Japan* (New York: Columbia University Press, 1965), p. 57.

30   John Meyer et al., "National Economic Development, 1950–70," in John Meyer and Michael Hannan (eds.), *National Development and the World System* (Chicago: University of Chicago Press, 1979), chap. 6.

31   Smelser and Lipset, op. cit., p. 37.

32   Ibid.; see also June Kronholz, "In Third-World India College Students Study Humanities, Not Skills," *Wall Street Journal,* May 7, 1982.

33   Halpern, op. cit., p. 122.

34   Henry A. Landsberger (ed.), *Latin American Peasant Movements* (Ithaca, N.Y.: Cornell University Press, 1969).

35   For Latin America, see Robert E. Scott, "Political Elites and Political Modernization: The Crisis of Transition," in S. M. Lipset and Aldo Solari (eds.), *Elites in Latin America* (New York: Oxford University Press, 1967), p. 133.

36 John Paxton (ed.), *The Statesman's Yearbook, 1980–81* (New York: St. Martin's Press, 1980).

37 The figure for Dar es Salaam is from Leslie, op. cit., p. 210, and that for Tanzania from Bruce Russett et al., *World Handbook of Political and Social Indicators* (New Haven: Yale University Press, 1964), tables 74 and 75.

38 Fraenkel, p. 154; and Russett et al., tables 74 and 75.

39 From J. A. K. Leslie, *A Survey of Dar es Salaam* (Oxford: Oxford University Press, 1963), p. 211. By permission of the Oxford University Press.

40 Ibid., pp. 210–211.

41 Fraenkel, pp. 158 and 162.

42 Hunter, p. 74, provides numerous examples.

43 Carter, pp. 433–434. Copyright 1962 by Cornell University. Used by permission of Cornell University Press.

44 See, for example, Vittorio Lanternari, *The Religions of the Oppressed: A Study of Modern Messianic Cults,* translated by Lisa Sergio (New York: Knopf, 1963), chap. 1; or Lucy Mair, *Primitive Government* (Baltimore: Penguin, 1962), p. 171ff.

45 L. A. Fallers (ed.), *The King's Men: Leadership and Status in Buganda on the Eve of Independence* (New York: Oxford University Press, 1964), p. 99.

46 Leslie, op. cit., pp. 27–29.

47 Ibid., pp. 60–61; or Fraenkel, op. cit., p. 127ff.

48 See, for example, June Kronholz, "Kenyans Say Missionaries Who Tried to Stop Polygamy Caused Baby Boom," *Wall Street Journal,* April 11, 1983.

49 For example, see Jane Perlez, "Elite Kenyan Women Avoid a Rite: Marriage," *New York Times,* March 3, 1991; James Brooke, "A Rape Case Fuels Debate across Brazil," ibid., July 5, 1992; Jane Perlez, "Uganda's Women: Children, Drudgery and Pain," ibid., Feb. 24, 1991; "In Parts of India, Families Kill Baby Girls Rather Than Raise Them," *Los Angeles Times,* Feb. 27, 1994; Masland et al.., op. cit.; Wallace, op. cit.; Emily MacFarquar, "The War against Women: Violence, Poverty, and Abuse," *U.S. News & World Report,* March 28, 1994, pp. 42–48; ibid., "The Echoes of Sita: A Lethal Age-Old Contempt for Women Persists," pp. 54–55. Toni Nelson, "Violence Stalks Women Worldwide," pp 134–135 in Lester R. Brown, Christopher Flavin, and Hal Kane, *Vital Signs 1996* (New York: Norton, 1996); and Kate Chalkey, "Female Genital Mutilation: New Laws, Programs Try to End Practice," *Population Today,* 25, no. 10, (October, 1997) Population Reference Bureau.

50 See, for example, Andre Gunder Frank, *Capitalism and Underdevelopment in Latin America* (New York: Monthly Review Press, 1969); Theotonio Dos Santos, "The Structure of Dependence," *American Economic Review,* 60 (1970), pp. 231–236; or Celso Furtado, *Economic Development of Latin America* (Cambridge: Cambridge University Press, 1970).

51 Compare, for example, Frank, op. cit., with Johan Galtung, "A Structural Theory of Imperialism," *Journal of Peace Research,* 8 (1971), pp. 81–117.

52 See, for example, W. W. Rostow, *The Process of Economic Growth* (New York: Norton, 1962); Wilbert Moore and David Feldman, *Labor Commitment and Social Change in Developing Areas* (New York: Social Science Research Council, 1960); S. N. Eisenstadt, *Modernization* (Englewood Cliffs, N.J.: Prentice-Hall, 1966); Talcott Parsons, *The System of Modern Societies* (Englewood Cliffs, N.J.: Prentice-Hall, 1971); or Alex Inkeles and David Smith, *Becoming Modern* (Cambridge, Mass.: Harvard University Press, 1974).

53 See Nasar, op. cit., Jan. 17, 1993.

54 Population Reference Bureau, Datafinder (www.worldpop.org/datafinder.htm).

Chapter 15

1 Robert Osborn, *Soviet Social Policies* (Homewood, Ill.: Dorsey, 1970), p. 139.

2 Ibid, p. 140.

3 See, for example, Aleksandr Solzhenitsyn, *The Gulag Archipelago* (New York: Harper & Row, 1973), or Andrei Amalrik, *Involuntary Journey to Siberia* (New York: Harcourt, Brace, 1970).

4 See, for example, Harrison Salisbury, *The New Emperors* (Boston: Little, Brown, 1992), on the lifestyle of the Chinese Communist elite; or Michael Voslensky, *The Soviet Ruling Class* (Garden City, N.Y.: Doubleday, 1984) on the Soviet elite.

5 Jeri Laber, "The Bulgarian Difference," *New York Review of Books,* May 17, 1990, pp. 34–36.

6 *Washington Post,* May 6, 1990.

7 Mervyn Matthews, *Privilege in the Soviet Union* (London: Allen & Unwin, 1978).

8 Vladimir Shlapentokh, *Public and Private Life of the Soviet People* (New York: Oxford University Press, 1989); "The Soviet Economy," *The Economist,* April 9, 1988, pp. 3–18; Leonard Silk, "Soviet Crisis Worse, Economists Declare," *New York Times,* March 15, 1990; Henry Kamm, "Hungarians Shocked by News of Vast Poverty in Their Midst," *New York Times,* Feb. 6, 1989; T. Anthony Jones, "Work, Workers and Modernization in the USSR," *Sociology of Work,* 1 (1981), pp. 249–283; Michael Scammel, "Yugoslavia: The Awakening," *New York Review of Books,* June 28, 1990, pp. 42–47; Leo Huberman and Paul Sweezy, *Socialism in Cuba* (New York: Modern Reader Paperbacks, 1967); Maurice Zeitlin, *Revolutionary Politics and the Cuban Working Class* (New York: Harper & Row, 1970).

9 For example, see Stephen Jay Gould, *Hen's Teeth and Horse's Toes: Further Reflections on Natural History* (New York: Norton, 1980), pp. 134–144.

10 Maurice Duverger, *Political Parties: Their Organization and Activity in the Modern State,* translated by Barbara North and Robert North (London: Methuen, 1959), pp. 118–119. Quoted by permission of Methuen & Company, Ltd.

11 Solzhenitsyn, op. cit.; Roy Medvedev, *Let History Judge* (New York: Knopf, 1971).

12 Robert Conquest, *The Great Terror: A Reassessment* (New York: Oxford University Press, 1990), p. 486, and *New York Times,* Dec. 14, 1997.

13 Jasper Becker, *Hungry Ghosts: Mao's Secret Famine* (New York: Free Press, 1996), p. 183; and *New York Times,* Dec. 14, 1997.

14 *New York Times,* Dec. 14, 1997.

15 William Ellis, "A Soviet Sea Lies Dying," *National Geographic,* 177, no. 2 (February 1990), pp. 71–93.

16 Ibid., p. 88.

17 Vladimir Kostakov, "Employment: Scarcity or Surplus?" in Anthony Jones and William Moskoff (eds.), *Perestroika and the Economy* (Armonk, N.Y.: Sharpe, 1989), pp. 159–175; Hedrick Smith, *The Russians* (New York: Quadrangle, 1976); and Steven Greenhouse, "Can Poland's Dinosaur Evolve?" *New York Times,* Nov. 27, 1989.

18 Elrad Parkhovmosky, "Can't Anybody Here Make Shoes?" *Izvestia.* Reprinted in *World Press Review,* July 1982, p. 36.

19 Grigorii Medvedev, *Chernobyl'skaia Kronika* (Moscow: Sovremennik, 1989). Cited by David Holloway, "The Catastrophe and After," *New York Review of Books,* July 19, 1990, p. 5; and Zhores Medvedev, *The Legacy of Chernobyl* (New York: Norton, 1990).

20 "The Soviet Economy," *The Economist,* April 9, 1988, p. 11.

21 John Emerich, Lord Acton, letter to Mandell Creighton, Apr. 5, 1887.

Chapter 16

1 See, for example, Jacques Ellul, *The Technological Society,* translated by John Wilkinson (New York: Vintage Books, 1967).

2 George R. Scott, *The History of Capital Punishment* (London: Torchstream Books, 1950), pp. 39–40.

3 Dover Wilson, *The Essential Shakespeare,* as quoted by Ivor Brown in *Shakespeare* (New York: Time Books, 1962), p. 112.

4   See, for example, Colin Turnbull, *The Forest People* (New York: Simon & Schuster, 1961); or John Garvan, *The Negritos of the Philippines* (Vienna: Ferdinand Berger, 1964).

5   Rene Dubos, *So Human an Animal* (New York: Scribner's, 1968), p. 270.

6   See, for example, Friedrich Engels, as cited by D. G. Brennan in Foreign Policy Association (ed.), *Toward the Year 2018* (New York: Cowles, 1958), p. 2.

7   Bill McKibben, "Reaching the Limit," *New York Review of Books,* May 29, 1997, pp. 32–35.

8   After ibid., recalculated with data from U.S. Bureau of the Census, *International Data Base,* updated July 17, 2003.

9   *World Population Data 2003* (Population Reference Bureau, www.worldpop.org/datafinder.htm).

10   Ibid.

11   Lester R. Brown, et al., *Vital Signs 1997* (NY: Norton, 1997); and United Nations, "World Urbanization Prospects: The 2001 Revision."

12   *Statistical Abstract of the U.S., 1993,* table 1377; and United Nations, "World Urbanization Prospects: The 2001 Revision."

13   Stephen Budiansky, "The Doomsday Myths," *U.S. News & World Report,* Dec. 13, 1993.

14   Worldwatch Institute, *Vital Signs, 2003,* pp. 28–29.

15   Ibid.

16   Worldwatch Institute, *Vital Signs, 2002,* p. 18.

17   Ibid.

18   Priit J. Vesilind, "Water: The Middle East's Critical Resource," *National Geographic,* 183, no. 5 (May 1993), pp. 38–71.

19   See especially the special issue of *National Geographic,* "Water: The Power, Promise, and Turmoil of North America's Fresh Water" (November 1993).

20   Associated Press, March 22, 2003.

21   R. E. Rhoades, "The World's Food Supply at Risk," *National Geographic,* 181, no. 4 (April 1991), pp. 74–105.

22   *Vital Signs, 2002,* p. 51.

23   *Vital Signs, 2003,* p. 84.

24   J. T. Houghton et al., eds., *Climate Change 2001: The Scientific Basis* (Cambridge: Cambridge University Press, 2001); World Meteorological Organization, "WMO Statement on the Status of the Global Climate in 2001."

25   S. Fred Singer, "Hit and Myth of Global Warming, *Washington Times,* July 7, 2002.

26   Ibid.

27   *Vital Signs, 2003,* p. 38.

28   *New York Times,* June 5, 2003.

29   Ibid.

30   Stewart Boyle, "Daze in the Sun," *Tomorrow Magazine,* June 2001, pp. 64–67.

31   *Vital Signs, 2002,* pp. 44–45.

32   Elias P. Gyftopolous, "Energy: Everybody's Business," *Forbes,* Oct. 27, 1980, p. 86.

33   *Vital Signs, 1997.*

34   Ibid.

35   *Statistical Abstract of the U.S., 1993,* table 373; *Statistical Abstract 1997,* table 385; and *Statistical Abstract, 2002,* table 351.

36   William K. Stevens, "When Trash Leaves the Curb: New Methods Aid Recycling," *New York Times,* May 2, 1989.

37   *Consumer Reports,* "Recycling: Is It Worth the Effort?" February 1994, pp. 92–98.

38   *Newsweek,* Sept. 22, 1980, p. 90; and *Wall Street Journal,* June 22, 1992.

39   Thomas Canby, "Bacteria: Teaching Old Bugs New Tricks," *National Geographic,* 184, no. 2 (August 1993), pp. 36–60.

40   *Vital Signs, 2003,* p. 30.

41   Statistic for 1995 in *Vital Signs, 1997,* adjusted to reflect growth in world meat production between 1995 and 2002 as reported in *Vital Signs, 2003.*

42   *Statistical Abstract of the U.S., 1997,* table 1353, and *Vital Signs, 2002,* p. 28.

43   Ibid., and "Changing Chinese Diet May Beef Up Global Trade," *Baltimore Sun,* March 6, 1994.

44   Anne Platt McGinn, "Promoting Sustainable Fisheries," *State of the World 1998* (New York: Norton, 1998), p. 60.

45   *Vital Signs, 2002,* p. 25.

46   William Broad, "The Incredible Shrinking Transistor . . . ," *New York Times,* Feb. 4, 1997.

47   John Markoff, "New Wave in High Tech: Tiny Motors and Sensors," *New York Times,* Jan. 27, 1997.

48   Jessica Tuchman Mathews, "Factories Too Tiny to See," *Washington Post,* Jan. 23, 1980.

49   Sandra Blakeslee, "Human Genes Turn Plants into Factories for Medicines," *New York Times,* Jan. 16, 1990.

50   Our calculations from *World Development Indicators* Online Database (www.worldbank.org/data/onlinedatabases/onlinedatabases.html).

51   Ibid.

52   Robert Heilbroner, *An Inquiry into the Human Prospect* (New York: Norton, 1974).

53   Ibid., pp. 121–122.

Photo Credits

Chapter 1

1-1a, Colin G. Butler/Photo Researchers
1-1b, William Stephens/Photo Researchers
1-1c, Clem Haagner/Photo Researchers
1-1d, James R. Holland/Stock Boston
1-2, Baron Hugo Van Lawick/National Geographic Society
1-3, Canada Transport, Canadian Government
1-4, American Foundation for the Blind

Chapter 2

2-1, T. D. Lovering/Stock Boston
2-2, Jeffry Myers/Stock Boston
2-3a, American Museum of Natural History
2-3b, right, Lynn McLaren/Photo Researchers
2-4, Courtesy of Dept. of Antiquities, Ashmolean Museum, Oxford
2-5, Henri Cartier-Bresson/Magnum
2-6, Reuters/Sunil Malhotra/Archive Photos
2-7, Mike Mazzaschi/Stock Boston
2-8, Martha Swope Photography
2-9, The Bridgeman Art Library International Ltd.

Chapter 3

3-1, Peter Southwick/Stock Boston
3-2, Corbis-Bettmann
3-3, *The Plague* by Marcantio Raimondi (ca. 1515–1516), University of Michigan Museum of Art
3-4, Peter Menze/Stock Boston

Chapter 4

4-1, Australian Information Services/Photo Researchers
4-2, Will & Deni McIntyre/Photo Researchers

Chapter 5

5-1, From Grahame Clark, *The Stone Age Hunters,* © 1967 by Thames and Hudson, Ltd., London
5-2, American Museum of Natural History
5-3, Topham/The Image Works
5-4, Prehistoric Division, Museum of Natural History, Vienna
5-5, By permission of Peter J. Ucko and Andrea Rojenfeld, *Paleolithic Cave Art,* 1967, Wiedenfeld Publishers
5-6, By permission of John Marshall, Peabody Museum, Harvard University.
5-7, Penny Tweedle/Woodfin Camp & Associates
5-8, By permission of John Marshall, Peabody Museum, Harvard University
5-9, American Museum of Natural History
5-10, Colonel Charles W. Furlong
5-11, National Anthropological Archive, Smithsonian Institution.

Chapter 6

6-1, American Museum of Natural History
6-2, American Museum of Natural History
6-3, From Napoleon A. Chagnon, *Yanomano: The Fierce People* © 1968 by Holt, Rinehart, Winston, Inc. Reprinted by permission of CBS College Publishing.
6-4, From W. Watson, *Early Civilization in China,* © 1970, Thames & Hudson, Ltd., London
6-5, American Museum of Natural History
6-6, United Nations
6-7, United Nations
6-8, American Museum of Natural History
6-9, Courtesy of the University Museum, University of Pennsylvania, Philadelphia

6-10, From Jacques Maquet, *Africanity, The Cultural Unity of Black Africa,* Oxford U. Press, 1972, p. 112

Chapter 7

7-1, From *Standard Cyclopedia of Horticulture,* MacMillan, 1916
7-2, Evans/Three Lion Photos
7-3, Corbis-Bettmann
7-4, Courtesy of the Metropolitan Museum of Art, Museum Excavations, 1919–1920, Rogers Fund, supplemented by contribution of Edward S. Harkness
7-5, Courtesy of the Metropolitan Museum of Art, Museum Excavations, 1919–1920, Rogers Fund, supplemented by contribution of Edward S. Harkness
7-6, United Nations
7-7, Courtesy of Exxon Corporation
7-8, United Nations
7-9, Corbis-Bettmann
7-10, United Nations
7-11, Courtesy of the Metropolitan Museum of Art, Bashford Dean Memorial Collection, Funds from various donors, 1929
7-12, United Nations
7-13a, Nabel Turner/Tony Stone Images
7-13b, Reuters/Vincenzo Pinto/Archive Photos
7-13c, Paul Chesley/Tony Stone Images
7-14, Alinari/Art Resource, NY

Chapter 8

8-1, United Nations
8-2, Pietro F. Mele/Photo Researchers
8-3, Paolo Koch/Photo Researchers
8-4, By Permission of Institut Français d'Archéologie, Beirut, Lebanon
8-5, Courtesy of the Metropolitan Museum of Art, Rogers Fund, 1906.

Chapter 9

9-1, The Smithsonian Institution
9-2, No credit needed, public domain
9-3, Edward L. Bafford Photography Collection, Albin O. Kuhn Library & Gallery, U. of Maryland, Baltimore Gallery

Chapter 10

10-1, USDA Online Photography Center
10-2, Reuters/Peter Morgan/Archive Photos
10-3, Courtesy of the New York Public Library, Astor, Lenox and Tilden Foundations

Chapter 11

11-1, Courtesy of the New York Public Library, Astor, Lenox and Tilden Foundations
11-2, Independence National Historic Park Collection
11-3, Courtesy of the New York Public Library, Astor, Lenox and Tilden Foundations
11-4, V. Zufarov/V. Repik/Tass from Sovfoto
11-5, Brown Alumni Magazine

Chapter 12

12-1, Brad Markel/Liaison International
12-2, NATO Photos

Chapter 13

13-1, German Information Center
13-2, n/a

Chapter 14

14-1, United Nations
14-2, United Nations
14-3, United Nations
14-4, United Nations
14-5, Alfred/SIPA Press
14-6, Reuters/Corbis-Bettmann
14-7, U.S. Embassy, Tanzania

Chapter 15

15-1, A. Kuzyarin/Tass from Sovfoto
15-2, Jill Hartley/Photo Researchers
15-3, Patrick Forestier/Sygma

Chapter 16

16-1, UN Photos
16-2, USAID Photo/Agency for International Development
16-3, UPI/Corbis-Bettmann

Name Index

Subject Index